Informatik aktuell

Herausgeber: W. Brauer
im Auftrag der Gesellschaft für Informatik (GI)

Springer
Berlin
Heidelberg
New York
Barcelona
Budapest
Hongkong
London
Mailand
Paris
Singapur
Tokio

Jürgen Dassow Rudolf Kruse (Hrsg.)

Informatik '98

Informatik zwischen Bild und Sprache

28. Jahrestagung der
Gesellschaft für Informatik
Magdeburg, 21.–25. September 1998

Herausgeber

Jürgen Dassow
Rudolf Kruse
Institut für Wissens- und Sprachverarbeitung
Fakultät für Informatik
Otto-von-Guericke-Universität Magdeburg
Universitätsplatz 2, D-39106 Magdeburg

Die Deutsche Bibliothek - CIP-Einheitsaufnahme

Informatik '98 : Informatik zwischen Bild und Sprache ; Magdeburg, 21. - 25. September 1998 / Jürgen Dassow ; Rudolf Kruse (Hrsg.). - Berlin ; Heidelberg ; New York ; Barcelona ; Budapest ; Hongkong ; London ; Mailand ; Paris ; Singapur ; Tokio : Springer, 1998
(... Jahrestagung der Gesellschaft für Informatik ; 28) (Informatik aktuell)
ISBN-13:978-3-540-64938-0 e-ISBN-13:978-3-642-72283-7
DOI: 10.1007/978-3-642-72283-7

CR Subject Classification (1998): A.0, D.0, E.0, F.0, H.0, I.0, J.0, K.0

ISBN-13:978-3-540-64938-0

Satz: Reproduktionsfertige Vorlage vom Autor/Herausgeber

SPIN: 10573306 33/3142-543210 – Gedruckt auf säurefreiem Papier

Vorwort

Die Gesellschaft für Informatik veranstaltet vom 21.–25. September 1998 in Magdeburg ihre 28. Jahrestagung, die *Informatik'98*. Die Tagung steht in diesem Jahr unter dem Motto *Informatik zwischen Bild und Sprache.* Die Organisation hat die Fakultät für Informatik der Otto-von-Guericke-Universität in Magdeburg übernommen. In diesem Tagungsband sind die Beiträge des Hauptprogramms sowie Kurzübersichten über die anderen Programmteile enthalten.

Das Ziel der Tagung besteht darin, einen Überblick über neue Trends in den Gebieten *Bild und Sprache* zu geben, die für die weitere Entwicklung der Informatik eine Schlüsselrolle spielen. In sechs Hauptvorträgen werden Resultate aus der Spitzenforschung präsentiert, Anforderungen aus der Industrie formuliert sowie die gesellschaftliche Relevanz dieser Themengebiete beleuchtet:

Hans Ulrich Block (Siemens AG München): *Maschinelle Übersetzung in der technischen Dokumentation — Anforderungen und Lösungen,*

José Luis Encarnação (Technische Universität Darmstadt): *Digital Story Telling — Die nächste API-Generation für Multimedia-Anwendungen,*

Steven K. Feiner (Columbia University New York): *Wearing it Out: First Steps Toward Mobile Augmented Reality Systems,*

Peter Glotz (Rektor der Universität Erfurt): *Die Informationsgesellschaft: Deutsche Rahmenbedingungen, deutsche Hemmungen,*

Claus Heinrich (Vorstand SAP AG Walldorf): *User-Centric Business Computing,*

Wolfgang Wahlster (DFKI und Universität Saarbrücken): *Adaptive Informationspräsentation: Zur Koordination von Visualisierung und Verbalisierung.*

Den Hauptteil des Tagungsprogramms bilden 28 Beiträge aus Wirtschaft und Wissenschaft, die aus 45 Einreichungen ausgewählt wurden. Diese sorgfältig referierten Beiträge präsentieren neue Forschungsresultate aus den Bereichen *Bild und Sprache.* Ergänzt wird dieser Tagungsteil durch die Vorstellung wichtiger Großprojekte in diesen Fachgebieten sowie durch ein *Minisymposium*, in dem neue Informatik-Studiengänge (wie die Computer-Visualistik oder die Medien-Informatik) diskutiert werden. In einem *Computer Animation Festival* im Magdeburger Theater werden zusätzliche Beiträge vorgestellt, die diese innovativen Techniken bereits intensiv nutzen.

Wie immer sind mit der Haupttagung auch *Tutorien* und *Workshops* verbunden, in denen Spezialthemen vertieft werden. Hierzu zählen insbesondere auch spezielle Veranstaltungen für Studierende, da Firmen wegen des Mangels an Informatik-Absolventen die Studierenden derzeit besonders umwerben. Bei den Workshops handelt es sich zum Teil um umfangreiche Veranstaltungen, in denen aktuelle Forschungsthemen in größerem Umfang vorgestellt werden, als es auf der Haupttagung möglich ist. Verweise auf die Workshop-Ergebnisse finden sich in den Kurzdarstellungen in diesem Tagungsband.

Die Organisation einer solchen Tagung erfordert einen erheblichen Aufwand, den nur zahlreiche Helfer gemeinsam bewältigen können. Wir danken den Autoren, den weiteren Mitgliedern des Programmkomitees Hinrich Bonin, Rüdiger Buck-Emden, Oliver Burgert, Werner Burhenne, Ralf Cordes, Ulrich Furbach, Peter Gorny, Manfred Grauer, Walther von Hahn, Erik Maehle, Nadia Magnenat Thalmann, Max Mühlhäuser, Heinrich Müller, Thomas Ottmann, Karl-Heinz Rödiger, Dietmar Rösner, Detlev Ruland, Michiel Smid sowie den Organisatoren der Workshops, Tutorien, Podiumsdiskussionen und Minisymposien. Dem GI-Präsidium und der GI-Geschäftsstelle danken wir für vielfältige Unterstützungen. Besonderer Dank gilt den Herren D. Nauck und B. Reichel für die sorgfältige Vorbereitung dieses Tagungsbandes und nicht zuletzt dem Springer-Verlag für die fruchtbare Zusammenarbeit.

Magdeburg, im Juli 1998

Jürgen Dassow
Rudolf Kruse

Inhalt

Fachbeiträge Bild und Sprache

Innovative Anwendungen von Bildern I

Innovative Anwendungen von Bildern II

Bildanalyse

Visuelle Programmierung

Sprachverarbeitung

Gestik I

Gestik II

Laser Display Technologien

Technologie-Diskussionen

Sonderforschungsbereiche und Schwerpunktprogramme

CAVE

Informatik-Ausbildung

Electronic Commerce

Workshops, Tutorien, Computer Animation Festival

Fachbeiträge
Bild und Sprache

Visual Cryptography – How to Use Images to Share a Secret

Ingrid Biehl[1], Bernd Meyer[2] and Susanne Wetzel *[3]

[1] Technische Universität Darmstadt, Fachbereich Informatik, Alexanderstraße 10, D–64283 Darmstadt, Germany, email: ingi@cdc.informatik.tu-darmstadt.de
[2] Siemens Corporate Technology, Otto-Hahn-Ring 6, D–81730 München, Germany, email: bernd.meyer@mchp.siemens.de
[3] Daimler Benz AG, FTK/A, HPC 0507, D–70546 Stuttgart, Germany, email: swetzel@acm.org

Abstract. In this paper, we give a survey of **visual cryptography schemes**, a new type of cryptographic schemes which was first introduced by Naor and Shamir [9] in 1994. Visual cryptography schemes can be considered as encryption schemes based on graphical data. In visual cryptography schemes as special instances of **secret sharing schemes**, the secret information is encoded by the construction of several fragments, called *shares* which are distributed secretly to different, not necessarily trustworthy parties. In order to reconstruct the secret image, a *qualified* subset of these parties has to combine their shares. For example, in (k, n)–threshold schemes there are n different parties and each subset of at least k parties is qualified. Visual cryptography schemes are *perfect*, i.e., *forbidden* (i.e., not qualified) subsets of parties learn no information at all about the encrypted image (in the information–theoretic sense). In contrast to conventional encryption (resp. secret sharing) schemes, visual cryptography schemes allow the decryption to be done directly by the **human visual system**, i.e., without performing any sophisticated cryptographic computations.

1 Introduction

This paper gives a survey of visual cryptography schemes, a new cryptographic paradigm which was recently introduced by Naor and Shamir [9] as a visual variant of *secret sharing schemes*. In secret sharing schemes, the secret information is encoded by the construction of several *shadow images*, called *shares*. In other words, the secret information is distributed among the shares. These shares are then given secretly to different, not necessarily trustworthy parties. In order to reconstruct the secret, a *qualified* subset of these parties has to combine their shares. For example, in (k, n)–threshold secret sharing schemes (see [11]), there are n different parties and only subsets of at least k parties are qualified, i.e.,

* This work was done while the author was a member of the Graduiertenkolleg Informatik at the University of Saarbrücken, a fellowship program of the DFG (Deutsche Forschungsgemeinschaft).

only subsets of at least k parties can reconstruct the original image and no subset of less than k parties is able to obtain any information about the secret image. A special feature of visual cryptography schemes is the way decryption can be done: By printing the shares of a qualified subset of share-holders on transparencies and stacking them, the original image can be seen. Thus, decryption can simply be done by the *human visual system*, i.e., a visual cryptography scheme can be used by everyone without any knowledge of cryptography. In the most simple case, i.e., if the image is encoded in two shares, the basic system can be thought of as a private key cryptosystem where one share serves as ciphertext while the other one is the private key. To encode data different from graphical data, one has to embed the secret information for example into a black–and–white picture and apply the visual cryptography scheme to this image.

In this paper, we will first present the basics of visual cryptography schemes as introduced in [9]. Then, we will focus on its improvements and extensions. In [1, 2, 3, 4], Ateniese et al. extend the model introduced by Naor and Shamir to any general access structure specifying all qualified subsets of participants who can reveal the secret by stacking their transparencies. Moreover, in their work they present new techniques for constructing visual cryptography schemes, provide bounds for particular parameters of the systems and extend their capabilities. Also in [7], a new construction principle is proposed, new bounds on relevant parameters are developed and an extension of the original system is presented such that every combination of transparencies can reveal independent information. In a recent paper, Hofmeister et al. [8] show how to compute not only an upper bound but the exact maximum of one of the system parameters. In [5], the idea of traceable visual cryptography is introduced which allows to track down possible saboteurs of the system.

2 (k, n)-Visual Cryptography Schemes

In the sequel, we assume that the images to be encoded (shared) are black-and-white. Each pixel is handled separately, appears in n modified versions (shares) - one for each transparency - and is represented by m *sub-pixels*. In Figure 1, we illustrate this by an example given by Naor and Shamir (see [9]) where $m = 9$ and $n = k = 4$. When printing in close proximity, the human visual

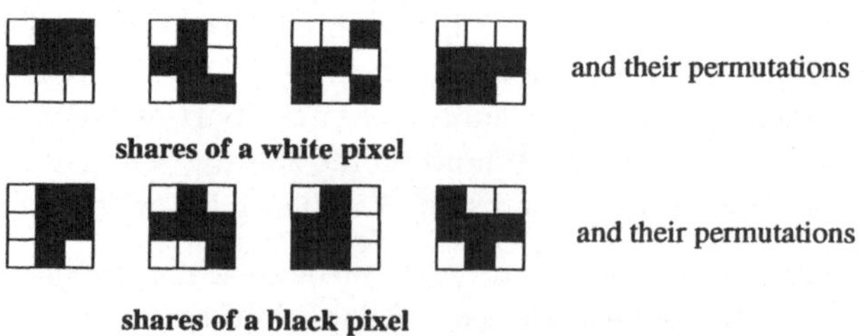

Fig. 1. Example for a (4, 4)-VCS

system averages the individual black and white contributions of the sub-pixels. Therefore, a black pixel has to be represented by more black sub-pixels than a white pixel. Hence, the *contrast* of a picture depends on the difference of the number of black sub-pixels used for the representation of a black pixel and the number of black sub-pixels used for a white pixel. The contrast should be as high as possible. However, due to security reasons, the obvious model in which a white pixel is represented by a collection of only white sub-pixels and a black one is represented by m black sub-pixels, is ruled out.

The basic construction idea is as follows: A k out of n visual cryptography system can be described by an $n \times m$ Boolean matrix $B = (b_{ij})$. For a set $I \subseteq \{1, \ldots, n\}$, $\text{Shares}_B(I) = \{b_{i\cdot} \ : \ i \in I\}$ is the set of all rows $b_{i\cdot}$ of B whose row numbers i are in I. With $v = \text{OR}(s_1, \ldots, s_l)$ we denote the OR of a set of Boolean vectors s_i $(1 \leq i \leq l,\ l \in \mathbb{N})$ consisting of m components. For $B = (b_{ij}) \in \{0,1\}^{n \times m}$, a row $b_{i\cdot}$ is interpreted as the encoding of the i-th share of a pixel p, i.e., $b_{ij} = 1$ if and only if the j-th sub-pixel of the i-th transparency is black. The Hamming weight of the OR of k corresponding rows of B (i.e., stacking the corresponding shares) determines the grayness of the stack of k transparencies. The grey level is interpreted to be *black* if $H(v) \geq b$ (Hamming weight of the OR) and as *white* if $H(v) \leq b - \alpha * m$ for some threshold $1 \leq b \leq m$ and *relative difference* $\alpha > 0$. Thus, the shared pixel p is black if $H(v) \geq b$ and it is white if $H(v) \leq b - \alpha * m$. When stacking less than k transparencies, the original black as well as white pixels have to be represented by the same combinations of sub-pixels in order to guarantee security. The problem in the construction of a (k,n)-threshold-VCS consists in the creation of sets of matrices C_0 and C_1 such that the matrices in C_0 are used for the creation of shares of white pixels and those in C_1 are used for black pixels. To be more precise, a visual cryptography scheme is defined as follows:

Definition 1 [9]. Two collections of $n \times m$ Boolean matrices C_0 and C_1 are called a k out of n visual cryptography scheme ((k,n)-VCS), if there are constants $\alpha \geq \frac{1}{m}$ and $b \in \{1, \ldots, m\}$ such that the following conditions hold:

1. For any B in C_0, the OR v of any k of the n rows of B has a Hamming weight $H(v) \leq b - \alpha * m$.
2. For any B in C_1, the OR v of any k of the n rows of B has a Hamming weight $H(v) \geq b$.
3. For any subset $\{i_1, i_2, \ldots, i_q\}$ of $\{1, 2, \ldots, n\}$ with $q < k$, the two collections of $q \times m$ matrices B_j for $j \in \{0,1\}$ obtained by restricting each $n \times m$ matrix in C_j $(j \in \{0,1\})$ to the rows $\{i_1, i_2, \ldots, i_q\}$ contain the same matrices with the same frequencies.

Hence, the n shares (transparencies) are generated from the original secret picture by choosing a matrix of the set C_0 or C_1 equally distributed and independently for every pixel, depending only on the color of the pixel. I.e., to share a white pixel (resp. black pixel), a matrix is chosen from the collection C_0 (resp. C_1) and the rows are distributed to the participants as the shares of this pixel.

The first two conditions of the definition are called *contrast*, ensuring that stacking k transparencies will reveal the original color of the pixel. The last condition is called *security*, implying that inspecting less than k transparencies will not give any information on the original pixel. The value m is the loss in resolution from the original picture to the shared one and should be as small as possible. α is the *relative contrast* and determines how well k transparencies will reveal the secret. The *minimal greyness* of a black pixel is determined by the parameter b. Note that the size of $\mathcal{C}_0$ and $\mathcal{C}_1$ do not have to be the same.

In the following, we will present the construction of a (k,n)-VCS as introduced in [9]. We will start with a (k,k)-VCS, where the sets $\mathcal{C}_0$ and $\mathcal{C}_1$ consist of all matrices obtained by permuting the columns of two Boolean *base matrices* K^0 and K^1, respectively.

2.1 A (k,k)-VCS

In [1], a (k,k)-VCS is presented where K^0 is the matrix whose columns are all the Boolean vectors of length k having an even number of 1's and K^1 is the matrix where the columns are the Boolean vectors of length k with an odd number of 1's. Note that the Hamming weight of each row in K^0 and K^1 is $m/2 = 2^{k-2}$. The collections $\mathcal{C}_0$ and $\mathcal{C}_1$ consist of all possible permutations of the columns of the corresponding base matrix. As long as one obtains at most $k-1$ rows of a matrix in $\mathcal{C}_0$ or $\mathcal{C}_1$, it cannot be decided whether the original matrix belongs to $\mathcal{C}_0$ or to $\mathcal{C}_1$ since for each submatrix of at most $k-1$ rows of some permutation of the columns of K^0 there is a permutation of the columns of K^1 which contains the identical submatrix. The Hamming weight of the OR of all rows of some matrix in $\mathcal{C}_0$ (resp. $\mathcal{C}_1$) is $2^{k-1}-1$ (resp. 2^{k-1}). Thus, this construction results in a (k,k)-VCS with $|\mathcal{C}_0| = |\mathcal{C}_1| = 2^{k-1}!$ and parameters $m = 2^{k-1}$, $\alpha = 1/2^{k-1}$. These parameters are optimal in the sense that m is as small as possible and α is as large as possible (as shown in [9]).

With K^0 as the matrix whose columns are all the Boolean k-vectors having an even number of 1's, K^1 can be chosen such that $k-1$ rows $a_{i_1}, \ldots, a_{i_{k-1}}$ are identical in both matrices and the i_k-th row of K^1 is the complement of the corresponding row of K^0. In the sequel, the complement of a_{i_k} will be denoted by $\overline{a_{i_k}}$.

Example 1.

$$K^0 = \begin{bmatrix} 0\,0\,0\,0\,1\,1\,1\,1 \\ 0\,0\,1\,1\,0\,0\,1\,1 \\ 0\,1\,0\,1\,0\,1\,0\,1 \\ 0\,1\,1\,0\,1\,0\,0\,1 \end{bmatrix} \text{ and } K^1 = \begin{bmatrix} 0\,0\,0\,0\,1\,1\,1\,1 \\ 0\,0\,1\,1\,0\,0\,1\,1 \\ 0\,1\,0\,1\,0\,1\,0\,1 \\ 1\,0\,0\,1\,0\,1\,1\,0 \end{bmatrix}$$

are the black and white base matrices for a $(4,4)$-VCS.

2.2 A (k,n)-VCS

Using the (k,k)-VCSs of Section 2.1, one can now construct (k,n)-VCSs with $k \leq n$ using an $n \times \ell$ matrix $SH(n,\ell,k)$ whose entries are elements of a ground set $\{a_1,\ldots,a_k\}$ (see [1, 2, 9]).

The $n \times \ell$ matrix $SH(n, \ell, k)$ has the property that for any subset of k rows there exists at least one column such that the entries in the k given rows of that column are all distinct. One constructs the base matrices S^0 and S^1 for (k,n)-VCS by replacing the symbols $a_1, \dots, a_k$ with the 1-st, ..., k-th row of the corresponding base matrices K^0 and K^1 of the (k,k)-VCS (see Section 2.1). The collections $\mathcal{C}_0$ (respectively $\mathcal{C}_1$) obtained by permuting the columns of the corresponding base matrix S^0 (respectively S^1) in all possible ways form a (k,n)-VCS with $m = \ell \times 2^{k-1}$.

In the construction of (k,n)-VCSs, the $n \times \ell$ matrix SH is a representation of a *hash family* H, a collection of ℓ k-wise independent hash functions (see [6, 9, 12]) which means that for any k distinct elements $x_1, \dots, x_k \in \{1, \dots, n\}$ and any k (not necessarily distinct) elements $y_1, \dots, y_k \in \{1, \dots, k\}$ the probability that for a randomly chosen $h \in \mathcal{H}$ follows $h(x_j) = y_j$(for all $1 \leq j \leq k$) is the same. If one uses the rows of the base matrices K^0 and K^1 to fill the SH matrix, one obtains a (k,n)-VCS. The following lemma shows that Condition 3 of Definition 1 is satisfied.

Lemma 2. *Let B be some matrix in $\mathcal{C}_0 \cup \mathcal{C}_1$, $p < k$ and P_0, P_1 be two subsets of p rows of B. Then, there is a permutation of the columns which applied to P_0 results in P_1.*

Proof. It is sufficient to look at the base matrices. Each p-tuple of values as entries of p rows in a single column of the SH matrix appears in each set of p rows with the same frequency. This is guaranteed by the k-wise independence of the hash functions. □

Because the properties of K^0 and K^1 and H it follows that Conditions 1 and 2 of the Definition 1 are satisfied, too.

In the following example we show a part of a SH matrix and the corresponding base matrix S^0 of a $(3,4)$-VCS (see also [1, 2, 9]). (For the definition of K^0 see Section 2.1.)

Example 2.

$$SH = \begin{bmatrix} \cdots a_1\ a_2 \cdots \\ \cdots a_1\ a_3 \cdots \\ \cdots a_2\ a_1 \cdots \\ \cdots a_2\ a_3 \cdots \\ \cdots a_3\ a_1 \cdots \\ \cdots a_3\ a_2 \cdots \end{bmatrix} \qquad S^0 = \begin{bmatrix} \cdots & 0011 & 0101 & \cdots \\ \cdots & 0011 & 0110 & \cdots \\ \cdots & 0101 & 0011 & \cdots \\ \cdots & 0101 & 0110 & \cdots \\ \cdots & 0110 & 0011 & \cdots \\ \cdots & 0110 & 0101 & \cdots \end{bmatrix}$$

3 Bounds on the Pixel Expansion and the Relative Contrast in (k,n)-VCS

We recall from [7, 9] that in general, the relative contrast α is at most 2^{-k+1} and m is at least 2^{k-1} for a (k,n)-VCS. While Ateniese et al. [1, 2, 3, 4] were focusing on improving solely the pixel expansion, Droste [7] was looking for an improvement of both relevant system parameters. Droste presents a new construction technique for (k,n)-VCS for which the following theorem holds:

Theorem 3. *If C_0 and C_1 are a (k,n)-VCS, then α is at most $\frac{1}{MIN(k,n)}$ and m is at least $\lceil MIN(k,n)\rceil$, where $MIN(k,n)$ is the minimal value of the objective function of the following linear programming problem:*

$$\text{minimize } m_0^0 + \ldots + m_n^0 \text{ under the constraints:}$$
$$m_0^0 + \ldots + m_n^0 = m_0^1 + \ldots + m_n^1$$
$$m_0^0, \ldots, m_n^0, m_0^1, \ldots, m_n^1 \geq 0$$
$$\forall \text{ even } q \in \{0,\ldots,k\} : \sum_{i=q}^{n-k+q} \binom{n-i}{k-q} \cdot \binom{i}{q} \cdot m_i^0 \geq \binom{n}{k} \cdot \binom{k}{q}$$
$$\forall \text{ odd } q \in \{0,\ldots,k\} : \sum_{i=q}^{n-k+q} \binom{n-i}{k-q} \cdot \binom{i}{q} \cdot m_i^1 \geq \binom{n}{k} \cdot \binom{k}{q}$$
$$\forall q \in \{0,\ldots,k-1\} : \sum_{i=q}^{n-k+1+q} \binom{n-i}{k-1-q} \cdot \binom{i}{q} \cdot (m_i^0 - m_i^1) = 0$$

The m_i^t are the number of columns in $\mathcal{D}(C_t)$ with exactly i 1's where $\mathcal{D}(C_t)$ is the concatenation of all matrices of C_t in arbitrary order ($t \in \{0,1\}$).

In [8], these results are improved such that for general k and n not only an upper bound but the exact value of the maximum possible relative contrast α can be computed.

A completely different approach for achieving a better contrast is taken by Naor and Shamir in [10]. In the original model, the combination of black and white subpixels determines the grey level of the original pixel. The underlying structure is an *OR semigroup*, i.e., a black subpixel in one of the transparencies cannot be undone by the same subpixel in another share. To improve the achievable contrast, the model is changed such that there are two opaque colors, e.g., yellow and red, as well as a completely transparent one. When stacking the shares, the top opaque color will always win. The structure is called *COVER semigroup.* Obviously, it is not commutative, i.e., the order in which the transparencies are stacked is significant. Another change is that instead of using single transparencies, each one consists of c sheets. Due to these changes, the contrast for (2,2)-VCS can be improved significantly. We know from [9] that in the original model, the maximal achievable relative contrast is $\frac{1}{2}$. In comparison, the new model allows the achievement of a contrast as $1 - \frac{1}{c}$. However, it turns out that for (k,n)-VCS, in general the application of the COVER semigroup is not the appropriate tool for improving the contrast, no matter how many sheets are used. For further details we refer to [10].

4 General Access Structures

In [1, 2], the original model of visual cryptography schemes is extended to *general access structures*:

Let $\mathcal{P} = \{1,\ldots,n\}$ be the set of participants. Then, the qualified (resp. forbidden) sets are denoted by $\Gamma_{Qual} \subseteq 2^{\mathcal{P}}$ (resp. $\Gamma_{Forb} \subseteq 2^{\mathcal{P}}$) with $\Gamma_{Qual} \cap$

$\Gamma_{Forb} = \emptyset$. The pair $(\Gamma_{Qual}, \Gamma_{Forb})$ is the so-called *access structure.* If Γ_{Qual} is monotone increasing, i.e., $A \in \Gamma_{Qual}$ and $A \subseteq A' \subseteq \mathcal{P}$ implies $A' \in \Gamma_{Qual}$, then Γ_{Forb} is monotone decreasing, $\Gamma_{Qual} \cup \Gamma_{Forb} = 2^{\mathcal{P}}$ and the access structure is said to be *strong* with basis $\Gamma_0 = \{A \in \Gamma_{Qual} : A' \notin \Gamma_{Qual} \ \forall A' \subset A\}$ (collection of minimal qualified sets). Thus, the generalized visual cryptography scheme can be defined as follows:

Definition 4 [1, 2]. Let $(\Gamma_{Qual}, \Gamma_{Forb})$ be an access structure on a set of n participants. Two collections of $n \times m$ Boolean matrices $\mathcal{C}_0$ and $\mathcal{C}_1$ are called a $(\Gamma_{Qual}, \Gamma_{Forb}, n)$-VCS, if there is a value $\alpha \geq \frac{1}{m}$ and a set $\{(X, b_X)\}_{X \in \Gamma_{Qual}}$ (set of thresholds) such that the following conditions hold:

1. For any qualified set $X = \{i_1, \ldots, i_p\} \in \Gamma_{Qual}$, the following holds: For any B in $\mathcal{C}_0$, the OR v of the rows of $i_1, \ldots, i_p$ has Hamming weight $H(v) \leq b_X - \alpha * m$. And for any B in $\mathcal{C}_1$, the OR v has Hamming weight $H(v) \geq b_X$.
2. For any forbidden set $X = \{i_1, i_2, \ldots, i_q\} \in \Gamma_{Forb}$, the two collections of $q \times m$ matrices B_j for $j \in \{0, 1\}$ obtained by restricting each $n \times m$ matrix in $\mathcal{C}_j$ $(j \in \{0, 1\})$ to the rows $\{i_1, i_2, \ldots, i_q\}$ contain the same matrices with the same frequencies.

Based on this definition, Ateniese et al. present two new techniques for constructing visual cryptography schemes. While the first one is based on so-called cumulative arrays (see [1, 2]), in the second one, large VCSs are constructed by using small schemes as building blocks. Applying the construction principle introduced by Naor and Shamir for building generalized schemes will result in a decrease of the pixel expansion m. While the pixel expansion in the original system is shown to be $m = \log n 2^{O(k \log k)}$, in [1, 2] it is proven to be $m = \Omega(k \log n)$ for the generalization. This is due to relaxing the condition that all thresholds are required to be equal. Among other results, Ateniese et al. prove the following theorem:

Theorem 5. *For a strong access structure* $(\Gamma_{Qual}, \Gamma_{Forb})$ *having basis* Γ_0 *there exists a* $(\Gamma_{Qual}, \Gamma_{Forb}, m)$*-VCS where* $m = \sum_{X \in \Gamma_0} 2^{|X|-1}$.

In [3], an extended visual cryptography scheme along with possible constructions also in combination with general access structures is proposed. Extension is meant in respect to the fact that the original image is not encoded in random looking shares but rather innocent looking meaningful images.

A different kind of extension, called *s-extended* n out of n schemes is presented in [7] where each possible combination of shares reveals a different image.

5 Traceable Visual Cryptography Schemes

In [5], a new k out of n visual cryptography scheme is presented which does not only meet the requirements of a basic visual cryptography scheme as defined by Naor and Shamir (see Section 2) but is also traceable. Thus, no information about the original secret can be revealed if less than k share-holders combine their shares. In those systems, it is inherently assumed that even if there are k or more share-holders with an interest in the abuse of the secret, then it is almost impossible that they can meet up as an entirety (e.g., because they are to cautious to inform too many others about their intentions) and combine their shares to misuse the secret. But in real scenarios it might not be too unlikely that the betrayers find together in small groups. Even though each one of these groups is too small to compute the original secret, the betrayers of such a group can impose a major security risk on the system by publishing the information about their shares. Suppose for example that $k-1$ betrayers find each other and do the publishing. Then, all the other $n-k+1$ share-holders can potentially reveal the secret without ever meeting up with at least $k-1$ other share-holders as is intended by the system.

For example, a practical scenario is given by a key escrowing system, realized as a k out of n threshold secret sharing scheme with a large number n of escrow agencies (which is discussed by the cryptographic research community nowadays) where the agencies share the secret keys for encryption or electronic signatures for participating parties. Then, if for instance $k-1$ agencies are traitors and combine their shares of the parties' keys and publish this information, every other single escrow agent can retrieve the secret keys and illegally eavesdrop the communication of the parties using the system. This is a major lack of security and definitely will not help to build up some confidence of the general public in the system.

Obviously, it is important to provide mechanisms which allow the tracing of the publishing saboteurs so that they can appropriately be punished.

Based on the definition of a visual cryptography scheme (see Definition 1), we will now present the traitor model as introduced in [5]. It is assumed that $0 < t < k$ share-holders try to sabotage the system by stacking their shares and publishing the resulting information. Note that one is not interested in keeping other coalitions from stacking their shares on top of the published information and thus revealing the secret illegally. One is solely interested in tracing the traitors who have started the sabotage act by publishing the information. In order to guarantee that the traitors can be traced, markings are inserted in the picture.

Prior to defining a traceable (k,n)-VCS, we shall first introduce some additional notations: Given a visual cryptography scheme with $\mathcal{C} = (\mathcal{C}_0, \mathcal{C}_1)$ (where $\mathcal{C}_0$ and $\mathcal{C}_1$ are collections of $n \times m$ matrices) with threshold constants α and b and a vector v, the predicate $\text{Threshold\_Decision}_{\mathcal{C}_0,\mathcal{C}_1}(v)$ is 0 if the Hamming weight of v is at most $b - \alpha m$ and is 1 if the Hamming weight of v is at least b. Let $\mathcal{K}$ be a collection of Boolean $n \times m$ matrices B, $t \in \mathbb{N}$ and S be an $t \times m$ matrix. Then, $\mathcal{B}_{\mathcal{K}}(S)$ is the set of all matrices $B \in \mathcal{K}$ such that $\{s_{i\cdot} \mid 1 \leq i \leq t\}$ (set of rows of S) is a subset of $\{b_{i\cdot} : 1 \leq i \leq n\}$ (set of rows of B).

Definition 6. A *traceable (k,n)-VCS with (ε, δ)-security* is a set of three collections of Boolean $n \times m$ matrices $\mathcal{C}_0, \mathcal{C}_1$ and $\mathcal{C}_M$, denoted by $\mathcal{C} = (\mathcal{C}_0, \mathcal{C}_1, \mathcal{C}_M)$. The matrices of the set $\mathcal{C}_M$ are called *marking matrices* and for each marking matrix $B \in \mathcal{C}_M$ there is a special row $1 \leq r = r(B) \leq n$, called *marking row*, which can be used for tracing. The collections $\mathcal{C}_0, \mathcal{C}_1$ and $\mathcal{C}_M$ have to satisfy the following properties:

1. $(\mathcal{C}_0, \mathcal{C}_1)$ is a (k,n)-VCS.
2. For any subset $\{i_1, i_2, \ldots, i_q\}$ of $\{1, 2, \ldots, n\}$ with $q < k$, the three collections of $q \times m$ matrices B_j for $j \in \{0, 1, M\}$ obtained by restricting each $n \times m$ matrix in $\mathcal{C}_j$ ($j \in \{0, 1, M\}$) to the rows $\{i_1, i_2, \ldots, i_q\}$ contain the same matrices with the same frequencies.
3. There is a *tracing algorithm Trace* such that the following holds: Take the information which is published by $t < k$ saboteurs (holding the shares $S = \{s_1, \ldots, s_t\}$) as the description of a Turing machine $\mathcal{A}$. If for $\mathcal{A}$ there is an integer u such that for all $U \subseteq \{1, \ldots, n\}$ with $|U| = u$ and $U \cap S = \emptyset$ there is a subset $S' = \{s'_1, \ldots, s'_{k-u}\} \subseteq S$ such that for all $B \in \mathcal{B}_{(\mathcal{C}_0 \cup \mathcal{C}_1 \cup \mathcal{C}_M)}(S)$

   $$\mathcal{A}(\text{Shares}_B(U)) = \text{Threshold\_Decision}_{\mathcal{C}_0, \mathcal{C}_1}(\text{OR}(s'_1, \ldots s'_{k-u}, \text{Shares}_B(U)))$$

   then the following is true:

   (a) (Protection against saboteurs)

   $$\sum_{B \in \mathcal{B}_M(S)} Pr\{B\} \cdot Pr\{Shares_B(\{r\}) \in S \Rightarrow \text{Trace}(\mathcal{A}, B) = r\} \geq 1 - \varepsilon$$

   (b) (Security for innocent share-holders)

   $$\sum_{B \in \mathcal{B}_M(S)} Pr\{B\} \cdot Pr\{Shares_B(\{r\}) \notin S \text{ and } \text{Trace}(\mathcal{A}, B) = r\} \leq \delta$$

The first condition of a traceable visual cryptography scheme guarantees that it is also a visual cryptography scheme. The second one ensures that a coalition of less than k share-holders cannot decide whether they have obtained their shares from a matrix corresponding to a white or a black pixels or even from a marking matrix. The third condition describes the traceability property. The motivation of the chosen formalization is as follows: For the attack scenario in [5] it is assumed that the saboteurs publish some information $\mathcal{A}$ which can be interpreted as the description of a Turing machine. Note that the information $\mathcal{A}$ does not necessarily consist of $v = \text{OR}(s_1, \ldots, s_t)$. For example, the saboteurs might somehow combine their t shares to some kind of information which corresponds to less than t shares. For any sufficiently large subset of share-holders U with $|U| = u$, those share-holders can use the published information $\mathcal{A}$ in combination with their shares to reveal the correct information about the shared pixel. The *correct* information about the shared pixel is the value which the share-holders get if they would obtain $k - u$ shares from the saboteurs. Property 3.(a) guarantees that a saboteur holding the marking row can be traced with high probability and 3.(b) ensures that it is very unlikely that an innocent share-holder will be found guilty.

Due to the space limitations, we refer to the original paper [5] for the actual construction of a traceable (k,n)-VCS with (ε, δ)-security based on visual cryptography schemes as well as the explanations of the traceable sharing of a picture.

6 Summary

In this paper we have presented a brief survey of the research done in respect to the new cryptographic paradigm of visual cryptography schemes which was first introduced by Naor and Shamir [9]. In [1, 2, 3, 4, 7, 8, 10], the original scheme is extended (e.g., for general access structures), new constructions are proposed and improved bounds on relevant system parameters are proven. In [5], a new approach is taken by introducing traceability for visual cryptography schemes.

References

1. Ateniese, G., Blundo, C., De Santis, A., and Stinson, D.R.: *Visual Cryptography for General Access Structures.* Information and Computation, Vol. 129, No. 2, pp. 86–106, 1996 and ECCC, Electronic Colloquium on Computational Complexity (TR96-012), 1996.
2. Ateniese, G., Blundo, C., De Santis, A., and Stinson, D.R.: *Constructions and Bounds for Visual Cryptography.* Proc. 23rd International Colloquium on Automata, Languages and Programming (ICALP '96), Springer Lecture Notes in Computer Science, pp. 416–428, 1996.
3. Ateniese, G., Blundo, C., De Santis, A., and Stinson, D.R.: *Extended Schemes for Visual Cryptography.* Preprint, 1995.
4. Ateniese, G., Blundo, C., De Santis, A., and Stinson, D.R.: *New Schemes for Visual Cryptography.* Preprint, 1996.
5. Biehl, I., and Wetzel, S.: *Traceable Visual Cryptography.* Proc. ICICS '97, Springer Lecture Notes on Computer Science, pp. 61–71, 1997.
6. Carter, J.L., and Wegman, M.N.: *Universal Classes of Hash Functions.* Journal of Computer and System Sciences 18, pp 143–154, 1979.
7. Droste, S.: *New Results on Visual Cryptography.* Proc. CRYPTO '96, Springer Lecture Notes in Computer Science, pp. 401–415, 1996.
8. Hofmeister, T., Krause, M., and Simon, H.U.: *Contrast-Optimal k out of n Secret Sharing Schemes in Visual Cryptography.* Proc. COCOON '97, Springer Lecture Notes in Computer Science, pp. 176–185, 1997.
9. Naor, M., and Shamir, A.: *Visual Cryptography.* Proc. EUROCRYPT '94, Springer Lecture Notes in Computer Science, pp. 1–12, 1995.
10. Naor, M., and Shamir, A.: *Visual Cryptography II: Improving the Contrast via the Cover Base.* Proc. Security Protocols: International Workshop 1996, Springer Lecture Notes in Computer Science, pp. 69–74, 1997.
11. Shamir, A.: *How to Share a Secret.* Comm. of the ACM, Vol. 22, pp. 612–613, 1979.
12. Wegman, M.N., and Carter, J.L.: *New Hash Functions and their Use in Authentication and Set Equality.* Journal of Computer and System Sciences 22, pp 265–279, 1981.

'Begriffliche Rückkopplung' zur Behandlung temporärer Verdeckungssituationen in der Bildfolgenauswertung von Straßenverkehrsszenen

Michael Haag[1] und Hans-Hellmut Nagel[1,2]

[1] Institut für Algorithmen und Kognitive Systeme, Fakultät für Informatik der Universität Karlsruhe (TH), Postfach 6980, D-76128 Karlsruhe, Germany
[2] Fraunhofer-Institut für Informations- und Datenverarbeitung (IITB), Fraunhoferstr. 1, D-76131 Karlsruhe, Germany, EPost: hhn@iitb.fhg.de

Zusammenfassung Ein Bildfolgenauswertungssystem zur Verfolgung sich bewegender Objekte in Straßenverkehrsszenen und zur begrifflichen Charakterisierung ihrer Verkehrssituation wird um die Behandlung zeitweise vollständig verdeckter Objekte ergänzt. Typische Verkehrssituationen werden hierzu begrifflich modelliert und unter Ausnutzung von automatisch extrahierten geometrischen Verfolgungsergebnissen schritthaltend ausgeprägt. Solch begriffliches Zusatzwissen gestattet die Erschließung von Zusammenhängen, die (etwa aufgrund vollständiger Verdeckungen) nicht explizit im Bild zu sehen sind. Begriffliches Wissen über typische Objektbewegungen in bestimmten Verkehrssituationen wird wieder auf die geometrische Auswertungsebene rückgekoppelt, um eine geometrische Zustandsschätzung auch während Phasen vollständiger Verdeckung plausibel fortschreiben zu können. Die so gewonnene rechnerinterne Repräsentation bildet den Ausgangspunkt für eine natürlichsprachliche Beschreibung der in einer Bildfolge erfaßten Geschehen.

1 Einleitung

Das Bildfolgenauswertungssystem Xtrack dient der Verfolgung bewegter Objekte in digitisierten Videoaufnahmen von Straßenverkehrsszenen und einer anschließenden begrifflichen Beschreibung der extrahierten Objektbewegungen. Bereitgestellte Grauwertbildfolgen sollen auch unter *verschiedenen* und *ungünstigen* Bedingungen mit einem *einheitlichen* Ansatz ausgewertet werden. Anstatt den Verfolgungsansatz oder seine Parameter an die jeweiligen Aufnahmebedingungen (Blickwinkel der Kamera auf die Szene, Größe der Objektabbilder, Schattenwurf, Kontrastverhältnisse, Verdeckungen) anzupassen, wird ein *modellgestützter* Ansatz realisiert. Der Vorteil besteht darin, daß veränderte Aufnahmebedingungen keine Modifikation des Ansatzes oder seiner Parameter erforderlich machen, sondern nur eine Erweiterung des eingesetzten Modellwissens.

Im Rahmen einer konsequenten Erweiterung des (bisher ausschließlich geometrischen) Modellwissens, wird in [4, 5] Wissen über den zeitlichen Verlauf von

Verkehrssituationen *begrifflich* modelliert. Eine robuste geometrische Auswertung von Objekttrajektorien bildet dabei eine wichtige Voraussetzung für eine automatische Ausprägung generisch beschriebener Situationsschemata. Die resultierenden begrifflichen Beschreibungen von Verkehrssituationen bilden ihrerseits wieder den Ausgangspunkt für eine sich anschließende Erzeugung *natürlichsprachlicher* Beschreibungen der aufgezeichneten Geschehnisse [1, 2].

In vorliegendem Beitrag wird jedoch die schrittweise Abstraktion geometrischer Auswertungsergebnisse nicht als „Einbahnstraße" von einer Bildfolge hin zu einer natürlichsprachlichen Beschreibung aufgefaßt. Vielmehr wird das auf begrifflicher Ebene zusätzlich zur Verfügung stehende Wissen für eine Rückkopplung auf die geometrische Auswertungsebene genutzt. Dies wird anhand einiger Beispiele von temporär vollständig oder fast vollständig verdeckten Fahrzeugen demonstriert (vgl. Abb. 1). Anstatt die Heuristik zu bemühen, daß ein Objekt seinen Bewegungszustand unmittelbar vor der Verdeckung für die gesamte Dauer der Verdeckung beibehält, werden mit Hilfe einer Situationsanalyse für das verdeckte Fahrzeug plausible Handlungen des Fahrers ermittelt. Solche zunächst begrifflich spezifizierten Handlungen, wie *hinter einem Fahrzeug anhalten*, werden dann in eine Aktualisierung der geometrischen Zustandsschätzung (z. B. Reduktion der geschätzten Fahrzeuggeschwindigkeit) umgesetzt.

Nur wenige Ansätze der uns bekannten Literatur beschäftigen sich mit der Verfolgung signifikant verdeckter Fahrzeuge (vgl. Literaturüberblick in [3]). So nutzen [8] eine spezielle Kameraperspektive aus, bei welcher (partiell verdeckte) Fahrzeuge mit zunehmender Entfernung von der Kamera in der Abbildung weiter oben erscheinen. [10] verfolgen Fahrzeuge im 2D–Bildbereich mit Hilfe von Differenzbildern und detektieren Bildregionen, in welchen Verdeckungen auftreten können. Ein Hintergrundmodell der Szene wird ständig aktualisiert. [11] verwenden räumlich–zeitliches Schließen, um gegebene, durch Verdeckungen unterbrochene Fahrzeugtrajektorien einem einzelnen Objekt zuzuordnen.

Während sich einige Ansätze mit der begrifflichen oder natürlichsprachlichen Beschreibung von Abläufen in Videosequenzen beschäftigen, gibt es nur wenige Beispiele für eine Rückkopplung des auf begrifflicher Ebene gewonnenen Wissens auf die signalnäheren Auswertungsebenen. [7] diskutieren den Unterschied zwischen dem passiven und aktiven Beobachten einer Szene, welcher sich in der Entwicklung zweier Systeme (*HIVIS–MONITOR* und *HIVIS–WATCHER*) manifestiert. Im ersten Fall wird eine datengetriebene Vorgehensweise realisiert. Es wird eine Datenbank mit sämtlichen erkannten Ereignissen aufgebaut, an welche a–posteriori Anfragen gestellt werden können. Das aktive System wird umgekehrt mit einer Anfrage gestartet und fokussiert seine Auswertung auf die für die Anfrage relevanten Aspekte. Begriffliches Wissen wird hingegen nicht zur Gewinnung von Aussagen über zeitweise nicht sichtbare Objekte genutzt.

Der umgekehrte Weg der graphischen Visualisierung einer begrifflichen Szenenbeschreibung wird in [9] beschritten. Die entstehenden synthetischen Bilder oder Bildfolgen werden mit der begrifflichen Beschreibung verglichen und erlauben insofern eine Bewertung der Angemessenheit der verwendeten Modelle.

Abb. 1. Oben: Halbbilder #1070 und #1071 der Bildfolge „Karl–Wilhelm–Straße“ (jedes Vollbild besteht aus zwei zeilenverschränkten Halbbildern). Der PKW, welcher von oben auf der linken Geradeausfahrspur fährt, muß hinter dem an der Kreuzung stehenden hellen Transporter anhalten. Währenddessen wird er von dem großen Wegweiserschild fast vollständig verdeckt. Unten: Halbbilder #2480 und #2481 der Rheinhafen–Bildfolge. Der von rechts hinter dem Abschleppwagen kommende PKW wird partiell durch eine Lichtzeichenanlage und durch Verkehrszeichen verdeckt. Anschließend wird er vollständig von dem gerade nach rechts abbiegenden hellen Transporter verdeckt.

Während sich die genannten Ansätze jeweils auf Teilaspekte konzentrieren, ist uns kein durchgängiges System bekannt, welches (1) unter *verschiedenen* Bedingungen aufgenommene *Realwelt*-Videoaufnahmen auswertet, (2) den Diskursbereich *umfassend* geometrisch *und* begrifflich modelliert, (3) begriffliche Schemata *automatisch* ausprägt und (4) das so gewonnene begriffliche Wissen wieder auf die geometrische Ebene *rückkoppelt.*

2 Geometrische Auswertung

Grundlage für eine automatische Ausprägung begrifflich spezifizierter Situationsschemata bildet eine geometrische Zustandsschätzung für alle relevanten Szenenobjekte. Während statische Szenenkomponenten, wie Fahrspuren, Masten oder Verkehrsschilder, explizit modelliert werden, wird der Bewegungszustand von sich bewegenden Fahrzeugen automatisch geschätzt. Eine solche geometrische Zustandsbeschreibung enthält für jeden Zeitpunkt die geschätzte (x, y)–Position eines Referenzpunktes des zu verfolgenden Fahrzeugs bezüglich der Fahrbahnebene, die geschätzte Orientierung θ der Fahrzeuglängsachse, die Fahrzeuggeschwindigkeit v sowie die zeitliche Änderungsrate $\dot{\theta}$ der Fahrzeugorientierung.

Eine initiale Schätzhypothese über einen Fahrzeugzustand wird durch eine bewegungsbasierte Segmentierung des Bildbereichs zu einem Initialisierungszeitpunkt gewonnen. Eine A–Priori–Schätzung wird dann mit Hilfe des in [6] beschriebenen Modellanpassungsverfahrens aktualisiert. Mittels einer Maximum–A–Posteriori (MAP) Schätzung wird eine Korrektur der Zustandsschätzung ermittelt, welche die Messungen im Bild am besten erklärt. Als Messung wird dabei eine Kombination von Kantenelementen (Bildpunkte mit einem lokalen Maximum des Gradientenbetrages in Gradientenrichtung) und Optischem–Fluß (scheinbare Verschiebungsgeschwindigkeit von Grauwertstrukturen im Bild) genutzt. Eine A–Priori–Zustandsschätzung für den Folgezeitpunkt wird mit Hilfe eines physikalischen Bewegungsmodells vorhergesagt. Die eingangs beschriebene automatische Initialisierung ist also für jedes zu verfolgende Objekt nur einmal durchzuführen.

Signifikante Verdeckungen von zu verfolgenden Fahrzeugen durch andere Szenenkomponenten führen zu Fehlanpassungen bei der Zustandsaktualisierung. Während kleinere partielle Verdeckungen, wie beispielsweise durch Masten, durch die robuste Kombination von Kantenelement– und Optischer–Flußanpassung i. a. toleriert werden, können großflächigere Verdeckungen zum Scheitern einer Verfolgung führen. *Statische* Szenenkomponenten, die signifikante Verdeckungen hervorrufen können, werden deshalb wie in [3] explizit modelliert. Bei der Aktualisierung gehen dann nur Messungen in die Modellanpassung ein, die tatsächlich zu Bildpunkten des Objektabbilds gehören.

Verdeckungen durch *bewegungsfähige* Szenenkomponenten werden automatisch berücksichtigt. Mit Hilfe einer Tiefenkarte wird zu jedem Zeitpunkt eine Bearbeitungsreihenfolge so ermittelt, daß zuerst der Zustand unverdeckter Objekte aktualisiert wird. Diese Schätzung wird bei der anschließenden Zustandsaktualisierung verdeckter Objekte berücksichtigt.

3 Begriffliche Rückkopplung

Wie in [4, 5] beschrieben, werden die von der geometrischen Auswertungsebene zu jedem Zeitpunkt und für jedes zu verfolgende Szenenobjekt ermittelten Zustandsbeschreibungen herangezogen, um begrifflich spezifizierte Situationsschemata automatisch auszuprägen. Jedes Schema enthält eine Handlungsanweisung, welche die in der betreffenden Situation vorgesehene Handlung des Fahrzeugführers beschreibt. In vorliegendem Beitrag werden solche Handlungsanweisungen als plausible Hypothesen über das Verhalten eines Fahrers während einer totalen Verdeckung des beobachteten Fahrzeugs verwendet.

Die Verkehrssituationen für das Überqueren einer Straßenkreuzung werden folgendermaßen modelliert: Eine allgemeine Kreuzungssituation wird spezialisiert in das Hinfahren, das Überfahren und das Verlassen der Kreuzung. Das Hinfahren selbst wird weiter unterteilt in ein Hinfahren hinter einem anderen Fahrzeug und das alleinige Zufahren auf eine Kreuzung. Im ersten Fall hängt das Verhalten des Fahrers des hinteren Fahrzeugs im wesentlichen vom voranfahrenden Fahrzeug ab: fährt dieses, so folgt man ihm, steht es dagegen, so nähert man sich dem Fahrzeug, hält hinter ihm an und wartet. Sobald das vordere Fahrzeug schließlich wieder losfährt, fährt das hintere ebenfalls an. Fährt man dagegen alleine auf eine Kreuzung zu, gibt es nur zwei Möglichkeiten: entweder man hält vor der Kreuzung an (weil die Lichtsignalanlage rot zeigt oder um Vorfahrt zu gewähren) oder man überquert die (freie) Kreuzung zügig.

Die genannten Situationstypen wurden gemäß dieser Überlegungen modelliert. Sobald von der geometrischen Auswertungsebene eine so signifikante Verdeckung des zu verfolgenden Fahrzeugs festgestellt wird, daß aufgrund fehlender Messungen keine geometrische Schätzaktualisierung mehr möglich ist, wird das in der gerade ausgeprägten Situationsbeschreibung spezifizierte Handlungsschema ausgeführt und damit die Zustandsschätzung für die Zeit der Verdeckung fortgeschrieben. Für die im nächsten Abschnitt gezeigten Ergebnisse wurden folgende Handlungsschemata implementiert:

sich_dem_vorderen_Fahrzeug_nähern: Das vordere Fahrzeug steht und der Fahrer des hinteren Fahrzeugs wird seine Geschwindigkeit so reduzieren, daß er kurz hinter dem anderen Fahrzeug zum Stehen kommt. Die hierzu erforderliche Geschwindigkeitsänderung wird aus der zuletzt geschätzten Eigengeschwindigkeit und dem Abstand zum vorderen Fahrzeug berechnet.

hinter_dem_vorderen_Fahrzeug_warten: Das Fahrzeug steht (Geschwindigkeit null).

hinter_dem_vorderen_Fahrzeug_anfahren: Das Fahrzeug beschleunigt. Dies wird durch eine gleichmäßige Beschleunigung von $1.25\frac{\mathrm{m}}{\mathrm{s}^2}$ modelliert.

Bei allen Handlungsschemata wird außerdem die Orientierungsänderung des Fahrzeugs so bestimmt, daß sich die Fahrzeuglängsachse parallel zur Richtung des gerade benutzten Fahrspursegments ausrichtet. Da der Fahrer selbst nur die Möglichkeit hat, den Bewegungszustand seines Fahrzeugs durch Beschleunigen bzw. Bremsen und durch Lenken zu beeinflussen, sind durch die implementierten Handlungsschemata auch nur die beiden Schätzgrößen v und $\dot{\theta}$ betroffen.

4 Ergebnisse

Der skizzierte Ansatz wird nun auf die Beispiele aus Abb. 1 angewendet. Das große Wegweiserschild in der Bildfolge „Karl–Wilhelm–Straße“ sowie die rechte Lichtzeichenanlage samt Verkehrsschilder der Rheinhafen–Bildfolge werden hierzu explizit modelliert, um die Verdeckung während der Verfolgung von Fahrzeugen berücksichtigen zu können. Die Abbildungen 2 und 3 zeigen für die hier betrachteten Beispiele jeweils die Modellanpassung des zu verfolgenden Objekts vor, während und nach der Verdeckung sowie den zeitlichen Verlauf des automatisch ermittelten Verdeckungsgrades. Die geometrische Zustandsaktualisierung wird ausgesetzt, sobald mindestens 80 Prozent des Fahrzeugabbilds verdeckt wird. In dieser Zeit erfolgt die Zustandsschätzung nicht mehr mit Hilfe einer MAP–Schätzung auf Basis von Messungen im Bildbereich, sondern durch Ausführung der für die erkannte Situation vorgegebenen Handlungsschemata.

Die Verfolgung des hellen Transporters der Bildfolge „Karl–Wilhelm–Straße“ wurde zum Halbbildzeitpunkt #50 initialisiert. Aufgrund seiner Größe wird er von dem Wegweiserschild nur zu höchstens 55 Prozent verdeckt (vgl. Abbildung 2 (b)), so daß er während seiner gesamten Fahrt mit Hilfe der in Abschnitt 2 beschriebenen geometrischen Zustandsaktualisierung verfolgt werden kann. Beginnend mit dem Halbbildzeitpunkt #1000 (während der Transporter bereits an der Kreuzung steht) wird das ins Bild fahrende Objekt 6 initialisiert. Bei diesem PKW treten am Wegweiserschild Verdeckungen von bis zu 97 Prozent auf (vgl. Abbildung 2 (b)), so daß eine geometrische Zustandsaktualisierung während der Verdeckungsphase nicht möglich ist. Obwohl der PKW während der Verdeckung praktisch nicht zu sehen ist, wird durch die begriffliche Rückkopplung erkannt, daß er sich dem Transporter nähert, anhält (Abbildung 2 (c))und wieder beschleunigt, sobald der helle Transporter anfährt (Abbildung 2 (d)). Abbildung 4 zeigt den geschätzten Geschwindigkeitsverlauf des PKW und des Transporters im Vergleich.

In der Rheinhafen–Bildfolge dürfte sich die Geschwindigkeit des PKW während der Verdeckung leicht reduzieren, da das Fahrzeug hinter einem vor der Kreuzung wartenden Abschleppwagen anhalten muß. Dies wird bei dem Ansatz mit begrifflicher Rückkopplung auch erkannt. Abb. 5 zeigt den gesamten geschätzten Geschwindigkeitsverlauf für beide Fahrzeuge.

5 Diskussion

In diesem Beitrag ist es gelungen, explizit modelliertes begriffliches Wissen über den Verlauf von Verkehrssituationen zu nutzen, um plausible Hypothesen über Fahrzeugbewegungen während vollständiger Verdeckungen auf die geometrische Zustandsschätzung rückzukoppeln. Erst eine umfassende geometrische und begriffliche Modellierung des Diskursbereiches sowie eine robuste geometrische Verfolgung von Fahrzeugbewegungen ermöglicht das Schlußfolgern auf einem begrifflichen Niveau. Kurze Phasen vollständiger Verdeckung lassen sich zwar in vielen Fällen auch durch die Heuristik eines konstanten Fortschreibens des Zustands

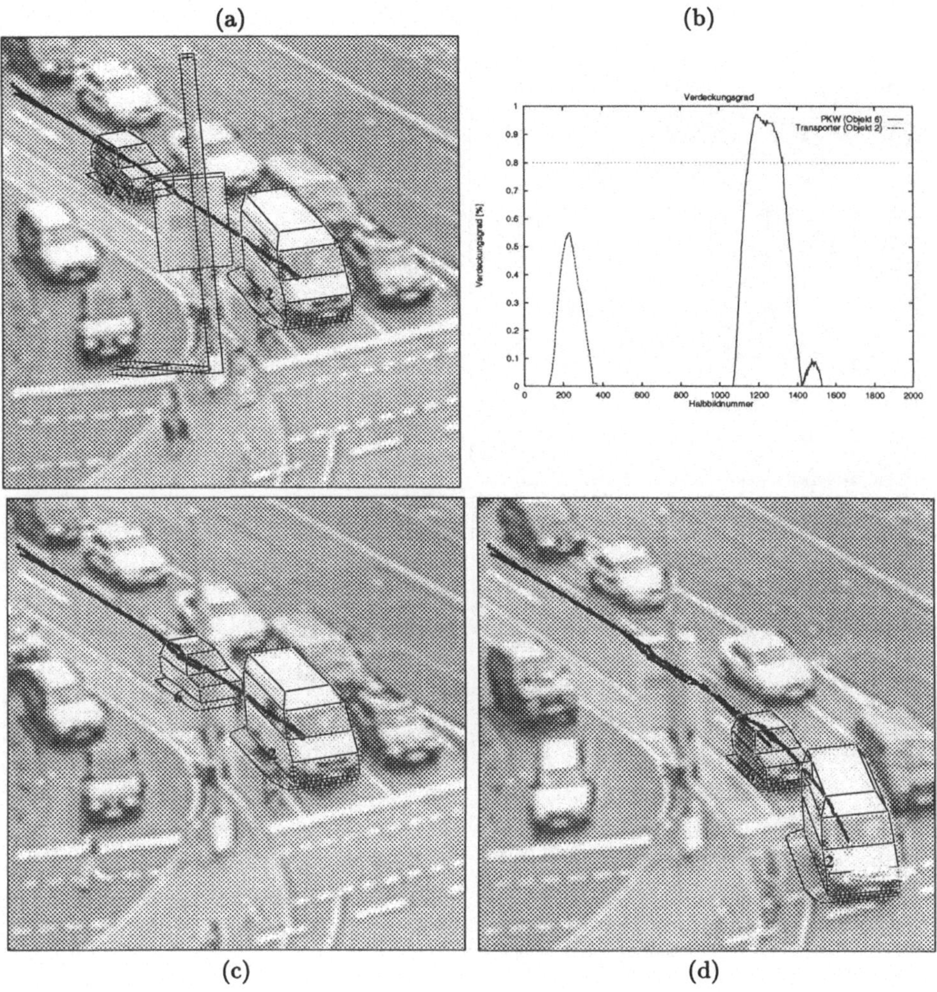

Abb. 2. (a) Modellüberlagerung aufgrund der automatischen Zustandsschätzung für den PKW und den hellen Transporter zum Halbbildzeitpunkt #1080 (vor der totalen Verdeckung) sowie Überlagerung des Wegweisermodells. (b) Geschätzter zeitlicher Verlauf des Verdeckungsgrades (Anteil der verdeckten Bildpunkte am gesamten Fahrzeugabbild) für beide Objekte. Ab einem Verdeckungsgrad von 0.8 wird die geometrische Schätzaktualisierung ausgesetzt. Der PKW wird im Zeitintervall #1065–#1420 vom Wegweiserschild verdeckt. Anschließend tritt bis zum Zeitpunkt #1529 eine leichte Verdeckung durch den abbiegenden Transporter auf. (c) Modellüberlagerung zum Halbbildzeitpunkt #1200 während der Verdeckung des PKWs. Das Anhalten des PKWs hinter dem an der Kreuzung stehenden Transporter wurde mit Hilfe der begrifflichen Rückkopplung richtig erkannt. (d) Modellüberlagerung zum Halbbildzeitpunkt #1450 nach Auflösung der Verdeckung. Das Anfahren des PKWs hinter dem anfahrenden Transporter wurde erkannt. Nach Abnahme des Verdeckungsgrads des PKWs erfolgt die Zustandsschätzung wieder auf Basis von Messungen.

Abb. 3. (a) Modellüberlagerung für drei verfolgte Fahrzeuge zum Halbbildzeitpunkt #2500 sowie für die modellierten Verkehrszeichen. (b) Geschätzter zeitlicher Verlauf des Verdeckungsgrades für den PKW. Dieser wird zu Beginn nur von den Verkehrszeichen und kurz darauf von dem hellen abbiegenden Transporter vollständig verdeckt. Anschließend wird er wieder nur von den modellierten Verkehrszeichen verdeckt, bis er schließlich hinter dem Abschleppwagen anfährt, um die Kreuzung zu überqueren (vgl. Abb. 5). (c) Modellüberlagerung für den PKW zum Halbbildzeitpunkt #2590, *nach* Auflösung einer vollständigen Verdeckung durch den hellen Transporter. Die geschätzte Geschwindigkeit und Orientierungsänderung wurden während der Verdeckung konstant fortgeschrieben. (d) Modellüberlagerung nach begrifflicher Rückkopplung während der Verdeckung. Zwischen den Ergebnissen in (c) und (d) sind kaum Unterschiede festzustellen.

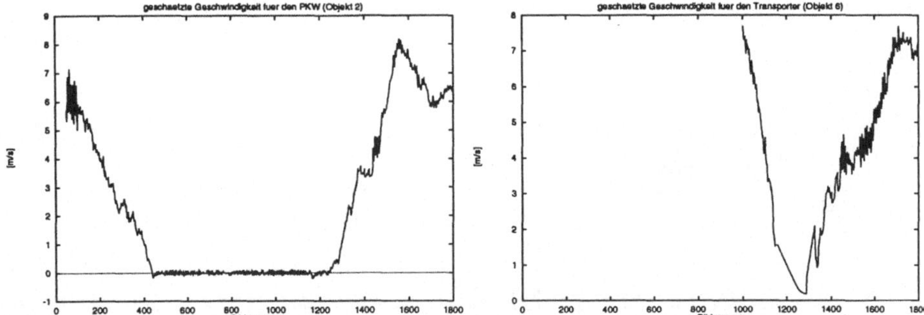

Abb. 4. Vergleich der geschätzten Geschwindigkeit des Transporters (links) und des PKWs (rechts) aus der Bildfolge „Karl–Wilhelm–Straße“. Während der totalen Verdeckung des PKWs wird die Geschwindigkeit bis zum Stehen reduziert. Nach dem Anfahren des Transporters wird vom System eine Beschleunigung des PKWs angenommen.

überbrücken (vgl. das Beispiel der Rheinhafen–Sequenz). Eine begriffliche Rückkopplung liefert jedoch eine plausiblere Fortsetzung der Zustandsschätzung auch in nicht–trivialen Fällen, wenn sich etwa der Bewegungszustand des Fahrzeugs während der Verdeckungsphase ändert (Beispiel „Karl–Wilhelm–Straße“) und dies aus der sichtbaren Umgebung erschlossen werden kann. Ferner dienen die ausgeprägten begrifflichen Schemata als Ausgangspunkt für eine sich anschließende natürlichsprachliche Beschreibung der auftretenden Geschehen [2].

Literatur

1. R. Gerber und H.–H. Nagel: *Berechnung natürlichsprachlicher Beschreibungen von Straßenverkehrsszenen aus Bildfolgen unter Verwendung von Geschehens– und Verdeckungsmodellierung.* In B. Jähne, P. Geißler, H. Haußecker und F. Hering (Hrsg.), Mustererkennung 1996, 18. DAGM–Symposium, Heidelberg/Germany, 11.–13. September 1996, Springer–Verlag Berlin, Heidelberg 1996, pp. 601–608.
2. R. Gerber and H.–H. Nagel: *(Mis?)–Using DRT for Generation of Natural Language Text from Image Sequences.* Proc. Fifth European Conference on Computer Vision (ECCV'98), Freiburg/Germany, 2–6 June 1998; H. Burkhardt and B. Neumann (Eds.), Lecture Notes in Computer Science **1407**, Springer–Verlag Berlin, Heidelberg 1998, pp. 255–270.
3. M. Haag, Th. Frank, H. Kollnig, and H.–H. Nagel: *Influence of an Explicitly Modelled 3D Scene on the Tracking of Partially Occluded Vehicles.* Computer Vision and Image Understanding **65**:2 (1997) 206-225.
4. M. Haag, W. Theilmann, K. Schäfer, and H.–H. Nagel: *Integration of Image Sequence Evaluation and Fuzzy Metric Temporal Logic Programming.* KI–97: Advances in Artificial Intelligence, 21st Annual German Conference on Artificial Intelligence, Freiburg/Germany, 9–12 September 1997, G. Brewka, Ch. Habel, and B. Nebel (Eds.), Lecture Notes in Artificial Intelligence **1303**, Springer–Verlag Berlin a. o. 1997, pp. 301–312.

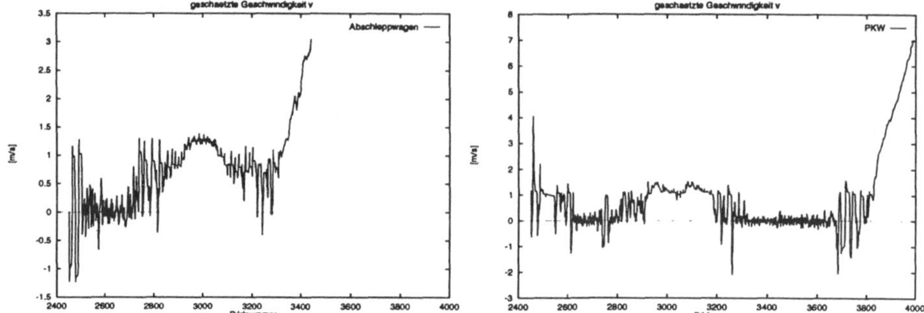

Abb. 5. Gesamter geschätzter Geschwindigkeitsverlauf für den Abschleppwagen (links) und den PKW (rechts) der Rheinhafen–Sequenz. Der Abschleppwagen steht zu Beginn an der Kreuzung, der PKW hält hinter ihm an. Etwa ab Halbbild #2800 ziehen beide Fahrzeuge zur Kreuzung vor. Der Abschleppwagen bewegt sich anschließend über die Kreuzung, bis er den Bildbereich etwa in Halbbild #3500 verläßt. Der PKW hält abermals an, um ein vorfahrtsberechtigtes Fahrzeug passieren zu lassen, und fährt erst ab ca. Halbbild #3800 über die Kreuzung.

5. M. Haag and H.–H. Nagel: *Incremental Recognition of Traffic Situations from Video Image Sequences.* Proc. ICCV'98 Workshop on Conceptual Descr. of Images (CDI-98), 2 January 1998, Bombay/India, H. Buxton and A. Mukerjee (Eds.), pp. 1–20.
6. M. Haag and H.–H. Nagel: *Beginning a Transition from a Local to a More Global Point of View in Model-Based Vehicle Tracking.* Proc. Fifth European Conference on Computer Vision (ECCV'98), Freiburg/Germany, 2–6 June 1998; H. Burkhardt and B. Neumann (Eds.), Lecture Notes in Computer Science **1406**, Springer–Verlag Berlin, Heidelberg 1998, pp. 812–827.
7. R.J. Howarth and H. Buxton: *Conceptual Descriptions from Monitoring and Watching Image Sequences.* Proc. ICCV'98 Workshop on Conceptual Descriptions of Images (CDI-98), 2 January 1998, Bombay/India, H. Buxton and A. Mukerjee (Eds.), pp. 21–38.
8. T. Huang, D. Koller, J. Malik, G. Ogasawara, B. Rao, S. Russell, and J. Weber: *Automatic Symbolic Traffic Scene Analysis Using Belief Networks.* Proc. 12th National Conf. on Artificial Intelligence, Seattle/WA, 31 July – 4 August 1994, pp. 966–972.
9. A. Mukerjee, K. Gupta, S. Nautiyal, M.P. Singh, and N. Mishra: *Conceptual Description of Visual Scenes from Linguistic Models.* Proc. ICCV'98 Workshop on Conceptual Descriptions of Images (CDI-98), 2 January 1998, Bombay/India, H. Buxton and A. Mukerjee (Eds.), pp. 83–96.
10. M.K. Teal and T.J. Ellis: *Spatial–Temporal Reasoning Based on Object Motion.* Proc. 7th British Machine Vision Conference (BMVC'96), 9–12 September 1996, Edinburgh/UK, R.B. Fisher and E. Trucco (Eds.), Vol. **2** (ISBN 0 9521898 5 2) 1996, pp. 465–474.
11. A.F. Toal and H. Buxton: *Spatio–Temporal Reasoning within a Traffic Surveillance System.* Proc. Second European Conference on Computer Vision 1992 (ECCV'92), 18–23 May 1992, S. Margherita/Italy, G. Sandini (Eds.), Lecture Notes in Computer Science **588**, Springer–Verlag Berlin, Heidelberg 1992, pp. 884–892.

Verwendung von Bildern zur Exploration und Analyse großer Datenmengen

Daniel A. Keim
Institut für Informatik, Martin-Luther-Universität Halle-Wittenberg
Kurt-Mothes-Str. 1, 06120 Halle (Saale)
keim@informatik.uni-halle.de

Durch den rasanten technologischen Fortschritt steigt die Menge an Daten, die in heutigen Computersystemen gespeichert ist, sehr schnell an. Damit wird die Suche nach interessanter Information innerhalb der Datenbestände immer schwieriger. In diesem Beitrag wird ein neuer Ansatz zur Datenexploration und -analyse vorgestellt, der auf neuartigen Visualisierungstechniken basiert und für die Exploration und Analyse sehr großer Datenbanken entwickelt wurde. Die prinzipielle Idee dabei ist die gleichzeitige Darstellung möglichst vieler Datenobjekte am Bildschirm, wobei jeder Datenwert durch ein Pixel des Bildschirms repräsentiert wird.

1 Einleitung

Bei Entscheidungen ist es wichtig, im richtigen Augenblick die richtigen Informationen zur Hand zu haben. Durch den rasanten technologischen Fortschritt steigt die Menge an Daten, die in gespeicherter Form verfügbar und für die Entscheidungsfindung potentiell von Bedeutung ist, sehr schnell an. Nach neuesten Schätzungen verdoppelt sich die Menge an Daten, die weltweit vorhanden ist, alle 20 Monate. Eine Ursache für die ständig ansteigenden Datenmengen ist die Automatisierung fast aller Vorgänge in Wirtschaft, Wissenschaft und Verwaltung. In der heutigen Zeit werden selbst einfache Vorgänge wie das Bezahlen mit Kreditkarte oder das Telefonieren durch Computer erfaßt. Versuchsreihen in Physik, Chemie und Medizin erzeugen große Mengen an Daten, die zumeist automatisch mit Hilfe von Sensoren gesammelt werden. Beobachtungssatelliten werden schon bald täglich Datenmengen im Terabytebereich (1 TeraByte = 10^{12} Bytes) sammeln und zur Erde übermitteln. Die gesammelten Daten gleichen Heuhaufen, in denen die Stecknadeln wichtiger Informationen versteckt sind. Die großen Mengen gespeicherter Daten stellen eine wichtige Informationsressource dar; es ist in den meisten Fällen aber recht schwer, die relevanten Informationen zu finden.

Die Speicherung großer Datenmengen erfolgt in der Regel mit Hilfe von Datenbanksystemen. Heute verfügbare Datenbanksysteme unterstützen den Benutzer bei der Speicherung und Verwaltung der Daten sowie bei der Suche nach exakt spezifizierten Daten. Sie sind im allgemeinen aber ungeeignet, um die unexakt spezifizierte Suche nach interessanten Zusammenhängen, den sogenannte 'Data Mining'-Prozeß, zu unterstützen. Zum 'Data Mining' (Datenexploration und -analyse) verwendet man Techniken aus den Bereichen multivariate Statistik (z.B. die Hauptkomponenten-, Faktor- und Cluster-Analyse), Soft-Computing (Neuronale-Netze, Fuzzy-Systeme), Knowledge Discovery sowie Information Retrieval. Die in diesen Bereichen entwickelten Techniken eignen sich im allgemeinen nur eingeschränkt für die Datenexploration und -analyse von großen

Datenbanken mit Hunderttausenden oder sogar Millionen von Datensätzen. Erste Ergebnisse bei der Anwendung dieser Techniken auf großen Datenmengen zeigen, daß die Nutzung der Fähigkeiten des Computers allein nicht ausreicht, um überzeugende Ergebnisse zu erzielen.

Eine effektive Unterstützung von Datenexploration und -analyse großer Datenmengen ist derzeit nur unter Einbeziehung des Menschen und seiner Fähigkeiten möglich. Insbesondere seine unübertroffenen Fähigkeiten der Wahrnehmung erlauben es dem Menschen, in kürzester Zeit komplexe Sachverhalte zu analysieren, wichtige Informationen zu erkennen und Entscheidungen zu treffen. Das menschliche Wahrnehmungssystem kann flexibel die verschiedensten Arten von Daten verarbeiten, wobei es intuitiv ungewöhnliche Eigenschaften erkennt, bekannte Eigenschaften dagegen ignoriert. Menschen können leichter und besser mit vagen Beschreibungen und unscharfem Wissen umgehen als heutige Systeme, und ihr Allgemeinwissen erlaubt es ihnen, ohne große Anstrengung komplexe Schlußfolgerungen zu ziehen.

Das Ziel unseres Ansatzes der Datenexploration und -analyse ist es deshalb, den Menschen in den 'Data Mining'-Prozeß mit einzubeziehen und seine Fähigkeiten auf die großen, in heutigen Computersystemen verfügbaren Datenbestände anzuwenden. Da weder Mensch noch Computer allein das Problem der Datenexploration sehr großer Datenbanken lösen kann, ist eine möglichst enge Kooperation zwischen Mensch und Computer erforderlich. Es gilt, die immense Speicherkapazität und Rechenleistung heutiger Computer mit Intuition, Flexibilität, Kreativität und Allgemeinwissen des Menschen zu vereinen. Dabei ist die Entwicklung von Techniken wichtig, die den Menschen nicht einfach mit Daten überhäufen, sondern einen guten Überblick über die wesentlichen Daten ermöglichen.

Unser Ansatz zur Datenexploration und -analyse großer Datenmengen basiert auf neuartigen Visualisierungstechniken für multidimensionale Daten. Die prinzipielle Idee ist die gleichzeitige Darstellung möglichst vieler Datenwerte am Bildschirm, wobei jeder Datenwert durch ein Pixel des Bildschirms repräsentiert wird. Die Farbe des Pixels entspricht jeweils einem Datenwert (bzw. der Distanz zwischen Datenwert und Anfragewert bei anfrageabhängiger Visualisierung). Die Anordnung der Pixel hängt von der gewählten Visualisierungstechnik ab und ist entweder durch eine vorgegebene Sortierung der Daten oder durch die Gesamtdistanz der Datensätze in Bezug auf die Anfrage gegeben. Durch ein graphisches Benutzerinterface kann der Benutzer seine Anfragen schrittweise ändern, wobei er durch das visuelle Feedback, das er bei Änderungen bekommt, in der Verfeinerung seiner Anfragen unterstützt wird.

Bei unseren Betrachtungen gehen wir zunächst von einer einfachen Strukturierung der Daten, dem relationalen Datenmodell, aus. Eine einfache relationale Datenbank (z.B. eine Personendatenbank) kann man sich als eine große Tabelle vorstellen, in der die Zeilen den Datensätzen (Personen) entsprechen und die Spalten spezielle Eigenschaften der Datensätze angeben (für Personen z.B. Name, Geburtsdatum, Alter, etc.). In unserem Kontext werden die Spalten auch als Attribute der Datensätze bezeichnet.

2 Visualisierungstechniken multidimensionaler Daten

In vielen Bereichen von Forschung und Industrie werden Visualisierungen von geographischen bzw. geometrischen Daten, die eine inhärente zwei- oder drei-dimensionale

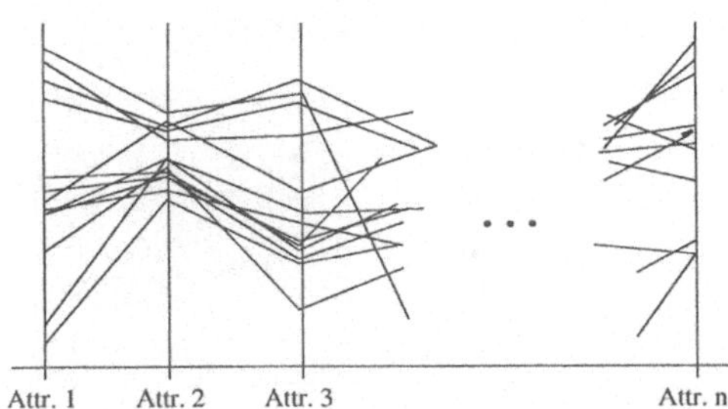

Abb. 1: Visualisierung von multidimensionalen Daten durch die Technik der parallelen Koordinaten - Die vertikalen Achsen entsprechen den Attributen und sind vom Minimum- bis zum Maximumwert der Attribute linear skaliert. Jeder Datensatz wird als polygonale Linie dargestellt, die jede Achse an dem Punkt schneidet, dessen Wert dem jeweiligen Attribut entspricht.

Semantik haben, verwendet. Eine Übersicht über solche Techniken ist beispielsweise in den bekannten Büchern von Edward R. Tufte [1] zu finden. Bis vor kurzem gab es jedoch nur wenige Techniken, die eine Visualisierung multidimensionaler Daten ohne inhärente zwei- oder drei-dimensionale Semantik erlauben. Erste Ansätze sind beispielsweise Matrizen von X-Y-Diagrammen [2] [3] oder die Chernoff'sche Gesichter-Darstellung [4]. Durch die zunehmende Verfügbarkeit von Grafik-Workstations mit hoher Rechenleistung wurden in den letzten Jahren zahlreiche neue Visualisierungstechniken entwickelt. Um einen Einblick in das Gebiet der Visualisierung multidimensionaler Daten zu geben, sollen im folgenden beispielhaft einige Techniken, die für die Visualisierung großer Datenmengen geeignet sind, vorgestellt werden.

2.1 Geometrische Projektionen

Das Ziel geometrischer Projektionstechniken ist es, aussagekräftige Projektionen multidimensionaler Daten zu finden. Die Klasse der geometrischen Projektionen umfaßt Techniken zur Dimensionsreduzierung wie z.B. Hauptkomponenten-Analyse [5], Faktor-Analyse [6] und multidimensionales Skalieren [7], sowie eine Reihe von Techniken, die unter dem Begriff 'projection pursuit' zusammengefaßt werden [8]. Da die Anzahl der Möglichkeiten, multidimensionale Daten mit hoher Dimension auf zwei Dimensionen abzubilden, sehr groß ist, versuchen 'projection pursuit'-Systeme (z.B. das Grand Tour System [9]), automatisch aussagekräftige Projektionen zu finden oder wenigstens den Benutzer bei der Suche nach geeigneten Projektionen zu unterstützen.

Eine andere geometrische Projektionstechnik ist die Technik der Parallelen Koordinaten (parallel coordinates) [10]. Diese Technik stellt den k-dimensionalen Raum mit Hilfe von k äquidistanten Achsen dar, die parallel zu einer der Bildschirmachsen liegen. Die Achsen entsprechen den Dimensionen und sind vom Minimum- bis zum Maximumwert der Dimensionen linear skaliert. Jeder Datensatz wird als polygonale Linie dargestellt, die jede Achse an dem Punkt schneidet, dessen Wert der jeweiligen Dimension entspricht (vgl. Abbildung 1). Obwohl die Grundidee der 'Parallelen Koordinaten'-Technik einfach ist, ermöglicht sie das Erkennen eines weiten Spektrums von Datencharakteristika, wie z.B. verschiedene Datenverteilungen und funktionale Abhängigkeiten. Wegen der Überlappungen der Linien ist jedoch die Anzahl der Datensätze, die gleichzeitig visuell darstellbar ist, auf ca. 1.000 begrenzt.

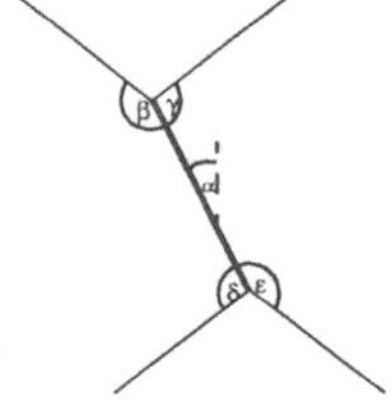

a. Strichmännchen

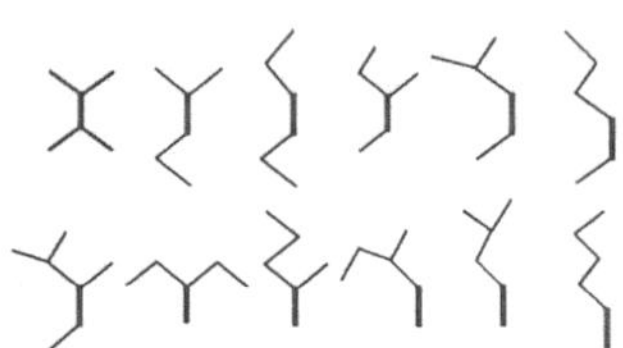

b. Eine Familie von Strichmännchen

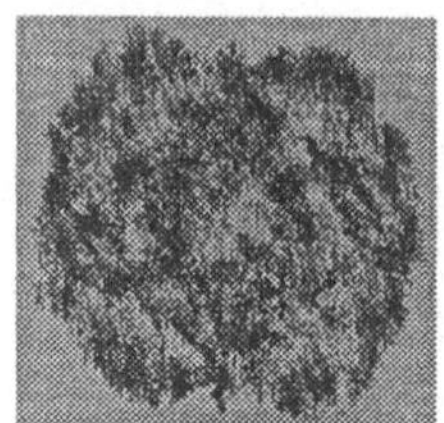

c. Visualisierung von achtdimensionalen Oberflächendaten von Molekülen

Abb. 2: Visualisierung von multidimensionalen Daten durch die 'Strichmännchen-Technik' - Die Winkel und Längen der Arme und Beine eines Strichmännchens entsprechen den Attributswerten eines Datensatzes.

2.2 Pixeldiagramme (Iconic Displays)

Eine andere Technik zur visuellen Darstellung multidimensionaler Daten sind Pixeldiagramme (iconic displays), bei denen jedes multidimensionale Datenelement durch ein Icon dargestellt wird. Erste Ansätze der 'iconic display' Technik sind die bereits erwähnten Chernoff'schen Gesichter [4] [11], bei denen zwei Dimensionen durch die zwei Bildschirmdimensionen und die restlichen Dimensionen durch Merkmale des Gesichts (Form von Nase, Mund, Augen und des Gesichts selbst) dargestellt werden. Die Chernoff'sche Visualisierungstechnik basiert auf der Fähigkeit des Menschen, Gesichter bzw. Gesichtszüge zu unterscheiden.

Eine weitere bekannte Pixeldiagramm-Visualisierungstechnik ist die sog. Strichmännchen (stick figure)-Technik [12]. Wie der Name bereits sagt, sind die verwendeten Icons eine Art Strichmännchen, wobei die Winkel und Strichlängen die Datendimensionen repräsentieren (vgl. Abbildung 2a). Wenn die Datensätze im Bezug auf die Bildschirmdimensionen verhältnismäßig dicht beieinander liegen, zeigt die resultierende Visualisierung Strukturmuster, die gemäß der Datencharakteristika variieren. Als Strichmännchen können verschiedene Icons mit unterschiedlicher Dimensionalität verwendet werden (vgl. Abbildung 2b). In Abbildung 2c ist eine Visualisierung von achtdimensionalen Oberflächendaten von Molekülen dargestellt, die mit Hilfe der Strichmännchen-Technik generiert wurde. Deutlich erkennbar in der Visualisierung ist eine markante Stelle in der Mitte des Moleküls. Diese Stelle ist eine Einbuchtung, die für das sogenannte Docking von Molekülen von besonderer Bedeutung ist. An dieser Stelle sei angemerkt, daß sowohl bei der Strichmännchen-Technik als auch bei den Chernoff'schen Gesichtern die Anzahl der gleichzeitig darstellbaren Dimensionen begrenzt ist.

Anders ist dies bei der sog. 'shape coding' Technik [13]. Bei der 'shape coding' Technik wird jeder Dimension ein kleines Pixel-Array zugeordnet, wobei die Farbe bzw. Graustufe der Pixel dem Wert der Dimension entspricht. Die Pixel-Arrays, die zu den Dimensionen eines Datensatzes gehören, werden dann nacheinander in einem kleinen Quadrat oder Rechteck angeordnet. Die kleinen Quadrate oder Rechtecke, die den Datensätzen entsprechen, werden zeilenweise angeordnet.

2.3 Sonstige Techniken

Neben den Geometrischen Projektionen und Pixeldiagrammen gibt es noch eine Reihe weiterer Visualisierungstechniken, die an dieser Stelle aus Platzgründen nicht weiter er-

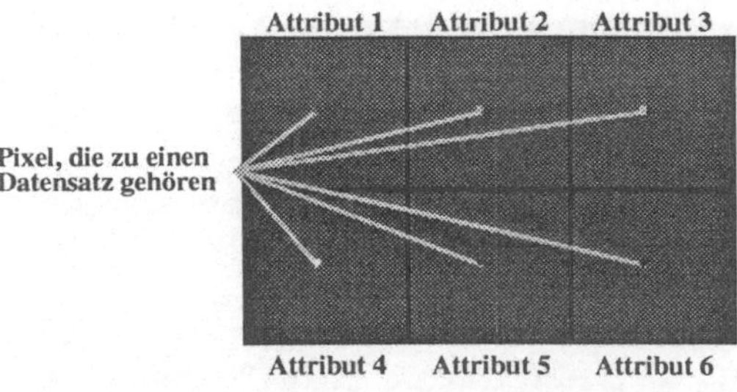

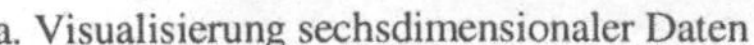

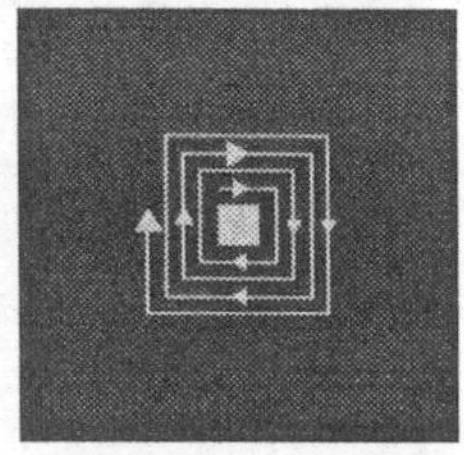

a. Visualisierung sechsdimensionaler Daten

b. Spiralanordnung eines Attributs

Abb. 3: Pixel-orientierte Visualisierungstechniken - Jedes Pixel entspricht einem Attributswert. Die Pixel sind attributweise gruppiert, d.h. ein Datensatz besteht aus je einem Pixel in jedem der Attributbereiche. Innerhalb der Attributbereiche sind verschiedene Anordnungen möglich. Bei der Spiraltechnik ist es eine spiralförmige Anordnung um den Mittelpunkt.

läutert werden können. Dazu gehören beispielsweise hierarchische Techniken [14] [15], Graph-basierte Techniken [16] [17] sowie Verzerrungstechniken (Distortion Techniques) [18] [19]. Von großer Wichtigkeit bei der Datenexploration sind ferner Interaktionstechniken wie z.B. 'Interactive Linking and Brushing' [20], 'Interactive Zooming' [21], 'Interactive Data-to-Visualization-Mappings' [22], oder 'Interactive Drill Down'. Für einen ausführlichen Überblick über diese Techniken sei auf ein Tutorial zum Thema Datenbanken und Visualisierung [23] verwiesen.

3 Pixel-orientierte Visualisierungstechniken

In den bisher vorgeschlagenen und im letzten Abschnitt vorgestellten Visualisierungstechniken für multidimensionale Daten ist die Anzahl der gleichzeitig am Bildschirm darstellbaren Datensätze auf maximal 100 bis 1.000 begrenzt. Im folgenden sollen einige neue Visualisierungstechniken, die sich auch für sehr große Datenmengen (bis 1.000.000 Datensätze) eignen, vorgestellt werden.

Bei den pixel-orientierten Visualisierungstechniken wird jeder Datenwert durch ein farbiges Pixel dargestellt. Die Pixel für die einzelnen Attribute werden in separaten Fenstern repräsentiert (vgl. Abbildung 3a). Eine wichtige Frage ist, wie die Pixel, die einem Attribut entsprechen, innerhalb des Fensters angeordnet werden. Eine einfache Anordnung ist beispielsweise eine einfache zeilen- oder spaltenweise Anordnung. Eine solche Anordnung führt in der Regel zu wenig aussagekräftigen Visualisierungen. Bei unserer 'Recursive Pattern' Visualisierungstechnik verwenden wir deshalb eine strukturierte Anordnung, die vom Benutzer gemäß der Semantik der Daten über die Parameter (h_i, w_i) wählbar ist. Die Anordnung ist eine rekursive Verallgemeinerung zeilen- und spaltenorientierter Anordnungen. Die Parameter (h_i, w_i) geben dabei die Höhe (h_i) und Breite (w_i) der Pixelmuster auf der Rekursionsebene i in Pixeln an. Die Anordnung erfolgt dann nach folgendem Algorithmus. Auf der ersten Rekursionsebene werden h_1-mal w_1 Pixel abwechselnd von links nach rechts und von rechts nach links angeordnet. Das entstehende Pixelmuster sei ein *Ebene1*-Pixelmuster. Auf den nächsten Rekursionsebenen werden die *(Ebene-1)*-Pixelmuster wieder gemäß dem gleichen Schema angeordnet. Sei w_i die Anzahl der Pixelmuster, die auf Rekursionsebene i in links-rechts Richtung an-

Abb. 4: 'Rercusive Pattern' Visualisierung der täglichen Aktienkurse des FAZ Index für den Zeitraum Januar '74 bis April '95 (insgesamt 532.900 Datenwerte).

geordnet werden sollen und h_i die Anzahl der Zeilen auf Rekursionsebene i. Auf jeder Rekursionebene werden w_i *(Ebene-1)*-Pixelmuster h_i-mal abwechselnd von links nach rechts und von rechts nach links angeordnet. Die w_i und h_i müssen vom Benutzer vorgegeben werden.

Das Beispiel in Abbildung 4 zeigt eine 'Recursive Pattern' Visualisierung der täglichen Aktienkurse des Frankfurter Aktien Indexes von Januar 1994 bis April 1995, was insgesamt 532900 Datenwerten entspricht. Die gewählten Parameterwerte für w_i und h_i sind $(w_1, h_1) = (1, 22)$ und $(w_2, h_2) = (243, 1)$. Eine Spalte mit 22 Pixel entspricht dabei ungefähr einem Monat. Die Farbkodierung der Datenwerte bildet hohe Datenwerte auf helle Farben und niedrige Werte auf dunkle Farben ab. Das Farbspektrum durchläuft die Farben gelb, hellgrün, blau, rot bis dunkelbraun. Die Visualisierung in Abbildung 4 erlaubt eine Reihe interessanter Beobachtungen, die an dieser Stelle nur angedeutet werden können. Interessant sind beispielsweise die ähnlichen Entwicklungen der Aktienkurse bei der ersten, vierten, achten, zehnten und fünfzehnten Aktie in der vierten Spalte (Südzucker, Thyssen, Veba, Volkswagen, Bayr. Hypobank). Bemerkenswert ist dabei insbesondere, daß es sich um Firmen handelt, die in völlig unterschiedlichen Branchen arbeiten. Eine weitere interessante Beobachtung ist, daß in mehr als 50% der Fälle ein heller grüner Streifen an ungefähr der gleichen Position zu sehen ist. Der grüne Streifen bedeutet eine allgemeine Phase besonders hoher Aktienkurse, wie sie etwa im Frühjahr 1990 zu beobachten war. Aus der Visualisierung kann man nun leicht ablesen, daß sich viele Aktien nicht mehr vollständig von dem Einbruch der Aktienkurse erholen konnten der auf die Phase der hohen Aktienkurse folgte. Ebenso leicht sind die Aktien zu identifizieren, die sich gegen den allgemeinen Trend entwickelt haben. Beispiele dafür sind die elfte und neunzehnte Aktie in der ersten Spalte (Daimler-Benz, DYWIDAG), die

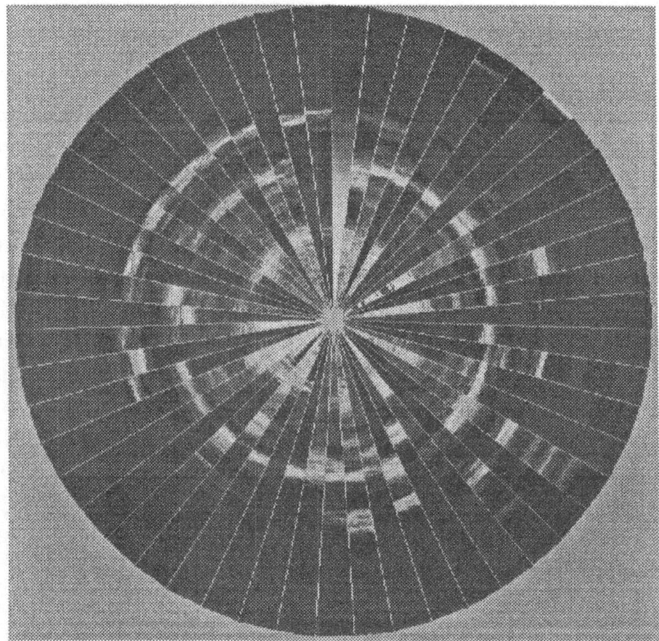

Abb. 5: 'Circle Segments' Visualisierung der täglichen Aktienkurse des FAZ Index für den Zeitraum Januar '74 bis April '95.

beide in den letzten Jahren keinen größeren Kursanstieg mehr verzeichnen konnten. Weitere Details der 'Recursive Pattern' Technik sind in [24] zu finden.

In Abbildung 5 ist eine weitere pixel-orientierte Visualisierungstechnik, die sogenannte 'Circle Segments' Visualisierungstechnik dargestellt. Im Gegensatz zur 'Recursive Pattern' Visualisierungstechnik sind die Dimensionen bei der 'Circle Segments' Technik als Segmente eines Kreises angeordnet. Die Pixel werden der Reihe nach senkrecht zur Winkelhalbierenden der Segmente angeordnet. Vorteil im Vergleich zur 'Recursive Pattern' ist, daß die Dimensionen leichter miteinander verglichen werden können. Die Details zur effizienten Berechnung der 'Circle Segments' Visualisierungen sind in [25] zu finden.

4 Anfrageabhängige Visualisierungstechniken

Neben einer statischen Visualisierung der Daten ist es beim 'Data Mining' aber auch wichtig, die Daten in Abhängigkeit von einer gestellten Anfrage zu visualisieren. Im folgenden werden wir eine anfrageabhängige Visualisierungstechnik, die sogenannte Spiraltechnik, vorstellen. Um diese Technik beschreiben zu können, betrachten wir die Relationen einer relationalen Datenbank als Mengen von Tupeln (Vektoren) der Form $(a_1, a_2,..., a_k)$, wobei $a_1, a_2,..., a_k$ die Attributswerte eines Datensatzes darstellen. Anfragen an relationale Datenbanken können als Anfrageregion(en) im k-dimensionalen Raum, der durch die k Attribute einer Relation aufgespannt wird, verstanden werden. Alle Datensätze, die innerhalb der Anfrageregion(en) liegen, stellen die Antworten auf die Anfrage dar und werden als Ergebnis der Anfrage ermittelt. Die Menge der Antworten kann sehr groß, sie kann aber auch leer sein. In beiden Fällen ist es für den Benutzer schwierig, die Antwort zu verstehen und die Anfrage entsprechend zu modifizieren. Um dem Benutzer mehr Feedback auf seine Anfrage zu geben, werden durch unsere Visualisierungstechniken nicht nur die Datensätze visualisiert, die innerhalb der Anfrageregion(en) liegen und damit die Anfrage erfüllen, sondern auch solche, die 'in der Nähe' der Anfrageregion(en) liegen und damit die Anfrage nur approximativ erfüllen.

Unabhängig davon, ob ein Datensatz die Anfrage erfüllt oder nicht, kann für jedes Attribut die Distanz[1] vom vorgegebenen Anfragewert (oder -intervall) berechnet werden. Macht man dies für jedes Attribut, so erhält man Tupel $(d_1, d_2,..., d_k)$, die die Distanzen der Datenwerte bezüglich der Anfrage beinhalten. Verändert man die Anfrageregion, so ändern sich die Distanztupel entsprechend. Das Distanztupel kann um einen (k+1)-ten Werte erweitert werden, der die Gesamtdistanz des Datensatzes bezüglich der Anfrage darstellt. Der Wert von d_{k+1} ist '0', falls der Datensatz die Anfrage erfüllt; ansonsten gibt d_{k+1} die Distanz des Datensatzes bezüglich der Anfrage wieder. Die Menge der Distanztupel $(d_1, d_2,..., d_k, d_{k+1})$ wird nach dem Wert d_{k+1} (Resultat) aufsteigend sortiert, d.h. am Anfang stehen die Tupeln mit $d_{k+1} = 0$ (falls vorhanden) und am Schluß die Tupel mit den größten Distanzen.

Anstatt der Datenwerte werden bei den anfrageabhängigen Techniken die Distanzen bezüglich der Anfrage visualisiert. Die Distanzen für jedes Attribut inklusive des Gesamtresultats werden dabei auf eine spezielle Farbskala abgebildet. Die Farbskala ist so entworfen, daß dem Distanzwert '0' die Farbe gelb zugeordnet ist; Distanzwerte größer '0' werden in aufsteigender Reihenfolge immer dunkler. Die gelbe Farbe ist besonders hervorgehoben und zeigt an, daß der zugehörige Datenwert innerhalb des vorgegebenen Anfrageintervalls liegt; die übrigen Farben zeigen die relative Entfernung des Attributswertes von dem Intervall an. Für eine einfache Zuordnung von Datenwerten zu den Farbpixeln sorgt eine Option des interaktiven Interfaces: Durch Anklicken von Pixeln können die zugehörigen Datenwerte abgefragt werden. Details des interaktiven Interfaces sind in [26] und [27] beschrieben.

Ähnlich wie bei der 'Recursive Pattern' Technik wird auch bei der Spiraltechnik jedem Wert ein Pixel zugeordnet. Ebenso werden die einzelnen Attribute sowie das Gesamtergebnis in separaten Fenstern dargestellt (vgl. Abbildung 3a). Die Anordnung der Pixel erfolgt bei der Spiraltechnik spiralförmig um die Mitte der Fenster herum (vgl. Abbildung 3b). Die Reihenfolge der Pixel entspricht dabei der Sortierung entsprechend der Gesamtdistanz. Im Fenster für das Gesamtergebnis sind in der Mitte die gelben Pixel; weiter nach außen verlaufen die Farben kontinuierlich von hellgrün bis dunkelbraun. Die Fenster für die einzelnen Attribute weisen keine kontinuierlichen Farbübergänge auf, da die Pixel der Attribute in derselben Reihenfolge angeordnet sind wie im Fenster für das Gesamtergebnis. Die Farben der Pixel sind von den Attributswerten abhängig und daher nicht gleichmäßig verteilt. Die Visualisierung einer Datenbank mit k Attributen besteht damit aus insgesamt k+1 Fenstern der gleichen Größe, wobei jedes Fenster eine Dimension des R^k (bzw. R^{k+1}) repräsentiert. Die Pixel, die zu den Attributs-

1. Die Distanzfunktionen hängen vom Datentyp und der Anwendung ab. Für numerische Attribute wird beispielsweise die Differenz zwischen Attribut- und Anfragewert verwendet.

Abb.6: Anfrageabhängige Visualisierung von 100.000 fünfdimensionalen Datensätzen (insgesamt 500.000 Datenwerte). Die verschiedenfarbigen Bereiche, die sich an der gleichen relativen Position in den Attributbereichen befinden, stellen Mengen von Datensätzen mit ähnlichen Datenwerten (Cluster) dar.

werten eines Datensatzes gehören, liegen in verschiedenen Fenstern. Da sie jedoch in jedem Fenster die gleichen Koordinaten haben, können leicht Zusammenhänge zwischen den Attributswerten eines Datensatzes hergestellt sowie Cluster erkannt werden (vgl. Abbildung 6). Für eine detaillierte Beschreibung des visuellen Datenexplorations- und Analysesystems *VisDB*, das neben der Spiraltechnik auch weiterer pixel-orientierte Visualisierungstechniken implementiert sei auf die Literatur verwiesen [27][28][1].

5 Ausblick

Visualisierungstechniken können bei der Exploration und Analyse sehr großer multidimensionaler Daten hilfreich sein, um interessante Daten und ihre Eigenschaften zu finden. Unser Ansatz der Datenexploration zielt auf eine adäquate Unterstützung des Menschen durch den Computer ab und kombiniert Datenbankanfrage- und Information Retrieval-Techniken mit neuartigen Visualisierungstechniken. Die Anzahl der Datenwerte, die zu einem Zeitpunkt am Bildschirm dargestellt werden können, ist dabei nur durch die Auflösung des Bildschirms beschränkt und liegt für die uns heute zur Verfügung stehenden 19 Zoll Bildschirme mit einer Auflösung von 1.024 x 1.280 bei etwa 1.3 Millionen Pixel. Ziel zukünftiger Forschungsarbeiten ist es, die Menge der gleichzeitig darstellbaren Datensätze noch weiter zu erhöhen sowie die Qualität und Aussagekraft der Visualisierungen zu verbessern. Eine Möglichkeit ist beispielsweise, durch Verschieben der Anfrageregion im k-dimensionalen Raum Sequenzen von Visualisie-

1. Neben den Pixel-orientierten Visualisierungstechniken sind im *VisDB*-System auch die Technik der Parallelen Koordinaten sowie die Strichmännchentechnik implementiert.

rungen zu erzeugen. Dadurch können zum einen größere Datenmengen visualisiert werden, zum anderen werden durch die Veränderung der Bilder aber auch Abhängigkeiten innerhalb der Daten besser wahrnehmbar.

Literatur

[1] Tufte E. R.: *'Envisioning Information'*, Graphics Press, Cheshire, CT, 1990.

[2] Andrews D. F.: *'Plots of High-Dimensional Data'*, in: Biometrics, Vol. 29, 1972, pp. 125-136.

[3] Cleveland W. S.: *'Visualizing Data'*, AT&T Bell Laboratories, Murray Hill, NJ, Hobart Press, Summit NJ, 1993.

[4] Chernoff H.: *'The Use of Faces to Represent Points in k-Dimensional Space Graphically'*, Journal Amer. Statistical Association, Vol. 68, pp. 361-368.

[5] Dunn G., Everitt B.: *'An Introduction to Mathematical Taxonomy'*, Cambridge University Press, Cambridge, MA, 1982.

[6] Harman H. H.: *'Modern Factor Analysis'*, University of Chicago Press, 1967.

[7] Shepard R. N., Romney A. K., Nerlove S. B.: *'Multidimensional Scaling'*, Seminar Press, New York, 1972.

[8] Huber P. J.: *'Projection Pursuit'*, The Annals of Statistics, Vol. 13, No. 2, 1985, pp. 435-474.

[9] Asimov D.: *'The Grand Tour: A Tool For Viewing Multidimensional Data'*, SIAM Journal of Science & Stat. Comp., Vol. 6, 1985, pp. 128-143.

[10] Inselberg A., Dimsdale B.: *'Parallel Coordinates: A Tool for Visualizing Multi-Dimensional Geometry'*, Visualization '90, San Francisco, CA, 1990, pp. 361-370.

[11] Tufte E. R.: *'The Visual Display of Quantitative Information'*, Graphics Press, Cheshire, CT, 1983.

[12] Pickett R. M., Grinstein G. G.: *'Iconographic Displays for Visualizing Multidimensional Data'*, Proc. IEEE Conf. on Systems, Man and Cybernetics, IEEE Press, Piscataway, NJ, 1988, pp. 514-519.

[13] Beddow J.: *'Shape Coding of Multidimensional Data on a Mircocomputer Display'*, Visualization '90, San Francisco, CA, 1990, pp. 238-246.

[14] LeBlanc J., Ward M. O., Wittels N.: *'Exploring N-Dimensional Databases'*, Visualization'90, San Francisco, CA, 1990, pp. 230-239.

[15] Shneiderman B.: *'Tree Visualization with Treemaps: A 2D Space-Filling Approach'*, ACM Transactions on Graphics, Vol. 11, No. 1, pp. 92-99, 1992.

[16] Becker R. A., Eick S. G., Wilks A. R.: *'Visualizing Network Data'*, Transactions on Visualization and Computer Graphics, Vol. 1, No. 1, 1995.

[17] Hendley R. J., Drew N. S., Wood A. M., Beale R.: *'Narcissus: Visualizing Information'*, Proc. Int. Symp. on Information Visualization, Atlanta, GA, 1995, pp. 90-94.

[18] Sarkar M., Brown M.: *'Graphical Fisheye Views'*, Communications of the ACM, Vol. 37, No. 12, 1994, pp. 73-84.

[19] Lamping J., Rao R., Pirolli P.: *'A Focus + Context Technique Based on Hyperbolic Geometry for Visualizing Large Hierarchies'*, Proc. Human Factors in Computing Systems CHI'95 Conf., Denver, CO, 1995, pp. 401-408.

[20] Ward M. O.: *'XmdvTool: Integrating Multiple Methods for Visualizing Multivariate Data'*, Visualization'94, Washington, DC, 1994, pp. 326-336.

[21] Bederson B.: *'Pad++: Advances in Multiscale Interfaces'*, Proc. Human Factors in Computing Systems CHI '94 Conf., Boston, MA, 1994, p. 315.

[22] Beshers C., Feiner S.: *'AutoVisual: Rule-Based Design of Interactive Multivariate Visualizations'*, IEEE Computer Graphics and Applications, Vol. 13, No. 4, 1993, pp. 41-49.

[23] Keim D. A.: *'Databases and Visualization'*,Tutorial, Int. Conf. on Management of Data (SIGMOD'96), 1996 (postscript file available at http://www.informatik.uni-halle.de/~keim).

[24] Keim D. A., Kriegel H.-P., Ankerst M.: *'Recursive Pattern: A Technique for Visualizing Very Large Amounts of Data'*, Visualization '95, Atlanta, GA, 1995, pp. 279-286.

[25] Ankerst M., Keim D. A., Kriegel H.-P.: *'Circle-Segments: A Technique for Visually Exploring Large Multidimensional Data Sets'*, Visualization '96, Hot Topic Session, San Francisco CA, 1996.

[26] Keim D. A., Kriegel H.-P., Seidl T.: *'Supporting Data Mining of Large Databases by Visual Feedback Queries'*, Proc. 10th Int. Conf. on Data Engineering, Houston, TX, 1994, pp. 302-313.

[27] Keim D. A.: *'Visual Support for Query Specification and Data Mining'*, Dissertation, Ludwig-Maximilians-Universität München, 1994.

[28] Keim D. A., Kriegel H.-P.: *'VisDB: Database Exploration using Multidimensional Visualization'*, Computer Graphics & Applications, Sept. 1994, pp. 40-49.

Sprache zwischen Visualisierung und Benutzer

Thomas Strothotte und Bernhard Preim

Otto-von-Guericke-Universität Magdeburg
Institut für Simulation und Graphik
{tstr|bernhard}@isg.cs.uni-magdeburg.de

1 Einleitung

Was unternehmen eigentlich Benutzer, nachdem sie informierende Visualisierungen betrachtet haben, die ihnen ein interaktives System präsentiert hat? Diese Frage ist von entscheidender Bedeutung für die Gestaltung der Visualisierung an sich. Dabei gibt es Situationen, die nur einen Zwischenschritt in der Arbeit darstellen und zur Auswahl weiterer Visualisierungen führen. Andere Visualisierungen werden von Benutzern als "mentale Bilder" verinnerlicht, ohne daß eine Verbalisierung im Vordergrund steht. Eine Vielzahl von Visualisierungen erfüllt aber ihren Zweck genau dann besonders gut, wenn sie zu geeigneten Verbalisierungen von Seiten der Betrachter führt.

Eine Verbalisierung wird vor allem in Anwendungen durchgeführt, bei denen das Betrachten einer Visualisierung zu einer bewußten kognitiven Handlung führt. Beispiele dafür sind Lehr-/Lernsysteme sowie Entscheidungsunterstützungssysteme. Hier müssen Benutzer Erkenntnisse aus Bildern gewinnen, diese in bereits vorhandenes Wissen einordnen und Schlußfolgerungen ziehen. Dieser Prozeß ist oft mit einer Verbalisierung des den Visualisierungen entnommenen Wissens verbunden. Dies gilt besonders dann, wenn darüber mit anderen Personen gesprochen werden muß, sei es mit einem anderen Lernenden, einem Lehrenden, einem Prüfer oder jemandem, der von einem Sachverhalt überzeugt werden soll.

Dieser Beitrag geht von der Hypothese aus, daß es ein lohnenswertes Ziel ist, die einer Visualisierung zu entnehmenden Erkenntnisse zu verbalisieren. Dieses wirft sogleich die Frage auf, wie eine Visualisierung gestaltet werden kann, um den Prozeß der Verbalisierung zu begünstigen. Darüber hinaus ergibt sich die Frage, wie Benutzer bei der Verbalisierung unterstützt werden können. Schließlich bietet die Behandlung dieser Fragen einen Ansatz, um über grundlegende Probleme des Verhältnisses zwischen Bildern und Sprache nachzudenken.

Der Beitrag ist wie folgt gegliedert. Kapitel 2 beschäftigt sich mit Situationen, in denen die Verbalisierung von Visualisierungen eine wichtige Rolle spielt. Grundlegende Verfahren zur Beeinflussung der Verbalisierung werden in Kapitel 3 diskutiert. Es werden vier Ebenen der Unterstützung dieses Prozesses eingeführt, die in den darauffolgenden Kapiteln 4 bis 7 nacheinander beleuchtet werden. Ein Ausblick wird in Kapitel 8 gegeben.

2 Verbalisierung von Visualisierungen

In vielen Situationen verbalisiert der Betrachter einer Visualisierung die aus der bildlichen Darstellung gewonnenen Erkenntnisse. Dieses sind insbesondere Situationen, in denen entweder andere Personen in eine Diskussion über die Ergebnisse einer Bildanalyse einbezogen werden sollen oder das Bild bei der Verwendung dieser Ergebnisse durch den Betrachter selbst dann nicht mehr zur Verfügung steht. Beispiele von Situationen, in denen Verbalisierungen durchgeführt werden, sind:

1. *Ein Befund muß für einen Bericht schriftlich erfaßt werden.* Diese Situation ergibt sich beispielsweise bei bildgebenden Verfahren in der Medizin (Röntgen- oder Ultraschalluntersuchung).
2. *Mehrere Benutzer wollen über eine Visualisierung sprechen.* Die aus einer Visualisierung zu entnehmenden Erkenntnisse sind in der Regel nicht eindeutig. So können von verschiedenen Benutzern unterschiedliche Schlußfolgerungen gezogen werden. Die Benutzer müssen ihre Schlußfolgerungen vergleichen und diskutieren. Dieses erfolgt in jedem Falle über Verbalisierungen des Sachverhalts aus der jeweiligen Perspektive.
3. *Weitere Visualisierungen werden vom Benutzer benötigt und abgefordert.* Die Analyse einer Visualisierung führt oft dazu, daß eine neue Visualisierung angefertigt werden muß, in der bestimmte Details besser dargestellt werden können. Obwohl es Möglichkeiten zur direktmanipulativen Handhabung von Visualisierungen gibt (z.B. Skalieren und Bewegen), ist das Abfordern weiterer Visualisierungen oft mit einer verbalen Beschreibung der von der neuen Visualisierung erwünschten Eigenschaften oder der an alten Visualisierung bemängelten Merkmale verbunden.

Insgesamt kann über diese Situationen gesagt werden, daß sie alle einen Kommunikationsbedarf erzeugen, und somit ein kognitiver Prozeß von Seiten des Betrachters eingeleitet wird. Ein derart bewußter kognitiver Prozeß ist in der Regel unmittelbar mit einer Verbalisierung des Sachverhalts verbunden.

Die Verbalisierung des Inhalts eines Bildes ist auch Grundlage für die Zweiteilung der Aussagen in *gelieferte* bzw. *mitgelieferte* Information (Strothotte [1994] sowie Strothotte et al. [1997]). Dabei wird unter gelieferter Information einer Präsentation die Information verstanden, die mit den darin verwendeten Wortsymbolen oder deren Substituten direkt verbunden ist. Mitgelieferte Informationen sind dann solche, die nur auf der Grundlage eines Schlußfolgerungsprozesses vom Empfänger „errechnet" werden können. Bei aussagekräftigen Visualisierungen kann davon ausgegangen werden, daß der Anteil an mitgelieferten Informationen hoch und möglicherweise nicht eindeutig ist. Die Auseinandersetzung über die mitgelieferte Information kann praktisch nur über deren Verbalisierung erfolgen.

3 Beeinflussung des Verbalisierungsprozesses

Bei interaktiven Systemen ist es möglich, den Verbalisierungsprozeß des Benutzers zu beeinflussen. Eine Beschäftigung mit diesem Thema ist schon deshalb nötig, da es für praktisch jeden Sachverhalt viele Möglichkeiten der Visualisierung gibt, die nicht alle zur gleichen Verbalisierung führen (Helms [1994]). Somit kann durch Beeinflussung der Visualisierung auch Einfluß auf eine anschließende Verbalisierung durch den Benutzer genommen werden.

Es wird zwischen vier verschiedenen Methoden der Beeinflussung einer Visualisierung zur Unterstützung des Verbalisierungsprozesses unterschieden:

1. *Anpassung der Visualisierung.* Obwohl die Erzeugung möglichst realistischer Graphiken seit Jahrzehnten ein wichtiges Ziel in der Computergraphik ist, gibt es einen Trend zu nichtphotorealistischen Graphiken (Saito und Takahashi [1990], Winkenbach und Salesin [1994], Strothotte et al. [1994]). Dabei gibt es Belege dafür, daß die Gestaltung der Graphik einen entscheidenden Effekt auf die Bereitschaft von Benutzern hat, diese zu kommentieren, und auch darauf, in welcher Form sie diese Kommentare abgeben (Schumann et al. [1996]). Dabei kann zur Verdeutlichung eines Sachverhaltes sogar von der Maßstabstreue des darzustellenden Objekts abgewichen werden. Außerdem kann die Detailtreue innerhalb einer Visualisierung variiert werden. Für solche interpretativen Weiterentwicklungen von Visualisierungen wird der Begriff der *Abstraktion* verwendet (Strothotte [1998]) und im weiteren Verlauf dieses Artikels aufgegriffen.
2. *Einfügen von Text in Visualisierungen.* Um einen unmittelbaren Zugang zu Vokabeln zu bieten, die Benutzer für die Verbalisierung nutzen können, sowie ihnen Orientierungshilfen zu bieten, können Beschriftungen in gerenderte Bilder eingefügt werden (Preim [1998], Preim et al. [1997]). Dazu müssen geeignete Bezeichner gefunden werden, und es muß eine geeignete Auswahl der einzubeziehenden Beschriftungen vorgenommen werden.
3. *Ergänzung von Visualisierungen durch Texte.* Während Texte in Visualisierungen dazu geeignet sind, auf Einzelheiten gesondert hinzuweisen, werden in herkömmlichen Printmedien ergänzende Bildunterschriften genutzt, um Lesern zu helfen, Abbildungen insgesamt zu interpretieren und einzuordnen. In Anlehnung an diese Praxis wurden Methoden und Werkzeuge entwickelt, um automatisch Bildunterschriften zu gerenderten Computergraphiken zu erzeugen (Preim et al. [1998]).
4. *Interaktion mit Visualisierungen.* Oft können Benutzer das Wesen eines Sachverhalts besonders gut dadurch begreifen, daß sie dessen Visualisierung editieren und die Änderungen sorgfältig beobachten. Dabei kommt den oben genannten Texten in und als Ergänzung von Visualisierungen entscheidende Bedeutung zu, da Änderungen in dem einen Medium oft notwendigerweise zu korrespondierenden Änderungen im anderen führen. Dadurch gestaltet sich die Interaktion mit angereicherten Visualisierungen wesentlich komplexer als die Interaktion mit Visualisierungen oder Texten allein. Dennoch bietet gerade die Abhängigkeit der Medien voneinander den Betrachtern die Gelegenheit, die zugrundeliegenden Modelle zu erkunden (Preim et al. [1995]; Preim et al. [1997]).

In den folgenden Kapiteln wird nacheinander auf diese vier Methoden eingegangen.

4 Anpassung von Visualisierungen

Für die Computergraphik besteht die Herausforderung nun darin, Visualisierungen zu generieren, die an das Ziel der Visualisierung angepaßt sind. Diese Visualisierungstechniken können sich an handgemachten Illustrationen orientieren.

Generell können die Techniken danach eingeteilt werden, ob sie auf einer hohen Ebene oder einer elementaren Ebene arbeiten.

4.1 Techniken der Bildkomposition

Die Techniken auf der hohen Ebene zur Unterstützung von Verbalisierungen betreffen die Spezifikation einer Sicht, von der abhängt, welche Objekte sichtbar und erkennbar sind. Diese Techniken beeinflussen also die Bildkomposition. Rist und André [1990] (wissensbasierte Perspektivenwahl) sowie Seligman und Feiner [1991] (gezielte Anwendung von Illustrationstechniken, wie z.B. die Erzeugung von Aufrissen) haben zu diesem Ziel wichtige Beiträge geleistet. Die Generierung von Explosionsdarstellungen und von Insets (vergrößerten Darstellungen eines Details in einer Gesamtansicht) sind weitere Techniken, die nach dem Vorbild von Illustratoren auf dieser Ebene angewendet werden können (Li [1996], Raab und Strothotte [1998]). Die Spezifikation von (globalen) Lichtquellen, von denen die Ausleuchtung d Szene, die Erzeugung von Schatten und die Erkennbarkeit der gesamten Sze abhängt, ist eine weitere Aufgabe auf dieser globalen Ebene.

4.2 Elementare Techniken der Visualisierung

Zu den elementaren Visualisierungstechniken gehört die Anpassung von Präse tationsvariablen (vgl. Noik [1994]). Dazu zählen Farben, Texturen sowie bei linie haften Graphiken Linienstile und Schraffurstile. Diese Attribute sind in der Regel einem geometrischen Modell codiert, können aber auch bei der Visualisieru angepaßt werden, z.B. durch eine Nachbearbeitung (Hoppe [1998]).

Die Präsentationsvariablen beeinflussen Kontraste und damit die Unterscheidbarkeit von Objekten. Die Grenze zwischen Visualisierungstechniken auf der hohen und der elementaren Ebene ist fließend. So ist die Transparenz eines Objektes zwar eine Präsentationsvariable – diese beeinflußt aber auch die Sichtbarkeit anderer Objekte.

Zu den Techniken, die auf der elementaren Ebene angesiedelt sind, aber auch die Sichtbarkeit von Objekten betreffen können, zählt die selektive Vergrößerung von Objekten zum Zweck der Hervorhebung. So kann ein Fisheye-Algorithmus genutzt werden, um kleine graphische Details in ihrem Kontext zu vergrößern, wobei zugleich andere Objekte zur Seite gedrängt werden (Raab und Rüger [1996]).

4.3 Veranschaulichung von räumlichen Verhältnissen

Ein wichtiger Aspekt der Visualisierung von Bildern für Lehr- und Lernzwecke ist die Veranschaulichung von räumlichen Verhältnissen in gerenderten Bildern. Diese spielen in vielen Anwendungen eine bedeutende Rolle für die Verbalisierung wesentlicher Bildinhalte. Dabei ist neben der Darstellung von Schatten auch die Darstellung der Objekte wichtig (Wanger et al. [1992]).

Der Beitrag von Saito und Takahashi [1990] zeigt, wie durch Visualisierungstechniken auf der elementaren Ebene dieses Ziel wirkungsvoll unterstützt werden kann. Unter dem Titel „Comprehensible Rendering of 3D-Shapes" wird die Veranschaulichung räumlicher Zusammenhänge mittels Linien beschrieben. Linien mit geometrischer Bedeutung werden bestimmt, indem Daten über die geometrischen Eigenschaften der Oberflächen beim Rendern gespeichert werden. Die Speicherung erfolgt in G(eometry)-Buffern, die für jedes Pixel Informationen enthalten. Dazu zählt das zugehörige Objekt, der Tiefenwert (Z-Buffer) und die Oberflächennormale. G-Buffer stellen eine Verbindung zwischen dem Bild und dem zugrundeliegenden Modell dar. Dadurch werden Bildverarbeitungsoperationen ermöglicht, die auch Informationen über das Modell auswerten. Hervorzuheben ist die Generierung von gekrümmten Schraffurlinien. Abb. 1 zeigt eine Anwendung dieser Technik auf medizinische Daten.

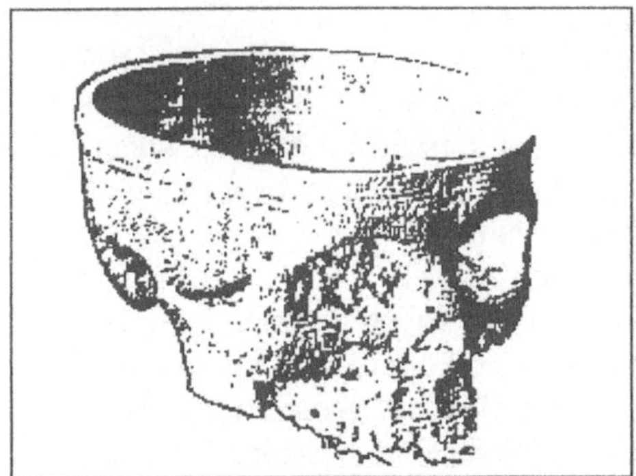
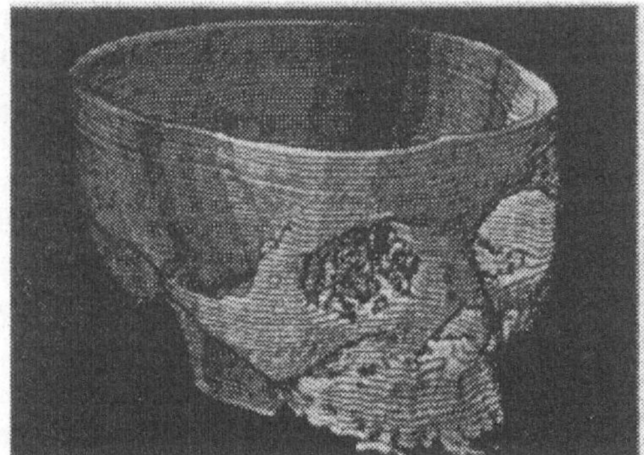

Abb. 1: Ein geshadetes Modell, das aus einer CT-Rekonstruktion entstanden ist. Rechts: Verstärkung des räumlichen Effektes durch gekrümmte Schraffuren, Quelle: Saito und Takahashi [1990], S. 205, © ACM 1990

5 Automatische Beschriftung von Graphiken

Viele interaktive Systeme basieren auf einer graphischen Darstellung der Anwendung, z.B. in Form einer Landkarte, eines Diagrammes oder einer schematischen Darstellung. Benutzer können in diesen graphischen Darstellungen beispielsweise Objekte selektieren und direkt-manipulativ eine Aktion initiieren. Dabei tritt allerdings das Problem auf, daß der Benutzer wissen muß, was diese Teile der graphischen Darstellung bedeuten. Dies kann durch eine geeignete Beschriftung erreicht werden. Allerdings ist die Beschriftung oft von mehreren Randbedingungen gekennzeichnet. Die Beschriftung muß lesbar sein und darf trotzdem nicht zuviel Platz beanspruchen, sie darf sich nicht mit andern Beschriftungen oder wichtigen Bildteilen überlagern. Beschriftungen sollten möglichst nahe an dem Objekt zu finden sein, das sie beschriften, was häufig mit der Symboldichte in bestimmten Regionen kollidiert. Schließlich sollen die Beschriftungen einheitlich aussehen und zu einer ausgewogenen graphischen Darstellung beitragen. Bei komplexen graphischen Darstellungen kommt ein weiteres Problem hinzu: eine einzelne Beschriftung oder eine Beschriftungslinie reicht häufig nicht aus, um den Verlauf eines komplexen Objektes hinreichend zu veranschaulichen. So werden Flüsse oder Straßen in Landkarten an mehreren Stellen beschriftet, falls sie mehrfach abbiegen, verzweigen oder einfach so lang sind, daß es für den Betrachter mühsam ist, eine weit entfernte Beschriftung zu suchen.

Bei komplexen graphischen Darstellungen, die zudem dynamisch generiert werden, ist eine manuelle Beschriftung aber kaum möglich. Daher werden Verfahren der automatischen Beschriftung immer wichtiger. Es zeigt sich dabei, daß diese Verfahren auf die jeweilige Domäne und die Art der Zeichnungen zugeschnitten sein müssen. So werden Objekte in kartographischen Illustrationen häufig so beschriftet, daß sich die Beschriftung an den Verlauf der in der Regel dünnen langgezogenen Objekte (Flüsse, Straßen) „anschmiegt".

Dabei sind verschiedene Varianten möglich. Das ANNA-System von Zimmermann erzeugt automatisch beschriftete CAD-Umriß-Zeichnungen (Zimmermann [1994]). Die Beschriftungen erfolgen teilweise in den Objekten, teilweise in unmittelbarer Nähe und teilweise durch die Verbindung mit einer Beschriftungslinie, wobei das System diese Auswahl automatisch trifft und zugleich „versucht", benachbarte oder anderweitig ähnliche Objekte auf die gleiche Weise zu beschriften.

Die Strategien zur Beschriftung von technischen Modellen sind allerdings nicht ohne weiteres übertragbar auf andere Domänen, um topographisch komplizierte Modelle, so wie sie in der Medizin oder der Biologie vorkommen, zu beschriften. Im Gegensatz zu technischen Modellen, die zum großen Teil aus geometrisch einfachen Objekten, wie Zylindern, Quadern und Kugeln, aufgebaut sind, bestehen Modelle von natürlichen Phänomenen oft aus konkaven, mehrfach verzweigenden Objekten. Um diese Objekte adäquat zu beschriften, sind oft mehrere Beschriftungslinien erforderlich, die auf verschiedene Zweige eines derart komplizierten Objektes verweisen. So ist in Abb. 2 die Beschriftung eines Muskels dargestellt, der sich an einem Punkt in vier Teile verzweigt. Zugleich wird dieser Muskel durch zwei Bänder teilweise verdeckt – ein Band verdeckt gerade den Verzweigungspunkt. Eine einzige Beschriftungslinie würde in keinem Fall ausreichen, damit der Betrachter erkennt, daß der im oberen Bildteil beginnende Muskel sich in vier Teile teilt, die jeweils an den Zehen enden. Um diese Beschriftungen automatisch zu generieren, ist eine Analyse der Topologie des zu beschriftenden Objektes erforderlich (wo verzweigt das Objekt?). Zusätzlich muß die Sichtbarkeit analysiert werden, damit Linien generiert werden können, die auf jeden sichtbaren Abschnitt eines teilweise verdeckten Objektes verweisen.

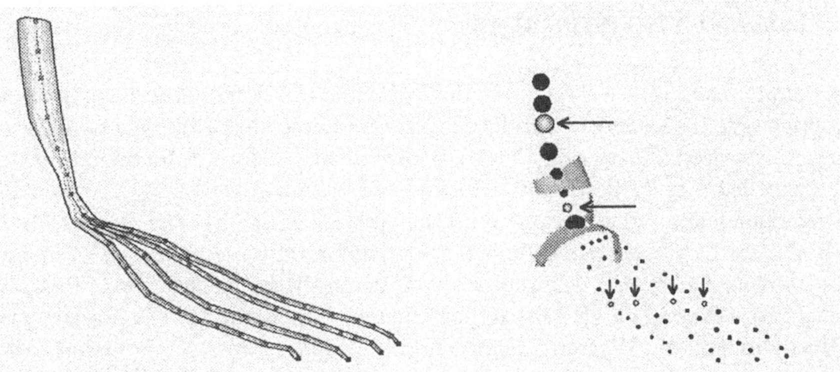

Abb. 2: Analyse eines Muskels und seiner Sichtbarkeit mit dem Ziel, geeignete Punkte für eine Beschriftung zu finden. Durch Pfeile werden rechts die Punkte angedeutet.

Abb. 3 zeigt das Ergebnis der Analyse eines Muskels und der verdeckenden Bänder. Die algorithmischen Details sind in Preim und Raab [1998] beschrieben.

Automatische Beschriftungen von Graphiken haben eine Vielzahl von Anwendungen in interaktiven Systemen. So können Beschriftungen eingeblendet werden, wenn nach einer Skalierung die Zahl der dargestellten Objekte unter eine gewisse Grenze fällt und der Platz für weitere Beschriftungen ausreicht.

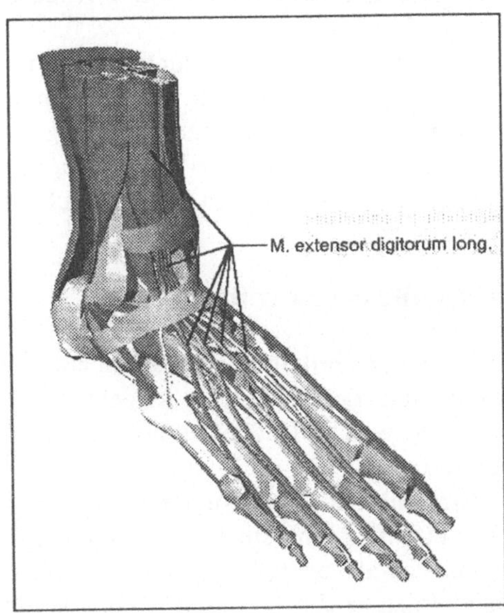

Abb. 3: Automatische Beschriftung eines topographisch komplizierten Muskels auf der Basis einer topologischen Analyse des zu beschriftenden Muskels und einer Sichtbarkeitsanalyse.

6 Texte zu Visualisierungen

„No Picture Tells its own Story“ – der berühmte Ausspruch des Kunstphilosophen Gombrich gilt insbesondere für Bilder, die zu Lern- und Dokumentationszwecken eingesetzt werden (Gombrich [1984]). Gerade bei diesen Bildern geht es darum sicherzustellen, daß bestimmte Inhalte vermittelt werden. Der Pädagoge Weidenmann leitet – unter Bezug auf das Gombrich-Zitat – daraus die Notwendigkeit ab, Bilder im Lernkontext z.B. durch Bildunterschriften sorgfältig zu kommentieren (Weidenmann [1989]). Ausgehend von gerenderten Bildern ist dieses Thema erstmalig von Preim et al. [1998] aufgegriffen worden (siehe auch Preim [1998]).

Illustrationen in Büchern sind durch Bildunterschriften begleitet, die die Bildinterpretation erleichtern, auf ungewöhnliche Details der Visualisierung oder besonders wichtige Aspekte eines Bildes hinweisen. Gerade bei komplexen unvertrauten Bildern geben sie eine wichtige Orientierung.

In vielen Anwendungen ist es nötig, Visualisierungen an den verfügbaren Platz anzupassen, damit die Symboldichte nicht zu hoch ist. Dabei müssen Informationen eventuell verzerrt dargestellt werden, oder Teile des Informationsraumes werden ausgeblendet. All diese Techniken sind auch in manuell erzeugten Visualisierungen üblich. Sie werden in unterschiedlichen Bereichen mit dedizierten Namen versehen. So spricht Weidenmann von der Didaktifizierung von Bildern, die an Lehrzwecke angepaßt sind. Bei der Visualisierung von kartographischen Daten wird der Prozeß der Generalisierung angepaßt, um eine Karte aus einem Maßstab an einen anderen anzupassen. Bei diesen Anpassungsvorgängen werden Symbole vereinfacht oder weggelassen und auch Präsentationsvariablen, wie z.B. die Farbe, verändert, so daß die wichtigen Elemente gut erkennbar sind.

In manuellen Illustrationen nutzt man Bildunterschriften, textuelle Kommentare, um die Interpretation der Bilder zu erleichtern. So findet man in Anatomieatlanten – in stark bebilderten Büchern zur Anatomieausbildung – Formulierungen, wie <*Objekt*$_1$> wurde {entfernt|zur Seite gezogen} um <*Objekt*$_2$> zu zeigen. Dadurch wird nicht nur die Veränderung, sondern auch deren Zweck erläutert.

6.1 Klassifikation von Bildunterschriften

Bei weitem nicht alle Bildunterschriften können automatisch aus einem strukturierten Modell und der Interaktion des Benutzers abgeleitet werden. Die folgende Klassifikation macht klarer, welche Bildunterschriften für den interaktiven Umgang mit Bildern wesentlich sind.

Der Pädagoge Bernard führt die Begriffe deskriptive und instruktive Bildunterschriften ein (Bernard [1990]). In Anlehnung an diese Begriffe betrachten wir deskriptive Bildunterschriften als textuelle Kommentare, die ein Bild als die Sicht auf ein Modell beschreiben. Dazu gehört die Beschreibung des dargestellten Modells, der Sichtrichtung, wichtiger Objekte, die im Bild zu sehen sind, aber auch die Beschreibung von verdeckten oder bewußt entfernten Objekten, sofern diese für das

Verständnis wichtig sind. Somit werden Aspekte des Bildinhaltes und des (räumlichen) Kontextes beschrieben.

Instruktive Bildunterschriften erklären, wie eine Handlung durchgeführt werden kann, wie etwas gehandhabt oder repariert wird. Dazu wird häufig eine Serie von Bildern eingesetzt, die unterschiedliche Stadien der Handlung repräsentieren. Pfeile werden genutzt, um zu zeigen, wie Hebel bewegt oder Knöpfe gedrückt werden.

Instruktive Bildunterschriften enthalten oft Informationen, die über die Beschreibung von Bildinhalten hinausgehen: So wird auf kausale Abhängigkeiten hingewiesen, es werden Voraussetzungen von Aktionen erklärt und beschrieben, welche Komplikationen bei der Handlung auftreten können und wie darauf reagiert werden kann. Instruktive Bildunterschriften werden z.B. in technischen Dokumentationen und in Büchern über Chirurgie eingesetzt. Die automatische Generierung von instruktiven Bildunterschriften erfordert aufwendige Wissensbasen (Wahlster et al. [1993]).

6.2 Bildunterschriften

Bildunterschriften können auch die Interpretation von computergestützten Visualisierungen erleichtern, in dem sie darauf hinweisen, inwieweit die Visualisierung von einer maßstabsgetreuen und realistischen Darstellung (z.B. in bezug auf Farben) abweicht. Die für diese Bildunterschriften nötigen Daten können bei der computergestützten Visualisierung als Seiteneffekt der Generierung abgeleitet werden. Als weitere Voraussetzung ist eine linguistische Analyse des Anwendungsgebietes erforderlich, um zu typischen Formulierungen zu gelangen. Abb. 4 zeigt ein Beispiel derartiger Bildunterschriften aus dem Bereich der Anatomie. Die Details der linguistischen Realisierung sind in Preim et al. [1998] beschrieben.

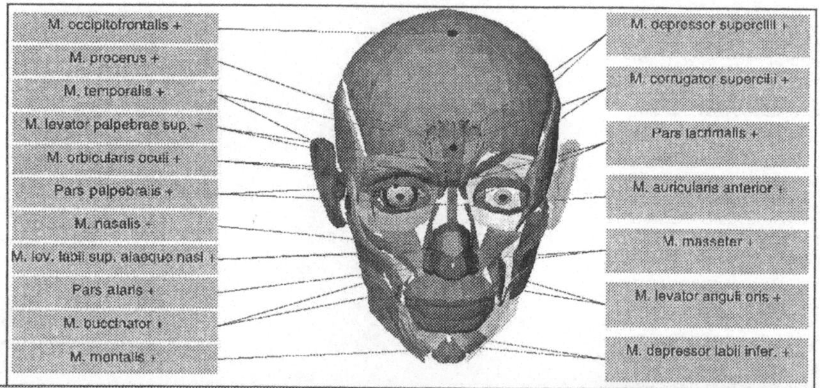

Abb. 4: Eine Bildunterschrift beschreibt, was von wo zu sehen ist. Insbesondere wird die unterschiedliche Gestaltung der beiden Hälften eines vertikalsymmetrischen Modells beschrieben.

7 Interaktion

Interaktive Systeme, die Bilder und Texte integrieren, bieten oft Interaktionsmöglichkeiten, die sich auf die bildliche Darstellung beziehen und solche, die sich auf den Text beziehen. So können in einem Lernprogramm textuelle Erklärungen angefordert oder Querverweise innerhalb der Textstruktur verfolgt werden. Zusätzlich können Bilder (z.B. eines Autos) manipuliert werden, z.B. indem das Modell gedreht wird, Teile bewegt oder entfernt werden. Die textuellen Informationen und die Bilder sind aber nicht unabhängig voneinander. Insofern sollten sich die bildhaften Informationen und die Texte aneinander anpassen, so daß eine Reaktion im jeweils anderen Medium erfolgt.

Eine einfache Form dieser Anpassung besteht darin, daß die Interaktion mit einer Beschriftung dazu führt, daß der korrespondierende Teil eines Bildes eingefärbt und dadurch hervorgehoben wird. Die Einfärbung ist aber nur dann wirksam, wenn im Ergebnis ein klarer Kontrast zur Umgebung entsteht, z.B. wenn eine Farbe für Hervorhebungen reserviert ist. Andernfalls müßte die Abgrenzung zu umgebenden Objekten durch eine Betonung der Kontur, durch eine entsprechende Musterung oder eine andere Form der Kontrastverstärkung erreicht werden (siehe Hoppe [1998] für eine Bewertung von Kontrasten in gerenderten Bildern). Die farbliche Hervorhebung ist aber nur dann ausreichend, wenn der entsprechende Bildteil tatsächlich sichtbar (bei einem komplexen 3D-Modell keine triviale Voraussetzung) und hinreichend groß ist. Eine ausreichende Größe eines Objektes kann durch einen 3D-Fisheye-Zoom sichergestellt werden (siehe Preim et al. [1997] und Abb. 5).

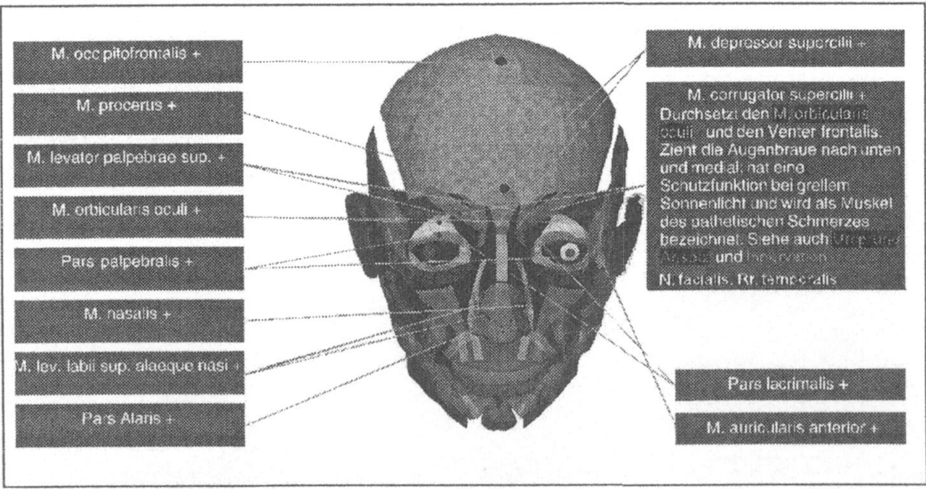

Abb. 5: Ein textuell erklärter Muskel (oberhalb der Augen) ist zur Hervorhebung eingefärbt und mit dem 3D-Fisheye-Zoom vergrößert worden.

Um ein Objekt hervorzuheben, das nicht sichtbar ist, kann das 3D-Modell rotiert werden oder die Objekte, die das interessierende Objekt verdecken, können entfernt oder abgeschnitten oder zur Seite gezogen werden. Es bedarf noch aufwendiger Untersuchungen, um diese Verfahren gezielt einzusetzen und zu einem befriedigenden Ergebnis zu kommen.

Die heute verbreiteten Multimedia-Systeme bieten diesbezüglich nur wenig. Oft werden gescannte Bilder und Videos verwendet, mit denen keinerlei Interaktion möglich ist. Nur selten werden Bilder aus 3D-Modellen generiert und diese erlauben zumeist lediglich Interaktionen mit dem 3D-Modell (Rotation, Manipulation von Teilen), die sich nicht auf textuelle Bestandteile einer Illustration auswirken. So kann das Verständnis eines 3D-Modelles erhöht werden, indem z.B. Beschriftungen eingeblendet werden, die daran angepaßt sind, welche Bestandteile zu sehen sind und wie weit diese vom Betrachter entfernt sind.
Bildunterschriften in interaktiven Systemen bieten gegenüber Bildunterschriften in Printmedien einige zusätzliche Möglichkeiten. So kann die Inhaltsauswahl vom Benutzer über einen entsprechenden Dialog angepaßt werden, wobei z.B. eingestellt werden kann, welche Objekte eines Modells oder welche Aspekte den Benutzer besonders interessieren. Darüber hinaus können Bildunterschriften dazu genutzt werden, um das Bild zu manipulieren. Abb. 6 zeigt, wie durch Selektion eines sensitiven Bereiches einer Bildunterschrift, ein Popup-Menü eingeblendet wird, das alternative Werte für ein Attribut der Graphikgenerierung (in dem Fall für die Sichtrichtung) enthält, die auf diese Weise angepaßt werden können, was zu einer Rotation des Bildes führt.

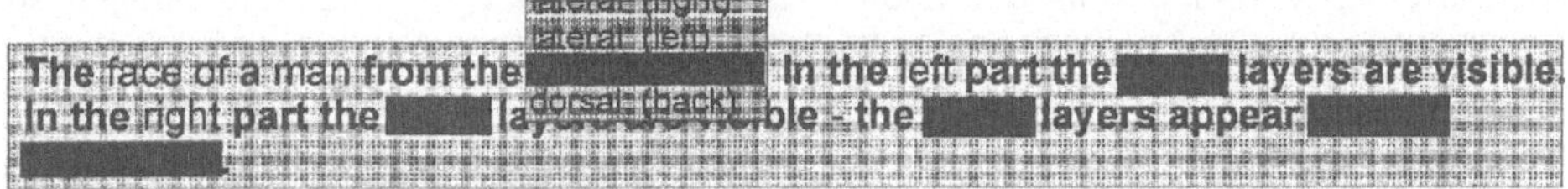

Abb. 6: Beispiel einer interaktiven Bildunterschrift, mit der Attribute der Graphikgenerierung – z.B. die Sichtrichtung geändert werden können.

Bildunterschriften können breit angewendet werden, um Visualisierungen von strukturierten Daten zu beschreiben. Hartmann et al. [1998] diskutiert Bildunterschriften für interaktive technische Dokumentationen. Mittah et al. [1995] erläutern die Codierung von mehreren Variablen in komplexen Diagrammen mit erklärenden Bildunterschriften. Routenplanungssysteme können durch automatisch generierte Wegbeschreibungen ergänzt werden, wobei die Beschreibung an die Präferenzen und Bedürfnisse des Benutzers angepaßt werden können (welche Punkte sind für sie oder ihn von besonderem Interesse und als Orientierungspunkte gut geeignet).
Es gibt eine Vielzahl von Anwendungsszenarien für Bildunterschriften: die Beschreibung von automatisch generierten Visualisierungen, die Beschreibung der Effekte von interaktiven Handlungen (z.B. was ist nach einer Rotation sichtbar geworden?), die automatische Beschreibung von Bildschirmabzügen und die Generierung von Bookmarks, die ein Zurücksetzen zu einer generierten Visualisierung ermöglichen.

8 Zusammenfassung und Ausblick

Dieser Artikel hat zunächst begründet, daß die Verbalisierung von Visualisierungen häufig eine wichtige Rolle bei interaktiven Systemen spielt. Dabei hat die Form der Visualisierung einen entscheidenden Einfluß darauf, ob Benutzer geeignete Verbalisierungen erlangen. Um die Verbalisierung zu beeinflussen bzw. zu begünstigen, werden mehrere Methoden vorgestellt. Diese sind der Einsatz von nichtphotorealistischen Computergraphiken, Beschriftungen, Bildunterschriften und Interaktion.

Im Ergebnis dieses Artikels wird eine Reihe neuer Fragestellungen aufgeworfen. Zum einen bietet die Verbalisierung einen Ansatzpunkt, um die Qualität von Visualisierungen zu messen. Dabei könnten in Untersuchungen die Verbalisierungen verschiedener Personen, die Aufgaben anhand von Visualisierungen bearbeiten sollen (siehe auch Helms [1994]), verglichen werden. Damit ist auch eine Grundlage gegeben, um Visualisierungen hinsichtlich ihrer Aufgaben- und Benutzeradaptierbarkeit zu analysieren.

Ein anderes Feld für weitere Untersuchungen betrifft die Visualisierung von Informationen, die spekulativer Natur sind. So gelten beispielsweise in der Archäologie bei Ausgrabungen oft gewisse Informationen als erwiesen (z.B. wo ein Fundament war), andere Informationen aber eher als spekulativ (z.B. wieviele Stockwerke ein Gebäude hatte). Zwischen diesen zwei extremen Sicherheitsgraden können auch andere Informationen liegen, die beispielsweise als plausibel oder wahrscheinlich gelten. Der Sicherheitsgrad könnte einer Visualisierung abzulesen sein und sich dann auch in einer Verbalisierung des Sachverhaltes niederschlagen. Untersuchungen zu diesem Thema werden derzeit angestellt (Masuch [1998]).

Obwohl (kurze) Bildunterschriften als Methode zur Unterstützung der Verbalisierung vorgestellt wurden, ist nicht geklärt, inwiefern längere generierte Begleittexte zu gerenderten Bildern die Verbalisierung einer Visualisierung beeinflussen.

Die Schlußfolgerungen der Arbeit lassen sich wie folgt zusammenfassen:

- Flexible Renderingverfahren sind vonnöten, um Visualisierungsziele umzusetzen. Dabei kommen unterschiedlich realistische Visualisierungen zum Einsatz.
- Nicht nur Methoden der Computerlinguistik sind geeignet, um Verbalisierungen an Rechnerbenutzer zu vermitteln, sondern auch Methoden der Computervisualistik.
- Im Bereich der Mensch-Computer Interaktion lohnt es sich, dem flexiblen Umgang mit dynamischen Visualisierungen Aufmerksamkeit zu widmen. Dabei ist besonders auf Nuancen bei Bildaussagen zu achten.

Danksagung

Die Autoren möchten sich bestens bei ihren Kollegen im Institut für Simulation und Graphik bedanken, die zur vorliegenden Arbeit Beiträge geleistet haben. Darunter seien insbesondere Andreas Raab und Michael Rüger (3D Zoom) genannt. Petra Specht sei herzlich gedankt für die redaktionelle Überarbeitung des Textes.

Literatur

Bernard, R. M. (1990) „Using Extended Captions to improve learning from instructional illustrations", *British Journal of Educational Technology*, Band 21 (3), S. 215-225

Feiner, S. K. und K. R. McKeown (1993) „Automating the Generation of Coordinated Multimedia Explanations", In: M. T. Maybury (Hrsg.) *Intelligent Multimedia Interfaces*, Menlo Park, CA: AAAI Press, S. 117-138

Furnas, G. W. (1986) „Generalized Fisheye Views", *Proc. of the ACM CHI'86 Conference on Human Factors in Computing Systems* (Boston, Massachusettes, April), S. 16-23

Gombrich, E. H. (1984) *The Sense of Order – A study in the psychology of decorative art*, Zweite Auflage, Phaidon Press, London

Hartmann, K., B. Preim und Th. Strothotte (1998) „Describing Abstraction in Rendered Images through Figure Captions", In *Proc. of ECAI'98 Workshop on Combining AI and Graphics for the Interface of the Future* (Brighton, UK, August), erscheint

Helms, C. (1994) *Sichtbeschreibungen für die Mensch-Computer Interaktion am Beispiel der Computersimulation*, Dissertation, Otto-von-Guericke Universität Magdeburg, Fakultät für Informatik

Hoppe, A. (1998) *Validierung und Nachbearbeitung von gerenderten Bildern*, Dissertation, Otto-von-Guericke Universität Magdeburg, Fakultät für Informatik

Krüger, A. (1998) „Automatic Graphical Abstraction in Intend-Based 3D-Illustrations", In *Proc. of the Working Conference on Advanced Visual Interfaces*, AVI'98 (L'Aquila, Italien, Mai), ACM Press, S. 47-56

Li, M. (1996) *Ein wissensbasiertes System zur automatischen Generierung von Explosionszeichnungen*, Phd Thesis, Universität des Saarlandes, Technische Fakultät

Masuch, M. und Th. Strothotte (1998), Visualising Ancient Architecture using Animated Line Drawings ", Information Visualisation '98, London (erscheint)

Mittah, V. O., S. Roth, J. D. Moore, J. Mattis und G. Carenini (1995) „Generating Explanatory Captions for Information Graphics", *Proc. of IJCAI'95*, Montreal, Dezember, S. 1276-1283

Noik, E. (1994) „A Space of Presentation Emphasis Techniques for Visualizing Graphs", *Proc. of Graphics Interface'94* (Banff, Alberta, Mai), S. 225-233

Preim, B., A. Ritter, Th. Strothotte, D. R. Forsey, L. Bartram und T. Pohle (1995) „Consistency of Rendered Images and Their Textual Labels", *Proc. of CompuGraphics* (Alvor, Portugal, Dezember), S. 201-210

Preim, B., A. Raab und Th. Strothotte (1997) „Coherent Zooming of Illustrations with 3D-Graphics and Text", *Proc. of Graphics Interface* (Kelowna, BC., Mai), S. 105-113

Preim, B. (1998) *Interaktive Illustrationen und Animationen zur Erklärung komplexer räumlicher Zusammenhänge*, Dissertation, Otto-von-Guericke-Universität Magdeburg, Fakultät für Informatik

Preim, B. und A. Raab (1998) „Annotation von topographisch komplizierten 3D-Modellen", *Proc. of Simulation und Visualisierung* (Magdeburg, März), SCS-Verlag, S. 128-140

Preim, B., R. Michel, K. Hartmann und Th. Strothotte (1998) „Figure Captions in Visual Interfaces", In *Proc. of the Working Conference on Advanced Visual Interfaces*, AVI'98 (L'Aquila, Italien, Mai), ACM Press, S. 235-246

Raab, A. und M. Rüger (1996) „3D-Zoom: Interactive Visualization of Structures and Relations in Complex Graphics", *Proc. of Bildanalyse und -synthese*, Infix-Verlag, Erlangen, November, S. 123-132

Raab, A. und Th. Strothotte (1998) „Interactively Exploring Geometric Models", *Proc. of "8th International Conference on Engineering Computer Graphics and Descriptive Geometry"*, (erscheint)

Rist, T. und E. Andrè (1990) „Wissensbasierte Perspektivenwahl für die automatische Erzeugung von 3D-Objektdarstellungen", *GI-Workshop über Graphik und Künstliche Intelligenz*, (Bonn, April), Springer Verlag, Berlin-Heidelberg-New York, S. 48-57

Saito, T. und T. Takahashi (1990) „Comprehensible Rendering of 3-D Shapes", *Proc. of SIGGRAPH'90, Computer Graphics* (Dallas, Texas, Juli), Band 24 (4), S. 197-206

Schumann, J., Th. Strothotte, A. Raab und S. Laser (1996) „Assessing the Effect of Non-Photorealistic Images in Computer-Aided Design", *Proc. of the ACM Conference on Human Factors in Computing Systems* (Vancouver, April), S. 35-41

Seligmann, D. D. und S. K. Feiner (1991) „Automated Generation of Intent-Based 3D Illustrations", *Proc. of SIGGRAPH'91* (Las Vegas, Juli), *Computer Graphics* , Band 25 (4), S. 123-132

Strothotte, Th., B. Preim, A. Raab, J. Schumann, und D. R. Forsey (1994) „How to Render Frames and Influence People", *Proc. of Eurographics*, (Oslo, September), *Computer Graphics Forum*, Band 13 (3), S. 455-466

Strothotte, Th. (1994), „Informationsfluß durch Bilder in der Mensch-Computer-Interaktion", in B. Weidenmann (Hrsg.), *Wissenserwerb mit Bildern*, Verlag Hans-Huber, Bern, S. 195-213

Strothotte, C. und Th. Strothotte (1997) *Seeing Between the Pixels: Pictures in Interactive Systems*, Springer-Verlag, Berlin-Heidelberg-New York

Strothotte, Th. (Hrsg.) (1998) *Abstraction in Interactive Computer Visualizations: Exploring Complex Information Spaces*, Springer-Verlag, Berlin-Heidelberg-New York (erscheint)

Wahlster, W., W. Finkler, E. André, H.-J. Profitlich und T. Rist (1993) „Plan-Based Integration of Natural Language and Graphics Generation", *Artificial Intelligence*, Band 63, S. 387-427

Wanger, L., J. Ferwerda und D. Greenberg (1992) „Perceiving Spatial Relationships in Computer-Generated Images", *IEEE Computer Graphics & Applications*, Band 8 (5) S. 44-58

Weidenmann, B. (1989) „Informative Bilder – Was sie können, wie man sie didaktisch nutzen und wie man sie nicht verwenden sollte", *Pädagogik*, September, S. 30-34

Winkenbach, G. und D. H. Salesin (1994) „Computer-Generated Pen-and-Ink Illustration", *Proc. of SIGGRAPH'94, Computer Graphics* (Orlando, Florida, Juli), Band 28 (4), S. 91-100

Zimmermann, D. (1994) *AnnA II: Ein wissensbasiertes System zur automatischen Annotation von Graphiken*, Diplomarbeit der Universität des Saarlandes FB14

TREEBAG – Baum-basierte Generierung und Transformation von Objekten*

Frank Drewes

Fachbereich 3 – Mathematik und Informatik, Universität Bremen
Postfach 33 04 40, D–28334 Bremen
drewes@informatik.uni-bremen.de

Zusammenfassung. Es wird ein Software-System namens TREEBAG (*Tree-Based Generator*) vorgestellt, welches der Generierung, Transformation und Visualisierung unterschiedlicher Typen von Objekten (z.B. Bildern, Bäumen, Zeichenketten oder Zahlen) dient. Das Grundprinzip ist, Terme zu erzeugen, die von geeignet gewählten Algebren interpretiert werden. Die dadurch erhaltenen Objekte können durch passende Visualisierungskomponenten dargestellt werden.

1 Einleitung

Ein Formalismus zur Generierung von Termen kann zur Erzeugung beliebiger Typen von Objekten benutzt werden, indem die generierten Terme durch geeignet gewählte Algebren interpretiert werden. Darüber hinaus können die so erhaltenen Objekte durch Transformation der zugrundeliegenden Terme in andere Objekte überführt werden: Ein Term t, der ein Objekt O repräsentiert, wird in einen Term t' transformiert, der das gewünschte Objekt O' repräsentiert – wobei t und t' von möglicherweise unterschiedlichen Algebren interpretiert werden (vgl. [7, 3, 2]).

Im folgenden wird ein auf der Grundlage dieser Beobachtungen entwickeltes Software-System namens TREEBAG (*Tree-Based Generator*) vorgestellt, das der Erzeugung, Transformation und Visualisierung von Objekten unterschiedlicher Art dient. Es erlaubt die interaktive Erstellung eines Netzes aus Baumgrammatiken, Baumtransformationen, Algebren und Visualisierungskomponenten (im weiteren *Displays* genannt).[1] Baumgrammatiken und Baumtransformationen liefern Ausgabeterme, die wiederum als Eingabe für Baumtransformationen und Displays verwendet werden können. Jedes Display kann außerdem mit einer Algebra verknüpft werden. Die dem Display als Eingabe übergebenen Terme werden dann entsprechend interpretiert, und das Resultat wird in einem dem Display zugeordneten Fenster angezeigt.

Zur Zeit sind im wesentlichen folgende Baumgrammatiken, Baumtransformationen, Algebren und Displays implementiert:

---

* Ich bedanke mich für die finanzielle Unterstützung durch die Europäische Kommission im Rahmen des TMR Netzwerks GETGRATS (*General Theory of Graph Transformation Systems*).

[1] Der Begriff *Baum* ist hier als Synonym für *Term* zu verstehen.

- reguläre Baumgrammatiken (siehe [12]),
- *Top-Down Tree Transducer* (siehe z.B. [18, 20, 6, 12]) und die sog. YIELD-Transformation [9], und
- Algebren mit entsprechenden Displays für Wahrheitswerte, Zeichenketten, ganze Zahlen und Terme (die freie Termalgebra und die YIELD-Algebra), für Kettenkode-Bilder (siehe [14]) und die Schildkröten-Geometrie [17], sowie für den Typ von Bildern, der durch Collagengrammatiken [13] und iterative Funktionensysteme [1, 16] erzeugt wird.

Wie oben angedeutet, können in TREEBAG reguläre Baumgrammatiken mit beliebigen Sequenzen von Baumtransformationen der genannten Typen komponiert werden. Damit steht eine sehr große Klasse erzeugbarer Baumsprachen zur Verfügung (vgl. [9, 10, 2]). Insbesondere enthält diese Klasse die sog. IO-Hierarchie von Baumsprachen, deren unterste Ebenen die regulären und die IO-kontextfreien Baumsprachen sind, und es können diverse Varianten regulierter Ersetzung simuliert werden (siehe [8]). Durch geeignete Kombination von regulären Baumgrammatiken, Baumtransformationen und Algebren können somit in TREEBAG u.a. reguläre, kontextfreie, indizierte, ETOL und viele andere Wortsprachen, die erwähnten Typen von Baumsprachen, kontextfreie und andere Kettenkode-Bildsprachen, durch ETOL-Systeme auf Basis der Schildkröten-Geometrie erzeugbare Bildsprachen, kontextfreie Collagensprachen, und mittels iterativer Funktionensysteme erzeugbare Bildsprachen generiert werden.

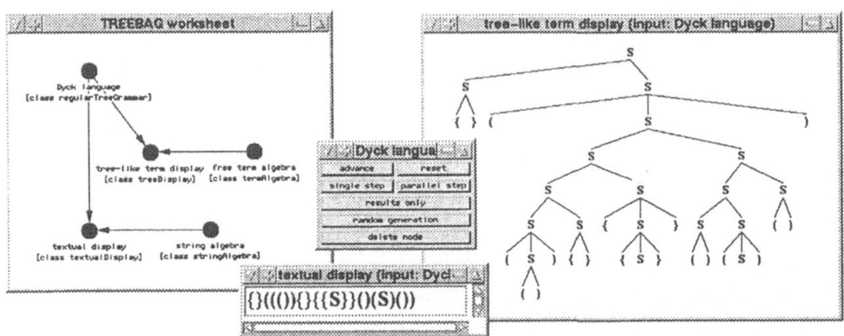

Abbildung 1. Erzeugung einer Dyck-Sprache in TREEBAG

Durch Einfügen von Displays an geeigneten Stellen ist es auf einfache Weise möglich, Ableitungsprozeße zu visualisieren. Abbildung 1 verdeutlicht dies an einem sehr einfachen Beispiel: Eine reguläre Baumgrammatik liefert die Ableitungsbäume der bekannten kontextfreien Grammatik zur Erzeugung einer Dyck-Sprache. Die durch den jeweiligen Ableitungsbaum gegebene Satzform wird durch ein textuelles Display angezeigt. Gleichzeitig wird mittels eines anderen Displays der Ableitungsbaum selbst visualisiert. Die Eingabe des Kommandos „single step“ würde jetzt z.B. dazu führen, daß eines der beiden Nichtterminale

S sowohl im Ableitungsbaum als auch, korrespondierend dazu, in dem dargestellten Wort ersetzt wird.

TREEBAG dient in erster Linie der Demonstration theoretischer Konzepte. Einer der Beweggründe für seine Entwicklung war der Wunsch, für die Lehre in theoretischer Informatik über ein flexibles System zu verfügen, das die Veranschaulichung von Konzepten und Begriffen der Theorie formaler Sprachen (im weitesten Sinne) erlaubt. Erste Erfahrungen scheinen anzudeuten, daß TREEBAG sich in der Tat für eine solche Verwendung eignet, wenngleich ein wirklich ernsthafter Versuch in dieser Richtung noch aussteht.

Diese Arbeit ist im wesentlichen eine gekürzte und ins Deutsche übersetzte Version von [5]. In den folgenden Abschnitten werden kurz die Grundlagen von TREEBAG erläutert sowie dessen Funktionsweise skizziert, und es werden einige Beispiele vorgestellt. Aufgrund der Platzbeschränkung mußte auf die meisten Details verzichtet werden. Interessierte Leser seien auf die ausführlichere Darstellung in [5] verwiesen. TREEBAG selbst ist in Java implementiert und im WWW über http://www.informatik.uni-bremen.de/~drewes/treebag erhältlich.

2 Baumgrammatiken und Baumtransformationen

In diesem Abschnitt werden die zum Verständnis des Weiteren benötigten Begriffe eingeführt – insbesondere reguläre Baumgrammatiken und Top-Down Tree Transducer[2]. Auf die Diskussion der YIELD-Transformation muß aus Platzgründen leider verzichtet werden.

Eine (einsortige) *Signatur* ist eine Menge Σ von *Symbolen* $f{:}\,n$, wobei f der Name des Symbols und $n \in \mathbb{N}$ seine Stelligkeit ist. Statt $f{:}\,n$ wird auch einfach f geschrieben. Für eine (möglicherweise leere) Menge T von Termen bezeichnet $\mathrm{T}_\Sigma(T)$ die Menge aller Terme über Symbolen aus Σ, mit Untertermen in T: die kleinste Menge, so daß $T \subseteq \mathrm{T}_\Sigma(T)$ und $f[t_1, \ldots, t_n] \in \mathrm{T}_\Sigma(T)$ für alle $f{:}\,n \in \Sigma$ und $t_1, \ldots, t_n \in \mathrm{T}_\Sigma(T)$. T_Σ steht für $\mathrm{T}_\Sigma(\emptyset)$, und $\Sigma(T)$ bezeichnet die Menge aller Terme der Form $f[t_1, \ldots, t_n]$ mit $f{:}\,n \in \Sigma$ und $t_1, \ldots, t_n \in T$. Statt $f[\,]$ wird auch f geschrieben, d.h. ein nullstelliges Symbol wird mit dem nur aus diesem Symbol bestehenden Term identifiziert.

Sei $X = \{x_1, x_2, \ldots\}$ eine Signatur nullstelliger, paarweise verschiedener *Variablen* x_i. Ein (linkslineares) *Termersetzungssystem* ist eine endliche Menge R von $s \to t$ geschriebenen Paaren (s, t), wobei s und t Terme sind, jede Variable höchstens einmal in s vorkommt und jede Variable aus t auch in s zu finden ist. Die durch R gegebene Termersetzungsrelation $\to_R$ und deren reflexive, transitive Hülle $\to_R^*$ sind in der üblichen Weise definiert.

Eine *Σ-Algebra*, kurz *Algebra*, ist ein Paar $\mathcal{A} = (\mathbb{A}, (f_\mathcal{A})_{f \in \Sigma})$ bestehend aus einer *Trägermenge* $\mathbb{A}$ und einer partiellen *Operation* $f_\mathcal{A}\colon \mathbb{A}^n \to \mathbb{A}$ für jedes Symbol $f{:}\,n \in \Sigma$. Der *Wert* eines Termes $t = f[t_1, \ldots, t_n] \in \mathrm{T}_\Sigma$ bezüglich $\mathcal{A}$ ist gegeben durch $val_\mathcal{A}(t) = f_\mathcal{A}(val_\mathcal{A}(t_1), \ldots, val_\mathcal{A}(t_n))$.

[2] Dieser Begriff und die hier verwendete Schreibweise mögen für einen deutschen Text seltsam anmuten; eine passendere Alternative ist mir aber leider unbekannt.

Eine *reguläre Baumgrammatik* ist ein Tupel $g = (N, \Sigma, P, S)$, wobei N eine Signatur nullstelliger *Nichtterminale*, Σ mit $\Sigma \cap N = \emptyset$ eine Signatur von *Ausgabesymbolen*, $P \subseteq N \times \mathrm{T}_\Sigma(N)$ eine Menge von *Produktionen* und $S \in N$ das *Startsymbol* ist. Zusätzlich wird von N, Σ, und P Endlichkeit verlangt. Die von g erzeugte Sprache ist $\mathrm{L}(g) = \{t \in \mathrm{T}_\Sigma \mid S \to_P^* t\}$.

Ein *Top-Down Tree Transducer* ist ein Tupel $td = (\Sigma, \Sigma', \Gamma, R, \gamma_0)$, wobei Σ die *Eingabe-* und Σ' die *Ausgabesignatur*, Γ mit $\Gamma \cap (\Sigma \cup \Sigma') = \emptyset$ eine Signatur einstelliger *Zustände*, $R \subseteq \Gamma(\Sigma(X)) \times \mathrm{T}_{\Sigma'}(\Gamma(X))$ ein linkslineares Termersetzungssystem und $\gamma_0 \in \Gamma$ der *initiale Zustand* ist. Von den Signaturen Σ, Σ' und Γ wird Endlichkeit verlangt. Die von td berechnete Baumtransformation wird ebenfalls mit td bezeichnet und ist definiert als die Menge aller Paare $(s, t) \in \mathrm{T}_\Sigma \times \mathrm{T}_{\Sigma'}$, so daß $\gamma_0[s] \to_R^* t$.

Die Begriffe der regulären Baumgrammatik sowie des Top-Down Tree Transducers verallgemeinernd, wird im folgenden der Begriff *Baumgenerator* benutzt, um einen jeglichen Mechanismus zu bezeichnen, der eine Menge von Ausgabetermen defininiert. Eine *Baumgrammatik* ist ein Baumgenerator, der Ausgabeterme liefert, ohne dabei auf Eingabeterme angewiesen zu sein, während eine *Baumtransformation* ein Baumgenerator ist, der Eingabeterme in Ausgabeterme transformiert.

3 TREEBAG

TREEBAG ist ein in Java implementiertes System, das interaktiv Baumgeneratoren mit Algebren und Displays zu kombinieren gestattet, um Terme zu erzeugen, zu transformieren und zu interpretieren, sowie die jeweiligen Resultate anzuzeigen. Es existieren vier Grundtypen von Komponenten, die im Rahmen des Sinnvollen frei arrangiert werden können: Baumgrammatiken, Baumtransformationen, Algebren und Displays. Diese vier Typen von Komponenten sind implementierungstechnisch als abstrakte Java-Klassen realisiert, von denen jede konkrete Implementierung einer TREEBAG-Komponente eine Unterklasse bildet. Eine solche Implementierung legt u.a. eine Syntax fest, in der Komponenten dieser Klasse definiert werden können. Komponenten werden von Dateien geladen, wozu im Bedarfsfall zunächst die Implementierung der entsprechenden Klasse dynamisch geladen wird. Dies macht es möglich, neue Klassen von Baumgeneratoren, Algebren und Displays hinzuzufügen, ohne am System selbst Änderungen vornehmen zu müssen.

Das TREEBAG-*Worksheet* ist das Hauptfenster des Systems. In ihm werden die geladenen Komponenten als Knoten eines Graphen angezeigt. Die Benutzerin kann mit der Maus Ein-/Ausgabebeziehungen zwischen den Komponenten herstellen, die durch Kanten dargestellt werden (vgl. Abbildung 1). Baumtransformationen und Displays erhalten ihre Eingabe von Baumgeneratoren. Displays können darüber hinaus mit Algebren verbunden werden (und zwar mit jeweils einer zur Zeit), wodurch die Interpretation der als Eingabe erhaltenen Terme bestimmt wird.

Zweifaches Klicken auf einen Display-Knoten öffnet das eigentliche Display in einem separaten, diesem Knoten zugenordneten Fenster. Ist das Display bereits geöffnet, oder handelt es sich um eine Komponente anderen Typs, so wird ein kleines Fenster mit Steuerbefehlen für diese Komponente geöffnet.

4 Beispiele

Wie bereits in der Einleitung bemerkt, kann TREEBAG u.a. zur Visualisierung der Funktionsweise von kontextfreien Wortgrammatiken, ETOL-Systemen, Baumgrammatiken und Baumtransformationen verwendet werden. Einfache Beispiele dieser Art werden in [5] diskutiert. Die folgenden Beispiele demonstrieren die in TREEBAG realisierten Möglichkeiten zur Bildgenerierung.

4.1 Schildkröten-Algebren

Eine bekannte Methode der Erzeugung von Bildern besteht darin, mit Lindenmayer-Systemen Zeichenketten zu erzeugen, die mittels der sog. Schildkröten-Interpretation als Liniengrafiken interpretiert werden (siehe [17]). Derselbe Effekt kann in TREEBAG durch Top-Down Tree Transducer erreicht werden, deren Ausgabeterme durch *Schildkröten-Algebren* interpretiert werden. Dies liegt in erster Linie an dem in [8] eingehend untersuchten engen Zusammenhang zwischen ETOL-Sprachen und den durch Top-Down Tree Transducer mit monadischer Eingabesignatur[3] erzeugten Baumsprachen.

Eine Liniengrafik im hier betrachteten Sinne ist ein Paar, bestehend aus einer Menge von Einheitslinien und einem Punkt, dem Endpunkt der Grafik. Der Endpunkt ermöglicht die Konkatenation zweier Liniengrafiken durch Vereinigung, wobei zuvor der Ursprung der zweiten an den Endpunkt der ersten verschoben wird.

Schildkröten-Algebren interpretieren bis auf einige Symbole mit besonderer Bedeutung alle Symbole als Konkatenationsoperationen entsprechender Stelligkeit. Symbole mit abweichender Bedeutung sind die folgenden: $F{:}\,0$ wird interpretiert als die Liniengrafik, die aus dem Intervall $[(0,0),(0,1)]$ mit Endpunkt $(0,1)$ besteht. Die Interpretation von $f{:}\,0$ liefert das „unsichtbare" Gegenstück $(\emptyset,(0,1))$. Die Symbole $+{:}\,1$ und $-{:}\,1$ drehen ihr Argument um den Ursprung, und zwar um einen festen Winkel α bzw. $-\alpha$, während $enc{:}\,1$ den Endpunkt auf $(0,0)$ setzt. Die Symbole $+\mathit{branch}{:}\,1$ und $-\mathit{branch}{:}\,1$ werden wie $+$ and $-$ als Rotation interpretiert, wobei aber zusätzlich der Endpunkt auf $(0,0)$ gesetzt wird. Somit können $+\mathit{branch}[t]$ und $-\mathit{branch}[t]$ als Abkürzungen für $enc[+[t]]$ bzw. $enc[-[t]]$ betrachtet werden. Der Winkel α, auf den die Rotationsoperationen Bezug nehmen, ist für jede Schildkröten-Algebra fest zu wählen. Da ansonsten die Interpretation von Symbolen fest vordefiniert ist, unterscheiden sich Schildkröten-Algebren also nur in diesem Winkel.

[3] Eine Signatur ist *monadisch*, wenn sie keine Symbole der Stelligkeit größer als 1 enthält.

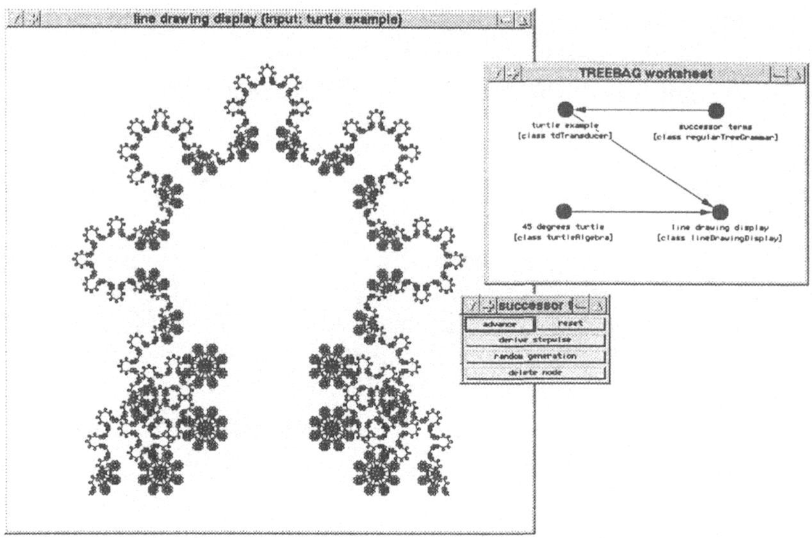

Abbildung 2. Erzeugung einer Liniengrafik unter Benutzung der Schildkröten-Algebra mit $\alpha = 45^o$.

Der Kürze halber erlauben Schildkröten-Algebren auch die Benutzung der Symbole $n{+}{:}\,1$, $n{-}{:}\,1$, $n{+}\mathit{branch}{:}\,1$, und $n{-}\mathit{branch}{:}\,1$ mit $n \in \mathbb{N}$. Die Interpretation entspricht derjenigen ohne die Zahl n, bis auf die Tatsache, daß der Winkel $n \cdot \alpha$ anstelle von α zugrunde gelegt wird.

Ein Beispiel ist in Abbildung 2 dargestellt. Um den parallelen Ableitungsmodus von Lindenmayer-Systemen zu simulieren, werden die Terme nicht direkt von einer regulären Baumgrammatik erzeugt, sondern durch einen Top-Down Tree Transducer mit Eingabetermen der Form $s[s[\cdots s[0]\cdots]]$:

$$
\begin{aligned}
(\ &\{\ s{:}\,1,\ 0{:}\,0\ \},\\
&\{\ F{:}\,0,\ \mathit{empty}{:}\,0,\ \mathit{conc}{:}\,13,\ +{:}\,1,\ 2{+}{:}\,1,\ 3{+}{:}\,1,\ -{:}\,1,\ 2{-}{:}\,1,\ 3{-}{:}\,1\ \},\\
&\{\ \mathit{start},\ A\ \},\\
&\{\ \mathit{start}[0] \to \mathit{empty},\ \mathit{start}[s[x_1]] \to -[-[A[x_1]]],\ A[0] \to F,\\
&\quad A[s[x1]] \to\\
&\qquad \mathit{conc}[A[x_1], +[A[x_1]], 2{+}[A[x_1]], 3{+}[A[x_1]], 2{+}[A[x_1]], +[A[x_1]],\\
&\qquad A[x_1], -[A[x_1]], 2{-}[A[x_1]], 3{-}[A[x_1]], 2{-}[A[x_1]], -[A[x_1]], A[x_1]]\ \},\\
&\mathit{start}\ ).
\end{aligned}
$$

Der jeweilige Eingabeterm bestimmt also die Rekursionstiefe und damit den Verfeinerungsgrad des Bildes.

Eine andere, hier nicht weiter diskutierte Methode, in TREEBAG Liniengrafiken zu erzeugen, bietet die sog. Kettenkode-Algebra. Diese enthält im Gegensatz zu den Schildkröten-Algebren keine Rotationsoperationen. Statt dessen werden die Symbole $n{:}\,0$, $e{:}\,0$, $s{:}\,0$ und $w{:}\,0$ als Einheitslinien vom Ursprung nach oben, rechts, unten bzw. links interpretiert. Die zentrale Operation ist auch hier die

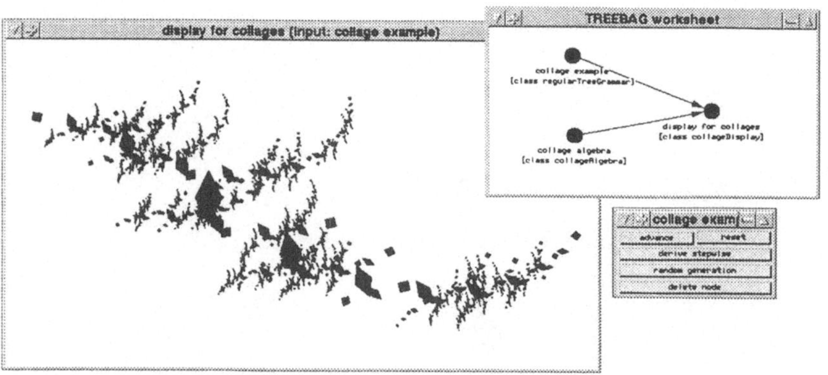

Abbildung 3. Beispiel einer Collagengrammatik in TREEBAG

Konkatenation von Liniengrafiken.

4.2 Collagengrammatiken und iterative Funktionensysteme

Collagengrammatiken im zweidimensionalen Raum (siehe [13] und, für die hier benutzte Form, [3, 4]) können in TREEBAG mit Hilfe entsprechender Algebren und Displays visualisiert werden. Eine *Collage* ist eine endliche Menge geometrischer Objekte. Eine Collagen-Algebra besteht aus nullstelligen Symbolen, die für einzelne Collagen stehen, und Symbolen $F{:}\,n$, die für Operationen der Form $<f_1,\ldots,f_n>$ stehen. Dabei sind $f_1,\ldots,f_n$ affine Transformationen und $<f_1,\ldots,f_n>(C_1,\ldots,C_n)$ ist definiert als $f_1(C_1)\cup\cdots\cup f_n(C_n)$ für Collagen $C_1,\ldots,C_n$ (wobei $f_1,\ldots,f_n$ kanonisch auf Collagen zu erweitern ist). Die syntaktische Beschreibung einer Collagen-Algebra besteht aus einer Menge von Definitionen, die jeweils ein Symbol mit einer solchen, durch n affine Transformationen angegebenen Operation assoziieren (bzw. mit einer Collage, im Fall einer nullstelligen Operation).

Eine mit Hilfe einer solchen Algebra erzeugte Collage ist in Abbildung 3 zu sehen. Die benutzte reguläre Baumgrammatik ist $(\{S\},\{F{:}3,C{:}0\},\{S\to C, S\to F[C,S,S]\},S)$. In Abbildung 4 ist dieses Beispiel um ein Display erweitert worden, das zusätzlich den jeweiligen Term als Baum anzeigt. Beachte außerdem die Darstellung der Instanzen des Nichterminals S, welche mittels einer Interpretation dieses Symbols durch die Collagen-Algebra auf einfache Weise zu erzielen ist.

Wie in Abschnitt 4.1 gezeigt, erhält man eine gleichförmigere Art der Ersetzung, wenn statt einer regulären Baumgrammatik ein Top-Down Tree Transducer mit der Eingabesignatur $\{s{:}\,1,0{:}\,0\}$ benutzt wird. Dies liefert eine Klasse von Systemen, die äquivalent ist zu hierarchischen (auch verschränkt rekursiv genannten) iterativen Funktionensystemen mit Kondensation (siehe [1, 16]). Das Resultat einer entsprechenden Modifikation des vorliegenden Beispiels ist in Abbildung 5 gezeigt, wobei zusätzlich noch ein textuelles Display mit einer Algebra

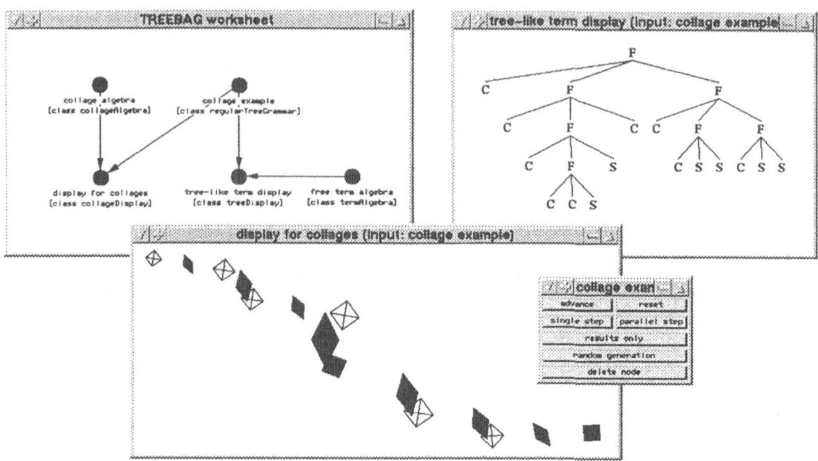

Abbildung 4. Das Beispiel aus Abbildung 3 mit einem zusätzlichen Baum-Display

über den ganzen Zahlen (die 0 als Null und s als Nachfolger-Funktion interpretiert) hinzugefügt ist, um den Verfeinerungsgrad des Bildes anzuzeigen.

4.3 Kachelungen

Collagen-Algebren können in Verbindung mit Top-Down Tree Transducern auch verwendet werden, um (endliche Ausschnitte von) Kachelungen der Ebene herzustellen. Periodische Kachelungen sind sehr einfach zu erzeugen, aber auch andere sind möglich. Das in Abbildung 6 zu sehende Beispiel stammt aus [11, Abbildung 9.5.5] (siehe auch [15]).

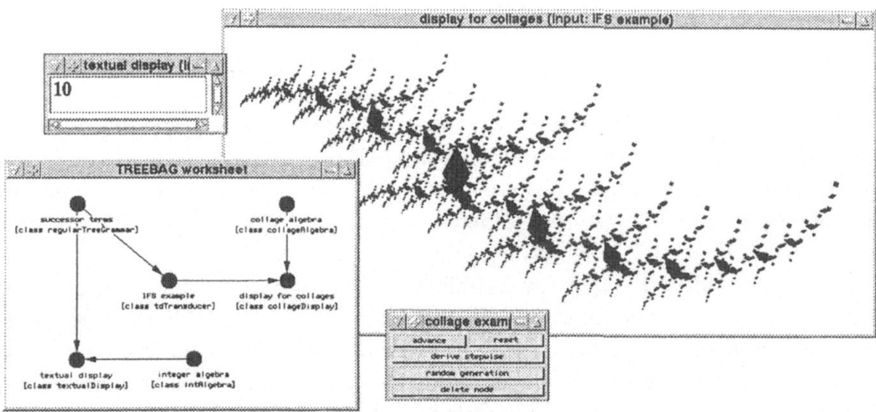

Abbildung 5. Das Beispiel aus Abbildung 3 als iteratives Funktionensystem

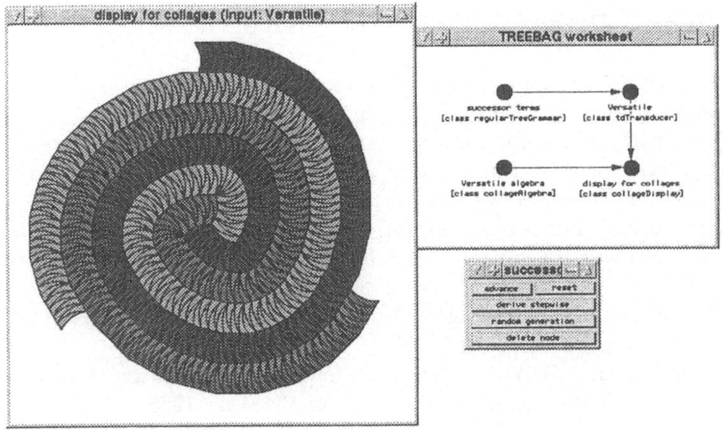

Abbildung 6. Eine in TREEBAG erzeugte Kachelung

5 Schlußbemerkungen

Dank seiner offenen Architektur ist TREEBAG ein leicht erweiterbares System. Interessant wäre sicherlich eine Erweiterung um die sog. Macro-Tree-Transducer [9]. Eine andere naheliegende Aufgabe besteht in der Implementierung von Algebren und Displays für dreidimensionale Collagen. Außerdem sollte über die Erzeugung von Graphen mittels Hyperkanten- oder Knotenersetzung (siehe [19, Kaptitel 1 und 2]) in TREEBAG nachgedacht werden. Entsprechende Algebren sind wohlbekannt und leicht zu implementieren; schwierig ist allerdings bekanntermaßen die Implementierung geeigneter Displays, da dies ein gutes Layout von Graphen voraussetzt. Schließlich sollte auch über ein Konzept nachgedacht werden, das die interaktive Auswahl und Anwendung von Regeln in TREEBAG erlaubt und dabei weitgehend unabhängig vom Typ der dargestellten Objekte ist.

Aus theoretischer Sicht wäre es sicher interessant, zu untersuchen, welche Bildsprachen sich mit Hilfe der in TREEBAG zur Verfügung stehenden Algebren durch reguläre Baumgrammatiken, Top-Down Tree Transducer und YIELD-Transformationen (oder Kompositionen davon) beschreiben lassen.

Literatur

1. Michael Barnsley. *Fractals Everywhere.* Academic Press, Boston, 1988.
2. Frank Drewes und Joost Engelfriet. Decidability of the finiteness of ranges of tree transductions. Erscheint in *Information and Computation.*
3. Frank Drewes. Computation by tree transductions. Dissertation, Univ. Bremen, 1996.
4. Frank Drewes. Language theoretic and algorithmic properties of d-dimensional collages and patterns in a grid. *Journal of Computer and System Sciences*, 53:33–60, 1996.

5. Frank Drewes. TREEBAG—a tree-based generator for objects of various types. Report 1/98, Univ. Bremen, 1998.
6. Joost Engelfriet. Bottom-up and top-down tree transformations—a comparison. *Mathematical Systems Theory*, 9(3):198–231, 1975.
7. Joost Engelfriet. Some open questions and recent results on tree transducers and tree languages. In R.V. Book, Hrsg., *Formal Language Theory: Perspectives and Open Problems*, Seite 241–286. Academic Press, New York, 1980.
8. Joost Engelfriet, Grzegorz Rozenberg und Giora Slutzki. Tree transducers, L systems, and two-way machines. *Journal of Computer and System Sciences*, 20:150–202, 1980.
9. Joost Engelfriet und Heiko Vogler. Macro tree transducers. *Journal of Computer and System Sciences*, 31:71–146, 1985.
10. Joost Engelfriet und Heiko Vogler. High level tree transducers and iterated pushdown tree transducers. *Acta Informatica*, 26:131–192, 1988.
11. Branko Grünbaum und G.C. Shephard. *Tilings and Patterns*. Freeman, New York, 1987.
12. Ferenc Gécseg und Magnus Steinby. Tree languages. In G. Rozenberg and A. Salomaa, Hrsg., *Handbook of Formal Languages. Vol. III: Beyond Words*, Kapitel 1, Seite 1–68. Springer, 1997.
13. Annegret Habel und Hans-Jörg Kreowski. Collage grammars. In H. Ehrig, H.-J. Kreowski und G. Rozenberg, Hrsg., *Proc. Fourth Intl. Workshop on Graph Grammars and Their Application to Comp. Sci.*, *Lecture Notes in Computer Science* 532, Seite 411–429. Springer, 1991.
14. H.A. Maurer, Grzegorz Rozenberg und Emo Welzl. Using string languages to describe picture languages. *Information and Control*, 54:155–185, 1982.
15. Roger Penrose. *The Emperor's New Mind. Concerning Computers, Minds, and the Laws of Physics.* Oxford University Press, Oxford, 1989.
16. Heinz-Otto Peitgen, Hartmut Jürgens und Dietmar Saupe. *Chaos and Fractals. New Frontiers of Science.* Springer-Verlag, New York, 1992.
17. Przemyslaw Prusinkiewicz und Aristid Lindenmayer. *The Algorithmic Beauty of Plants.* Springer-Verlag, New York, 1990.
18. William C. Rounds. Mappings and grammars on trees. *Mathematical Systems Theory*, 4:257–287, 1970.
19. Grzegorz Rozenberg, Hrsg. *Handbook of Graph Grammars and Computing by Graph Transformation. Vol. I: Foundations.* World Scientific, 1997.
20. James W. Thatcher. Generalized^2 sequential machine maps. *Journal of Computer and System Sciences*, 4:339–367, 1970.

VRML-basierte Präsentation raum-zeitlicher Geschäfts- und Wissenschaftsdaten mit WWW-Browsern

Hartmut Luttermann und Manfred Grauer

Universität-GH Siegen, Wirtschaftsinformatik, Hölderlinstr. 3, D-57068 Siegen
{hartmut,grauer}@fb5.uni-siegen.de; http://www-winfo.uni-siegen.de/

Zusammenfassung Bei der visuellen Exploration mehrdimensionaler, insbesonders raum-zeitabhängiger Daten entstehen häufig zeitliche 3D-Animationen. Die Speicherung und Visualisierung dieser Darstellungen ist bislang auf den Nutzerkreis spezieller wissenschaftlicher Visualisierungssoftware beschränkt. In diesem Beitrag wird daher ein ASCII-Dateiformat zur Beschreibung von raum-zeitabhängigen Präsentationen vorgestellt, das die standardisierte Virtual Reality Modeling Language (VRML) erweitert. Die damit erzeugten Dateien können in World Wide Web (WWW)-Seiten eingebunden und von jedem VRML-fähigen WWW-Browser interpretiert und visualisiert werden. Die VRML-basierte Realisierung unterstützt den Betrachter mit einer erweiterten Navigations- und Interaktionstechnik für die zeitliche Dimension der Präsentation.

1 Einleitung

Große Mengen mehrdimensionaler, insbesonders raum-zeitabhängiger Daten werden in wissenschaftlichen Experimenten, Prozeßsimulationen generiert [DG93], in GIS-Anwendungen erfaßt bzw. archiviert [LB95,LL96] oder in Data Warehouse- und OLAP-Systemen von Geschäftsanwendungen zusammengefaßt [CG98,GE97]. Zur Auswertung werden diese Daten häufig mit Methoden der wissenschaftlichen Datenvisualisierung in computer-generierte Bilder transformiert [NHM97,KK95]. Es ist ein Verfahren, mehrdimensionale Daten auf effiziente Weise zu betrachten, zu analysieren und in ihnen interessante Muster zu entdecken [BEJV95].

Darstellungen mit hohem Informationsgehalt sind das Ergebnis eines iterativen und rechenaufwendigen Visualisierungsprozesses. Die Daten werden problembezogen selektiert, transformiert, mit statistischen Methoden ausgewertet und mit verschiedenen Visualisierungsmethoden, die bzgl. Schwellwerte, Perspektive, Farb- und Texturauswahl optimiert werden, in Darstellungen überführt. Es besteht deshalb der Wunsch die resultierenden Darstellungen zu vielfältigen Zwecken (Marketing, Werbung, Wissensverbreitung, effiziente Entscheidungsfindung, kooperatives Arbeiten) zu speichern, auszutauschen und zu veröffentlichen. Das World Wide Web (WWW) spielt dabei eine wichtige Rolle, weil es durch leicht bedienbare Visualisierungstools (z.B. WWW-Browser), die das Hyperlink-Konzept und eine integrierte Datenvisualisierung realisieren, sowohl als Publikationsmedium als auch zur Informationsbeschaffung von einem sehr großen Nutzerkreis verwendet wird [RS97].

Die zu publizierenden Darstellungen lassen sich wie folgt klassifizieren:

- *Statische Darstellungen (Bilder/Grafiken):*
  Die Berechnung von z.B. Strömungslinien, Flußgrafiken, Isooberflächen [NHM97] aus räumlichen Daten oder z.B. Zeitschnitten und flow maps in kartographischen Anwendungen [HU94] führen zu statischen 2D- bzw. 3D-Darstellungen.
- *Dynamische Darstellungen (Animationen):*
  Komplexe oder zeitvariante Daten werden zumeist in dynamischen 2D- bzw. 3D-Darstellungen visualisiert, die Veränderungen über der Zeit wiedergeben. Diese Darstellungen lassen sich in zwei weitere Formen unterteilen [Dran95]:
  - *Kartographische Animationen:*
    Statische Darstellungen werden zur Hervorhebung bestimmter Informationen durch Ausnutzung der in der Kartographie und Animation identifizierten dynamischen Variabeln (z.B. Größe, Kamerastandpunkt, Textur, Farbe) kartographisch animiert [Each94,MTT90,Pet95,Shep95]. Ein wichtiges Kriterium ist, daß die Veränderung animierter Objekte nicht relativ zur Zeit sondern zu zeitunabhängigen Variabeln stattfindet.
  - *Zeitliche Animationen:*
    Die Veränderung eines räumlichen Objekts findet relativ zur Zeit statt. Dabei wird zwischen einer "realen Zeit" als Teil der Darstellung (in unserem Fall ist damit die Gültigkeitszeit gemeint) und der Präsentationszeit, wann die Animation gezeigt wird, unterschieden.

Zur Speicherung und Publikation von 2D-Darstellungen existiert eine große Zahl von WWW-fähigen Bild- und Filmformaten [GM97]. Für statische und dynamische (kartographische) Animationen bietet sich die Ende 1997 von der ISO standardisierte Virtual Reality Modeling Language (VRML) [VRML97] an, eine plattformunabhängige Skriptsprache und textbasiertes Dateiformat zur Beschreibung von interaktiven, animierten 3D- und Multimedia-Objekten im WWW [Dieh97,Lut97]. Mittlerweile existieren zu VRML verschiedene Visualisierungstools für WWW-Browser sowie Editoren und Konverter [VRMLRep].

Zeitliche 3D-Animationen sind bislang nur in den diese Darstellungen generierenden Visualisierungssystemen präsentierbar und speicherbar. Sobald die Datenstrukturn erhalten werden soll, die verschiedene Navigations- und Explorationstechniken erlaubt (z.B. Rotation, Zoom, letzter Zeitschnitt), ist der Verbreitung dieser Darstellungen enge Grenzen gesetzt.

In diesem Beitrag wird daher eine Erweiterung von VRML vorgestellt, die Konstrukte zur Beschreibung von zeitliche 3D-Animationen enthält und im Rahmen des Standards mit Java implementiert ist. Die damit erzeugten Darstellungen sind von jedem VRML-fähigen WWW-Browser mit einer integrierten zeit-orientierten Navigationstechnik visualisierbar.

Der Inhalt gliedert sich in folgende Abschnitte: Nach einer Übersicht zu der bisherigen Vorgehensweise bei der Publikation von zeitlichen 3D-Animationen werden die Konzepte zur Zeit-Erweiterung von VRML beschrieben. Anschließend werden einige Ergebnisse vorgestellt und diskutiert.

2 Speicherung zeitlicher 3D-Animationen

Verschiedene Datenanalyse- und Visualisierungssysteme (z.B. Grape [GRA97], vtk [SML97], Vis5D [Hib97], Khoros [KR93], AVS [UFK89]) generieren zeitliche 3D-Animationen. Zur Speicherung werden i.a. zwei Verfahren verwendet:

- *Speicherung der Grunddaten und der Generierungsvorschrift:* In datenfluß-orientierten Visualisierungssystemen (sog. Pipeline-) wird neben den zeitabhängigen Grunddaten die Vorschrift (Skript) abgespeichert, nach der aus den Grunddaten die Darstellung generiert wurde (z.B. in vtk, AVS, Khoros). Bei der Visualisierung werden dann sukzessiv die Grunddaten eingelesen und nach der Generierungsvorschrift visualisiert. Obwohl mit diesem Verfahren der Empfänger mit den publizierten Daten weiterarbeiten, d.h. eine andere Visualisierungsmethode anwenden kann, ist die notwendige Freigabe der Grunddaten für den Absender problematisch.
- *Speicherung in einem systemspezifischen Dateiformat:* Mittlerweile existieren Ansätze zu Dateiformaten, die eine Beschreibung dieser Darstellungen speichern (z.B. in Grape, AVS). Diese erlauben eine Visualisierung ohne eine erneute Berechnung aus den Grunddaten.

Beide Verfahren sind systemspezifisch realisiert und beschränken damit die Publikationsmöglichkeiten. Ebenso sind die realisierten Navigations- und Explorationstechniken (z.B. Rotation, Zoom, vorheriger Zeitschnitt, Annotation, 3D-Schnitt) systemspezifisch. Die Kosten für den Erwerb dieser Visualisierungssysteme sowie der Lernaufwand für die Bedienung (des Systems und der Visualisierungstechniken) stehen damit in keinem Verhältnis zu dem Wunsch einer einfachen Visualisierung von zeitlichen 3D-Animationen.

Datenvisualisierungssysteme bieten daher die Möglichkeit, zeitliche Darstellungen in *datenstruktur-ärmere* Dateiformate zu transformieren. Bei Vernachlässigung der Dynamik werden i.a. 3D-Geometrieformate (z.B. VRML) eingesetzt. Mit erhöhtem Aufwand werden aus dynamischen Darstellungen Filme (z.B. MPEG) erzeugt. In den meisten Fällen jedoch werden die Darstellungen in die bekannten Bildformate (z.B. GIF, JPEG) transformiert, obwohl dabei die Möglichkeit zur Navigation in räumlicher oder zeitlicher Dimension verloren geht.

Andere Datenformate sind nur begrenzt einsetzbar: Moderne *3D-Grafik-Toolkits/-APIs* bieten komprimierte (z.B. Java3D) oder textbasierte Dateiformate (z.B. OpenInventor [OIV]) an, die neben der 3D-Szenenbeschreibung z.T. auch kleine Animationsskripts abspeichern. Die Integration zeitabhängiger Daten ist bislang nicht vorgesehen.

Der für das textbasierte 3D-Geometrie-Dateiformat *OOGL* [OOGL] entwickelte Browser *GeomView* kann durch ein zusätzliches Skript gesteuert zeitabhängige Daten dynamisch einlesen und visualisieren.

Zur Beschreibung von Animationen und der Ereignisverarbeitung in 3D-Szene wurden *Animationssprachen* entwickelt (z.B. AniLan [FK96]). Sie sind in Verbindung mit einer geometrischen 3D-Szenenbeschreibung die Eingabe für einen Graphik-Renderer, der daraus eine zeitliche 3D-Animationen produziert. Eine Navigation ist dabei zumeist nur in zeitlicher Dimension möglich.

3 Anforderungen an Dateiformat und Visualisierungstool

Folgende Anforderungen werden an ein Dateiformat für zeitliche 3D-Animationen gestellt: Grundsätzlich ist aus Gründen der Wissenserhaltung, Lernbarkeit und Wiederverwendbarkeit keine Neuentwicklung sondern eine Weiterentwicklung bekannter Technologien anzustreben. Für jede Erweiterung ist es notwendig, die ursprüngliche Definition in der neuen Spezifikation vollständig zu integrieren. Inhaltlich hat ein Dateiformat sowohl kartographisch als auch zeitliche Animationen zu unterstützen. Gefordert werden Konstrukte für zeitabhängige Geometrien, Materialeigenschaften (z.B. Farbe, Textur), Umgebungsparameter (z.B. Licht) und zeitabhängige Generierung von Ereignissen. In allen Fällen ist auf eine effiziente, d.h. kurze aber ausdrucksstarke Beschreibung zu achten. Daneben gilt es verschiedene spezielle Formen zeitabhängiger Daten zu unterstützen: zustandsverändernde (Zeitreihen), zustandserhaltende und ereignis-orientierte Objektrepräsentationen.

Das Visualisierungstool sollte ebenfalls bestehende Technologien nutzen (z.B. integrierte Datenvisualisierung in WWW-Browsern). Zur Rezipation der zeitabhängigen Veränderung ist es nötig, daß der Betrachter zeitlich navigierend verschiedene diskrete Objektzustände, deren Existenzzeit, die Reihenfolge und die Übergange identifizieren, sie in einen Zeitbezug setzen sowie die Geschwindigkeit der Änderung feststellen kann. Zu jedem angesteuerten Zeitpunkt beliebiger Granularität sollte eine Repräsentation, falls definiert, existieren. Ereignis-orientierte Repräsentationen sind im Zeitverlauf erkennbar zu halten. Ein weiterer Aspekt ist die Gewährleistung der Synchronität zeitabhängiger Daten. Bei Präsentationen raum-zeitabhängiger Daten ist eine Information zum Zeitbezug der visualisierten Daten essentiell, um von der technisch bedingten Zeit zum Aufbau der Visualisierung unterscheiden zu können.

Als Ausgangspunkt für eine Erweiterung bietet sich hier das standardisierte VRML an. Viele Konstrukte zur Beschreibung kartographischer Animationen sind vorhanden und es existieren verschiedene Visualisierungstools für die bekanntesten WWW-Browser.

4 Konzepte zur zeitlichen Erweiterung von VRML

4.1 Überblick zu VRML

VRML geht von einem realzeit-basierten drei-dimensionalen Raum aus, in dem Geometrieobjekte Lichtquellen, Kamerapositionen, verschiedene Multimedia-Objekte (z.B. Sound, Bilder, Video), Sensorobjekte sowie Hyperlink-Objekte zu z.B. Text oder anderen VRML-Welten hierarchisch in einen Szenegraphen organisiert sind. Der Szenegraph entscheidet durch Ableitung von Koordinatentransformationen über die Position im Raum und die Sichtbarkeit der definierten Objekte. Alle Objekte (in VRML Knoten) können über frei definierbare Pfade Mitteilungen (Ereignisse mit Datenwerten) an andere Knoten versenden und von diesen empfangen. Sensor-Knoten erzeugen aufgrund bestimmter Systemzustände

Ereignisse, die durch Weiterleitung an die im Pfadnetz miteinander verbundenen Knoten der Start jeder Animation sind. In Form des *Script*-Knotens besitzt VRML einen Mechanismus mit Hilfe einer Programmier- (z.B. Java) oder Skriptsprache (z.B. JavaScript) individuelle Verhaltensweisen von Knoten zu definieren. Dies setzt auf Nutzerseite (d.h. in dem VRML-fähigen WWW-Browser) eine entsprechende Steuerungsmaschine voraus (z.B. Java Runtime Environment).

4.2 Systemzeit und Gültigkeitszeit

In VRML97 wird der Verlauf der Zeit durch die Folge der in einem Zeitsensor generierte Ereignisse simuliert. Die Geschwindigkeit der Zeit ist vom Visualisierungstool abhängig, aber i.a. wird die reale Zeit approximiert. Der aktuelle Zeitpunkt t_{now} dieser Zeit ist der Moment, in dem der Betrachter die Abbildung der VRML-Szene im Visualisierungstool sieht. Alle in der VRML-Welt zu einem Zeitpunkt t_e definerten Ereignisse werden aktiv, wenn zum ersten Mal $t_{now} >= t$ gilt. Demnach werden vergangene Ereignisse ($t < t_{now}$) nie aktiv und zukünftige Ereignisse ($t > t_{now}$) erst, wenn zum ersten Mal $t_{now} >= t$ gilt. Zur Unterscheidung wird diese Zeit *Systemzeit* oder *Präsentationszeit* genannt.

Zur Aktivierung vergangener oder zukünftiger Ereignisse zur aktuellen Präsentationszeit t_{now} wird daher eine neue Zeitdimension v, *Gültigkeitszeit* (valid time [Snod95] oder kartographische Zeit [Lan92]) genannt, eingeführt. Sie markiert die Zeit, wann ein Ereignis oder Zustand gültig war, ist oder sein wird. Sie ist unabhängig von der Präsentationszeit und kann ein weiterer Parameter von in VRML definierten Objekten sein. Die Gültigkeitszeit basiert auf einem linearen und kontinuierlichen Zeitmodell. Die Granularität von diskreten Zeitpunkten bzw. die Zeiteinheit (z.B. Sekunden, Tag, Jahr) ist anwendungsabhängig. Parallel zum aktuellen Präsentationszeitpunkt t_{now} existiert somit ein aktueller Gültigkeitszeitpunkt v_{now}, zu dem die VRML-Szene dargestellt wird. Die aktuelle Gültigkeitszeit wird auf jedes Objekt einer VRML-Welt angewendet. Zur Steuerung der Gültigkeitszeit durch den Betrachter existiert ein Navigationsparadigma, das es erlaubt, den aktuellen Gültigkeitszeitpunkt zu verändern.

4.3 Zeitinvariante und zeitvariante Objekte

Jede VRML-Szene kann *zeitinvariante* und *zeitvariante* Objekte beinhalten. Zeitinvariante Objekte besitzen nur eine, über den gesamten Bereich der Gültigkeitszeit gültige Repräsentation. Eine Änderung des aktuellen Gültigkeitszeitpunkt hat daher keinen Einfluß auf diese Objekte. Jedes in der VRML97-Spezifikation definierte Objekt ist automatisch zeitinvariant.

Zeitvariante Objekte besitzen verschiedene Repräsentationen (*Versionen*), die jeweils zu einer bestimmten Zeitperiode (*Versionszeitperiode*) gültig sind. Während einer Versionszeitperiode ist nur eine Repräsentation möglich, die zu jedem Zeitpunkt innerhalb der Versionzeitperiode gilt. Das Objekt ist unsichtbar, falls zu einer Zeitperiode keine Repräsentation definiert ist. Normalerweise existiert ein zeitvariantes Objekts zwischen zwei spezifischen Zeitpunkten, der Entstehung und der Dekonstruktion. Vor bzw. nach diesen Zeitpunkten existiert das Objekt nicht, d.h. es gibt keine Informationen zu dem Objekt. Die Existenzzeit wird *Gültigkeitsperiode* des Objekts und die zeitlich geordnete Reihe der aufeinanderfolgenden Repräsentationen, die ein Objekt während der Gültigkeitsperiode annehmen kann, wird *Historie* genannt. Die Historie eines zeitvarianten Objekts kann eine Folge von diskreten Zuständen, Ereignissen oder eine Zeitreihe bezeichnen (Folge von diskreten Meßwerten mit dazugehörigen Zeitpunkten, die eine sich in der Zeit kontinuierlich verändernde Eigenschaft beschreiben).

5 Vorschlag zur zeitlichen Erweiterung von VRML

Die Syntax und die Parameter der im folgenden vorgestellten Knoten des Erweiterungsvorschlags **VRML History** kann in [VRMLH] nachgelesen werden. Der Inhalt der VRML97-Spezifikation wird dabei als bekannt vorausgesetzt.

Definition der Gültigkeitsperiode: Der Knoten *ValidPeriod* definiert alle Start- und Endzeitpunkte der zeitlich aufeinanderfolgenden Versionszeitperioden eines zeitvarianten Objekts und spezifiziert somit dessen Gültigkeitsperiode. Da die Versionszeitperioden die Intervalle einer Partition der Gültigkeitsperiode sind, ist der Endzeitpunkt einer Versionszeitperiode identisch mit dem Startzeitpunkt der darauffolgenden Periode. Auch punktuelle Versionszeitperioden sind möglich. Da alle Zeitpunkte in dem ValidPeriod-Knoten als Intervallwerte in Bezug zu einem Basiszeitpunkt definiert werden, sind auch periodische Gültigkeitsperioden möglich; z.B. zur Definition periodischer Phänomene (z.B. Gezeiten, Temperaturschwankungen).

Definition zeitvarianter, zustandserhaltender Objekte: Die Knoten *HistoryShape* und *HistoryAppearance* definieren zu ihren Gültigkeitsperioden die Liste der zeitlich aufeinanderfolgenden Geometrie- bzw. Texturbeschreibungen zeitvarianter Objekte. Die Beschreibung i ist während der dazugehörigen Versionszeitperiode i gültig, d.h sie wird visualisiert, wenn der aktuelle Gültigkeitszeitpunkt v_{now} in der Versionszeitperiode i enthalten ist.

Zur Spezifikation zeitabhängiger Objektgruppen definiert ein *History*-Knoten als Version zu einer Versionszeitperiode nicht nur einzelne sondern eine Menge von Beschreibungsobjekten. Dabei richtet der History-Knoten eine Ableitungshierarchie für die Gültigkeitszeit ein: Die Versionszeitperiode eines History-Knotens für dessen Version i ist die Zeitperiode, die jedes Objekt dieser Version i als Gültigkeitsperiode maximal annehmen kann. Dies gilt auch für zeitinvariante Objekte, die in der Version i definiert sind.

Definition von zeitvarianten, zustandverändernden Objekteigenschaften: Zeitlich kontinuierlich verändernde Objekteigenschaften werden meistens durch Zeitreihen beschrieben. Während zu den Zeitpunkten der Stützstellen der Eigenschaftswert bekannt ist, werden zu Zeitpunkten zwischen den Stützstellen Interpolationswerte angenommen. Der *ValidTimeSensor*-Knoten definiert in seiner Gültigkeitsperiode mit den Versionszeitperioden die Zeitpunkte der Stützstellen der Zeitreihe. Die Datenwerte zu den Stützstellen werden in einem in VRML97 spezifizierten Interpolator-Knoten definiert. Während der ValidTimeSensor den Anteil bestimmt, den die aktuelle Gültigkeitszeit in den Versionszeitperioden der Gültigkeitsperiode belegt und diesen als Mitteilung an den Interpolator-Knoten übergibt, kann dieser daraus den dazugehörigen Eigenschaftswert interpolieren. Die Trennung der Zeitdefinition (ValidTimeSensor-Knoten) von der Datenwertdefinition (Interpolator-Knoten) hat den Vorteil, daß die Zeitdefinition für andere Interpolator-Knoten wiederverwendet werden kann.

Navigation in der Gültigkeitszeit: Eine VRML-Welt besitzt prinzipiell Viewpoints (Betrachterstandpunkte), von denen aus die Welt betrachtet werden kann. Die Navigation bezeichnet Aktionen, die die Position, Orientierung *oder* den aktuellen Gültigkeitszeitpunkt des Viewpoints und damit die Sicht des Betrachters auf die Welt verändern. Dies erlaubt dem Benutzer, sich individuell oder durch ein Skript geführt in der Welt räumlich wie auch zeitlich zu bewegen. Der *Viewpoint*-Knoten spezifiziert Schlüsselpositionen, zu denen der Benutzer via Skripts oder Browser-spezifischer Benutzungsoberfläche steuern kann. Die Möglichkeiten der Navigation sind durch verschiedene Navigationsparadigmen (im *NavigationInfo*-Knoten definierbar) näher spezifiziert. Neben räumlichen Navigationsparadigmen (WALK, FLY, EXAMINE) wird zur Änderung des aktuellen Gültigkeitszeitpunkts v_{now} eines Betrachterstandpunkts das zeitliche Navigationsparadigma TIMEWALK eingeführt. Eine animierte Navigation in der Gültigkeitszeit wird in Kombination mit einem *TimeInterpolator*-Knoten durch die Animierung des Gültigkeitszeitparameters des aktuellen Viewpoints realisiert.

Zeitabhängige Umgebungs-/Sensor-Knoten: Die zeitabhängigen Umgebungsknoten *Background* und *Fog* spezifizieren Umgebungsparameter für VRML-Welten, deren Gültigkeit auf die Zeit ihrer Gültigkeitsperiode reduziert ist. Zeitabhängige Sensor-Knoten spezifizieren raum-zeitabhängige Regionen in der Welt, die auf die Navigation des Betrachters reagieren können. Sie produzieren Ereignisse, sobald im Falle eines *ProximitySensor*-Knotens der Betrachter in die Region hineinnavigiert und im Falle eines *VisibilitySensor*-Knotens die Region in das raum-zeitabhängige Sichtfeld des Betrachters kommt.

6 Implementierung und Ergebnisse

Eine Implementierung von **VRML History** ist das Packet *vrmlHistory* [VRMLH]. Zur Definition der Knotenschnittstellen wurde das in VRML für diese Aufgabe vorgesehene Sprachkonstrukt der *Prototypisierung* verwendet. Die Definition der Prototypen ist in externen Dateien realisiert, die ein WWW-Browser wie eine Programmbibliothek nur bei Bedarf einlädt. Zur Implementierung des Knotenverhaltens wurde die Programmierschnittstelle der *Script*-Knoten zu Java verwendet (Java Scripting Autoring Interface). Das alternativ in vielen Browsern unterstützte interpretative JavaScript wurde aus Gründen längerer Ausführungszeiten, geringerer Sicherheitsanforderungen, größerer VRML-Prototypdateien und damit längerer Dateiladezeiten nicht genutzt. Sobald ein VRML-fähiger WWW-Browser den Hyperlink einer WWW-Seite folgend eine auf der Basis von VRML History beschriebene Präsentation einliest, werden die entsprechenden Knotenrealisierungen geladen und bei der Visualisierung angewendet. Dabei wird in dem WWW-Browsern automatisch eine Navigationsmöglichkeit für die zeitliche Dimension der Präsentation bereitgestellt.

Eine erste Anwendung war die Aufgabe, die raum-zeitabhängigen Ergebnisdaten einer FEM-Simulation zu visualisieren und im Internet zu publizieren. Für eine Entwässerungsmaßnahme wurde in Abhängigkeit von verschiedenen Pumpstrategien und der zeitabhängigen Grundwasserneubildung die Veränderung des Grundwasserspiegels über ein Jahr berechnet. Die Bildfolge (Abb.1)(visualisiert mit Netscape Navigator und SGI CosmoPlayer) zeigt den aus verschiedenen Blickrichtungen und zu unterschiedlichen Zeitpunkten im Jahr visualisierten Grundwasserspiegel [VRMLH]. Die in der VRML-Datei gespeicherte Datengrundlage für diese Präsentation umfaßt die berechneten Koordinaten eines 3D-Flächennetzes zu 34 ausgewählten Zeitschnitten. Die Repräsentation zu den übrigen Zeitschnitten wird automatisch interpoliert.

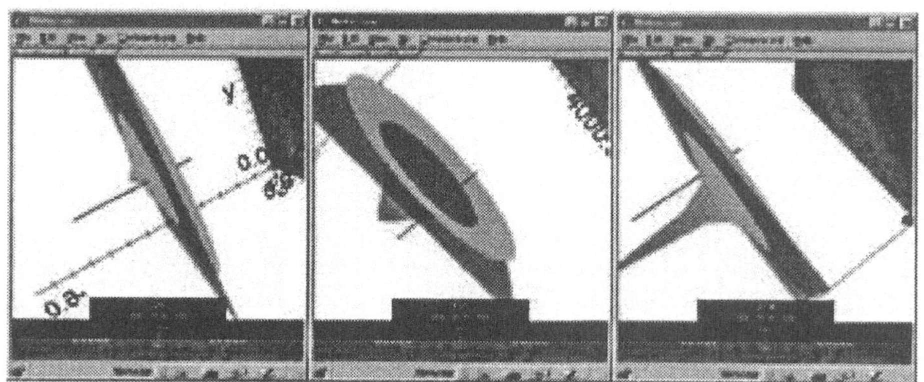

Abbildung1. *Bildfolge zum Ergebnis der FEM-Grundwassersimulation*

Die in **VRML History** definierten Knoten unterstützen eine effiziente Speicherung der zeitabhängigen Daten, da die aus dem Forschunggebiet der temporalen Datenbanken bekannten Speicherstrukturen Tuple-Timestamping und Attribute-Timestamping [TCGJ93] sowohl einzelnd als auch in Kombination anwendbar sind. Das Tuple-Timestamping ist im *History*-Knoten enthalten, das ein zeitabhängiges Objekt durch eine Folge von mit der Gültigkeitszeit parametrisierten Objektversionen beschreibt. Das Attribut-Timestamping, das jeden Attributdatenwert mit der Gültigkeitszeit parametrisiert, wird durch den Verbund eines *ValidTimeSensors* mit einem Interpolator realisiert. Damit kann, unabhängig von der Visualisierung, situationsabhängig die günstigste Speicherstruktur für die zeitabhängigen Daten gewählt werden.

Jede VRML-Datei ist eine ASCII-Textdatei und damit auch nach einer automatischen Generierung editierbar (z.B. Koordinatenkreuz, Texte) sowie problemlos für einen Austausch im Internet geeignet. Da zur Visualisierung der Dateien ein VRML-fähiger WWW-Browser ausreicht, der fast auf jeder Rechnerplattform angeboten wird, bestehen keine Hindernisse (in Hardware oder Software) zeitliche 3D-Animationen im Internet, auf Messen, Konferenzen oder beim Projektpartner einem großen Publikum zu zeigen.

7 Zusammenfassung

Ein Problem heutiger Visualisierungssysteme besteht darin, zeitliche 3D-Animationen, die im Zusammenhang mit der Visualisierung von raum-zeitabhängigen Daten häufiger auftreten, nicht speichern, austauschen oder im WWW publizieren zu können, ohne daß die für eine umfangreiche Navigations- und Interaktionstechnik notwendige Datenstruktur verloren geht. Mit diesem Beitrag wird ein Dateiformat und Skriptsprache zur Beschreibung solcher Darstellungen vorgestellt (VRML History), das die standardisierte VRML um die Gültigkeitszeit erweitert. Eine Visualisierung solcher mit VRML Historie beschriebenen Präsentationen kann sehr einfach mit den bekannten VRML-fähigen WWW-Browsern erreicht werden. Die Implementierung von VRML Historie stellt dafür innerhalb der WWW-Browser eine Möglichkeit zur Navigation und Interaktion in räumlicher und zeitlicher Dimension der Präsentation zur Verfügung.

Zukünftige Schritte sehen vor, das Dateiformat in den VRML-Standardisierungsprozeß einzubringen und das Laufzeitverhalten der Implementierung an verschiedenen raum-zeitabhängigen Szenebeschreibungen zu untersuchen.

Literatur

[BEJV95] J.R. Brown, R.Earnshaw, M. Jern, J. Vince: *Visualization*, John Wiley & Sons, 1995.

[CG98] P. Chamoni, P. Gluchowski (Hrsg.): *Analytische Informationssysteme: Data Warehouse, Online Analytical Processing Data Mining*, Springer, 1998.

[Dieh97] S. Diehl: VRML, in *Informatik Spektrum*, Nr. 20, S. 294-295, Springer, 1997.

[DG93] H.-J. G. Diersch, R. Gründler: GIS-based groundwater flow and transport modeling - the simulation system FEFLOW, *HYDROGIS'93*, Wien, 1993.

[Dran95] D. Dransch: *Temporale und nontemporale Computer-Animation in der Kartographie*, Selbstverlag FB Geowissenschaften, FU Berlin, 1995.

[Each94] A. MacEachren: Time as a Cartographic Variable, in [HU94], pp. 115-130.

[FK96] A. Formella, P.P. Kiefer: ANILAN: An Animation Language, in *IEEE Computer Animation'96*, pp. 184-189, 1996.

[GE97] N. Gershon, S.G. Eick: Information Visualization, in *IEEE Computer Graphics and Applications*, pp. 29-31, Jul/Aug 1997.

[GM97] M. Grauer, U. Merten: *Multimedia: Entwurf, Entwicklung und Einsatz in betrieblichen Informationssystemen*, Springer, 1997.

[GRA97] *GRAPE Manual*, Inst. für Angew. Mathematik, Universität Bonn und Universität Freiburg, 1997.

[Hib97] B. Hibbard: *Vis5D User's Guide*, Space Science and Engineering Center, Madison, 1997.

[HU94] K.M. Hearnshaw, D.J. Unwin (Eds.): *Visualization in GIS*, John Wiley & Sons, 1994.

[KK95] D.A. Keim, H.-P. Kriegel: Visualisierungstechniken zur Exploration und Analyse sehr großer Datenbanken, in *Proc. Datenbanksysteme in Büro, Technik und Wissenschaft (BTW)*, Dresden, 1995.

[KR93] K. Konstantinides, J. Rasure: The Khoros Software Development Environment for Image and Signal Processing, in *IEEE Journal of Image Processing*, 1993.

[Lan92] G. Langran: *Time in Geographical Information Systems*, Taylor & Francis, 1992.

[LB95] H. Luttermann, A. Blobel: CHRONOS: A Spatio-Temporal Data Server for GIS, in H. Kremers, W. Pillmann (Hrsg.): *Space and Time in Evironmental Information Systems*, CSEP'95, pp. 135-142, Metropolis-Verlag, 1995.

[Lut97] H. Luttermann: Analyse von VRML zur Visualisierung von FEM-Simulationsdaten, Arbeitsbericht Nr. 27, Universität-GH Siegen, Wirtschaftsinformatik, 1997.

[LL96] H. Lessing, U.W. Lipeck (Hrsg.): *Informatik für den Umweltschutz*, 10. Symp. CSEP, Hannover, Metropolis-Verlag, 1996.

[MTT90] N. Magnenat-Thalmann, D. Thalmann: *Computer-Animation: Theory and Practice*, Springer, 1990.

[NHM97] G.M. Nielsen, H. Hagen, H. Müller (Hrsg.): *Scientific Visualization: Overview, Methodologies, Techniques*, IEEE Computer Society Press, 1997

[OIV] Silicon Graphics: *Open Inventor*, *http://www.sgi.com/Technology/Inventor.html.*

[OOGL] University of Minnesota: *GeomView*, *http://www.geom.umn.edu/software/.*

[Pet95] M.P. Peterson: *Interactive and Animated Cartography*, Prentice Hall, 1995.

[RS97] R.M. Rohrer, E. Swing: Web-Based Information Visualization, in *IEEE Computer Graphics and Applications*, pp. 52-59, Jul/Aug 1997.

[Shep95] I.D.H. Shepherd: Putting Time on the Map: Dynamic Display in Data Visualization and GIS, in P. Fischer (Eds.): *Innovation in GIS 2*, Taylor & Francis, 1995.

[SML97] W.J. Schroeder, K.M. Martin, W.E. Lorensen: *The Visualization Toolkit: An object-Oriented Approach To 3D Graphics*, Prentice Hall, 1997.

[Snod95] R.T. Snodgras: *The TSQL2 Temporal Query Language*, Kluwer Academic Press, 1995.

[TCGJ93] A.U. Tansel, J. Clifford, S.K. Gadia, S. Jajodia, A. Segev, R.T. Snodgras (Eds.): *Temporal Databases: Theory, Design, and Implementation*, Benjamin/Cummings, 1993.

[UFK89] C. Upson, T. Faulhaber, D. Kamins, u.a.: The Application Visualization System: A Computational Environment for Scientific Visualization, in *IEEE Comp. Graphics and Appl.*, 9(4):30-42, 1989.

[VRML97] VRML Architecture Group (VAG): The Virtual Reality Modeling Language Specifications ISO/IEC DIS 14772-1, 1997, *http://www.vrml.org/Specifications/VRML97/.*

[VRMLRep] San Diego Super Computing Center: The VRML Repository, *http://www.sdsc.edu/vrml/.*

[VRMLH] Universität-GH Siegen: The VRML History Homepage, *http://www-winfo.uni-siegen.de/vrmlHistory/docs/index.html.*

Interaktive Visualisierung von Geoinformationen

Dipl.-Inform. Kai Pollermann*
Prof. Dr.-Ing. habil. H. Rothe

Universität der Bundeswehr
Fachbereich Maschinenbau
Holstenhofweg 85
22043 Hamburg

Zusammenfassung Durch den Einsatz von interaktiven Computergrafiken ergeben sich neue Möglichkeiten bei der Analyse geographischer Daten. In diesem Paper wird gezeigt, wie die Informationen aus einer Datenbasis so in einer Grafik dargestellt werden können, daß der Anwender die für ihn interessanten Zusammenhänge im Bild erkennen kann. Weiter wird gezeigt wie dies durch verschiedene Interaktionstechniken noch effizienter gestaltet werden kann. Im Gegensatz zur Künstlichen Intelligenz wird bei dieser Vorgehensweise nicht versucht, die Fähigkeiten des Menschen nachzubilden, sondern es werden seine Fähigkeiten gezielt unterstützt. Realisiert wurden diese Konzepte und Ideen im Programm "3D-Server".

1 Einleitung

Der Mensch verfügt über ausgezeichnete Fähigkeiten im Bereich Mustererkennung und der Verarbeitung von unvollständigem bzw. unsicherem Wissen. Da es schwierig ist, menschliches Wissen und Denkprozesse mathematisch exakt zu formulieren, gibt es trotz aller Bemühungen aus der KI-Forschung kein System mit vergleichbaren Leistungen. Gerade bei komplexen Aufgabenstellungen arbeiten die meisten Menschen nicht mit exakten logischen Methoden, sondern mit ihrer *Intuition*, d. h. mit Wissen und Schlußfolgerungen, die ihnen selbst nicht bewußt sind. Daher ist es erfolgversprechender, dieses Vorgehen durch geeignete Tools zu unterstützen, als zu versuchen dieses versteckte Wissen zu extrahieren und ein gleichwertiges Expertensystem mit entsprechend aufwendigen Deduktionsmechanismen zu erstellen[1]. Howard Rheingold spricht in diesen Zusammenhang auch von "Intelligenzverstärkung"[2].

Beispielsweise sind bei Bauvorhaben neben den gut berechenbaren bautechnischen und betriebswirtschaftlichen Faktoren auch soziale bzw. politische Randbedingungen sowie Aspekte des Landschafts- und Umweltschutzes zu berücksichtigen. Die verschiedenen Einflüsse und die langfristigen Auswirkungen können hierbei nur schwer analytisch erfaßt und bestimmt werden. In den Entscheidungsprozeß müssen alle Betroffenen einbezogen werden. Da diese nicht immer logisch und vernünftig denken und handeln, ist an eine automatische Entscheidungsfindung nicht zu denken. Wer aber in diesem Bereich schon Erfahrungen gesammelt hat, kann die Folgen solcher Projekte gut abschätzen und seine Entscheidungen danach richten.

* Tel.: 040 6541 3351, Email: pollermann@acm.org

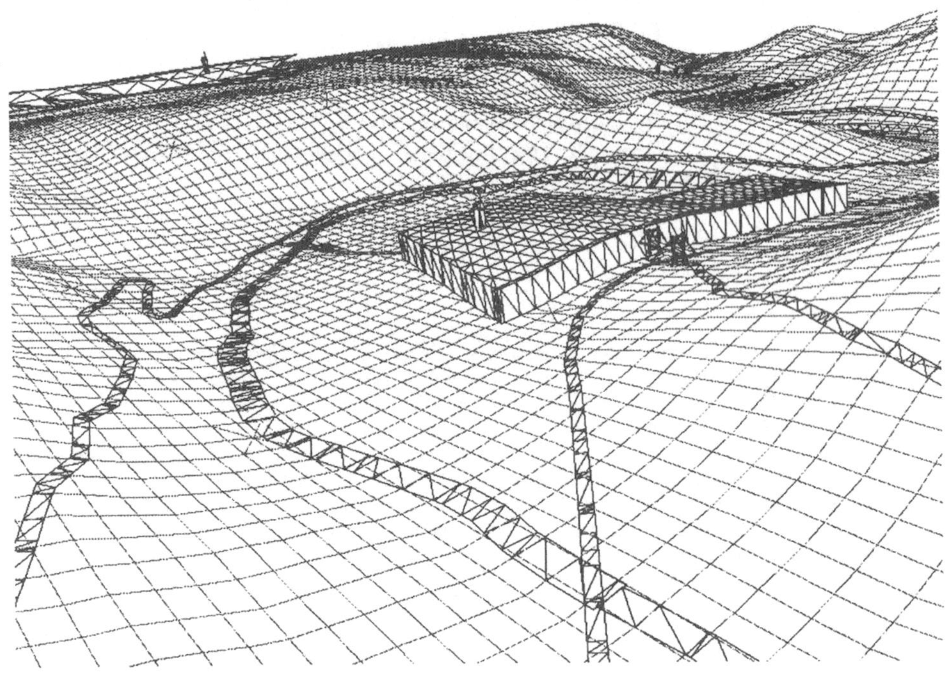

Abbildung 1. Drahtgittermodell

Aus den vorangegangenen Ausführungen geht hervor, daß bei der Erstellung eines Informationssystems der Schwerpunkt auf die Präsentation der Daten, d. h. die *Informationsvermittlung*[3], gelegt werden soll und nicht auf ihre Analyse und Auswertung. Wenn der Entscheidungsträger alle relevanten Daten schnell zur Verfügung hat, kann er seine eigenen Erfahrungen voll ausspielen. Dabei ist aber darauf zu achten, daß die Daten sinnvoll aufbereitet sind und er nicht von einer Informationsflut erschlagen wird. Für das Design solcher Systeme ist also viel Hintergrundwissen über die jeweilige Anwendung notwendig.

Am besten kann der Mensch Informationen aufnehmen, wenn sie als *Bild* vorliegen. Die Informationsvermittlung ist mit Bildern, z. B. in Form von Businessgrafiken, wesentlich effektiver als mit Texten und Tabellen. Daher liegt es nahe die entscheidungsrelevanten Daten in ein Bild umzusetzen.

Am Lehrstuhl für Meß- und Informationstechnik wurde das Programm *3D-Server*[4] entwickelt, das die hier beschriebene Vorgehensweise für Aufgabenstellungen mit einem geographischen Kontext demonstriert. Der 3D-Server ist ein Forschungsprototyp, der in Zusammenarbeit mit Anwendern weiter ausgebaut werden soll.

2 Geodaten

Geodaten werden bereits seit den 60er Jahren mit Hilfe von Geoinformationssystemen (GIS) elektronisch verarbeitet[5, 6]. Allgemein versteht man unter dem Begriff "Geodaten" bzw. "Geoinformationen" alle Daten über die Erde und ihre Bewohner. Geodaten zerfallen in zwei Klassen, *räumliche* und *thematische* Daten. Die räumlichen Daten beschreiben die Topographie des Geländes sowie die Geometrie der in dem Gelände vorhandenen Objekte. Typische Repräsentationen für die Geländeform sind Höhenraster oder Triangulated Irregular Networks (TINs). Die Geometrie der im Gelände vorhandenen Objekte, wie z. B. Häuser, Städte, Straßen, Wälder, Gewässer u. s. w., wird in einer separaten vektororientierten Datenbank beschrieben. Die thematischen Daten enthalten die nicht-geometrischen Eigenschaften dieser Objekte. Ein Objekt kann beispielweise die Eigenschaften "Dorf", "Luftkurort" und "3500 Einwohner" haben. Die thematischen Daten werden auch Sachdaten genannt.

Eine weitere Form von Geodaten sind Karten oder Luft- bzw. Satellitenbilder. Zwar können diese Daten nicht durch den Computer interpretiert werden, ein menschlicher Betrachter kann diese Informationen aber sofort auswerten. Dies gilt insbesondere für Karten, da diese bereits so gestaltet sind, daß sie einfach interpretiert werden können. Somit liefern sie einen wichtigen Beitrag zur Informationsvermittlung.

3 Visualisierung

Unter "Visualisierung" versteht man die Erzeugung einer grafischen Darstellung aus einer Datenbasis. Die genaue Art der Darstellung hängt von der zugehörigen Anwendung ab. Der 3D-Server verwendet als Datenbasis für die Visualisierung DTED[7] (Höhenraster), DFAD[8] (Oberflächenbeschreibung) und Rastergrafiken (RGB und TIFF). Die Objekte in der Oberflächenbeschreibung, auch Features genannt, liegen als 2D Vektordaten vor und sind in Punkt-, Linien- und Flächenobjekte unterteilt. Jedes Objekt hat außer der geometrischen Beschreibung eine Klassifikation, die angibt, um was für ein Objekt es sich handelt. Aus diesen Daten wird ein *Drahtgittermodell* des Geländes konstruiert werden (Abbildung 1). Dieses Drahtgittermodell ist die Grundlage für die Visualisierung.

Bei der Konstruktion des Drahtgittermodells liegt die Hauptaufgabe in der Integration der 2D Vektordaten in die $2\frac{1}{2}$D Höhendaten. Aus den Höhendaten wird direkt ein reguläres Quadmesh berechnet, in das die Featuremodelle plaziert werden. Das Quadmesh wird bei jedem Bildaufbau neu berechnet, so daß kein zusätzlicher Hauptspeicher benötigt wird. Dies ist in Echtzeit möglich, weil die Berechnung der einzelnen Modellpunkte aus den Rasterdaten mit wenigen Rechenoperationen in konstantem Zeitaufwand erfolgen kann.

Punktobjekte, wie z. B. Häuser oder Strommasten, werden je nach gewünschtem Detaillierungsgrad als Quader oder mit einem VRML-Modell dargestellt. Bei Linienobjekten, wie z. B. Straßen, können sich die Höhenwerte des Geländes im Verlauf der Linie ändern. Bei Flächenobjekten gilt dasselbe für die Höhenwerte innerhalb der Fläche. Daher müssen zusätzliche Punkte in das Drahtgittermodell eingefügt werden. Die neu eingefügten Punkte liegen immer auf den Gitterlinien des Höhenrasters.

In Abhängigkeit von der Anwendung wird das Drahtgittermodell mit geeigneten Materialeigenschaften und Texturen versehen. Soll eine möglichst realitätsnahe Darstellung erreicht werden, so werden Luftbilder und fotorealistische Texturen verwendet (Abbildung 2). Steht hingegen die Analyse räumlicher Strukturen und Zusammenhänge im Vordergrund, so werden die Methoden aus der thematischen Kartographie verwendet[9], um dem Benutzer ein optimales Bild von der Situation zu geben. Dabei sind auch Erkenntnisse aus den Bereichen Raumkognition und Wahrnehmungspsychologie zu berücksichtigen[10], da eine schlechte Visualisierung zur Verfälschung der Tatsachen führen kann[11].

Für den Import der Daten und für die Konstruktion des Geländemodells wurden alle Algorithmen selbst entwickelt, so daß außer dem OpenInventor[12, 13] und OpenGL[14] keine zusätzlichen Fremdprodukte benötigt werden. OpenGL ist eine weit verbreitete Grafikbibliothek und stellt grundlegende Funktionen zum Zeichnen texturierter 3D Grafiken zur Verfügung. Der OpenInventor ist eine objektorientierte Kapselung von OpenGL. Beim OpenInventor werden die zur Visualisierung benötigten Daten mit Hilfe eines Szenengraphen verwaltet. Zusätzlich bietet er Funktionen zur Interaktion an.

Der 3D-Server, von dem auch die hier abgebildeten Screenshots stammen, bietet dem Anwender zahlreiche leicht konfigurierbare Möglichkeiten bei der Darstellung an. Der Anwender kann z. B. in Symboltabellen angeben, wie die einzelnen Objekte dargestellt werden sollen. Für die Seitenwände und für das Dach der Featuremodelle können jeweils Materialeigenschaften, Farbe und Textur angeben werden. Für Punktobjekte kann außerdem ein 3D-Modell (z. B. eine VRML–Datei) angegeben werden.

4 Interaktion

Der wesentliche Vorteil des hier beschriebenen Verfahrens gegenüber den herkömmlichen ist die Möglichkeit der Interaktion. Wenn man bei der Arbeit mit Papierkarten ein Objekt entdeckt, über das man mehr Informationen benötigt, dann muß man entweder über den Namen oder die Koordinaten des Objektes auf eine externe Tabelle zugreifen. Durch den Einsatz von elektronischen Karten bzw. Computermodellen der Landschaft ergibt sich eine wesentlich effizientere Möglichkeit. Wenn man am Bildschirm ein Objekt ausgewählt hat, über das man mehr Informationen benötigt, dann kann der Computer die gewünschten Informationen automatisch aus einer Datenbank herauslesen.

Im Programm wurde dies realisiert indem eine neue OpenInventor–Klasse (`SoFeature`) definiert wurde, die zusätzlich Identifikatoren bzw. Zeiger enthält,

Abbildung2. Realitätsnahe Geländedarstellung

die auf das entsprechende Objekt in der Datenbasis verweisen. Klickt der Betrachter mit der Maus auf den Bildschirm, dann liefert eine Funktion des Viewers den Pfad auf das geometrische Objekt im Szenengraphen zurück, das an dieser Stelle sichtbar ist. Das `SoFeature`-Objekt wird bei der Konstruktion des Szenengraphen vor das entsprechende geometriesche Objekt plaziert. Ausgehend von dem gefundenen geometrischen Objekt wird dann im Pfad solange zurückgegangen, bis man auf das `SoFeature`-Objekt trifft. Dieses Objekt enthält dann die Referenz auf den gesuchten Datenbankeintrag. Das Auswerten der Zusatzinformationen geschieht dann mittels eines extern defnierbaren Callbacks.

In Abbildung 3 ist der Schattenwurf dargestellt, den ein Sendemast erzeugt. Ein Auswerter ist dadurch in der Lage, gezielt nach Städten zu suchen, die im Funkschatten liegen. Anhand von Zusatzinformationen (Einwohnerzahl, Anzahl der Betriebe etc.) kann er entscheiden ob es sich lohnt, einen höheren Sendemast zu bauen bzw. einen anderen, unter Umständen teureren, Standort zu suchen.

Weiter besteht die Möglichkeit, verschiedene Ansichten des Geländes zu betrachten. Beim 3D-Server kann man das Geländemodell mit der Maus drehen oder heranzoomen. Dadurch kann man beispielweise von der Gesamtansicht zu

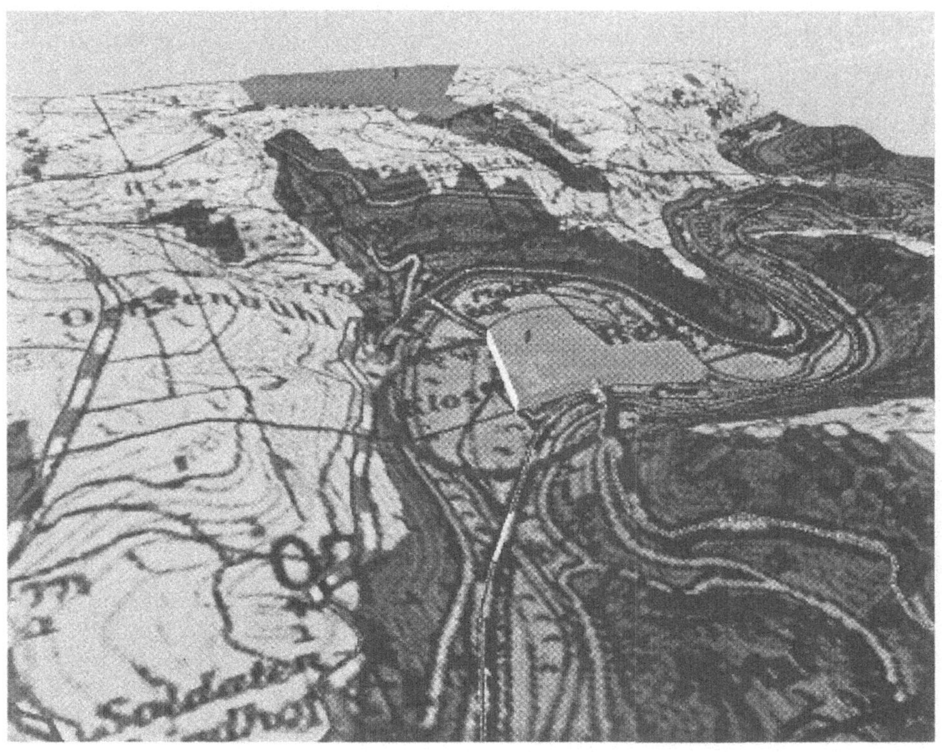

Abbildung3. Anwendungsorientierte Geländedarstellung

einer Detailansicht und wieder zurück gehen. Hierfür wird der in den OpenInventor integrierete Viewer verwendet, der entsprechende grafische Kontrollelemente enthält. Eine flüssige Bewegung setzt jedoch zur Zeit noch teure spezielle Grafikhardware voraus. Durch den rapiden Preisverfall in diesem Sektor dürften entsprechende Systeme aber bald Allgemeingut werden.

Ebenfalls wichtig ist die Möglichkeit zwischen verschiedenen Darstellungsmodi umzuschalten. Dadurch kann man sehr viel mehr verschiedene thematische Daten in die Grafik integrieren, als mit herkömmlichen Medien möglich ist. Diese Möglichkeit ist wichtig, wenn man die Entscheidungsfindung in mehrere Phasen unterteilen will, die jeweils auf verschiedene thematische Schichten zurückgreifen. Das Umschalten geschieht, indem die verschiedenen Attribute in den Szenengraphen eingebunden werden und dann je nach Bedarf aktiviert oder ausgeschaltet werden können.

Um die Interaktionsmöglichkeiten besser an die Anwendung und den aktuellen Kontext anzupassen wird auch mit wissensbasierten Techniken gearbeitet[15, 16].

5 Anwendungsbeispiele

Anwendungsmöglichkeiten ergeben sich in den Bereichen Landschaftsgestaltung, Touristik, Planung, Logistik und Überwachung. Ein Landschaftsplaner kann in einem Geoinformationssystem (GIS) die ihm vorschwebenen Änderungen vornehmen und diese sofort in einer realitätsnahen Darstellung sichtbar machen. Diese Vorgehensweise bietet zwei Vorteile. Auf der einen Seite kann der Planer seine ihm bekannten Tools verwenden, die ihm die benötigten Funktionen zur Aufbereitung und Analyse der Daten zur Verfügung stellen. Auf der anderen Seite können die Auswirkungen der Änderungen durch die interaktive 3D-Darstellung mit Personen diskutiert werden, die an der Entscheidung beteiligt sind, aber nicht über das entsprechende Fachwissen verfügen. Ähnliche Möglichkeiten ergeben sich im Touristikbereich bei der Verwendung von Multimedia-Informationssystemen. Der Kunde kann, bevor er sich für eine Reise entscheidet, virtuell in der Landschaft bewegen und beispielsweise Skiabfahrten simulieren. Wenn er dann das Gebiet weiter eingrenzt, kann er im Bild gezielt nach Hotels o. ä. suchen und sich ggf. online mit einem Hotelbuchungssystem verbinden lassen.

Während in den vorherigen Anwendungsbeispielen eine realitätsnahe Darstellung erforderlich war, sind für die Bereiche Planung, Logistik und Überwachung eher solche Darstellungen wichtig, die möglichst viele verschiedene Informationen übersichtlich zusammenfassen. Die räumliche Verteilung der verschiedenen thematischen Daten kann durch entsprechende Farben, Muster und Symbole dargestellt werden. Insbesondere geht die Möglichkeit, zwischen verschiedenen Ansichten per Knopfdruck umzuschalten, weit über das hinaus, was mit Papierkarten möglich ist.

Realisiert sind z. Z. in Zusammenarbeit mit Dornier Anwendungen aus den Bereichen Bild- und Signalauswertung sowie der Flugroutenplanung.

6 Zusammenfassung

Die Automatisierung von Entscheidungsprozessen scheitert bei komplexeren Aufgaben an der Formalisierung des benötigten Wissens. Daher sollte auf eine automatische Entscheidungsfindung verzichtet werden. Das Programm 3D-Server stellt Geodaten grafisch dar und bietet zahlreiche Interaktionsmöglichkeiten, um die Darstellung zu verändern oder Zusatzinformationen über Einzelobjekte im Bild abzufragen. Dadurch können zum einen räumliche Strukturen und Zusammenhänge gut erkannt werden, und zum anderen wird der Zugriff auf die zur Entscheidungsfindung benötigten Informationen optimiert. Dieses Vorgehen verbindet traditionelle Arbeitsmethoden mit modernen Technologien und dürfte somit in Zukunft weite Verbreitung finden.

Literatur

1. K. Pollermann
Visualisierung von Geoinformationen in Decision Supporting Systems
Diplomarbeit am FB Informatik, Univ. Hamburg

2. H. Rheingold
Virtuelle Welten – Reisen im Cyberspace
Rowohlt, Hamburg 1992

3. H. Preuß
Informationsvermittlung -
eine wichtige Aufgabe moderner Geoinformationssysteme
in G. Buziek (Hrsg.)
GIS in Forschung und Praxis
Wittwer, Stuttgart 1995

4. K. Pollermann, A. Kasper, H. Rothe, J. Geppert
Interaktive 3D-Realzeitgrafiken für die Bildauswertung
"Neue Technologien in der wehrtechnischen Simulation"
Symposium beim BAkWVT, Mannheim 1997

5. R. Bill, D. Fritsch
Grundlagen der Geo-Informationssysteme, Bd. 1
Wichmann, Heidelberg 1994

6. R. Bill
Grundlagen der Geo-Informationssysteme, Bd. 2
Wichmann, Heidelberg 1996

7. Defence Mapping Agency Specifications for
Digital Terrain Elevation Data
DMA Aerospace Center, 1986

8. Defence Mapping Agency Specifications for
Digital Feature Analysis Data
DMA Aerospace Center, 1986

9. D. Grünreich
Aufgabe und Bedeutung der kartographischen Visualisierung
in Geo-Informationssystemen (GIS)
in G. Buziek (Hrsg.)
GIS in Forschung und Praxis
Wittwer, Stuttgart 1995

10. H. Couclelis
People Manipulate Objects (but Cultivate Fields)
Beyond the Raster-Vektor Debate in GIS
in A. U. Frank et al (Hrsg.)
Theories and Methods of Spatial-Temporal Reasoning
in Geographic Space
Lecture Notes in Computer Science
Spinger, Berlin 1992

11. M. von Rimscha
Lügen mit GIS
`http://www.bio-geo.uni-karlsruhe.de/Buch/Aufsatz/MR/kgr-mr1.htm`

12. J. Wenecke
The Inventor Mentor
Addison Wesley, Reading 1994

13. J. Wenecke
The Inventor Toolmaker
Addison Wesley, Reading 1994

4. J. Neider, T. Davis, M. Woo
OpenGL Programming Guide Addison Wesley, Reading 1993

5. M. Lindholm, T. Sarjakoski
User models and information theory
in the design of a query interface for GIS
in A. U. Frank et al (Hrsg.)
Theories and Methods of Spatial-Temporal Reasoning
in Geographic Space
Lecture Notes in Computer Science
Springer, Berlin 1992

6. G. Gegg
Wissensbasierte Beratungssysteme für
Fernerkundung und Geo-Informationssyseme im Forstwesen
in M. Schilcher (Hrsg.)
Geo–Informatik
Anwendungen, Erfahrungen, Tendenzen
Siemens-Nixdorf AG, München 1991

Integriertes Patientenmodell für chirurgische Eingriffe

J. Raczkowsky, H. Grabowski, J. Münchenberg, C. Burghart, U.Rembold, H. Wörn

Institut für Prozeßrechentechnik, Automation und Robotik (IPR), Universität Karlsruhe, 76128 Karlsruhe, email: rkowsky@ira.uka.de

Zusammenfassung. Die präoperative Modellierung des individuellen Patienten bzw. seiner für die Operation relevanten Aspekte bildet die Grundlage für die Automatisierung von Vorgängen im Operationssaal. Insbesondere der Einsatz eines Roboters bei chirurgischen Eingriffen ist ohne diese Daten nicht möglich. Häufig existieren verschiedenste Daten über einen Patienten; sehr oft in nicht kompatibler Form und sie erfüllen nicht die spezifischen Anforderungen chirurgischer Modelle. Im folgenden wird ein Ansatz für ein integriertes Patientenmodell vorgestellt, das sich im Moment auf Anforderungen der Mund-, Kiefer- und Gesichtschirurgie beschränkt.

1 Einleitung

Chirurgische Eingriffe erfordern neben dem hohen manuellen Geschick des operierenden Arztes eine sehr gute räumlicher Vorstellung der im Operationsfeld liegenden Gewebestrukturen. Trotz der sehr langen und intensiven Ausbildung von Chirurgen sind nur sehr wenige Spezialisten in der Lage, aus den meist zweidimensionalen Daten, z.B. Röntgenaufnahmen, Tomographieschichtbildern, Ultraschallbildern etc., eine präzise dreidimensionale Rekonstruktion der interessierenden Patientenregion in ihrem Kopf vorzunehmen. Verschiedene Systeme für die Unterstützung manuell ausgeführter Operationen bieten eine rechnerbasierte 3D-Rekonstruktion aus den zweidimensionalen Schichtdaten eines Tomograhieverfahrens zusammen mit Navigationssystemen an [9]. Sogenannte Matching-Verfahren [15] können eine solche Darstellung aus einer Modalität zu einer mehrere (komplementäre) Gewebearten enthaltenden Visualisierung erweitern. Dies ist der erste Schritt zu einem integrierten Patientenmodell, das alle relevanten Aspekte für die anstehende Operation des Patienten enthält. Im Rahmen des Sonderforschungsbereiches 414: „Rechner- und sensorgestützte Chirurgie" wird ein solches Patientenmodell entwickelt, welches neben der manuellen Operation auch roboterunterstützte Operationen verbessert bzw. erst ermöglicht. Durch die enge Zusammenarbeit zwischen Ingenieuren, Naturwissenschaftlern und Medizinern ist die Basis für ein profundes und stabiles Patientenmodell gegeben.

2 Anforderungen an das Patientenmodell

Das Patientenmodell für die Unterstützung eines chirugischen Eingriffes ist Teil einer Datensammlung über den Patienten, die in Zukunft in einer sogenannten „Elektronischen Patientenmappe“ in der Datenbank eines PAC-Systems gespeichert wird [18]. Allerdings muss das chirurgische Modell bis zu seiner endgültigen Archivierung so gestaltet sein, daß es einfach erweiterbar ist. Die initiale Datenbasis stellen präoperative Aufnahmen des Patienten dar. Liegen mehrere Aufnahmen vor, so kann eine dreidimensionale Rekonstruktion errechnet werden. Obwohl diese Vorgehensweise prinzipiell auch mit, aus mehreren Richtungen aufgenommenen, Röntgenaufnahmen möglich ist, sind tomographische Schichtbilder heutzutage gängig. Je nach Modalität (CT, MRT, PET etc.) lassen sich so bestimmte Gewebestrukturen als Volumenmodelle darstellen. Als nächster Schritt folgt die Klassifikation der einzelnen Volumenelemente: die Segmentierung. Die Volumenelemente werden dabei mit Organ- bzw. Teilorgan-Indizes belegt. Bis heute ist noch kein Verfahren für eine vollständig automatische Segmentierung bekannt; sie erfolgt interaktiv durch einen Mediziner. Da für verschiedene Bearbeitungsschritte die Oberflächen von Organen wichtig sind, sind Oberfächenmodelle neben den Volumenmodellen von hoher Relevanz. Mit Hilfe von Triangulationsverfahren lassen sie sich aus den Volumenmodellen errechnen. Je nach erwünschtem Approximationsgrad bestehen sie aus einer großen Zahl Polygone. Daneben werden Funktionale Modelle immer wichtiger, um in einer präoperativen Simulation den Erfolg eines Eingriffs besser beurteilen zu können. Bild 1 zeigt das Patientenmodell als Kern der Automatisierungsbestrebungen im Operationssaal.

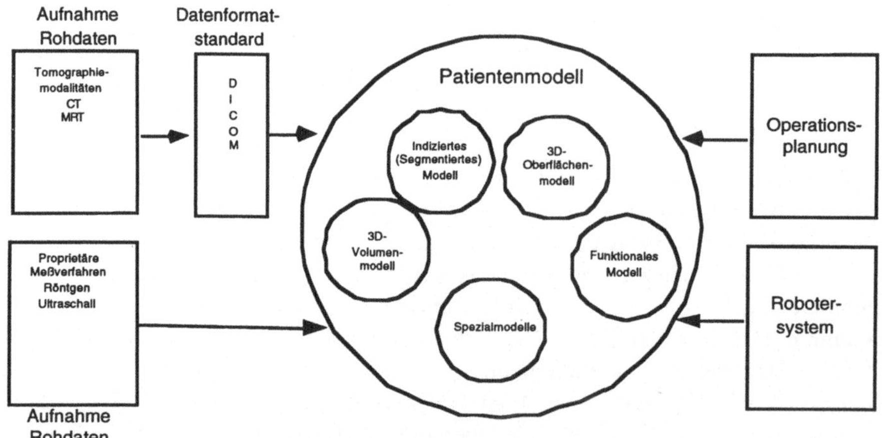

Bild 1. Patientenmodell als Kern der Automatisierung im Operationssaal

Strukturelle Änderungen auf den präoperativ gewonnenen Daten des Patienten finden in zwei Phasen statt:

- Präoperativ während der Planung
  Neben der reinen Visualisierung, die heute meist als Planung verstanden wird, soll dem planenden Arzt die Möglichkeit gegeben werden, Operationsschritte in einer Simulation auszuführen und somit auf das zu erwartende Operationsergebnis zu schließen. Dabei sind Schnitte auszuführen und Gewebe zu bewegen.
- Intraoperativ anhand neuer Daten
  Während einer Operation verschieben sich insbesondere Weichgewebe, deren genaue Lage mit Hilfe intraoperative Messungen bestimmt werden soll. Mit den von den verschiedenen Modalitäten (Ultraschall, Offener Kernspintomograph, Röntgen etc.) registrierten Daten läßt sich das aus präoperativen Daten bestehende Patientenmodell aktualisieren.

Die meisten bisherigen Modelle aus Patientendaten dienten rein der Visualisierung und lassen sich nur mühsam ändern bzw. aktualisieren. Planungsmodelle, beispielsweise für Knochenverschiebungen, beschränken sich auf sehr wenige markante Punkte und stellen deshalb eine zu grobe Approximation dar.

3 Modellierung der Patientendaten

Im Gegensatz zu den meisten industriellen Werkstücken sind in der Medizin die zu handhabenden Objekte durch die Eigenschaften Verformbarkeit, komplexe Formgebung und Individualität gekennzeichnet. Die Basis für die Nutzung eines Roboters für chirurgische Eingriffe ist somit eine individuelle und je nach Operation präzise Modellierung des Operationsfeldes. Bei komplexen chirurgischen Eingriffen sind jedoch über die reine Darstellung hinausgehende Simulationsverfahren gefordert. So ist z. B. bei der präoperativen Planung der Frontal Orbital Advancement (FOA) Operation der Volumengewinn von Interesse, der durch die Knochenverlagerung erreicht wird. Um solche komplexen Eingriffe mit Hilfe des Computers simulieren zu können, müssen die Schichtaufnahmen, insbesondere verschiedener Aufnahmemodalitäten zunächst untereinander in Relation gesetzt werden. Anschließend müssen aus den so gewonnenen multimodalen Bilddaten geometrische Modelle erzeugt werden, die zum einen die anatomischen Strukturen genau repräsentieren, zum anderen die Simulation der für die Operation relevanten Eingriffe wie z.B. Bohren, Sägen, Fräsen oder Verformen effizient unterstützen. Neben den geometrischen Modellen müssen Methoden zur Interaktion bereitstehen, die dem Chirurgen eine exakte und intuitive Eingabe der chirurgischen Eingriffe ermöglicht.

In der medizinischen Diagnostik fallen mittlerweile umfangreiche Mengen von Bilddaten an. Für eine effiziente Nutzung dieser Daten müssen die Bilder verschiedener Modalitäten registriert werden, so daß ein schnelles Umschalten zwischen verschiedenen Modalitäten und das Betrachten von Mischbildern ermöglicht wird (Bild 2).

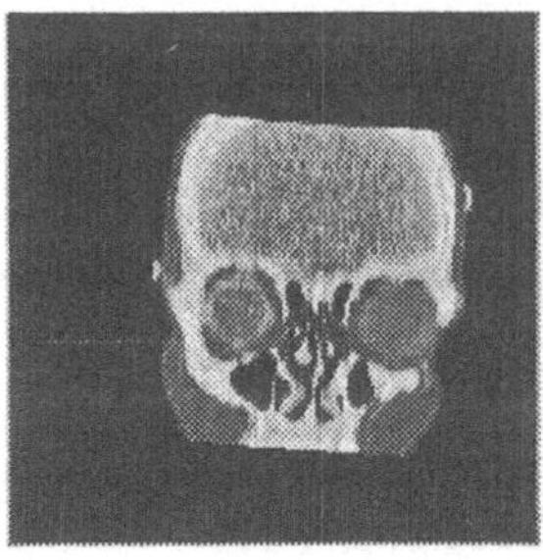
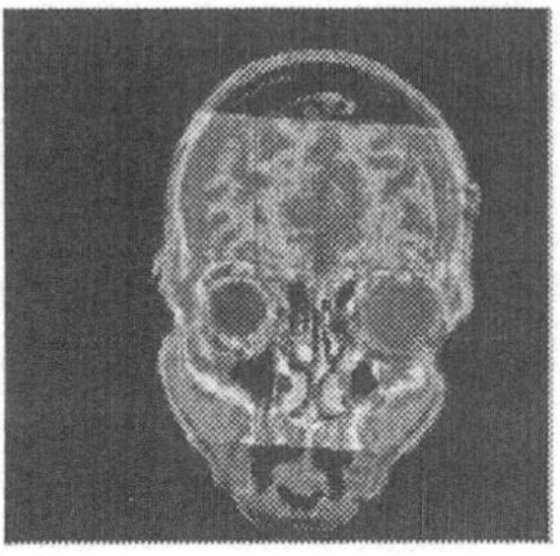
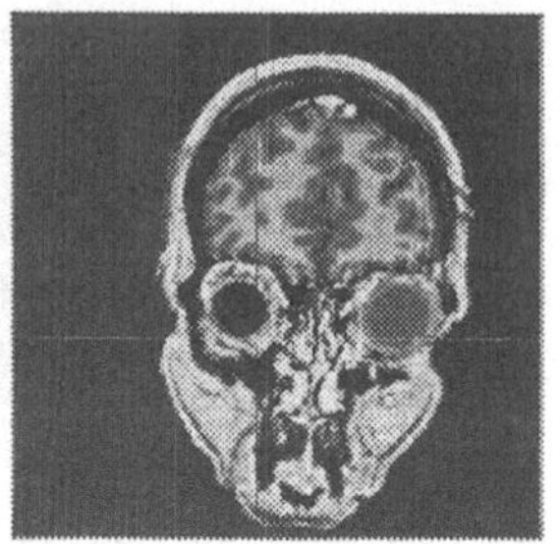

Bild 2. Erzeugung von Mischbildern aus registrierten CT und MR Bilddaten.

Um solche Ansichten zu ermöglichen, ohne die Originaldaten zu verändern, wird für jedes Tomogramm eine *Normierungsmatrix* bestimmt, mit deren Hilfe eine metrisch korrektes dreidimensionales Bild berechnet werden kann. Anschließend wird für jedes Tomogramm durch ein automatisches Registrierungsverfahren [15] eine *Positionierungsmatrix* berechnet, in der die für die synchrone Ausrichtung notwendigen Rotationen und Translationen enthalten sind (Bild3). Mit dem Konzept der Normierungs- und Positionierungsmatrizen kann dann für jeden Bildpunkt seine Lage im Raum berechnet werden und umgekehrt aus der Lage eines Punktes im Raum sofort die ihm entsprechende Originalschicht bestimmt werden.

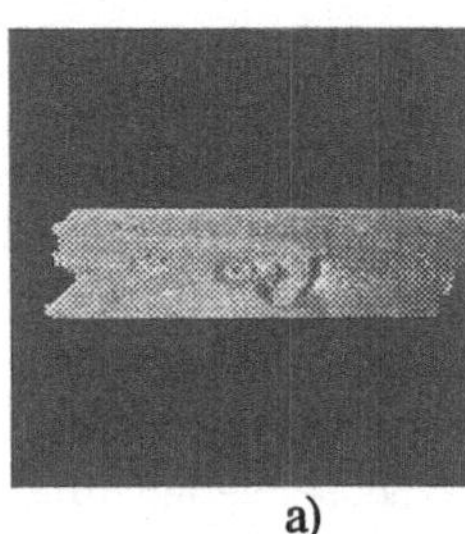
a)

b)

c)

Bild 3. a) Normierungsmatrix b) 3D-Datensatz c) Ausrichten mit Hilfe der Positionierungsmatrix.

Für die Erzeugung geometrischer Modelle wurden zahlreiche Verfahren entwickelt, die aus den Schichtbildern Oberflächenmodelle erzeugen [2] [11]. Manche Verfahren, wie z.B. die Simulation von Schneideoperationen oder die Simulation von Deformationen, erfordern jedoch komplexere Modelle; in ihnen kann auf Eigenschaften innerhalb der Modellstrukturen zurückgegriffen werden. Deshalb werden hier Finite Element-Modelle verwendet, die die Simulation von Deformationen ermöglichen und die Berechnung virtueller Schnitte [12] erleichtern.

Für die Simulation solcher Modelle haben wir ein Verfahren entwickelt, welches aus den Volumendaten ein klassifiziertes Tetraedernetz erzeugt. Das Verfahren kann in folgende vier Teilschritte aufgeteilt werden:

- *Segmentierung:* Das Bild wird in verschiedene homogene Grauwertbereiche zerlegt. Jeder Grauwertbereich repräsentiert eine anatomische Struktur, die durch ein aus Tetraedern bestehendes Modell ersetzt wird.

• *Konturpunkterzeugung*: Für jeden Grauwertbereich wird eine Menge von Punkten erzeugt, die auf der Oberfläche der segmentierten Strukturen liegen. Die Anzahl der erzeugten Punkte kann dabei individuell den Regionen angepaßt werden.
• *Triangulierung:* Die verschiedenen Punktmengen werden in einer Menge vereinigt. Diese Menge wird dann der dreidimensionalen Delaunay-Triangulierung unterzogen.
• *Klassifizierung:* Die erzeugten Tetraeder werden entsprechend der segmentierten Bereiche klassifiziert. Für jeden Tetraeder wird eine Punktmenge generiert, an Hand derer entschieden wird, ob der Tetraeder eindeutig einer Klasse zugeordnet werden kann oder ob er rekursiv in zwei kleinere Tetraeder zerlegt wird.

Als Ergebnis erhält man ein aus Tetraedern bestehendes Netz, in dem jeder Tetraeder einer Klasse zugeordnet ist. Bild 4 zeigt die vier Teilschritte des Algorithmus.

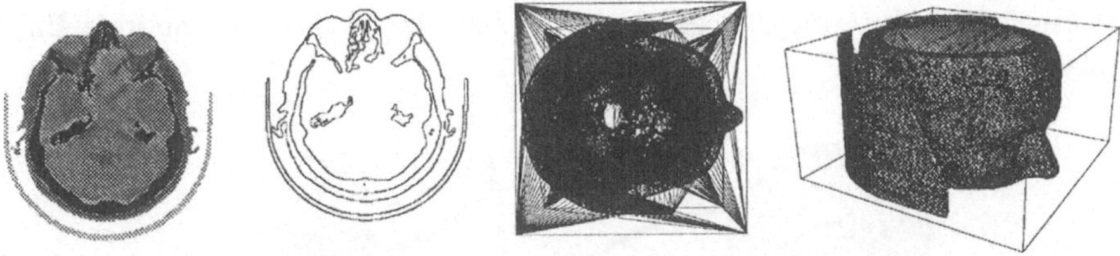

Bild 4. Aus den segmentierten Grauwertbereichen (links) wird das Tetraedernetz (rechts) erzeugt.

Um die verschiedenen Strukturen (Knochen, Gewebe, etc.) sichtbar zu machen, können die verschiedenen Tetraederklassen ein- und ausgeblendet werden. Die der Modellerzeugung zugrundeliedenden Bilddaten können dabei in das Modell eingeblendet werden, so daß eine Validierung des Modells durch den Rückgriff auf die Originaldaten jederzeit möglich ist.

4 Planung medizinischer Eingriffe

Operationplanungen in der Mund-, Kiefer- und Gesichtschirurgie basieren bisher nahezu ausschließlich auf den Erfahrungswerten des operierenden Arztes. Die Planung wird durch die Auswertung zweidimensionaler statischer Informationsquellen wie Röntgenbilder und kephalometrische Vermessungen und deren Vergleich mit Normdaten unterstützt. In der präoperativen Planung bearbeitet der Chirurg das Patientenmodell interaktiv. Es steht dabei die Markierung von Fremdkörpern, Resektionsgrenzen und Osteotomielinien im Vordergrund. Die Position von Implantaten soll präoperativ festgelegt werden können. Darüber hinaus muß festgelegt werden, wie die präoperativ generierten Pläne intraoperativ umgesetzt werden können. Dabei ist beispielsweise die Vermeidung und Überwachung von Risikoregionen von großer Bedeutung [3].

Mit Hilfe der im vorherigen Kapitel beschriebenen Tetraedernetze können die einzelnen Operationsschritte geplant werden. Wichtig hierbei ist, dem planenden Mediziner ein geeignetes Werkzeug zur dreidimensionalen Eingabe verschiedener Elementaroperationen wie Bohren, Sägen, Fräsen, Knochenverlagerung, etc. zur Verfügung zu stellen. Herkömmliche Eingabegeräte beruhen hauptsächlich auf visuellen Feedback. Dementsprechend sind sie für die genannten Planungsschritte ungeeignet, da erfahrungsgemäß die Eingabe von Punkten oder Schnittrajektorien im freien Raum ohne Auflagefläche schwierig ist.

Anders verhält es sich bei einem dreidimensionalen Eingabewerkzeug mit Kraftrückkopplung (haptisches Interface), welches von immer mehr medizinischen Forschungsgruppen eingesetzt wird. Der Chirurg wird hierbei zusätzlich durch ein taktiles Feedback bei der Planungseingabe unterstützt. Durch die Kraftrückkopplung wird dem Mediziner das Gefühl suggeriert, als ob er auf der Oberfläche einer der Klassen des oben erzeugten Modells entlanggleiten würde. Folglich erzeugt die Kraftrückkopplung die bisher fehlende Auflagefläche, durch die erst eine exakte und intuitive Eingabe erfolgen kann.

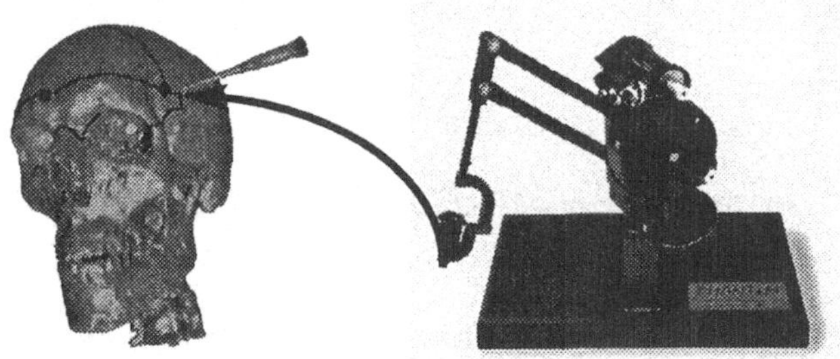

Bild 5. Schnitteingabe mit dem haptischen Interface PHANToM

Am IPR wurde ein Verfahren entwickelt, das den Mediziner bei der Segmentierung des Originaldatensatzes des Patientenmodells unterstützt. Hierbei kann der Mediziner wie bisher ein Grauwertfenster festlegen, in dem sich der Grauwert des zu segmentierenden Gewebes befindet. Allen Werten innerhalb dieses Fensters wird eine starre, allen außerhalb eine elastische Materialeigenschaft zugewiesen. Der Mediziner kann somit zu der zu untersuchenden Region vordringen und hat dennoch eine grobe Orientierung bezüglich des gesamten Tomogramms. Das zu extrahierende Objekt kann durch Abfahren der „harten“ Oberfläche segmentiert werden.
Desweiteren wurde von uns ein Verfahren für die Eingabe von Landmarken, Schnittrajektorien, Knochenverlagerungen, etc. entwickelt, welches dem Mediziner ermöglicht, die Eingabe sowohl auf den unsegmentierten Originaldatensatzes, als auch auf den oben erzeugten segmentierten Modellen durchzuführen [13]. Klassen aus dem oben erzeugten Modell können jederzeit in die haptische Umgebung hinzugefügt und wieder entfernt werden, so daß es z. B. möglich ist, direkt auf dem Knochen zu planen. Zusätzlich kann jeder Klasse eine bestimmte Materialeigenschaft zugewiesen werden, so daß unterschiedliche Gewebearten taktil differenziert werden können.

Die Schnitteingabe z. B. für die temporäre Entfernung des Stirnbeins bei der FOA-Operation wird zunächst, wie in Bild 5 zu sehen, auf der Klasse „Knochen“ ausgeführt. Anschließend wird das Stirnbein vom restlichen Schädel getrennt, indem die zwei neuen Klassen „Stirnbein“ und „restlicher Schädel“ mit Hilfe entsprechender Algorithmen generiert werden. Diese beiden Klassen können beliebig zueinander verschoben werden.

Das Ergebnis der Planung sind zum einen Schnittrajektorien, zum anderen Transformationsmatrizen, die die Verschiebung der einzelnen Klassen zueinander beschreiben. Diese Parameter werden vom Robotersystem für die intraoperative Umsetzung benötigt.

5 Patientenmodell für einen Operationsroboter

Bezüglich ihrere Eigenständigkeit existieren in der Robotik zwei Ansätze: Telerobotik und Autonome Roboter. Die Telerobotik [7] [17] stellt die Verlängerung des Benutzers dar. Er ist die intelligente Zentrale des Systems. Eine Weiterentwicklung der Eingabeschnittstelle für Telerobotikanwendungen stellen die Ansätze der Virtuellen Realität dar. Der Benutzer wird mit seinen sensorischen Fähigkeiten vollständig in die der Aufgabe entsprechenden Umgebung eingebettet [14] [16] etc. Dazu ist ein komplettes Modell der Umwelt zur Visualisierung aller Objekte notwendig, in dem der Benutzer seine Manipulationen durchführt. Das Konzept des Chirurgieroboters am IPR geht dagegen in die Richtung eines autonomen Robotersystems [6], das der Chirurg als „intelligentes“ Werkzeug einsetzt. Unabhängig vom Konzept ist in beiden Fällen ein Patientenmodell notwendig.

Der Einsatz eines chirurgischen Roboters ist an eine Reihe von Bedingungen geknüpft. So ist eine adäquate Modellierung des Operationsfeldes, eine kollisionsfreie Bahnplanung, eine Kalibrierung des Roboters, eine geeignete Darstellung der zu bearbeitenden Aufgabe und eine kontinuierliche Überwachung des Geschehens mit redundanter Sensorik vonnöten, um eine hinreichende Sicherheit für Patient und Operationsteam zu gewährleisten. Voraussetzung für die obigen Bedingungen ist ein geeignetes Patientenmodell, das eine Integration von Sensor- und Positionsdaten zuläßt, und das in geeigneter Weise in eine Umweltmodellierung integriert werden kann. [4] [5] [8].

Wie in der vorhergehenden Kapitel schon beschrieben, wurde am IPR ein Patientenmodell entwickelt, das einerseits eine Volumendarstellung aus den Tomographiedaten und andererseits ein trianguliertes Oberflächenmodell beinhaltet. Eine Rückrechnung von Punkten auf dem Oberflächenmodell zu den korrespondierenden Volumenelementen ist ebenfalls möglich. Die Planung chirurgischer Eingriffe erfolgt auf dem Oberflächenmodell, die Planungsdaten und eine Referenz auf das Oberflächenmodell werden an die Robotersteuerung weitergegeben. Das bearbeitete Oberflächenmodell des Patienten ist ebenfalls Teil der Modellierung des Operationsfeldes.

Um einen Roboter intraoperativ einsetzen zu können, muß jederzeit die Position des Roboters in Relation zum Patienten bekannt sein. Dies erfolgt durch die Kalibrierung, indem mindestens drei geeignete natürliche oder künstliche Landmarken auf dem Patienten mit dem Roboter angefahren werden. Das bekannteste Robotersystem für orthopädische chirurgische Eingriffe, ROBODOC [1], benutzt hierzu zwei Pins, die vor der Operation in den Oberschenkelknochen des Patienten implantiert worden sind. Die Pins können im CT segmentiert und ihre Position kann berechnet werden. Während des chirurgischen Eingriffs werden die freigelegten Pins mit Hilfe eines speziellen, am Roboter befestigten Kalibrierungswerkzeuges angefahren. Da zusätzliche Bewegungen des Patienten nicht detektiert werden können, bzw. der Roboter dann nicht mehr kalibriert ist, muß der zu bearbeitende Knochen während des Eingriffs fixiert und fest mit der Roboterbasis verbunden werden.

Das IPR verfolgt einen ähnlichen Ansatz, wobei dem Patienten präoperativ vier Titanminischrauben implantiert werden, die später im Tomogramm segmentiert werden können. Während der Operation werden Infrarotdioden auf die Pins gesetzt, so daß die Position des Patienten, der nicht fixiert werden muß, jederzeit von den Infrarot-CCD-Kameras des Navigationssystems festgestellt werden kann [10]. Des gleichen wurde ein mit Dioden bestückter Körper entwickelt, der zusammen mit dem Werkzeug an den Flansch des Roboters angebracht ist und die Position des Tool Center Points angibt. Da die Position des TCP zusätzlich mittels der Encoder in den Gelenken des Roboters ermittelt wird, ist die Transfomation vom Koordinatensystem des Navigationssystems in das Koordinatensysstem des Roboters und umgekehrt bekannt. Das gleiche gilt für die Transfomation vom Volumen- und vom Oberflächenmodell des Patienten in das Koordinatensystem des Infrarotsystems. Zusätzlich zum Patienten und zum Roboter kann noch die Position weiterer chirurgischer Instrumente, beispielsweise eines Infrarotpointers, die mit Infrarotdioden ausgestattet sind, detektiert werden (Bild6).

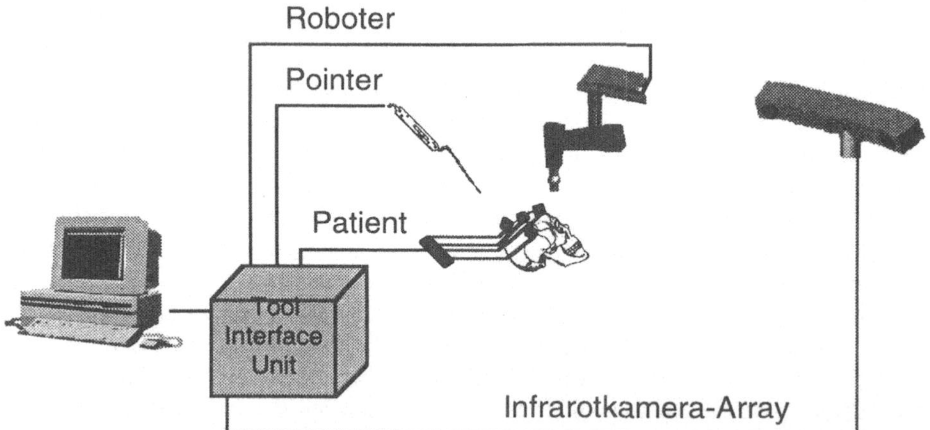

Bild 6. Simultane intraoperative Überwachung von Patient, Roboter und Instrument des Chirurgen mit Hilfe eines Infrarotnavigationssystems

Die Modellierung des Operationsfeldes berücksichtigt das Weichgewebe des Patienten indirekt über die die Operationswunden aufhaltenden chirurgischer Haken. So werden der Kopf des Patienten und die chirurgischen Haken, die das Weichgewebe vom freipräparierten Knochen zurückhalten, mittels Infrarotnavigationssystem detektiert. Zusätzlich gibt der Chirurg mit dem Infrarotpointer die höchsten Punkte sowie die

Grenzen des Patienten an. Es wird eine konvexe Hülle berechnet, in der auch die Operationswunde modelliert ist. Der Knochen des Patienten ist im triangulierten Ausschnitt innerhalb der Wundenöffnung zu sehen. Das erzeugte Modell des Operationsfeldes wird in eine in ROBCAD simulierte OP-Umgebung eingebunden, die einem Bahnplaner als Basis zur Berechnung einer geeigneten kollisionsfreien Trajektorie dient (Bild 7).

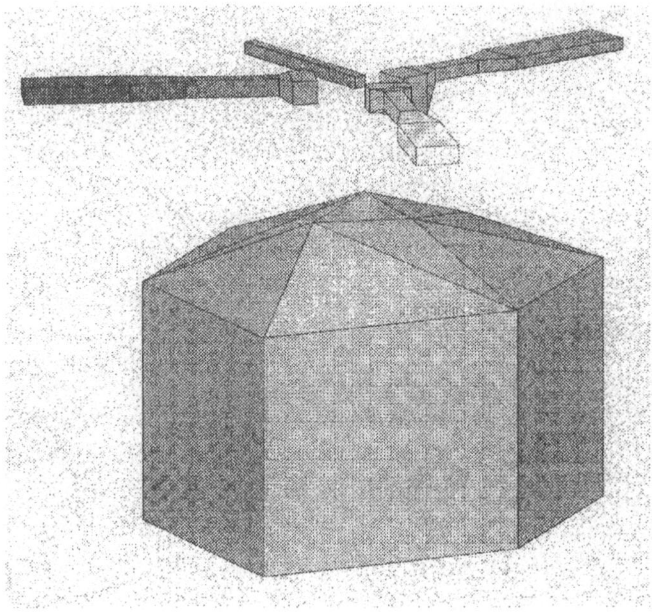

Bild 7. Modellierung des Operationsfeldes unter Zuhilfenahme der Wundhaken in ROBCAD.

6 Zusammenfassung

Die obigen Ausführungen zeigen, daß ein integriertes Patientenmodell für die Unterstützung des Chirurgen notwendig ist. Bisher mußten für die Akquisition und Nutzung von Patientendaten jeweils separate Prozeßketten aufgebaut werden. Die Nutzung von Robotern für eine Operation stellt sehr hohe Anforderungen an Umfang und Qualität der genutzten Daten. In einem integrierten Patientenmodell lassen sich alle für eine Operation relevanten Daten zusammenfassen. Nur mit seiner Hilfe sind die verschiedenen Sichten auf den Patienten verwaltbar. Der von der Deutschen Forschungsgemeinschaft eingerichtete Sonderforschungsbereich 414 bildet mit der Möglichkeit für interdisziplinäres Arbeiten mit Medizinern aus verschiedenen Fächern die Voraussetzung für die oben beschriebenen Arbeiten.

Literatur

1. BauerA., Börner M., Lahmer A.,: ROBODOC-animal experiment and clinical evaluation. First Joint Conf. on Comp. Vision, Virt. Reality and Rob. in Medicine and Med. Robotics and Comp. Ass. Surg. (CVRMed-MRCAS'97), Grenoble, France (1997).
2. Bajaj, C. L., E. J. Coyle, K. N. Lin: Surface and 3D triangular meshes from cross planar sections. 5th International Meshing Roundtable, Pittsburgh, Pennsylvania, U.S.A., on October 10-11, 1996
3. P. Bohner, S. Hassfeld, C. Holler, M. Damm, J. Schloen, J. Raczkowsky: *Operation planning in cranio-maxillo-facial surgery*, Second Int. Symposium on Medical Robotics and Computer Assisated Surgery (MRCAS'95), Baltimore, Maryland, 1995.
4. Brandt G., Radermacher K., Rau G., Staudte H.-W.: Development of a x-ray image-guided parallel robot for orthopaedic surgery, in proceedings of the IARP 2nd Interantional Workshop on Medical Robtics, Heidelberg, Germany (1997).
5. Burckhardt, C., P. Flury, and D. Glauser (1995). Stereotactic brain surgery - integrated minerva system meets demanding robotic requirements. IEEE Engineering in Medicine and Biology, 14(3):314-317.
6. Burghart C., Münchenberg J., Rembold U.: A System for Robot Assisted Maxillofacial Surgery. Medicine Meets Virtual Reality 6 (MMVR'98), San Diego (1998).
7. P.S. Green, J.W. Hill, J.F. Jensen, A. Shah. Telepresence Surgery. IEEE Engineering in Medicine and Biology Magazine Vol. 14, No. 3 May/June 1995, S. 321-329.
8. Harris, S., W. Lin, R. Hibberd, J. Cobb, R. Middleton and B. Davies (1997). Experiences with Robotic Systems for Knee Surgery. CVRMed-MRCAS '97, Grenoble, France.
9. Haßfeld S, Zöller J, Wirz C R, Knauth M and Mühling J: Intraoperative navigation in maxillofacialsurgers-clinical experiences, demands and developments CAR '1996-Computer Assisted Radiology, S.739-744 (1996)
10. Haßfeld S., Burghart C., Bertovic I., Raczkowsky J., Rembold U., Wörn H., Mühling J.: Intraoperative Navigation Techniques: Accuracy Tests and Clinical Report. accepted for Computer Assisted Radiology and Surgery (CAR'98), Tokyo (1998).
11. Lorensen, W., H. E. Cline: Marching Cubes: A high resolution 3D surface construction algorithm. Computer Graphics, 21(4):163-169
12. Mazura, A., S. Seifert: Virtual cutting in medical data. MMVR 5, San Diego, January 1997
13. Münchenberg J., Haßfeld S., Raczkowsky J., Rembold U., Wörn H.: Expert supported Operation Planning in Maxillofacial Surgery. accepted for Computer Assisted Radiology and Surgery (CAR'98), Tokyo (1998).
14. A. Perneczky: Eine Reise durch das Gehirn: die intelligente Endoskopie. Medicine Goes Electronic, 1. Innovativer Medizinkongress, Nürnberg, 14.- 17.Sept.1995
15. Pokrandt, P.: Probabilistisches Matchen Medizinischer Bilddatensätze, Diss., Universität Karlsruhe, Institut für Prozeßrechentechnik und Robotik, Nov. 1996
16. J.M. Rosen, H. Soltanian, D.R. Laub, A. Mecinski, W.K. Dean: The Evolution of Virtual Reality from Surgical Training to the Development of a Simulator for Health Care Delivery: Proc. of MMVR 4, San Diego, CA, Jan. 17-20, 1996
17. Voges U., Holler E., Neisius B., Schurr M., Vollmer Th.: Evaluation of ARTEMIS, the Advanced Robotics and Telemanipulator System for Minimally Invasive Surgery, IARP 2nd Interantional Workshop on Medical Robtics, Heidelberg, Germany (1997).
18. Wanchoo, V.: Full Component PACS, Data Collection, Archive, and Display Devices. PACS, Teleradiology and Computed Radiography, Charleston Harbor Hilton, Mount Pleasant, SC, USA, Oct. 26 - 29, 1997

Nondeterminism and Motion Compensation for Weighted Finite Automata

Jürgen Albert and Ullrich Hafner

Department of Computer Science, University of Würzburg
Am Hubland, D-97074 Würzburg, Germany
{albert,hafner}@informatik.uni-wuerzburg.de

Abstract. Nondeterministic finite automata with states and transitions labeled by real numbers as weights have turned out to be powerful tools for compression of still images and video sequences. These Weighted Finite Automata (WFA) as introduced and studied by Culik II, Kari, Karhumäki and others can exploit self-similarities within single pictures, between colour components and also sequences of pictures. Thus, as a coding-method WFA has much in common with fractal encoding algorithms like Barnsley's Iterated Function Systems, but it can be viewed as well as a generalization of gain-shape vector quantization. WFA-coding is particularly effective for low bit-rates and our current implementation clearly outperforms the video standard H.263. This paper discusses the control of nondeterminism – i.e. the fan-out of states in the WFA labeled by the same input-symbol – and of motion compensation and shows how both features are handled as two facets of a coding decision taken during WFA-inference.

1 Introduction

Although definitions of finite automata, where transitions are labeled by real numbers can be found already in the classical textbooks on formal language theory like [1], this was mainly for the purposes of describing probabilistic behaviour of finite state acceptors or for the study of formal power series [2]. The generation of digitized images from finite automata appears then later independently in [3] and specifically in [4] and [5], where a recursive WFA-inference algorithm with remarkable compression-results had been presented. Since then several improvements have led to competitive WFA-codecs with performance-figures in general superior to the JPEG image compression standard and on a par with advanced wavelet codecs like embedded zerotree wavelet coding [6, 7, 8, 9, 10]. Due to the simple mathematical structure of the WFA approximation, the image reconstruction can be done faster here than in wavelet based codecs which have to rely on an inverse fast wavelet transform. This makes the WFA-approach a promising choice for low bit-rate video coding e.g. in the rapidly growing field of WWW applications [10]. And there are some first experiments underway to adapt WFA-codecs to the specific characteristics of audio-data.

In the following sections we will present Weighted Finite Automata in an informal manner and refer the interested reader to [4] and [11] for a more rigorous mathematical treatment and for fundamental results about the families of real-valued functions that can be generated by WFA.

2 Preliminaries

To avoid messy detail in the beginning we consider the basic principles of WFA for the one-dimensional case first, i.e. for WFA generating only one row of pixels of an image (or equivalently a sequence of digitized audio data). We can assume that the current resolution is 2^k for some nonnegative k and that the total width of the picture is 1. Pixels are then addressed by their numbers in binary notation. Thus, pixel with address $x = x_1x_2 \dots x_k$ starts at position $0.x_1x_2 \dots x_k$ of the unit interval $[0, 1)$ and has width 2^{-k}. As an example consider 101 which addresses the interval $[\frac{5}{8}, \frac{6}{8})$.

For any WFA we can assume the input-alphabet $\Sigma := \{0, 1\}$ fixed, since addresses for higher dimensions can also be formed in binary notation as we will see later. Now, given any address x as an input-sequence a WFA computes a real value as the greyness-value of the corresponding pixel by following every path in the (nondeterministic) automaton labeled by x. Along those paths the weights of the transitions are multiplied and results are summed up. Intuitively, each state of a WFA corresponds to a multi-resolution image and therefore computing the complete image for a given resolution 2^k means "unrolling" the WFA from its start state to depth k.

To obtain a compatible set of images at different resolutions, the weights of the states themselves (the so-called final distribution) have to match the average greyness-values of the images they generate.

Now, more formally, we define a quintuple $A = (Q, \Sigma, W, s, F)$ to be a Weighted Finite Automaton (WFA), if for some $n \in \boldsymbol{N}$

1. $Q = \{0, 1, \dots, n-1\}$ is the set of states
2. $\Sigma = \{0, 1\}$ is the input alphabet
3. W_0 and $W_1 \in \boldsymbol{R}^{n \times n}$ are the weight matrices for transitions and the input-symbols 0 and 1 resp.
4. $n - 1 \in Q$ is the start state
5. $F \in \boldsymbol{R}^n$ is the final distribution.

Let $[C]_i$ denote the element in row i of any column vector $C \in \boldsymbol{R}^n$. For each state i, each given resolution 2^k and each address $x = x_1x_2 \dots x_k$ the WFA A generates a real value as greyness-value of the corresponding pixel, i.e. a function $\Phi_i : \Sigma^* \to \boldsymbol{R}$, in the following manner:

$$\begin{aligned} \Phi_i(\epsilon) &= [F]_i \quad \text{for all} \quad i \in Q \\ \Phi_i(x_1x_2 \dots x_k) &= [W_{x_1} \times W_{x_2} \times \dots \times W_{x_k} \times F]_i \qquad (1) \\ & \text{for all} \quad x_j \in \Sigma; i \in Q, k \in \boldsymbol{N}. \end{aligned}$$

As an example consider a WFA A with states $Q = \{0, 1, 2, 3, 4\}$, weight matrices W_0, W_1 and final distribution F together with the corresponding transition-graph.

$$W_0 = \begin{pmatrix} 1 & 0 & 0 & 0 & 0 \\ 0 & \frac{1}{2} & 0 & 0 & 0 \\ 0 & 0 & \frac{1}{4} & 0 & 0 \\ 1 & 0 & -1 & 0 & 0 \\ 0 & 0 & 0 & 1 & 0 \end{pmatrix}, W_1 = \begin{pmatrix} 1 & 0 & 0 & 0 & 0 \\ \frac{1}{2} & \frac{1}{2} & 0 & 0 & 0 \\ \frac{1}{4} & \frac{1}{2} & \frac{1}{4} & 0 & 0 \\ 0 & -2 & 1 & 0 & 0 \\ 0 & 0 & 0 & -1 & 0 \end{pmatrix}, F = \begin{pmatrix} 1 \\ \frac{1}{2} \\ \frac{1}{3} \\ 0 \\ 0 \end{pmatrix}$$

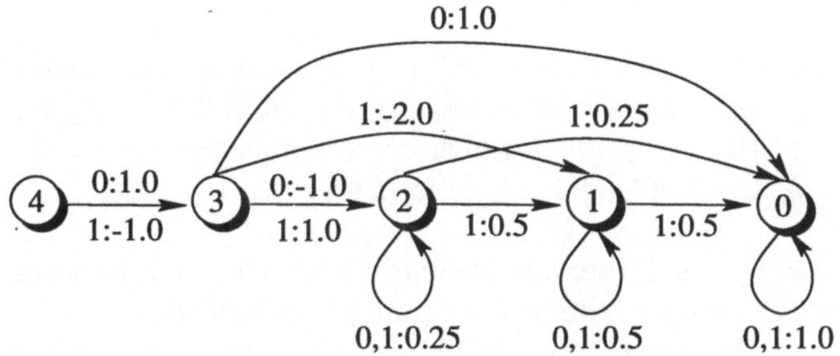

Fig. 1. Transition-graph for A

If we assume a resolution of 32 pixels, i.e. considering input strings of length 5, then A produces the following set of output values, which are also depicted as greyscale values below. For example, 10000 was mapped to -1.0, which we draw as totally black.

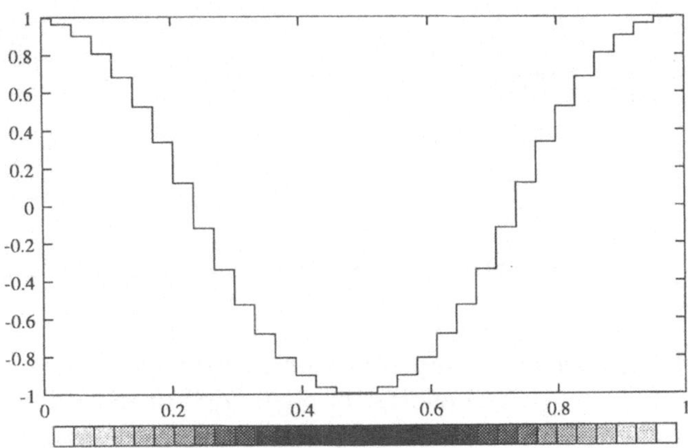

Fig. 2. Output for resolution 32

A closer look at A reveals that the subautomata of A defined by the new start states $0, 1$ and 2 represent the functions $f_0(t) = 1$, $f_1(t) = t$ and $f_2(t) = t^2$ resp. The self-similarity of the polynomials expresses itself here in that they can be written as linear combinations of scaled versions of themselves and polynomials of lower degrees.

For the binary sequences $x = x_1x_2 \ldots x_k$ we consider the real values $0.x$, together with $0.0x = \frac{1}{2}0.x$ and $0.1x = \frac{1}{2} + \frac{1}{2}0.x$ of the unit interval $[0, 1)$. Thus it holds $f_0(0.0x) = f_0(0.1x) = f_0(0.x) = 1$, and then $f_1(0.0x) = \frac{1}{2}f_1(0.x)$, $f_1(0.1x) = \frac{1}{2} + \frac{1}{2}f_1(0.x)$ and also $f_2(0.0x) = \frac{1}{4}f_2(0.x)$, $f_2(0.1x) = \frac{1}{4} + \frac{1}{2}f_1(0.x) + \frac{1}{4}f_2(0.x)$ exactly as noted in our weight matrices W_0, W_1.

The functions for the states 3 and 4 are composed from these in a simple way by scaling and taking mirror images, e.g. $f_3(0.0x) = f_0(0.x) - f_2(0.x)$, $f_3(0.1x) = -2f_1(0.x) + f_2(0.x)$ which corresponds to $f_3(t) = 1 - 4f_2(t)$ for $t \in [0, \frac{1}{2})$ and $f_3(t) = -4f_1(t) + 4f_2(t)$ for $t \in [\frac{1}{2}, 1)$.

The addressing of subintervals in binary notation – via bintrees – as shown above carries over to higher dimensions (images, volume-data, ...) in a straightforward manner. To obtain the bintree representation for 2-dimensional data (images) we have to alternatingly apply a horizontal and a vertical subdivision as in Fig. 3.

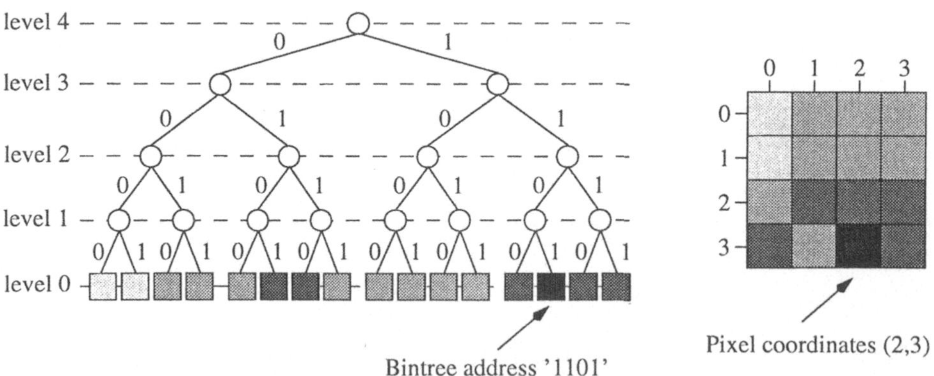

Fig. 3. Bintree addresses and pixel coordinates

Note that there exists a simple conversion between bintree addresses and array indices. E.g. the bintree address of pixel $(2, 3)$ of the 2-dimensional array in Fig. 3 is given by the word "1101". Thus the two coordinates are merged into one address in "zipper-like" fashion.

We now treat Weighted Finite Automata as a generalization of bintrees and show how WFA can achieve good compression-results for images and videos.

In this paper we use a modified version of the WFA definition that is already adapted to the compression task. For the original definition of WFA refer to [4].

For every state i function Φ_i is a generalization of a function f of fixed resolution (it's table-size). The functions $\Phi_i(0)$ and $\Phi_i(1)$ have to be composed by linear combinations of other multi-resolution state functions. The coefficients of such a linear combination of a state function $\Phi_i(z)$ are stored in row i of the matrices W_z, $z \in \Sigma$. The multi-resolution state function Φ_s of start state s is representing the function f_A of WFA A.

Assume that we are given the coefficients F and W_z of a WFA A. Then the image f_A of the WFA A can be computed for any desired resolution 2^k using the formula (1). At first glance the inverse problem seems to be more complex: how should we construct a WFA that computes a given image f? Contrasting IFS based fractal image encoders the inverse problem (termed WFA inference problem) has a trivial solution, which just uses the image and its bintree graph. Weights for transitions and the final distribution for states are attached there in an obvious way, weight 1.0 for all bintree-transitions and the average greyness values of the corresponding subimages as final distribution for all states. This WFA inference algorithm will in general give no compression of the input data, since any existing self-similarities are ignored. But it produces an especially simple deterministic WFA, from which one can start to infer a more efficient (nondeterministic) WFA which approximates the input picture.

3 WFA Inference Algorithm

First, according to the bintree-structure, the image f has to be subdivided recursiveley into a set of non-overlapping regions. Following the conventions of IFS based fractal encoders these subimages are termed range images.

Since the WFA definition allows nondeterminism every range image may be computed as a linear combination of subimages of arbitrary state images. Moreover, it is not required that a given linear combination computes the corresponding range image exactly, the WFA compression is intended to be a lossy compression scheme. Just under the start state we will still have a deterministic part in the WFA from the bintree, defining a image partitioning with range images but any approximation of range images may take advantage of nondeterminism now.

3.1 Recursive Inference Algorithm

During the encoding process the images currently available for linear combinations are called domain images. Obviously this domain pool is growing after each approved approximation of a range image. The result of such an adaptive bintree partitioning is given in Fig. 4. For to start, the domain pool is initialized with a small set of basis functions (e.g. polynomial functions — represented by WFA states), and the entire image is considered as the first range block. Then two different approximation methods are tested for every range block. First the block

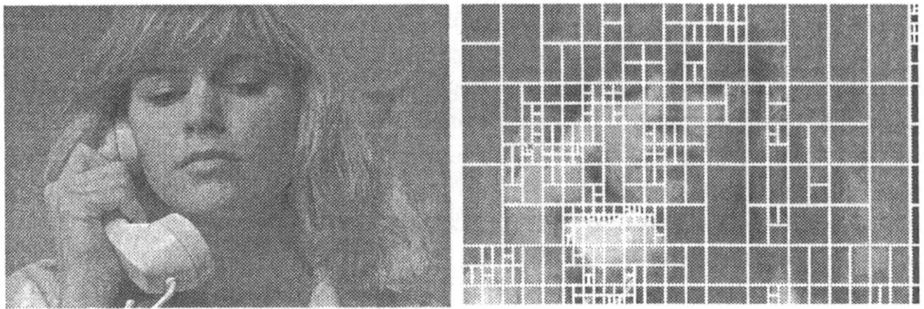

Fig. 4. Adaptive partitioning of one frame of the SUSIE sequence

is approximated with a linear combination of the domain images available up to now. We use a rate-distortion constrained version of a greedy algorithm called orthogonal matching pursuit [12, 13] to obtain a (suboptimal) approximation of a given range block. Thereafter, the range block is subdivided and the coder tries to find recursively approximations for the new range blocks. After recursion has terminated both alternatives are compared and the better one is used.

The decision whether to use a subdivision or a linear combination is found by a controlling cost function C:

$$C(\Phi, \hat{\Phi}, T) := q\|\Phi - \hat{\Phi}\|^2 + \mathbf{sizeof}(T) \tag{2}$$

where Φ is the current range block, $\hat{\Phi}$ is the approximation of Φ (subdivision or linear combination resp.). The set T consists of all parameters and coefficients that are necessary to code the computed approximation (number of subranges, domains and coefficients used to approximate these subranges). Parameter q controls the quality of the encoding; large values of q will produce good approximations while small values will produce high compression ratios and also higher distortions. Since T is entropy-coded, note that a strong connection with the entropy coding module has to ensure that the number of bits used to store the approximation coefficients T on disk is close to the estimated value $\mathbf{sizeof}(T)$. This cost function is also used in the matching pursuit algorithm: a linear combination is composed step by step with respect to the cost function C.

If the recursive subdivision yields the lower costs then we obtain an approximation of the current range Φ with its subimages $\Phi(0)$ and $\Phi(1)$ (Equation (1)). Then Φ can be assigned to a new WFA state. Thus, the domain pool is increased by another multi-resolution image which can be computed with formula (1) Generating the domain pool step by step during run time ensures that we do not have error propagation like IFS based fractal codecs which construct the domain pool at the beginning of the computation [14].

3.2 Predictive Coding

Using nondeterminism to approximate ranges and determinism to specify the image subdivision yields compression results for WFA comparable to wavelet

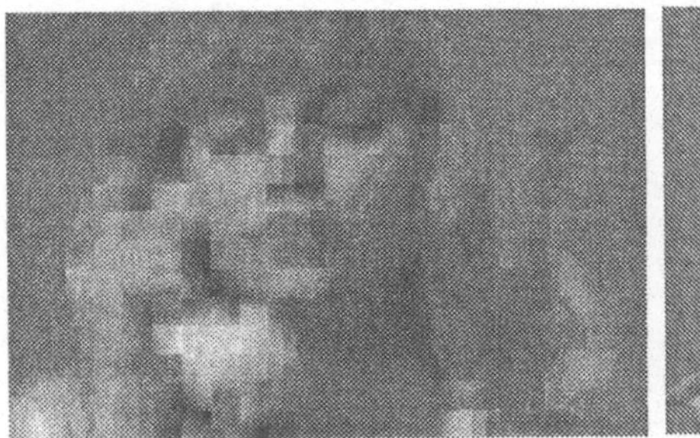 

Fig. 5. Coarse approximation (left image) and refinement (right image) of SUSIE

codecs [8]. This can be improved even if we extend the usage of nondeterminism in our WFA inference coder, i.e., not only "leaf-states" but also "inner-states" are allowed to use nondeterminism. One can think of this extended concept as of generating a coarse prediction of a subimage and then to continue subdividing the image of the prediction until the required quality criterion is met.

Therefore, our algorithm is modified in the following way: an adaptive coarse subdivision of the image into non-overlapping range blocks is computed in a first step. These ranges are approximated with linear combinations. At this time a high quality approximation of these range blocks is not yet required, hence we can use specially tuned models. Currently, only a few domains are allowed in such linear combinations, hence reducing the entropy of the indices. Finally, the prediction error (difference of the original image and the coarse approximation) is further approximated with the standard WFA algorithm. Fig. 5 shows both approximation types for one frame of the SUSIE sequence. Testing all existing combinations is not feasible (and not necessary). Currently, only one coarse approximation and one subsequent refinement is allowed in order to give an acceptable relation between compression performance and coding time. Also in our linear combinations the subsequent entropy coding of the (sparse) weight matrices favors short linear combinations, i.e. low bounds on the degree of nondeterminism in the constructed WFA; typical are 2 or 3 elements only.

3.3 Video Coding

Of course, not only images but also video streams can be coded with the WFA inference algorithm described above. In our current implementation we use a data structure similar to the one found in the MPEG-1 standard: image sequences consist of several groups of pictures (GOP). Each GOP contains one intra-frame encoded picture (I-frame) and a given number of inter-frame encoded pictures. Inter-frame encoding may use forward prediction (P-frame) as well as backward or bi-directional prediction (B-frame).

We integrated a block matching motion compensation with variable block sizes into the WFA coder to exploit inter-frame redundancies. In fact these temporal redundancies can be handled nearly the same way as spatial redundancies

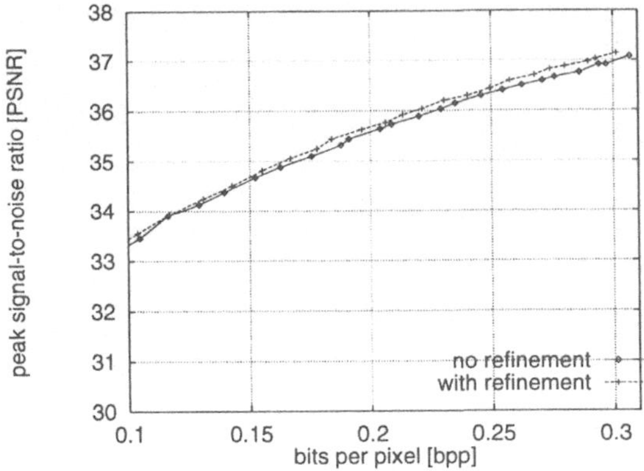

Fig. 6. Rate-distortion ratios of the SUSIE frame

in intra-frame coding. The general concept of the WFA compression is thus retained since it already provides a hierarchical subdivision of the image. In addition, one further approximation method is tested for each range block Φ: the previous and next reference frame are searched for a block $\tilde{\Phi}$ that closely matches Φ (i.e., $\|\Phi - \tilde{\Phi}\|$ is minimal). The motion compensation prediction error $\Phi - \tilde{\Phi}$ is then considered as a new range image and recursively approximated as described in the last section. Of course, a further motion compensation of predicted frames is not allowed. After this, the generated set of motion vectors is joined with set T of the cost function C in equation (2). Thus, the range approximation that minimizes the new extended cost function is used.

4 Experimental results

First a comparison of the standard WFA codec of [8] and the new coder described in this paper is shown in Fig. 6 (two levels in the bintrees have been used for nondeterminism). There is a noticable improvement of the rate-distortion ratios of the SUSIE image (720 × 480, 8 bpp) obtained with the new approximation method.

Moreover, we compared the results of our software codec with Telenor's [15] implementation of the H.263 coding standard [16]. All results were computed on a DEC Alpha-Station 600 (266 MHz, 256MB RAM). The first 20 frames of the SUSIE sequence (original resolution 720 × 480, 24 bpp, RGB) have been used for the comparison (scaled to the 4CIF, CIF and QCIF format). Note that our codec converts the RGB stream internally into the YCbCr color space without subsampling while the H.263 codec requires the already converted and subsampled input in YCbCr color space. Thus, there are already some roundoff errors introduced in the H.263 codec.

The rate-distortion ratios of our WFA codec and the H.263 codec are shown in Table 1.

Table 1. Rate-distortion ratios of the WFA and H.263 coded SUSIE sequence

stream	codec	I-frame				P-frame			
		bits/frame	PSNR [dB]			avrg. bits/frame	avrg. PSNR [dB]		
			Y	Cb	Cr		Y	Cb	Cr
4CIF	WFA	30464	33.1	42.8	42.9	3653	33.1	42.7	42.9
	H.263	90824	32.8	43.3	43.0	8232	33.6	43.5	43.4
CIF	WFA	12768	32.0	41.9	41.5	1252	32.1	42.0	41.7
	H.263	24248	31.6	42.3	41.3	1548	32.4	42.7	41.7
QCIF	WFA	7544	31.9	40.8	40.2	827	31.6	41.1	40.7
	H.263	8136	31.7	40.4	39.3	354	31.6	40.6	39.7

In all experiments we used the standard options for the H.263 codec. The video streams have been subdivided into one I-frame and 19 P-frames both in the WFA and in the H.263 codec. The WFA codec generates lower bit rates for I-frames than the DCT based algorithm as already shown in [8]. Moreover, the compression performance increases with image size. E.g. the filesize of the WFA encoded I-frame of the 4CIF sequence is only one third of the H.263 codec. The main reason for this behavior is that more domain images are available for approximation due to the larger image size. Similar results hold for predicted frames: due to the usage of hierarchical motion compensation we get better results for larger images. Our movie player uses as back-end process the dithering and display module of the MPEG-1 player version 2.0 of the University at Berkeley. On the DEC Alpha-Station described above a real-time decoding of the WFA stream is possible for the QCIF (50 frames/sec) and the CIF (16 frames/sec) sequences.

5 Conclusion

Within the WFA-framework spatial and temporal redundancies as appearing in video-sequences are captured by linear combinations and motion compensation for range images. Since this encoding is controlled by a cost function which favors sparse transition-matrices, the degree of nondeterminism used in the resulting WFA is usually very small. First experiments showed that using an adaptive image partitioning with coarse approximations and refinements for the range images still improves the rate-distortion ratios of the WFA codec noticable. Moreover, we described that the clear advantage of WFA compression against DCT-based methods for intra-frame coding (at low bit-rates, WFA encoded images are typically half the size of comparable JPEG images) has been preserved for video coding. WFA compression seems to be well suited for image- and video-archives due to the asymmetry of encoding and decoding speed. Together with its high compression capability, this makes WFA a good alternative for low bit-rate coding and e.g. net-based applications which have to cope with limited bandwidth.

References

[1] S. Eilenberg. *Automata, Languages and Machines, Vol. A.* Academic Press, New York, 1974.

[2] A. Salomaa and M. Soittola. *Automata-Theoretic Aspects of Formal Power Series.* Springer-Verlag, Berlin, 1978.

[3] J. Berstel and A. Nait Abdullah. Quadtrees generated by finite automata. In *AFCET 61-62*, pages 167–175, 1989.

[4] K. Culik and J. Kari. Image compression using weighted finite automata. *Computers and Graphics*, 17(3):305–313, 1993.

[5] K. Culik and J. Kari. Image-data compression using edge-optimizing algorithm for wfa interference. *Journal of Information Processing and Management*, 30:829–838, 1994.

[6] J. M. Shapiro. Embedded image coding using zerotrees of wavelet coefficients. *IEEE Transactions on Signal Processing*, 41(12):3445–3462, December 1993.

[7] J. Kari and P. Fränti. Arithmetic coding of weighted finite automata. *Theoretical Informatics and Applications*, 28(3-4):343–360, 1994.

[8] U. Hafner. Refining image compression with weighted finite automata. In J. A. Storer and M. Cohn, editors, *Proc. of Data Compression Conference*, pages 359–368, 1996.

[9] U. Hafner. Image and video coding with weighted finite automata. In *Proc. of the IEEE International Conference on Image Processing*, pages 326–329, 1997.

[10] U. Hafner, J. Albert, S. Frank, and M. Unger. Weighted finite automata for video compression. *IEEE Journal on Selected Areas in Communications*, 16(1):108–119, January 1998.

[11] K. Culik and J. Karhumäki. Finite automata computing real functions. *SIAM J. Comput.*, 23(4):789–814, 1994.

[12] S. G. Mallat and Z. Zhang. Matching pursuits with time-frequency dictionaries. *IEEE Transactions on Signal Processing*, 41(12), December 1993.

[13] M. Gharavi-Alkhansari and T. S. Huang. Fractal video coding by matching pursuit. In *Proc. of the IEEE International Conference on Image Processing*, 1996.

[14] Y. Fisher. Fractal image compression with quadtrees. In Yuval Fisher, editor, *Fractal Image Compression*, chapter 3, pages 55–77. Springer-Verlag, 1995.

[15] Telenor Research Digital Video Coding Group and Development. Telenor H.263 codec, version 2.0. http://www.nta.no/brukere/DVC/, June 1996.

[16] International Telecommunication Union (ITU), Geneva, Switzerland. *Video Coding for low bitrate communication*, May 1996. Recommendation H.263.

Über Binarisierung und Potentiale der Fuzzy-Ansätze

Hamid R. Tizhoosh
Otto-von-Guericke-Universität Magdeburg
Lehrstuhl für Technische Informatik
Postfach 4120, D-39016 Magdeburg

1 Einleitung

Segmentierung ist eine fundamentale Aufgabe der Bildverarbeitung. Kaum eine Aufgabenstellung kann ohne Segmentierung, sei es Pixelklassifikation, Binarisierung oder Kantendetektion, gelöst werden (die letztere Aufgabe hat sich in den letzen Jahren zu einem eigenen Bereich entwickelt, zählt jedoch ebenfalls zu segmentierenden Verfahren). Wir konzentrieren uns hier auf die Binarisierung, weil die Behandlung der Segmentierung ohne diese Beschränkung den Rahmen dieses Beitrags sprengen würde. Binarisierung, als die einfachste Form der Bildsegmentierung, ist eine der kritischsten Schritte der Bildverarbeitung. Obwohl sie eine relativ einfache Klassifikationsaufgabe darstellt (nämlich die Pixel entweder dem Hintergrund oder dem Objekt zuzuordnen), ist dieser Schritt mit diversen Problemen und Unsicherheiten behaftet. Oft läßt sich keine eindeutige bzw. klare Grenze zwischen Objekt und Hintergrund ziehen. Dies ist vor allem auf die inhärente Unschärfe digitaler Bilder zurückzuführen. Dies hat zur Folge, daß das Ergebnis der Binarisierung oft nicht optimal ist; eine eindeutige Trennung zwischen Objekt und Hintergrund kann nicht herbeigeführt werden (Abbildung 1). In der Praxis wird dies durch Störfaktoren wie ungleichmäßige Beleuchtung, Reflexionen an der Objektoberfläche, Schmutzpartikel usw. verstärkt.

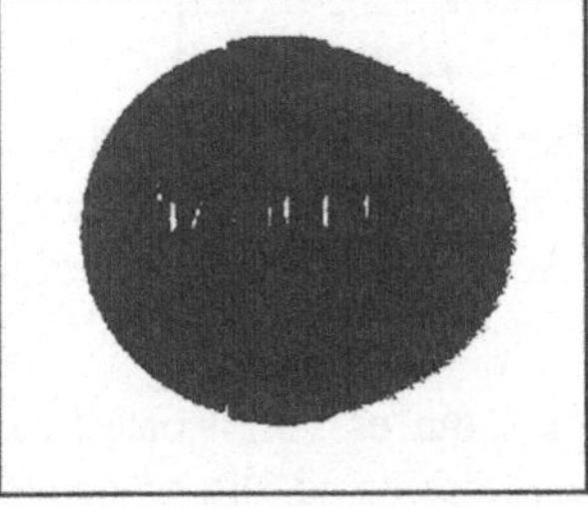

Abbildung 1. Das Ergebnis der Binarisierung ist oft nicht optimal

Die Fuzzy-Ansätze bieten neue Möglichkeiten zur Entwicklung bzw. Optimierung der Binarisierungsverfahren. In diesem Beitrag geben wir zunächst eine kurze Übersicht über die Potentiale der Fuzzy-Geometrie. Sie kann speziell in Anwendungen, in denen die digitale Bildgeometrie eine Rolle spielt, den Binarisierungsschritt und die damit verbundenen Probleme umgehen. Weiterhin wird eine kurze Übersicht der auf den Maßen der Unschärfe basierenden Algorithmen skizziert. Letztlich stellen wir einen neuen Algorithmus zur Binarisierung vor, der einen geeigneten Schwellwert als eine unscharfe Zahl interpretiert und nach maximaler Unschärfe sucht. Am Ende vergleichen wir die Ergebnisse untereinander und auch mit klassischen Methoden.

2 Ist die Binarisierung wirklich notwendig?

Die Frage, ob die Binarisierung entbehrlich ist, läßt sich nur anwendungsspezifisch beantworten. Ohne Zweifel ist eine scharfe Trennung zwischen Objekt und Hintergrund in vielen Anwendungen die einzige Möglichkeit, die gestellte Aufgabe zu lösen. In manchen Situationen jedoch führt eine explizite Segmentierung nicht unbedingt zur Lösung der Aufgabe. Ein Beispiel hierzu ist die Merkmalsextraktion. Will man Objekte erkennen, so müssen geeignete Merkmale aus dem Bild generiert werden, die eine Unterscheidung zwischen unterschiedlichen Objekten ermöglichen. Angenommen wir wollen durch die Binarisierung die Länglichkeit (engl. *elongatedness*) der Objekte berechnen, so ist die Binarisierung der einzige Weg, weil die digitale Bildgeometrie auf Schwarz-Weiß-Verhältnissen basiert. Die Binarisierung ist jedoch oft mit Verlust an Information behaftet. Dadurch können beim Übergang vom Grauwertbild zum Binärbild signifikante Bildstrukturen verloren gehen. Dies kann eine zuverlässige Merkmalsberechnung nachteilig beeinflussen (Abbildung 2).

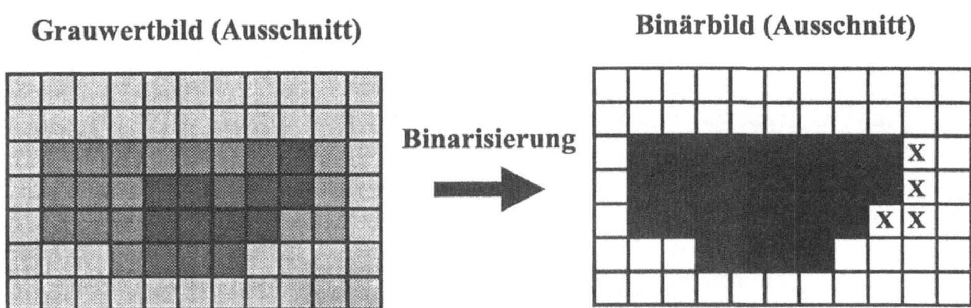

Abbildung 2. Zur Berechnung der Länglichkeit in Binär- und Grauwertbildern. Binarisierung ist oft mit Informationsverlust behaftet (die mit X markierten Bildpunkte sind infolge der Schwellwertbildung verlorengegangen)

In solchen Fällen kann es von Vorteil sein, auf eine eindeutige Objekt-Hintergrund-Trennung zu verzichten und die erforderlichen Merkmale in Grauwertbild selbst zu berechnen. Azriel Rosenfeld führte die Fuzzy-Geometrie ein, die die digitale Bildgeometrie auf die Fuzzy-Mengen erweitert [6,7,10]. Dadurch wird die Berechnung solcher Größen wie z.B. Objektfläche, -umfang, -länglichkeit usw. bereits in Grauwertbildern ermöglicht [6,7]. Bei vielen Anwendungen kann der Binarisierungsschritt hierdurch umgangen werden. Durch die Erfassung inhärenter Vagheit der Bildstrukturen können fuzzy-geometrische Größen auch dazu verwendet werden, neue und robustere Algorithmen zur Schwellwertbildung zu entwickeln [8].

Verbundenheit (engl. *connectedness,* [6,9]) ist beispielsweise eine Kategorie in der Bildverarbeitung, die bei vielen Aufgaben wie Konturverfolgung, Kantenrelaxation und generell Segmentierung eine wichtige Rolle spielt. Bei all diesen Aufgaben muß die Frage, ob zwei Bildpunkte miteinander verbunden sind, mehrfach und in unterschiedlichen Nachbarschaften beantwortet werden. Dies ist jedoch keine triviale Aufgabe, wenn man die auf Binärbilder zugeschnittene digitale Topologie zugrunde legt. Die Verbundenheit wird immer in einem gegebenen Nachbarschaftsverhältnis betrachtet. Aus diesem Grund ist die Frage, ob zwei Punkte P und Q in einem Bild miteinander verbunden sind, immer in Abhängigkeit von der gewählten Nachbarschaft zu beantworten. Im allgemeinen werden 4er und 8er Nachbarschaften zugrunde gelegt (Abbildung 3).

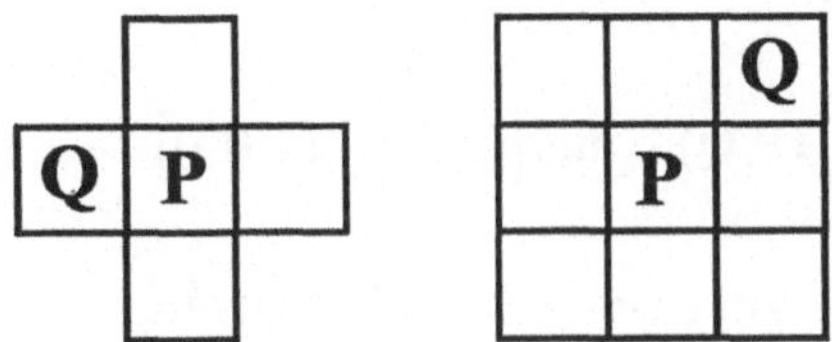

Abbildung 3. Die 4er und 8er Nachbarschaft zur Berechnung der Verbundenheit zwischen den Bildpunkten P und Q

Liegt das Binärbild X der Größe M×N vor, und eine Nachbarschaft $S \subset X$, dann sind die Punkte P und $Q \in S$ in S verbunden, falls ein Pfad δ von P zu Q existiert, der nur Punkte der Nachbarschaft S beinhaltet. Ein Pfad δ der Länge n von P zu Q ist eine Punktsequenz $P = P_0, P_1, ..., P_n = Q$, so daß P_i das Nachbarpixel von P_{i-1} ist $(1 \leq i \leq n)$. Die Binarisierung kann, analog zur Länglichkeit, auch im Falle der Verbundenheit zu einem Informationsverlust führen (Abbildung 4). Bildpunkte, die im Originalbild verbunden sind, werden infolge von Überbelichtung, Rauschen usw. durch die Schwellwertbildung getrennt.

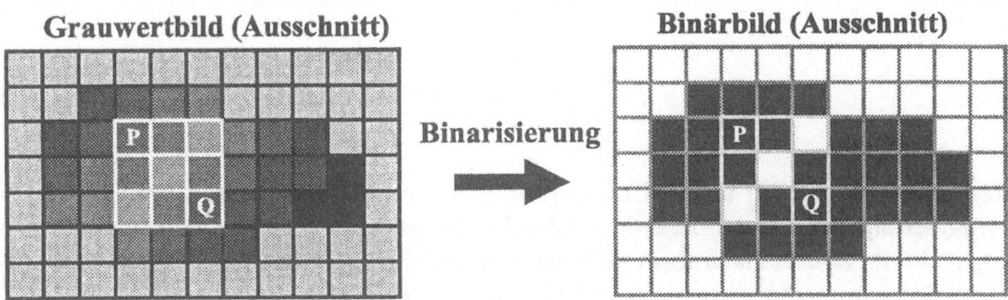

Abbildung 4. Zur Verbundenheit in Grauwert- und Binärbildern. Die Punkte P und Q sind im Grauwertbild zu einem gewissen Grad verbunden. Nach der Binarisierung sind sie jedoch in derselben Nachbarschaft nicht mehr verbunden, weil manche Pixel nicht richtig klassifiziert worden sind (beispielsweise infolge einer Überbelichtung bzw. Reflexion)

Ist das Bild X ein Grauwertbild und S eine Nachbarschaft der Zugehörigkeiten, so läßt sich der Begriff der Verbundenheit auf Fuzzy-Mengen erweitern [6,7]. Es seien P und

$Q \in S\ (\subset X)$ und die Zugehörigkeitsfunktion μ_X des Bildes X gegeben. Der *Grad der Verbundenheit* von P und Q mit Rücksicht auf μ_X ist wie folgt definiert:

$$V_\mu(P,Q) \equiv \max_{\delta_{PQ}} \left[\min_{r \in \delta_{PQ}} \mu_X(r) \right], \tag{1}$$

wobei δ_{PQ} alle möglichen Pfade zwischen P und Q sind. Die Punkte P und Q sind in μ_X verbunden, wenn gilt:

$$V_\mu(P,Q) \geq \min\left[\mu_X(P), \mu_X(Q)\right]. \tag{2}$$

3 Unscharfe Binarisierung: Eine Übersicht

Betrachtet man das Bild X der Größe M×N mit L Graustufen als eine unscharfe Menge der Grauwerte, deren Grad der Zugehörigkeit proportional zu ihrer Helligkeit ist, so kann man die Frage stellen, wie groß die Unschärfe des Bildes ist [9]. Um diese Unschärfe zu quantifizieren, kann man unterschiedliche Maße der Unschärfe einsetzen. De Luca und Termini [1] führten die unscharfe Entropie H ein, um diese Frage zu beantworten (μ_i gibt den Zugehörigkeitsgrad und h_i die Häufigkeit des i-ten Bildpunktes):

$$H = \frac{1}{MN \ln 2} \sum_{i=0}^{L-1} h_i \cdot [-\mu_i \ln(\mu_i) - (1-\mu_i)\ln(1-\mu_i)]. \tag{3}$$

Kaufmann [3] führte ein ähnliches Maß (Index der Unschärfe) ein:

$$\gamma = \frac{2}{MN} \sum_{i=1}^{L-1} h_i \cdot \min(\mu_i, 1-\mu_i). \tag{4}$$

Rosenfeld und Pal [8] und Pal und Murthy [5] verwendeten diese Maße, um durch Minimierung der Unschärfe einen Schwellwert der Binarisierung zu finden. Dabei legen die Autoren eine S-förmige Zugehörigkeitsfunktion fest (Abbildung 5). Zwischen den Parametern dieser Funktion herrscht folgende Beziehung:

$$B = (A + C)/2 \quad \text{und} \quad \Delta = B - A = C - B.$$

Der Algorithmus zur Binarisierung kann wie folgt angegeben werden:

1. Berechne das Histogramm
2. Initialisiere die Zugehörigkeitsfunktion

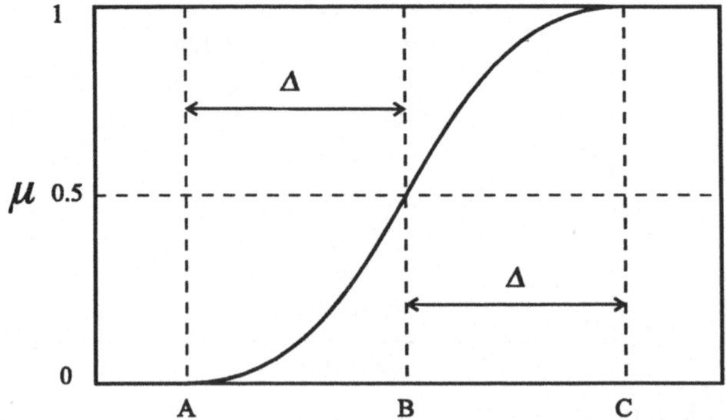

Abbildung 5. S-Funktion mit der Bandbreite Δ zur Schwellwertsuche [9]

3. Verschiebe die Zugehörigkeitsfunktion und berechne die Unschärfe für die aktuelle Position
4. Finde das Minimum der Unschärfe und den korrespondierenden Crossover-Punkt (der Punkt mit $\mu = 0.5$)
5. Binarisiere das Bild mit dem neuen Crossover-Punkt als Schwellwert

Dieser Ansatz weist einige Nachteile auf. Die Festlegung der Bandbreite Δ erfordert nähere Kenntnisse über das Histogramm und zur Detektion des Minimums der Unschärfe braucht man zusätzliche Rechenschritte. Huang und Wang [2] verfolgten die Idee der unscharfen Binarisierung, setzten jedoch eine andere Zugehörigkeitsfunktion ein, die die erwähnten Nachteile beseitigte (Abbildung 6):

$$\mu_i = \begin{cases} \dfrac{1}{1 + \dfrac{|i - m_1(T)|}{i_{max} - i_{min}}} & \text{falls } i \leq T, \\[2ex] \dfrac{1}{1 + \dfrac{|i - m_2(T)|}{i_{max} - i_{min}}} & \text{sonst.} \end{cases} \tag{5}$$

Hierbei sind i_{min} und i_{max} der minimale und maximale Grauwert des Bildes. Die Faktoren m_1 und m_2 werden in Abhängigkeit des aktuellen Schwellwertes T wie folgt berechnet:

$$m_1(T) = \frac{\sum_{i=0}^{T} i \cdot h_i}{\sum_{i=0}^{T} h_i}, \quad m_2(T) = \frac{\sum_{i=T+1}^{L-1} i \cdot h_i}{\sum_{i=T}^{L-1} h_i}. \tag{6}$$

h_i gibt die Häufigkeit des i-ten Grauwertes wieder.

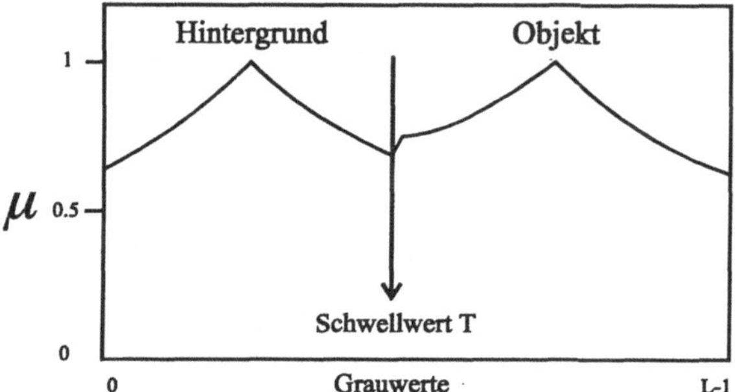

Abbildung 6. Zugehörigkeitsfunktion zur Binarisierung nach Huang/Wang

4 Schwellwert als unscharfe Zahl: Ein neuer Algorithmus

Die Binarisierung ist in der Praxis alles andere als ein trivialer Schritt. Ungleichmäßige Beleuchtung und verrauschte Bilddaten erschweren die eindeutige Bestimmung eines Schwellwertes. In solchen Fällen kann es sinnvoll sein, den Schwellwert nicht als eine exakte Zahl sondern als eine unscharfe Zahl zu definieren. Selbstverständlich muß der Algorithmus am Ende eine konkrete Zahl als Schwellwert liefern und keine Funktion. Durch Modellierung des Schwellwertes als unscharfe Zahl kann man jedoch versuchen, die Unsicherheit zu reduzieren. Eine unscharfe Zahl ist eine konvexe Fuzzy-Menge, die stückweise stetig ist und für genau ein Element die Zugehörigkeit 1 aufweist. Die LR-Zahlen sind solche unscharfen Zahlen, deren linke (L) und rechte (R) Hälfte getrennt definiert wird. Wir benutzen unscharfe Zahlen folgender Form:

$$\mu_i = \begin{cases} 0 & \text{falls } i \le i_{min}, \\ R(i) = \left(\dfrac{i - i_{min}}{T - i_{min}} \right)^{\alpha} & \text{falls } i_{min} < i \le T, \\ L(i) = \left(\dfrac{i_{max} - i}{i_{max} - T} \right)^{\beta} & \text{falls } T < i \le i_{max}, \\ 0 & \text{falls } i > i_{max}. \end{cases} \tag{7}$$

Die Exponenten α und $\beta \in (0, \infty)$ stellen linguistische Modifikatoren dar [11]. Durch die geeignete Wahl dieser Parameter kann die Form des unscharfen Schwellwertes an das vorliegende Bild angepaßt werden. Abbildung 7 stellt den Schwellwert T = 90 als unscharfe Zahl schematisch dar ($\alpha = 0.5$ und $\beta = 2$). Für unsere folgenden Betrachtungen setzen wir ohne Beschränkung der Allgemeinheit $\alpha = \beta = 1$. Die Aufgabe besteht nun darin, diese unscharfe Zahl so festzulegen, daß der Scheitelpunkt (die Position mit $\mu = 1$) den gesuchten (scharfen) Schwellwert markiert.

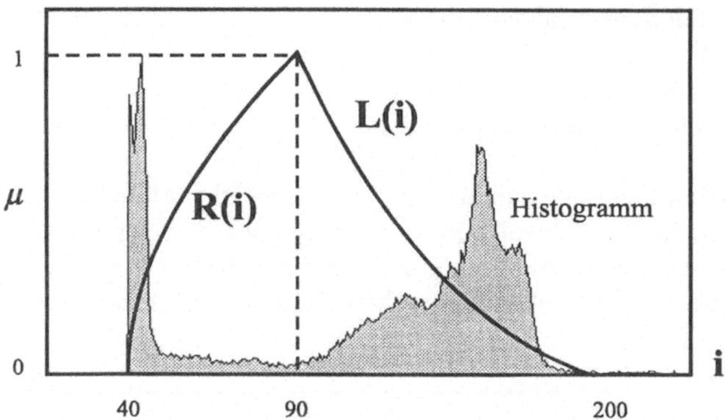

Abbildung 7. Schwellwert 90 als unscharfe Zahl ($\alpha = 0.5$ und $\beta = 2$)

Verschiebt man den Scheitelpunkt der Funktion über den gesamten Grauwertbereich (Abbildung 8) und berechnet in jeder Position die Unschärfe nach Gleichung (3) oder (4), so sinkt die Unschärfe, falls der Scheitelpunkt eher zum Objekt bzw. Hintergrund gehört, und steigt, falls der Scheitelwert die Übergangsgrauwerte darstellt. In der Position, wo der Scheitelpunkt einen existierenden Schwellwert markiert, erreicht die Unschärfe ihr Maximum.

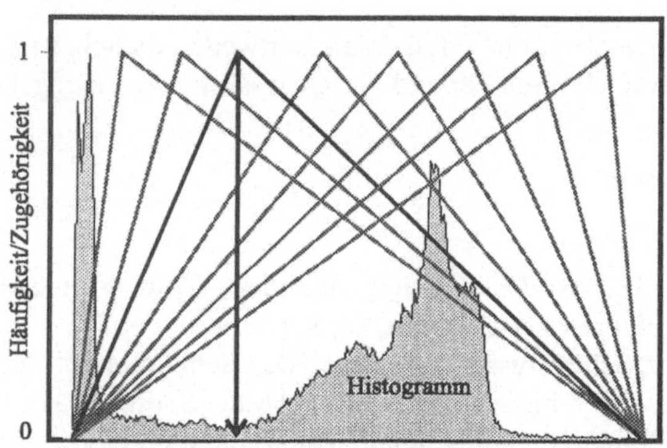

Abbildung 8. Zur Schwellwertdetektion mit unscharfen Zahlen. Eine Dreiecksfunktion wird über den gesamten Grauwertbereich verschoben. In jeder Position wird die Unschärfe berechnet. Der Scheitelpunkt der Funktion, für den die Unschärfe maximal wurde, markiert den gesuchten Schwellwert

Der Algorithmus zur Binarisierung mit unscharfen Zahlen kann wie folgt formuliert werden:

1. Berechne das Histogramm
2. Lege eine unscharfe Zahl fest (Dreiecks- oder π-Funktion)

3. Verschiebe den Scheitelpunkt der unscharfen Zahl und berechne die Unschärfe für die aktuelle Position
4. Finde das Maximum der Unschärfe und den korrespondierenden Scheitelpunkt
5. Binarisiere das Bild mit dem neuen Scheitelpunkt als Schwellwert

In manchen Fällen kann es sinnvoll sein, statt den Scheitelpunkt als Schwellwert zu nehmen, den unscharfen Schwellwert zu defuzzyfizieren (beispielsweise den Schwerpunkt der Funktion, siehe Abbildung 9). Über die Parametrisierung der unscharfen Zahl kann der Verlauf der linken und rechten Funktionshälfte an spezifische Anforderungen angepaßt werden.

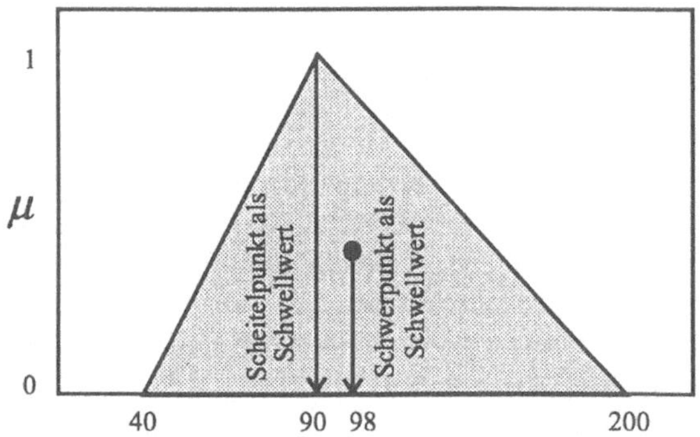

Abbildung 9. Der gesuchte Schwellwert kann entweder als Scheitelpunkt der unscharfen Zahl oder als ihr Schwerpunkt (*Defuzzyfizierung*) angegeben werden

5 Ergebnisse

Die Methoden wurden in MATLAB implementiert. Zum Vergleich der Ergebnisse wurde das Otsu-Verfahren [4] ebenfalls implementiert. Tabelle 1 zeigt einige Ergebnisse. Als gesuchter Schwellwert wurde hier der Scheitelpunkt der unscharfen Zahl angegeben. Die ausgewählten Bilder weisen keine optimale Bimodalität auf, weil entweder mehrere Objekte im Bild enthalten sind (erste und letzte Reihe in Tabelle 1), oder die Bimodalität wegen Rauschens und ungleichmäßiger Helligkeitsverteilung gestört ist (zweite und dritte Reihe in Tabelle 1). Unsere Untersuchungen zeigten auch, daß die unscharfen und klassischen Methoden bei optimalen Verhältnissen stets (fast) denselben Schwellwert liefern. Die Ergebnisse weisen jedoch große Abweichungen auf, sobald die Bimodalität gestört wird. Unsere Methode mit unscharfen Zahlen liefert in solchen Fällen akzeptable Ergebnisse, auch wenn die Parameter nicht an die spezifischen Histogramme angepaßt sind (für alle Bilder waren die linguistischen Modifikatoren α und β auf 1 gesetzt). Die weiteren Untersuchungen zeigten, daß unsere Methode sich besonders dann zur Binarisierung anbietet, falls das Bild einen Hintergrund, jedoch mehrere Objekte unterschiedlicher Helligkeiten besitzt.

Tabelle 1. Vergleich zwischen unterschiedlichen Binarisierungsalgorithmen (alle Methoden sind global implementiert).

	Methode		
Originalbild	Huang/Wang	Otsu-Verfahren	Unsere Methode
	T = 109	T = 125	T = 56
	T = 28	T = 52	T = 20
	T = 5	T = 41	T = 12
	T = 47	T = 80	T = 20

6 Zusammenfassung

Soll das Binärbild der Berechnung geometrischer Merkmale dienen, so kann man, soweit die Anforderungen der Aufgabenstellung dies erlauben, die Fuzzy-Geometrie heranziehen. Dadurch kann auf die Binarisierung verzichtet werden. Läßt sich eine explizite Pixelklassifikation nicht vermeiden, so bieten Maße der Unschärfe neue Möglichkeiten zur Entwicklung robuster Binarisierungsalgorithmen, die die inhärente Vagheit der Schwellwertsuche effizienter modellieren können.

Die Minimierung der Unschärfe nach Pal und Murthy [5] stellt eine Erweiterung des gleitenden Mittelwertes dar. Der Ansatz von Huang und Wang [2] kann als eine verbesserte Version angesehen werden, die einfacher zu implementieren ist. Unser Ansatz mit unscharfen Zahlen und Maximierung der Unschärfe eignet sich besonders dann, falls das Bild ein Hintergrund und mehrere Objekte beinhaltet, die unterschiedliche Helligkeiten aufweisen. Durch Verwendung parametrisierter unscharfer Zahlen kann ein lernfähiger Algorithmus entwickelt werden, der bei besonders schwierigen Fällen zum Einsatz kommen kann. In unserer weiteren Arbeiten werden wir die Leistung der Fuzzy-Methoden im bezug auf die Ortsabhängigkeit der Objekt-/Hintergrundpixel anhand lokal-adaptiver Implementierung dieser Methoden untersuchen.

7 Literatur

[1] De Luca, A., Termini, S. (1972): A definition of a nonprobabilistic entropy in the setting of fuzzy set theory. Information and Control 20, S. 301–312

[2] Huang, L. K., Wang, M. J. (1995): Image thresholding by minimizing the measure of fuzziness. Pattern Recognition 28, S. 41–51

[3] Kaufmann, A. (1975): Introduction to the Theory of Fuzzy Subsets – Fundamental Theoretical Elements, Band 1. Academic Press, New York

[4] Otsu, N. (1979): A threshold selection method from gray-level histogram. IEEE Transactions on System, Man and Cybernetics SMC-9 (1), S. 62–66

[5] Pal, S. K., Murthy, C. A. (1990): Fuzzy thresholding: mathematical framework, bound functions and weighted moving average technique. Pattern Recognition Letters 11, S. 197–206

[6] Rosenfeld, A. (1979): Fuzzy digital topology. Information and Control 40, S. 76–87

[7] Rosenfeld, A. (1984): The fuzzy geometry of image subsets. Pattern Recognition Letters 2, S. 311–317

[8] Rosenfeld, A., Pal, S. K. (1988): Image enhancement and thresholding by optimization of fuzzy compactness. Pattern Recognition Letters 7, S. 77–86

[9] Tizhoosh, H. R. (1997): Fuzzy-Bildverarbeitung, Einführung in Theorie und Praxis. Springer, Heidelberg

[10] Tizhoosh, H.R., Michaelis, B. (1977): Über den systematischen Einstieg in die Fuzzy-Bildverarbeitung. AFN-Jahrestagung 1997, Magdeburg, S. 39-45

[11] Zadeh, L. A. (1972): A fuzzy-set-theoretic interpretation of linguistic hedges. Journal of Cybernetics 2, S. 4–34

Extracting Symbols from the Environment – The Concept of Correspondence-Based Object Recognition

Rolf P. Würtz

Institute for Neurocomputing, Ruhr-University Bochum, Germany,
http://www.neuroinformatik.ruhr-uni-bochum.de/ini/PEOPLE/rolf/
E-mail: Rolf.Wuertz@neuroinformatik.ruhr-uni-bochum.de

Abstract. Current computer systems still suffer from the inability to transform sensory image data into a meaningful symbolic description of what the image contains. It is argued that such a capability is of paramount importance for robust AI systems. As a step in that direction, several systems for the recognition of human faces and technical objects are presented. They consist of three steps: feature extraction, solving the correspondence problem (matching), and the actual comparison with stored models of known objects. Two of them are implemented in the Dynamic Link Architecture and are, therefore, close to biological hardware, the others are more technical in nature but also have some biological plausibility.

1 Introduction

A central aspect of computer science between image and language is the question, *"how can we talk about what we see?"* Put that way, it is more a psychological or philosophical question. To add the slant towards computer science, it should be reformulated somehow, *"how can we build a machine that can talk about what it sees?"*.

This question can be answered in a trivial way. A computer can be equipped with a frame grabber and a camera, and after some programming can easily produce correct statements like "I have encountered an intensity of 156 at location (278,195)." This is probably not what was meant by the original question, and the crucial word is obviously the word "see". With seeing we mean more than the acquisition of raw data from some sensor, we expect the production of *abstract symbols* like "I see two green cubes and a red ball" or "This must be Dr. Meyer in front of my camera".

Why is this extraction important? Computer systems are good at manipulating abstract symbols and drawing conclusions from relations between abstract symbols. However, they are currently weak in producing these symbols. This is serious because because the best reasoning system is not able to predict what is going on in the real world. So even if it was once perfectly programmed the conclusions it keeps drawing will automatically get out of touch with what is going on "out there". Everyone who ever took a look at poorly maintained databases knows examples of that.

An alternative would be to equip the system with means to acquire information about the environment actively and match its internal processes with the data found out there. As the implementation of internal processes working on symbols produces good results and powerful systems, the gap that must be closed is extracting, or in technical terms, *grounding* symbols in the environment is the way to go. As symbols and relations between symbols are usually expressed in (some sort of) language this shows the importance of the question we started with.

Today I will present several algorithms that solve tiny subproblems of this general goal, namely the recognition of objects from a small number of known objects and the recognition of persons out of a small to medium number of known persons by their faces. The common feature of these algorithms is that they require *correspondence maps* between an *image* to be analyzed and several stored views of known objects, which we call *models.* This means that pairs of points in model and image must be found which are images of the same point on the physical face. This is not trivial and has acquired the name *correspondence problem.*

The difficulty of the correspondence problem depends on the choice of features. If, e.g., grey values of pixels are taken as local features, there is a lot of ambiguity, i.e., many points from very different locations share the same pixel value without being correspondent points. A possible remedy to that consists in combining local patches of pixels, which of course reduces this ambiguity. If this is done too extensively, i.e., if local features are influenced by a large area, the ambiguities disappear if identical images are used, but the features become more and more sensitive to distortions and changes in background.

2 Correspondence Based Recognition

Once a mapping is established the feature similarities of corresponding point pairs are added up (or averaged) over the whole mapping. This yields a similarity value for each stored model, and the highest similarity belongs to the recognized person. A measure for the reliability of the recognition is derived by a simple statistical analysis of the series of all similarity values.

3 Features

The processing of a retinal grey-level image in simple cells of the primary visual cortex can be modeled by a wavelet transform based on complex-valued Gabor functions [4, 15]. The single wavelet is parameterized by its two-dimensional spatial frequency vector. The responses of all spatial frequencies of some fixed length form a *frequency level*, which assigns a small feature vector to all image points on an appropriate sampling grid. These features have turned out to be a good compromise in the dilemma discussed above. Furthermore, the complex

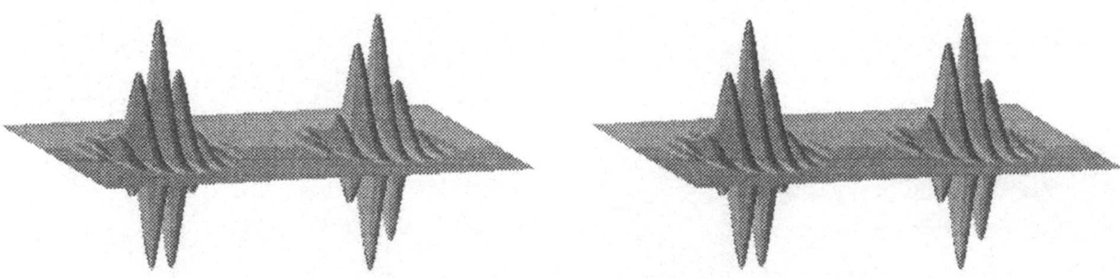

Fig. 1. The form of Gabor wavelets. The left figure shows the Gabor kernel as it is found as receptive field profile in the visual cortex and is used for feature extraction in [15–17]. On the left the real part is shown, on the right the imaginary part. The left figure shows a type of Gabor functions used in [4]. The complete wavelet transform consists of convolutions with scaled and rotated versions of these kernels.

numbers invite a splitting into modulus and phase which is very convenient for matching purposes. The systems I am describing differ in the *sampling* of this transform. The ones in [4, 12] need a sampling grid which is uniformly dense for all spatial frequencies, the one in [15, 16] uses a pyramidal arrangement.

The appeal of Gabor wavelets in comparison to the immense zoo of linear filters used in image processing is twofold. First, they model a certain type of nerve cells, which is found in the early visual processing of mammals (simple cells). Second, they have complex values, which makes it natural to represent the transform as amplitude and phase rather than real and imaginary part. This simple nonlinearity will have important (and pleasant) consequences in the algorithms. Again, the amplitudes are models for another type of visual cells (complex cells).

3.1 Corners

Corners are important image features because they are robust respect to changes in perspective and small distortions, and they allow efficient matching for recognition purposes. It is known that removing the corners from images impedes human recognition performance, while removing much of the edge information does not [2]. Robustness and speed of corner matching can be improved by adding attributes to the corners [8]. This makes computationally expensive detection algorithms attractive, which usually yield a variety of further information.

We followed known models for the early stages of vision and checked the performance of models for end-stopped (corner detecting) cells, which can be regarded as a suitable combination of complex cells. This compared poorly with the capabilities of the human visual system, especially in the presence of background texture and noise. The major problem was that those models act on a single scale only, whereas a robust systems must check for corners on a range of scales. So we proposed a scheme that combines the outputs of end-stopped cells over several scales.

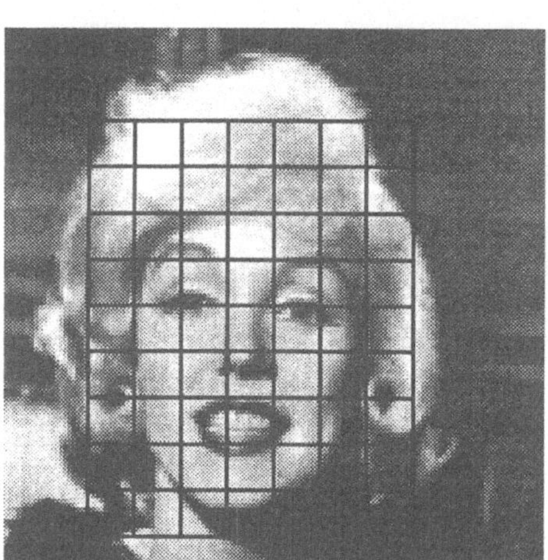

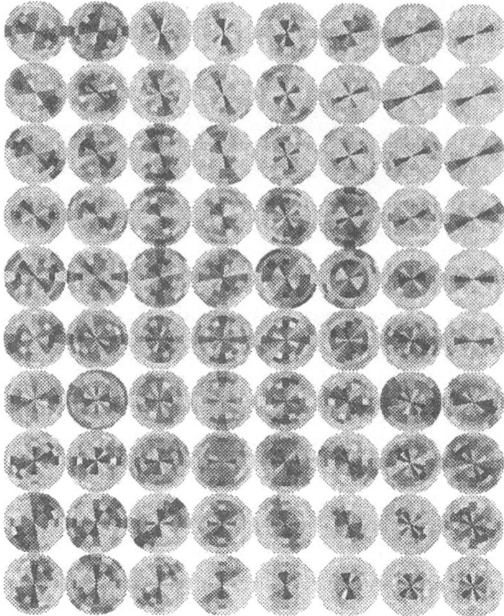

Fig. 2. Visualisation of Gabor features with frequency-independent sampling. Each point in the grid is assigned a little frequency space, which is visualized on the right hand side. The grey values of the little segments show the moduli of the Gabor responses as a function of the (two-dimensional) spatial frequency.

4 Topology

In order to overcome the feature ambiguity the *relative position* of the features must be taken into account. Three different ways to do this will be presented.

4.1 Elastic graphs

In the system described in [4, 12, 3] the model faces are represented by sparse graphs (see figure 2) which are vertex labeled with the Gabor features and edge labeled with the distance vector of the connected vertices. Matching is done by first optimizing the similarity of an undistorted copy of the graph in the input image and then optimizing the individual locations of the vertices. This results in a distorted graph whose vertices are at corresponding locations to the ones in the model graph (see figure 3). The rectangular model graph arrangement has been chosen in [4], in [12] the vertices have been carefully placed on salient points, thus yielding a larger recognition rate.

4.2 Bunch graphs

The major drawback of most correspondence-based recognition systems is that the computationally expensive procedure of creating a correspondence map must be done for *each* of the stored models. This has been overcome by the concept of

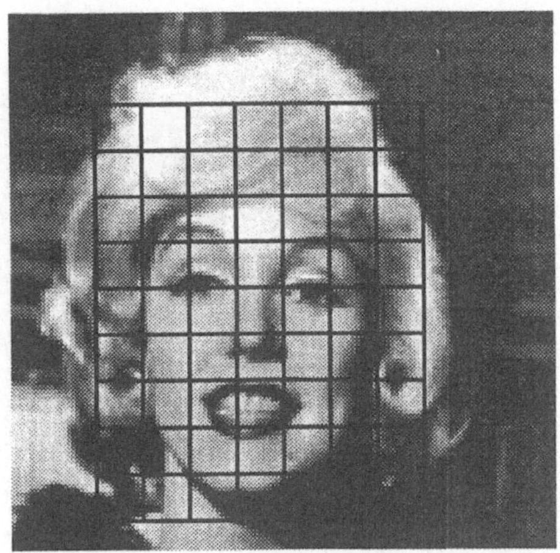

Fig. 3. The result of labeled graph matching. The right hand side shows the graph with maximal similarity to the one on the left.

bunch graphs [13]. The idea is that the database of models is arranged in such a way that corresponding graph nodes are already located at corresponding object points, e.g., a certain node lies on the left eye in all models. For large databases, this reduces the recognition time by orders of magnitudes. Although it is not easy to apply the bunch graph principle to object classes other than faces it has been applied successfully to hand gesture recognition [10, 9].

4.3 Coarse to fine matching

Pyramidal representations of image and model [15, 16] can be matched using the following modules:

1. The *coarse localization* of the counterpart of the model in the image is done by global template matching of the vectors of Gabor amplitudes on the lowest frequency level. This is not very expensive, because the resolution is low, and yields a first rough correspondence mapping.
2. Mappings acquired using only the amplitudes of the Gabor responses are not very precise, because the fine geometrical information resides in the phases. On the other hand, the phases or the full complex responses are not suitable for template matching because they depend strongly on the sampling grid. Therefore, a *local phase matching* has been implemented that enhances the accuracy of amplitude-based mappings. This can be done in parallel on all model points.
3. In order to cope with occlusion problems, it must be possible to *exclude points* from the mapping. This is done on the basis of poor similarity, which is also possible in parallel on all image points.
4. Finally, any mapping can be refined by local template matching with amplitudes from the next higher frequency level. For this, the model is split

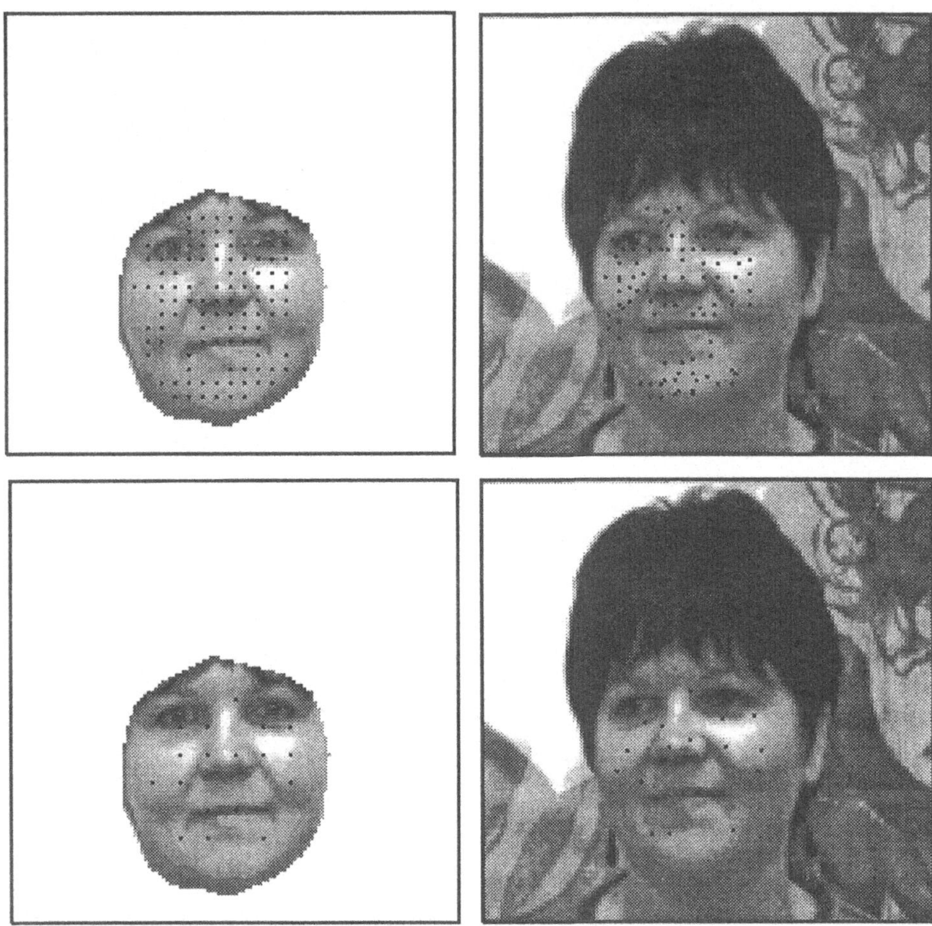

Fig. 4. Course-to-fine matching. The left column shows the model representation on the lowest and next higher frequency levels, the right column the matching points in the image. Due to phase matching correspondences are fairly accurate on the lowest level already.

up into several patches that independently search for correspondences in an area defined by the coarse mapping already known.

The pyramidal arrangement has the advantage that all responses in the stored model which are influenced by the background can be discarded, but the object (which here is the face without hair) still represented well enough for recognition. See figure 4 for an illustration. Note that the image to be analyzed consists of a full pyramid, a presegmentation is not required. The resulting invariance under changes in hairstyle and background constitutes an important advantage of this system as compared with the ones in [4] and [12].

4.4 Point distribution models

In addition to these advantages, the pyramidal system yields fairly dense and very accurate correspondence maps. The accuracy is mainly due to the phase adjustment. These can be used for tracking facial points. In this case, the coarse to fine matching becomes unpractical, and it has been replaced by a learned shape model in [7]. This sort of tracking can eventually lead to automatic measurement of emotions.

5 Neural Models

All the systems discussed here have been inspired by a biologically plausible framework, C. von der Malsburg's Dynamic Link Architecture. The basic idea is as follows. Neurons that have physical connections (with a long-term strength) have the possibility may also have a dynamic link between them, i.e. a connection which is modifiable on a very short time scale by a combination of Hebbian learning and competition.

This can be used to solve the correspondence problem as follows. Two layers of neurons that represent the image space in model and image, respectively, are fully interconnected by dynamic links. They have an internal wiring that supports moving localized blobs of activity. The development of links is supported by feature similarity and synchronous activation of the connected neurons. The link dynamics then converge to a correspondence mapping. In [14] this has been extended by a competition between a multitude of model layers to a full-blown neural face recognition system. In [15, 18] this system is sped up by a coarse to fine strategy working on the Gabor pyramid. The speedup (in principle) is due to the fact that all refinement steps can be done in parallel. That system also shows background invariance, because model- and image-representation are the same as for pyramid matching.

6 Matching of Edge Graphs

In the systems presented so far, features were local texture elements and graph edges or the pyramid structure carry the geometrical information about the relative locations. Applicability of such methods is limited to richly structured or textured objects like faces. Objects with homogeneous surfaces do not provide the sort of vertex labels required there and can only be matched using their outlines. Therefore, we have developed a somehow complementary matching scheme that matches corners and connecting edges [6, 5] with the idea that a combination of both approaches will yield a fairly general recognition method.

Images as well as stored models are represented as graphs whose vertices correspond to object corners and whose edges code for edges connecting corners in the image. The method is invariant under translation, rotation, and scaling and robust under changes in background, limited changes in perspective, and small distortions, but can not handle significant occlusion, due to the absence

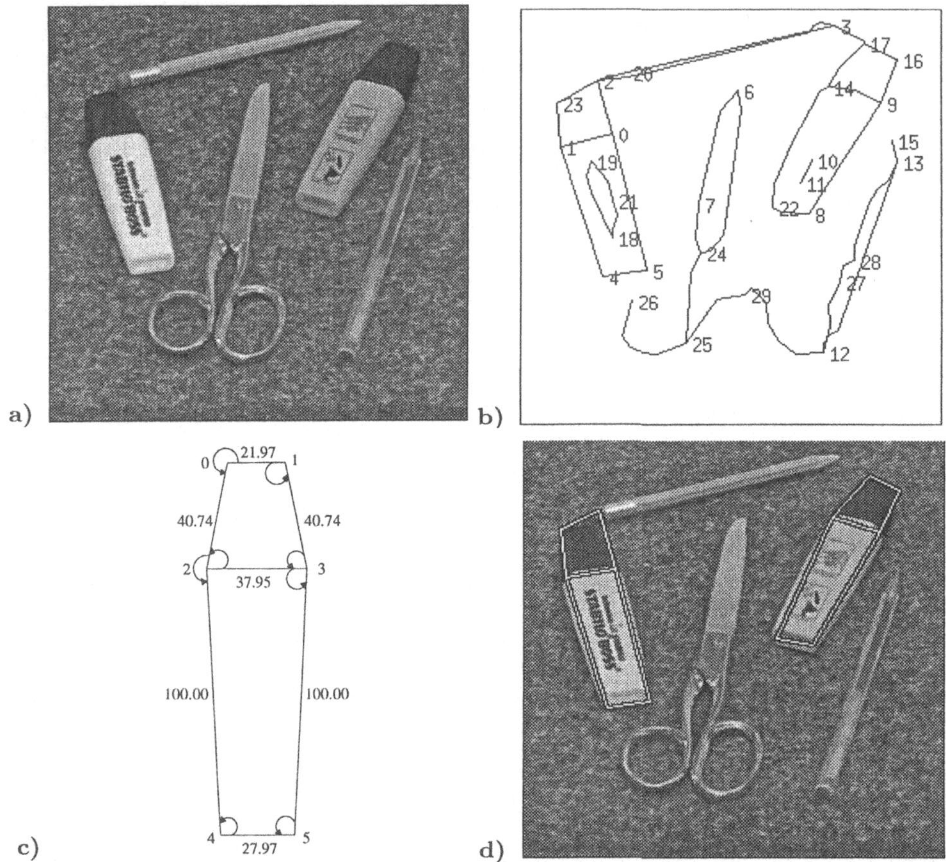

Fig. 5. a) Input image. **b)** Image graph extracted from **a)**, with numbered vertices. **c)** A model graph with implicit attributes, such a the (relative) length of an edge and the angle between two edges. **d)** Found matches of the markers. The used parameters are: maximum five edges to be added, ratio between two edge pairs $\delta r = 5$, average angle tolerance of 10%, maximum angle tolerance of 10%, maximum length tolerance of 50%, and an average length tolerance of 10%.

of area-based features. Graphs are constructed from detected corners by a line-following algorithm [5, 6]

For model matching it is assumed that corners can only be matched onto corners and connecting edges must match edges in the image. Therefore, subgraph isomorphisms must be found, which is, in full generality, NP-complete in the number of vertices. In our approach, the complexity is drastically reduced by demanding that the labels of matched vertices and edges, respectively, must be roughly equal. We have shown experimentally that the problem is so reduced to a tractable size [5].

Each corner is labeled with the angles between all pairs of adjacent line segments starting from it. The edges are labeled with the relative length of the line segments (i.e. the ratio of the length to the length of the longest line segment in the whole graph). This choice of labels automatically yields invariance under translation, rotation and changes in size.

The matching is done by a modified version of the algorithm for subgraph isomorphism is from Ullman [11] based on tree search with backtracking. To cut down evaluation expenses the above mentioned labels are assigned to vertices and edges.

7 Current and Future Work

After the presentation of so many attempts at invariant object recognition the question is in order, what has to be done next. Segmentation of the visual scene is an important prerequisite for robust object recognition and has not been dealt with. A problem that may have become obvious is that the matching algorithms for area-based features such as texture or structure elements are very different from the ones required for outline matching. However, it is easy to construct examples, where each method alone will fail. The incorporation of both is a challenging task.

Furthermore, we are currently working on a system that adds active components to the visual recognition task. This is an active camera system for changing views but, more importantly, a robot arm that can manipulate the objects in question [1]. We hope to automate the process of learning new objects with this robot and at a later point to present an artificial system that can actually talk about what it sees.

Acknowledgments: Most of the work described here has been done in close cooperation with other people. The author wishes to thank Christoph von der Malsburg, Jan C. Vorbrüggen, Laurenz Wiskott, Wolfgang Konen, Shaogang Gong, Stephen McKenna, and Tino Lourens for excellent cooperation.

References

1. Mark Becker, Efthimia Kefalea, Eric Maël, Christoph von der Malsburg, Mike Pagel, Jochen Triesch, Jan C. Vorbrüggen, Rolf P. Würtz, and Stefan Zadel. GripSee: A gesture-controlled robot for object perception and manipulation. *Autonomous Robots*, 1998. Submitted.
2. Irving Biedermann. Recognition-by-components: A theory of human image understanding. *Psychological Review*, 94(2):115–147, 1987.
3. W. Konen and E. Schulze-Krüger. ZN-Face: A system for access control using automated face recognition. In Martin Bichsel, editor, *Proceedings of IWAFGR95, Zürich, June 1995*, pages 18–23, 1995.
4. Martin Lades, Jan C. Vorbrüggen, Joachim Buhmann, Jörg Lange, Christoph von der Malsburg, Rolf P. Würtz, and Wolfgang Konen. Distortion invariant object recognition in the dynamic link architecture. *IEEE Transactions on Computers*, 42(3):300–311, 1993.
5. Tino Lourens. *A Biologically Plausible Model for Corner-based Object Recognition from Color Images.* Shaker, Maastricht, 1998.

6. Tino Lourens and Rolf P. Würtz. Object recognition by matching symbolic edge graphs. In Roland Chin and Ting-Chuen Pong, editors, *Computer Vision — ACCV'98*, volume 1352 of *Lecture Notes in Computer Science*, pages II–193 - II–200. Springer Verlag, 1998.
7. Stephen J. McKenna, Shaogang Gong, Rolf P. Würtz, Jonathan Tanner, and Daniel Banin. Tracking facial feature points with Gabor wavelets and shape models. In Josef Bigün, Gerard Chollet, and Gunilla Borgefors, editors, *Proceedings of the First International Conference on Audio- and Video-based Biometric Person Authentication Crans-Montana, Switzerland, March 1997*, volume 1206 of *LNCS*, pages 35–42. Springer Verlag, 1997.
8. Paul L. Rosin. Augmenting corner descriptors. *Graphical Models and Image Processing*, 58(3):286–294, May 1996.
9. J. Triesch and C. von der Malsburg. A gesture interface for robotics. In *FG'98, The IEEE Third International Conference on Automatic Face and Gesture Recognition*, 1998. In press.
10. Jochen Triesch and Christoph von der Malsburg. Robust classification of hand postures against complex backgrounds. In *Proceedings of the Second International Conference on Automatic Face and Gesture Recognition 1996, Killington, Vermont, USA, October 14–16*, pages 170–175. IEEE Computer Society Press, 1996.
11. J. R. Ullman. An algorithm for subgraph isomorphism. *Journal of the Association for Computing Machinery*, 23(1):31–42, 1976.
12. Laurenz Wiskott, Jean-Marc Fellous, Norbert Krüger, and Christoph von der Malsburg. Face recognition and gender determination. In Martin Bichsel, editor, *Proceedings of IWAFGR95, Zürich, June 1995*, pages 92–97, 1995.
13. Laurenz Wiskott, Jean-Marc Fellous, Norbert Krüger, and Christoph von der Malsburg. Face recognition by elastic bunch graph matching. *IEEE Transactions on Pattern Analysis and Machine Intelligence*, 19(7), 1997.
14. Laurenz Wiskott and Christoph von der Malsburg. Face recognition by dynamic link matching. In Joseph Sirosh, Risto Miikkulainen, and Yoonsuck Choe, editors, *Lateral Interactions in the Cortex: Structure and Function.* The UTCS Neural Networks Research Group, Austin, TX, Electronic book, ISBN 0-9647060-0-8, http://www.cs.utexas.edu/users/nn/web-pubs/htmlbook96, 1996.
15. Rolf P. Würtz. *Multilayer Dynamic Link Networks for Establishing Image Point Correspondences and Visual Object Recognition*, volume 41 of *Reihe Physik.* Verlag Harri Deutsch, Thun, Frankfurt am Main, 1995.
16. Rolf P. Würtz. Object recognition robust under translations, deformations and changes in background. *IEEE Transactions on Pattern Recognition and Machine Intelligence*, 19(7):769–775, 1997.
17. Rolf P. Würtz and Tino Lourens. Corner detection in color images by multiscale combination of end-stopped cortical cells. In Wulfram Gerstner, Alain Germond, Martin Hasler, and Jean-Daniel Nicoud, editors, *Artificial Neural Networks - ICANN '97*, volume 1327 of *Lecture Notes in Computer Science*, pages 901–906, Berlin, Heidelberg, New York, 1997. Springer Verlag.
18. Rolf P. Würtz and Christoph von der Malsburg. A hierarchical dynamic link network for correspondence maps between image points. 1997. In preparation.

Visualisierung von Programmabläufen*

Arne Frick

Tom Sawyer Software, 804 Hearst Avenue, Berkeley, CA 94710,
africk@tomsawyer.com

Zusammenfassung Das Thema dieses Beitrages ist die Visualisierung von Programmabläufen. Darunter versteht man die Darstellung dynamisch veränderlicher Datenstrukturen auf unterschiedlichen Abstraktionsstufen mit dem Ziel, einem Betrachter schnell und leicht Einsichten in funktionale und nicht-funktionale Eigenschaften von Programmen zu vermitteln.
Die Konstruktion solcher Visualisierungen mittels existierender Werkzeuge und Verfahren ist aus mehreren Gründen unbefriedigend. Die zentralen Probleme hierbei sind mangelnde Flexibilität und Erstellungseffizienz. Trotz ihres offensichtlichen Nutzens zu Zwecken der Präsentation, Analyse und Exploration von Programmen, Datenstrukturen und Algorithmen haben Ablaufvisualisierungen daher bislang nicht die erwartete Verbreitung erfahren. Der hier vorgestellte Lösungsansatz besteht in einer allgemeinen Konstruktionsmethode für Visualisierungen, einer flexiblen Software-Architektur sowie Werkzeugen und Techniken zur Unterstützung der effizienten Konstruktion flexibler Visualisierungen.

1 Einleitung

Als *Visualisierung* bezeichnen wir die graphische Repräsentation einer realen oder künstlichen Wissens-Domäne. Der klassischen Systemtheorie folgend, gehen wir davon aus, daß die Domänen aus diskreten Objekten und ihren Beziehungen bestehen. Software-Systeme zur Konstruktion und Betrachtung von Visualisierungen heißen *Visualisierungssysteme*. In diesem Zusammenhang unterscheiden wir mehrere Rollen, welche gegebenenfalls von unterschiedlichen Personen ausgefüllt werden können:

- den *Programmierer* des zu visualisierenden Programmes;
- den *Architekt* des Visualisierungssystems;
- den *Konstrukteur* als Benutzer des Visualisierungssystems; sowie
- den *Betrachter* einer mit Hilfe des Systems erstellten Visualisierung.

Im Unterschied zu statischen Darstellungen, etwa des Programmzustandes zu einem beliebigen, aber festen Zeitpunkt während des Ablaufes oder (von Teilen) des Kontrollflusses, sollte eine Ablaufvisualisierung die zeitlichen Veränderungen der Datenstrukturen sichtbar machen und so die Logik des Programms durchschaubar machen. Anwendungsbeispiele für Ablaufvisualisierungen sind Algorithmen-Animationen, die Aufdeckung algorithmischer Fehler sowie die Analyse von Laufzeitverhalten und Speicherplatzbedarf von Programmen. Dem Konstrukteur stehen die Hilfsmittel der Computer-Graphik und Animation zur Verfügung.

* Die Ergebnisse dieses Beitrages entstanden im Rahmen der Dissertation des Autors am Institut für Programmstrukturen der Fakultät für Informatik an der Universität Karlsruhe.

Programme basieren auf Modellen eines Realitätsausschnittes oder einer geschlossenen, künstlichen Welt. Der Nutzen einer Programmvisualisierung für den Betrachter und die Akzeptanz einer Visualisierung hängen entscheidend davon ab, wie gut und treffend der Konstrukteur

- die relevanten Objekte und Beziehungen des Modells erfaßt und in Bilder umsetzt, und
- die teilweise unbekannten Anforderungen von Betrachtern antizipieren kann.

Wir wollen davon ausgehen, daß der Konstrukteur über ein angemessenes Modell des Darstellungsgegenstandes verfügt. Die Umsetzung in eine Darstellung sollte Ergebnisse der Kognitionswissenschaften berücksichtigen. Sie kann aus Informatiksicht als gelöst angesehen werden, wenn der Architekt im Visualisierungssystem hierzu geeignete Werkzeuge und Hilfsmittel anbietet, das Visualisierungssystem also insbesondere *ausdrucksstark* genug ist, um (möglichst kurze) Beschreibungen von Sachverhalten und Zusammenhängen durch den Konstrukteur zu ermöglichen. Dies beinhaltet auch vorgefertigte Implementierungen häufig auftretender Probleme algorithmischer Natur oder aus dem Bereich der Benutzerschnittstellen.

Die Anforderungen von Betrachtern sind zur Konstruktionszeit nicht oder nur unvollständig bekannt. Nützlichkeit und Akzeptanz von Visualisierungen hängen also neben der Frage, wie gut der Konstrukteur diese Anforderungen trifft, insbesondere noch von der *Flexibilität* zur Anpassung an unbekannte oder wechselnde Anforderungen ab. Die vom Benutzer beeinflußbaren Teile der Darstellung bezeichnen wir als *Darstellungsstrategie*. Hierzu zählen die Navigation in der Darstellung sowie Wechsel der Abstraktionsstufe und der Plazierungsstrategie. Zur Flexibilität trägt ferner noch die *Skalierbarkeit* bezüglich der Problemgröße bei.

Der Rest des Beitrages ist wie folgt gegliedert. In Abschnitt 2 schlagen wir eine Konstruktionsmethode für Ablaufvisualisierungen vor, von der ausgehend in Abschnitt 3 eine Software-Architektur für Visualisierungssysteme beschrieben wird. Abschnitt 4 beleuchtet Werkzeuge und Techniken zur Erzielung von Effizienz und Flexibilität bei Erstellung und Betrachtung von Ablaufvisualisierungen. Verwandte Arbeiten sind Gegenstand von Abschnitt 5.

2 Eine Konstruktionsmethode für Ablaufvisualisierungen

In diesem Abschnitt diskutieren wir die Konstruktionsmethode aus [7]. Dort werden folgende Konstruktionsschritte vorgeschlagen, die nachfolgend näher erläutert wird:

1. Identifikation von *Phänomenen* im Programm;
2. Wahl eines *Programmodells*,
3. Wahl eines *Zeitmodells*,
4. Abbildung des *Programmzustandes* in den Zustandsraum des Programmodells;
5. Gruppierung der Phänomene zu *Sichten*;
6. Zuordnung von *Abstraktionsstufen* zu Sichten;
7. Konstruktion der *Bildorganisation* und *-dynamik*; sowie
8. Wahl bzw. Konstruktion von *Darstellungsstrategien*.

Phänomene Der Konstrukteur einer Visualisierung muß das Programm zumindest insoweit verstanden haben, daß er die zum Verständnis wesentlichen Phänomene identifizieren kann. Basierend auf seinem Verständnis des Programms, das auch als *mentales Modell* bezeichnet wird, kann er dann ein Modell des Programms konstruieren. Ziel der Modellkonstruktion ist die Erfassung der den Betrachter vermutlich interessierenden Phänomene, denn im allgemeinen können nur solche Einsichten und Zusammenhänge vermittelt werden, die Bestandteil des Modells sind. Dabei können sehr wohl auch Phänomene auftreten, die für die Funktionalität des Programms nicht erforderlich, aber für das Verständnis hilfreich sind. Beispielsweise dient in der Informatik das Problem der TÜRME VON HANOI oft als Beispiel zur Illustration des Konzeptes der Rekursion. Rekursive Implementierungen des Problems haben oft keinen expliziten Rekursionstiefenzähler. Diese Information muß also rekonstruiert werden, wenn die Rekursionstiefe als Funktion der Schrittanzahl darstellt werden soll.

Programmodell Durch explizite Konstruktion eines Programmodells wird die Abbildung vom Programmzustand in den Zustand der einzelnen Sichten in zwei einfachere Teilabbildungen zerlegt. Ferner werden dadurch die Flexibilität erhöht und die Konstruktionseffizienz durch Wiederverwendung gesteigert. Oftmals können einmal erstellte Programmodelle und Teilabbildungen wiederverwendet werden. Ein Beispiel möge dies verdeutlichen: Modelle verschiedener vergleichsbasierter Sortieralgorithmen enthalten in der Regel Operationen compare und exchange zum Vergleich bzw. zum Vertauschen von Elementen. Mit einer solchen einheitlichen Schnittstelle kann die zweite Teilabbildung vom Programmodell in die angeschlossenen Sichten unabhängig vom konkreten Sortieralgorithmus des Zielprogramms konstruiert werden und ist damit wiederverwendbar. Die Konstruktion der ersten reduziert sich im wesentlichen auf die Identifikation von Programmstellen, an denen die genannten (Modell-)Ereignisse eintreten.

Zeitmodell Die Darstellung zeitlicher Veränderungen erfordert die Berücksichtigung der Zeitdimension im Rahmen des Entwurfes. Die Wahl eines geeigneten Zeitmodelles hängt insbesondere davon ab, ob die Zeit im Rahmen des Programmodells eine *kardinale, ordinale oder metrische* Größe ist. Um die Kausalität von Veränderungen zu bewahren, genügt ein virtuelles Zeitmodell. Sind die Abstände zwischen aufeinanderfolgenden Zeitdifferenzen nicht gleich groß, so ist statt dessen das Zeitmodell der simulierten Echtzeit zu bevorzugen.

Abbildungen Nach Festlegung von Phänomenen und Programmodell kann der Konstrukteur *Triggerstellen* im Zielprogramm identifizieren, denen Zustandswechsel im Programmodell entsprechen, und mit diesen die erste der beiden Abbildungen gewinnen. Für nähere Einzelheiten sei aus Platzgründen auf [7] verwiesen.

Sichten Komplexe Modelle können nicht als Einzelbild dargestellt werden, da sonst der Betrachter durch die Fülle an Information überwältigt wird und vor lauter „Rauschen" die Information nicht mehr sieht. Daher ist es sinnvoll, die Menge der Phänomene in verträgliche Gruppen einzuteilen. Jede Gruppe stellt eine *Sicht* des Modells dar und wird als eigenes Bild dargestellt. Der Betrachter kann zwischen den angebotenen Sichten diejenigen auswählen, die seinen Intentionen am besten entsprechen. Wir illustrieren dies am Beispiel der TÜRME VON HANOI. Bild 1 zeigt drei unterschiedliche Sichten des Modells: eine natürliche Sicht, ein KIVIAT-Diagramm sowie eine Zeitlinie, die die Rekursionstiefe über der Zeit abträgt (vgl. auch 2).

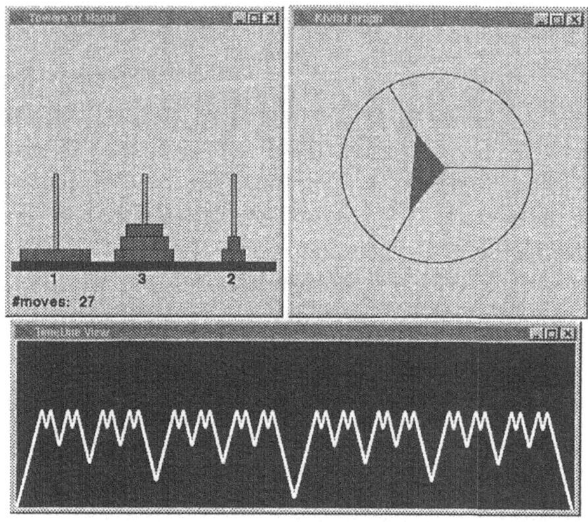

Abbildung1. Drei Sichten des Problems der TÜRME VON HANOI.

Abstraktionsstufen Jeder Sicht werden anschließend Abstraktionsstufen zugeordnet. Da dem Konstrukteur die genauen Anforderungen der Betrachter nicht vorab bekannt sind und diese auch während der Betrachtung wechseln können, sollte eine flexible Visualisierung in Abhängigkeit von antizipierten, denkbaren Anwendungsprofilen mehrere Abstraktionsstufen vorsehen. Beispielsweise sollten Visualisierungen von Netzwerkflußalgorithmen in der Lage sein, sowohl einen (algorithmusnahen und implementierungsunabhängigen) Graphen des Netwerks als auch eine (programmnahe und implementierungsabhängige) Darstellung der diesen realisierenden Datenstruktur zu zeigen. Ersteres ist hilfreich für das Verständnis des zugrundeliegenden Algorithmus, während letzteres beim Aufspüren von Fehlern hilfreich sein kann. Unterschiedliche Abstraktionsstufen dienen verschiedenen Zwecken. Während höhere Abstraktionsstufen sich auf die Semantik der Anwendung konzentrieren, zeigen niedrigere Stufen mehr und mehr Details der Implementierung. Der Betrachter sollte in der Lage sein, zwischen den angebotenen Ebenen willkürlich und unabhängig vom Konstruktionsprozeß auszuwählen.

Abstraktionen dienen schließlich noch einem weiteren Zweck, dem Verbergen überflüssiger Details. Der Betrachter ist damit in der Lage, die Granularität der Betrachtung seinen Anforderungen flexibel anzupassen. Als Beispiel diene ein Modell mit Hunderten von Objekten und Tausenden von Ereignissen auf unterster Stufe, die das Programmodell aktualisieren. Indem man das Modell zunächst eine zeitlang auf einer hohen Abstraktionsstufe betrachtet, können unerwünschte bzw. unnötige Teile der Visualisierung übersprungen werden, bevor man zu einer feingranularen, detaillierten Abstraktionsstufe übergeht. Diese Eigenschaft ist beispielsweise nützlich zum Auffinden von Programmfehlern, indem der Programmablauf zunächst für eine deutliche Zeitspanne voranschreitet, bevor die den Betrachter interessierenden Veränderungen sichtbar werden.

Bildorganisation und -dynamik In diesem Schritt wird festgelegt, wie die Phänomene und ihre zeitlichen Veränderungen dargestellt werden. Dies vervollständigt den zweiten Abbildungsschritt, in dem die in einer Sicht darzustellenden Teile des Modellzustandes abgebildet werden auf zugehörige Bildelemente (Symbole, Metaphern und Beziehungen zwischen diesen). Aus der in 1 gestellten Skalierbarkeitsanforderung resultiert, daß die Bildobjekte wo immer möglich automatisch plaziert werden sollten. Dies ist für statische Strukturen wie Reihungen und Datenfelder fester Struktur leicht, wird jedoch für dynamische Daten, deren Struktur zeitlichen Änderungen unterworfen ist, wie beispielsweise Graphen, nicht-trivial. Im letzteren Fall verwendet man typischerweise Algorithmen aus dem Forschungsgebiet des automatischen Zeichnens von Graphen (*graph drawing*) [1,4]. Zwei Beobachtungen rechtfertigen dies:

1. die meisten während des Ablaufs von Programmen auftretenden Daten sind nichtnumerischer Natur, und
2. Graphen eignen sich gut zur graphischen Repräsentation beliebiger Modelle und sind damit eine zweckmäßige Standarddarstellung.

Auf Verfahren zur Lösung des Plazierungsproblems für Graphen kommen wir im Zusammenhang mit der Diskussion von Werkzeugen und Techniken in 4 noch einmal zurück. Denkbare Alternativen zur algorithmisch möglicherweise schwierigen und aufwendigen automatischen Plazierung allgemeiner Graphen sind

1. fest vorgegebene Darstellungsstrategien für gut beherrschte Teilprobleme, beispielsweise für Datenreihungen, Binärbäume etc.. Diese sind zwar leicht zu implementieren, versagen jedoch für Strukturen unbekannter oder veränderlicher Natur.
2. das Abwälzen des Plazierungsproblems auf den Betrachter. Es ist klar, daß diese Vorgehensweise bereits für verhältnismäßig kleine Problemgrößen unakzeptabel wird.

Änderungen des Modellzustandes werden durch Wechsel des zugehörigen Programmzustandes hervorgerufen. Die daraus resultierenden Anforderungen an Ablaufvisualisierungen diskutiert Abschnitt 4. Ferner zeigen wir auf, wie Flexibilität durch interaktive Operationen erzielt werden kann, die zwar das graphische Bild verändern, jedoch das zugrundeliegende Modell unverändert lassen. Dies bedeutet einen weiteren signifikanten Fortschritt: Sichten können interaktiv verändert werden, während das Modell seinen Zustand und demzufolge auch seine Konsistenz beibehält.

Darstellungsstrategie Zusätzlich zur Plazierungsstrategie legt die Darstellungsstrategie weitere interaktiv veränderbare Teile der Visualisierung fest, wie etwa

1. Navigationsmechanismen zur Modifikation des räumlichen Bildaspektes, und
2. Selektionsmechanismen, die dem Betrachter die Konzentration auf bestimmte, von ihm festlegbare Bildteile ermöglichen.

Zusammenfassung Bild 2 zeigt die Struktur einer Architektur für Visualisierungssysteme als Hintereinanderschaltung von Bausteinen (*pipeline*), die durch Datenfilter und -transformationen miteinander verknüpft sind. Die notwendigen Filter und Transformationen mögen zunächst als Bestandteil des Visualisierungssystems angesehen werden.

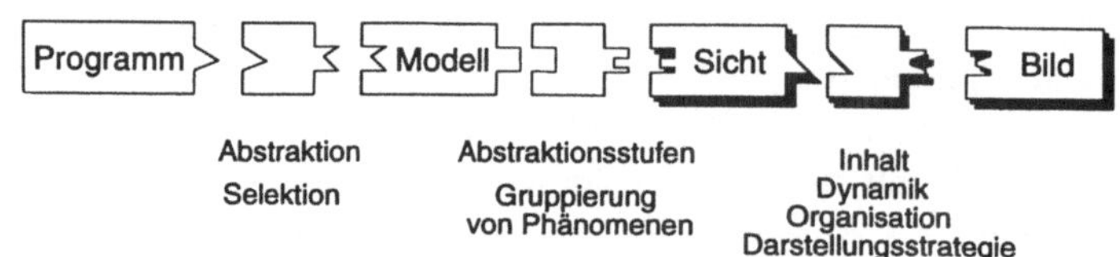

Abbildung2. Struktur der Architektur.

3 Architektur von Visualisierungssystemen

Dieser Abschnitt beschreibt eine Software-Architektur für Visualisierungssysteme namens DYNASTRUCT [6, 7], die auf der Konstruktionsmethode aus 2 beruht. Bild 3 zeigt, wie die Komponenten zusammengeschaltet werden. Zusätzlich zum flexiblen

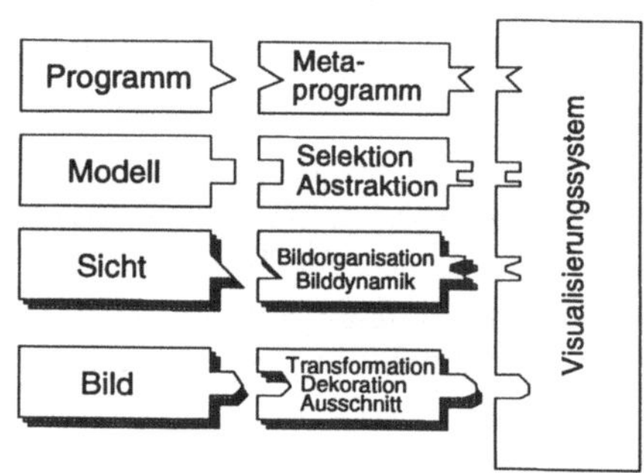

Abbildung3. Die DYNASTRUCT-Architektur.

Austausch von Programm, Modell, Sichten und Bildern sollte ein Visualisierungssystem, das der DYNASTRUCT-Architektur folgt, Schnittstellen zum dynamischen Wechsel der Darstellungsstrategie anbieten. Die Verwendung von *Architektur-* [3] und *Entwurfsmustern* [9] an Schlüsselstellen der Architektur ermöglicht die geforderte Flexibilität:

- Durch *Reflexion* wird eine Metaebene zum existierenden Programm hinzugefügt, so daß Zustandswechsel des Programmodells durch Ereignisse auf der Metaebene des Programms ausgelöst werden.

- Die Implementierung eines *Beobachter*-Musters legt fest, wie das Visualisierungssystem die Sichten verwaltet, sie mit Zustandswechseln im Programmodell assoziiert und Benachrichtigungen verteilt.
- Ein *Interpretierer*-Muster modelliert eine ausdrucksstarke Sprache mit Graphikbefehlen und Benutzerschnittstellenkommandos.

Es sei bemerkt, daß wir bislang keinerlei Annahmen über Implementierungen getroffen haben. Die Festlegung, wie diese Muster im Rahmen eines konkreten Visualisierungssystems implementiert werden sollen, bleibt dem Architekten überlassen.

4 Werkzeuge und Techniken

Ablaufvisualisierungen sollten das mentale Bild (*mental map*) [12] des Betrachters, die Rückwärtszuordnung zwischen Bildelementen und seinem mentalen Modell, nach Möglichkeit erhalten, um kognitive Verwirrung und Ablenkung zu vermeiden. Zu diesem Zweck sollten Zustandswechsel des Programmodells stets zu inkrementellen Bildänderungen führen.

In 2 haben wir argumentiert, daß die Skalierbarkeitsforderung durch automatische Plazierungsstrategien erfüllt werden kann. Hierzu sind entweder spezielle, der Struktur des Modells angepaßte Algorithmen zu implementieren, oder aber das Modell selbst kann als Graph aufgefaßt (Objekte=Knoten, Beziehungen=Kanten) und mit Hilfe automatischer Verfahren zum Zeichnen von Graphen dargestellt werden. Die dabei benutzten Kriterien fallen in zwei Klassen:

Konventionen (unbedingt einzuhalten), z.B. die Darstellung von Kanten als Strecken, Polygonzüge oder Splines, Verlauf von Polygonzügen auf Gitterlinien, ggf. Konventionen des Anwendungsgebietes.

Ästhetik (möglichst einzuhalten), z.B. Minimierung der Kantenkreuzungen, gute Flächenausnutzung, gleichmäßige Verteilung der Objekte, Anzeige von Symmetrien und weitere, nicht vollständig verstandene Kriterien.

Ein Visualisierungssystem sollte zumindest Techniken zur Darstellung der wichtigsten Unterklassen von Graphen wie Bäumen sowie von gerichteten und ungerichteten Graphen. Die Klasse der planaren Graphen ist zwar theoretisch interessant, sie taucht jedoch in der Praxis der Ablaufvisualisierung kaum auf. Ein realistisches Benutzungsszenario könnte etwa kräftegerichtete [5] und hierarchische [15] Darstellungsverfahren für ungerichtete und gerichtete Graphen umfassen. Abhängig von der Topologie des Graphen kann eine initiale Darstellungsstrategie dann automatisch bestimmt werden, wobei nachträgliche Strategiewechsel und -modifikationen durch den Betrachter möglich sind.

Während sich das automatische Zeichnen von Graphen vornehmlich mit Darstellungen theoretischer Graphen befaßt, stellt die Darstellung „realer Graphen“, mit denen wir es in der Ablaufvisualisierung von Programmen zu tun haben, oft weitergehende Anforderungen. Neben der Topologie sind die Ausdehnung von Bildobjekten sowie Kantenbeschriftungen zu berücksichtigen. Des weiteren werden in der Theorie oft Randfälle wie unverbundene Graphen sowie reflexive und Mehrfachkanten vernachlässigt. Für Zwecke der Ablaufvisualisierung von Programmen beschränken wir uns auf Darstellungen im $\mathbb{R}^2$ oder $\mathbb{R}^3$.

Neben Wechseln bzw. Modifikationen der Plazierungsstrategie sollte die Darstellungsstrategie einer Ablaufvisualisierung noch weitere interaktive Operationen zur Verbesserung der Flexibilität anbieten:

- Bildnavigation (z.B. Rollbalken und andere Techniken der direkten Manipulation) zur Wahl des Bildausschnittes, und
- Auswahl von Bildteilen zur Einschränkung des Betrachterfokus, z.B. durch *Faltung*, *Verstecken* und *Abschwächen* von Bildteilen [11].

Zur Verknüpfung des Zielprogramms mit dem Visualisierungssystem hat der Architekt mehrere Alternativen. Sie umfassen

- die statische Instrumentierung des Programms, etwa durch Programmannotationen, objektorientierte Vererbung sowie Modifikationen des benutzten Übersetzers oder der Laufzeitbibliothek, und
- dynamische Instrumentierung, etwa durch Haken, Entwurfsmuster, Laufzeitmodifikationen des Programms, Benutzung eines Debuggers.

Eine effiziente Konstruktion von Ablaufvisualisierungen kann durch Werkzeuge erreicht werden, die die Spezifikation der zu reflektierenden Programmstellen (*Annotationseditor*) oder der Abbildung zwischen den Ereignissen auf der Metaebene des Programms und dem Programmodell (*Abbildungseditor*) unterstützen. Ein Abbildungseditor ist natürlich abhängig vom Anwendungsgebiet des Programmes und muß daher für jedes Gebiet eigens angepaßt werden. Beispielsweise würde ein Abbildungseditor für vergleichsbasierte Sortieralgorithmen die Operationen compare und exchange auf dem Programmodell unterstützen. Analog sollte ein Abbildungseditor für die Domäne Graphen Operationen zum Hinzufügen und Löschen von Knoten und Kanten kennen sowie zum Verändern von Attributen.

5 Verwandte Arbeiten

Mit existierenden Visualisierungssystemen wie ZEUS [2], POLKA [14] und PAVANE [13] wurden teilweise bahnbrechende Fortschritte erzielt. Dennoch haben sie alle bislang nicht den Evolutionsschritt vom Werkzeug für Spezialisten in die tägliche Praxis geschafft. Die Tabellen 1 und 2 zeigen ausschnittsweise Ergebnisse einer Analyse existierender Systeme in [7] anhand der Kriterien Flexibilität und Erstellungseffizienz. So zeigt sich, daß die Systeme

- keine Unterstützung zur Unterscheidung von und Navigation zwischen unterschiedlichen Abstraktionsebenen bieten;
- keine oder geringe Werkzeugunterstützung für den Konstrukteur bieten;
- keine oder geringe Unterstützung mehrerer Zielsprachen leisten;
- keinerlei Unterstützung automatischer Plazierungsstrategien anbieten[1];

[1] Die Autoren des ALADDIN-Systems [10] diskutieren zwar einige der Anforderungen und erwähnen, daß sie künftigen Erweiterungen die automatische Plazierung unterstützen sollen, haben aber noch keine nennenswerten Ergebnissen vorgelegt.

- keine flexible Unterstützung zur Einbindung zusätzlicher Darstellungsstrategien wie Fischaugensichten [8] leisten; sowie
- die Betrachterinteraktion mit den dargestellten Bildern einschränken auf den Aspekt der Bildnavigation. Keine oder geringe Unterstützung existiert zur interaktiven Selektion von Bildteilen, beispielsweise durch Techniken der direkten Manipulation, durch reguläre Ausdrücke oder Bedingungen (*constraints*) sowie die anschließende Hervorhebung/Abschwächung der selektierten Objekte.

Insgesamt werden die Systeme den Kriterien nicht ausreichend gerecht. Dies deutet auf mögliche Ursachen der geringen Akzeptanz existierender Visualisierungssystem bei Benutzern hin. Wir sehen diese insbesondere in geringer Flexibilität und ineffizienter Konstruktionsunterstützung [7].

System	*Ausdrucksstärke*			*Efficienz*	
	graphische Sprache	mehrere Sichten	Abstraktion	Werkzeuge	Komponenten-Bibliotheken
ZEUS	✓	✓	–	(✓)	–
POLKA	✓	✓	–	–	–
PAVANE	(✓)	✓	–	–	–

Tabelle1. Ausdrucksstärke und Effizienz verbreiteter Visualisierungssysteme.

System	*Flexibilität* (Erstellung)		*Flexibilität* (Betrachtung)	
	mehrere Zielsprachen	Plazierungs-verfahren	Abstraktions-wechsel	Darstellungs-wechsel
ZEUS	–	–	–	(✓)
POLKA	–	–	–	(✓)
PAVANE	(✓)	–	–	(✓)

Tabelle2. Flexibilität verbreiteter Visualisierungssysteme.

6 Zusammenfassung und Ausblick

Ablaufvisualisierungen sind weithin akzeptierte Hilfsmittel zum Verständnis von Programmen, Datenstrukturen und Algorithmen. Die Erfahrung zeigt jedoch, daß existierende Visualisierungssysteme nicht dieser Einsicht entsprechend häufig für Zwecke der Präsentation, Analyse und Exploration von Programmen und der ihnen zugrundeliegenden Modelle eingesetzt werden. Wir haben einen Mangel an Flexibilität und Erstellungseffizienz konstatiert und vermuten, daß die festgestellten Mängel wesentlich dazu beitragen. Insbesondere erscheinen die fehlende Unterstützung unterschiedlicher Abstraktionsstufen und automatischer Plazierungsstrategien für dynamische Strukturen dazu geeignet, die fehlende Benutzerakzeptanz auf der Betrachterseite zu erklären, was durch fehlende Konstruktionswerkzeuge auf Erstellungsseite komplementiert wird.

Unser Lösungsvorschlag besteht in einer allgemeinen Konstruktionsmethode für Visualisierungen sowie einer flexiblen Software-Architektur namens DYNASTRUCT. Eine prototypische Implementierung dieser Architektur entstand im Rahmen der Dissertation des Autors [7]. Sie beinhaltet

- mehrere Sprachanbindungen;
- Konstruktionswerkzeuge auf der Grundlage *direkter Manipulation*;
- Unterstützung zur automatischen Bildorganisation; sowie
- Unterstützung des Wechels der Darstellungsstrategie.

Zusammenfassend halten wir die hier vorgestellte Konstruktionsmethode und die DYNASTRUCT-Architektur für eine geeignete Grundlage zum Entwurf eines erfolgreichen Visualisierungssystems, das den Erwartungen sowohl der Konstrukteure als auch der Betrachter besser als bisher gerecht wird.

Literatur

1. F. J. Brandenburg, M. Jünger und P. Mutzel. Algorithmen zum automatischen Zeichnen von Graphen. *Informatik Spektrum*, 20(4):199–207, 1997.
2. Marc. H. Brown. Zeus: A system for algorithm animation and multi-view editing. DEC SRC Technischer Bericht 75, Digital Systems Research Center, Digital Systems Research Center, 130 Lytton Avenue, Palo Alto, California 94301, February 1992.
3. Frank Buschmann, Regine Meunier, Hans Rohnert, Peter Sommerlad und Michael Stal. *Pattern-Oriented Software Architecture - A System of Patterns*. Wiley and Sons Ltd., 1996.
4. G. di Battista, P. Eades, R. Tamassia und I. Tollis. Algorithms for drawing graphs: An annotated bibliography. *Computational Geometry: Theory and Applications*, 4(5):235–282, 1994.
5. P. Eades. A heuristic for graph drawing. *Congressus Numerantium*, 42:149–160, 1984.
6. Arne Frick. Efficient specification techniques for software visualization. ACM SIGCHI'94 Workshop on Software Visualization, April 1994.
7. Arne Frick. *Visualisierung von Programmabläufen*. Dissertation, Universität Karlsruhe, Fakultät für Informatik, Karlsruhe, 1998.
8. George W. Furnas. Generalized fisheye views. In *Proceedings of the ACM SIGCHI Conference on Human Factors in Computing Systems*, pages 16–23, 1986.
9. Erich Gamma, Richard Helm, Ralph Johnson und John Vlissides. *Design Patterns: Elements of Reusable Software Components*. Addison-Wesley, 1995.
10. Esa Helttula, Aulikki Hyrskykari und Kari-Jouka Räihä. Graphical specification of algorithm animations using aladdin. In *Proc. of the 22nd Hawaii Int'l Conf. on System Sciences*, pages 892–901, January 1989.
11. Doug Kimelman, Burce Leba, Tova Roth und Dror Zernik. Dynamic graph abstraction for effective software visualization. *The Australian Computer Journal*, 27(4):129–137, 1995.
12. Kazuo Misue, Peter Eades, Wei Lai und Kozo Sugiyama. Layout adjustment and the mental map. *Journal of Visual Languages and Computing*, 6:183–210, 1995.
13. G.-C. Roman, K. Cox, C. Wilcox und J. Plun. Pavane: A system for declarative visualization of concurrent computations. *Journal of Visual Languages and Computing*, 3(2):161–193, 1992.
14. John T. Stasko. The POLKA Animation Designer's Package. Technischer Bericht. Georgia Institute of Technology, 1993.
15. K. Sugiyama, S. Tagawa und M. Toda. Methods for visual understanding of hierarchical system structures. *IEEE Transactions on Systems, Man and Cybernetics*, SMC-11(2):109–125, February 1981.

Formalisierung und visuelle Modellierung am Beispiel der UML-Statecharts

Franz Matejka, Andreas Schwald

Universität Salzburg, Institut für Computerwissenschaften, Jakob Haringer Straße 2, A-5020 Salzburg, Österreich
f.matejka@computer.org, schwald@compuserve.com

Zusammenfassung: Das Motiv dieser Arbeit ist eine möglichst einfache formale Beschreibung visueller Ausdrucksmittel am Beispiel der Harel'schen Statecharts. Diese bieten ein mächtiges Modellierungswerkzeug zur Spezifikation reaktiver Systeme und sind als Notation für die Zustandsdiagramme der Unified Modelling Language (UML) wichtig. Darüber hinaus sind sie gut beschrieben. Der Vergleich der hier skizzierten formalen Beschreibung, die zusammen mit einem Editor für Statecharts entwickelt wurde, mit der Statechart-Beschreibung der UML (Version 1.1) zeigt einige Abweichungen und Lücken auf, deren Interpretation diskutiert wird.

1 Einführung

1.1 Motivation

Das Zeichnen von Skizzen und Plänen ist eine weit verbreitete Abstraktionsmethode. Auch für den Software-Entwurf spielen graphische Spezifikationssprachen eine wichtige Rolle, obwohl diese Art der (oft primär anwendungsorientierten) Abstraktion scheinbar von einer ganz anderen Sichtweise geprägt ist als die Sprachmittel von formalen Spezifikations- oder von Programmiersprachen.

Insbesondere scheinen die Ziele visueller Spezifikation (intuitive Verständlichkeit) zumindest teilweise konträr zu den Zielen formaler Spezifikation (Korrektheit, Genauigkeit, Vollständigkeit). Der Einsatz formaler Methoden hat im Bereich von sicherheitskritischen Systemen zu wesentlichen Verbesserungen der Qualität geführt. Sie ermöglichen auch die rechnergestützte Prüfung und sind die Voraussetzung für die automatische Generierung von Programmen aus Spezifikationen, bei der Informationsverlust oder Fehlinterpretation vermieden wird [3]. Allerdings herrscht die Ansicht vor, daß derartige Methoden die Entwicklungszeit wesentlich verlängern und deshalb nur sehr hohe Qualitätsanforderungen ihren Einsatz rechtfertigen.

Den Anstoß zu dieser Arbeit bildete die Frage nach den Gemeinsamkeiten graphischer und mathematisch orientierter Spezifikationen von Software. Sie versucht, die Vorteile objekt-orientierter graphischer Modellierung ([1], [2]) und formaler Beschreibung gemeinsam zu nutzen. Ausgehend vom intuitiven Verständnis arbeitet der Benutzer mit der graphischen Darstellung und sieht zunächst nichts von dem darunter liegenden formalen Modell. Die formale Komponente kommt bei der Verifizierung der Entwicklungsergebnisse und beim Einsatz von Softwarewerkzeugen ins Spiel. Diese ermöglichen die Visualisierung und Simulation des Systems.

1.2 Zielsetzung

Es hat sich gezeigt, daß die formale Beschreibung der UML-Statecharts mit grundlegenden Ausdrucksmitteln aus der Mengenlehre und der Prädikatenlogik möglich ist. In [4] wird die Spezifikation vollständig ausgeführt und der UML-Definition kritisch gegenübergestellt. Diese Spezifikation diente auch als Basis für die Entwicklung eines Editors zum Entwickeln und Prüfen von UML-Statecharts.

Hier wird diese Beschreibung der Statechart-Semantik vorgestellt und mit der Beschreibung der UML-1.1 verglichen. Insbesondere wird dargelegt, wie durch diesen Ansatz die in der UML identifizierten Lücken geschlossen werden können.

2 Statecharts

2.1 Allgemeines

Statecharts ([5], [6], [7]), sind eine Erweiterung von Zustandsdiagrammen. In Statecharts können Zustände rekursiv in Unterzustände (UND/ODER) zerlegt werden. Transitionen können States[1] auf beliebigem Verfeinerungs-Niveau betreten und verlassen.

ODER-Verfeinerung bedeutet, daß ein Statechart im Inneren eines States eingebettet werden kann. UND-Verfeinerung bedeutet, daß ein State mehrere weitere Statecharts enthält. Diese Statecharts heißen orthogonal (auch: nebenläufig) und der aktuelle Systemzustand besteht aus je einem aktiven State jedes dieser eingebetteten Statecharts.

Transitionen werden durch eine textuelle Beschriftung genauer spezifiziert, die in der Nähe des Pfeils plaziert wird. Die Syntax dieser Beschriftung ist $e[g]a/s$. e ist das Ereignis, durch das die Transition ausgelöst wird. g gibt eine Bedingung an, die erfüllt sein muß, damit die Transition ausgeführt werden kann. Wird die Transition ausgeführt so gibt a die Aktionen an, die in diesem Falle auszuführen sind, und s besteht aus einer Menge von zu generierenden internen Ereignissen, die im nächsten Schritt vom Statechart verarbeitet werden. Detailliertere Ausführungen zur Syntax der Transitionsbeschriftung sind zu finden in [8].

[1] Hier wird generell der Begriff *State* verwendet, wenn das durch das grafische Rechtecksymbol dargestellte Konzept gemeint ist, *Zustand* für den Systemzustand

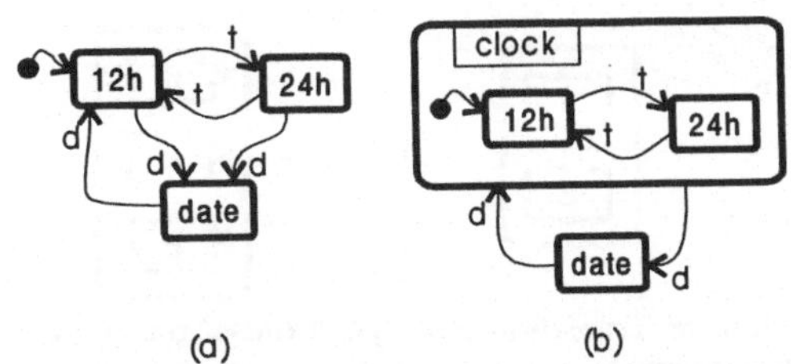

Abb. 1. Einfaches Beispiel einer ODER-Verfeinerung. Das gezeigte Statechart modelliert das Verhalten einer Uhr mit 2 verschiedenen Anzeigevarianten der Uhrzeit sowie einer Datumsanzeige. (a) zeigt das Zustandsdiagramm und (b) das äquivalente Statechart

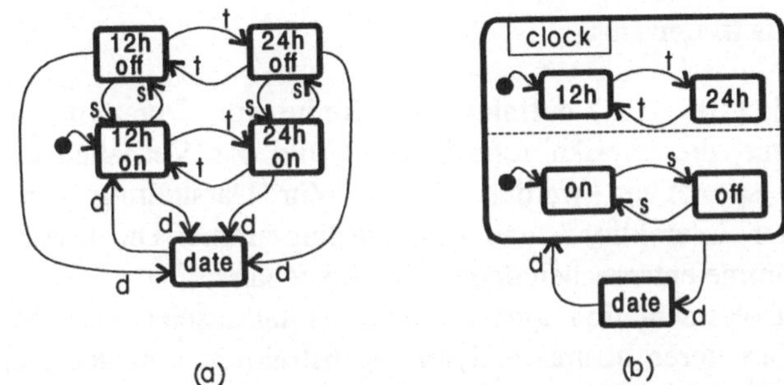

Abb. 2. zeigt die Erweiterung des obigen Systemmodels (Uhr) um die Möglichkeit, bei der Anzeige der Zeit die Darstellung der Sekunden ein- und auszuschalten. Das Zustandsdiagramm (a) zeigt bereits deutlich erhöhte psychologische Komplexität, viel übersichtlicher scheint das Statechart (b). [8]

Zustandsübergänge werden ausgelöst von Ereignissen. Wenn eine Transition ausgelöst wird, verläßt das System den aktuellen Zustand, führt die mit der Transition verbundene Aktion aus und geht in einen neuen Zustand. Bei einem Zustandsübergang können mehrere States verlassen und betreten werden.

Die Ausführung von Aktionen ist auch ohne Zustandsübergänge möglich. Zu diesem Zweck dienen interne Transitionen. Diese bestehen nur aus der Transitionsbeschriftung und sind einem State zugeordnet.

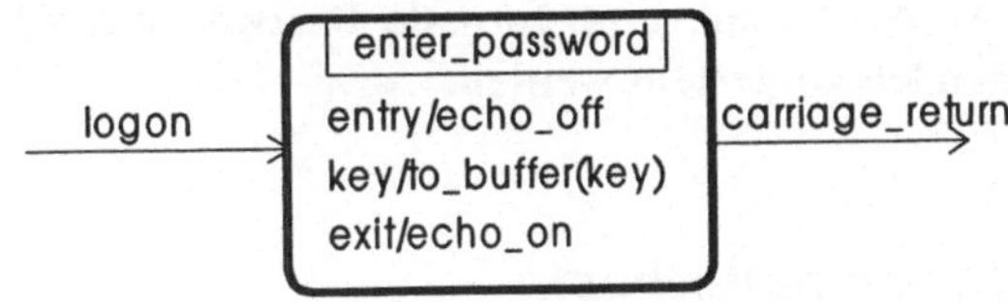

Abb. 3. Darstellung interner Transitionen im Inneren eines States. `entry` und `exit` sind spezielle Ereignisse, die beim Betreten bzw. Verlassen des States generiert werden, diese sind nur für den betreffenden State sichtbar (kein Broadcast-Mechanismus)

Synchronisation zwischen orthogonalen Statecharts kann durch komplexe Transitionen dargestellt werden. Diese führen von mehreren States weg und kommen bei mehreren States an.

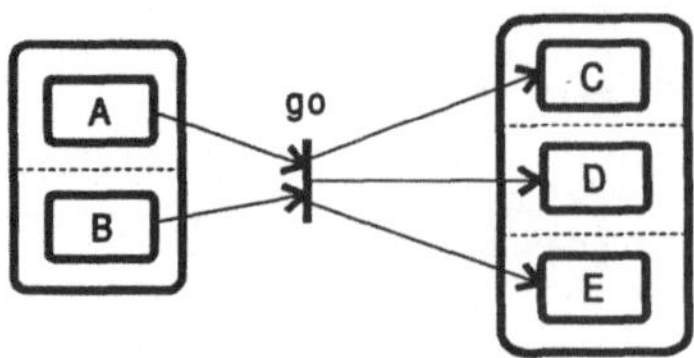

Abb. 4. zeigt eine komplexe Transition zur Synchronisation. Tritt das Ereignis go auf, so müssen die orthogonalen Zustände A und B aktiv sein damit die Transition ausgeführt werden kann (Synchronisation des States A mit dem State B)

2.2 Statecharts in der UML

Die UML ([9], [10], [11]) definiert eine Reihe von Diagrammen mit denen die logische Struktur, die physikalische Struktur und das Verhalten der Komponenten eines Systems spezifiziert werden können. Zur Darstellung von (dynamischem) Verhalten dienen Interaktions- und Zustandsdiagramme. Die Darstellungsmittel der Zustandsdiagramme entsprechen denen von Statecharts.

Die UML Dokumentation gibt für jedes Notationselement eine informelle Erklärung, definiert deren abstrakte Syntax (Abstraktion von der grafischen Darstellung), gibt eine statische Semantik an (Identifizierung möglicher Beziehungen zwischen Komponenten) und spezifiziert eine dynamische Semantik (zur Interpretation der graphischen Modelle). Für jeden Zweck werden unterschiedliche Darstellungsmittel verwendet, die Erklärung, die dynamische Semantik und die abstrakte Syntax werden in informeller textueller und graphischer Weise, oft unter Verwendung der UML selbst, definiert. Die statische Semantik wird mit Hilfe der Object Constraint Language (OCL) formal beschrieben [11].

In der UML dienen Statecharts zur Spezifikation des Verhaltens einer Klasse, des Protokolls einer Schnittstelle, der (zustandsabhängig) gültigen Operationen auf einem Datentyp und des Verhaltens einer Operation bzw. Methode.

Beim Entwurf eines graphischen Editors für UML-Statecharts [4] zeigte sich, daß die informellen Definitionen der UML dafür zu ungenau sind. Als Grundlage der Implementierung wurde deshalb eine formale Softwarespezifikation erstellt, deren Grundzüge im folgenden vorgestellt werden.

3 Die Semantik von Statecharts

3.1 Statecharts als Hierarchie von States

S sei die Menge aller States eines Statecharts. Ein ausgezeichneter Zustand *root* ist die Wurzel der States-Hierarchie (in der graphischen Darstellung repräsentiert durch den Zeichenhintergrund). Die Funktion *children*, angewandt auf einen State, liefert die Menge der States, die unmittelbar darin enthalten sind (direkte Nachkommen, $\wp$ bezeichnet die Potenzmenge): $children: S \rightarrow \wp(S)$ (1)

Die Funktion *parent* ist die Umkehrfunktion zu *child*. Sei $s \in S$,

$$parent: S \rightarrow S,\ parent(s) = p \Leftrightarrow s \neq root \wedge s \in children(p) \quad (2)$$

Falls ein State direkte Nachfolger hat, wird dieser als zusammengesetzt (composite), andernfalls als einfach (basic) bezeichnet. Sei $s \in S$,

$$basic(s) \Leftrightarrow children(s)=\varnothing,\ composite(s) \Leftrightarrow \neg basic(s). \quad (3, 4)$$

Die (reflexive) transitive Hülle aller Nachkommen eines States ist gegeben durch ($children^*$) $children^+$. Sei $s \in S$,

$$children^*: S \rightarrow \wp(S),\ children^*(s) = \bigcup_{i \geq 0} children^i(s), \quad (5)$$

$$children^+: S \rightarrow \wp(S),\ children^+(s) = \bigcup_{i \geq 1} children^i(s), \quad (6)$$

$$\text{wobei } children^0(s)=\{s\}, \text{ und für } i \geq 0,\ children^{i+1}(s) = \bigcup_{s' \in children(s)} children^i(s'). \quad (7)$$

Für $d \in children^*(a)$ heißt a der *Vorfahr* (*ancestor*) von d bzw. d der *Nachkomme* (*descendent*) von a. Ist ein State Vorfahr bzw. Nachkomme eines anderen, so stehen beide States in *Vorfahren-Beziehung* (*ancestrally related*). Seien $a, d, s_1, s_2 \in S$,

$$ancestor \subseteq S \times S,\ ancestor(a,d) \Leftrightarrow d \in children^*(a), \quad (8)$$

$$descendant \subseteq S \times S,\ descendant(d,a) \Leftrightarrow ancestor(a,d), \quad (9)$$

$$ancestrally\_related \subseteq S \times S,\ ancestrally\_related(s_1,s_2) \Leftrightarrow ancestor(s_1,s_2) \vee descendant(s_1,s_2) \quad (10)$$

Das *Niveau* eines States im Baum ist definiert durch: Sei $s \in S$, $niveau: S \rightarrow \mathbf{N}$,

$$niveau(s) = \begin{cases} 0 & falls\ \ s = root \\ niveau(parent(s))+1 & sonst \end{cases} \quad (11)$$

Jeder State erhält durch die Funktion *type* einen Typ zugewiesen. Die ODER Verfeinerung wird durch die direkten Nachkommen eines States vom Typ *or* (OR-State) dargestellt. Bei der UND Verfeinerung erhält der zu verfeinerne State den Typ *and* (AND-State). Für jedes enthaltene orthogonale Statechart wird ein State vom Typ *component* (AND-Komponente) als direkter Nachkomme (zusätzliches Niveau) eingesetzt. Die Nachkommen der AND-Komponenten sind die orthogonalen Statecharts.

$$type: S \rightarrow \{and, component, or, initial, final, history\},\ type(root)=or. \quad (12)$$

States vom Typ *initial* und *final* sind Pseudo-States, d.h. das System kann sich nicht in diesen befinden. Initial-States werden durch einen ausgefüllten Kreis dargestellt. Von einem Initial-State muß immer eine Transition zu einem State (OR oder AND) abgehen. Dieser State wird als der Default-State bezeichnet und wird eingenommen, wenn eine Transition an einem State endet, der Nachfolger hat. Seien $s, d \in S$, $type(s)=or$ oder $type(s)=component$, $default: S \rightarrow S$, (13)

Es gilt $default(s)=d$ genau dann, wenn es einen Initial-Pseudo-State i gibt mit $child(i,s)$ und $child(d,s)$ und es eine Transition von i nach d gibt.

Der *gemeinsame Vorfahr* einer Menge von States X ist der State x, dessen Nachkommensmenge X enthält und der selbst Nachkomme jedes anderen Zustands mit dieser Eigenschaft ist. Diese Funktion ist total, d.h. für alle $X \in \wp(S)$ definiert. Sei $X \subseteq S$,

$$lca: \wp(S) \rightarrow S,\ lca(X)=x \Leftrightarrow ancestor(x,X) \wedge \forall s \in S: X \subseteq children^*(s) \Rightarrow x \in children^*(s). \tag{14}$$

wobei: $ancestor \subseteq S \times \wp(S)$, $ancestor(x,X) \Leftrightarrow X \subseteq children^*(x)$

Einschränkung auf OR-States gibt den *Scope*. Sei $X \subseteq S$,

$$scope: \wp(S) \rightarrow S,\ scope(X)=x \Leftrightarrow lca(x) \wedge type(x)=or \tag{15}$$

Zwei States sind *orthogonal*, wenn sie nicht in Vorfahren-Beziehung stehen und ihr niedrigster gemeinsame Vorfahre ein AND-State ist. Eine Menge von States ist *orthogonal*, wenn ihre Elemente paarweise orthogonal sind. Man schreibt für $orthogonal(s_1,s_2)$ auch $s_1 \perp s_2$. Seien $s_1,s_2 \in S$, $X \subseteq S$,

$$orthogonal \subseteq S \times S,\ orthogonal(s_1,s_2) \Leftrightarrow \neg ancestrally\_related(s_1,s_2) \wedge (type(lca(\{s_1,s_2\}))=and),$$

$$orthogonal \in \wp(S),\ orthogonal(\{X\}) \Leftrightarrow \forall s_1,s_2 \in X : (s_1=s_2) \vee orthogonal(s_1,s_2). \tag{16}$$

Zwei States sind *konsistent* (*consistent*), wenn sie in Vorfahren-Beziehung (s. (10)) stehen oder orthogonal sind. Eine Menge von States ist *konsistent* (*consistent*), wenn ihre Elemente paarweise konsistent sind. Eine konsistente Menge von States ist *partiell konsistent* (*partial consistent*) in Bezug auf den State *r*, falls durch Hinzunahme eines Nachkommens von *r* die Konsistenzeigenschaft verloren ginge. Seien $s_1,s_2,r \in S$, $X \subseteq S$,

$$consistent \in S \times S,\ consistent(s_1,s_2) \Leftrightarrow ancestrally\_related(s_1,s_2) \vee orthogonal(s_1,s_2), \tag{17}$$

$$consistent \in \wp(S),\ consistent(X) \Leftrightarrow \forall s_1,s_2 \in X : consistent(s_1,s_2),$$

$$partial\_consistent \in \wp(S) \times S,\ partial\_consistent(X,r) \Leftrightarrow consistent(X) \wedge \forall s \in (children^*(r) \backslash X): \neg consistent(X \cup \{s\}), \tag{18}$$

$$maximally\_consistent \in \wp(S),\ maximally\_consistent(X) \Leftrightarrow partial\_consistent(X,root). \tag{19}$$

Bemerkung: Die Menge aller Konfigurationen die ein Statechart einnehmen kann, ist gegeben durch alle maximal konsistente Mengen.

T sei die Menge aller *Transitionen* eines Statechart. $T \subseteq \wp(S) \times \wp(S)$. Die *Quellmenge* einer Transition sind jene States, von denen die Transitionspfeile abgehen. Die *Zielmenge* einer Transition sind die States, an denen die Transitionspfeile enden. Sei $t \in T$, $t=(s,d)$, wobei $s,d \in \wp(S)$,

$$source,\ destination: T \rightarrow \wp(S),\ source(t)=s,\ destination(t)=d. \tag{20}$$

Sei *E* die Menge aller *Ereignisse* (*events*), auf die ein gegebenes Statechart reagieren kann. Ereignisse, die von außen kommen, heißen *externe Ereignisse* (*external events*). Ereignisse die bei der Abarbeitung des Statecharts generiert werden, heißen *interne Ereignisse* (*internal events*).

Jeder Transition ist entweder kein (gekennzeichnet durch ε) oder genau ein Event zugeordnet. Dieser Event wird *Trigger* der Transition genannt.

$$trigger: T \rightarrow E \cup \varepsilon. \tag{21}$$

Um zu prüfen, ob zwei Transitionen *nicht in Konflikt* (*non conflicting*) zueienander stehen, ermittelt man für jede Transition den Scope (s. (15)) der Vereinigung von

Quell- und Zielstates. Sind diese beiden Scopes orthogonal zueinander, dann stehen beide Transitionen nicht in Konflikt. Für die Statechartsemantik bedeutet das, daß beide Transitionen gleichzeitig ausgeführt werden können. Eine Menge von Transitionen steht *nicht in Konflikt*, wenn die Transitionen dieser Menge paarweise nicht in Konflikt zueinander stehen. Seien $t_1, t_2 \in T$, $T_3 \in \wp(T)$,

$$non\_conflicting \subseteq T \times T,\ non\_conflicting(t_1,t_2) \Leftrightarrow t_1=t_2 \vee$$
$$scope(source(t_1) \cup destination(t_1)) \perp scope(source(t_2) \cup destination(t_2)),$$
$$conflicting \subseteq T \times T,\ conflicting(t_1,t_2) \Leftrightarrow \neg non\_conflicting(t_1,t_2),$$
$$non\_conflicting \subseteq \wp(T),\ non\_conflicting(T_3) \Leftrightarrow$$
$$\forall t_{31},t_{32} \in T_3 : (t_{31}=t_{32}) \vee non\_conflicting(t_{31},t_{32}). \quad (22)$$

Eine Transition wird *Initial-Transition* genannt, wenn ihre Quell- und Zielmengen nur je ein Element enthalten und der Quellstate ein Initial-Pseudo-State ist. Sei $t \in T$,

$$initial\_transition \subseteq \mathrm{T},\ initial\_transition(t) \Leftrightarrow$$
$$|source(t)|=|target(t)|=1 \wedge (\forall s \in source(t): type(s)=initial). \quad (23)$$

Die vorangegangenen Definitionen genügen um UML-Statecharts unabhängig von ihrer graphischen Darstellung beschreiben zu können. Darüber hinaus ist es mit diesen Mitteln möglich sowohl die statische als auch die dynamische Semantik von UML-Statecharts zu definieren.

3.2 Statische Semantik

3.2.1 Hierarchische Einschränkungen

S sei die Menge aller States mit $root \in S$. Für jeden State müssen die folgenden Bedingungen erfüllt sein. Sei $s \in S$,

H1: Der *root*-State ist vom Typ *or*: $s=root \Rightarrow type(s)=or$

H2: Nur der *root*-State ist nicht Kind eines anderen States.

$$(s \in S \wedge \neg(\exists r \in S: s \in children(r))) \Rightarrow s = root$$

H3: AND-States und AND-Komponenten haben immer Nachkommen.

$$type(s) \in \{and, component\} \Rightarrow composite(s)$$

H4: Ein State darf dann und nur dann eine AND-Komponente sein, wenn sein Vater-State ein AND-State ist. Das heißt auch, daß ein AND-State nur AND-Komponenten als Kinder haben darf.

$$type(s)=component \Leftrightarrow type(parent(s))=and$$

H5: Ein AND-State muß mindestens zwei Nachkommen haben.

$$type(s)=and \Rightarrow |children(s)| \geq 2$$

H6: Pseudo-States dürfen keine Nachkommen haben. Nur OR-States oder AND-Komponenten dürfen Pseudo-States als Kinder haben.

$$type(s) \in \{initial, final, history\} \Rightarrow (\ type(parent(s)) \in \{or, component\} \wedge basic(s)\ )$$

H7: Jeder State darf von jedem Pseudo-State maximal einen als Kind haben.

$$\neg\exists p_1,p_2 \in children(s) : (\ p_1 \neq p_2 \wedge type(p_1)=type(p_2) \wedge type(p_1) \in \{initial, final, history\})$$

Eine Hierarchie von States, die alle diese Prädikate erfüllt, ist gültig.

3.2.2 Transitionen

Eine Menge von gültigen Transitionen T erfüllt die folgenden Bedingungen:

T1: Eine AND-Komponente darf weder Quelle noch Ziel einer Transition sein.

$$\forall s \in (source(t) \cup destination(t)) : type(s) \neq component$$

T2: Ein Initial-State kann nur Quelle einer einfachen Transition sein. Initial-State und Ziel der zugehörigen Initial-Transition müssen denselben direkten Vorgänger haben.

$$\forall t \in T : ((\exists s \in source(t) : type(s)=initial) \Rightarrow (|source(t)|=|destination(t)| = 1 \wedge \forall s \in source(t), d \in destination(t) : parent(s) = parent(d)))$$

T3: Ein Initial-State darf nicht Ziel einer Transition sein.

$$\forall t \in T : s \in destination(t) : type(s) \neq initial$$

T4: Von jedem Initial-State muß genau eine Transition abgehen.

$$\forall s \in S : type(s)=intial \Rightarrow \exists_1 t \in T : s \in source(t)$$

T5: An jedem State darf maximal eine Initial-Transition ankommen.

$$\forall s \in S : |\{ t \in T \mid initial\_transition(t) \wedge destination(t) = \{s\} \}| = 1$$

T6: Eine Transition zu einem Final-State darf kein anderes Ziel haben.

$$\forall t \in T : ((\exists s \in destination(t) : type(s)=final) \Rightarrow |destination(t)| = 1)$$

T7: Ein Final-State darf nicht Quelle einer Transition sein.

$$\forall t \in T : s \in source(t) : type(s) \neq final$$

T8: An jedem Final State muß genau eine Transition ankommen.

$$\forall s \in S : type(s)=final \Rightarrow \exists_1 t \in T : s \in destination(t)$$

T9: Von einem History-State können keine Transitionen abgehen.

$$\neg \exists t \in T : \exists s \in source(t) : type(s)=history$$

In manchen Situationen müssen Initial-States und Initial-Transitionen angegen werden; siehe Abb. 5 (a). Bei tiefer geschachtelten Statecharts könnten Initial-States auch auf einem höheren Niveau angegeben werden, siehe Abb. 5 (b), dies führt jedoch zu Problemen.

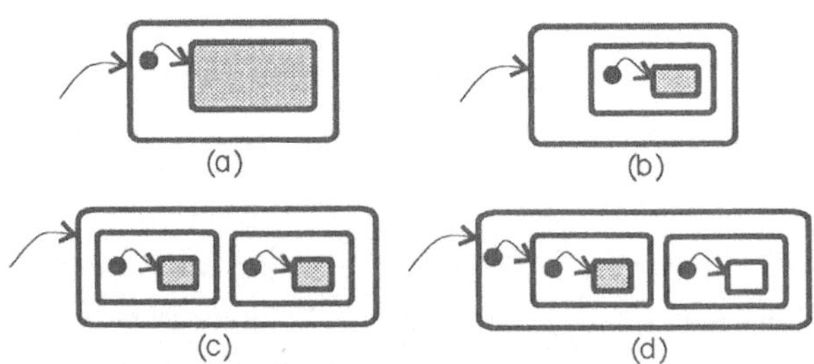

Abb. 5. Initial-Transitionen

Die Transition, die am äußeren Rand des umgebenden States endet, hat in beiden Fällen eine eindeutige Semantik. Dies ist leicht zu sehen, indem man gedanklich diese Transition bis zum grauschattierten State verlängert und den Initial-State mit seiner Initial-Transition wegläßt.

Allerdings kann das Statechart (b) so erweitert werden, daß das nicht mehr möglich ist; siehe Abb. 5 (c). Im Statechart (c) ist die Fortsetzung der von außen

kommenden Transition nicht mehr eindeutig (nicht deterministisch). Das Statechart muß, wie in (d) gezeigt, ergänzt werden.
Als hinreichende Bedingungen für die Gültigkeit von Transitionen wird deshalb folgende Einschränkung definiert:
T10: Ein OR-State, der Ziel einer Transition ist, muß entweder ein Basic-State sein oder als direkten Nachfolger einen Initial-State enthalten.

$$\forall s \in S : (\ \exists t \in T : s \in destination(t) \wedge type(s)=or) \Rightarrow$$
$$basic(s) \vee (\exists s_1 \in children(s) : type(s_1)=intial)$$

T11: Die Quellmenge muß orthogonal sein. $\forall t \in T : orthogonal(source(t))$
T12: Die Zielmenge muß orthogonal sein. $\forall t \in T : orthogonal(destination(t))$
T13: (Zielstateskriterium). Jede Zielmenge einer Transition muß sich in eine in Bezug auf den Scope (s. (15)) der Transition partiell-konsistente Menge (s. (18)) erweitern lassen. Für jeden State aus dieser Menge, der zwar Kinder hat, von denen aber keines Element der Menge ist, wird der Default-State zur Menge hinzugenommen. Das folgende Prädikat gibt an, ob eine solche Erweiterung existiert.

$$\exists X \subseteq children^*(scope(destination(t) \cup source(t))) : destination(t) \subseteq X \wedge$$
$$partial\_consistent(X, scope(destination(t) \cup source(t))) \wedge$$
$$\forall s \in X : ((destination(t) \cap children(s)=\emptyset) \wedge$$
$$((type(s)=or \vee type(s)=component) \wedge \neg basic(s))) \Rightarrow default(s) \in X.$$

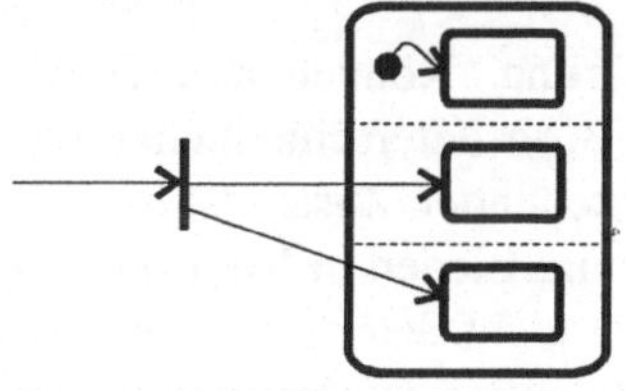

Abb. 6. Zielstateskriterium. die oberste AND-Komponente enthält einen Initial-Pseudo-State mit einer Initial-Transition nach einem Default-State. Ohne diesen Initial-Pseudo-State wäre die gezeigte Transition ungültig.

Die vorangegangenen syntaktischen Bedingungen, insbesondere das Zielstateskriterium T13, bieten weitreichende Möglichkeiten für Softwarewerkzeuge das erstellte Statechart auf seine Korrektheit hin zu überprüfen. Dies kann geschehen noch bevor das Statechart zur Ausführung gebracht wird.

3.3 Dynamische Semantik

Die vorgestellte Beschreibung der statischen Semantik wurde in [4] auch als Basis für die Definition der dynamischen Semantik von UML-Statecharts verwendet. Das Ziel war die Definition eines Algorithmus', der die dynamische Abarbeitung (Zustandsübergänge) eines Statecharts ausdrückt. Dieser Algorithmus ist in Form einer Funktion definiert, die 4 Eingabegrößen auf eine Ausgabegröße abbildet. Die Eingaben dieser Funktion sind: (1) die Menge der States und ihre hierarchische Struktur, (2) die Menge der Transitionen, (3) der aktuelle Zustand (Konfiguration = die aktiven States), (4) das aufgetretene Ereignis. Abgebildet wird diese Eingabemenge auf den neuen Zustand des Statecharts (Makroschritt).

Da durch ausgelöste Transitionen weitere Ereignisse generiert werden können, geschieht die Abarbeitung eines Statecharts möglicherweise in mehreren Teilschritten (Mikroschritt). In jedem Teilschritt führt die vorliegende Menge von Ereignissen zu Zustandsübergängen (ausgelöste Transitionen) die weitere Ereignisse generieren können. Die in einem Schritt generierten Ereignisse werden im jeweils darauffolgenden Schritt abgearbeitet. Dieser Prozeß terminiert, wenn in einem Schritt keine weiteren Ereignisse mehr generiert wurden.

Diese Form der Semantikdefinition führt zu Statecharts deren Verhalten intuitiv nachvollziehbar ist, stellt allerdings die Terminierung des Abarbeitungsalgorithmus nicht sicher. Dieser Algorithmus wird in [4] in deklarativer Form als Pseudocode unter Verwendung von Konstrukten aus der Mengenlehre und der Prädikatenlogik gegeben. Er kann in weiterer Folge zur grafischen Animation der Abarbeitung eines Statecharts bzw. zur Implementierung eines Codegenerators verwendet werden.

Hier soll nur die Ausführung eines Mikro-Schritts verbal erklärt werden. Ein Mikro-Schritt wird in 4 sequentiellen Stufen abgearbeitet.

(1) Bestimme die Transitionen, die von der aufgetretenen Ereignismenge betroffen sind. Von dieser Transitionsmenge werden wiederum nur jene Transitionen weiter betrachtet, deren Quellstates Teil der aktuellen Konfiguration (Menge der aktiven States) sind.

(2) Führe Transitionen aus.
   (a) gleichzeitige Ausführung. Können alle Transitionen gleichzeitig ausgeführt werden (wenn sie z.B. in unterschiedlichen orthogonalen Komponenten sind) so werden die entsprechenden Zustandsübergänge ausgeführt.
   (b) priorisierte Ausführung. Liegen in Konflikt stehende Transitionen vor (s. (22), d.h. das Statechart ist nicht determinstisch), so wird versucht, diesen Konflikt aufzulösen. Jeder Transition wird aufgrund ihrer Position in der Stateshierarchie (Niveau) eine Priorität zugewiesen. Besteht ein Konflikt zwischen einer Menge von Transitionen, so wird nur jene mit der höchsten Priorität ausgeführt.
   (c) implementierungsabhängige Ausführung. Liegen in Konflikt stehende Transitionen gleicher Priorität vor, so wird (implementierungsabhängig) eine zufällige Auswahl getroffen bzw. eine Fehlermeldung generiert.

(3) Transitionen die keine Beschriftung tragen, sogenannte Komplettierungs-Transitionen, können ausgelöst werden auch wenn kein äußeres Ereignis vorliegt. Es genügt, wenn alle Quellstates aktiv sind. Der Algorithmus prüft ob solche Transitionen vorhanden sind und führt diese gegebenenfalls aus.

Interne Transitionen werden gesondert betrachtet und haben Priorität gegenüber anderen Transitionen. Den internen Ereignissen entry und exit kommt dabei eine Sonderrolle zu.

Eine ausführliche Darstellung und Diskussion des Algorithmus findet sich in [4].

4 Vergleich mit UML

4.1 Statische Semantik

Die Definition der Statecharts in der UML [12] besteht aus drei Teilen: dem Metamodell, den „Well-Formedness Rules“ und der Semantik.

Das Metamodell der UML wird durch ein Klassendiagramm dargestellt, d.h. die UML wird durch die UML definiert. Das mag teilweise intuitiv verständlich sein, den formalen Anforderungen für die Implementierung eines Werkzeugs kann damit allerdings nicht entsprochen werden. Die in dieser Arbeit gewählte Ausdrucksform (Mengenlehre und Prädikatenlogik) bildet eine ausreichend formale Basis für eine präzise Softwarespezifikation als Grundlage der Implementierung.

Alle „Well-Formedness Rules“ der UML entsprechen den unter 3.2. angegebenen Regeln. Für eine genaue Gegenüberstellung siehe [4]. Zusätzlich wurden zusätzliche Bedingungen gefunden,die für ein korrektes Statechart notwendig sind. Diese sind: H3, H4, T1, T2, T3, T4, T6, T8, T10, T11, T12, T13. Diese Auflistung zeigt, daß die UML-Regeln für gültige Transitionen aus unserer Sicht recht unvollständig sind.

4.2 Dynamische Semantik

Die UML definiert die dynamische Statechartsemantik in informeller Form. Die gewählte Darstellungsform der UML ist keine präzise Definition, gibt also nur den Rahmen des zu implementierenden Verhaltens vor. Durch die in dieser Arbeit gewählte mathematische Ausdrucksform wurde die Basis für die Implementierung eines Werkzeugs geschaffen und die Aussagen der UML insbesondere in folgenden Punkten präzisiert:

(1) Die UML unterscheidet nicht zwischen Mikro- und Makro-Schritt. Wann die Reaktion auf ein externes Ereignis abgeschlossen ist, bleibt unklar. Der in [4] gegebene Algorithmus klärt diese Frage.

(2) Der Begriff einer *legal state configuration* wird in [12] auf Seite 110 definiert. In [4] wird diese informell gegebene Definition präzisiert.

(3) Auf Seite 108 in [12] wird über *completion transitions* gesprochen, die präzise Bedeutung dieses Begriffes wird nicht genau klar. Die Intention dieses Modellierungselements scheint intuitiv klar (siehe [12], ab Seite 103). Die Definition wird allerdings dadurch erschwert, daß eine Transition ohne Auftreten eines Ereignisses ausgeführt wird. In [4] wird eine präzise Semantik für *completion transition* gegeben.

(4) [12] gibt auf Seite 108 eine Definition für in Konflikt stehende Transitionen. Die Definition läßt zu viele Sonderfälle offen, reicht deshalb als Vorgabe für eine Implementierung nicht aus. Die in dieser Arbeit gegebene Definition (22) beschreibt genau, wann Transitionen in Konflikt stehen.

(5) Prioritäten werden in [12] verwendet, um Konflikte zwischen Transitionen nach Möglichkeit aufzulösen. Diese informelle Beschreibung wird in [4] genauer ausgeführt und, was wesentlich ist, auch für interne Transitionen definiert. Dies

ermöglicht eine Formulierung des Algorithmus, die nicht zwischen internen und anderen Transitionen unterscheiden muß.

(6) Auf Seite 109 in [12] wird ein Algorithmus zum Selektieren (UML Bezeichnung für Konfliktauflösung) von Transitionen angegeben. Diese Regeln berücksichtigen keine eventuell auszuführenden Initial-Transitionen. Der in [4] gegebene Algorithmus liefert eine Formalisierung dieses Algorithmus und berücksichtigt auch Initial-Transitionen.

Die bei der Implementierung des graphischen Editors gemachten positiven Erfahrungen haben unsere Annahme bestätigt, daß der Entwurf von Softwareentwicklungswerkzeugen durch eine formale Spezifikation deutlich erleichtert wird.

5 Andere Arbeiten

Die Idee der Statecharts wurde durch Harel erstmals in [16] beschrieben. In [5] wird die formalisierbarkeit visueller Darstellungen aufgezeigt. Erste Ansätze einer formalen Semantikdefinition finden sich in [17], die dort dargestellte Semantik wird in [13] weiter präzisiert und formalisiert.
Weitere, im Rahmen dieser Arbeit wichtige Ideen zur Statechartsemantik sind in [14], [18] und [19] beschrieben. [15] führt systematisch in die Variationsmöglichkeiten bei der Wahl einer Statechartsemantik ein.
Für ein Softwareentwicklungswerkzeug ist das Thema der Codegenerierung besonders wichtig siehe dazu [20] und [21].

6 Zusammenfassung

In dieser Arbeit wurde mit Hilfe einfacher mathematischer Ausdrucksmittel die statische Semantik von UML-Statecharts formal definiert. Im Zuge des Umsetzungsprozesses wurden Lücken in der UML Definition erkennbar, die geschlossen werden mußten. Eine Auflistung aller gefundenen Schwachstellen wurde gegeben.

Auf die Möglichkeit, mit denselben Ausdrucksmitteln eine dynamische Semantik zu definieren, wurde kurz eingegangen.

In [4] findet sich eine ausführlichere Darstellung der Formalisierung sowie Ausführungen zur Implementierung dieser Spezifikationen. Die vorliegende Implementierung des Softwarewerkzeugs beschränkt sich derzeit auf das Editieren von Statecharts und die Überprüfung der statischen Semantik. Die Regeln der dynamischen Semantik sollen in einer zukünftigen Version umgesetzt werden, z.B. in der Form einer Animation der Statechartabarbeitung bzw. als Codegenerator.

7 Literatur

1. Booch, G.: *Object Oriented Analysis and Design*, 2nd Edition, Benjamin/Cummings, Redwood City CA, 1994.
2. Rumbaugh, J., Blaha, M., Premerlani, W., Eddy, F., Lorensen, W.: *Object-Oriented Modeling and Design*, Prentice Hall, Englewood Cliffs NJ, 1991.
3. Day, N.: A Model Checker for Statecharts (Linking CASE Tools with Formal Methods), TR 93-35, Univ. of British Columbia, Vancouver Canada, 1993.
4. Matejka, F.: *Ein Ansatz zur Formalisierung und Werkzeugunterstützung von Statecharts im Rahmen der Unified Modeling Language*. Diplomarbeit, Univ. Salzburg, Institut für Computerwissenschaften, http://www.edvz.sbg.ac.at/~mafr/home.htm, Februar 1998.
5. Harel, D.: „On Visual Formalisms". *Comm. ACM*, Vol.31 Nr.5 Seiten 514-530, 1988.
6. Harel, D., Gery, E.: „Executable Object Modeling with Statecharts", *IEEE Comp.*, 1997.
7. Harel, D., Naamad, A.: „The STATEMATE Semantics of Statecharts", *ACM Trans. on Software Eng. and Methodology*, Vol. 5, No. 4, Seiten 293-333, October 1996.
8. Leveson, N., Heimdahl, M., Hildreth, H., Reese, J.: „Requirements specification for process-control systems", *IEEE Trans. on Software Eng.*. Vol. 20, No.9, 684-707, 1995.
9. Rumbaugh, J.: „To form a more perfect union: Unifying the OMT and Booch methods", *Journal of Object Oriented Programming*, pp.14-18, January 1996.
10. http://www.omg.org/. *Object Management Group*.
11. UML Documentation Set, Version 1.1, *Rational Software Corporation*, Septemper 1997.
12. UML Semantics, Version 1.1, *Rational Software Corporation*, Septemper 1997.
13. Pnueli, A., Shalev, M.: „What is in a step: On the semantics of statecharts". *Proc. of the Symposium on Theoretical Aspects of Computer Software*, LNCS Vol. 526, Springer, Berlin, Seiten 244-264, 1991.
14. Nazareth, D., Regensburger, F., Scholz, P.: Mini-*Statecharts: A Lean Version of Statecharts*, TU München, Institut für Informatik, TUM-I9610, Februar 1996.
15. von der Beek, M.: „A comparison of statechart variants", In *Formal Techniques in Real-Time and Fault-Tolerant Systems*, LNCS Vol.863, Springe, NY, Seiten 128-148, 1994.
16. Harel, D.: „Statecharts: A Visual Formalism for Complex Systems", *Science of Computer Programming*, Seiten 231-274, 1987.
17. Harel, D., Pnueli, A., Schmidt, J., Sherman, R.: „On the formal semantics of statecharts", In Proc. *First IEEE Symp. on Logic in Comp. Sc.*, pp 54-64, 1986.
18. Huizing, C., Gerth, R.: *On the Semantics of Reactive Systems*, Department of Mathematics and Computer Science, Eindhoven Univ. of Technology, January 1991.
19. Maraninchi, F.: *Operational and Compositional Semantics of Synchronous Automaton Compositions*: LNCS, vol.650, Springer-Verlag, Berlin, Seiten 550-564, 1992.
20. Selic, B.: *High-Performance Implementations from ROOM Models*, ObjecTime Limited, Kanata, Ontario Canada, http://www.objectime.com/, 1995.
21. Martin, R.: *The Care and Feeding of The State Map Compiler*, R.C.M. Consulting Inc., June 1993.

Intelligente Editoren - ein innovatives Konzept für die Erstellung von schematischen Darstellungen[1]

M. Pleßow, M. Pocher
Gesellschaft zur Förderung angewandter Informatik
Rudower Chaussee 5, D - 12 484 Berlin
email :{plessow,pocher}@gfai.de

Zusammenfassung

Zur Beschreibung der Struktur oder des Verhaltens komplexer Systeme finden häufig nichtmaßstäbliche schematische Darstellungen Verwendung. Die Herstellung und Bearbeitung solcher Schemata ist aber ein zeitaufwendiger und fehleranfälliger Prozeß. Im vorliegenden Beitrag wird deshalb ein Ansatz vorgestellt, der für eine gewisse Klasse von Schemata sowohl deren grafische Gestaltung unterstützt (automatisiertes Layout), als auch deren Korrektheit unter bestimmten Aspekten garantiert. Das dabei zugrundeliegende Modell, die für die Gestaltung der Schemata auftretenden Layoutprobleme und die entwickelten Lösungswege werden erläutert. Die Anwendung der Forschungsergebnisse erlaubt die Herstellung von Grafikeditoren und Dokumentationssystemen mit neuen Eigenschaften. Als beispielhaftes Resultat dieser Arbeiten wird ein intelligenter Editor für Funktionspläne, wie sie in der Prozeßleittechnik zum Einsatz kommen, vorgestellt.

Motivation

Schematische Darstellungen spielen als wesentlicher Bestandteil von technischen Dokumentationen eine große Rolle. Ein wichtiger Grund dafür liegt darin, daß die immer komplexer werdenden technischen Systeme nur noch durch eine adäquate Dokumentation für den Menschen überschaubar bleiben. Zur Auflösung der Komplexität werden Abstraktionsebenen eingeführt, in denen der betreffende Sachverhalt

---

[1]Das diesem Bericht zugrundeliegende Vorhaben wird mit Mitteln des Bundesministeriums für Bildung, Wissenschaft, Forschung und Technologie unter dem Förderkennzeichen 01 IN 507 C gefördert.

eine schematisierte Darstellung erhält. Dabei werden den jeweils interessierenden Bestandteilen (Komponenten) des Systems abstrakte Visualisierungsformen (Symbole) zugeordnet, während die Beziehungen der Komponenten untereinander durch Verbindungen (z.B. in Form achsenparalleler, sich eventuell verzweigender Streckenzüge) zwischen den Symbolen wiedergegeben werden.

Ein typisches Beispiel einer nichtmaßstäblichen schematischen Darstellung zeigt Abbildung 1.

Für die Erzeugung schematischer Darstellungen stehen heute verschiedene computergestützte Verfahren zur Verfügung. Beginnend bei einfachen Grafiksystemen (Zeichensystemen) bis hin zu hochspezialisierten CAD-Lösungen (z.B. für den Entwurf von integrierten Schaltungen) findet man eine breite Palette. Im allgemeinen wird dabei der Weg von der Zeichnung zum fertigen Produkt gegangen. Allerdings ist die Konsistenzsicherung zwischen Dokumentation und Produkt, bedingt durch häufig auftretende Iterationsstufen innerhalb des Planungs- / Produktionsprozesses, nur schwer zu garantieren. Außerdem ist die Herstellung der Schemata ein arbeitsaufwendiger und fehleranfälliger Prozeß.

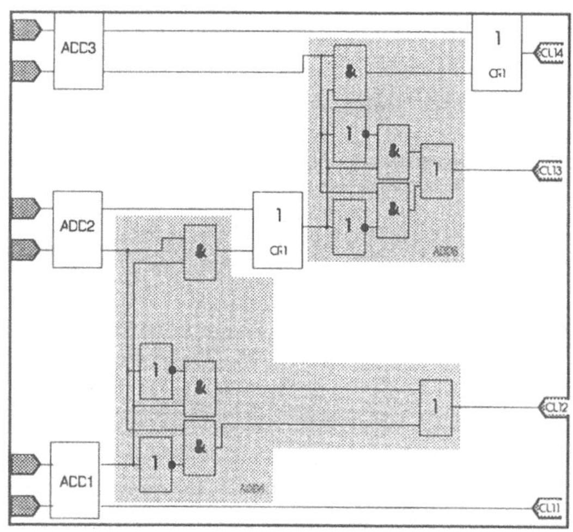

Abbildung 1 Logikplan

Hier setzen die im Beitrag vorgestellten Arbeiten an. Gelingt es, die Kernaussage eines Schemas zu formalisieren, kann unter Umständen die schematische Darstellung *automatisiert* erzeugt werden. Wird diese Information auch als Basis der Produktion verwendet, so ist gleichzeitig gewährleistet, daß das Schema das herzustellende Objekt *richtig* widerspiegelt. Umgekehrt kann in einem solchen Fall auch aus Daten über das Produkt, also zum Beispiel nach Modifikationen während der Produktionsüberführung, die Dokumentation automatisiert aktualisiert werden.

Betrachtet man das obige Beispiel genauer, erkennt man eine *netzartige Struktur* innerhalb der mit dem Logikplan dargestellten Funktion.

Das Problem der automatisierten Erzeugung von Dokumenten aus der Kenntnis der zugrundliegenden Struktur ist im Kern ein Layoutproblem und wird der generativen Computergrafik zugeordnet. Es gibt sehr viele Arbeiten, die sich mit dem verwandten

Gebiet des Graph Drawings befassen. Eine Übersicht findet man in [BaTaET 94].
Bei der GFaI wurden spezielle Untersuchungen zur Dokumentation allgemeiner netzartiger Strukturen vorgenommen. Im Rahmen dieser Arbeiten entstand eine Toolbox (**CASTool**), die in Form von Klassenbibliotheken konzipiert und implementiert wurde. Durch ihren objektorientierten Ansatz ist sie leicht an verschiedenste Applikationen anpaßbar (siehe [PPS 96]). Sie erlaubt die Herstellung *intelligenter* Editoren bzw. Dokumentationssysteme, die dem Benutzer vielfältige Unterstützung sowohl in der Interaktionsphase (Editoren) als auch beim automatisierten Erstellen von Zeichnungen (Dokumentationssysteme) bieten. Dazu zählen vor allem eine Interaktions-/Layoutunterstützung, eine möglichst umfassende semantische Prüfung des Sachverhaltes, den das Schema darstellt, sowie vielfältige Import- und Exportmöglichkeiten. Ermöglicht wird dies durch die Abbildung des Schemas in einem speziell entwickelten Netzwerkmodell, das innerhalb verschiedener Schichten Struktur-, Layout- und Grafikinformationen enthält.
Großes Augenmerk wurde auf einen adaptierbaren, erweiterbaren Systemansatz gerichtet. Er garantiert, daß der Aufwand für die Herstellung verschiedenster Applikationen aus unterschiedlichen Anwendungsgebieten durch den Einsatz der Toolbox minimiert wird.

Netzwerkmodell

In erster Näherung sind netzartige Systeme durch den mathematischen Begriff des Graphen abgedeckt. In Abbildung 2 werden am Beispiel eines Energieversorgungsnetzes die zwei Sorten von Graphelementen, Knoten (Komponenten) und Kanten (Verbindungen von jeweils zwei Knoten), dargestellt. In Abbildung 3 treten gerichtete sowie verzweigte (netzartige) Verbindungen auf. Beide Verbindungsarten sind noch Begriffe der Graphentheorie (gerichtete Kanten, Hyperkanten). Die Tatsache, daß Komponenten als räumlich ausgedehnte Symbole dargestellt werden und daß die Verbindungen

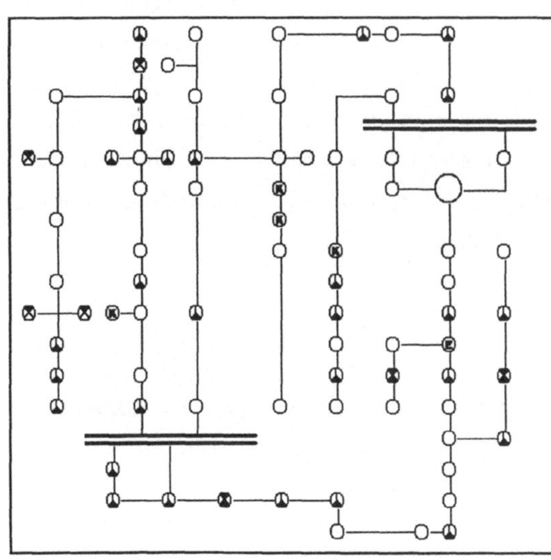

Abbildung 2 Komponenten und Verbindungen

an speziellen Punkten (den Pins) auf die Komponenten treffen (Abbildung 1 und 3), geht jedoch über den Begriff des Graphen hinaus. Pins können als Ein- oder Ausgänge der Komponenten spezifiziert sein (Richtungspfeil). Eine weitere Verfeinerung des Graphenbegriffes wird in Abbildung 3 hervorgehoben. Die Komponenten können hierarchisch verschachtelt sein, d.h. sie können in ihrem Innern weitere netzartige Systeme aufweisen. Die Pins spielen dabei die Rolle der Vermittler zwischen inneren und äußeren Netzen.

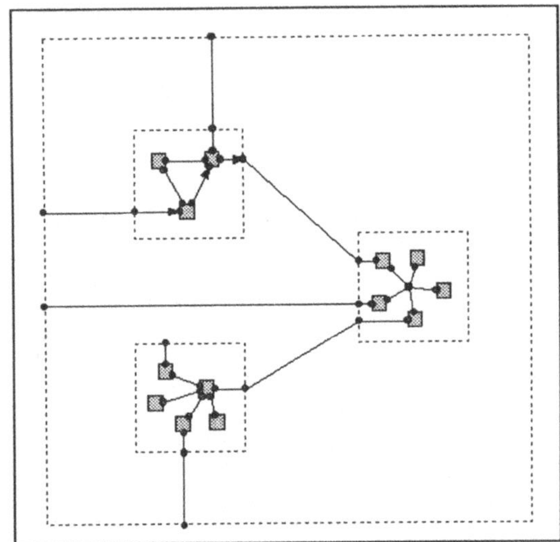

Abbildung 3 Hierarchisches Netzschema mit verzweigten/gerichteten Verbindungen und Pins

Um die genannten Eigenschaften von Netzwerken beschreiben und verarbeiten zu können, wurde ein allgemeines Modell für Netzwerke ELADO (**E**rweitertes **La**yout-**D**aten-M**o**dell) konzipiert und implementiert.

Neben den strukturellen Eigenschaften des Netzwerkes (*Sturkturschicht*) dient eine weitere Schicht des Modells der Abbildung von Layoutinformationen, zu denen Positionen und Größe des Shapes (umrandendes Rechteck) von Symbolen sowie Angaben über die Linienzüge zur Visualisierung der Netze gehören. Zusätzliche Informationen für einzelne Schemaelemente, wie z.B. Annotationen an Komponenten oder Netzen, werden innerhalb einer speziellen *Informationssicht* verwaltet. Um eine grafische Darstellung des Schemas zu ermöglichen, werden in einer *Grafiksicht* Informationen über die grafische Darstellung der Schemaelemente gehalten.

Layoutunterstützung

Unter Layout von Netzwerken wird allgemein die geometrische Anordnung der Netzwerkelemente verstanden, d.h. die Struktur eines Netzwerkes ist in ein begrenztes *Layout-Gebiet* innerhalb eines *Layout-Raumes* einzubetten

Die Layout-Aufgabe besteht in der Positionierung der Komponenten und dem Realisieren der Netze durch linienartige Gebilde, also in der *Plazierung* und dem *Routing*. Dabei ist eine Vielzahl von Layout-Bedingungen und Optimierungszielen zu beachten, welche von dem jeweiligen Anwendungsgebiet abhängig sind. Diese Grundaufgaben sind mit dem Layout elektronischer Schaltkreise auf einem Chip oder einer Leiterplatte vergleichbar. Dort besteht allerdings ein wichtiges Optimierungsziel darin, die Elemente eng zu packen. Dieses Ziel entfällt beim Netzwerk-Layout für Dokumentationszwecke und wird durch die Forderung nach einer übersichtlichen und ästhetischen Anordnung ersetzt [Goetze 97].

Hinsichtlich der Ausgangssituation für das Layout gibt es drei grundsätzlich verschiedene Fälle: generelles Layout ohne Anfangslayout, generelles Layout mit einem Anfangslayout und partielles Layout.

Der erste Fall tritt dann ein, wenn die reine Strukturinformation eines Schemas z.B. zum Zweck einer Rückdokumentation aus einer Datenbank extrahiert wird.

Der zweite Fall liegt vor, wenn im Editormodus ein Schema erstellt wird, dessen Layout aber hinsichtlich ästhetischer Anforderungen oder bestimmter Normen noch nicht befriedigend ist.

Der dritte Fall, der des partiellen Layouts, tritt bei intelligenten Editoren auf. Der Editor reagiert auf lokale Benutzereingriffe in das Netzwerkschema mit lokal begrenzten Layoutaktionen.

Von besonderer Wichtigkeit für das Layout netzartiger Schemata sind von der jeweiligen Applikation abhängige Anforderungen (Design-Regeln). Diese können sowohl struktureller (nur bestimmte Symbole dürfen miteinander verbunden werden) als auch grafischer Art (die Anordnung bestimmter Symbole ist vorgeschrieben) sein.

Um das Layout von schematischen Darstellungen möglichst komfortabel steuern und konfigurieren zu können, wurde ein *planbasierter* Layout-Manager entwickelt, der in der Lage ist, für verschiedene Situationen vorgedachte Abfolgen von Layoutoperationen (Layoutpläne) anzuwenden.

Im Folgenden werden einige der genannten Schwerpunkte näher erläutert.

Generelles Layout

Wie angedeutet wurde, erzeugt ein generelles Layout eine Darstellung des gesamten Schemas. Dabei kann entweder bereits ein Anfangs-Layout vorliegen oder das Layout muß aus den vorliegenden Strukturinformationen generiert werden. Im ersten Fall kommt neben der Forderung nach einem guten ästhetischen Gesamteindruck und bestimmten domänenspezifischen Bedingungen noch hinzu, daß die *topologische Stabilität* des bereits vorhandenen Schemas gesichert werden soll. Dies bedeutet, daß ein Layoutverfahren so wenig Änderungen wie möglich am bisherigen Layout vornehmen soll. Anderenfalls wird die Wiedererkennung von Teilen des Schemas erschwert.

In der GFaI wurden im Laufe der letzten Jahre verschiedenste Layoutverfahren entwickelt. Dazu zählen Plazierungsverfahren, Routingverfahren und Kombinationen aus beiden. Insbesondere wurde untersucht, welche Layoutverfahren auf bestimmten Strukturen von Schemata gute Ergebnisse liefern. Beispielhaft sei hier auf das Layout von Reihen-Parallel-Strukturen (R-P-Struktur) verwiesen. Strukturen dieser Art lassen sich in sehr vielen Beispielanwendungen finden. Sie sind dadurch gekennzeichnet, daß Symbole oder Symbolgruppen in Anlehnung an die E-Technik als seriell oder parallel geschaltet betrachtet werden können (Abbildung 4). Die in der GFaI entwickelten Layoutverfahren arbeiten jedoch auch auf Strukturen, die den Reihen-Parallel-Strukturen verwandt sind, bzw. gewisse Abweichungen von dieser Struktur aufweisen (Baumstrukturen, Mischstrukturen). Außerdem lassen sich in vielen Anwendungen Teilstrukturen finden, nach deren temporärer Zusammenfassung (hierarchische Strukturierung) und lokaler Behandlung, eine Reihen-Parallel-Struktur verbleibt. Dies ist zum Beispiel bei den Funktionsplänen (s.u.) der Fall.

Partielles Layout

Beim Editieren netzartiger Schemata soll durch das System eine intelligente Layout-Unterstützung geleistet werden. Sie hat das Ziel, Layout-Restriktionen (z.B. Schnittfreiheit) oder einfache ästhetische Anforderungen (z.B. Achsenparallelität der Netzrealisierungen) zu garantieren. Da der Bearbeiter eine gewisse Stabilität des Bildes sowie kurze Reaktionszeiten erwartet, können die Layoutaktionen sich nur auf einen kleinen Ausschnitt des Schemas beschränken. Die hierbei angewandten Verfahren werden wegen ihres Zeitverhaltens auch als Quick-Layoutverfahren bezeichnet.

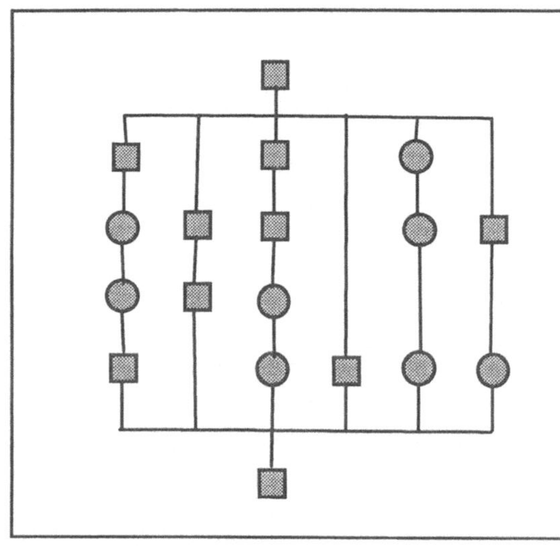

Abbildung 4 Reihen-Parallel-Struktur

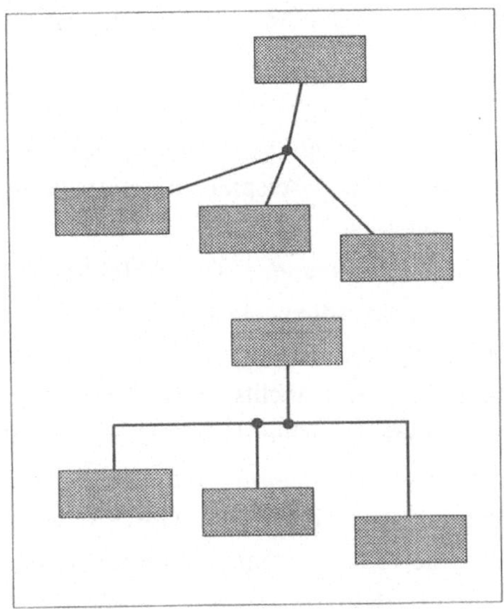

Abbildung 5 Gummiband- und Busrouting

Eine einfache, aber wirkungsvolle Unterstützung besteht im automatischen Nachziehen der Netze beim Verschieben von Komponenten. Hierbei wird die Möglichkeit gegeben, verschiedene schnelle Routingverfahren zum Erzeugen der Netzvisualisierungen zu verwenden. Abbildung 5 zeigt beispielhaft zwei verschiedene Routingverfahren für Mehr-Pin-Netze.

Eine weitere wichtige Forderung ist i.a. die Überlappungsfreiheit der Symbole. Auch hier wird seitens des Systems Hilfestellung gegeben, indem Kollisionen sofort erkannt und entsprechende Reaktionen ausgelöst werden. Dazu werden die Symbole, die sich unter einem zu plazierenden Symbol befinden, entweder verschoben oder das zu plazierende Symbol sucht sich selbständig einen freien Platz in der Nähe des gewünschten Zielortes.

Weitere wichtige Aufgaben der Quick-Layoutverfahren beziehen sich auf die Erfüllung von Layout-Constraints (siehe nächsten Abschnitt).

Design-Regeln

In vielen Anwendungsfällen bestehen hinsichtlich der Erstellung von schematischen Darstellungen bestimmte, teilweise durch Normen o.ä. vorgegebene, Bedingungen. Diese können als Constraints formuliert werden. Sie lassen sich in strukturelle und grafische Constraints unterteilen. So wird in dem als Anwendungsbeispiel vorgestellten Funktionsplan-Editor während der Editierphase überwacht, ob wie in Abbildung 6 eine Verbindung von einem *Schritt*-Symbol (Rechteck mit Nummer im Inneren) zu einem *Übergangs*-Symbol (dicke waagerechte Linie, mit x beschriftet) führt. Die

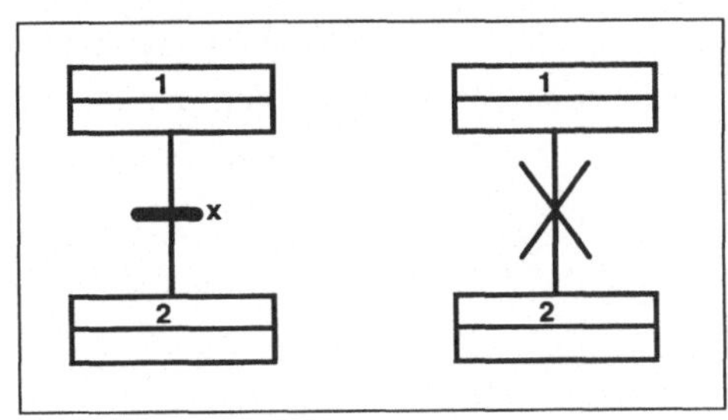

Abbildung 6 Strukturelle Constraints

Verbindung zweier Schritte wird abgelehnt (rechter Teil der Abbildung). Dies ist ein Beispiel eines *strukturellen* Constraints.

Der im Zusammenhang mit dem Layoutmanagement interessantere Fall bezieht sich auf die Einhaltung von *grafischen* Constraints. Im Beispiel der Funktionspläne werden den bereits erwähnten Schritten *Kommandos* (in Abbildung 7 rechts) zugeordnet. Dabei besteht die Forderung, die Kommandos wie in der Abbildung (also rechts vom Schritt und übereinander) anzuordnen. Diese nicht besonders komplizierte Anordnung kann mit einem einfachen Quick-Layout-Verfahren hergestellt werden, das sofort nach einer entsprechenden Interaktion des Benutzers angestoßen wird.

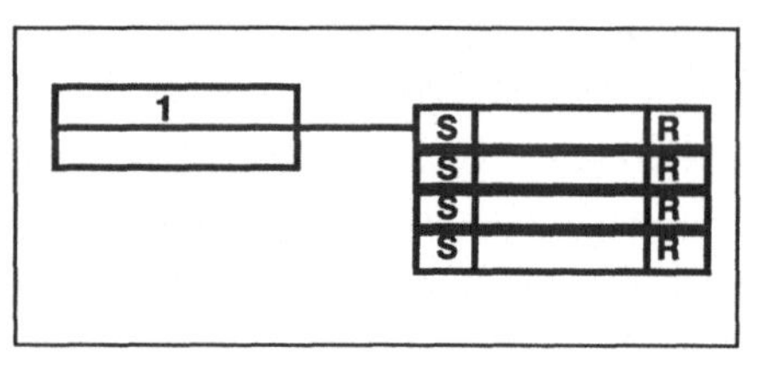

Abbildung 7 Grafische Constraints

Planbasierter Layout-Manager

Die Steuerung des Layouts eines Schemas erfolgt durch einen Layout-Manager. Er arbeitet mit Layoutplänen. Diese bestehen aus Scripten, die von einem Interpreter innerhalb des Layout-Managers abgearbeitet werden. Innerhalb der Scripte können nicht nur Layoutschritte (einzelne Layoutverfahren), sondern auch Schemaanalyse- und Layoutbewertungsverfahren angesprochen werden, die innerhalb der Toolbox entwickelt wurden. Als eine grundsätzliche Möglichkeit, ein Layout durchzuführen ergibt sich somit der im Folgenden beschriebene Ablauf.

Zuerst wird auf dem zu gestaltenden Schema eine Analyse durchgeführt. Sie kann einen Verweis auf die vorhandene Struktur des Schemas liefern. Anhand dieses Ergebnisses wird ein Layoutverfahren ausgewählt, welches mit den entsprechenden Strukturen arbeiten kann. Nach erfolgtem Layout wird eine Layoutbewertung durchgeführt. Sie kann nach verschiedensten Gesichtspunkten erfolgen (Platzverteilung, Netzlänge, ...). Ist das Bewertungsergebnis nicht zufriedenstellend, kann der Prozeß nach Auswahl eines anderen Layoutverfahrens oder der Modifikation der Verfahrensparameter wiederholt werden.

Beispielapplikation Funktionsplan-Editor

Unter Anwendung der beschriebenen Konzepte wurde im Rahmen des Projektes VERMEIL [GOPP 96] ein Editor für **Funktionspläne** aus der Prozeßleittechnik realisiert. Hierzu wurde die CASTool-Toolbox um Funktionen erweitert, die es gestatten, die besondere Struktur eines Funktionsplanes zu beachten und dabei die Einhaltung der strukturellen und grafischen Constraints zu garantieren.

Konkret wurde hier u. a. ein Layoutverfahren integriert, welches die weiter oben erläuterten Reihen-Parallel-Strukturen verarbeiten kann. Vorher ist es notwendig, störende Strukturelemente zu temporären Teilstrukturen zusammenzufassen. Diese werden mit jeweils speziellen eigenen Layoutverfahren bearbeitet. Konkret werden in Funktionsplänen jeweils Schritte und zugehörige Kommandos zu einem temporären Layoutelement zusammengefaßt. So entstand das in Abbildung 8 vorgestellte Layout. Generell kann für Funktionspläne nicht sichergestellt werden, daß das Reihen-Parallel-

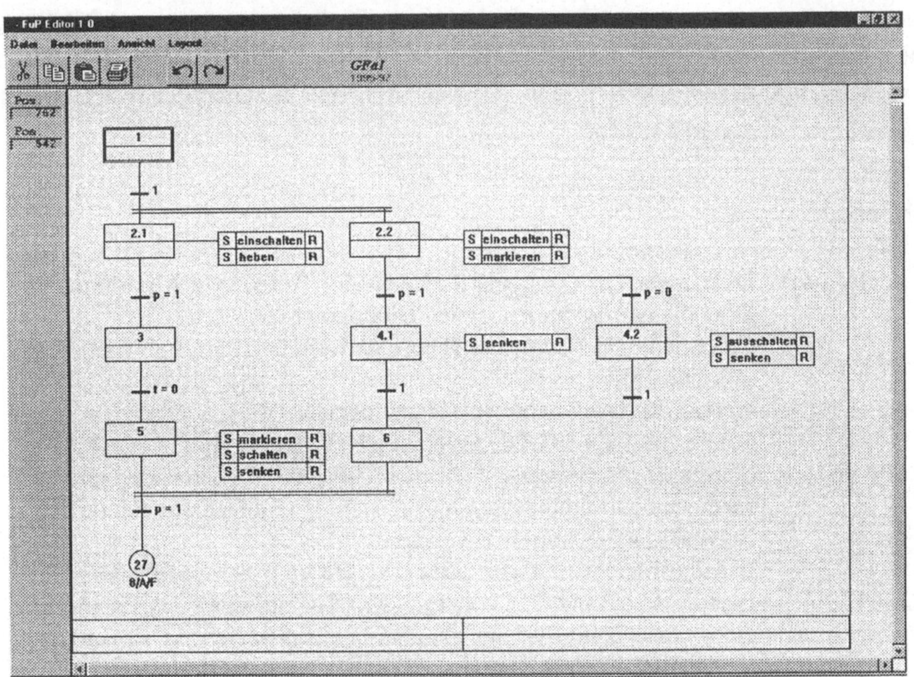

Abbildung 8 Funktionsplan-Editor mit Layout eines Funktionsplanes

Layout immer eingesetzt werden kann. Führen z.B. nicht mehr alle Verbindungen zu dem im unteren Teil der Abbildung befindlichen Konnektor, so ist keine R-P-Struktur mehr vorhanden. Statt dessen ist eine Baumstruktur (im Sinne der Graphentheorie) entstanden. Diese wird mit einem darauf spezialisierten Verfahren bearbeitet.

Zusammenfassung und Ausblick

Mit Hilfe des entwickelten Ansatzes ist es möglich, intelligente Editoren zu realisieren, die sich durch folgende Eigenschaften auszeichnen:

- Layoutunterstützung,
- Unterstützung der Einhaltung von Design-Rules (Constraints),
- modellbasierte Arbeitsweise.

Solche Editoren ermöglichen eine nach qualitativen und quantitativen Gesichtspunkten optimierte Arbeitsweise. So wird am Beispiel des Funktionsplan-Editors deutlich, daß es dem Benutzer nicht möglich ist, unerlaubte Strukturen zu erstellen. Außerdem ist automatisch sichergestellt, daß eine bestimmten Normen entsprechende grafische Darstellung erzeugt wird.

Zur Zeit wird an der Qualifizierung des Editors (und der Toolbox) in Hinblick auf eine seitenweise Strukturierung (Multi-View-Aspekt) der Funktionspläne gearbeitet.

Für die Erweiterung des Einsatzfeldes der Toolbox ist die Bereitstellung entsprechender zusätzlicher Layoutverfahren notwendig. Wegen des großen damit verbundenen Aufwandes ist zu prüfen, wie sich Verfahren des Graph Drawings in den Systemansatz integrieren lassen.

Literatur

[BaTaET 94] Di Battista, G.; Tamassia, R.; Eades, P.; Tollis, I.G.: Algorithms for Drawing graphs: an Annotated Bibliography. Computational Geometry: Theory and Applications, vol. 4, no. 5. pp. 235-282 (1994).

[Goetze 97] Goetze, B.: Das Layout von Netzschemata, Studie GFaI-CASTOOL-6-96, GFaI e.V. Berlin, 1997.

[GoPP 96] Goetze, B.; Pleßow, M.; Pocher, M.:VERMEIL- Verfahren und Methoden zur intelligenten Visualisierung und Dokumentation des Entwurfes leittechnischer Anlagen. In Jahresbericht 1996 der GFaI e.V., Berlin, 1997, pp. 91-94.

[PPSCH 96] Pleßow, M.; Pocher, M.; Schmid, M.: Konzipierung und Entwicklung einer Toolbox für Systeme zum automatischen Generieren von schematischen Darstellungen. Proc.: 2. GI-Workshop Entwurf und Dokumentation im rechnergestützten Facility-Management, 9.-11.10.1996, Eisenach (Wartburg), IIEF-Institut für Informatik in Entwurf und Fertigung zu Berlin GmbH, 1997, pp. 25-38.

Incremental Speech Translation: A Layered Chart Approach

Jan W. Amtrup

Computing Research Lab
New Mexico State University, Las Cruces, NM
jamtrup@crl.nmsu.edu
http://crl.nmsu.edu/Lab/Personnel/jamtrup.html

Abstract. Human speech understanding works incrementally. We begin to process acoustic input before the speaker's utterance has ended. A system capable of performing sophisticated communication in a natural dialogue or simultaneous interpreting, has to work incrementally, too. The architecture of such a system should be modular, uniform and integrated. We present an architectural framework that suits these three requirements by implementing layered charts, a multi-purpose data structure intended to represent several competing hypotheses about linguistic content of utterance intervals based on hypergraphs. We demonstrate the feasibility by presenting results from an actual interpreting system.

1 Introduction

Human natural language comprehension and production is inherently incremental in nature. Incrementality means to begin the processing of parts of the input (or even to generate output) before the input is complete. We do this by understanding spoken words while or even before they are being uttered. This mode of operation enables us to follow an almost continuous stream of speech signals. Simultaneous conference interpreters take a step further and even generate the content of what they understood incrementally in another language [12, 15]. Psycholinguistic research isolated many processes and features that demonstrate the incremental operation. The applicability of the concept ranges from the early stages of speech recognition, e.g. described by the cohort model [25, 24], to context influences on word recognition [31] and syntactic analysis [27].

The application of incremental principles within systems designated to process natural human speech seems to be appropriate in this light. Only if speech understanding is performed incrementally, one can expect performance similar to human speech comprehension, like dialog systems which interrupt the user, or simultaneous translators. But even if this approach is not taken to mimick the human model, incrementality offers significant advantages compared to non-incremental operation. First of all, it enables the introduction of inter-modular parallelism into a speech understanding application without the need of two independent components operating on the same data. Second, modules may influence the operation of other modules working on the same interval of the input by exploiting top-down interactions. Third, a system may already start to analyze input even if the speaker still continues to utter words.

Thus, incrementality is a natural and useful paradigm for natural language processing systems which has been mostly explored punctually so far [14, 17]. It is highly convenient to constitute an architecture for NLP systems which reflects the properties of incremental processing and which minimizes redundancy to reduce the negative effects of incrementality. The sources of those negative effects are twofold: First, the amount of data to be processed increases. This is due to the fact that a system never knows if a partial hypothesis can be extended into the future because it does only know the left context. Second, the structure of search spaces is much less strict compared to the non-incremental case. Any ranking must be done locally and thus is suboptimal from a global point of view.

We are going to present an approach to architecture that is modular, uniform and integrates information of all modules in a convenient way. *Layered Charts* are used to represent partial hypotheses throughout an application. They are centered around the assumption that every partial result describes some interval of the input to the system. The content of the description may vary from hypotheses about what words were spoken during a specific interval in time to hypotheses about what should be the translation of a part of the input utterance. The representation schema captures the differences of several types of linguistic knowledge by allowing any kind of feature structure description while simultaneously retaining the common ground of results, namely time.

Two successful existing incremental systems are TDMT [22], which takes an example-based approach to translation on large scale parallel machines and INTARC [16], which at least partly uses a chart-based method for the analysis phase. The transfer and generation modules, however, deviate from this schema by being oriented at dialogue act transfer and schema-based generation [19]. One recent attempt to design an architectural framework for NLP systems, white-boards [8], is able to emulate incremental operation. But, since the control schema for white-boards is centralized, a parallel, distributed system can not easily been built.

2 Layered Charts Based on Hypergraphs

Every hypothesis being processed in a speech understanding system is strongly connected with the underlying input: It describes some property of an interval of the speech signal. The range of different types of descriptions is broad. There are hypotheses about which word was actually spoken during some time, what kind of syntactic structure has to be assigned to a sequence of words presumably spoken, what semantic content is included, etc. We assume, however, that the temporal extension within the input speech signal represents the common ground for all information.

The lowest level of representation we take into account are *word graphs* [7]. These graphs are able to represent a huge number of utterance hypotheses in a very compact manner. For example, the graph in Fig. 1 is built out of only 461 edges, but contains $1.2 \cdot 10^{23}$ paths. This compactness and the number of potential candidates are highly advantageous and yet problematic. On one hand, the probability of the correct utterance hypothesis being part of the graph rises with the number of paths, but on the other hand, the amount of input data to linguistic processing reduces performance drastically.

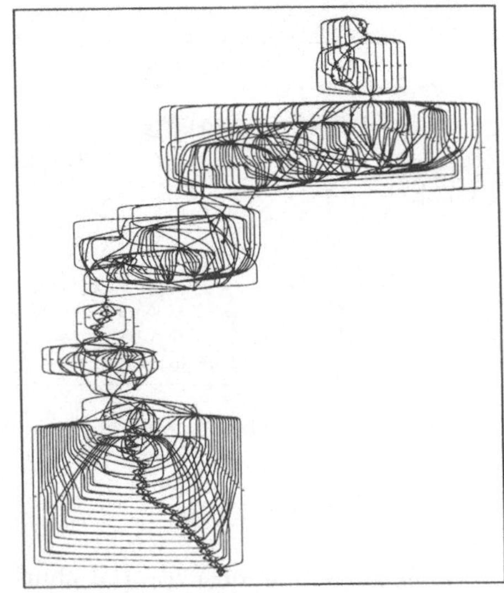

Fig. 1. A word graph

One simple, yet efficient, approach to increase efficiency is to make use of the fact that word graphs usually contain bundles of similar word hypotheses, bearing the same label, but having slightly different start and end times. The processing burden can be greatly reduced if one does not treat these word edges independently, but groups *families of edges* together as hyperedges in a hypergraph [6]. Now, edges do not connect two distinct vertices (points in time), but rather two sets of vertices.

Word graphs and their generalizations to hypergraphs are instances of a chart-like structure [20] or a generalized chart with hyperedges. Charts are directed, acyclic graphs that are used to store partial and completed results of some linguistic processing. The origins can be found in the domain of parsing [20], where charts are used extensively, and in many systems. Additionally, charts have been proposed as central data structure for generation [21] and transfer in machine translation [5]. Usually, edges of a chart carry data related to the specific task at hand, be that structural information used for parsing, semantic content for transfer or generation information.

Layered charts offer a method to separate information of different origin. Starting from the hyperedges representing word hypotheses, each component in a distributed system may add knowledge to the current state of processing by adding edges containing information relevant for that component (cf. Fig. 2). Depending on criteria defined individually for each module, edges are considered useful for other components. In that case, they are transmitted to components which can utilize them. Thus, using a layered chart, a distributed system can be constructed in an integrated fashion. The amount of data each component has to store individually is minimized, yet at the same time every bit of data a component may need is presented to it.

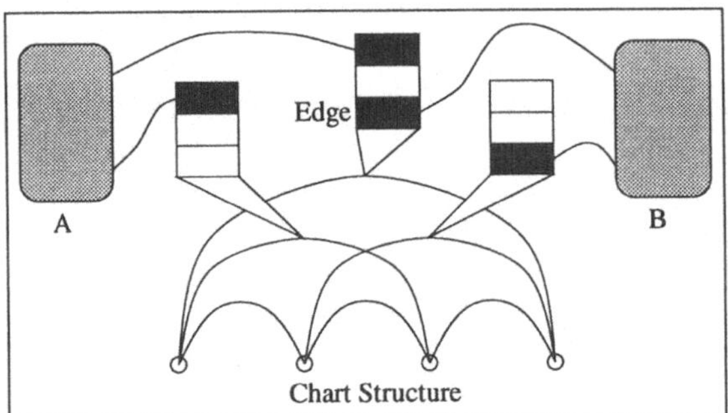

Fig. 2. The principal layout of layered charts

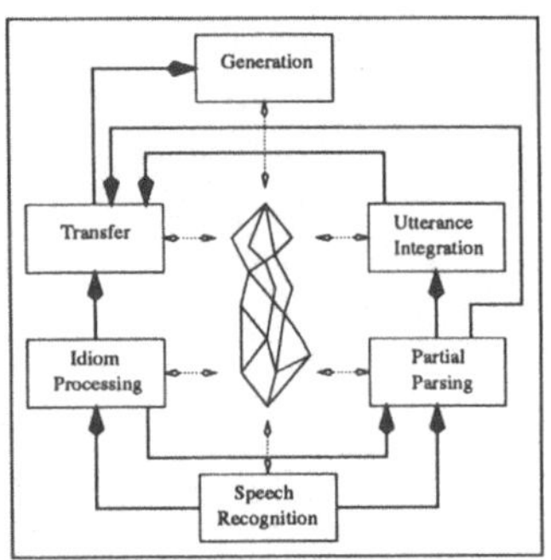

Fig. 3. The architecture of the prototypical interpreting system

The uniformity of a layered chart system is guaranteed by using a unique formalism throughout. We developed a linguistic description language capable of representing well-typed feature structures with appropriateness [10]. Since we assume that a large proportion of the feature structures in a system has to be transmitted to some other component during its lifetime, we implemented feature structures using an automaton-like approach [29]. All references are local to a feature structure, leading to a memory-position independent representation. That way, the transmission does not require linearization in the source component and reconstruction in the target component, but a feature structure can be directly sent as stream of bytes by retaining its semantics [4].

Using an integrated, uniform representation enables easy exchange of data between components. But layered charts are more than a measure for information reuse within natural language processing systems. They provide a direct way to view the union of all edges as the current state of processing. Naturally, there is no global state of a distributed system, but given the edges present in all components one can always get a notion of the progress of each component. This progress can be visualized with an additional component performing no linguistic task, but only user interface functions. Figure 4 shows a screen-dump of some results using the system described here. Since each hypothesis covers a certain interval in time, the relation between edges is always evident. This orientation at a common scale is an important advantage for incremental architectures. It allows the easy introduction of feedback loops which can be used to let a component influence the behavior of another one. For example, the search space of a component may be restricted due to work done by the component receiving the results; it is even possible to influence the order in which search spaces are explored. This concerns the crucial speech-language interface [17] as well as interactions which possibly result from higher-level knowlegde [13].

The micro structure of layered charts is given by the individual word hypotheses, as already mentioned. Those are assigned a score which measures the acoustic correspondence between the model for a word and the incoming speech

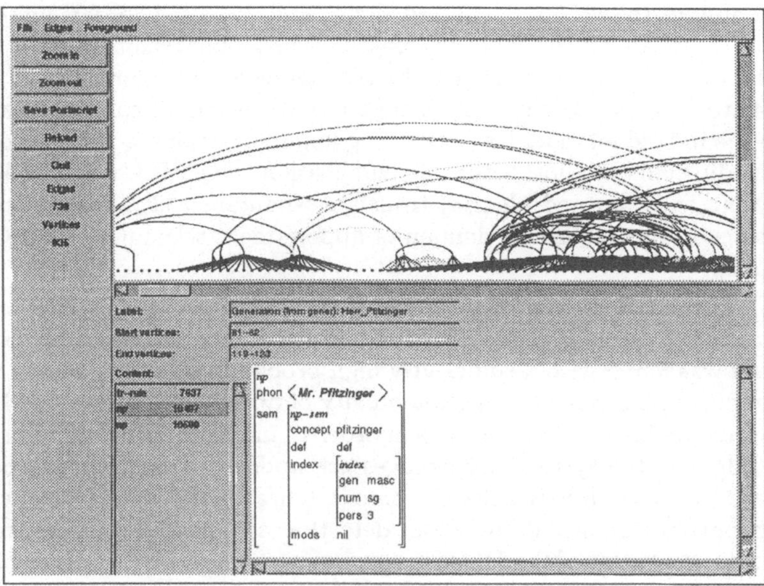

Fig. 4. A layered chart with some hyperedges

signal. The design of layered charts opens the possibility to introduce additional scores into the application. This begins with language model scores and can be possibly extended to the probability of syntactic rule applications, the preferences for specific translations, or the specificity of generation rules.

Furthermore, work done by different modules on neighboring paths within the application can be combined. This feature can be used to establish a selection function to choose between several results computed by modules using different approaches, e.g. to chose between the results of a deep analysis and some shallow understanding [9]. But even more complicated schemata can be implemented. It is possible to modify scores of certain edges based on the evidence available in one component. At present, this is used to prevent a parser from searching for compositional interpretations of idiomatic expressions (see below).

From a software-engineering point of view, layered charts form an architectural framework for natural language processing applications. Distributed systems comprising of several specialized components can easily be built, since they all share the same data structures. Communication between modules takes place, if needed, using a message-passing paradigm [3] which lets the system yield overall system performance in a cooperative way.

3 Architecture

In this section, we will present the architecture and components of an incremental system designed to translate spontaneous conversational speech. It is centered around the notion of layered charts and was used to demonstrate the feasibility of our approach and to evaluate it. The global architecture of the system is shown in Fig. 3 in section 2. In the center of the figure, the graph-like data structure of the layered chart symbolizes its use in all components. Boxes indicate the individual modules performing linguistic analysis, while arrows represent the directed data flow within the application. The MILC system (*M*achine *I*nterpreting with *L*ayered *C*harts) translates spontaneously spoken utterances from dialogs in the Verbmobil domain of appointment scheduling from German into English.

The first component is a HMM-based speech recognizer [18], which produces word graphs incrementally, i.e., they contain dead ends where no further word hypothesis was found with a sufficiently high probability. In fact, we use preproduced graphs with a word recognition quality of about 76%. These word graphs are converted online into hypergraphs in order to model incremental distribution of word edges to the system. Hyperedges are updated if new word hypotheses arise that fit into an already existing context. These hyperedges are delivered to two components responsible for idiom detection and partial parsing according to the 10ms resolution of the HMM-recognizer.

The Idiom processor searches for lexically defined, fixed expressions such as greetings (guten Tag) or utterance parts that are used to continue the dialog flow (einen Moment bitte). Currently, we do not model inflected variants of idioms (like, e.g., support-verb constructions). After detection of an idiom it is sent to transfer and is treated as one atomic construction. Thus, the non-compositional character of idioms is taken into account. Additionally, information about the idiom is delivered to partial parsing, which renders two effects: First, the idiom can be integrated into larger constituents. Second, and evenly important, the word hypotheses the idiom is made of receive a penalty score. This reflects the assumption that in general it is fruitless to try to compositionally analyze an idiom. Because idiom recognition is much faster that parsing, this should also add to the performance of the system.

Syntactic and semantic interpretation are divided into two stages, partial parsing and utterance integration. This is due to the fact that spoken language shows a wide range of phenomena not usually covered by a standard grammar designed with written language in mind. Second, the construction of complement complexes where verbs are yet unknown (e.g. in German subordinate clauses) leads to complexity problems [4]. Consequently, we introduced two modules: The partial parser builds relatively small constituents (noun phrases, prepositional phrases, date expressions etc.), while the utterance integrator selects verbs and tries to construct verb expressions based on the relevant subcategorization information. Furthermore, PP attachment is handled here. The integrator is able to perform island analyses.

The next component in the application is incremental transfer. The transfer stage in a machine interpreting system has to obey incremental operation if the system as a whole is to meet the criteria set out in the introduction [5]. Transfer in MILC is based on chart processing algorithms, too. This enables the reuse of already constructed target language constructions. The mapping algorithm is based on semantic knowledge, functor-argument structures are transferred from German into English.

Transfer starts with the smallest semantic object available from the integrator, the partial parser or the idioms processor. Typically, these are small NP constituents, mostly stemming from pronouns which tend to be short and are often recognized spuriously. As soon as richer semantic content is present in transfer, recursive equations in transfer rules are explored. Then, reuse of already constructed parts comes into play. The result of transfer is in any case a semantic description of the source language utterance parts in terms of the target language semantics. This selection is passed to generation.

The generation is chart-based like all components of the MILC system. The behavior of the generator is a mixture between [28], who binds the generator tightly into the domain of time present in analysis, and [21], who uses a chart to represent which part of the semantic content has already been taken care of. Our approach retains the temporal structure of the source language utterance. This entails that the extension in time is recorded for all edges that are received from transfer. But this does not extend to subsequent smaller parts that have to be generated according to generation rules. Here, the relative position of edges can be neglected, since they are only used to be integrated into larger chunks, and will never reach the system surface.

Nowhere in the system a requirement exists that one single edge has to cover the whole input. This is in contrast to most existing systems; only recently the incorporation of units smaller than a sentence or utterance has begun [1, 23, 30]. One consequence of this procedure is the presence of multiple solutions of the translation task within the generation component. There is a whole graph of possible partial surface forms that could be given to the user by synthesis. The approach we are taking here is to incrementally present growing optimal sub-paths of the solution graph. For the time being, the search criterion is the acoustic score of the source language words, combined with a penalty for skipping vertices of the solution graph (which results in a preference for one single long edge over several small ones). This selection schema means that we search for generation results of well recognized word sequences that can be translated.

4 Experiments

We have carried out preliminary experiments using the system described in the previous section. We used dialogs taken from the Verbmobil corpus of spontaneous speech. The results presented stem from an experiment covering one dialog (m123n) of eleven utterances, which was also used to construct the grammars of the system. The average utterance length was 16.4 words and 5.25 seconds speaking time. We used pregenerated incremental word graphs with an average number of 4157 edges, which corresponds to a hypothesis density of 253 edges per reference word. The utterances have not been previously used for training of the word recognizer. The overall acoustic recognition rate was approximately

76% based on the best matching word sequence compared to a reference. The linguistic knowledge sources consisted of a type hierarchy of 453 types, grammars with 99 rules and lexicons with 720 word forms (ca. 80% analysis, 20% generation, a hint to the sometimes schematic type of generation). Processing time was 15.25 seconds of CPU time per utterance on the average, system elapsed time was 12.55 s on a 2-processor SUN Ultra-4.

To give an impression of the kind of operation, consider the utterance guten Tag Herr <NIB> Klitscher hier ist wieder Fringes ich möchte gerne diesmal einen Termin <NIB> für das Arbeitstreffen in der Filiale <SPELL> in Potsdam mit Ihnen vereinbaren <NIB> (m123n000). The output presented by the generator starts with several small constituents as shown in Tab. 1. The vertical lines (|) denote edge boundaries and demonstrate the incremental search for a best path through the solution graph. Finally, the best path for the completed generation graph is Hello |Mr. Pfitzinger |it |from you |it |my |it |appointment for the work meeting in the branch |I |in the Potsdam |up to tuesday |I.

Table 1. The first lines generated by MILC

Hello	Hello |Mr. Quell
Hello |it	Hello |Mr. Quell |it
Hello |me	Hello |it |Mr. Pfitzinger
Hello |me |we	Hello |Mr. Pfitzinger
Hello |me |Mr. Kopp	Hello |Mr. Pfitzinger |it
Hello |Mr. Kopp	Hello |Mr. Pfitzinger |it |you
Hello |in Mr. Kopp	Hello |Mr. Pfitzinger |it |to you
Hello |me |Mr. Quell	Hello |Mr. Pfitzinger |it |from you

We evaluated the translations to be approximately correct to 64%. This is a preliminary evaluation as the utterances were used to construct the grammars of the system, but experiments with unseen data are underway. Moreover, a strict evaluation should cover a larger amount of test data. What we did was simply to judge if the central intention of the source language speaker and certain central propositional content like dates could be transported successfully into the target language. In the future, we will carry out a more thorough evaluation using a methodology similar to that used in [11]. But even now, it is obvious that the translation accuracy is too low for practical purposes and that the style of the translation needs to be improved. Measures to take into account are for example the utilization of prosody and dialog management, which have been deliberately left out in our experimental system, but which nevertheless have a great impact on the performance of a system [26,2]. Moreover, the word recognition rate was only 76%, which should be increased. And finally, we need to model the selection process from the sets of generation candidates in a more suitable way. The reduction to acoustic evidence from the source language is not enough to guarantee a smooth output. At the moment, the quality of the combination of generation edges is neglected. A better selection schema could, for example, try to reanalyze the generation output to grade the legibility in a "hearing while speaking" model.

5 Conclusion

We have presented layered charts, a architectural framework for distributed, incremental systems for natural language processing, especially in the area of speech. They enable the construction of large, parallel applications that allow the exploration of complex interactions between speech processing components. We described an experimental interpreting system based on layered charts which demonstrated the feasibility of the approach. Further improvement is necessary by integrating prosodic interpretation and dialogue management, but the performance of less than threefold real time seems promising.

References

1. Steven Abney. Partial Parsing via Finite-State Cascades. In *Proceedings of the ESSLLI '96 Robust Parsing Workshop*, 1996.
2. Jan Alexandersson, Norbert Reithinger, and Elisabeth Maier. Insights into the Dialogue Processing of Verbmobil. In *Proc. of the 5th Conference on Applied Natural Language Processing*, Washington, D.C., 1997.
3. Jan W. Amtrup. ICE: A Communication Environment for Natural Language Processing. In *Proceedings of the International Conference on Parallel and Distributed Processing Techniques and Applications (PDPTA97)*, Las Vegas, NV, July 1997.
4. Jan W. Amtrup. Layered Charts for Speech Translation. In *Proceedings of the Seventh International Conference on Theoretical and Methodological Issues in Machine Translation, TMI '97*, Santa Fe, NM, July 1997.
5. Jan W. Amtrup. Perspectives for Incremental MT with Charts. In Christa Hauenschild and Susanne Heizmann, editors, *Machine Translation and Translation Theory. Perspectives of Co-operation*, Text, Translation, Computational Processing (TTCP), number 1. Mouton de Gruyter, 1997.
6. Jan W. Amtrup and Volker Weber. Time Mapping with Hypergraphs. In *Proc. of the 17 th COLING*, Montreal, Canada, 1998.
7. Xavier Aubert and Hermann Ney. Large Vocabulary Continuous Speech Recognition Using Word Graphs. In *ICASSP 95*, 1995.
8. Christian Boitet and Mark Seligman. The "Whiteboard" Architecture: A Way to Integrate Heterogeneous Components of NLP systems. In *COLING-94: The 15th International Conference on Computational Linguistics*, Kyoto, Japan, 1994.
9. Thomas Bub, Wolfgang Wahlster, and Alex Waibel. Verbmobil: The Combination of Deep and Shallow Processing for Spontaneous Speech Translation. In *Proc. of the IEEE International Conference on Acoustics, Speech and Signal Processing, ICASSP*, pages 1/71–1/74, Munich, Germany, 1997.
10. Bob Carpenter. *The Logic of Typed Feature Structures.* Tracts in Theoretical Computer Science. Cambridge University Press, Cambridge, 1992.
11. David Carter et al. Translation Methodology in the Spoken Language Translator: An Evaluation. In *ACL Workshop on Spoken Language Translation*, 1997.
12. G. V. Chernov. Message redundancy and message anticipation in simultaneous interpretation. In Lambert and Moser-Mercer, editors, *Bridging the Gap: Empirical Research in Simultaneous Interpretation*, pages 139–153. John Benjamins, 1994.
13. Michael Finke, Maria Lapata, Alon Lavie, Lori Levin, Laura Mayfield Tomokiyo, Thomas Polzin, Klaus Ries, Alex Waibel, and Klaus Zechner. CLARITY: Inferring

Discourse Structure from Speech. In *Proceedings of the AAAI 98 Spring Symposium: Applying Machine Learning to Discourse Processing*, pages 23–32, Stanford, CA, 1998.
14. Wolfgang Finkler and Anne Schauder. Effects of Incremental Output on Incremental Natural Language Generation. In *Proc. of the 10 th ECAI*, pages 505–507, Vienna, Austria, August 1992.
15. D. Gerver. Empirical studies of simultaneous interpretation: A review and a model. In R.W. Brislin, editor, *Translation: Applicatons and Research*, pages 165–207. Gardner Press, New York, 1997.
16. Günther Görz, Marcus Kesseler, Jörg Spilker, and Hans Weber. Research on Architectures for Integrated Speech/Language Systems in Verbmobil. In *Proc. of the 16 th COLING*, pages 484–489, Copenhagen, Denmark, August 1996.
17. Andreas Hauenstein and Hans Weber. An Investigation of Tightly Coupled Speech Language Interfaces Using an Unification Grammar. In *Proceedings of the Workshop on Integration of Natural Language and Speech Processing at AAAI '94*, pages 42–50, Seattle, WA, 1994.
18. Kai Huebener, Uwe Jost, and Henrik Heine. Speech Recognition for Spontaneously Spoken German Dialogs. In *ICSLP96*, Philadelphia, 1996.
19. Susanne J. Jekat. Automatic Interpretation of Dialogue Acts. In Christa Hauenschild and Susanne Heizmann, editors, *Machine Translation and Translation Theory. Perspectives of Co-operation*, Text, Translation, Computational Processing (TTCP), number 1. Mouton de Gruyter, 1997.
20. Martin Kay. Algorithmic Schemata and Data Structures in Syntactic Processing. Technical Report CSL-80-12, Xerox Palo Alto Research Center, Palo Alto, 1980.
21. Martin Kay. Chart generation. In *Proc. of the 34 nd ACL*, pages 200–204, Santa Cruz, CA, June 1996.
22. Hiroaki Kitano. *Speech-to-Speech Translation: A Massively Parallel Memory-Based Approach.* Kluwer Academic Publishers, Boston, 1994.
23. Marc Light. CHUMP: Partial Parsing and Underspecified Representations. In *Proceedings of the ECAI-96 Workshop: Corpus-Oriented Semantic Analysis*, 1996.
24. W.D. Marslen-Wilson. Functional Parallelism in Spoken Word Recognition. *Cognition*, 25:71–102, 1987.
25. W.D Marslen-Wilson and A. Welsh. Processing Interactions during Word Recognition in Continuous Speech. *Cognitive Psychology*, 10:29–63, 1978.
26. Heinrich Niemann, Elmar Nöth, Andreas Kiessling, Ralf Kompe, and Anton Batliner. Prosodic Processing and its Use in Verbmobil. In *Proc. of the IEEE International Conference on Acoustics, Speech and Signal Processing, ICASSP*, 1997.
27. Michael Niv. *A Computational Model of Syntactic Processing: Ambiguity Resolution from Interpretation.* PhD thesis, Univ. of Pennsylvania, 1993.
28. Manny Rayner and David Carter. Hybrid Language Processing in the Spoken Language Translator. In *Proc. of the IEEE International Conference on Acoustics, Speech and Signal Processing, ICASSP*, Munich, Germany, 1997. http://www.cam.sri.com/tr/crc064/paper.ps.Z.
29. Shuly Wintner and Nissim Francez. Parsing with Typed Feature Structures. In *Proceedings of the 4th International Workshop on Parsing Technologies (IWPT95)*, pages 273–287, Prague, September 1995. Charles University.
30. Klaus Zechner and Alex Waibel. Using Chunk Based Partial Parsing of Spontaneous Speech in Unrestricted Domains for Reducing Word Error Rate in Speech Recognition. In *COLING98P*, COLING98L, 1998.
31. P. Zwitserlood. The Locus of Effects of Sentential-Semantic Context in Spoken-Word Processing. *Cognition*, 32:25–64, 1989.

Sehen und Verstehen: Der Beitrag bildlicher Information zur robusten Sprachverarbeitung

Wolfgang Menzel

Fachbereich Informatik, Universität Hamburg
Vogt-Kölln-Straße 30, 22527 Hamburg, Germany

Zusammenfassung Sprachverstehen ist in hohem Maße situativ beeinflußt. Um diese Charakteristik des menschlichen Vorbilds in technische Lösungen zu übertragen, wird eine Verarbeitungsarchitektur entwickelt, die in der Lage ist, sehr unterschiedliche informationelle Beiträge in einem einheitlichen Entscheidungsverfahren zusammenzufassen. Am Beispiel eines Einsatzes in Lehrsystemen für den Fremdsprachenunterricht wird gezeigt, wie propositional repräsentierte piktorielle Information eine robuste Analyse von möglicherweise hochgradig gestörten sprachlichen Äußerungen unterstützen kann.

1 Einführung

Technische Lösungen zur Integration von Bild- und Sprachverstehen beruhen üblicherweise auf der relativ losen Kopplung von zwei weitgehend eigenständigen Komponenten (vgl. Bild 1a). Da eine solche Anordnung keinerlei direkten Informationsaustausch zwischen den parallelen Verarbeitungssträngen erlaubt, erfolgt die Analyse von Bild- und Sprachdaten praktisch unabhängig von dem aktuellen Informationsstand auf der jeweils komplementären Wahrnehmungsebene und die Resultate dieser Berechnungsprozesse werden erst auf einer relativ tiefen Verarbeitungsstufe miteinander in Beziehung gesetzt. Demgegenüber zeichnet sich die Kopplung der Sinnesmodalitäten beim menschlichen Vorbild durch ein erheblich stärkeres Zusammenwirken aus.

Bereits auf der rein phonetischen Ebene läßt sich eine sehr starke Beeinflussung der sprachlichen Perzeption durch die visuelle Beobachtung des Sprechvorgangs nachweisen. Einerseits führen etwa desynchronisierte Videoaufzeichnungen der Lippenbewegungen systematisch zu fehlerhaften Lautwahrnehmungen [9], während andererseits unter Rückgriff auf den Informationsbeitrag der Lippenbewegungen auch im Fall eines extrem gestörten akustischen Kanals (verminderte Hörfähigkeit, starke Umgebungsgeräusche usw.) eine Verständigung noch ermöglicht werden kann.

Durch eine erhebliche Verfeinerung der Techniken zur Verfolgung von Augenbewegungen konnte eine enge Kopplung von Sprach- und Bildverarbeitung auch für die höheren Ebenen der Sprachverarbeitung nachgewiesen werden [22]. So erfolgt die visuelle Identifizierung der sprachlich vermittelten Objektreferenzen auch im Falle komplexer sprachlicher Konstruktionen unmittelbar, sobald ausreichend viel Information verfügbar ist. Zudem läßt sich zeigen, daß die durch den visuellen Kontext bereitgestellte Information die syntaktische Verarbeitung in einer Weise beeinflußt, wie dies für sprachliche Kontexte bereits von Steedman und Crain [1] behauptet worden war. Insbesondere folgt die Aufmerksamkeitssteuerung in den Fällen eindeutiger Referenzbedingungen nicht den durch das Sprachsystem vorgegebenen Präferenzen, was mit der Annahme einer weitgehend autonomen syntaktischen Verarbeitung im sprachlichen Verarbeitungskanal [5] nicht verträglich ist.

Da vermutet werden kann, daß die enge Kopplung des Sprachverstehens mit der visuellen Wahrnehmung auch auf den höheren Ebenen der Sprachverarbeitung einen erheblichen Beitrag zur Robustheit des Gesamtsystems erbringt [11], stellt sich die Frage nach geeigneten Systemarchitekturen, die ein derartiges Zusammenwirken bereits zu einem relativ frühen Zeitpunkt überhaupt ermöglichen. Ein spezieller Bedarf an derartigen Lösungen ergibt sich vor allem im Bereich der Verarbeitung gesprochener Sprache, sowie bei der Analyse fehlerhafter sprachlicher Konstruktionen, die etwa im Kontext des Fremdsprachenunterrichts besonders häufig auftreten.

Aufbauend auf einer Analyse existierender Lösungsansätze aus diesen beiden Anwendungsfeldern werden allgemeine Anforderungen an eine geeignete Systemarchitektur identifiziert und in einen Lösungsvorschlag umgesetzt, der auf einem Verfahren zum eliminativen Parsing in Mehrebenenrepräsentationen beruht. Eine erste experimentelle Umsetzung erfolgt in einem Lehrsystem für den Fremdsprachenunterricht.

2 Sprachsignalerkennung

Tatsächlich finden sich erste Lösungsansätze zur wechselseitigen Beeinflussung von Bild- und Sprachverarbeitung vorrangig in Szenarien zur (gesprochen-) sprachlichen Interaktion mit autonomen Robotern, wo von dem Zusammenwirken u.a. eine Reduktion der Erkennungsunsicherheit in beiden Wahrnehmungskanälen erwartet wird. Naeve u.a. [17] nutzen die aus dem visuellen Kanal resultierenden Angaben über mögliche Referenzobjekte, um spezielle, der jeweiligen Situation angepaßte Sprachmodelle (in Form von endlichen Automaten) zu generieren. Auf diese Weise gelingt es, die Gesamtperplexität fast um einen Faktor zwei zu reduzieren und die entsprechenden visuell induzierten Erwartungen auf die Ebene der Sprachsignalerkennung abzubilden. Die Kopplung der visuellen und sprachlichen Information erfolgt auf der Ebene der Domänenkonzepte über die eine bidirektionale Ausbreitung von Informationsbeiträgen aus den beiden Wahrnehmungskanälen erfolgen kann.

Handelt es sich bei diesem Verfahren um einen Lösungsansatz zur Steigerung der Erkennungssicherheit für Objektbenennungen, wendet sich Socher [21] dem Problem der Objektidentifizierung zu. Bayes'sche Netze werden benutzt, um visuelle und sprachliche Informationsbeiträge zur Referenzidentifikation zusammenzuführen. Wegen der bidirektionalen Arbeitsweise der Netze, die den Transport kausaler und diagnostischer Evidenz unterstützt, ist auch hier eine Kopplung der beiden Modalitäten über die Konzeptebene möglich.

Für den jeweils ausgewählten Teilbereich liegt beiden Ansätzen eine Anordnung der Verarbeitungskomponenten zugrunde, die über die gerichtete In-

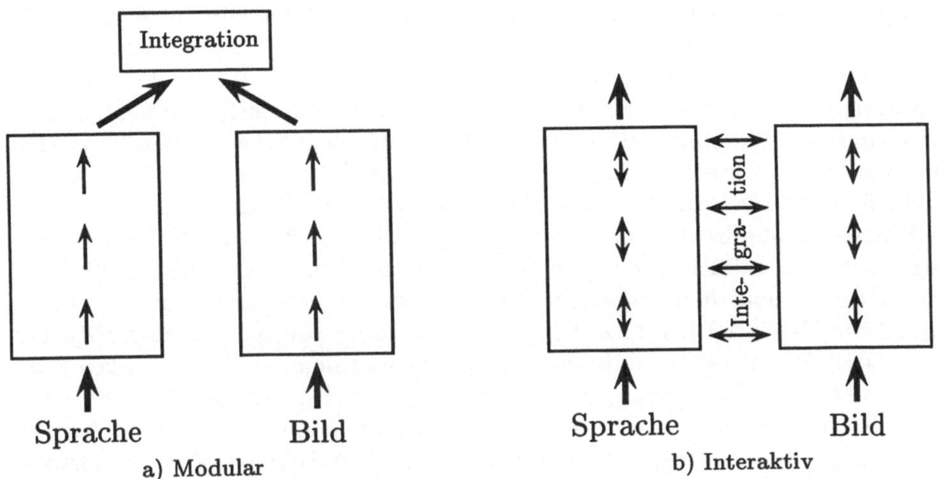

Abbildung1. Systemarchitekturen für die Integration komplementärer Informationsbeiträge

formationausbreitung in Bild 1a hinausgeht. Damit bieten sie tatsächlich die notwendigen Voraussetzungen für die gewünschte Integration von visueller und sprachlicher Information zumindest für isolierte Phänomenbereiche. Basis dafür ist jedoch eine allein auf Hypothesenprädiktion abzielende, strikt generative Sichtweise. Gegen deren Erweiterbarkeit beim Übergang von einfachen Prädikationen auf komplexe relationale Zusammenhänge oder gar temporale Abläufe spricht vor allem die Tatsache, daß die rein generative Sicht

- bei größeren Domänen sehr schnell auf prinzipielle Realisierungsschwierigkeiten stößt und
- die Perspektive des Systementwicklers sehr starr[1] auf die sprachliche Realisierung abbildet.

Komplementär hierzu sind die eher analytisch ausgerichteten Ansätze angelegt, die sich an den klassischen Parsingverfahren orientieren, allerdings kaum auf die Erfordernisse einer Interaktion mit externen Wissensquellen Rücksicht nehmen. Beispiele hierfür sind die Systemrealisierungen in [16] und [2], denen aber wiederum eine Systemarchitektur nach Bild 1a zugrunde liegt. Die Kopplung der beiden unidirektionalen Wahrnehmungskanäle erfolgt erst nach dem Parsing, wodurch eine direkte Beeinflussung der Sprachverarbeitung durch die visuellen Befunde ausgeschlossen ist.

3 Sprachlehrsysteme

Recht ähnlich stellt sich die Situation im Bereich der Lehrsysteme für den Fremdsprachenunterricht dar. Hier besteht bereits aus didaktischen Überlegungen heraus die Notwendigkeit, sprachliche Interaktion in einen Kontext einzubetten, um einerseits die Aufgabenstellung für den Schüler zu motivieren und andererseits

[1] Mit Ausnahme der Möglichkeit zum Ignorieren von Signalabschnitten.

einen kommunikativen Zusammenhang herzustellen. Besonders gut eignen sich hierfür direkt manipulierbare virtuelle Welten, in denen Schüler und Lehrsystem gleichzeitig sprachlich und grafisch agieren. Wiederum ist eine Integration und Abstimmung der verschiedenen Informationsbeiträge gefordert. Insbesondere besteht aber die Hoffnung, daß die vom Lehrsystem ohnehin verwaltete grafische Information zur Unterstützung der Analyse und der Diagnose der oftmals hochgradig fehlerhaften Spracheingabe herangezogen werden kann.

Klassische unidirektionale Parser (z.B. [4], aber auch [6, 19, 20, 23, 25]) orientieren sich ebenfalls an einer modularen Architektur nach Bild 1a. Um die erforderliche Robustheit gegenüber Schülerfehlern zu erreichen, kommen unterschiedliche Varianten der Idee des *minimal distance parsing* [18] zum Einsatz. Dabei wird die zur Fehlererklärung herangezogene Diagnose aus derjenigen validen Strukturbeschreibung abgeleitet, die eine möglichst geringe Distanz zu der vorgefundenen Schülerlösung aufweist. Das Abstandsmaß ist dabei über Anzahl und Art der zur Lösungsfindung ggf. erforderlichen Fehlerregeln bzw. Bedingungsrücknahmen definiert. Da beide Techniken die zur Suchraumbegrenzung zwingend erforderlichen Einschränkungen neutralisieren, ist eine Generalisierbarkeit problematisch, solange hierfür keine adäquate Kompensation z.B. durch Restriktionen aus dem visuellen Kontext erfolgt.

Eine (rudimentäre) Steuerung durch den (sprachlichen) Kontext ist nur über die Zuweisung von Straffaktoren zu Grammatikregeln möglich. Da Grammatikregeln aber kaum direkte Korrelationen mit den außersprachlichen Gegebenheiten des visuellen Kontexts aufweisen, ist dieser Mechanismus für die Integration visueller Information kaum geeignet.

Wesentlich bessere Voraussetzungen für die Einbeziehung außersprachlicher Bedingungen ergeben sich in einem erwartungsgesteuerten Ansatz, wie er beispielsweise in [3] realisiert wurde. Ausgehend von einem durch das finite Verb des Satzes instanziierten Prädikat werden die Argumentstellen durch das sprachliche Material gefüllt, wobei wiederum ein geeignet zu definierendes Ähnlichkeitsmaß für die Auswahl einer bestimmten Zuordnung maßgeblich ist (*predication-driven parsing*). Die Integration visuell präsentierter Informationen in diesen Auswahlprozeß erscheint prinzipiell möglich, wenn es gelänge, den zugrundeliegenden Abbildungsmechanismus auf mehrere alternative Prädikate zu erweitern und bei der Selektion der zu erwartenden Prädikate auch außersprachliche Information zu berücksichtigen.

4 Anforderungen an integrative Architekturen

Ausgehend von den bisherigen Beobachtungen in den genannten Anwendungsbereichen können eine Reihe von Anforderungen an eine Architektur zur integrativen multimodalen Verarbeitung formuliert werden:

Mehrebenenrepräsentation: Die Architektur muß die Verwaltung mehrerer zueinander komplementärer (d.h. parallel aufzubauender) Repräsentationsebenen unterstützen, zwischen denen ein Informationsaustausch erfolgen kann.

Feinkörnige Interaktion: Die wechselseitige Bezugnahme zwischen den beteiligten Repräsentationen muß auf allen Ebenen der hierarchischen Dekomposition erfolgen. Es reicht hierbei nicht aus, komplette Analyseergebnisse des visuellen und sprachlichen Kanals zu kombinieren, vielmehr muß auch für Teilergebnisse eine unmittelbare Wechselwirkung möglich sein.

Omnidirektionale Informationsausbreitung: Unterstützende Information muß zwischen allen Repräsentationsebenen austauschbar sein, ohne daß ein explizites Umschalten zwischen verschiedenen Ausbreitungsrichtungen erforderlich ist. Dies ist insbesondere deshalb notwendig, weil die Qualität der jeweils zur Verfügung stehenden Information (z.B. sichere vs. unsichere, aber auch relevante vs. irrelevante Information) nicht a priori bewertet werden kann, sondern sich üblicherweise erst im Verlaufe der Integration ergibt.

Behandlung widersprüchlicher Aussagen: Sowohl innerhalb einer Repräsentationsebene als auch ebenenübergreifend müssen Inkonsistenzen zwischen Informationsbeiträgen toleriert werden, um einerseits der inhärenten Unsicherheit der Kategorienwahrnehmung Rechnung zu tragen, aber auch um potentielle Widersprüche zwischen visueller Realität und sprachlicher Äußerung detektieren und diagnostizieren zu können.

Damit ergibt sich eine Systemarchitektur nach Bild 1b. Zwei parallele Verarbeitungskomponenten mit jeweils separaten Repräsentationen für bildliche und sprachliche Information sind über Interaktionspfade so miteinander gekoppelt, daß die entsprechenden Strukturen auf allen jeweils verfügbaren Repräsentationsebenen unmittelbar aufeinander abgebildet werden können. So sollte das Vorliegen einer bestimmten räumlichen Relation (z.B. ein Buch liegt auf dem Tisch) bestimmte präpositionale Konstruktionen (z.B. *"Buch auf dem Tisch"*) im sprachlichen Kanal präferieren und umgekehrt. Gleichzeitig muß aber vermieden werden, den Informationsbeitrag einer Verarbeitungskomponente der jeweils komplementären Repräsentation aufzuzwingen, weil dann Widersprüche (z.B. das Buch liegt in Wirklichkeit gar nicht auf dem Tisch, sondern im Regal) nicht mehr kommunikativ behandelbar sind. Zudem kann ja niemals mit Sicherheit davon ausgegangen werden, daß sich der Sprecher auf die Verwendung der visuell erfaßbaren Objekte beschränkt. In solchen Fällen ist die visuell verfügbare Information irrelevant für die Verarbeitung der sprachlichen Konstruktion und darf den Sprachanalyseprozeß nicht negativ beeinflussen.

5 Informationsintegration im eliminativen Parsing

Auf der Grundlage eines Verfahrens zum eliminativen Parsing wurde eine Mehrebenenarchitektur zur Integration von komplementären Wissensquellen realisiert [12, 8, 14]. Um die wechselseitige Abbildung der Repräsentationsstrukturen zu unterstützen, wird auf allen Ebenen ein einheitliches, hierarchisch strukturiertes relationales Darstellungsformat verwendet, das sich an dem Formalismus einer Dependenzgrammatik orientiert.

Modelliert wurden die Ebenen Syntax, Semantik und Domänenwissen (Bild 2). Lokale Konfigurationen aus maximal zwei Dependenzrelationen werden durch gewichtete Constraints lizensiert, wobei die Gewichte den Grad widerspiegeln, zu dem eine Verletzung eines Constraints noch akzeptabel erscheint. Auf diese Weise können sehr unterschiedliche sprachliche und außersprachliche Wissensbestandteile modelliert werden:

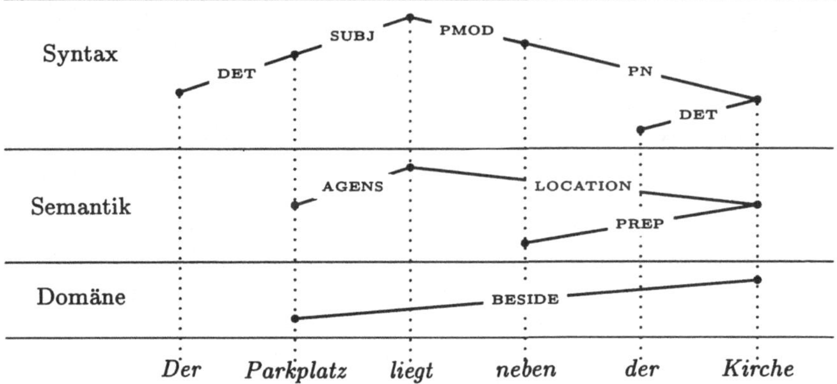

Abbildung2. Mehrebenenrepräsentation für eine Schüleräußerung.

Harte Constraints müssen von jeder Strukturbeschreibung erfüllt werden. Sie dienen in erster Linie dazu, Wohlgeformtheitsbedingungen für Strukturbeschreibungen zu formulieren (z.B. Relationen wie SUBJECT-OF oder OBJECT-OF modifizieren immer ein Verb).

Defaults sind mögliche, aber hart bestrafte Strukturbeschreibungen, die nur dann "überleben", wenn im Hypothesenraum keine Alternative mehr verbleibt (z.B. kann bei Bedarf auch ein Nomen als Spitzenknoten einer nichtsatzwertigen Äußerung verwendet werden). Auf diese Weise wird die Möglichkeit zum partiellen Parsing problemlos in den Ansatz integriert.

Korrektheitsbedingungen stellen die Wohlgeformtheit der sprachlichen Ausdrücke auf den verschiedenen Ebenen sicher (z.B. Obligatheitsforderungen, Kongruenz- und Rektionsbedingungen, selektionale Restriktionen, Domänenwissen usw.). Die Bewertung variiert in Abhängigkeit von der Verläßlichkeit der jeweiligen Forderungen.

Präferenzen differenzieren zwischen sprachlichen Optionen innerhalb des Bereiches der Wohlgeformtheit (z.B. Subjekt-vor-Objekt-Präferenz).

Beginnend mit einer vollständig unterspezifizierten Ausgangsstruktur, die grundsätzlich alle durch das Relationeninventar definierten Dependenzrelationen in einer kompakten Form enthält, wird durch die Anwendung von Constraints der Raum möglicher Lösungen sukzessive eingeschränkt, bis nur noch eine eindeutige Strukturbeschreibung auf den verschiedenen Repräsentationsebenen vorliegt. Dabei erlaubt die parallele Verfügbarkeit aller Strukturbeschreibungen eine vergleichende Bewertung für lokale Strukturkonfigurationen. In Abhängigkeit von den Ergebnissen der Constraintanwendung werden diejenigen Dependenzrelationen gelöscht, für die ein Maximum an negativer Evidenz akkumuliert wurde.

Da auch die bidirektionale Abbildung zwischen Dependenzrelationen auf den verschiedenen Repräsentationsebenen durch gewichtete Constraints erfolgt, kann so der gewünschte ebenenübergreifende Abgleich von Evidenz erfolgen. Steht die ermittelte Strukturbeschreibung im Widerspruch zu einer oder mehreren Korrektheitsbedingungen, so können diese Constraintverletzungen auch als Diagnose

Abbildung3. Ausschnitt aus einem Kleinstadt-Szenario.

der Schüleräußerung interpretiert und in geeignete Fehlererklärungen umgewandelt werden [15]. Dieser enge Bezug zwischen den Parsingresultaten und der Diagnosefähigkeit bildet die Grundlage für eine Integration des Verfahrens in ein prototypisches Sprachlehrsystem [13]. Dazu wurde die Domänenebene durch das propositional repräsentierte Wissen aus der bildlichen Darstellung einer Szenerie modelliert (Bild 3), wobei sich der Prototyp durch eine Reihe sehr gravierender Vereinfachungen auszeichnet:

- Es handelt sich um eine statische Welt.
- Es wird von einer einfachen Referenzauflösung ausgegangen, d.h. nominale Bezeichner stehen für die Objektinstanzen.
- Es wird ausschließlich eine extrinsische Perspektive zugrundegelegt.
- Es werden ausschließlich relativ einfache, narrative Sprachäußerungen betrachtet.

Tatsächlich stellt sich bei geeigneter Modellierung sehr schnell das angestrebte kompensatorische Verhalten ein, wobei insbesondere für fehlerhafte Äußerungen eine wechselseitige Unterstützung der Repräsentationsebenen zu beobachten ist. Im Normalfall wird semantische und domänenspezifische Information benutzt, um die syntaktische Diagnose zu steuern, etwa zur Subjekt-Objekt-Disambiguierung in Fällen wie

**Dort entdeckt Verkäuferin ein kleines Hund.*

oder aber zur Klärung der PP-Anbindung in

**Mich gefällt Auto auf das Parkplatz.*

Wegen des bidirektionalen Charakters der ebenenübergreifenden Constraints entsteht hier allerdings keine einseitige (und damit in einigen Fällen fatale) Abhängigkeit von einer bestimmten Ebene, wie sie etwa für semantisch gesteuerte Ansätze durchaus typisch ist. Solange ausreichend stabile syntaktische Kriterien vorhanden sind, stützen diese die Disambiguierung auf den komplementären Ebenen, so daß bei (relativ zum Domänenwissen) unbekannten Sachverhalten in Fällen wie

Der Parkplatz liegt neben dem Krankenhaus.

eine Extraktion des (noch unbekannten) propositionalen Gehalts versucht werden kann. Darüberhinaus bietet das Verfahren aber auch bei (relativ zum Domänenwissen) sachlich fehlerhaften Beschreibungen der Art

Die Bäckerei liegt hinter dem Parkplatz.

eine Diagnose der vorliegenden Inkonsistenzen an, die dann im Dialog mit dem Schüler weiter thematisiert werden kann. Das Verfahren realisiert somit eine durch den visuellen Kontext gesteuerte Sprachanalyse, ohne jedoch das Analyseergebnis durch die Spezifikation der Kontextinformation vollständig zu determinieren, so daß ein Verlassen des vorgegebenen Szenarios unter bestimmten Bedingungen (u.a. ausreichende lexikalische Abdeckung) immer noch möglich ist.

6 Bildliche Information in Sprachlehrsystemen

Mit dem Vorliegen eines Verfahrens, das einen bidirektionalen Informationsaustausch zwischen visueller und sprachlicher Information vermittelt, sind die Voraussetzungen für eine ganze Reihe von didaktisch interessanten Interaktionsformen im Kontext eines Sprachlehrsystems gegeben. Hamburger [7] unterscheidet acht Interaktionstypen, für die aus der hier betrachteten Sprachanalysesicht vor allem die folgenden fünf von Bedeutung sind:

Quizmaster: Das System fragt und der Schüler antwortet.

Movecaster: Das System generiert eine (animierte) Grafik und der Schüler erzählt, was er sieht.

In beiden Fällen überprüft das System die Akzeptabilität der Schüleräußerung in sprachlicher und pragmatischer Hinsicht, wobei die grafisch präsentierte Information als Stütze bei der Behandlung fehlerhafter Konstruktionen dient. Als Interaktionsformen, bei denen die Initiative überwiegend beim Schüler liegt, kommen in Frage:

Oracle: Der Schüler fragt und das System antwortet.

Servant: Der Schüler gibt Kommandos und das System führt sie aus.

Interpreter: Der Schüler erzählt etwas und das System generiert eine entsprechende Animation.

Darüberhinaus kann die interaktive Manipulation einer grafischen Repräsentation aber auch als alternativer Kommunikationskanal benutzt werden, falls wegen der eventuell noch mangelhaften Sprachbeherrschung eine sprachliche Verständigung nicht mehr möglich ist. Indem der Schüler seine sprachliche Äußerung gleichzeitig direktmanipulativ visualisiert, enthält das System zusätzliche Informationen, die zur Steuerung der Diagnose verwendet werden können. Mealing und Yazdani [10, 24] schlagen für diesen Zweck eine kompositionelle, und teilweise animierte Piktogramm-Sprache vor, die eine eindeutige Visualisierung sprachlicher Äußerungen gestattet.

7 Schlußfolgerungen

Unter Verwendung von Techniken des eliminativen Parsings konnte eine Systemarchitektur realisiert werden, die die Forderung nach Mehrebenenrepräsentation, feinkörniger Interaktion, omnidirektionalem Informationsfluß und Behandlung widersprüchlicher Information erfüllt. Sie gestattet die Beinflussung der Sprachverarbeitung durch visuell gegebene Information, ohne daß dadurch eine einseitige Dominanz des visuellen Kanals in Kauf genommen werden muß. Wesentlicher Vorteil dieses integrativen Ansatzes ist seine Robustheit gegenüber fehlerhaftem sprachlichen Input, verbunden mit der Fähigkeit zur Diagnose von Inkonsistenzen auf allen Repräsentationsebenen. Dies erlaubt die Entwicklung von Lehrsystemen für den Fremdsprachenunterricht, die wegen der situativen Verankerung der Sprachverwendung eine deutlich gesteigerte kommunikative Relevanz der Schülerübungen vorweisen können.

Eindeutig unbefriedigend ist zur Zeit noch die Ausdruckskraft der visuellen Repräsentationsebene. Hier wird eine sukzessive Erweiterung der Möglichkeiten im Hinblick auf die Behandlung komplexerer Szenarien erforderlich sein, wobei jedoch darauf zu achten ist, daß die vorteilhaften Eigenschaften der Integrierbarkeit erhalten bleiben.

Literatur

1. S. Crain and M. Steedman. On not being led up the garden path. In D. R. Dowty, L. Kartunen, and A. M. Zwicky, editors, *Natural Language Parsing: Psychological, computational, and theoretical perspectives*, pages 320–358. Cambridge University Press, Cambridge, 1985.
2. C. Crangle and P. Suppes. *Language and Learning for Robots*, volume 41 of *CSLI Lecture Notes*. CSLI, Stanford, CA, 1994.
3. W. H. DeSmedt. Herr Kommissar: An ICALL conversation simulator for intermediate german. In V. M. Holland, J. D. Kaplan, and M. R. Sams, editors, *Intelligent Language Tutors: Theory Shaping Technology*, chapter 9, pages 153–174. Lawrence Erlbaum Ass., Mahwah, NJ, 1995.
4. S. Felshin. The Athena language learning project NLP system: A multilingual system for conversation-based language learning. In V. M. Holland, J. D. Kaplan, and M. R. Sams, editors, *Intelligent Language Tutors*, chapter 14, pages 257–272. Lawrence Erlbaum Associates, Hillsdale, NJ, 1995.
5. L. Frazier. Theories of sentence processing. In J. L. Garfield, editor, *Modularity in Knowledge Representation and Natural Language Understanding*, pages 291–307. MIT-Press, Cambridge MA, 1987.
6. L. K. Hagen. Unification-based parsing applications for intelligent foreign language tutoring systems. *CALICO Journal*, 12(2/3):5–30, 1995.

7. H. Hamburger. Tutorial tools for language learning by two-medium dialogue. In V. M. Holland, J. D. Kaplan, and M. R. Sams, editors, *Intelligent Language Tutors*, chapter 10, pages 183–199. Lawrence Erlbaum Associates, Hillsdale, NJ, 1995.
8. J. Heinecke, J. Kunze, W. Menzel, and I. Schröder. Eliminative parsing with graded constraints. In *Proceedings 17th International Conference on Computational Linguistics, 36th Annual Meeting of the ACL, Coling-ACL '98*, Montreal, Canada, 1998.
9. H. McGurk and J. MacDonald. Hearing lips and seeing voices. *Nature*, 264(5588):746–748, 1976.
10. S. Mealing and M. Yazdani. A computer-based iconic language. In M. Yazdani, editor, *Multilingual Multimedia: Bridging the Language Barrier with Intelligent Systems*. Intellect Books, Oxford, 1993.
11. W. Menzel. Robust parsing of natural language. In *KI-95: Advances in Artificial Intelligence*, pages 19–34, Berlin, 1995. Springer-Verlag.
12. W. Menzel. Constraint satisfaction for robust parsing of natural language. *Theoretical and Experimental Artificial Intelligence*, 10(1):77–89, 1998.
13. W. Menzel and I. Schröder. Constraint-based diagnosis for intelligent language tutoring systems. In *Proceedings IT & KNOWS, XV. IFIP World Computer Congress*, Wien und Budapest, 1998.
14. W. Menzel and I. Schröder. Decision procedures for dependency parsing using graded constraints. In S. Kahane and A. Polguere, editors, *Proc. Coling-ACL Workshop on Processing of Dependency-based Grammars*, Montreal, Canada, 1998.
15. W. Menzel and I. Schröder. Model-based diagnosis under structural uncertainty. In *Proceedings 13th European Conference on Artificial Intelligence*, pages 284–288, Brighton, 1998.
16. J.-T. Milde, K. Peters, and S. Strippgen. Situated communication with robots. In *Proc. 1st. Int. Workshop on Human-Computer Conversation*, Bellagio, Italy, 1997.
17. U. Naeve, G. Socher, G. A. Fink, F. Kummert, and G. Sagerer. Generation of language models using the results of image analysis. In *4th European Confence on Speech Communication and Technology*, pages 1739–1742, Madrid, 1995.
18. C. P. Rosé and A. Lavie. An efficient distribution of labor in a two stage robust interpretation process. In *Proceedings EMNLP-2*, 1997.
19. C. B. Schwind. An intelligent language tutoring system. *International Journal of Man-Machine Studies*, 33:557–579, 1990.
20. C. B. Schwind. Error analysis and explanation in knowledge based language tutoring. *Computer Assisted Language Learning*, 8(4):295–324, 1995.
21. G. Socher. *Qualitative Scene Descriptions from Images for Integrated Speech and Image Understanding*, volume 170 of *Dissertationen zur Künstlichen Intelligenz*. Infix, Sankt Augustin, 1997.
22. M. K. Tanenhaus, M. J. Spivey-Knowlton, K. M. Eberhard, and J. C. Sedivy. Integration of visual and linguistic information in spoken language comprehension. *Science*, 268:1632–1634, 1995.
23. A. Weinberger, J. Garman, J. Martin, and P. Merlo. A principle-based parser for foreign language tutoring in german and arabic. In V. M. Holland, J. D. Kaplan, and M. R. Sams, editors, *Intelligent Language Tutors*, chapter 2, pages 23–44. Lawrence Erlbaum Associates, Hillsdale, NJ, 1995.
24. M. Yazdani and S. Mealing. Communicating through pictures. Technical report, Department of Computer Science, Exeter, 1993.
25. M. Yazdani and J. Uren. Generalising language tutoring systems. In M. Yazdani, editor, *Multilingual Multimedia: Bridging the Language Barrier with Intelligent Systems*. Intellect Books, Oxford, 1993.

Osiris: Qualitative Fortschritte bei der Literaturrecherche

Marc Ronthaler
Marc.Ronthaler@CL-KI.uni-osnabrueck.de
Institut für Semantische Informationsverarbeitung
Universität Osnabrück
49069 Osnabrück

Zusammenfassung Nachdem in beinahe allen großen Bibliotheken der alte Zettelkatalog durch den OPAC[1] abgelöst wurde, sind die Nachteile dieses Systems inzwischen offenkundig. Die Suchmöglichkeiten sind nicht am Bedarf des Endbenutzers orientiert und die Suchergebnisse oft interpretationsbedürftig, womit Endbenutzer überfordert sind. Statt in Benutzerschulungen zu investieren, will das OSIRIS[2]-System die Literaturrecherche mit natürlicher Sprache auf einer automatisch generierten Wissensbasis ermöglichen. Die mit OSIRIS erzielten Ergebnisse sind zudem von besserer Qualität, die Zahl der relevanten Treffer liegt in der neuen Version 2.0 oft um den Faktor 10 über der des OPAC.

1 Einleitung

Seit Mitte 1996 fördert die Deutsche Forschungsgemeinschaft (DFG) mit dem Projekt OSIRIS an der Universitätsbibliothek Osnabrück die Neukonzeption des Bibliothekszugangs mit Hilfe multilingualer, natürlichsprachlicher Retrievaltechniken.

Nach einer kurzen Darstellung der besonderen Problematik des Anwendungsbereiches „Universitätsbibliothek" wird es um die Neuerungen gehen, die nach sechs Monaten hochschulöffentlichen Betriebes in die nun vorliegende Version 2.0 eingegangen sind.

Im Anschluß daran soll anhand einiger Beispiele der Fortschritt demonstriert werden, den die in OSIRIS eingesetzten Techniken dem Bibliotheksbenutzer bringen.

2 Die Problemlage

In den vergangenen Jahren wurde in den meisten wissenschaftlichen Bibliotheken der klassische Zettelkatalog als Recherchemöglichkeit für den Endbenutzer vom sog. OPAC abgelöst. Ein typischer OPAC, und dazu zählt das Osnabrücker System, ist über eine Telnetverbindung mit VT100-Oberfläche zu erreichen. Der Benutzer kann nach folgenden Aspekten suchen: *Titelstichwörter*, *Personennamen*, *Körperschaften*, *Kongreßtitel*, *Serientitel*, *Systematik*, *Nummern* (ISBN etc.) und *Signaturen.*[3]

[1] **O**nline **P**ublic **A**ccess **C**atalog

[2] **O**snabrück **I**ntelligent **R**esearch **I**nformation **S**ystem

[3] Auf die besondere Problematik des Suchaspekts *Schlagwort*, der an einigen Bibliotheken angeboten wird, wird weiter unten eingegangen.

In vielen Bibliotheken ist der OPAC inzwischen die einzige Möglichkeit, im aktuellen Bestand zu recherchieren. So wird in der Universitätsbibliothek Osnabrück, mit ca. 1 Million Büchern eine mittelgroße Bibliothek, der Zettelkatalog seit 1996 nicht mehr aktualisiert. Laut einer Nutzerbefragung, die im Rahmen der die OSIRIS-Entwicklung begleitenden Evaluationsmaßnahmen[4] durchgeführt wurde, wird der Zettelkatalog von vielen immer noch dem OPAC vorgezogen, auch wenn die gesuchten Titel bereits im OPAC verzeichnet sind. Ein Grund hierfür ist in der ausgesprochen benutzerunfreundlichen VT100-Oberfläche zu sehen. Deshalb gibt es zahlreiche Ansätze, die OPAC-Oberflächen zu überarbeiten, z.B. sie WWW-konform zu gestalten. Doch auch eine sinnvolle, an softwareergonomischen Gesichtspunkten orientierte Oberflächengestaltung ändert nichts an der eigentlichen Schwäche des OPAC-Systems als Rechercheinstrument für den Endbenutzer: Der OPAC ist auf die Bedürfnisse der Bibliothekare zugeschnitten. Endbenutzer, die den OPAC zur Literaturrecherche benutzen, verstehen nachweislich die Bedeutung der meisten Suchmöglichkeiten nicht.[5] In der Folge verwenden sie daher beinahe ausschließlich nur die Suchaspekte *Titelstichwörter* und *Personennamen.*

Es ist zwar einfach, mit diesen beiden Optionen das Vorhandensein eines Werkes, dessen Titel und Verfasser sowie deren genaue Schreibweise bekannt sind, zu überprüfen, die Suche nach Literatur zu einem Thema aber gestaltet sich damit frustrierend. Die Ergebnisse solcher Suchanfragen sind sehr oft viel zu groß, oft so groß, daß das OPAC-System deren Darstellung verweigert (Bsp. Stichwort *Chemie*, *Geschichte* oder *Deutschland* an einem deutschen OPAC).

Ebenso leicht geschieht es, daß Benutzer überhaupt kein Ergebnis erhalten. Da Stichwortsuche im OPAC reines pattern matching ist, haben nur die Suchanfragen Erfolg, die genau die im Titel vertretenen Ausdrücke verwenden. Darüber hinaus befindet sich kaum weiteres sprachliches Material in den Datensätzen, so daß laut Schulz[6] jede zweite bis dritte Stichwortsuche überhaupt keinen Treffer erzielt. Hinzu kommt die mangelnde Robustheit und Flexibilität gegenüber den Benutzereingaben: Allein aufgrund unerkannter (!) Fehler in der Eingabe enden nach Schulz 10% aller Anfragen mit einem Nulltrefferergebnis.

Benutzer, die mit Hilfe von Titelstichwörtern Literatur zu einem Thema suchen und denen es gelingt, durch geschickte Formulierung sowohl leere als auch übergroße Ergebnismengen zu vermeiden, geraten in die eigentlich bedrohlichste Lage: Wie möchten sie sichergehen, daß die gefundenen Titel wirklich alle für die Themenstellung relevanten Titel im Bestand sind?

Sucht ein Benutzer im OPAC der Bibliothek Osnabrück bspw. nach Literatur zum Thema *Sport im Alter*, so ist er gezwungen, einen Ausdruck in der Booleschen Logik der Anfragesprache zu konstruieren, etwa wie folgt:. `sport AND alter`. Das Ergebnis dieser Anfrage sind fünf Bücher. Benutzer, die erwartungsgemäß dem System vertrauen, ärgern sich, daß ihre Interessen nicht in der Beschaffungspolitik der Bibliothek repräsentiert sind. Benutzer, die (zu Recht)

---

[4] Siehe auch Abschnitt 5.

[5] vgl. [Dre94] und [Sch94]

[6] [Sch94, :299]

an der Zuverlässigkeit des Systems zweifeln, beginnen nun, Ausweichstrategien zu entwickeln, um die Bücher zu finden, die der OPAC ihnen vorenthält. Eine Suche im semantischen Umfeld mit *Seniorensport* oder *Alterssport* fördert schon mehr zu Tage, aber auch mit den geschicktesten Strategien werden sie nie sicher sein können, alle für ihre Suchanfrage inhaltlich relevanten Werke der Bibliothek gefunden zu haben.

2.1 Traditionelle Lösungsansätze

Angesichts der genannten Probleme wurden bislang zwei Lösungsstrategien angeführt, *Schlagwörter* und *Trunkierung*. Beide Vorschläge sind allerdings untauglich, die beschriebene Lage zu verbessern.
Einige Bibliotheken bieten ihren Benutzern im OPAC die Möglichkeit, mit einer Suchoption *Schlagwort* nach inhaltlichen Kriterien und nicht nach Stichwörtern zu suchen. Schlagwörter werden intellektuell durch ausgebildete Fachkräfte einem Datensatz angefügt. Die hohen Kosten dieser personalintensiven Erschließung haben dazu geführt, daß nur etwa 50% der Bestände der Universitätsbibliothek Osnabrück unsystematisch mit Schlagwörtern versehen sind. In dieser Hinsicht unterscheidet sich die Universitätsbibliothek Osnabrück nicht von den meisten anderen deutschen Bibliotheken. Eine Suchoption *Schlagwort* arbeitet also von vornherein nur auf einem Bruchteil des eigentlichen Bestandes, weshalb in Osnabrück auf eine solchen Option im OPAC verzichtet wurde. Auch erscheint eine Benutzung der Schlagwörter aufgrund der enormen Komplexität der Ansetzungsregeln[7] durch einen bibliothekarischen Laien kaum möglich. Nur eine regelkonforme Anwendung garantiert aber Erfolg: *Hund* trifft keine inhaltlich relevanten Einträge, denn die Regel vom „engen Schlagwort" sorgt dafür, daß die entsprechenden Datensätze mit *Dackel*, *Terrier* usw. versehen werden. Da aber auch auf Schlagwortmaterial nur mit pattern matching gesucht wird, bleibt auch in einem zu hundert Prozent verschlagworteten Bestand die Suche nach Literatur zu *Hund* ohne Erfolg.
Trunkierung, das ist die Suche mit sog. Wildcards oder Jokerzeichen, um beliebige Wortendungen zu treffen, kann von den Benutzern nicht erwartet werden, denn diese haben „erhebliche Schwierigkeiten mit der Verwendung von Maskierungsmöglichkeiten"[8] und würden sie daher meiden. Schulz schreibt: *„Der Zweck von Trunkierungsmöglichkeiten wird offensichtlich nicht verstanden, die Funktion folglich nicht genutzt."*[9]
Außerdem ändert Trunkierung nichts am Fehlen von Schlagwörtern und führt in der Stichwortsuche noch eher zu den erwähnten übergroßen Treffermengen. Die Ergebnisse werden durch Trunkierung darüber hinaus sehr unpräzise, weil *beliebige* Wortfortsetzungen getroffen werden. Für semantische Phänomene (bspw. Synonyme und Ambiguitäten) stellt Trunkierung ebenfalls keine Lösung dar.
In dieser Situation, die durch bloße Oberflächengestaltung nicht zu verbessern ist, erscheint es angesichts der Kosten einer möglichen Vervollständigung der

[7] Regeln für den Schlagwortkatalog
[8] [Sch94, :300]
[9] siehe dort

sachlichen Erschließung sowie derem zweifelhaften Nutzen für die Recherche sinnvoll zu versuchen, auf der Grundlage des vorhandenen Datenbestandes eine qualitative Verbesserung der Sachrecherche des Endbenutzers zu erreichen. Dies ist der Ausgangspunkt des OSIRIS-Systems.

3 Das Osiris-System

OSIRIS trägt mit zwei Dingen zur Verbesserung der geschilderten Lage bei: Einerseits mit einer robusten, natürlichsprachlichen Endbenutzerschnittstelle zur Datenbank und andererseits mit einer intelligenten, automatischen Aufbereitung des verfügbaren Datenbestandes. In dieser Kombination und mit der Betonung automatischer, regelbasierter Verfahren, hebt sich das OSIRIS-System von allen uns bekannten Ansätzen zur Rechercheverbesserung ab.

3.1 Die Eingabeverarbeitung

Die in OSIRIS eingesetzte Endbenutzerschnittstelle hat die Aufgabe, natürlichsprachliche Anfragen des Benutzers syntaktisch und semantisch so zu analysieren, daß mit dem Ergebnis der Analyse eine Suche auf der Datenbank erfolgreich durchgeführt werden kann. Phrasen müssen erkannt und die sie konstituierenden Teile semantisch zueinander in Relation gesetzt werden. Komposita müssen in ihre Bestandteile zerlegt, flektierte Formen müssen normalisiert werden. Je nach Ansetzungspraxis muß Plural auf Singular (für das Deutsche) oder Singular auf Plural zurückgeführt werden. Weiterhin müssen, als Vorbereitung einer eventuell mehrstufigen Datenbankanfrage, Synonyme, Hypo- und Hyperonyme sowie eventuell einfache Kategorieninformationen bereitgestellt werden.
Die verwendeten Komponenten sind auf ihr Einsatzgebiet in der Bibliothek hin ausgelegt: Morphologie, Grammatik und Semantik wenden einfache und effiziente Techniken an und nutzen die Vorteile des prinzipiell eingeschränkten Aufgabenbereiches.
Um robust gegenüber fehlerhaftem Input zu sein, muß OSIRIS die häufigsten und einfachsten Eingabefehler erkennen und selbsttätig beheben können. Fehler dieser Art sind einfache Buchstabenvertauschungen, Verdoppelung einzelner Buchstaben sowie Fehlschreibungen durch Benutzung von auf der Tastatur benachbarten Tasten. Insbesondere wird OSIRIS so tolerant gegenüber beliebigen Reformen der Rechtschreibung. Ohne Änderung der Daten ist OSIRIS in der Lage, beispielsweise *Schifffahrt* (mit drei *f*, geplante neue Rechtschreibung) auf *Schiffahrt* (bislang mit zwei *f*) abzubilden.
Flexibilität meint aber auch, daß OSIRIS dem Benutzer im Bereich der notorisch schwierigen Schreibung von Namen hilft. Ganz im Gegensatz zu klassischen OPAC-Systemen ist es in OSIRIS möglich, erfolgreich eine Autorin Namens *Isabelle Ebers* zu suchen, obwohl die betreffende Person *Isabella Schneider-Eberz* heißt. Darüber hinaus sind Benutzer nicht mehr gezwungen, wie OPAC-Systeme es vorschreiben, nach *Mulen, Alice van* zu suchen, sondern können Namen auch in der natürlichen Reihenfolge *Alice van Mulen* eingeben. Und dabei werden

sie auch noch Erfolg haben, wenn die gesuchte Person in Wirklichkeit *Alice ter Meulen* heißt.
Hinsichtlich des Sprachumfangs der zu erwartenden Eingaben stellt das Einsatzgebiet „wissenschaftliche Bibliothek" in struktureller Hinsicht eine echte Einschränkung dar, in lexikalischer aber nicht. Die an OSIRIS gerichteten Anfragen werden stets Suchanfragen nach bestimmten Büchern oder Büchern zu einem Thema sein – OSIRIS ist kein allgemeines Bibliotheksauskunftssystem. Als Input sind also durchweg Nominalphrasen zu erwarten, wie sie als Titel wissenschaftlicher Arbeiten oft verwendet werden: *Mathematikunterricht in der gymnasialen Oberstufe*, *Subventionspolitik und Steuerreform* oder *Automatische Datenerfassung in deutschen Bibliotheken*. OSIRIS kann also problemlos eine eingeschränkte Syntax in der Anfrage voraussetzen, was auf der Oberfläche durch Vorgabe eines Satzanfanges realisiert wird. Im Fall der thematischen Literatursuche wird bspw. vom Benutzer erwartet, daß er den Satz *Ich suche Literatur zum Thema ...* vervollständigt. So wird intuitiv die Eingabe von Nominalphrasen angeregt, ohne daß der Benutzer in seinen Möglichkeiten beschränkt würde.
Trotz Ausbildung von Bestandsschwerpunkten muß in einer wissenschaftlichen Bibliothek aber mit Literatur zu *allen* Wissensgebieten und das in einem Spektrum vom einführenden Werk bis hin zu Tagungsbänden und Dissertationen gerechnet werden. Deshalb muß OSIRIS mit dem gesamten aktuellen wissenschaftlichen Vokabular vertraut sein. Die Schwierigkeiten an dieser Stelle liegen dabei nicht nur in der bloßen Menge des Vokabulars, sondern auch in der zu gewährleistenden Aktualität. Manuell zu wartende Wörterbücher erscheinen uns hier unrealistisch. Wir setzen auf regelbasierte Ansätze, inkrementelle und automatische Lexikonerweiterung, sowie in vielen Bereichen (wie z.B. der Kompositazerlegung) auf Heuristiken. So sind wir in der Lage, auch mit Lexika, die mehrere hunderttausend Einträge umfassen, noch effizient zu arbeiten.

3.2 Die Aufbereitung der Daten

Der zweite Aspekt, mit dem OSIRIS zur Verbesserung der Literaturrecherche beiträgt, ist die Generierung einer Wissensbasis, auf der im laufenden Betrieb gesucht wird. Diese Wissensbasis wird einmal automatisch generiert und später regelmäßig inkrementell erweitert. Die Informationen, die in dieser Wissensbasis zur Verfügung stehen, stammen im wesentlichen aus dem OPAC, in dem mehr Informationen enthalten sind, als sie der Endbenutzer normalerweise sieht. Neben den üblichen Angaben zu Verfasser und Titel finden sich im Idealfall noch deutsche wie fremdsprachige Schlagwörter, Notationen nicht lokaler Klassifikationssysteme und anderes mehr. Daß diese verborgen bleiben, liegt einerseits daran, daß der Endbenutzer bereits mit den jetzt im OPAC verfügbaren Möglichkeiten überfordert ist. Andererseits, und dies ist ein noch viel wichtigerer Grund, liegen die genannten Informationen zumeist nicht flächendeckend vor, wie am Beispiel der Schlagwörter bereits erörtert. Diese Informationen werden von OSIRIS vollständig gesammelt und ausgewertet.
Die Auswertung der Daten beruht darauf, daß bspw. ein Buch mit dem Titel *Lie groups and quantum mechanics*, das von einem Autor namens *Peter Cunning-*

ham veröffentlicht wurde, von einem Fachreferenten der Bibliothek in die lokale Systematik eingeordnet wird, in diesem Fall unter der Notation *TEN*. Dieselbe Arbeit aber hat in einer anderen Bibliothek eventuell auch jemand getan: So ist es gut möglich, daß z.B. in der Deutschen Bibliothek in Frankfurt dem Datensatz die Information angehängt wurde, daß das Buch inhaltlich mit den Themen *Quantenmechanik* und *Lie´sche Gruppe* zu tun hat. Eventuell wurde das Buch auch schon bei Erscheinen klassifiziert. Dann wird in der Library of Congress ein Mitarbeiter festgestellt haben, daß der Autor sich in diesem Werk mit den Gebieten *quantum mechanics* und *lie groups* beschäftigt.
OSIRIS wertet diese Informationen systematisch aus und stellt fest, daß von den Büchern, die in Osnabrück in der Systemstelle *TEN* stehen und Schlagwörter tragen, signifikant viele mit dem Schlagwort *Quantenmechanik* versehen sind. Deutlich weniger Exemplare tragen fremdsprachige Schlagwörter, unter diesen aber sind wiederum signifikant viele mit dem Schlagwort *quantum mechanics* versehen. Offenbar werden in der Systemstelle *TEN* die Bücher klassifiziert, die sich inhaltlich mit dem beschäftigen, was im Deutschen *Quantenmechanik* und im Englischen *quantum mechanics* genannt wird. Das gilt dann natürlich auch für die Bücher, für die keine Schlagwörter vergeben wurden, die aber ebenfalls unter *TEN* klassifiziert wurden. Damit OSIRIS auf dem gesamten Buchbestand suchen kann, ist es also nicht notwendig, daß alle Bücher tatsächlich mit Schlagwörtern versehen sind. Wir schätzen, daß ein Anteil von etwa 30% verschlagworteten Titeln ausreicht, damit OSIRIS erfolgreich eine Wissensbasis aufbauen kann.
Hilfestellung leisten bei den genannten Auswertungen natürlich die computerlinguistischen Komponenten, die für jede Suchanfrage neben der morphologischen Reduktion auch passende Synonyme, Hyponyme und Hyperonyme bereitstellen. So werden auch die genannten Nachteile einer schlagwortbasierten Suche umgangen. Diese computerlinguistische Funktionalität ist herkömmlichen bibliothekarischen Bemühungen um normgerechte Ansetzungen, normiertes Vokabular und manuelle Vervollständigung von Schlagwortmaterial hinsichtlich der Kosten, der Flexibilität, der Verfügbarkeit und Aufgabenangemessenheit weit überlegen.

3.3 Realisierung

OSIRIS ist modular aufgebaut: Alle Komponenten kommunizieren über Internet-Sockets miteinander, so daß die gesamte Anwendung verteilt in einem Netz unter Einbeziehung verschiedener Betriebssysteme (derzeit Linux und Solaris) arbeitet.
Seit der Version 2.0 arbeitet OSIRIS in der Eingabeverarbeitung auf einer Blackboardarchitektur, deren Kernkomponenten der Task Manager, der Parser und das Lexikon sind.
Der Task Manager ist für die syntaktische Vorverarbeitung verantwortlich. Er erhält die Benutzereingaben und kommuniziert mit dem Lexikon- und dem Parserserver. Zu den Aufgaben des Task Managers gehört dabei die wortweise Befragung des Lexikons sowie die Reduktion und Wiedervorlage von als unbekannt zurückgewiesenen Worten. Allgemein finden im Task Manager die Manipulationen statt, die nicht direkt während des Lexikonzugriffs realisiert werden können.

Die Ergebnisse des Lexikonprozesses werden zudem durch den Task Manager sortiert und bewertet und eine Auswahl dem Parserserver übergeben. Das Ergebnis des Parsingprozesses wird mit den Ergebnissen der lexikalischen Analyse vom Task Manager der OSIRIS-Wissensbasis übergeben.

Das Lexikon enthält Stammformeneinträge, wobei Endungen und ggf. erforderliche Umlautungen Bestandteil der lexikalischen Information im Eintrag sind. Beim Lexikonzugriff wird eine morphologische Reduktion vorgenommen, das Ergebnis ist die Zerlegung in Endung und Lemma, erkannte Affixe sowie Kongruenzinformationen. Kompositazerlegungen, Endungsanalyse und Korrektur einfacher Fehlschreibungen erfolgen ebenfalls in diesem Schritt. OSIRIS benötigt große Lexika mit mehr als 300.000 Stammformeneinträgen. Um diesen Anforderungen zu genügen, werden in OSIRIS die Lemmata als Suchschlüssel in einem Buchstabenbaum kodiert und die Inhalte der Einträge separat in einer Datenbank gespeichert. Dabei wird die morphologische Information von einer zugekauften Software erzeugt.[10]

Im Deutschen ist die Beziehung zwischen Konstituenten von Komposita sehr vage und kann daher nur auf der Basis von Heuristiken analysiert werden. So stützt sich die in OSIRIS verwendete Strategie auf die Beobachtung, daß der größtmögliche im Lexikon vorhandene rechte Rand eines Wortes als das spezifischste darin enthaltene bekannte Konzept das geeignete Objekt für die Suche in der Wissensbasis ist. Die Art der Beziehung zu den weiter links stehenden Teilen wird, falls bekannt, als eine unspezifische Modifikationsrelation interpretiert.

Zur Behandlung der notorisch schwierigen Semantik von Präpositionen wird ein einfaches Modell verwendet. Wenn Präpositionen mit einem zeitlichen oder räumlichen Aspekt annotiert sind, „restringieren“ sie das vom Nomen vertretene zentrale Konzept in Raum oder Zeit, andernfalls „modifizieren“ sie es. Anfragen wie „Datenverarbeitung in Bibliotheken“ werden daher semantisch genauso interpretiert wie „Datenverarbeitung in der Bibliothek“, nämlich als „Datenverarbeitung modifiziert-durch Bibliothek“.

Der Parserprozeß analysiert auf der Grundlage einer kontextfreien Grammatik mit Merkmalsannotationen und unter Berücksichtigung der durch den Task Manager gefilterten und sortierten Ergebnisse des Lexikonprozesses die syntaktische Struktur der Eingabe. Die Anforderungen, die OSIRIS an den Parser stellt, bestehen vor allen Dingen in einer optimierten Behandlung von Nominalphrasen sowie geringen Ressourcenansprüchen. Prinzipiell ist OSIRIS nicht auf die Verwendung eines bestimmten Parsers festgelegt. Derzeit wird eine Reimplementation des GEPARD-Parsers[11] eingesetzt, der bereits auf PCs auch mit umfangreichen Lexika und Grammatiken eine hohe Performanz erzielt. Dazu wird eine deklarative Grammatik mittels eines mehrstufigen parametrisierbaren Compilers in ein C-Programm übersetzt, so daß im Ergebnis ein sehr effizienter, für die jeweils gegebene Eingabegrammatik optimierter Chartparser zur Verfügung steht.

---

[10] „GERTWOL“ (deutsch) und „ENGTWOL“ (englisch) der Firma Lingsoft Inc., Helsinki, Finnland.

[11] [Lan96]

In der OSIRIS-Wissensbasis werden mit den Ergebnissen der Eingabeanalyse passende Klassen und Titel gesucht. Das Ergebnis der Suche wird in Abhängigkeit von der Größe der Ergebnismenge bewertet und ggfs. die Darstellung einzelner Klassen unterdrückt. Entspricht die Eingabe einem Buchtitel, so wird dieser Titel auch dann präsentiert, wenn die entsprechende Klasse insgesamt nicht als zur Anfrage passend betrachtet wird. Personennamen sind phonetisch kodiert und in Namensbestandteile zerlegt abgelegt. Der Zugriff auf Namen ist somit weder an die lineare Ordnung der Eingabe noch (in gewissen Grenzen) an die korrekte Schreibweise gebunden. Auch ist es möglich, mit Teilen des Namens, z.B. bei Doppelnamen, erfolgreich zu suchen.
Die OSIRIS-Wissensbasis ist mit jeder Standard-SQL-Datenbank zu realisieren, für den Einsatz von OSIRIS in der Universitätsbibliothek Osnabrück verwenden wir z.Z. Oracle.

4 Beispiele für Retrievalverbesserung

Die deutlichen Verbesserungen der Recherchemöglichkeiten durch OSIRIS zeigen sich nicht nur in einem höheren Recall, sondern auch in der Präzision der Suchergebnisse. Im OPAC sind aufgrund von pattern matching Suchergebnisse hinsichtlich der Benutzeranfrage nicht immer inhaltlich relevant (siehe das Beispiel *Rom* weiter unten). Hingegen werden in OSIRIS Suchergebnisse in der Regel in Form von Klassen präsentiert, denen Bibliothekare Bücher aufgrund ihres Inhaltes zuordnen. Die sich daraus ergebenden Vorteile sollen anhand einiger Beispiele veranschaulicht werden.
So liefert OSIRIS für das bereits erwähnte Beispiel *Sport im Alter* die Klasse *Seniorensport* mit 49 Titeln, sowie die Klassen *Sport und Heilpädagogik* und *Motorisches Lernen.* Im OPAC trifft die Frage nach *Sport im Alter* gerade 5 Titel.
Das ebenfalls bereits angeführte Beispiel *Datenverarbeitung in Bibliotheken* führt im OPAC auf 5 Titel, OSIRIS präsentiert verschiedene Unterklassen von *Buch- und Bibliothekswesen*, darunter auch *Automatisierte Datenerfassung und Datenverarbeitung in der Bibliothek.* Ein Klick auf diese Klasse liefert bereits 38 Titel, die aufgrund der Klassenzugehörigkeit natürlich alle relevant sind. Ein weiterer Klick auf einen der Titel präsentiert denselben in der Vollanzeige. Hier besteht auch die Möglichkeit, das entsprechende Buch in eine eigene Literaturliste zu legen sowie zu überprüfen, ob es eventuell ausgeliehen ist.
Eine Anfrage wie *Chemie* wird am OPAC nicht beantwortet: Die Zahl der Treffer liegt im Bereich von mehreren Tausend, und solche Treffersets werden nicht mehr dargestellt. OSIRIS liefert für die Frage nach *Chemie* genau eine Antwort: Ein Symbol für die Klasse *Chemie.* Klickt der Benutzer auf das die Klasse repräsentierende Symbol, so findet er natürlich nicht alle Titel der chemischen Literatur vor, sondern die Unterklassen des Faches Chemie, *Organische Chemie*, *Anorganische Chemie* usw.
Sucht ein Benutzer nach *machine learning with neural networks*, so findet der OPAC nur ein Buch, in dessen Titel genau die gesuchten Stichworte vorkommen:

Machine learning: neural networks, genetic algorithms, and fuzzy systems. Alle anderen Bücher, insbesondere die deutschsprachigen, werden nicht gefunden. Das ist in der Praxis durchaus ein Problem, denn die deutschen Entsprechungen zu Fachtermini wie bspw. *loop space* oder *string theory* sind ungebräuchlich und deshalb dem Suchenden meist unbekannt. OSIRIS liefert auf die oben genannte Anfrage neben besagtem Werk, dessen Titel mit der Suchanfrage übereinstimmt, weitere Klassen aus Informatik, Künstlicher Intelligenz und Wirtschaftwissenschaften (Statistik). Diese Anfrage wird in OSIRIS nicht mit Hilfe einer Übersetzung bearbeitet, sondern mit den englischsprachigen Schlagwörtern, die in der OSIRIS-Wissensbasis vorhanden sind.

Sucht ein Benutzer im OPAC nach *Morphologie*, so findet er in Osnabrück 289 Titel. Vielen Benutzern ist zunächst unklar, daß ihre Suchbegriffe in anderen Disziplinen mit ganz anderer Bedeutung verwendet werden können (*Morphologie*, *Gruppentheorie* ...). Anhand der unstrukturierten Titelliste, die der OPAC als Ergebnis präsentiert, ist es für den Benutzer schwer zu erkennen, aus welchen Bereichen (Medizin, Biologie, Linguistik usw.) die Treffer stammen. Versucht er dann die hinsichtlich seiner Interessen inhaltlich relevante Teilmenge zu identifizieren, muß er jeden einzelnen Titel betrachten. Dieselbe Anfrage an OSIRIS liefert als Ergebnis die entsprechenden einschlägigen Unterklassen, u.a. für die *Computerlinguistik* die Klasse *Lexikalisches Wissen, Morphologie, Phonetik*, für die *Biologie* in der *Zoologie* und in der *Botanik* die entsprechenden Klassen, für die Einzelsprachen die jeweiligen Unterklassen *Morphologie* usw. usf.

Sucht ein Bibliotheksbenutzer nach Literatur zur Programmiersprache *C*, so wird er im OPAC nicht fündig: *C* ist ein sog. Stoppwort und wird von vornherein nicht zur Suche zugelassen. Die Suche in OSIRIS führt u.a. in der *Informatik* in die Unterklasse *Problemorientierte Programmiersprachen*.

Eine Suche nach Literatur zur Stadt *Rom* endet im OPAC mit einer Liste von 470 Titeln. Da die Suche auf pattern matching basiert, haben etwa 20% der gefundenen Titel nichts mit *Rom* zu tun: Ihnen liegt eine *CD-**Rom*** bei oder der Begriff wird im Titel genannt. OSIRIS liefert eine Klasse *Rom* als Ergebnis.

Neben der Themensuche und der oben bereits erwähnten Autorensuche, können in OSIRIS natürlich auch bestimmte Werke gesucht werden. Im Gegensatz zum OPAC reicht es hier allerdings, wenn man seine Anfrage wie in einer Buchhandlung notiert: *Shoham: Reasoning about Change* findet das entsprechende Werk, *Chomsky Syntactic Structures* findet neben dem englischen Original auch die deutsche Übersetzung.

5 Osiris in der Praxis

Die Laufzeit des OSIRIS-Projektes endet im August 1998. Seit dem Herbst 1997 steht das OSIRIS-System allen Mitgliedern der Universität Osnabrück zur Literaturrecherche zur Verfügung. Seit April 1998 ist die Version 2.0 universitätsweit freigegeben. Interessierte von außerhalb können sich unter `http://www.ub.uni-osnabrueck.de` registrieren lassen, um einen Zugang zu erhalten.

Neben der Literaturrecherche für Endbenutzer wird OSIRIS auch bei der Katalogisierung eingesetzt werden. Für neuerworbene Titel macht das System dem Bibliothekar einen Vorschlag, wie das betreffende Buch lokal klassifiziert werden soll. Die Informationen in der OSIRIS-Wissensbasis über den vorhandenen Bestand sowie eventuell vorliegende Fremddaten für das neu erworbene Buch, machen einen solchen Vorschlag möglich. Diese Technik wird bereits jetzt im experimentellen Betrieb eingesetzt: OSIRIS erzeugt automatisch eine nach Fachgebieten klassifizierte Liste der bestellten und der neu erworbenen Titel, die im WWW für alle Benutzer einsehbar ist.
Die DFG hat bereits Anfang des Jahres eine Verlängerung des Projektes bis Mitte 1999 beschlossen.

Seit Beginn des öffentlichen Betriebes wird das OSIRIS-System von Angehörigen des Fachbereiches Psychologie der Universität Osnabrück unter der Leitung von Dr. Kai-Christoph Hamborg nach software-ergonomischen Gesichtspunkten und hinsichtlich der ISO 9241/10 evaluiert. Ziel dieser Evaluation ist die konkrete Verbesserung der Oberfläche und der derzeitigen Funktionalität auf der Grundlage von Untersuchungen, die Aufschluß geben sollen über die Wünsche und Arbeitsstrategien der Benutzer. Dazu finden Befragungen von Endbenutzern wie von Experten statt, die die Recherchemöglichkeiten von OSIRIS sowie die des OPAC kommentieren sollen. Parallel dazu geht es in Laborexperimenten mit Versuchspersonen darum, anhand komplexer Aufgaben, Suchstrategien bei der Literaturrecherche experimentell zu ermitteln.
Darüber hinaus haben die Evaluationen das Ziel, im OSIRIS-Projekt einen langfristigen Entwicklungszyklus zu induzieren, der die Beobachtung des Einflusses von begleitenden Evaluationsmaßnahmen auf die Softwareentwicklung ermöglicht.

Danksagung Dieser Artikel beschreibt die Arbeit vieler Menschen. Ich danke Helmar Gust, Ingrid Recker, Claus Rollinger, Andreas Rother, Ulrich Sauer, Wilfried Teiken und Hartmut Zillmann für die Zusammenarbeit und hilfreiche Kritik. Für hilfreiche Kommentare danke ich weiterhin zwei anonymen Gutachtern.

Literatur

[Dre94] G. Dreis. *Benutzerverhalten an einem Online-Publikumskatalog für wissenschaftliche Bibliotheken: Ergebnisse und Erfahrungen aus dem OPAC-Projekt der Universitätsbibliothek Düsseldorf.* No. 57 in Zeitschrift für Bibliothekswesen und Bibliographie, Sonderhefte. Klostermann, 1994.

[Lan96] H. Langer. Disambiguierung von Präpositionalkonstruktionen mit einem Syntaktischen Parser. In S. Mehl, A. Mertens und M. Schulz, Hrsg., *Präpositionalsemantik und PP-Anbindung.* Uni Duisburg, 1996.

[RRZ96] I. Recker, M. Ronthaler und H. Zillmann. OSIRIS (Osnabrück Intelligent Research Information System) - ein Hyperbase Front End System für OPACs. *Bibliotheksdienst*, 30(5):833–848, 5 1996.

[Sch94] U. Schulz. Was wir über OPAC-Nutzer wissen: Fehlertolerante Suchprozesse in OPACs. *ABI-Technik*, 14(4):299–310, 1994.

Moderne Informationstechnologie und ihre Auswirkungen auf die korpus-basierte Forschung

P. Wittenburg, H. Brugman, D. Broeder, A. Russel

Max-Planck-Institut für Psycholinguistik
Wundtlaan 1, NL 6525 XD Nijmegen
Peter.Wittenburg@mpi.nl

Zusammenfassung. Die technologische Entwicklung ermöglicht es den Sozialwissenschaften, distribuierte multi-mediale Korpora mittels Internet-Technologien aufzubauen. Das EUDICO Projekt hat das Ziel, kooperierenden, jedoch an verschiedenen Orten arbeitenden Wissenschaftlern eine einheitliche, format-unabhängige Schnittstelle zu den verschiedenen sprach- und video-basierten Korpora zu bieten. Zur Erreichung dieses Zieles wurde eine moderne Softwarearchitektur implementiert, die die in den Korpora vorhandenen gemeinsamen linguistischen Konzepte abbildet. Die Verwendung von Java-APIs wie dem JavaMediaFramework und modernen Streaming-Protokollen erlaubt die Realisierung einer interaktiven Schnittstelle. Mit EUDICO wurde eine Architektur geschaffen, die einen Schritt hin zu einem universellen Werkzeug für die korpus-basierte Forschung darstellt, zumal es in einfacher Weise möglich ist, weitere Objektklassen hinzuzufügen.

1 Einleitung

In Forschungsdisziplinen wie z.B. der Linguistik wurden in den letzten Jahrzehnten große Text-Korpora gebildet, die der Ausgangspunkt zur Theoriebildung und zu deren Überprüfung mittels computationeller Methoden waren. Beispiele hierfür sind das Kindersprachkorpus (CHILDES) [1], das Zweitsprachserwerbskorpus (ESF) [2], das British National Corpus (BNC) [3], und das Korpus gefährdeter Sprachen [4]. In diesen Korpora waren Verweise angebracht, um auf die auf Kassetten gespeicherten Sprach- und Video-Materialien zurückgreifen zu können. Faktisch wurde jedoch von dieser Möglichkeit kein Gebrauch gemacht, was bei den größeren Korpora zu einem umfassenden, teuren und fehlerbehafteten Transkriptions- und Codierungsprozeß führte. Insbesondere die fehlerbehafteten und subjektiven Codierungen schafften immer wieder Probleme bezüglich der Gültigkeit wissenschaftlicher Aussagen.

Die durch die technologischen Entwicklungen der letzten Jahre ermöglichte Verwendung rechnergestützter Multi-Media-Techniken erlaubt jeweils einen direkten Zugriff des Wissenschaftlers auf die interessierende Sequenz des Originalsignals. Für die korpus-basierte Forschung stellt dies einen wesentlichen Entwicklungssprung dar, was mit Systemen wie den am MPI entwickelten MED (MediaEditor) [5], TED (TranscriptionEditor) and MT (MediaTagger) [6] nachgewiesen werden konnte. Allerdings gehören derartige Spezialsysteme mit ihrer Bindung an bestimmte Hardware- und Software-Plattformen und dem zur Installation und zum Betreiben erforderlichen Spezialwissen nicht zur selbstverständlichen Ausrüstung in sozialwissenschaftlichen Abteilungen. Ebenfalls sind diese Spezialsysteme gebunden an die jeweiligen speziellen Korpusformate, d.h sie sind keine Werkzeuge, mit denen auf die verschiedenen die Wissenschaftler interessierenden Korpora zugegriffen werden kann. Für viele Korpora wurden eigenständige Formate gewählt und eigene Zugriffswerkzeuge entwickelt, die auf die Formate aufbauen, also kaum übertragbar sind.

Diese und andere Beschränkungen wurden von verschiedenen Gruppen im Bereich der Grundlagenwissenschaft aber auch des Language Engineering erkannt. Verschiedene Lösungsvorschläge wurden inzwischen präsentiert. Die auf SGML basierenden Standardisierungsvorschläge der TEI (Text Encoding Initiative) [7] sollten helfen, Korpora mit einheitlichen Tags zu entwickeln. Allerdings zeigt es sich in der Praxis, daß dort, wo viel Flexibilität und viele Annotationsschichten erforderlich sind, SGML-basierte Strukturen zu großen Problemen führen. Im Rahmen europäischer Initiativen wurden die EAGLES Standards [8] entwickelt. Hierbei handelt es sich um Vorschläge für einheitliche Korpora vor allem für den Bereich der Automatischen Spracherkennung und des Language Engineering. Diese Codierungsvorschläge müssen bei zukünftigen Projekten sicherlich berücksichtigt werden. Allerdings muß sich ihre Anwendbarkeit noch in der Praxis zeigen.

Neben den bereits genannten Entwicklungen am Max-Planck-Institut haben sich auch andere Gruppen aktiv mit der Frage der Extension der Korpora um sprachliche Informationen und Bewegtbilder befaßt. Zu nennen sind hier die Projekte des IDS (SERGES [9]), die sprachliche Informationen zu ihren Korpora hinzufügen wollen, allerdings auf sehr spezielle Lösungen vertrauen, verschiedener Gruppen im Bereich der Zeichensprache (NSDSK [10], SignStream [11]), die aufgrund ihrer speziellen Anwendung ebenfalls zu speziellen Lösungen kommen, *der Informedia Digital Video Library* Vorschlag [12] und der *Networking Linguistic Information* Vorschlag [13], der der NSF zur Entscheidung vorliegt. Beide zuletzt genannten Vorschläge sind sehr breit angelegt, fokussieren zu einem Teil auch auf die Entwicklung neuartiger Basistechnologien wie z.B. der Verwendung von Methoden der Bilderkennung zum automatischen Inidizieren von Video-Material.

Die Aufgabe, Korpora im Internet verfügbar zu machen, wurde inzwischen von mehreren Gruppen anerkannt. Allerdings nur wenige haben dies mit den Forderungen nach Format-Unabhängigkeit, Plattform-Unabhängigkeit, der Möglichkeit des Zugriffs auf distribuierte Korpora und der Wiederverwendbarkeit von Softwarekomponenten verknüpft. Hier sind zu nennen die Tipster-Architektur [14], die ein flexibles, auf Datenbank-Technologien beruhendes Annotationsformat vorgeschlagen und implementiert hat (jede Annotation wird mit einem Span im Text assoziiert) und von mehreren Projekten als Basis genommen wird, das ALEP-Projekt [15], das einen allgemeinen Werkzeugkasten für Linguisten und Sprachtechnologen zur Verfügung stellt, dessen Architektur jedoch einer allgemeineren Verwendbarkeit im Wege steht, die GATE Architektur [16], die auf Tipster basiert, den Gedanken der Wiederverwendbarkeit von Software-Komponenten in den Vordergrund gestellt hat und nunmehr ebenfalls die Forderung nach einem *Common Linguistic Object Model* erhoben hat, und das Calypso-Projekt [17], das ebenfalls auf Tipster und GATE Komponenten basiert und bereits für eine spezielle Anwendung Erfahrungen mit distribuierten und linguistisch motivierten Objektklassen gesammelt hat.

Das EUDICO Projekt des Max-Planck-Instituts [18] ist in mehrerer Hinsicht neben dem *Networking Linguistic Information* Projekt [13] am allgemeinsten formuliert, da es die oben-genannten Forderungen enthält und auch konsequent davon ausgeht, daß Korpora heute multi-medial sind, d.h. die multi-mediale Information wird nicht nur als ein Zusatz angesehen. Es ist auch am weitesten fortgeschritten, da bereits ein Objektklassen-Modell entworfen und implementiert wurde. Allerdings muß hinzugefügt werden, daß dieses Modell nur beanspruchen kann, die linguistischen Konzepte der im Institut zur Anwendung kommenden Korpora abzubilden, während andere Projekte [13,16,17] diesbezüglich weitergehen wollen.

2 Multi-Media Korpora

Existierende Text-Korpora wurden inzwischen mit Sprachinformationen ergänzt, wobei im allgemeinen das existierende Text-basierte Format als Ausgangspunkt genommen wurde. In einer Annotationsschicht (tier) wird einer Äußerung ein entsprechendes Segment aus dem Sprachsignal zugewiesen. Das im MPI entwickelte Werkzeug gestattet es dem Benutzer, durch ein einfaches Kommando eine Sprachanalysesoftware zu starten, wobei das Fenster genau das Sprachsegment umfaßt, das zu der gerade betrachteten Äußerung gehört. Wichtig für den Wissenschaftler ist die enge Synchronisation der Cursor und die Mächtigkeit der Operatoren in den beiden Domänen. So erwartet er in der Sprachdomäne z.B. die Verfügbarkeit eines Grundfrequenzdetektors, da gerade diese Information für linguistische Analysen auf höheren Ebenen von großer Bedeutung ist.

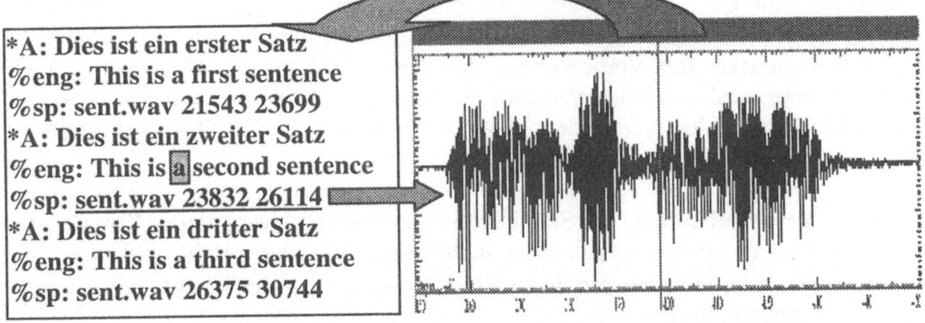

Abb. 1: Im linken Fenster ist ein Abschnitt aus einer typischen Textdatei im CHAT-Format [1] enthalten. Beim Aufruf der Sprachumgebung wird das zu dieser Äußerung gehörende Sprachsegment sichtbar gemacht, zu dem in einem abhängigen Tier eine Referenz existieren muß. Umgekehrt muß die Cursorposition in der Sprachumgebung für die Editierumgebung verfügbar sein.

Bei neuen Korpora wie z.B. dem Gestikulationskorpus-Projekt am MPI mußten neben der sprachlichen Information auch die entsprechenden Videosequenzen direkt zugreifbar sein. Da es in diesem Projekt keine existierenden Formatvorschriften gab, wurde aufgrund einer Reihe von Kriterien eine relationale Datenbank als Backend-Struktur gewählt. Die digitalisierten Sprach- und Videosignale sind in Quicktime Containern enthalten. In Echtzeit werden die verschiedenen selektierten Tiers (Sound, Video, Texttiers) derart zusammengeführt, daß sie synchron auf dem Bildschirm erscheinen. In diesem Projekt war es möglich, konzeptuell neue Wege zu gehen und von der durch das Videosignal fest vorgegebenen Zeitachse auszugehen. Auf diese können sich alle Annotationen beziehen, d.h. alle Codierungen in einem Tier haben jeweils eine Anfangs- und eine Endzeitmarke. Diese Art der Codierung gestattet es in einfacher Weise, zeitliche Relationen zwischen Aktivitäten zu codieren und auch zu erfragen. Die Vielzahl der Tiers (bis über 40), die Trennung zwischen den Codierungen verschiedener kooperierender Wissenschaftler und vor allem die Tatsache, daß das Korpus fortwährenden Anpassungen unterliegen wird, waren ein weiteres Argument für die Verwendung einer Datenbankstruktur. Obwohl im Tipster-Projekt [14] lediglich Textbestände zu verwalten sind, kam man unabhängig von der Arbeit am MPI zu der gleichen Backend-Struktur. Alle Annotationen werden in Tipster einem Span zugeordnet, wobei hier die Byte-Positionen im ursprünglichen Text angegeben werden. Die bisherigen Erfahrungen zeigen die Überlegenheit dieser Struktur gegenüber traditionelleren Methoden.

Die durch den MediaTagger zur Verfügung gestellte Benutzerschnittstelle mit der synchronen Darstellung der verschiedenen Informationen, einer flexiblen Datenbank inklusive des dazugehörigen flexiblen und graphisch unterstützten Querybuilders, der Interaktion zwischen einer Datenbank, die formale Suchfragen auf den Codierungen gestattet, und der multi-media Umgebung mittels einer Liste von gefundenen Sequenzen, und der interaktiven Dateneingabe können als Vorbild für weitere Projekte dienen.

3 Verteilte multi-mediale Korpora

3.1 Anforderungen

Obwohl mit der direkten Verfügbarmachung multi-medialer Informationen ein erheblicher Beitrag zur Verbesserung der wissenschaftlichen Methodik geleistet werden konnte, sind mit den gegenwärtigen Systemen MED und MT eine Reihe von erheblichen Nachteilen verbunden. Daher wurde das EUDICO Projekt mit den folgenden Zielsetzungen begonnen:

- Vereinheitlichung der Schnittstelle unabhängig davon, ob der Korpus neben Texttiers Sprach- oder auch Video-Informationen beinhaltet
- Realisierung eines mit den jetzigen Systemen vergleichbaren Benutzerkomforts
- plattform-unabhängige Zugriffswerkzeuge
- format-unabhängige Zugriffswerkzeuge, d.h. Entwurf einer Klassenhierarchie basierend auf den linguistischen Konzepten unabhängig von den diversen Korpusformaten
- Verwendung von Standard-Internet Benutzerschnittstellen, um die ersten Interaktionen durchzuführen, d.h. "browsable" Korpora
- Erzeugung verschiedener sinnvoller Visualisierungen
- Unterstützung möglichst weitgehender Zeichensätze (UNICODE)
- Ermöglichung eines zentralen Daten- und Software-Managements und eines Zugriffs auf die Korpora von im Intranet und Internet verteilten Arbeitsplätzen
- Verwendung moderner Software-Technologie (Java Multi-Media APIs, RMI)

- Verwendung aktueller Streaming-Protokolle
- Ausführung der für die Korpora bereits existierenden Programme

Benutzerschnittstelle. Bezüglich des Entwurfs der Benutzerschnittstelle konnte auf die Erfahrungen und Entwürfe aus früheren Projekten zurückgegriffen werden. Allerdings ist der Einsatz der Browser-Technologie heute für nahezu alle Benutzer ein Standard, so daß eine neue anwendungsorientierte Schnittstelle in der Wissenschaft nur in den durch die Browser allgemein definierten Rahmen eingebettet sein kann. Sie ermöglicht es dem Benuzter, sich ohne weiteren Lernaufwand mit einem Informationssystem zu befassen, und bei Korpora handelt es sich um wissenschaftliche Informationssysteme.

Linguistisch motivierte Klassenhierarchie. Die Wissenschaftler werden heute mit verschiedenen Formaten und auch Codierungssystemen konfrontiert, die es z.B. faktisch unmöglich machen, die Gemeinsamkeiten zwischen mehreren Korpora in wissenschaftlichen Fragestellungen auszunutzen. Dies liegt vor allem an den existierenden format-spezifischen Zugriffsprogrammen, die nur mit großem Aufwand erweiterbar wären. Die existierenden Korpusformate sind ein Fakt, da die Korpora ständig ergänzt werden und sich die existierenden vielfältigen Zugriffswerkzeuge nicht kurzfristig neu entwickeln lassen. Wie oft in der praktischen Informatik liegt die in Abbildung 2 skizzierte Situation vor.

Abb. 2: Die in EUDICO definierten und linguistisch motivierten Objektklassen bilden alle relevanten Korpora mittels Filter ab. Auf diese können neue einheitliche Werkzeuge aufsetzen. Die Benutzerschnittstelle und auch die Systemarchitektur müssen jedoch derartig sein, daß auch die existierenden Werkzeuge anwendbar sind, soweit sie nicht durch neue obsolet geworden sind. Die Filter definieren ein API.

In gleicher Weise wie im Gate- [16], im Calypso-Projekt [17] und auch im *Networking Linguistic Information* Vorschlag [13] wurde zum Erreichen einer Format-Unabhängigkeit der Weg gewählt, eine abstrakte und flexibel erweiterbare Schicht von Objektklassen zu entwerfen, die ausgeht von den in den für uns relevanten Korpora zu findenden linguistischen Konzepten. Eine solche Vorgehensweise erübrigt auch den bisherigen Unterschied zwischen Textkorpora, Korpora mit Spracherweiterung und solchen mit Videoerweiterung. In EUDICO müssen die folgenden Formate berücksichtigt werden: CHAT-Format [1], Shoebox-Format [19], Tabellen einer relationalen Datenbank und SGML/XML-Format. Die typischen abzubildenden Korpus-Entitäten sind: Korpus, Subkorpus, Transkription, Tiers, Tags, Mediaobjekt. Bei einem Tag handelt es sich um ein komplexes Objekt, das eine geordnete Gruppe von Codierungen (die Annotationen) umfaßt und mittels eines Zeitintervals auf die durch den Mediastrom vorgegebene Zeitachse referiert.

Eine internationale Kooperation der erwähnten Entwicklungsgruppen muß absichern, daß ein hohes Maß an Einheitlichkeit bezüglich der Objektklassen-Definitionen geschaffen wird. Nur diese garantiert, daß das Ziel wiederverwendbarer und austauschbarer Software erreicht werden kann. Im EUDICO Projekt wurden bisher lediglich die abstrakteren Korpuskonzepte abgebildet, andere wie z.B. Syntaxbeschreibungen und semantische Codierungen sind noch zu modellieren, lassen sich jedoch einfach in den vorhandenen Rahmen als Spezialisierungen einfügen.

Die optimale Integration existierender Werkzeuge ist noch nicht vollständig ausgearbeitet. Diese sind zum großen Teil batch-orientiert, d.h. operieren auf einer oder mehreren Korpusdateien. Eine volle Integration würde erfordern, daß sie z.B. auch über einer Selektion von Korpusteilen ausführbar sein müßten und ihre Ausgaben auch über die Filter in die Klassenhierarchie eingefügt werden kann.

Plattformunabhängigkeit. Die Forderung nach Plattformunabhängigkeit ist evident, im Detail aber schwer zu realisieren. Als Beispiel sei hier die in der Wissenschaft erforderliche Flexibilität bezüglich des Satzes der phonetischen Zeichen genannt. Diese Zeichensätze sind gegenwärtig nicht standardisiert. Die größten Anforderungen bezüglich des Zeichensatzes stellen in unserem Bereich die Konversations-Analytiker, die z.B. Pfeile zur Darstellung prosodischer Merkmale verwenden. Die Standardisierung auf den UNICODE ist ein großer Fortschritt.

Visualisierungen. Für z.B. Linguisten sind verschiedene Visualisierungen wünschenswert, um Korpora lesbar zu machen. So mag die Verwendung von SGML zur Erzeugung eines sauber strukturierten Korpus und als Austauschformat interessant sein, für den wissenschaftlichen Benuzter sind tag-behaftete Formate nicht lesbar. Für die Linguisten sind z.B. spaltenorientierte Darstellungen oder Partiturschemata von großer Bedeutung. Diese müssen an der Benutzerschnittstelle erzeugt werden können. Die Definition einer Klassenhierarchie ermöglicht es, die Visualisierungen ausgehend von den linguistischen Konzepten einheitlich vorzunehmen.

Java-Technologie. Andere Anforderungen ergeben sich aus der Sicht der modernen Informatik und aus Kostenüberlegungen. Ein zentrales Daten- und Software-Management würde den gegenwärtigen, zum Teil großen Aufwand für die Distribution und Fehlerbehebung beseitigen. Natürlich muß ein solches Projekt auf den neuesten Standards wie z.B. Java und seinen APIs aufsetzen. Insbesondere das Java Media Framework bietet sehr viele Möglichkeiten, indem es z.B. die Synchronisation verschiedener Mediaströme als ein Option beinhaltet. Für jeden der Mediaströme (diverse Texttiers, Sprache, Video) wird ein Media-Player instanziiert und mit einfachen Aufrufen können wir diese Ströme, die von verschiedenen Servern erzeugt werden können, auf dem Client zur Synchronisation bringen. Java gibt uns auch die Möglichkeiten, eine weitgehende Plattform-Unabhängigkeit zu realisieren und die Software-Distribution mittels Applets elegant zu lösen. Auch auf den Servern laufen Java-Applikationen, so daß eine objekt-orientierte Kommunikation zwischen Client- und Server-Programmen einfach implementiert werden kann.

Netzwerkprotokolle. Eine andere wichtige Frage ist die nach der Verwendung der zum Einsatz kommenden Netzwerk-Protokolle. Von großer Wichtigkeit sind RTP

(Realtime Protokoll) [20] und RTSP (Real Time Streaming Protokoll) [21]. Während RTP lediglich jedem Datagram einen Zeitstempel mitgibt, bietet RTSP mehrere Eigenschaften auf der Protokoll-Ebene, die sonst durch die Anwendungsprogramme gelöst werden müßten. Als Beispiel sei hier der Buffermechanismus auf der Client-Seite genannt, der bei schwankenden Bitraten und aus Effizienzüberlegungen von großer Bedeutung ist. RTSP kann sowohl auf das unzuverlässige Datagram Protokoll (UDP), auf das zuverlässige Datagram Protokoll (RDP) oder ein zuverlässiges Protokoll wie TCP aufsetzen. RTP basiert auf dem effizienten UDP. Das unter HTTP standardmäßig zum Einsatz kommende TCP kann aufgrund seiner Ineffizienz nicht zur Übertragung von Mediadaten empfohlen werden. RTSP ist noch nicht standardisiert und an proprietäre Lösungen wie RealVideo gebunden, die für EUDICO nicht in Frage kommen. Gegenwärtig wird daher eine RTP-basierte Kommunikation getestet, da auch JMF dieses Protokoll unterstützt.

3.2 System Architektur

Ausgehend von den Anforderungen wurde die Architektur des Systems entworfen (siehe Abbildung 3).

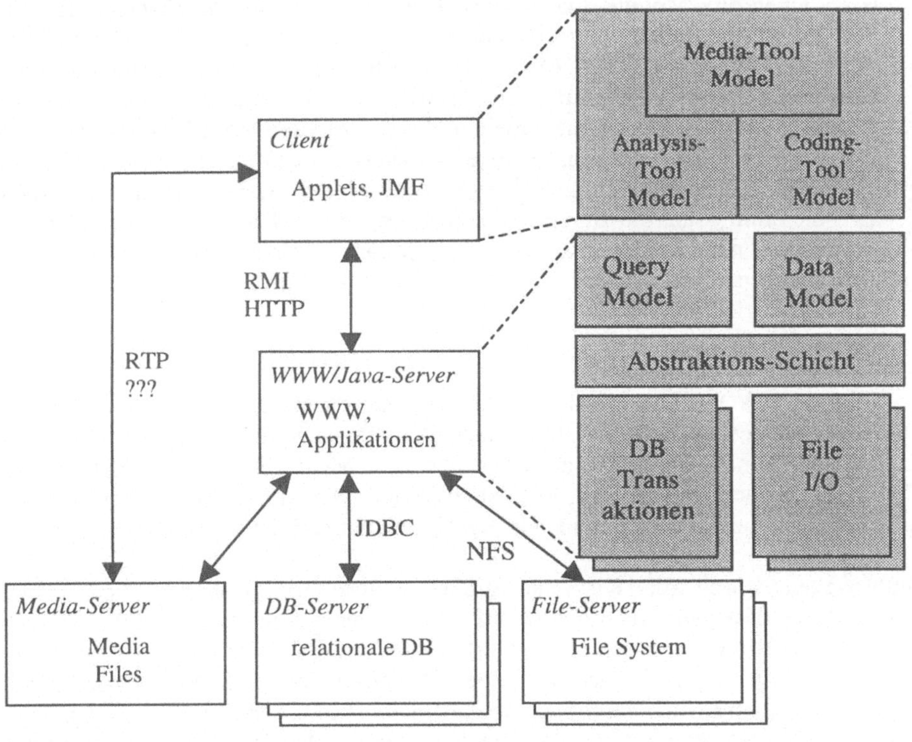

Abb. 3 stellt die Systemarchitektur von EUDICO schematisch dar. Dabei deuten die hellen Blöcke auf logische Serversysteme hin, die in verschiedener Weise auf physikalische Server abbildbar sind. Die dunklen Blöcke beschreiben wesentliche Software-Module, die den verschiedenen Server-Ebenen zugeordnet werden können.

Verschiedene (logische) Server können involviert sein, um die Multi-Media Korpora für die Clients verfügbar zu machen. Der zentrale Server ist der WWW-Server, er stellt die Eingangsseiten zur Verfügung, mit dessen Hilfe der Benutzer seine

Interaktion starten und seine Korpusauswahl vornehmen kann. Bei Bedarf sendet dieser Server Applets zum Client und startet selbst Java-Programme. Diese kommunizieren untereinander mit Hilfe von RMI (Remote Method Invocation), das in einfacher Weise den Zugriff auf remote Java-Objekte gestattet. Bei Bedarf wird der WWW-Server einen Datenbank-Server ansprechen, auf dem sich die Datenbank befindet. Hierbei kommt die JDBC-Middleware zum Einsatz. Da andere Korpora auf traditionellen File-Systemen aufbauen, wird der WWW/Java-Server mittels NFS auch auf derartige Bestände zugreifen. Ebenfalls wird er dafür sorgen, daß der Media-Server, auf dem sich die Sprach- bzw. Videodaten befinden, angestoßen wird. Zur Übermittlung der Media-Daten wird ein geeignetes Protokoll wie z.B. RTP zum Einsatz kommen.

Wie bereits beschrieben wird eine Abstraktionsschicht die verschiedenen Korporaformate (relationale DB, traditionelle Formate wie zB. CHAT, aber auch SGML-Dateien) einheitlich abbilden, so daß die höheren Schichten mittels eines einzigen API auf die Korpora zugreifen können. Auf dem WWW-Server werden die Suchfragen behandelt und die Resultate werden übernommen. Auf dem Client laufen im wesentlichen drei Module. Das Coding Tool Model umfaßt Werkzeuge, die dem Benutzer die Korpus-Inhalte in geeigneter Form präsentieren und deren Manipulation erlauben. Das Analysis Tool Model beschreibt alle Interface und diejenigen Interaktionen, die Suchfragen auf dem Korpus erlauben. Beide Module werden mit dem Media Tool Model zusammenarbeiten, das die Media-Darstellung in geeigneter Form übernimmt und durchaus andere spezialisierte Programme für z.B. die Sprachanalyse aufrufen kann. Das Media Tool Model muß auch alle wichtigen Mechanismen umfassen, die zum effizienten Umgang mit den Media-Daten gehören, jedoch noch nicht von Netzwerk-Protokollen gelöst werden wie z.B. Buffermechanismen und eine Prüfung der Kapazität der Verbindung zur Bestimmung optimaler Strategien.

3.3 Stand des Projektes

Ein Prototyp des Systems wurde erfolgreich getestet. Es umfaßt die wesentlichen Komponenten der Systemarchitektur unter Verzicht auf Teile des User-Interfaces. Insbesondere konnte die Verwendbarkeit des Java Media Framework API und der RMI-Mechanismen mit Erfolg getestet werden. Mehrere Media-Player konnten instanziiert und problemlos miteinander synchronisiert werden.

Mittlerweilen wurde die Klassenhierarchie vollständig spezifiziert und mittels verschiedener Beispiele theoretisch auf ihre Vollständigkeit überprüft. Für den Gestikulationskorpus wurde ein Filter mittels JDBC implementiert und die Funktionstüchtigkeit der Klassendefinitionen bewiesen. Wichtige Komponenten, wie z.B. eine allgemeine Suchmaschine zum Auffinden strukturierter Muster in den Text-Korpora, wurden entworfen und implementiert. Das Design der Benutzerschnittstellen wurde auf der Basis der Erfahrungen mit den jetzigen Systemen überarbeitet und ergänzt.

4 Ausblick

Die Einführung multi-medialer Techniken in den Sozialwissenschaften sowohl in der Forschung als auch in der Ausbildung stellt eine wesentliche Verbesserung dar, da es der analysierenden Person die reale Möglichkeit gibt, nicht nur auf der Basis abstrakter Zeichen zu operieren, sondern die ursprüngliche Sprach- oder Videoinformation mit einzubeziehen. Dadurch werden Aussagen über das zu analysierende Material wesentlich fundierter. Ebenfalls wird es jetzt möglich, nur genau die Transkriptionen bzw. Codierungen vorzunehmen, die für das jeweilige Projekt erforderlich sind. Die Möglichkeit der inkrementellen Ergänzung eines Korpus wird die Fehlerraten ebenfalls erheblich verkleinern.

Die vorhandenen Benutzerschnittstellen haben sich bewährt und können in neuen Lösungen wie z.B. EUDICO wiederverwendet werden. Es kann erwartet werden, daß wir am Ende des Jahres 98 Pilottests mit der EUDICO-Umgebung und dem darunter verfügbaren Gestikulations-Korpus ausführen können.

Wir erwarten auch aufgrund anderer ähnlicher Initiativen, daß multi-media Systeme wie EUDICO, die den Zugriff auf verteilte Korpora im Intranet/Internet erlauben, in wenigen Jahren die Wissenschaft stark beeinflussen und auch in die Ausbildung einziehen werden. Sie werden die Kooperation von Wissenschaftlern verstärken, die von verschiedenen Orten aus am gleichem Korpus arbeiten. Die zu erwartende zunehmende internationale Kooperation wird den Druck auf Standardisierungen erhöhen. Von dem sich jetzt abzeichnenden Trend zu einer einheitlichen linguistisch motivierten Klassenhierarchie kann viel erwartet werden. Die existierenden Korpusformate werden dabei als Fakt hingenommen und die Standardisierungsbemühungen werden auf die operationale Ebene verlagert. Bei geeigneten gemeinsamen Spezifikationen eröffnet sich die Möglichkeit der Entwicklung gemeinsamer Werkzeuge für die Analyse und die Visualisierung.

Die Verwendung multi-medialer Informationen wird neue Suchverfahren erfordern. Wissenschaftler werden mit Mustererkennungsalgorithmen ähnliche Laute oder auch Gesten (Bewegtbilder) im Korpus auffinden wollen. Für sprachliche Laute ist dies heute durchaus machbar, die Verfahren zum Auffinden ähnlicher Images bzw. Imagefolgen sind noch nicht ausreichend und sie kosten noch zu viel Rechenkapazität.

Wir werden eine Veränderung der Organisation des Wissenschaftsbetriebes erleben, wenn sich die genannten Techniken durchsetzen. Abhängig von den zur Verfügung stehenden Bandbreiten und deren Kosten werden sich Zentren herausbilden, die die Korpora pflegen, spezielle Kompetenzen anbieten und entsprechend leistungsfähige Server betreiben. Der Rücklauf der verschiedenen neuen Codierungen in das Korpus wird schneller als bisher erfolgen, allerdings muß ein Prozeß der kooperativen Qualitätsüberprüfung erarbeitet werden.

Anmerkung:
Das EUDICO Projekt wird u.a. von SURFNET, dem Betreiber des niederländischen Wissenschaftsnetzes, finanziert. Mehrere linguistische Abteilungen insbesondere niederländischer Universitäten unterstützen dieses Projekt.

Referenzen

[1] B. MacWhinney: The Childes Project. LEA Hillsdale, New Yersey. 1995
[2] C. Perdue: Adult Language Acquisition. Vol. 1: Field Methods. Cambridge University Press. 1993
http://www.mpi.nl/world/tg/lapp/esf/esf.html
[3] G. Aston, L. Bernard: The BNC Handbook. Edinburgh University Press. 1998
[4] Internal Documentation, MPI for Psycholinguistics
[5] http://www.mpi.nl/world/tg/spoken-childes/spoken-childes.html
[6] H.G. Brugman, S. Kita: Impact of digital video technology on transcription: A case of spontaneous gesture transcription. In Kodikas/Code, Volume 18 No 1-3, 95-112. 1995
http://www.mpi.nl/world/tg/CAVA/CAVA.html
[7] The Text Encoding Initiative. http://www-tei.uic.edu/orgs/tei
[8] http://coral.lili.uni-bielefeld.de/EAGLES/eagbook/eagbook
[9] http://www.ids-mannheim.de/ldo/serges.html
[10] T. Schermer: SignBase: a multi-media database for signed and spoken languages. Workshop on Constructing and Accessing Multi-Media Corpora. Nijmegen, 1998
[11] http://webdev.bu.edu/ASLLRP/SignStream
[12] http://www.informedia.cs.cmu.edu/info/project.html
[13] A. Akinlabi, St. Bird, P. Buneman, W. Leben, M. Liberman: Project Description: Creating and Disseminating Knowledge about the World's Languages. http://www.ldc.upenn.edu/myl/annotations.html
[14] http://www.tipster.org/arch.htm
[15] http://www.anite-systems.lu/alep
[16] H. Cunningham, W. Peters, C. McCauley, K. Bontcheva, Y. Wilks: Uniform Language Reource Access and Distribution. Workshop on Distributing and Accessing Linguistic Resources. Granada, 1998
[17] R. Zajac: Reuse and Integration of NLP Components in the Calypso Architecture. Workshop on Distributing and Accessing Linguistic Resources. Granada, 1998
[18] H. Brugmann, A. Russel, P. Wittenburg, R. Piepenbrock: Corpus-based Research using the Internet. Workshop on Distributing and Accessing Linguistic Resources. Granada, 1998
[19] http://www.sil.org
[20] ftp://ftp.ripe.net/rfc/rfc1889.txt
[21] http://www.real.com/rtsp/index.html

Real-Time 3-D Interaction from Monocular Video Image Flows

Ulrich Bröckl-Fox

Pape und Partner Media GmbH
Schottweg 3, D-22087 Hamburg
Email: ub@ppi.de

Abstract. Concepts of 3-D human-computer interaction based on 2-D images of the user's hand, obtained with a monocular vision system, are presented. From the images, 2-D parameters describing location and shape of the hand are extracted using moments and signatures. These parameters are mapped into 3-D movements to which intuitive metaphorical meanings are assigned. The resulting metaphors are evaluated using a network–distributed virtual squash game. Their effectiveness is compared with that of the space-ball, measuring the user's ability to translate, rotate and accelerate for each input device/metaphor. As an application, a remote control system is described that allows presentations using HTML-pages that are controlled by hand gestures. The system shows a robust behavior even under the rather weak light conditions imposed by the darkness needed for the video beamers.

1 Introduction

A large variety of 3D-input devices exists on the market. Among these the data-glove rules the virtual-reality market, and the space-ball the desktop market. The latter was shown in [7] to be nearly as efficient as the data-glove, and both are stated to be up to two times more effective than mouse-driven metaphors such as those described in [5]. However, according to [17], only 14% of desktop applications currently developed use 3-D graphics. Of these nearly none is pure 3-D: at least some choices, menu selections or options have to be entered, for which the mouse or keyboard are preferable devices. Hence, 2-D and 3-D input devices should be used simultaneously. This observation, however, has implications on the 3-D devices. For example, a data-glove is more likely to be a handicap than an advantage under this condition while the space-ball is well suited.

Another approach that is of interest in this setting is vision-based 3-D human-computer interaction. Cameras are becoming more and more a standard equipment for current multimedia workstations. This observation might be a main reason for the continuously increasing number of concepts and systems using video input as a device for human-computer interaction [14]. Like for the space-ball, for vision-based interaction the hands remain free, hence allowing an easy change to mouse and keyboard. In contrast to the space-ball device, vision offers the advantage of being often available without extra cost.

In this contribution, the possibilities of using a single camera for 3-D interaction are addressed, and compared to those of the space-ball. The particular challenge of the one-camera configuration is that a single camera limits the possibilities of spatial recognition. On the other hand, the costs and computational efforts are less than for multiple camera systems.

In section 2, a set of relevant 2-D parameters is suggested that can efficiently be calculated from the images of the camera. These parameters describe the location and the shape of the hand. Technically, the parameters are obtained from moments of the hand region in the image and the signature of the contour of the hand region. The advantage of the approach is that all these 2-D parameters can be won by integration, not by differentiation on the image, which makes the system less sensitive to noise. In section 3, the parameters are used for gesture classification of the observed shapes. In section 4, mappings of the parameters into 3-D movements are described to which intuitive metaphorical meanings are assigned. The resulting interactive "screw", "thumb", and "gear" metaphors serve for specifying 3-D translational and rotational movements of spatial objects by the user. In section 5, an evaluation of these metaphors is presented. The evaluation was performed using a virtual squash game. Main results are:

- In comparison to the space-ball, the precision of translations is slightly worse (factor 0.90), the number of hits (factor 1.19) and the velocity of the virtual squash-racket (factor 1.25) is slightly better, and the precision of rotations (factor 2.00) is supreme for the proposed metaphors.
- There is almost no need to provide six degrees of freedom at once with an input device: users, especially when untrained, tend to divide a manipulation task requiring both translation and rotation into several single-operation phases.
- Stable hand-shape recognition that notices switching between these phases can be guaranteed. Only under this condition, a change in hand-shape can be used as an event that triggers switching to a different operation.

In section 6, as an example of an application, a remote control system is described that allows presentations using HTML-pages that are controlled by hand gestures. The system shows a robust behavior even under the rather weak light conditions imposed by the darkness needed for the video beamers.

2 2-D Parameters

The first step of calculation of the 2-D parameters is to compute the contours from the given grey-scale images by a compass-mask algorithm. The integer-valued contours are transformed into real-valued ones by moving the contour points along the grey-scale gradient that is calculated by Sobel operators. The description of these steps can be found in [18]. Finally the real-valued contours are transformed into cubic B-spline curves which acts as a low pass filter [9].

From the cubic B-spline curves the *moments* $m_{p,q}$ up to the second order are calculated. This is done by a generalization for polynomials of the approach

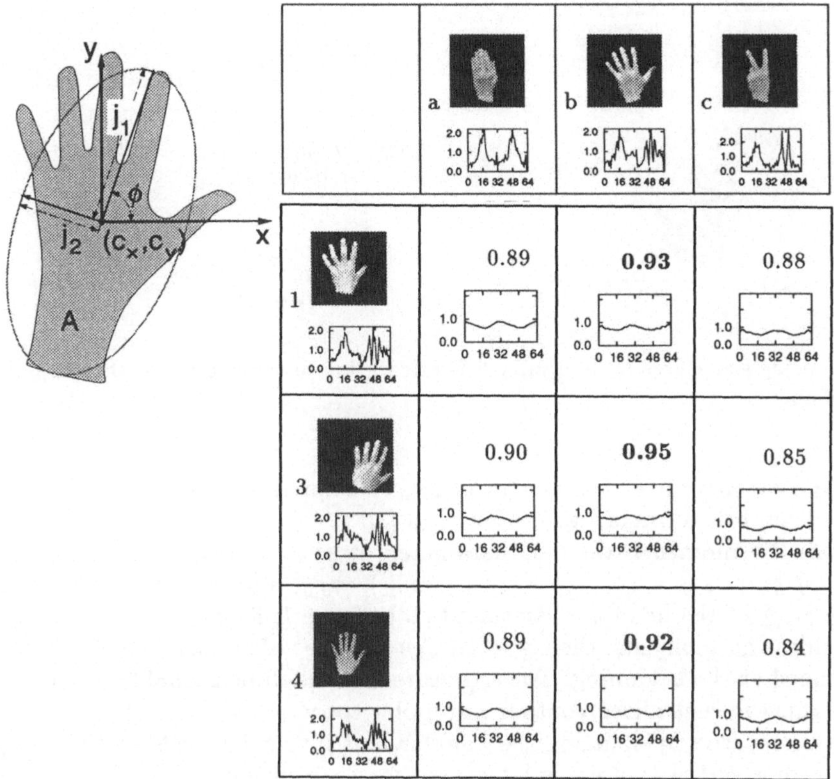

Fig. 1. Parameters of the hand (left) and examples of hand-shape classification (right).

described in [12]. It is based on Green's integral-theorem [11] saying that, if $B \in \mathbb{R}^2$ is a region, ∂B is the positively oriented boundary of B, and P and Q have continuous partial derivatives on B, then

$$\int_B \left(\frac{\partial Q}{\partial x} - \frac{\partial P}{\partial y} \right) d(x,y) \; = \; \int_{\partial B} P\,dx + Q\,dy.$$

Now, let be B a region bounded by n cubic polynomial segments $\gamma_1, \ldots, \gamma_n : \mathbb{R} \rightarrow \mathbb{R}^2$,

$$\gamma_i(t) = \begin{pmatrix} \gamma_{i,x}(t) \\ \gamma_{i,y}(t) \end{pmatrix}, \; t \in [0,1]$$

Then

$$m_{p,q}(B) = \sum_{i=1}^{n} \left(\int_0^1 \frac{\gamma_{i,x}^{p+1}(t)}{p+1} \, \gamma_{i,y}^{q}(t) \, \dot{\gamma}_{i,y}(t) \, dt \right)$$

This can be seen as follows. Assume that $P = 0$ in Green's theorem. Further let be $Q = \gamma_{i,y}^{q}(t)\,\gamma_{i,x}^{p+1}(t)/(p+1)$. Then $\partial Q/\partial x = x^p\,y^q$ which is equal to the definition of moments. If we finally set $dy = \dot{\gamma}_{i,y}(t)\,dt$ we obtain the result.

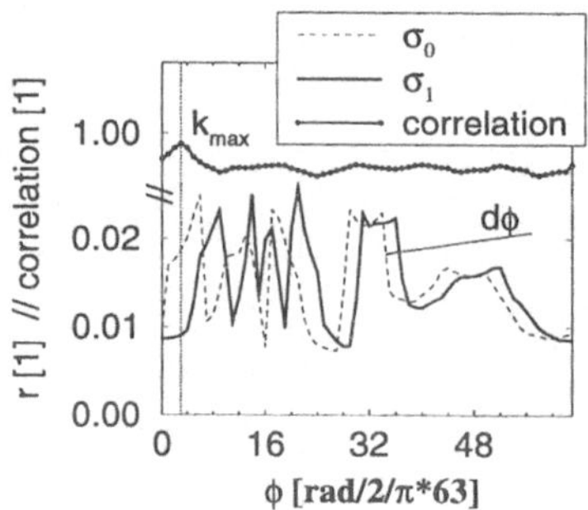

Fig. 2. Using signatures to determine 2-D orientation of the hand, and the class of the hand-shape.

The moments up to the second order, calculated with a computer algebra system from this formula, can be found in [3].

From the moments, the 2-D parameters *area* $A = m_{0,0}$, *contour length* l, *center of gravity* $c = (c_x, c_y) = (m_{1,0}, m_{0,1})/m_{0,0}$, and the *main moments of inertia* j_1, j_2 of the hand are calculated [13] (figure 1, left).

Besides the moments, the so-called *signature* is calculated from the contour determined at the beginning. The signature is a one-dimensional function which transforms the centralized contour into polar coordinates (figure 2). The signature is discretized by splitting the angular axis into n intervals and the length of the radius of the contour is integrated for each interval. The signatures are normalized by their autocorrelation.

From the signature, the further parameter ϕ is obtained which describes the *hand's 2-D angle of orientation* (figure 1, left). The underlying observation is that, if the contour is rotated as in figure 2, the shape of the signature remains similar, but it is phase-shifted. The phase shift yields ϕ. It is calculated as the quadratic interpolation of the maximum k_{max} of the correlation of the two signatures between the difference in orientation has to be determined. The correlation itself can be calculated efficiently applying the convolution theorem in $O(n \log n)$ steps [8]. The phase shift $d\phi$ i.e. the 2-D orientation calculated is much more robust with respect to noise and 3-D rotations of the hand than moment-based approaches.

The main use of signatures, however, is the classification of hand shapes that is described in the next section.

3 Stable Classification of Hand Shapes

To use the correlation of signatures as a means to classify hand-shapes, we use pre-learned signatures of sample-signs and correlate these with a given hand-shape of an unknown class. The correlation's maximum determines the class the hand-shape belongs to and gives a measurement for the fidelity of the classification process. It can be shown that this approach is (2-D) rotation-, translation and scaling-invariant und thus quite user-invariant.

Figure 1, right, shows the invariance of this simple algorithm for different users and different orientations of the hand-shape. The columns show the correlations for three shape samples. Each row stands for a hand sign given by different users in different 2-D orientations.

To evaluate this method it was used to classify dynamic hand-gestures such as hello- and bye-waving and pointing-gestures in the same arrangement as described in [6]. At a recognition speed of 14 Hz a recognition rate of 97.4 % was obtained on an *Intel 486* processor at a clock speed of 50 MHz. No false classifications occurred during the experiments. These results were obtained even though the training gestures were taken from *one* individual, whereas 19 different persons used the hand-gesture recognizer.

Even better recognition rates can be obtained if several differently defined signatures (e.g. the slope density function from [19] instead of radius versus angle) are used to feed a classification algorithm based on [20]. Here for eight different hand-shapes a recognition rate of 98.0 % was achieved. If we skip the user invariance, that is if we use the training-shapes individually, even 99.2 % can be achieved. Details can be found in [3].

4 3-D Metaphors

A central task of 3-D interaction is navigation in space. This means for instance translating and rotating an object in space, or translating or rotating the virtual camera determining the user's view on the spatial scene. Figure 3 shows a control panel of a gesture-based user interface for steering 3-D widgets that includes possibilities of spatial translation and rotation [2]. The control panel allows to switch between gesture-based and traditional mouse- and keyboard-based interaction.

Possible modes in 3-D interaction are *"Camera in hand"*, *"Scene in hand"* and *"Fly through scene"* with the same functionality as the metaphors described in [21]. The *"Nodo"* operation has the same meaning as lifting the mouse in 2-D graphical user interfaces, i.e., it enables the user to change the hand's position without performing any graphical actions and thus "walk" long distances through the 3-D scene.

In the following, three metaphors are outlined for the implementation of the operations of translation and rotation. Each of these metaphors allows both of these two modes. The translational and rotational modes are distinguished in the manner how the 2-D parameters are mapped to 3-D world parameters.

4.1 The Screw-Metaphor

In the translational mode of the screw-metaphor, the user translates in x- and z-direction by moving his hand into the appropriate direction. The y-translation is steered by turning the hand left or right: turning right means increasing

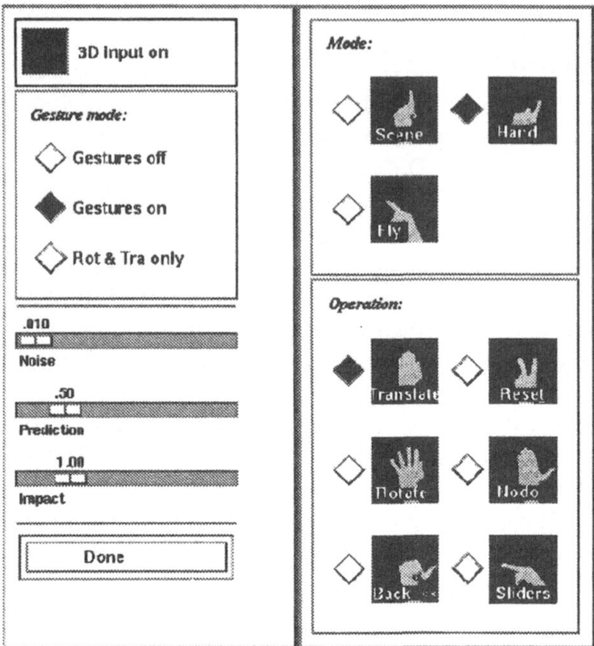

Fig. 3. Using several hand-shapes to steer a 3-D widget.

y-coordinates, turning left decreasing y-coordinates. This resembles turning a screw which gives the metaphor its name (right side of figure 4).

The rotational mode shown on the left of the figure is a straightforward adaptation of the rolling-ball metaphor [10] for three-dimensional input devices. The 2-D x- and y-translation of the center of gravity of the hand (c_x, c_y) steer the rotational angles α_y and α_x. The hands 2-D orientation ϕ is mapped directly onto the rotation α_z about the z-axis.

The metaphorical concepts, especially for translations, require some training time ($\approx$ 1 min) before they can be used efficiently. But once learned, the metaphor has a decisive advantage, especially for desktop applications. Since the hand rests for all manipulations in the x-y-plane it is quite un-fatiguing.

4.2 The Thumb-Metaphor

The metaphor is equal to the screw-metaphor in its rotational mode.

For translations the y-translation is specified by the abduction angle of the thumb. This angle again can be calculated by means of signature-correlation. Translations are then characterized by two sample hand-shapes: one for the totally closed hand (σ_1) and another one for the thumb abducted (σ_2). Let $\kappa_{\sigma_i,\sigma_k}$ denote the maximum correlation of two given hand-shapes. Then we are able to calculate the abduction angle (and likewise any other hand-shape alteration, in

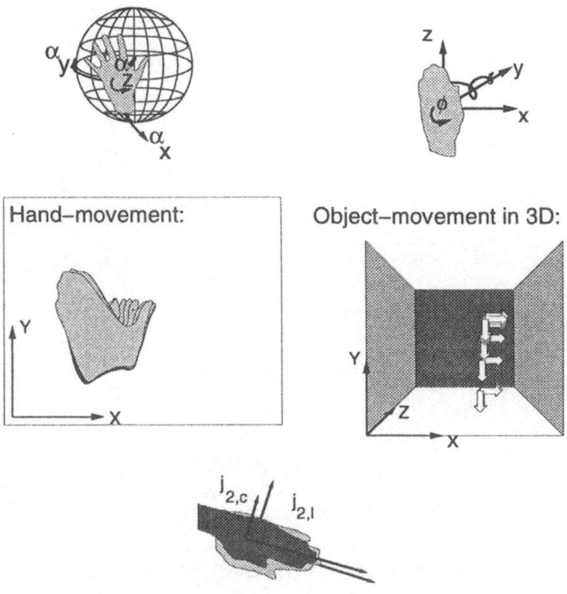

Fig. 4. Screw-metaphor (top), the thumb-metaphor (middle), and the gear metaphor.

particular finger movement) for a given signature σ_k by the two-class specific signature-distance

$$\tau(\sigma_k) := \left| \frac{\kappa_{(1),k} - \kappa_{(2),k}}{2 - 2\,\kappa_{(1),(2)}} + \frac{1}{2} \right| .$$

As for the screw-metaphor the hand rests for all manipulations in the x-y-plane. Furthermore the user has not to bother about un-voluntary changes of the 2D-orientation of the hand induced by x- and z-translations.

4.3 The Gear-Metaphor

The gear-metaphor is more intuitive. Translations are a 1:1 metaphor, that means, as the hand translates, the displayed geometries are translated. The changes in (x, y, z) coordinates are obtained from the changes of the center of gravity c_x, c_y and the area A of the depicted hand. For calculation, a camera-calibration algorithm is needed, see [4] for details of this algorithm.

The rotational mode of the metaphor gives the metaphor its name. It is a 1:4 metaphor, i.e. turning the hand about an angle of 45° implies a rotation of the displayed geometries about $4 \times 45° = 180°$. The reason for doing so is the fact that there is no means of determining the 3-D orientation from a 2-D image unambiguously [16]. But if the allowed rotations is restricted to an interval of $[-45°, 45°]$, the last $(j_{2,l})$ and current $(j_{2,c})$ inertia moments change with the rotation angle approximately linear to the sine of the angle, as the hand is rotated

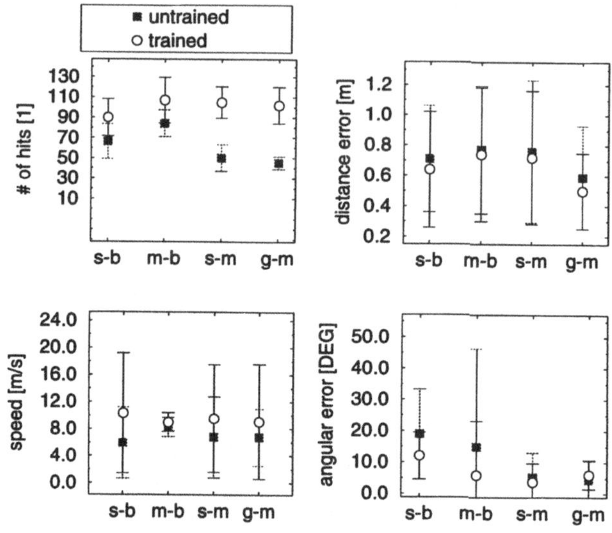

Fig. 5. The experimental results with the virtual squash court. results.

about its main inertia axis (figure 4). The same applies to rotations about the second inertia axis and all combinations of these rotations. The problem of the unknown sign of the rotation's sine is avoided by putting the camera at an Euler angle of $(-45°, -45°, 0)$ and restricting the allowed rotations to $[-45°, 45°]$. Now all rotations within that interval have a bijective effect on the inertia moments. Setting a to the sine of the rotation about the main axis of inertia, b likewise for the minor axis of inertia, and f to the unknown depth of the hand along the focal axis of the camera, we obtain the nonlinear system of equations

$$s_c = (a\ b\ s_l)/f,\ j_{1,c} = (a\ j_{1,l})/f,\ j_{2,c} = (b\ j_{2,l})/f,$$

where s_c and s_l stand for the current and last length of the hand contour, respectively. The solution of this system is

$$b = (s_c j_{1,l})/(j_{1,c} s_l),\ f = (s_c j_{2,l} j_{1,l})/(j_{1,c} j_{2,c} s_l),\ a = (s_c j_{2,l})/(j_{2,c} s_l).$$

Thus we are able to compute the angles of rotation about the axis of inertia from the moments of inertia and the contour length. Together with the 2-D hand orientation ϕ and the rotational part of the camera-calibration matrix we can transform these parameters into Euler angles in world coordinates.

5 Evaluation

To evaluate the vision-based 3-D input method it was compared directly to the space-ball, *the* alternative device for desktop 3-D interaction. Therefore a network-distributed *virtual squash game* was implemented. For the graphics output, the squash-rackets were modeled by polygons and superimposed onto a digitized picture of a real squash-court. In order to enhance the 3-D impression shadows of the rackets were plotted on the walls of the squash-court. To get sufficiently many contacts of the symbolic racket and target, the size of the rackets was chosen big.

The results of the squash experiment were obtained from 12 individuals during a 15-minute game composed of a training phase and three phases where the speed and the translations and rotations precision were used to calculate the final-score for each player. Figure 4 summarizes the results obtained for each phase, respectively. The abbreviations are: s-b = space-ball, s-m = screw-metaphor, g-m = gear-metaphor, and m-b = mirror-box.

The mirror-box is a 3-D input device that uses several camera views of the user's hand by a mirror construction. Details can be found again in [4]. One interesting result was found with this device: it was possible either to use translation and rotation isolated or in combination (i.e. 6 DOF), again triggered by different hand-shapes. The decision which variant should be taken was left to the user. Averaged for all users and operations in 3-D only in 20.3 % of all cases the 6 DOF variant was taken, all other operations were split into rotations (34.5 %) and translations(45.2 %). One explanation are the average Euler angles that were induced during translations by the rotational joints of the human arm and hand: for each translation an average of $(3.44, 3.83, 5.76)$ degrees of rotation was measured, for unique rotational tasks we found an average of $(4.51, 5.02, 7.56)$ degrees. Thus non-voluntary rotations during translations make up more than the half of those for voluntary rotations. Both facts together are a strong hint that there is almost no need to provide six degrees of freedom at once.

The implemented system achieves a frame rate of 10.6 Hz on an *Intel 486* processor at a clock speed of 50 MHz. This demonstrates its real-time capability.

6 Vision-Based Remote Control for HTML Presentations

To prove the robustness of our approach, we have developed a remote control for the Mosaic WWW-browser. The implemented remote control system enables presentations using HTML-pages that are browsed by hand gestures. That is possible even under the rather weak light conditions imposed by the darkness needed for the usage of video beamers. The system was flawlessly presented several times, in particular in the given environment of a real conference. To each of the five functions "page forward/backward", "pointer forward/backward", and "Launch 3-D experiment", an own gesture is assigned.

Besides simple navigation methods (forward, backward) there is the possibility to move a large blinking hand-shaped pointer in the presented HTML-documents in order to depict the current point of interest, just as it can be done with a laser pointer. Furthermore the presentation mode can be switched by the "Launch 3D-experiment" gesture. Then the thumb-metaphor is activated for 3D-manipulation of a VRML-object. The same gesture is used to switch back to HTML-mode.

References

1. R. Bolt and E. Herranz. Two-handed gesture in multi-modal natural dialog. In *Symposium on User Interface Software and Technology*, pages 7–14. ACM, 1992.
2. U. Bröckl, A. J. Klingert, and A. Schmitt. Towards standardized user interfaces for three-dimensional interaction: the development of 3D widgets based on PEX and motif. In *Proceedings of the Fourth Annual Conference of the European X User Group (EXUG)*, 1992.
3. U. Bröckl-Fox. *Untersuchung neuer, gestenbasierter Methoden für die 3D-Interaktion*. Verlag Shaker, Aachen, FRG, 1995.
4. U. Bröckl-Fox, L. Kettner, A. Klingert, and L. Kobbelt. *Artificial Life and Virtual Reality*, chapter XII, Using Three Dimensional Hand-Gesture Recognition as a New 3D Input Technique, pages 173–187. Wiley and Sons, 1994.
5. Michael Chen, S. Joy Mountford, and Abigail Sellen. A study in interactive 3-D rotation using 2-D control devices. *Computer Graphics*, 22(4):121–129, August 1988.
6. T. Darrell and A. Pentland. Space-time gestures. In *IEEE Conference Computer Vision and Pattern Recognition*, pages 294–299, New York City, June 15–17 1993.
7. Wolfgang Felger. How interactive visualization can benefit from multidimensional input devices. In *Proceedings of the SPIE - The International Society for Optical Engineering*, volume 1668, Visual Data Interpretation, pages 15–24, 1992.
8. R. C. Gonzalez and P. Wintz. *Digital Image Processing*. Addison-Wesley, Reading, MA, 2 edition, 1987.
9. A. Goshtasby, F. Cheng, and B. A. Barsky. B-spline curves and surfaces viewed as digital filters. *Computer Vision, Graphics, and Image Processing*, 52:264–275, 1990.
10. Andrew J. Hanson. The rolling ball. In David Kirk, editor, *Graphics Gems III*, pages 51–60. Academic Press, 1992.
11. H. Heuser. *Lehrbuch der Analysis, Teil 2*. B.G. Teubner Stuttgart, 1983.
12. X. Y. Jiang and H. Bunke. Ein konturbasierter Ansatz zur Berechnung von Momenten. In *Informatik Fachberichte 290*, pages 143–150. Bernd Radig, October 1991.
13. B. Klaus and P. Horn. *Robot Vision*. The MIT Press, McGraw-Hill Book Company, 1986.
14. M. Kohler and S. Schröter. Handgestenerkennung durch Computersehen. Informatik '98. In this volume.
15. M. W. Krueger. *Artificial Reality*. Addison-Wesley, 1981.
16. J. S. C. Yuan. Mukundan. Estimation of quaternion parameters from two dimensional image moments. *Graphical Models and Image Processing*, 54:345–350, 1992.
17. B. A. Myers and M. Rosson. *Survey on User Interface Programming*. Number (#77629) in RC 17624. IBM Research Division, January 1992.
18. M. Nadler. A note on coefficients of compass mask coefficients. *Computer Vision, Graphic, and Image Processing*, 51:96–101, 1990.
19. P. Nahim. The theory of measurement of a silhouette description for image processing and recognition. *Pattern Recognition*, 6(2):85–95, 1974.
20. D. Rubine. Specifying gestures by example. *Computer Graphics*, 25(4):329–337, 1991.
21. C. Ware and S. Osborne. Exploration and virtual camera control in virtual three dimensional environments. In *ACM Transactions On Computer Graphics*, pages 175–183, Oct. 1990.

Handgestenerkennung durch Computersehen

Markus Kohler und Sven Schröter

Universität Dortmund, Informatik VII (Graphische Systeme),
Otto-Hahn-Str. 16, D-44221 Dortmund
Email: {Markus.Kohler|Sven.Schroeter}@cs.uni-dortmund.de

Zusammenfassung Etwa im Jahr 1991 begannen intensive Forschungsaktivitäten im Bereich der computersehensbasierten Gestenerkennung, die momentan in vollem Gange sind. Dieser Beitrag gibt einen Überblick über bekanntgewordene Systeme, der auf einer Anfang 1998 durch die Autoren durchgeführten Umfrage beruht. Dabei werden die wesentlichen Ansätze, die diesen Systeme zugrundeliegen, generalisierend deutlich gemacht. Ferner wird auf die speziellen Anforderungen an die Bildverarbeitung eingegangen, die sich bei der computersehensbasierten Gestenerkennung ergeben und die auf der Erfahrung der Autoren bei der Entwicklung der Systeme ZYKLOP und ARGUS beruhen.

1 Einleitung

„Come as you are." war die einladende Aufforderung, mit der Myron W. Krueger Mitte der 70er Jahre eine neue Interaktionsform zwischen Mensch und Rechner propagierte. Wie in seiner Installation Videoplace [16] sollte der Mensch durch Bewegungen und Gesten mit dem Rechner kommunizieren, die vom Rechner über Kameras erkannt werden.

Vermutlich aufgrund der hohen Kosten für Videokomponenten, die erforderliche Rechenleistung und den Stand der Technik in der digitalen Bildverarbeitung wurden solche Ideen nicht breit weiterverfolgt. Die Entwicklung in bezug auf Interaktion durch Bewegung und Gestik ging vielmehr dahin, andere Arten von Sensoren zu deren Erfassung einzusetzen. Ein typisches Beispiel, das Verbreitung gefunden hat, ist der Datenhandschuh. Beim Datenhandschuh wird die Information über die aktuelle Handform etwa über Dehnstreifen erfaßt, die in den Handschuhfingern angebracht sind. Die Lage der Hand im Raum wird über Verfolgungssysteme etwa auf elektomagnetischer Basis durch geeignet angebrachte Sender und Empfänger bestimmt. Die aufgenommene Information wird an den Rechner weitergegeben, der diese dann zur Reaktionsberechnung verwendet. Der Nachteil gegenüber dem sehensbasierten Ansatz ist die Behinderung des Benutzers mit diesen speziellen Geräten, was im Gegensatz zu der Idee „Come as you are" steht.

Durch die technologische Entwicklung von Mikroprozessoren und Videosystemen ermöglicht und durch die zunehmende Verbreitung von Videokomponenten bei Multimedia-Systemen begünstigt, stehen mittlerweile preisgünstige und leistungsfähige Hardwarekomponenten zur Verfügung. Begünstigt wird die Handgestenerkennung durch die Tatsache, daß diese Systeme Farbsignale liefern. Durch den hohen Rotanteil der menschlichen Haut unabhängig von der Hautfarbe erleichtert dies die Trennung von menschlichen Körperteilen wir der Hand oder dem Kopf vom Hintergrund der aufgenommenen Bilder, einem der Kernprobleme der Bildverarbeitung in diesem Zusammenhang. Starke Einschränkungen an den Hintergrund oder markierende Hilfsmittel, wie etwa die von Krueger geschilderten speziell texturierten Handschuhe oder Anzüge, können dadurch vermieden werden.

Durch die geringer werdenden Einschränkungen an die Einsatzumgebung von Bildverarbeitungssystemen eröffnet sich ein weites Spektrum von Anwendungen für die computersehensbasierte Interaktion zwischen Menschen und Rechnern. Die Vision über Fernbedienung mittels Handbewegung, wie sie der Science-Fiction Autor Douglas Adams 1979 in seinem Buch *Per Anhalter durch die Galaxis* auf witzige Weise darstellt, wird nun im Prinzip möglich. Beispielsweise ist das Ziel des Dortmunder ARGUS-Projekts die Fernbedienung von Haushaltsgeräten durch Hinzeigen und Handgesten. Weitergehende Einsatzgebiete neben der intuitiven Steuerung aller möglichen Arten von Applikationen sind die Übersetzung von Gebärdensprachen und die Erkennung von Gesichtsmimik.

In den folgenden Kapiteln wird ein Überblick über dieses Gebiet und dessen Entwicklung gegeben. Probleme und Anforderungen an die Systeme, die beim Einsatz in komplexen Umgebungen auftreten werden im Kapitel 2 diskutiert. In Kapitel 3 werden aktuelle Systeme und deren Charakteristika zusammengestellt. Kapitel 4 skizziert Aspekte der Ergonomie und der Gestaltung von gestenbasierter Interaktion.

2 Bildverarbeitung für Handgestenerkennung

Bei der Handgestenerkennung spielen zwei Begriffe eine wesentliche Rolle, die Handpositur und der Handort. Unter einer *statischen Handpositur* versteht man eine gegebene Deformation der Hand, d.h. eine feste Konfiguration der gebogenen Finger und der Resthand. Eine *dynamische Handpositur* ist eine Deformationsvorgang der Hand, d.h. der Ablauf eines Prozesses des Verbiegens von Fingern und der Resthand. Der *Handort* beschreibt die Lage der Hand im Raum. Dabei wird zwischen *statischem* und *dynamische* Handort unterschieden, letzteres drückt einen zeitabhängigen Ortswechsel aus. Eine *Handgeste* ist eine Kombination aus Handpositur und Handort, der eine Bedeutung zugeordnet ist. Harling und Edwards [8] unterscheiden dabei die Gestentypen *SPSL* (statische Handpositur, statischer Handort), *DPSL* (dynamische Handpositur, statischer Handort), *SPDL* (statische Handpositur, dynamischer Handort) und *DPDL* (dynamische Handpositur, dynamischer Handort). Die SPSL-Gesten werden auch als *statische Gesten (SGE)*, die anderen Klassen als *dynamische Gesten (DGE)* bezeichnet.

Ziel der *Handgestenerkennung* ist das Identifizieren vorgegebener Handgesten aus Aufnahmen (je nach Typ ein Einzelbild oder eine Bildfolge), in der eine Hand zu sehen ist. Dabei ist es möglich, daß die Aufnahme mit nur einer Kamera erfolgt, aber auch, daß mehrere Aufnahmen vorliegen, die etwa von mehreren Kameras stammen, die für die Aufnahme verwendet werden. Letzteres kann durch mehrere Ansichten der Hand, die dadurch erhalten werden, die Erkennungsaufgabe vereinfachen. Ferner ist es einfacher möglich, auf die dreidimensionale Anordnung zurückzuschließen.

Bei der Lösung der Aufgabe der Handgestenerkennung wird üblicherweise nach der klassischen *Bildverarbeitungspipeline* vorgegangen. Im ersten Schritt, der *Bildaufnahme*, werden die von der Kamera aufgenommenen Bilder digitalisiert und zur weiteren Verarbeitung aufbereitet. Im darauffolgenden zweiten Schritt, der *Segmentierung*, werden die Gebiete im Bild, die die Hand repräsentieren, vom Hintergrund getrennt. Das Ziel des dritten Schritts, die *Merkmalsextraktion*, ist, eine möglichst kleine Menge von Merkmalen aus der segmentierten Region abzuleiten, anhand von denen sich die unterschiedlichen gegebenen Gesten unterscheiden lassen. Ferner wird, falls es der Gestentyp erfordert, der Handort bestimmt. Der vierte Schritt ist die *Klassifikation*, in der anhand von Merkmalen und vom Ort der Typ der Geste, die in der gegebenen Aufnahme zu sehen ist, bestimmt wird.

Eine wesentliche Randbedingung an die Bildverarbeitung bei der Handgestenerkennung ist, daß die Verarbeitung in Echtzeit erfolgen sollte, d.h. die ankommenden Bilder in dem Zeitintervall verarbeitet werden, das zwischen zwei aufeinanderfolgenden Bildern zur Verfügung steht, typischerweise 1/25 Sekunde. Falls dies nicht möglich ist, werden nicht alle Bilder der Bildfolge verarbeitet. Bei zu großen Abständen von verarbeiteten Bildern kann es vorkommen, daß Vorgänge übersehen werden und so die Fehlerhäufigkeit zunimmt.

Für die Durchführung der Bildverarbeitung hat es sich als zweckmäßig erwiesen, zwischen Handgestenerkennung in lokaler beziehungsweise globaler Umgebung zu unterscheiden. *Lokale Umgebung* meint, daß sich die Hand in einem kleinen, vorgegebenen Raumbereich bewegt. Dies hat zur Folge, daß die Segmentierung in einfacher Weise so geschehen kann, da im wesentlichen die Hand zu sehen ist. Bei *globaler Umgebung* kann die Hand in einem weiten Bereich geführt werden, etwa indem sich der Benutzer frei im Raum bewegt. Die lokale Situation tritt üblicherweise bei *Desktop-Anwendungen* und *Gebärdenspracherkennung* auf. Ein typisches Beispiel ist, die Hand als Ersatz für eine Maus zu verwenden, indem sie unter einer fest installierten Kamera bewegt wird. Über die Handbewegung wird der Cursor gesteuert, durch unterschiedliche Handposituren können Reaktionen ausgelöst werden, die etwa Mausklicks entsprechen. Die globale Situation ist gegeben, wenn Handgesten zur Fernsteuerung von Geräten eingesetzt werden oder wenn über Hinzeigen mit einer Videoprojektion interagiert wird.

Bei der Handgestenerkennung für lokale Umgebungen ist man mit folgenden Eigenschaften des zu erkennenden Objekte besonders konfrontiert:

1. unscharfe Objektabgrenzung: Übergang zwischen Hand und Unterarm;
2. glattes Objekt: die Berandung der Hand weist keine Ecken auf, allenfalls dort, wo der Unterarm abgetrennt wurde oder an Bildrändern;
3. deformierbares Objekt: die Hand verändert ihre Form;
4. variable Objektgröße und -lage.

Gestenerkennung in globalen Umgebungen muß zusätzlich mit dem natürlichen Verhalten des Benutzers und den Gegebenheiten des globalen Umfelds zurechtkommen. Besondere Schwierigkeiten sind hier:

1. Erfassung des weiten Umfelds;
2. perspektivische Verzerrung;
3. unterschiedliche, wechselnde Beleuchtung;
4. eventuell gleichzeitige Verfolgung mehrerer Objekte, z.B. beider Hände und des Kopfes;
5. verschwindende und wieder auftauchende Objekte;
6. Schätzungen von 3D-Positionen;
7. Bestimmung der Handorientierung, z.B. einer Zeigerichtung;

Insbesondere bei der Gestenerkennung in globaler Umgebung kann es notwendig sein, Objekte, z.B. Hände, über die Zeit zu verfolgen. Die Aufgabe der *Objektver-*

folgung besteht darin, Objekte, die in einem einzelnen Bild einer Bildfolge zu sehen sind, in weiteren Bildern der Bildfolge zu identifizieren. Eine wesentliche Teilaufgabe der Objektverfolgung ist die Aufgabe der *Vorhersage* der zukünftigen Lage eines Objekts aus den Bildern der bisher verarbeiteten Bildfolge.

Aus der Vorhersage ist es etwa möglich, den Bildausschnitt zu schätzen, in dem sich das gesuchte Objekt befindet. Durch die Beschränkung auf einen Bildausschnitt werden die nachfolgenden Bearbeitungsschritte, insbesondere die Segmentierung, weniger aufwendig. Bei der Verwendung rechnergesteuerter Bewegtkameras kann die Kamera entsprechend der Vorhersage mitgeführt werden, um so stets eine detaillierte Darstellung des interessanten Bereichs der Szenen zu haben.

Bei der Gestenerkennung in globaler Umgebung kann es weiterhin passieren, daß Objekte im Bild verschwinden z. B. dadurch, daß der Körper des Benutzers die Hände so verdeckt, daß sie von der Kamera nicht mehr gesehen werden können. Die Vorhersage der Bewegung kann helfen, die verdeckten Objekte schnell wiederzufinden, wenn sie wieder sichtbar werden.

Die Objektverfolgung und Lagevorhersage sind klassische Aufgaben der Bildverarbeitung, zu deren Lösung es zahlreiche Arbeiten gibt, die auch auf die Gestenerkennung angewendet werden können. Für eine recht umfassende Verwendung der Objektverfolgung auf die Handgesten, die die genannten Aspekte aufgreift, wird auf die Arbeit von Breig [2] verwiesen, die Teil des ARGUS-Systems ist.

3 Existierende Systeme

Anfang der Neunzigerjahre begann eine rasant wachsende Forschungs- und Entwicklungstätigkeit auf dem Gebiet der computersehensbasierten Mensch-Rechner-Interaktion. Die Tabellen 1 und 2 listen die Eigenschaften und Fähigkeiten von über 40 Systemen zur Gestenterkennung auf, die in dieser Zeit entstanden sind. Die aufgeführten Systeme sind dabei nicht auf Handgesten beschränkt. Ein Grund dafür ist, daß es bei der Gebärdenspracherkennung, die die Handgestenerkennung einschließt, zweckmäßig sein kann, eine globalere Analyse der Körperbewegung durchzuführen [25], um daraus Schlußfolgerungen für die Gebärde zu ziehen.

Die Übersicht basiert auf einem Artikel von Huang und Pavlovic [12] von 1995 und einer Umfrage, die Ende 1997 durchgeführt wurde[1]. Die Zusammenstellung zeigt die Vielfalt der laufenden Arbeiten und die eingesetzten Methoden.

In der Zusammenstellung wird zwischen Einkamerasystemen (Abb. 1) und Mehrkamerasystemen, (Abb. 2) unterschieden. Mehrkamerasysteme haben insbesondere bei der Gestenerkennung in globaler Umgebung den Vorteil, daß über mehrere Ansichten ein größerer Sichtbereich als mit einer Kamera abgedeckt werden kann, was die Größe der verdeckten Regionen mindert. Ferner ist es möglich, besser als mit einer Kamera auf die räumliche Lage zu schließen.

Bei den Einkamerasystemen ist das Konzept der *Spiegelbox* besonders erwähnenswert. Die Spiegelbox, die von Bröckl-Fox [3] entwickelt wurde und auch von Millar and Crawford [20] verwendet wird, erlaubt drei Ansichten der Hand mit einer einzigen Kamera. Obwohl es sich um ein Einkamerasystem handelt, besitzt die Spiegelbox Möglichkeiten, die der eines Mehrkamerasystems ähneln.

Ein anderer Aspekt ist der Einsatz von rechnergesteuerten, beweglichen Kameras mit steuerbarem Zoom. Solche Kameras erlauben, bei der Gestenerkennung

[1] Für umfassendere, aktuelle Information siehe http://ls7-www.informatik.uni-dortmund.de/html/englisch/gesture/vbgr-table.html

in globaler Umgebung den Benutzer und bei der Handgestenerkennung speziell die Hand besser im Auge zu behalten. Stationäre Kameras bieten trotz hoher Auflösung immer einen sehr eingeschränkten Interaktionsbereich innerhalb des Sichtkegels der Kamera. Bewegliche Kameras werden im System ARGUS von Kohler et al. [15] eingesetzt.

In den Tabellen 1 und 2 werden die Einkamera- bzw. Mehrkamerasysteme alphabetisch sortiert nach dem Autorennamen vorgestellt. Die zweite Spalte „Aufgabe" beschreibt die grundsätzliche Fähigkeit des Systems. Die nächste Spalte „Segmentierung" gibt Auskunft darüber, auf welcher Grundlage die Segmentierung erfolgt. In der Spalte „Merkmale" werden die durch die Bildanalyse extrahierten Merkmale aufgelistet, die nachfolgend von den Klassifikatoren verwendet werden, die in der nächsten Tabellenspalte „Klassifikation" aufgeführt sind. Soweit von den Autoren Einschränkungen an ihr System angegeben wurden, stehen diese in der nächsten Spalte „Bedingung". In der letzten Spalte werden erprobte Anwendungs- und Einsatzgebiete erwähnt. Die in den einzelnen Spalten verwendeten Kürzel sind in Tab. 3 zusammengestellt.

Im folgenden werden die genannten Aspekte näher beleuchtet.

3.1 Systemfähigkeiten

Ein wesentliches Merkmal in bezug auf Systemfähigkeit ist die Unterscheidung danach, ob statische (Kürzel SGE in der Tabelle) oder dynamische Gesten (DGE) erkannt werden. Es zeigt sich, daß beide Arten weit verbreitet sind.

Manche Systeme habe nicht die Erkennung von Gesten im Sinne der Klassifikation zum Ziel. Vielmehr geht es darum, eine Bewegung zu erfassen, die etwa dazu dienen kann, einen Gegenstand in einer rechnerintern gespeicherten Szene entsprechend zu bewegen. Dies wird auch als Verfolgung (engl. Tracking) bezeichnet. In der Tabelle wird zwischen Verfolgungsmöglichkeit als grundlegende Technik (V) und der Verfolgung spezifischer Objekte (HV = Handverfolgung, GV = Gliederverfolgung, BV = Bausteinverfolgung) unterschieden. Bausteinverfolgung meint, daß Gegenstände vor der Kamera bewegt werden, deren Bewegung und Lage über die Kamera erfaßt und auf eine rechnerintern gespeicherte Szene übertragen werden. So kann beispielsweise durch Manipulation einer realen Klötzchenwelt vor der Kamera ein im Rechner gespeichertes Abbild höherer Komplexität manipuliert werden. Rautenberg et al. setzen dies etwa zur Steuerung von Industrianlagen und Hoch zum Entwurf von Filmkulissen ein.

Manche Systeme bieten die Möglichkeit, durch Hinzeigen Objekte der Umwelt zu identifizieren. Diese sind durch einen Eintrag „Z" in der zweiten Spalte gekennzeichnet.

Schließlich gibt es Systeme, die ganz speziellen Anwendungen gewidmet sind, der Erkennung einer Gebärdensprache (GSE). Weitere Aspekte sind die Erkennung dynamischer Körpergesten (DKG) und die Erkennung spezifischer Gebärden (SSE).

3.2 Segmentierung

Die Segementierung stellt sowohl in lokalen als auch globalen Umgebungen eines der größten Probleme dar. Dieses Problem kann dadurch vereinfacht werden, daß Markierungen, bei der Handgestenerkennung beispielsweise auf Handschuhe aufgebracht, verwendet werden. Derartige Systeme sind in der dritten Spalte mit *(Marken)* und zusätzlich „MHS" bei der Verwendung von Handschuhen gekennzeichnet.

Autor	Aufg.	Segm.	Merkmale	Klassifikation	Bed.	Anwendung
S. Ahmad* (1)	HV	-	Fingerspitzenerkennung	-	-	-
S. Ahmad* (2)	SGE	-	-	Gaußsches Neuronales Netz		-
D. Banarse	SGE	Grau	Kantenerkennung	Neocognitron Neuronales Netz	-	-
U. Bröckl-Fox	HV, SGE, Z	Grau	Momente, Polare Segmentierung	Korrelation	OB, SB	3D GUI
R. Cipolla*	DGE	Marken	Fingerspitzenerkennung	-	-	-
K. Cho*	SGE	-	-	Lernen von lokalen Formeigenschaften	-	-
J. L. Crowley, J. Martin	HV, SGE, DGE, SSE	Grau, *Farbe*	Eigenräume	Distanz im Merkmalsraum, Endlicher Automat		Augmented Reality
T. Darrell*	DGE	-	-	Modell durch verschiedene Ansichten	-	-
J. Davis, M. Shah (1)	HV	Grau	Fingerspitzenerkennung, Punkte der Fingerspitzen, Punkte der Fingerwurzeln	zylindrisches 3D-Fingermodell	UH	-
J. Davis, M. Shah (2)	DGE	Marken, MHS	Fingerspitzenerkennung	Endlicher Automat, Modell-Vergleich	UH	-
A. Downton*	GV	-	-	zylindrisches 3D-Modell der Glieder	-	-
S. Eickeler, A. Kosmala, G. Rigoll	DGE	Grau	Momente aus Differenzbildern	kontinuierliche Hidden-Markov-Modelle	SH, BU	Fernbedienung, Robotersteuerung
W. Freeman*	DGE	-	Orientierungshistogramme	-	-	Fernbedienung für Fernseher
T. Heap, R. Bowden	HV, SGE	-	-	2D/3D-Punktverteilungsmodell	-	-
K. Grobel, H. Hienz	SGE, DGE, GSE	*Farbe*, MHS	konventionelle und spezielle Merkmale	Hidden-Markov-Modelle	UH, OB	Erkennung von Gebärdensprache
C. Kervrann*	HV	-	-	stochastisches, deformierbares Modell	-	-
R. Kjeldsen	Z, SGE, HV, DGE	*Farbe*	Pausen, Wendepunkte, grobe Richtung und Größe	ALVINN Neuronales Netz	keine	weiterentwickelte Maus in GUI
M. Krueger*	-	-	Silhouette	-	-	Objektmanipulation
J. Kuch*	DGE	-	-	3D-NURBS Handmodell	-	-
J. Lee*	DGE	-	-	3D Handskelett Modell	-	-
C. Maggioni* (1)	DGE	MHS	-	-	-	-
C. Maggioni (2)	Z, SGE	*LUT*	Fingerspitzenerkennung	-	-	virtueller Touchscreen
A. Makarov	DGE, GSE	Grau	Kanten in Binärbildern	Nullstellen höherer Ableitungen	BA	Alarmsensor
R. J. Millar, G. F. Crawford	HV, DGE, GSE	*Farbe*, MHS	Fingerspitzenerkennung	3D Handskelett Modell	SB	Erkennung von Gebärdensprache
C. Nölker, H. Ritter	Z, SGE	Grau	Fingerspitzenerkennung, Gaborfilter	Hierarchisches, lokales, lineares Neuronales Netz	UH	Verwendung in multimodalen Systemen, 3D-CAD
M. Rauterberg, M. Bichsel	BV	Grau	-	-	-	2D/3D Entwurf von Industrieanlagen, Steuerung von Robotern
J. Schlenzig*	DGE	-	Zernike Momente	Finite state estimation	-	-
J. Segen*	DGE	-	Silhouettenkanten	-	-	-
M. Stark, M. Kohler, S. Schröter et al	SGE, DGE	*Farbe*	Winkel-, Abstandssignaturen, Polare Segmentierung, Fingerspitzenerkennung, Momente	Multiklassifikation	-	3D GUI (ZYKLOP)
T. Starner*	DGE	-	Bildgeometrie Parameter, Blobs	Hidden-Markov-Modelle	-	-

Tabelle1. Merkmale und Eigenschaften von Einkamerasystemen zur Gestenerkennung. Die Zeilen, in denen der Autor mit „*“ markiert ist, wurden von Huang und Pavlovic übernommen. Die Abkürzungen sind in der Tabelle 3 beschrieben. *Farbe* in der Spalte Segmentierung markiert farbbasierte Segmentierung und *Grau* weist Systeme mit grauwertbasierter Segmentierung aus.

Autor	Aufg.	Segm.	Merkmale	Klassifikation	Bed.	Anwendung
M. Brand, N. Oliver, A. Pentland	V, DKG, GSE	*Farbe*	Zentrum, Masse, Dehnung, Flächen-Exzentrizität und Distanz zwischen Flächen und deren Änderungsrate	gekoppelte kontinuierliche Hidden-Markov-Modelle	-	Unterricht von T'ai chi-Bewegungen, Amerikanische Gebärdensprache
M. Etoh*	HV	-	-	zylindrisches 3D-Handmodell	-	-
M. Fukumoto*	Z	-	Erkennung der Fingerspitzen	Virtual Projection Origin	-	
M. Hoch	Z, SGE, GV	*Farbe*, *Marker*	Regionen, Blobs	Inverses Kinematikmodell	-	Filmplanung, Kunst
M. Kohler, M. Breig, B. Deimel, C. Esken et al	V, Z, SGE, DGE	*Farbe*, Bewegungserkennung	Abstandssignaturen, Polare Segmentierung, Erkennung der Fingerspitzen	Multi-Klassifikation	BU, BI	Fernbedienung im Heimbereich
J. Rehg*	DGE	-	-	zylindrisches 3D-Gliedmaßenmodell	-	-
A. Torige*	Z	MHS	-	-	-	-
J. Triesch, C. v. d. Malsburg	HV, SGE	*Farbe*, Bewegungserkennung	Gabor Filter	Elastic Graph Matching	keine	Fernbedienung, Robotersteuerung

Tabelle2. Merkmale und Eigenschaften von Mehrkamerasystemen zur Gestenerkennung. Die Zeilen, in denen der Autor mit „*“ makiert ist, wurden von Huang und Pavlovic übernommen. Die Abkürzungen sind in der Tabelle 3 erläutert. *Farbe* in der Spalte Segmentierung markiert farbbasierte Segmentierung und *Grau* weist Systeme mit grauwert-basierter Segmentierung aus.

Aufgabe	
V	Verfolgung
BV	Baustein -Verfolgung
HV	Hand-Verfolgung
GV	Glieder-Verfolgung
Z	Zeigen
SGE	Erkennung von statischen Gesten
DGE	Erkennung von dynamischen Gesten
GSE	Erkennung einer Gebärdenprache
SSE	Spezifische Spracherkennung (Gebärden)
DKG	dynamische Körpergesten

Anwendungen	
GUI	graphische Benutzeroberfläche

Segmentierung	
MHS	markierte Handschuhe
LUT	Farb-Lookup-Tabelle

Bedingungen	
BA	benutzerabhängig
BU	benutzerunabhängig
UH	uniformer Hintergrund
SH	statischer Hintergrund
OB	optimale Beleuchtung
SB	Spiegelbox

Tabelle3. Abkürzungen zu den Tabellen 1 und 2.

Die Segmentierung kann grauwertbasiert *(Grau)* oder farbbasiert *(Farbe)* geschehen. Die Verwendung von Farbe gegenüber der klassischen grauwertbasierten Bildverarbeitung erweist sich gerade bei der Gestenerkennung als sehr nützlich. Ein Ansatz für die farbbasierte Segmentierung besteht darin, Farbtabellen (LUT = Lookup Tables) zu bestimmen, in denen jedem Farbwerten das Gebiet zugeordnet wird, das er repräsentiert, z.B. „Hand“ oder „Hintergrund“. Die meisten aufgeführten farbbasierten Systeme scheinen ein starres, farbbasiertes Segmentierverfahren zu verwenden. Dies ist bei sich ändernden Lichtverhältnissen problematisch. So zeigt die Haut bei einem Weißabgleich bei Neonlicht und bewölktem Wetter den zu erwartenden, signifikanten Rot-Gelb-Anteil im Videosignal. Nach Ausschalten des Neonlichts erscheint die Hand jedoch blau-grün. Schröter [22,21] entwickelte eine adaptive, clusterbasierte Farbsegmentierung, die Objekt- und Hintergrundfarben zum Aufbau eine LUT berücksichtigt, die im ARGUS-System von Kohler et al. Anwendung findet.

Eine Möglichkeit, definierte Lichtverhältnisse herzustellen, ist bei der bereits erwähnten Spiegelbox von Bröckl-Fox durch eine Lampenanordnung in der Spiegelbox gegeben.

Bei der Gestenerkennung in globaler Umgebung ergibt sich die Schwierigkeit, daß die Hand in der Aufnahme so klein ist, daß die Handpositur nicht mehr erkennbar ist. Durch den Einsatz von Bewegtkameras wie im ARGUS-System von Kohler et al. kann dieses Problem gemindert werden, indem die Hand von einer Kamera in Großaufnahme verfolgt wird. Diese Aufnahme wird dann der Segmentierung unterworfen. Dies erleichtert die Segmentierung, wirft aber das Problem der Objektverfolgung auf.

Die allein auf Farbwerten basierende Segmentierung wir im allgemeinen Gebiete liefern, die das gesuchte Objekt nicht korrekt repräsentieren. Ein spezifisches Problem der Handgestenerkennung ist der Unterarm, der sich direkt an die Hand anschließt und sich nicht farblich davon abhebt. Die Länge des sichtbaren Unterarms kann von Bild zu Bild variieren, weil er durch ein Kleidungsstück oder auch durch den Bildrand abgeschnitten ist. Die Aufgabe der Unterarmabtrennung ist, von der segmentierten Region, die die Hand und den Unterarm überdeckt, den Teil zu erkennen und abzutrennen, der die Hand repräsentiert.

Eine Vorgehensweise zur Lösung dieser Aufgabe ist, die lokale Form des Gebietes zu analysieren. Als Möglichkeit hierfür bieten sich Schablonentechniken [11], aktive deformierbare Konturen [17] oder Skelettberechnung [23] an. Bei diesen Verfahren ist zum Teil der für die Echtzeitverarbeitung hohe Rechenaufwand problematisch. Das folgende Verfahren, das im ZYKLOP-System von Stark et al. und ARGUS-System von Kohler et al. Verwendung findet, hat sich als recht leistungsfähig erwiesen. Es basiert auf der Distanztransformationen [5] bzw. einer Approximationen davon [1]. Die Distanztransformation ermittelt zu jedem Punkt (x, y) des untersuchten Gebiets den minimalen Abstand $d(x, y) \in \mathbb{R}$ zum Gebietsrand. Das Mittel der Urbilder, in denen die Distanztransformation das absolute Maximum d_{max} annimmt, ist Mittelpunkt eines maximalen Kreises, der den Radius d_{max} hat und vollständig innerhalb der Handfläche liegt. Trägt man über diesem Kreis die Werte der Distanztransformation ab, und legt man eine Tangente in den Punkt, wo diese Werte maximal werden, erhält man in den meisten Fällen eine gute Trennlinie zwischen Hand und Unterarm. Weitere sicherere Kriterien für die Richtung des Unterarms erhält man über die um den Faktor $k \geq 1$ vergrößerten Kreise (optimale Werte sind $k = 1,58; 2,0$). Details dazu sind in [6] zu finden.

3.3 Merkmale und Klassifikation

Bezüglich der Klassifikation lassen sich im wesentlichen drei Systemtypen unterscheiden:

1. Systeme, die ein Hand/Arm-Modell verwenden, z.B. ein zylindrisches 3D-Hand- oder Gliedmaßenmodell;
2. Systeme, die direkt auf Bildeigenschaften, z.B. der geometrischen Form, arbeiten; dazu zählen Systeme, die Korrelation, Neuronale Netze, Elastic Graph Matching, Multiklassifikation einsetzen;

3. Systeme, zeitabhängige Parameter verwenden, z. B. statistisch beschreibbare Deformationen, wie sie in Hidden Markov Modellen (HMM) Verwendung finden.

Die in 3. erwähnten HMM sind vor allem in der Gebärdenspracherkennung gebräuchlich. Ein Beispiel für ein System, das HMM verwendet, ist *Ffinder* (*Flesh Finder*) von Campbell et al. [4]. *Ffinder* findet zunächst hautfarbene Regionen in zwei Kamerasichten. Die Regionen werden mit elliptischen *Blobs* überdeckt und die Zentren, die Haupt- und Nebenachsen, Position und Geschwindigkeit der Ellipsen in kartesischen und Polarkoordinaten, die Krümmung der Handtrajektorie und deren Ableitungen zurückgegeben. Zur Klassifikation werden HMM eingesetzt, mit denen sich 18 Körpergesten bei einer Erkennungsrate von 95 % erkennen lassen. Starner (siehe Tab. 1) verwendete Ffinder zur dynamischen Gestenerkennung.

In den Tabellen findet eine stichwortartige Charakterisierung der jeweils eingesetzten Merkmale und Klassifikationsmethoden statt. Die Methoden, die zur Klassifikation eingesetzt werden, sind so vielfältig, daß es unmöglich ist, sie im einzelnen hier zu beschreiben. Sie stammen aus dem mehr oder minder bekannten Repertoire der Mustererkennung und sind auf die speziellen Anforderungen adaptiert.

3.4 Systemeinschränkungen

Bei vielen Systemen sind Einschränkungen an die Umgebung notwendig, in denen das System betrieben wird. Die stärkste Einschränkung ist sicherlich die Spiegelbox (in der Spalte „Bedingung“ der Tabellen mit SK markiert), die die übliche Bilderfassungsumgebung durch eine weitere Konstruktion ergänzt. Andere Anforderungen sind, daß der Hintergrund uniform (UH) oder statische (SH) ist. Manche Systeme fordern auch eine spezielle optimale Beleuchtung (OB). Schließlich gibt es Systeme, die benutzerabhängig (BA) beziehungsweise benutzerunabhängig (BU) sind.

3.5 Anwendungs- und Einsatzgebiete

In der letzten Spalte der Tabellen werden erprobte Anwendungs- und Einsatzgebiete der Systeme aufgeführt. Einige Systeme sind als anwendungsunabhängige, dreidimensionale, graphische Benutzungsschnittstelle konzipiert. Ziel hierbei ist, die Beschränkungen der klassischen Maus/Tastatureingabe und der zweidimensionalen Menü/Fenster-Systeme zu überwinden.

Ein besonders erwähnenswertes System in diesem Zusammenhang ist der *Virtuellen Touchscreen*, der in die Gruppe der Desktop-Anwendungen fällt. Ein Videoprojektor projiziert ein Computerbild auf eine Tischplatte. Der Benutzer kann auf aufprojizierte Knöpfe zeigen, so als würde er einen Touchscreen verwenden. Das Gestenerkennungssystem bestimmt die Geste und Fingerspitzenposition und reagiert. Der Virtuelle Touchscreen beruht auf den Arbeiten von Maggioni [13,18,19]. Er findet kommerzielle Anwendung in einem Kioskinformationssystem der Firma Siemens und ist damit das wohl erste als in großem Umfang käufliches Produkt erhältliche, sehensbasierte Handgestenerkennungssystem. Der Vorteil dieses Systems ist, daß es gegen den an öffentlichen Plätzen möglichen Vandalismus im Gegensatz zu üblichen Touchscreens recht robust ist, da die Kamera und der Projektor sicher hinter Glas und unerreichbar weit über der Tischplatte angebracht werden können.

Ein Anwendungsbereich, bei dem besonders anspruchsvolle Anforderungen an die Benutzungsschnittstelle gestellt werden, ist der interaktive rechnergestützte Entwurf (CA), insbesondere wenn es um die Konstruktion dreidimensionaler Objekte geht. Unter den aufgeführten System treten in dieser Kategorie der Entwurf von

Industrieanlagensteuerungen und die Planung von Filmen auf. Das Filmplanungssystem von Hoch [9, 10] ermöglicht es einem Regisseur, virtuelle Schauspieler und Gegenstände in einer virtuellen Szene durch Zeigegesten interaktiv anzuordnen.

Als weiteres Anwendungsfeld ist die Verwendung der Gestenerkennung bei der Fernbedienung und Fernsteuerung von Geräten signifikant. Es gibt Systeme zur Fernbedienung von Robotern [24], Fernsehgeräten [7] und allgemein Heimgeräten [14].

Als weitere, speziellere Anwendungsgebiete treten die Erkennung von Gebärdensprachen und „Augmented Reality" auf.

4 Ergonomie und Interaktionsgestaltung

Bei der Interaktion mit Gesten gibt es zwei wesentliche Aspekte zu beachten. Der erste Aspekt ist die *Wahl der Gesten.* Dabei sind die anatomischen Möglichkeiten des Menschen, aber auch seine Merkfähigkeit und die Unterscheidbarkeit der Gesten zu beachten. Eine systematische Untersuchung von Bröckl-Fox [3] bezeichnet höchstens 24 statische Handgesten von 68 kombinatorisch möglichen (Aufsicht) als einfach ausführbar, wovon etwa die Hälfte als sehr leicht ausführbar klassifiziert wird.

Ein anderes Problem von gestenbasiertem Dialog insbesondere in globaler Umgebung ist die Interpretation von Bewegungen des Benutzers als Gesten, die nicht der Bedienung des Systems gegolten haben. Diese Schwierigkeit kann durch *multimodale Interaktion* gemindert werden, d.h. mehrere Kommunikationskanäle werden kombiniert werden. Beispielsweise kann die Kombination von Gestik und Spracheingabe nützlich sein, da auch bei der Spracheingabe die Gefahr der ungewollten Mißinterpretation besteht. Im Ausloten zweckmäßiger Kombinationen in Abhängigkeit der Anwendungssituation eröffnet sich neben der Perfektionierung der Bildverarbeitungstechnik ein weites Feld für zukünftige Arbeiten auf dem Gebiet der computersehensbasierten Gestikinteraktion.

Literatur

1. Gunilla Borgefors. Distance Transformations in Digital Images. *CVGIP*, 34:344–371, 1986.
2. Marcus Breig. Entwicklung einer Bewegungsdetektion und -vorhersage für den Einsatz zweier beweglicher Kameras bei menschlichen Bewegungen. Diplomarbeit, University of Dortmund, December 1997.
3. Ulrich Bröckl-Fox. *Untersuchung neuer, gestenbasierter Methoden für die 3D-Interaktion.* PhD thesis, Universität Karlsruhe, Februar 1995. Shaker-Verlag, ISBN 3-8265-0620-0.
4. L. W. Campbell, D. A. Becker, A. J. Azarbayejani, A. F. Bobick, and A. Pentland. Invariant Features for 3-D Gesture Recognition. In *Second International Conference on Face and Gesture Recognition*, pages 157–162, Killington VT, Oktober 1996. MIT Media Laboratory, IEEE Computer Society Press.
5. P. E. Danielson. Euclidean Distance Mapping. *CGIP*, 14(3):227–248, 1980.
6. Bernd Deimel. Entwicklung eines stabilen videobasierten Verfahrens zur Segmentierung der Hand am Unterarm. Diplomarbeit, Lehrstuhl Informatik 7, Universität Dortmund, Januar 1998.

7. W. T. Freeman and C. Weissman. Television control by hand gestures. In M. Bichsel, editor, *Proc. Intl. Workshop on Automatic Face- and Gesture-Recognition*, IEEE Computer Society, pages 179–183, Zürich, Switzerland, June 1995. http://www.merl.com/TR/TR94-24.
8. Phil A. Harling and Alistair D. N. Edwards. Hand tension as a gesture segmentation cue. In P. A. Harling and A. D. N. Edwards, editors, *Progress in Gestural Interaction*, pages 75–88, University of York, UK, March 19th 1996. Springer. ISBN 3540760946.
9. Michael Hoch. Object Oriented Desgin of the Intuitive Interface. In B. Girod, H. Niemann, and H.-P. Seidel, editors, *3D Image Analysis and Synthesis'96*, pages 161–167, Universität Erlangen-Nürnberg, November 18–19 1996. infix Verlag. ISBN 3-89601-000-X.
10. Michael Hoch. Human Body Tracking for the Intuitive Interface. In *3. Workshop Farbbildverarbeitung*, pages 73–79, Stuttgart, 1997. IRB-Verlag Fraunhofer Gesellschaft.
11. Chung-Lin Huang and Ching-Wen Chen. Human Facial Feature Extraction for Face Interpretation and Recognition. *Pattern Recognition*, 25(12):1425–1444, 1992.
12. Thomas S. Huang and Vladimir I. Pavlovic. Hand Gesture Modeling, Analysis and Synthesis. In M. Bichsel, editor, *Proc. Intl. Workshop on Automatic Face- and Gesture-Recognition*, IEEE Computer Society, pages 73–79, Zürich, Schweiz, Juni 1995.
13. B. Kämmerer and Ch. Maggioni. GestureComputer: Research and Practice. In *Proc. Interface to real and virtual Worlds*, Montpellier, France, June 1995.
14. Markus Kohler. Vision Based Remote Control in Intelligent Home Environments. In B. Girod, H. Niemann, and H.-P. Seidel, editors, *3D Image Analysis and Synthesis'96*, pages 147–154, University of Erlangen-Nuremberg/Germany, November 18–19 1996. infix Verlag. ISBN 3-89601-000-X; see also *Ein ergonomisches Dialogsystem zur Steuerung von technischen Systemen in Wohnbereichen mittels Gestenerkennung — Abschlußbericht* at Dep. f. CG/University of Dortmund.
15. Markus Kohler. System Architecture and Techniques for Gesture Recognition in Unconstraint Environments. In Nadia Magnenat Thalmann, editor, *International Conference on Virtual Systems and Multimedia VSMM'97*, pages 137–146, University of Geneva, Switzerland, September 10–12th 1997. IEEE Computer Society. ISBN 0-8186-8150-0.
16. Myron W. Krueger. *Artificial Reality II.* Addison-Wesley, Reading, 1991.
17. Kok Fung Lai. *Deformable Contours: Modelling, Extraction, Detection and Classification.* PhD thesis, University of Wisconsin-Madison, 1994.
18. Ch. Maggioni. GestureComputer: New Ways of Operating a Computer. In M. Bichsel, editor, *Proc. Intl. Workshop on Automatic Face- and Gesture-Recognition*, IEEE Computer Society, pages 166–171, Zürich, Schweiz, Juni 1995.
19. Ch. Maggioni and B. Kämmerer. GestureComputer: Die neue Art der Rechnersteuerung. *unix/mail magazine*, 1, 1996.
20. Richard J. Millar and Gordon F. Crawford. A Mathematical Model for Hand Shape Analysis. In P. A. Harling and A. D. N. Edwards, editors, *Progress in Gestural Interaction*, pages 235–245, University of York, UK, 19. März 1996. Springer. ISBN 3540760946.
21. Sven Schröter. Entwicklung von Verfahren zur automatischen Kalibration eines farbbasierten Objekterkennungssystems. Master's thesis, University of Dortmund, Oktober 16th 1996.
22. Sven Schröter. Automatic calibration of lookup-tables for color image segmentation. In B. Girod, H. Niemann, and H.-P. Seidel, editors, *3D Image Analysis and Synthesis'97*, pages 123–129, University of Erlangen-Nuremberg/Germany, November 17–18 1997. infix Verlag. ISBN 3-89601-007-7.
23. Jean Serra. *Image Analysis and Mathematical Morphology*, volume 1. Academic Press, London, 1982.
24. Jochen Triesch and Christoph von der Malsburg. Robotic Gesture Recognition. In Ipke Wachsmuth and Martin Fröhlich, editors, *Gesture and Sign Language in Human-Computer Interaction*, volume 1371 of *Lecture Notes in Artificial Intelligence*, pages 233–244. Universität Bielefeld, Springer-Verlag Berlin 1998, 17.–19. September 1997.

25. Christopher Wren, Ali Azarbayejani, Trevor Darrell, and Alex Pentland. Pfinder: Real-Time Tracking of the Human Body. *IEEE Transactions on Pattern Analysis and Machine Intelligence*, 19(7):780–785, July 1997. also as Technical Report No. 353.

GREFIT: Visuelle Erkennung kontinuierlicher Handposturen *

Claudia Nölker, Helge Ritter

Technische Fakultät, Neuroinformatik, Universität Bielefeld
Postfach 10 01 31, D-33501 Bielefeld
email: {claudia,helge}@techfak.uni-bielefeld.de

Zusammenfassung In GREFIT detektieren hierarchisch angeordnete künstliche neuronale Netze die Fingerspitzenorte in Grauwertbildern einer menschlichen Hand. Um hieraus die 3-dimensionale Handpostur zu gewinnen, wurden neuronale Netze trainiert, die Gelenkwinkel der Finger aus den Fingerspitzen-Positionen zu berechnen. Mit Hilfe eines Handmodells, welches der Form und den Bewegungsmöglichkeiten der menschlichen Hand nachempfunden ist, kann die 3-dimensionale Handpostur damit graphisch dargestellt werden. Im Unterschied zu anderen Systemen zur Handposturerkennung findet bei GREFIT keine Klassifikation in eine feste Anzahl von Handposturen statt, sondern beliebige Handstellungen werden erkannt und wiedergegeben.

1 Einführung

Bei dem Computer Vision Problem der Erkennung von Handstellungen (= Posturen) handelt es sich um eine anspruchsvolle Aufgabe, deren Schwierigkeit in der Vielzahl und Komplexität der möglichen Handposturen liegt. Eine wichtige Motivation für eine Lösung dieser Aufgabe liegt darin, Gestenerkennung als einfaches und intuitives Mittel zur Kommunikation zwischen Mensch und Maschine, zum Beispiel in der virtuellen Realität, einsetzbar zu machen.

In vielen Ansätzen werden als Hilfsmittel farbige oder mit Markern versehene Handschuhe verwendet [1,2], um aus der Position der "Handfragmente" die Handpostur zu bestimmen. Bei diesen Ansätzen wird stets eine Klassifikation durchgeführt, die Anzahl der zu erkennenden Posturen ist dadurch begrenzt.

In [3] wird ein System vorgestellt, das statt einer Klassifikation eine kontinuierliche Parametrisierung der Handpostur ausgibt und damit die Identifikation stufenloser Zwischenstellungen ermöglicht. Der dabei verwendete Ansatz basiert, wie in der vorliegenden Arbeit, auf trainierbaren neuronalen Netzen, benötigt jedoch Trainingsbeispiele bekannter 3-dimensionaler Handposturen, deren Gewinnung vergleichsweise aufwendig ist. Dagegen gelingt die Gewinnung von Trainingsbeispielen mit bekannten 2-dimensionalen Fingerspitzenorten mit

* Diese Arbeit wurde im Rahmen des Projektes 'Multimedia NRW: Die Virtuelle Wissensfabrik' vom Ministerium für Wissenschaft und Forschung des Landes Nordrhein-Westfalen unter der Nummer IV A3-107 031 96 gefördert.

wesentlich verringertem Aufwand. Dies motiviert, für die Erkennung von Handposturen von den 2d-Fingerspitzenorten auszugehen und diese Information zur Rekonstruktion der Handstellung zu verwenden.

Andere Verfahren zur Detektion von Fingerspitzen aus Grauwertbildern arbeiten modellbasiert und schränken die Erkennung auf solche Bilder ein, bei denen keine Überdeckungen vorkommen und der Bildbereich in der Nähe der Fingerspitzen sehr kontrastreich ist [10,13,14]. GREFIT (Gesture REcognition based on FIngerTips) findet Fingerspitzen unabhängig vom Kontrast, also auch wenn sie sich vor der Hand befinden.

Zur Rekonstruktion der Handpostur wird in [7] ein auf der Form und der Kinematik der Hand basierender Algorithmus eingesetzt, um aus manuell bestimmten 3-dimensionalen Positionen der 5 Fingerspitzen sowie des Handgelenks ein geometrisches Handmodell zu generieren. Die Visualisierung geschieht mit einem einfachen Strichmodell. Aus 16 Zylindern besteht das Handmodell in DigitEyes [10]. Wenn die Kinematik und die Geometrie der Benutzerhand bekannt sind, und keine Überdeckungen vorkommen, erkennt DigitEyes die Handstellung mit einer Framerate von bis zu 10 Hz.

In einem zweiten Schritt werden in GREFIT neuronale Netze eingesetzt, aus den 2d-Positionen der Fingerspitzen die Gelenkwinkelstellungen der Hand zu berechnen. Die Visualisierung geschieht mit Hilfe eines der Form und den Bewegungsmöglichkeiten der menschlichen Hand nachempfundenen Handmodell. Somit kann GREFIT *kontinuierliche*, also Handstellungen mit beliebigen Winkeln, erkennen und wiedergeben. Im Gegensatz zur Klassifikation, z.B. in Buchstaben des Fingeralphabets, ermöglicht es die Anwendung von Gestenerkennung überall dort, wo eine graduelle Auswahl stattfindet, z.B. im CAD oder bei der Navigation in virtuellen Welten.

2 Detektion der Fingerspitzen

Für die Detektion von Fingerspitzen verwenden wir einen hierarchischen Ansatz aus zwei hintereinandergeschalteten LLM-Netzen (s.u.), einem globalen Netz, welches die Grobpositionierung durchführt, sowie einem lokalen Netz, welches auf einem kleineren Bildausschnitt operiert und eine exaktere Lokalisation ermöglicht.

2.1 Vorverarbeitung

Die Eingabe in das System bilden monokulare Grauwertbilder (80x80 Pixel Auflösung) einer repräsentativen Anzahl von Handstellungen, bei denen die 2d-Fingerspitzenkoordinaten im Bild manuell bestimmt wurden.

In einem Vorverarbeitungsschritt wird zunächst die Beleuchtung normiert. Danach werden alle unterhalb einer Schwelle liegenden Pixelwerte auf 0 (= Schwarz) gesetzt, sowie der Armansatz maskiert und der Schwerpunkt der Pixelwertmenge der Hand auf einen festgelegten Punkt zentriert.

Aus dem so normierten Bild wird ein Merkmalsvektor für die LLM-Netze berechnet. Dies geschieht durch lokale Kreuzkorrelation mit richtungsempfindlichen Gaborfiltern [4]; im vorliegenden Fall verwenden wir eine Anordnung aus fünf "Gaborjets", die an fünf festen Punkten des Bildes (die Anordnung gleicht der einer Fünf auf einem Würfel) zentriert sind. Jeder "Jet" besteht aus je 3 Sinus- und Cosinus-Gaborfunktionen mit einer Orientierungsbandbreite von 30°, sowie einer richtungsisotropen Gaußfunktion (zusammen 7 Merkmale pro Punkt). Die Entfernung der Zentren und die Bandweite der Gaborfunktionen wurden entsprechend der Bildgröße gewählt. Dies führt auf 35-dimensionale Merkmalsvektoren. Eine Visualisierung des Ergebnisses der Anwendung des Gaborfilters ist in Abb. 1 dargestellt.

2.2 Hierarchischer Ansatz

Der Aufbau des hierarchischen Erkennungssystems ist in Abb. 1 schematisch wiedergegeben. Das globale Netz erhält einen Merkmalsvektor, der auf dem gesamten Bild berechnet wurde, und gibt einen ersten Näherungswert für die gesuchte Position aus. Diese ungefähre Lage wird der Mittelpunkt eines verkleinerten Bildausschnitts, aus dem der Merkmalsvektor für das nachfolgende, lokale Netz berechnet wird. Somit wird im ersten Schritt das Gesamtbild nur relativ grob ausgewertet, während im nachfolgenden Schritt der für die Suche interessantere Bildausschnitt mehr fokale Aufmerksamkeit erhält.

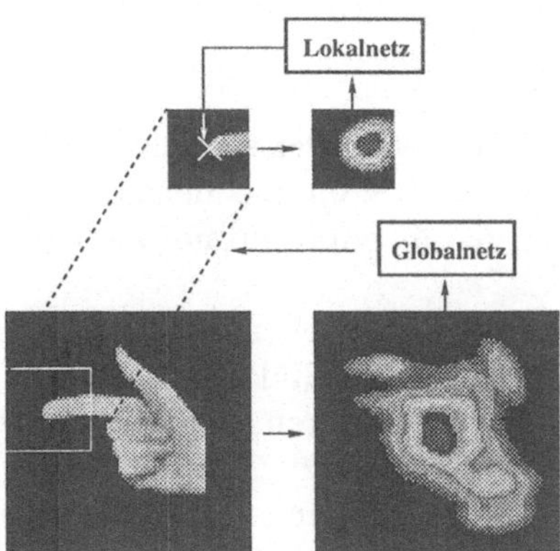

Abbildung 1. Hierarchischer Ansatz zur Detektion der Fingerspitze des Zeigefingers.

2.3 LLM-Netz

Bei dem verwendeten Netzwerk handelt es sich um ein LLM-Netz (Local Linear Mapping-Netz) [11]. Die Annäherung einer gesuchten Funktion wird durch

Vorgabe von Werten an einer festen Anzahl von Stützstellen (Knoten) und einer lokal linearen Abbildung in der Nähe jeder Stützstelle durchgeführt. Jedem Knoten r wird damit sowohl im Ein-, wie auch im Ausgaberaum je ein Referenzvektor $\boldsymbol{w}_r^{\mathrm{in}}$ bzw. $\boldsymbol{w}_r^{\mathrm{out}}$ und eine Matrix A_r zugeordnet. Im vorliegenden Fall ist der Eingaberaum durch den 35-dimensionalen Merkmalsraum und der Ausgaberaum durch die (für die nachgeschaltete Verarbeitungsstufe relativ zum Ursprung des Vorgängerbildes liegenden) 2d-Orte der Fingerspitzen gegeben.

In der Lernphase werden dem Netz Trainingsbeispiele bestehend aus Merkmalsvektor $\boldsymbol{x}$ mit zugehörigem Ausgabevektor $\boldsymbol{y}$ vorgelegt. Durch Vergleich von $\boldsymbol{x}$ mit den eingabeseitigen Referenzvektoren wird der Referenzvektor $\boldsymbol{w}_s^{\mathrm{in}}$ mit dem kleinsten euklidischen Abstand d_s ermittelt.

Bei einem Winner-takes-all-Netz bestimmt allein der $\boldsymbol{w}_s^{\mathrm{in}}$ ausgabeseitig zugeordnete Referenzvektor $\boldsymbol{w}_s^{\mathrm{out}}$ die Antwort $\boldsymbol{y}^{\mathrm{net}}$ im Ausgaberaum. Im Falle eines LLM-Netzes wird nun zusätzlich aus der Abweichung $\boldsymbol{x} - \boldsymbol{w}_s^{\mathrm{in}}$ zwischen Eingabewert und dem eingabeseitigen Referenzvektor mittels der lokal linearen Abbildung A_s ein linearer Korrekturterm berechnet:

$$\boldsymbol{y}^{\mathrm{net}} = \boldsymbol{w}_s^{\mathrm{out}} + A_s(\boldsymbol{x} - \boldsymbol{w}_s^{\mathrm{in}})$$

Während der Trainingsphase wird in jedem Schritt eine Fehlerkorrektur von w_s^{in}, w_s^{out} und A_s nach folgenden Regeln durchgeführt:

$$\Delta \boldsymbol{w}_s^{\mathrm{in}} = \varepsilon_1(\boldsymbol{x} - \boldsymbol{w}_s^{\mathrm{in}})$$

$$\Delta \boldsymbol{w}_s^{\mathrm{out}} = \varepsilon_2(\boldsymbol{y} - \boldsymbol{y}^{\mathrm{net}}) + A_s \Delta \boldsymbol{w}_s^{\mathrm{in}}$$

$$\Delta A_s = \varepsilon_3 (d_s^2)^{-1}(\boldsymbol{y} - \boldsymbol{y}^{\mathrm{net}})(\boldsymbol{x} - \boldsymbol{w}_s^{\mathrm{in}})^T$$

Im Laufe der Trainingsphase verteilen sich die Referenzvektoren so im Raum, daß sie sich in Regionen konzentrieren, aus denen besonders viele Trainingsbeispiele kommen. Sie bilden damit eine Voronoi-Zerlegung des Raums der Trainingsbeispiele.

In der Anwendung auf die beschriebene Aufgabe wurden 2 LLM-Netze hintereinandergeschaltet. Die Größe des Bildausschnitts des zweiten Netzes beträgt 20x20 Pixel. Das Zentrum des kleineren Bildausschnitts wird dabei durch die Ausgabe des Vorgängernetzes festgelegt. Zusätzlich wurde der Ausgabewert des globalen Netzes während jedes Trainingsschrittes um einen Zufallsvektor verschoben. Dadurch ergibt sich für das Training des lokalen Netzes ein künstlich vergrößerter Trainingsdatensatz, der zu einer verbesserten Generalisierungsfähigkeit führt. Abb. 2 zeigt die erhaltenen Resultate. Für quantitative Ergebnisse für ein vergleichbares Szenario siehe [8].

3 Erkennung und Visualisierung der 3d-Handpostur

Die 2d-Orte der Fingerspitzenpositionen werden nun zu einem 10-dimensionalen Merkmalsvektor für die Berechnung der Handpostur. Durch die in der Vorverarbeitung durchgeführte Zentrierung ist die Position der Handfläche im Bild fest,

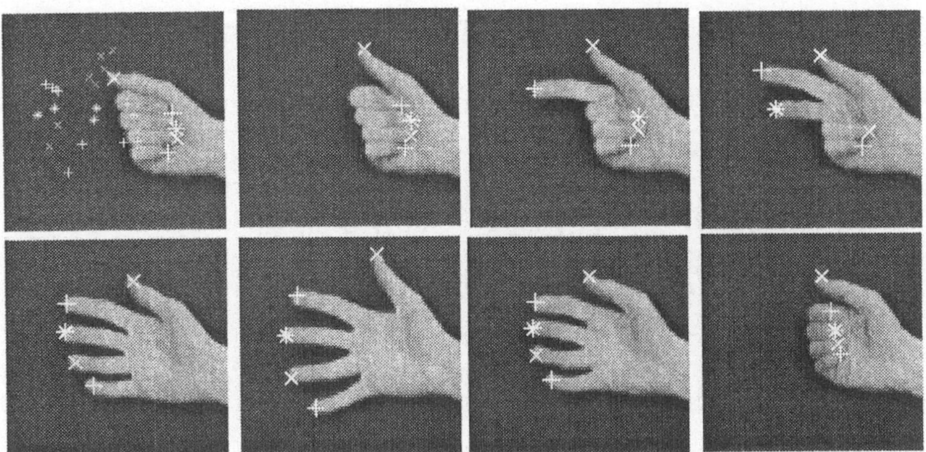

Abbildung 2. Erkennung von Fingerspitzen aus Einzelbildern einer Handbewegung. Die gefundenen Positionen sind mit einem Symbol im Bild markiert (oberes Kreuz = Daumen; oberes Plus = Zeigefinger; Stern = Mittelfinger; unteres Kreuz = Ringfinger; unteres Plus = Kleinfinger). Im Bild links oben sind zusätzlich die 5 Referenzvektoren im Ausgaberaum vom globalen Netz mit einem kleineren Symbol markiert.

die Gelenkwinkel der Finger und des Daumens werden jeweils einzeln mit einem neuronalen Netz berechnet.

Zur Visualisierung der Handpostur generieren wir ein virtuelles Handmodell, welches den Proportionen und Bewegungsmöglichkeiten einer menschlichen Hand nachempfunden ist. Mit diesem Handmodell können *beliebige* Handstellungen wiedergegeben werden, was für die Ausgabe von GREFIT essentiell ist. Bei Systemen, die nur eine Klassifikation in eine geringe Anzahl statischer Posturen durchführen, genügt eine einfache Repräsentation der Handpostur mit einem Synonym oder einem Symbol.

3.1 Dreidimensionales Modell der Hand

Das Handmodell besteht insgesamt aus 16 Elementen, eins für die Handfläche, sowie jeweils drei für die Glieder der Finger und des Daumens. Die Fingerlängen sind in Abb. 3 dargestellt. Sie wurden, ebenso wie die Fingerbreiten und die Handbreite, von einer durchschnittlich großen Hand auf das Modell übertragen. Die vielfältigen Bewegungsmöglichkeiten der Hand sind dadurch modelliert, daß jeder Finger (und der Daumen) 4 einstellbare Gelenkwinkel besitzen (siehe Abb.3). Im Grundgelenk des Fingers wird mit θ_0 die Seitbewegung (Abduktion/Adduktion) des Fingers eingestellt, die Winkel $\theta_1, \theta_2, \theta_3$ geben den Grad der Flexion der Gelenke wieder. Nicht in die Modellierung der virtuellen Hand integriert wurde die Krümmung der Handfläche (wie z.B. beim Greifen eines Balles), sowie die (minimale) Fähigkeit des mittleren Daumengelenks zur Seitbewegung.

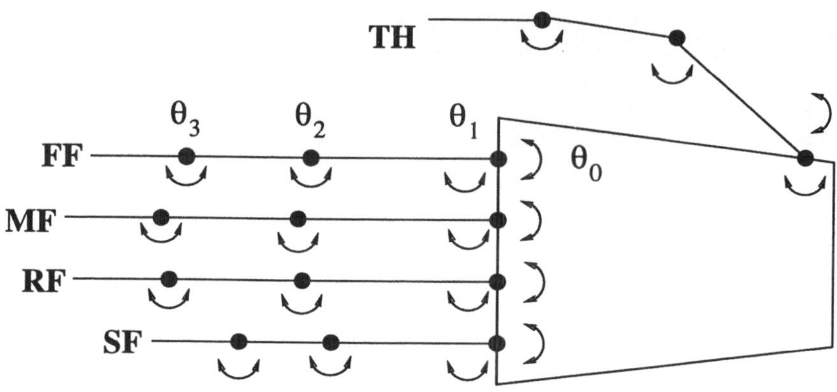

Abbildung 3. Freiheitsgrade der Finger

Damit erhalten wir 20 variable Parameter, die die Handpostur wiedergeben. Allerdings sind diese Gelenkwinkel einer menschlichen Hand teilweise miteinander korreliert und können nicht unabhängig voneinander bewegt werden [5]. Ein Beispiel hierfür sind die letzten beiden Gelenke der Finger, die von derselben Sehne bewegt werden. Annäherungsweise gilt zwischen ihnen die Beziehung

$$\theta_3 = \frac{1}{2}\theta_2.$$

Eine weitere Vereinfachung ergibt sich, wenn die Beugewinkel θ_2 und θ_1 gleich gesetzt werden

$$\theta_2 = \theta_1.$$

Erst diese Einschränkung auf zwei Freiheitsgrade pro Finger erlaubt die dreidimensionale Darstellung aus den zweidimensionalen Positionsdaten.

In Tab. 1 sind die Bereiche für die aktive Beugung und Streckung der Fingergelenke angegeben. Flexion und Extension des Daumens gehen dabei von einer Neutralnullstellung aus, bei der die Daumenmuskeln nicht aktiv sind. Die anderen Finger sind in Nullstellung gestreckt, ihre Fingerachsen verlaufen parallel.

Tabelle 1. Bewegungsbereiche der Fingergelenke (nach [5]).

	θ_0^{min}	θ_0^{max}	θ_1^{min}	θ_1^{max}
Daumen (TH)	-30	20	-20	30
Zeigefinger (FF)	-5	25	0	90
Mittelfinger (MF)	-10	10	0	90
Ringfinger (RF)	-15	5	0	95
Kleinfinger (SF)	-20	5	0	100

Ebenfalls in das Modell integriert wurde, daß die Beugeachsen der Finger- und Grundgelenke schräg verlaufen. Die Finger werden in einer zum Kleinfinger hin zunehmend schrägen Richtung gebeugt. Dies bewirkt, daß die Finger in Faust: stellung dicht nebeneinander liegen und ihre Achsen an einer Stelle zusammenlaufen.

3.2 PSOM

Wir verwenden eine PSOM (Parametrisierte Selbst-Organisierende Merkmalskarte) zur Berechnung der Gelenkwinkelstellungen aus der 2d-Position der Fingerspitzenorte.

Die PSOM ist, ebenso wie das LLM-Netz, eine Erweiterung der SOM (Selbst-Organisierende Merkmalskarte) von Kohonen [6]. Während das LLM-Netz eine lineare Approximation der gesuchten Funktion durchführt, verwendet eine PSOM eine Menge nichtlinearer Basismannigfaltigkeiten zur Konstruktion einer Abbildung durch die Referenzvektoren.

Eine PSOM benutzt eine Anzahl von Referenzvektoren w_r, die üblicherweise Punkten auf einem kartesischen Gitter A in einem Merkmalsraum V zugeordnet sind. Die Referenzvektoren müssen topologisch geordnet sein, d.h. Nachbarpunkte im Datenraum sind auch Nachbarpunkte auf dem Gitter. Nun wird eine Abbildungsmannigfaltigkeit S konstruiert, die durch die Gitterpunkte $a \in A$ hindurch verläuft. Dazu ist jedem Gitterpunkt $a \in A$ eine Basisfunktion $H(a, s)$, $s \in S$ zugeordnet, mit der die Interpolation $w : S \to M$ zwischen den Gitterpunkten realisiert wird:

$$w(s) = \sum_{a \in A} H(a, s)\, w_a. \tag{1}$$

Die Basisfunktionen müssen zwei Orthogonalitätsbedingungen erfüllen. Die erste Bedingung

$$H(a_i, a_j) = \delta_{ij} \quad \forall a_i, a_j \in A$$

bewirkt, daß die durch (1) gegebene Mannigfaltigkeit Mdurch die Gitterpunkte w_a, $a \in A$ hindurch verläuft. Weiterhin muß die Summe über alle Gewichtungsfaktoren eins ergeben

$$\sum_{a \in A} H(a, s) = 1 \quad \forall s \in S.$$

Die Anwendung der trainierten PSOM verläuft analog zur SOM: Zu einem Punkt x aus dem Merkmalsraum V wird der Punkt $s^* \in S$ bestimmt, für den gilt

$$s^* = min_s \|x - w(s)\|.$$

Die Ausgabe $w(s^*)$ der PSOM wird dann mittels (1) berechnet.

Die PSOM kann zur Approximation einer Abbildung $V \to M$ eingesetzt werden. Darüberhinaus ist sie jedoch auch zur assoziativen Vervollständigung von fragmentarischen Eingaben in der Lage. Für Details zur PSOM siehe z.B. [12,15].

3.3 Anwendung der PSOM

In GREFIT realisiert die PSOM die Abbildung von der 2d-Position einer Fingerspitze im Bild auf die Gelenkwinkelstellung des entsprechenden Fingers. Die Eingabe in das Netz bildete ein 4-dimensionaler Vektor, bestehend aus den beiden Gelenkwinkeln, sowie der resultierenden 2d-Position des Fingerspitzenortes im Bild. Während des Trainings variierten wir die Gelenkwinkel θ_0 und θ_1 in ihren Bewegungsbereichen (siehe Tab.1). Die resultierenden Positionen der Fingerspitze ergeben dann die Form einer "liegenden Eieruhr" (siehe Abb. 4, links oben), d.h. es liegt eine Überschneidung vor. An der Überkreuzungsstelle kann der 2d-Ort der Fingerspitze durch viele verschiedene Gelenkstellungen erreicht werden. Die Transformation zwischen 2d-Bildorten und Gelenkwinkeln ist daher an dieser Stelle singulär und kann von der PSOM nicht aufgelöst werden.

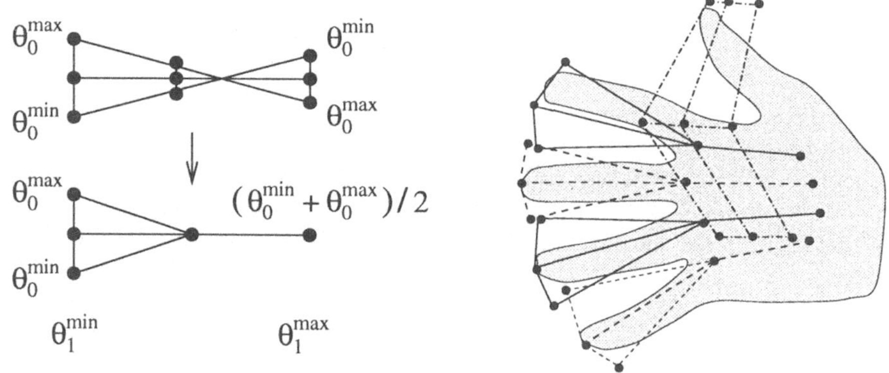

Abbildung 4. Links: Struktur der PSOM. Rechts: Bewegungsraum der Finger.

Diese Modellierung der Bewegungsmöglichkeiten des Fingers basierten allerdings auf der Annahme, daß die beiden Winkel θ_0 und θ_1 unkorreliert sind. Beobachtungen ergaben jedoch, daß nur eine geringe Bewegungsfreiheit in θ_0 vorhanden ist, falls θ_1 groß, der Finger also stark gekrümmt ist. Die volle Bewegungsfreiheit in θ_0 wird nur dann ausgenutzt, wenn der Finger annähernd gestreckt ist.

Da die Gitterstruktur für die Anwendung der PSOM erhalten bleiben sollte, wurden mehrere Gitterpunkte "zusammengezogen" und mit demselben Wert belegt. Damit ist der Bewegungsraum einer Fingerspitze nunmehr durch die Form eines "Hexenbesens" (siehe Abb. 4, links unten) gegeben.

Der Daumen nimmt eine Sonderrolle ein. Da in seinem Bewegungsbereich keine Singularitäten auftreten, basiert das Training der PSOM auf dem ursprünglichen 3 x 3 Gitter. Die resultierenden Bewegungsbereiche aller 5 Finger sind in Abb. 4 (rechts) dargestellt.

3.4 Ergebnisse

In Abb. 5 ist das Ergebnis von GREFIT bei der Anwendung auf 3 Beispielbilder dargestellt. Die Original-Handpostur und die Rekonstruktion mit dem Modell stimmen optisch gut überein. Eine genaue, quantitative Analyse erfordert eine Messung der Gelenkwinkel der Originalhand, wie sie beispielsweise mit einem Datenhandschuh erfolgen kann. Eine entsprechende Auswertung ist einer künftigen Untersuchung vorbehalten.

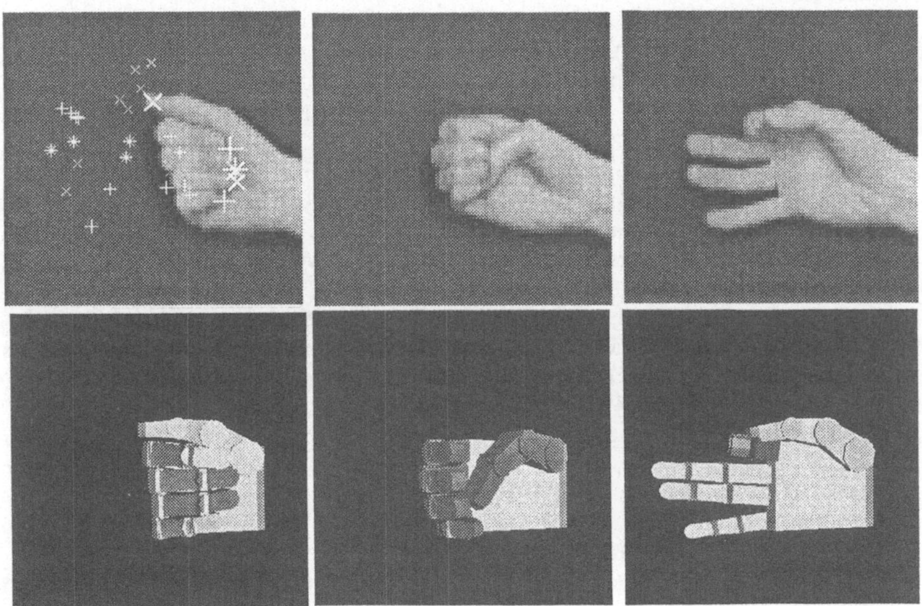

Abbildung 5. Visuelle Steuerung des Handmodells mittels natürlicher Handposturen.

4 Diskussion und Ausblick

Der vorgestellte, hierarchische Ansatz ist gut zur Detektion von Fingerspitzenorten geeignet. Im Unterschied zu modellbasierten Verfahren kann das erforderliche "Erkennungswissen" aus Trainingsbildern akquiriert werden. Die Rekonstruktion der dreidimensionalen Handstellung mit einem neuronalen Netz geschieht schnell und sicher. Die Berechnung der Gelenkwinkel aus dem Grauwertbild geschieht auf einem Pentium Pro (200 MHz) mit 10 Hz.

Es ist geplant, GREFIT auf die Verarbeitung von Stereo-Bildern zu erweitern, und damit die 3d-Position jeder Fingerspitze im Raum zu bestimmen. Liegt diese Information vor, kann die PSOM auf einem 3-dimensionalen Gitter trainiert werden, und jeder Finger kann mit einem dritten unabhängigen Freiheitsgrad ausgestattet werden.

Ein weiterer Schritt ist die Integration einer Evaluierungskomponente, die eine Einschätzung darüber liefert, wie sicher es ist, daß sich an der vom Lokalnetz gefundenen Position tatsächlich eine Fingerspitze befindet. Auf diese Weise können kurzfristige Überdeckungen der Fingerspitzen erkannt und mit einer bereits entwickelten Prädiktionskomponente [9] überbrückt werden.

Literatur

1. J. Davis and M. Shah. Visual gesture recognition. *IEE Proc.-Vis. Image Signal Processing*, 141(2):101–106, 1994.
2. B. Dorner and E. Hagen. Towards an American Sign Language interface. *Artificial Intelligence Review*, 8(2-3):235–253, 1994.
3. A. Drees. *Visuelle Erkennung von Handstellungen mit neuronalen Netzen.* PhD thesis, Universität Bielefeld, 1996. DISKI, Infix, Sankt Augustin.
4. B. Jähne. *Digitale Bildverarbeitung.* Springer Verlag, 1991.
5. I.A. Kapandiji. *Funktionelle Anatomie der Gelenke*, volume 1 of *Obere Extremität.* Enke Verlag Stuttgart, 1984.
6. T. Kohonen. The self-organizing map. In *Proc. IEEE 78*, pages 1464–1480, 1990.
7. R.J. Millar and G.F. Crawford. A mathematical model for hand-shape analysis. In P.A. Harling and A.D.N. Ewards, editors, *Progress in Gestural Interaction - Proceedings of Gesture Workshop'96*, pages 235–245. Springer, 1996.
8. C. Nölker and H. Ritter. Detektion von Fingerspitzen in Videobildern. In E. Paulus and F. Wahl, editors, *DAGM Mustererkennung 1997*, pages 97–104. Springer-Verlag Berlin Heidelberg New York, 1997.
9. C. Nölker and H. Ritter. Vorhersage der Bewegung von Fingerspitzen. In *Proc. Workshop Dynamische Perzeption*, Jun 1998.
10. J.M. Rehg and T. Kanade. Visual tracking of high DOF articulated structures: an application to human hand tracking. In J.-O. Eklundh, editor, *Computer Vision - ECCV'94*, pages 35–46, Berlin Heidelberg, 1994. Springer Verlag. Lecture Notes in Computer Science 801.
11. H. Ritter. Learning with the self-organizing map. In T. Kohonen, K. Mäkisara, O. Simula, and J. Kangas, editors, *Artificial Neural Networks*, pages 379–384. Elsevier Science Publishers B. V., 1991.
12. H. Ritter. Parametrized self-organizing maps. *Artificial Neural Networks*, 3, 1993.
13. N. Shimada, Y. Shirai, and Y. Kuno. Hand gesture recognition using computer vision based on model-matching method. *Advances in Human Factors Ergonomics*, 20:11–16, 1995.
14. A. Utsumi, T. Miyasato, F. Kishino, and R. Nakatsu. Hand gesture recognition system using multiple cameras. In *Proceedings of the International Conference on Pattern Recognition*, pages 667–671, 1996.
15. J. Walter. *Rapid learning in Robotics.* Cuvillier Verlag Göttingen, 1996.

Robotic Gesture Recognition by Cue Combination

Jochen Triesch[1] and Christoph von der Malsburg[1,2]

[1] Institut für Neuroinformatik
Ruhr-Universität Bochum, D-44780 Bochum, Germany
{Triesch,Malsburg}@neuroinformatik.ruhr-uni-bochum.de
[2] University of Southern California
Dept. of Computer Science and Section for Neurobiology
Los Angeles, CA, USA

Abstract. Automatic gesture recognition holds the promise of making man-machine interfaces more natural and intuitive. We discuss six requirements for gesture recognition by robots. We present computer vision techniques developed at our lab which are suited to meet the requirements. The techniques owe their robustness to the combination of several cues for a particular task instead of relying on a single cue alone. We demonstrate this in a sample application employing a real robot in a pick-and-place scenario.

1 Introduction

The idea of robots or computers communicating with humans naturally, i.e., by using speech and gesture, presumably is as old as the idea of building robots or computers at all. Clearly, using natural interfaces such as speech or gesture has great advantages over other modes of communication: it is very efficient and does not need special training of the human user. Yet the usual way of interacting with computers or robots is still by the keyboard and a pointing device such as the mouse. Only in the recent past with computers becoming faster and algorithms more refined significant progress has been made in the necessary computer vision techniques for gesture recognition, and first applications appear at the horizon. But there still is a huge amount of work to do. We are especially interested in vision-based gesture recognition for robots operating in real world environments. This poses a number of constraints to *human robot interaction* only some of which also apply for *human computer interaction* in controlled desktop environments:

1. **Real time constraint:** The robot must be capable of real time gesture recognition. If the robot's responses are slow, it is tiresome to use. However, with the increasing speed of standard hardware a system that falls short of real time performance today will work satisfactorily in a couple of years.
2. **Person independence:** The system must be person-independent. For most applications it is desirable that many potential users can operate the robot, even if the robot has never seen them before.

3. **"Come as you are" constraint:** The system must not require the user to wear special clothing (such as only long or short sleeves) or cumbersome devices such as colored markers or data gloves, since this is too tedious for the user.
4. **Naturalness constraint:** The gesture analysis must allow for natural intuitive gestures. If the user has to learn complicated artificial gestures he will not prefer the interface to using, e.g., a keyboard. Natural gestures would be those used in inter-human communication usually accompanying speech.
5. **Complex dynamic backgrounds:** The robot will face complex dynamic backgrounds against which a user operates it. A system requiring uniform or static background is not flexible enough for real world applications.
6. **Variable lighting:** The robot must cope with variable lighting situations. The requirement of constant studio-like illumination is too much of a restriction for any real world application.

While the first four constraints apply to all gesture interfaces the last two are more specific to the context of autonomous robots. Given these constraints a look at the recent research literature [3, 9, 16, 21, 14] reveals that hardly any published work acknowledges all the requirements stated above. A few examples shall illustrate this point. They are meant as providing a cross section of work being undertaken rather than giving a comprehensive review.

In the work of Franklin *et al.* [6] an attempt to build a robot waiter is presented, a domain which indeed poses all the above challenges. So far the robot's gesture analysis, however, only distinguishes between an empty hand and a hand holding an object based on how much skin color is visible. The system presented by Cui and Weng [5] recognizes different hand gestures in front of complex backgrounds. It reaches 93.1% correct recognition for 28 different gestures, but is not person independent and relies on a rather slow segmentation scheme taking 58.3 seconds per image. Heap and Hogg [7] present a method for hand tracking using a deformable model, which also works against complex backgrounds. The deformable model describes one hand posture and certain variations of it and is not aimed at recognizing different postures. The work presented by Campbell *et al.* [4] is an example of a system recognizing two-handed gestures. It allows only for motion based gestures, because it is not analyzing the shape of the user's hands. In Kjeldsen's and Kender's work [10] a real time gesture system for controlling a window-based computer user interface is presented. The posture analysis is indeed quite fast (2 Hz). A minor drawback of the system is that its hand tracking has to be specifically adapted for each user. The system presented by Maggioni [13] has a similar setup. It requires a constant background to the gesturing hand. For the systems developed by Kohler and coworkers [15, 11] it is unclear in how far they can cope with dynamic or complex (containing, e.g., skin color) backgrounds.

Most of the systems mentioned rely on a simple scheme for detecting and segmenting the gesturing body parts from the background such as motion detection or skin color. The implicit assumption is that there are no distractors with similar properties in the background of the scene, i.e., nothing in the back-

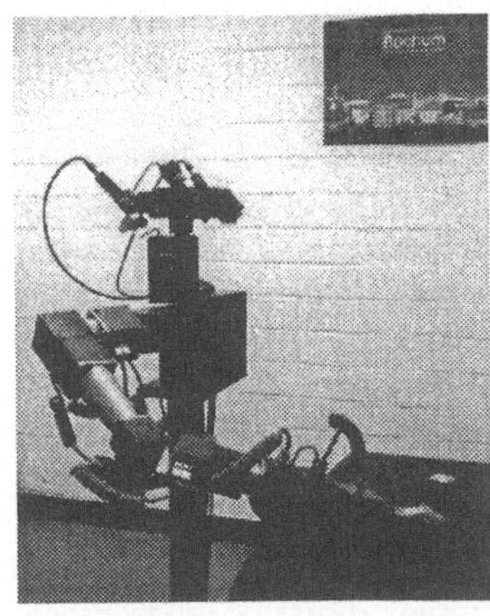

Fig. 1. Our robot (left) operates in a grasp put scenario and manipulates objects which are located on a table in front of it. The user points to objects with particular gestures (right) indicating how the robot shall manipulate the object.

ground is moving or has the color of skin. For robots operating in uncontrolled environments these assumptions clearly cannot be met. We are thus interested in the difficult cases where there is no simple way of segmenting the gesturing body parts, in our case the user's hand.

We are working with a real robot (section 2) and try to meet all the constraints mentioned. Our approach to tackle gesture recognition in difficult cases where segmentation is not possible by relying on a single cue is to combine multiple cues such as motion, color or stereo. The robustness reached by proper cue combination is much higher than for single cues (section 3). For the purpose of shape recognition we have developed techniques which do not require a bottom up segmentation of the target object but use top down processing in the form of template matching, where the templates may contain combinations of different feature types (section 4).

2 An Example Application

The robot at our lab has a kinematically redundant arm with seven degrees of freedom, which allows it to grasp an object from various directions (figure 1 left). On top of the arm a stereo camera head is mounted. It has three degrees of freedom, pan, tilt and vergence. The cameras yield images of 768 x 572 pixels and have a field of view of 35°.

There are at least three different ways for human robot interaction with gestures. First, the user may give explicit gestural commands to the robot. Second, the user may supplement spoken commands with gestures (e.g. saying "give me that object" while pointing to it). Third, the robot may be trained with imitation learning, i.e., it learns how to perform a particular action by observing the human teacher doing it and imitating his example.

So far we have only used the first type of interaction although it is perhaps the least interesting according to the naturalness constraint discussed in the introduction. However, work is in progress for the other types. We have designed an example application where the robot stands in front of a table with objects on it. The user tells it with gestures which object to grasp and how to grasp it, as well as where to put it (figure 1 right). The gestures are defined as pointing movements to the objects with a particular hand shape. The user's hand is tracked until it comes to rest using the techniques described in section 3. After tracking, the hand posture is analyzed as described in section 4. It tells the robot whether to grasp the object from, e.g., above, the side, the front, and so on. After the robot has grasped the object the user indicates with a second gesture where the object shall be placed and the robot puts it there.

We do not claim this being a particular useful application but it is well suited to study the problems of gesture recognition in a complex dynamic environment and demonstrating the dexterity of our robot. This application requires of course a number of other skills needed by the robot, e.g., recognition of shape and orientation of the object pointed to, grip planning and grip execution, which are discussed elsewhere [1, 2].

3 Tracking of Head and Hands

A prerequisite for the successful recognition of gestures is tracking the head and hands of the gesturing person. We combine motion, color and stereo cues to reach the robustness demanded by real world applications. Let us first consider a hand pointing to some objects on a table in front of the robot (figure 1 right). We work on low resolution images with a size of 96 x 71 pixels in HSI (hue, saturation, intensity) color format. The tracking currently runs at a maximal speed of 8 Hz using stereo and 12.5 Hz using only one camera on a standard PentiumPro PC without any special image processing hardware.

3.1 Color Cue

Skin color detection is based on the hue (H) and saturation (S) components of the image. We distinguish two types of processing. The first uses a very coarse and unrestrictive model of skin color, defined as a prototypical point in the HS plane. For each pixel of the input image we compute its Euclidean distance to this point, where the axes are appropriately rescaled. The closer the pixel is to the prototype, the higher is its likelihood of stemming from the head or hands of a person. When the lighting situation changes, e.g., due to the spotlights of a TV team, the prototypical point may no longer be appropriate. In order to deal with such cases we have introduced a second scheme which works with an adapted skin color table. Before actually using the system, its color table is adapted to the current lighting situation (and the subjects particular skin color) by the subject showing his or her hand to the robot for a couple of frames. With this scheme the color cue can be made much more restrictive. A result for the

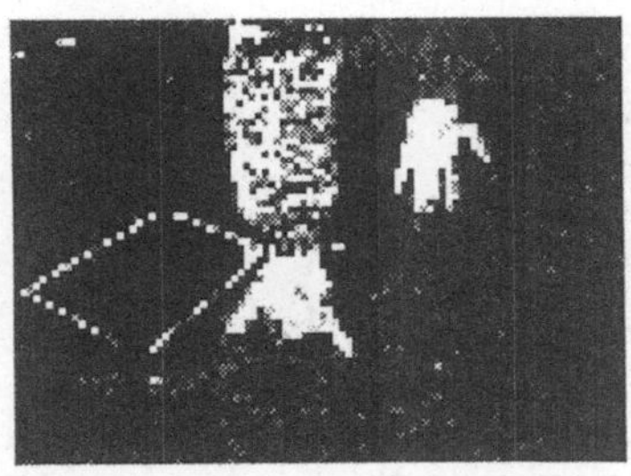
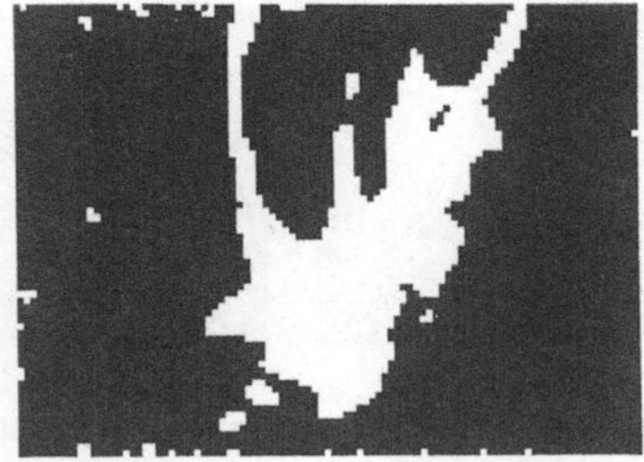

Fig. 2. Typical results of color cue (left) and motion cue (right) in a difficult situation where a distractor (the person's other hand) is moving in the background.

unrestrictive color cue is depicted in figure 2 left. There is a lot of noise in the cue since it reacts to any object approximately skin colored. For the future, it would be desirable to have an online recalibration taking place while the robot is performing, which detects changes in the lighting situation and automatically adapts to them.

3.2 Motion Cue

We compute a thresholded version of the absolute-difference images of the intensity (I) components of consecutive images. Afterwards, we apply a local regularization algorithm which switches on pixels that have a high number of direct neighbors which are on and which switches off isolated pixels being on. The result of such processing is depicted in figure 2 right. The motion cue responds to all moving image regions, i.e., to all moving objects and to some extent also to their shadows falling over still objects, producing artifacts. It would, of course, also be fooled by motions of the camera head itself resulting in perceived motion almost everywhere if this is not suppressed on the basis of known camera motion.

3.3 Attention Maps and Stereo Cue

We compute attention maps for each camera by combining the motion and color cue. For each camera the result of the color cue and the motion cue are added with appropriate weighting factors. The additive combination of cues ensures that the system will keep working (although in a deteriorated fashion) if one of the cues breaks down. Attention maps are then computed by convolving the summation results with a Gaussian kernel in order to smooth them and emphasize larger blobs. For the scene of figure 2 the attention maps of the left and right camera are depicted in figure 3. In both attention maps there are two strong blobs of activity belonging to the left and right hands of the subject.

The stereo cue is intended to select only objects that are in the plane of fixation of the robot. For this purpose, the attention maps of left and right image are simply added (figure 3). This highlights only the responses of objects

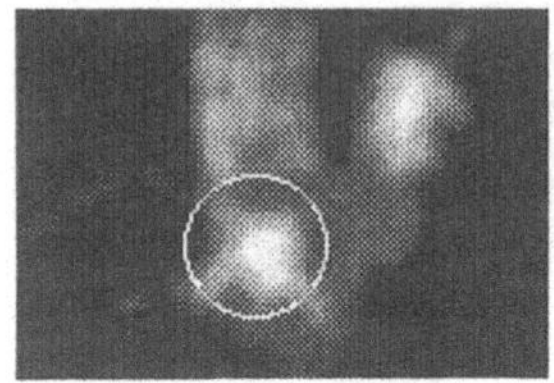
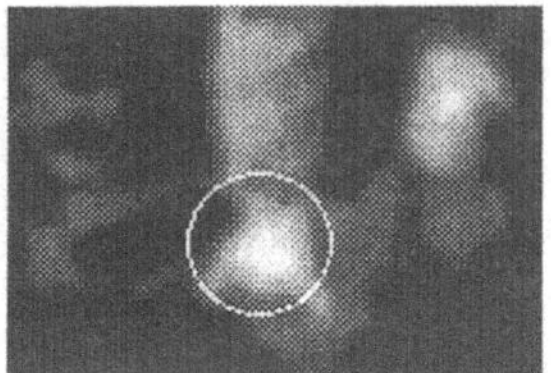
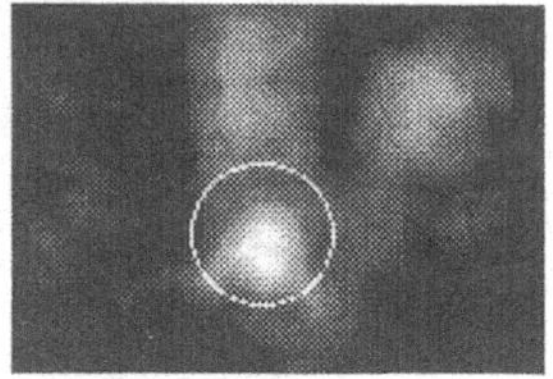

Fig. 3. Left: Two attention maps extracted from left and right camera. Each attention map contains two strong blobs of activity referring to the two hands of the subject. Right: When the two attention maps are added only objects in the plane of fixation pop out. The hand in the background is smeared out. The circles are drawn around the hand selected due to the stereo cue.

in the plane of fixation because only for these do the contributions of the left and right attention map overlap in image space.

The point with the highest response in the sum of the attention maps is the assumed position of the target hand. Starting from its coordinates, a gradient ascent is performed in the attention maps of the left and right image until the local maxima corresponding to the selected hand are reached. The spatial position of the hand can now be easily computed by triangulation.

3.4 Extensions

For some applications, e.g., sign language recognition, head and both hands of the subject have to be tracked simultaneously. We have demonstrated this for the case of a single camera by simply looking for targets in the current frame in the vicinity of targets detected in previous frames, i.e., the continuity of the targets' motion is exploited. This simple scheme has of course problems with mutually overlapping targets. If, for instance, both hands overlap strongly and then move apart again, tracking will not be able to tell which one was which. The incorporation of techniques for explicitly modeling the motion of the hands and predicting their future positions (e.g., Kalman filters) can attenuate this problem although they cannot solve it altogether.

We have also experimented with active tracking, where the camera head makes saccadic eye movements in order to keep a target fixated. Details on this can be found in [19].

4 Hand Posture Classification

The second important building block of a gesture recognition system is the analysis of hand postures. Our posture recognition is based on *elastic graph matching*, which has already been successfully applied to object and face recognition [12, 22]. For some applications such as sign language recognition, the analysis of facial expressions is important. This can also be done with elastic graph matching (e.g., [8]), but we will not discuss this point any further here.

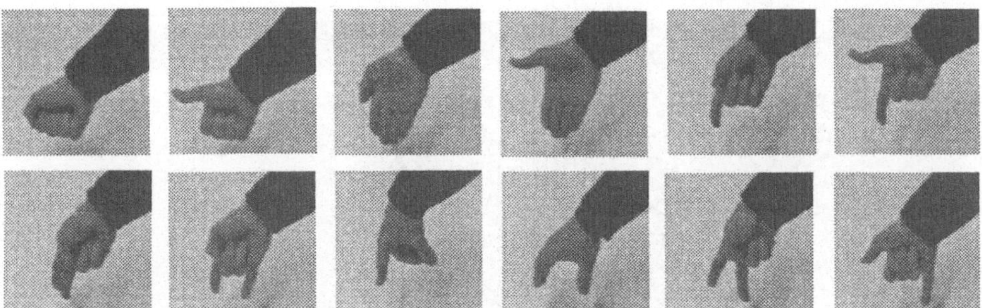

Fig. 4. Twelve postures used in a recent study [17] to determine the usefulness of color features for the hand posture analysis.

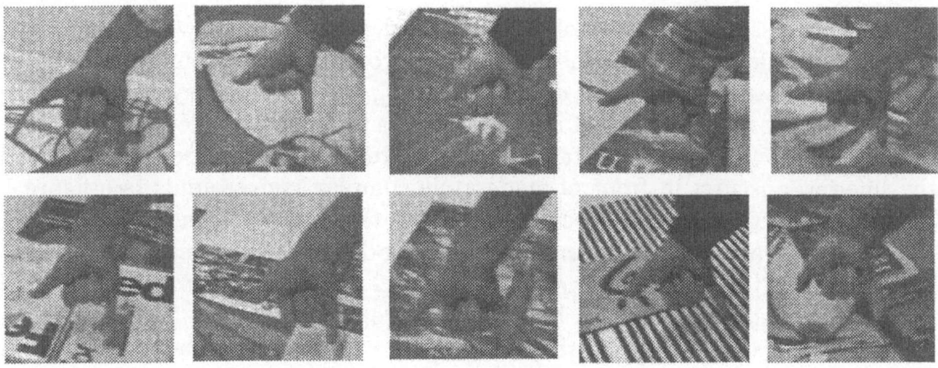

Fig. 5. Examples of one posture performed by different persons against different complex backgrounds. Most of the backgrounds contain skin color.

In elastic graph matching, objects are represented as labeled graphs, where the nodes carry local image information and the edges contain information about the geometry. One model graph is created for each object. The local image information at each node is often represented by a vector of responses to Gabor-based kernels called a *jet*. In recent experiments we also added color information to the nodes resulting in highly improved performance [17]. We fuse the graphs obtained from several persons performing the posture into a single *bunch graph* for each posture; for details on the bunch graph concept see [22]. A graph representing a particular posture is matched onto an image by moving it across the image until the jets at each node fit best to the regions in the image they come to lie on. During the matching process we allow for certain geometrical transformations of the graph such as scaling and rotation in plane. For recognition of a posture, the graphs of all postures are sequentially matched onto the images of left and right camera and the posture whose graph obtains the highest total similarity (sum of similarities in left and right image) is selected as the winner.

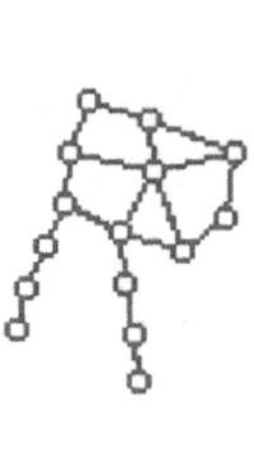
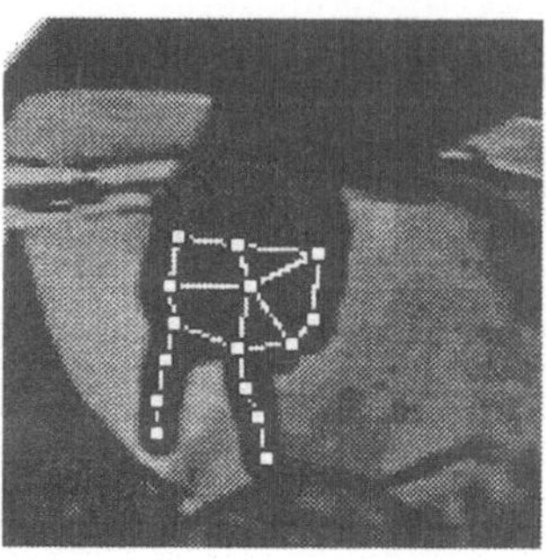
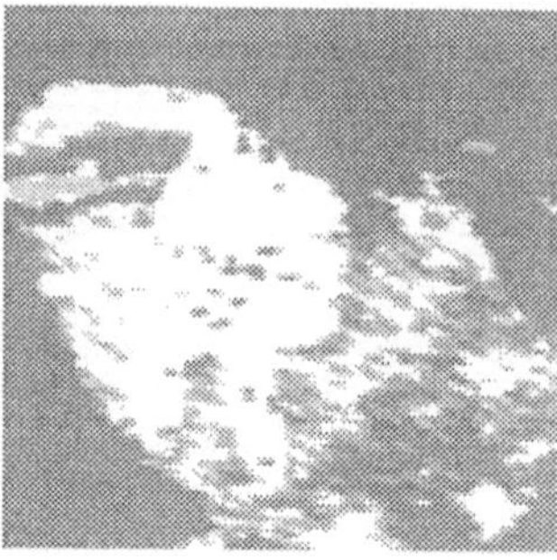

Fig. 6. Example of a model graph being matched onto an input image. Although the background has large regions of skin color the graph is positioned properly.

We have designed a series of systems which have been shown to work in a person-independent way and despite varying complex backgrounds. The older systems are described in more detail in [18, 20]. Our previous system [20] only used shape information in the form of responses to Gabor wavelets to the intensity distribution of the image. It performed correctly in four out of five times for six different postures in front of moderately complex backgrounds (see figure 1 right). Recognition time was between two and three seconds. In a recent study [17] we added also color information to the nodes of the graphs. Experiments were performed on images of an alphabet of 12 different postures (depicted in figure 4) against very complex backgrounds (depicted in figure 5). We reached 86 % correct recognition with the combination of color and Gabor information, where Gabor information alone could only account for 70 % correct recognition. However, the recognition time increased to between 10 and 20 seconds. The result of a matching process is depicted in figure 6.

5 Discussion and Outlook

We have discussed the requirements for gesture interfaces of robots operating in the real world. We have presented vision-based techniques for tracking the head and hands of a person, as well as for the analysis of hand shapes taking these real world requirements into account. Both the tracking and the hand posture recognition are purely vision-based and work by combining several cues such as shape, color or stereo. They do not require the user to wear gloves or other devices. They function in a person-independent way and despite dynamic complex backgrounds. The tracking is capable of real time performance. For the computationally more extensive posture analysis, there is a complex tradeoff between the allowed number of postures, the accuracy and the speed of the matching process. While the older version using only shape information [20] was not far from real time performance for distinguishing six postures, the most recent version integrating also color features currently takes between 10 and 20 seconds for distinguishing twelve postures.

For the future, we intend to study other forms of gestural communication such as imitation learning or speech supplementing gestures. Also we would like to close the gestural communications loop by letting the robot perform gestures itself, e.g., by pointing to unfamiliar objects whose names the user then supplies to the robot.

Acknowledgements

This work was in part supported by a grant from the German Federal Ministry for Science and Technology (01 IN 504 E9).

References

1. M. Becker, E. Kefalea, E. Maël, C. v.d. Malsburg, M. Pagel, J. Triesch, J. C. Vorbrüggen, R. P. Würtz, and S. Zadel. GripSee: A gesture-controlled robot for object perception and manipulation. *(submitted to) Autonomous Robots: Special Issue on Perception-Based Intelligent Robots*, 1998.
2. M. Becker, E. Kefalea, E. Maël, C. v.d. Malsburg, M. Pagel, J. Triesch, J. C. Vorbrüggen, and S. Zadel. Gripsee: a robot for visually-guided grasping. Accepted for publication at: ICANN'98, International Conference on Artificial Neural Networks, 1998.
3. Martin Bichsel, editor. *Proceedings of the International Workshop on Automatic Face- and Gesture- Recognition.* IEEE Computer Society, 1995.
4. L. W. Campbell, D. A. Becker, A. Azarbayejani, A. F. Bobic, and A. Pentland. Invariant features for 3-D gesture recognition. In *Proceedings of the Second International Conference on Automatic Face and Gesture Recognition 1996, Killington, Vermont, USA, October 14-16*, 1996.
5. Y. Cui and J. J. Weng. Hand sign recognition from intensity image sequences with complex backgrounds. In *Proceedings of the Second International Conference on Automatic Face and Gesture Recognition 1996, Killington, Vermont, USA, October 14-16*, 1996.
6. D. Franklin, R. E. Kahn, M. J. Swain, and R. J. Firby. Happy patrons make better tippers — creating a robot waiter using Perseus and the animate agent architecture. In *Proceedings of the Second International Conference on Automatic Face and Gesture Recognition 1996, Killington, Vermont, USA, October 14-16*, 1996.
7. T. Heap and D. Hogg. Towards 3D hand tracking using a deformable model. In *Proceedings of the Second International Conference on Automatic Face and Gesture Recognition 1996, Killington, Vermont, USA, October 14-16*, 1996.
8. H. Hong, H. Neven, and C. v. d. Malsburg. Online facial expression recognition based on personalized gallery. Proceedings of FG'98, The IEEE Third International Conference on Automatic Face and Gesture Recognition.
9. Mary E Kavanaugh, editor. *Proceedings of the Second International Conference on Automatic Face and Gesture Recognition.* IEEE Computer Society, 1996. ISBN 0-8186-7713-9.
10. R. Kjeldsen and J. Kender. Toward the use of gesture in traditional user interfaces. In *Proceedings of the Second International Conference on Automatic Face and Gesture Recognition 1996, Killington, Vermont, USA, October 14-16*, 1996.

11. Markus Kohler. Technical Details and Ergonomical Aspects of Gesture Recognition applied in Intelligent Home Environments. Technical Report 638, Informatik VII, University of Dortmund/Germany, January 1997.
12. M. Lades, J. C. Vorbrüggen, J. Buhmann, J. Lange, C. v.d. Malsburg, R. P. Würtz, and W. Konen. Distortion invariant object recognition in the dynamic link architecture. *IEEE Transactions on Computers*, 42:300–311, 1993.
13. C. Maggioni. Gesturecomputer — new ways of operating a computer. In *Proceedings of the International Workshop on Automatic Face- and Gesture Recognition 1995, Zürich, Switzerland, June 26-28*, 1995.
14. V. I. Pavlovic, R. Sharma, and T. S. Huang. Visual interpretation of hand gestures for human-computer interaction: A review. *IEEE Trans. PAMI*, 19 7, 1997.
15. Michael Stark and Markus Kohler. Videobasierte Mensch-Maschine-Interaktion. *Informationstechnik und Technische Informatik*, 38(3):15–20, June 1996. More Details in english *Video Based Gesture Recognition for Human Computer Interaction*, TR 593 and *Projektgruppe 247: ZYKLOP — Visueller Mensch-Rechner-Dialog — Abschlußbericht (1995)* at Department for Computer Graphics/University of Dortmund.
16. Penny Storms, editor. *Proceedings of the Third International Conference on Automatic Face and Gesture Recognition*. IEEE Computer Society, 1998. ISBN 0-8186-8344-9.
17. J. Triesch and C. Eckes. Object recognition with multiple feature types. Accepted for publication at: ICANN'98, International Conference on Artificial Neural Networks, 1998.
18. J. Triesch and C. v.d. Malsburg. Robust classification of hand postures against complex backgrounds. In *Proceedings of the Second International Conference on Automatic Face and Gesture Recognition 1996, Killington, Vermont, USA, October 14-16*, 1996.
19. J. Triesch and C. v.d. Malsburg. Robotic gesture recognition. In *GW 97, Gesture Workshop in Bielefeld, Germany*, Lecture Notes in Artificial Intelligence 1371, pages 233–244. Springer, 1997.
20. J. Triesch and C. v.d. Malsburg. A gesture interface for human-robot-interaction. In *Proceedings of the Third International Conference on Automatic Face and Gesture Recognition*, pages 546–551. IEEE Computer Society, 1998.
21. Ipke Wachsmuth and Martin Fröhlich, editors. *Gesture and Sign Language in Human-Computer Interaction*. Number 1371 in Lecture Notes in Artificial Intelligence. Springer, 1997.
22. L. Wiskott, J.-M. Fellous, N. Krüger, and C. v.d. Malsburg. Face recognition by elastic graph matching. *IEEE Trans. PAMI*, 19 7, 1997.

Videobasierte Eingabekomponente eines Schreibsystems für Gebärdensprache

Hermann Hienz und Kirsti Grobel

Lehrstuhl für Technische Informatik
Rheinisch-Westfälische Technische Hochschule Aachen (RWTH)
Ahornstr. 55, D-52074 Aachen
Telefon: +49-241-8026105, Fax: +49-241-8888308
hienz@techinfo.rwth-aachen.de
http://www.techinfo.rwth-aachen.de

Zusammenfassung In dieser Arbeit wird ein System zur videobasierten Erkennung von Gebärden präsentiert. Das Erkennungssystem stellt die natürlichste und intuitivste Eingabemodalität für ein Schreibsystem für Gebärdensprache dar, welches im Rahmen des europäischen Projekts SignPS[1] entwickelt wurde. Das Ziel des Projekts ist es, Gehörlosen den Zugang zu geschriebenen Informationen durch die schriftliche Darstellung von Gebärden zu ermöglichen. Das videobasierte Erkennungssystem erlaubt die automatische Erkennung der manuellen Parameter der Gebärdensprache. Diese lassen sich durch vier Chereme beschreiben: die Handform, die Handorientierung, die Handbewegung und die Ausführungsstelle im Gebärdenraum. Das System benötigt lediglich eine einzelne Farbvideokamera für die Bilddatenerfassung. Die explizite Bestimmung der manuellen Ausdrucksmittel erfolgt durch verschiedene Module, in denen unterschiedliche Erkennungsverfahren eingesetzt werden. Das videobasierte Erkennungssystem wurde mit 19 Probanden validiert, um die Gebrauchstauglichkeit und die Erkennungsleistung zu bestimmen. Das System erreicht Erkennungsraten von über 80% bei einer Vokabulargröße von 300 Gebärden.

Schlüsselwörter: Videobasierte Gebärdenerkennung, Farbbildverarbeitung, visuelle Mensch-Maschine-Kommunikation, Mustererkennung, Gebärdensprache, Gebärdenschreibsystem.

1 Einleitung

Das Ziel des SignPS-Projekts ist es, Gehörlosen den Zugang zu geschriebenen Informationen durch die schriftliche Darstellung von Gebärden zu ermöglichen. Etwa 0,2% der Bevölkerung in Europa sind gehörlos und somit selbst mit den

[1] SignPS - The Development of an Interactive Printing System for Sign Languages. Dieses Forschungsprojekt wurde von der Europäischen Union im Rahmen des TIDE (Technology Initiative for Disabled and Elderly People) Programms finanziell gefördert.

besten Hörhilfen nicht in der Lage, an lautsprachlicher Kommunikation teilzunehmen. Da ihnen die Wahrnehmung der gesprochenen Sprache unmöglich ist, sind ebenfalls die Sprechmöglichkeiten der Gehörlosen sehr begrenzt. Deshalb kommt die Mehrheit der Gehörlosen nicht über das Schreib-Leseniveau eines Drittkläßlers hinaus und ist somit nicht in der Lage, Zeitungen und Bücher zu lesen. Eine gleichberechtigte Teilnahme an der Kommunikation innerhalb der hörenden Gesellschaft ist daher unmöglich. Das entwickelte Schreibsystem erlaubt Gehörlosen, Texte in Gebärdensprache zu schreiben. Ferner stellt die Verwendung eines videobasierten Gebärdenerkennungssystems die natürlichste Art und Weise dar, um Gebärden in das Schreibsystem einzugeben.

Die Gebärdensprache ist die natürliche Sprache der Gehörlosen. Die Kommunikationsfunktion und kulturelle Bedeutung der Gebärdensprache sind vergleichbar mit jener der Lautsprache. Sie ist eine vollwertige, historisch gewachsene Sprache und wird von Gehörlosen auf der ganzen Welt verwendet, z.B. DGS (Deutsche Gebärdensprache) in Deutschland oder ASL (American Sign Language) in den Vereinigten Staaten. Bei der Gebärdensprache handelt es sich ferner um eine visuell-gestische, nichtverbale Sprache, die sich manueller (Hände und Arme) und nichtmanueller Ausdrucksmittel (Oberkörper, Kopf, Augen, Gesicht, Mund) bedient [1]. Eine Gebärde kann einhändig oder zweihändig sein. Bei einhändigen Gebärden wird die ausführende Hand als dominante Hand bezeichnet, während bei zweihändigen Gebärden die Bezeichnungen dominante und nichtdominante Hand Verwendung finden. Den Raum, in dem die gebärdende Person die Gebärde ausführt, bezeichnet man als Gebärdenraum.

Neben der videobasierten Eingabekomponente, besteht das Schreibsystem in der Hauptsache aus den folgenden Komponenten[2]:

- Vorhersage- und Vervollständigungssystem (PCS – Prediction and Completion System)
- Gebärdentextverarbeitungsprogramm (Document Editor)
- Zeichensatz für Gebärden (Sign Font)

Abbildung 1 verdeutlicht den Aufbau des Systems zum Verfassen eines Textes in Gebärdensprache mit Hilfe der videobasierten Eingabekomponente. Die Gebärde wird mit einer Farbvideokamera aufgenommen. Anschließend führt das Eingabesystem die Erkennung der manuellen Gebärdenparameter durch. Das Vorhersage- und Vervollständigungssystem benötigt die Gebärdenparameter als Grundlage für die Erkennung der wahrscheinlichsten Gebärden. Es vergleicht die erkannten Gebärdenparameter auf Gebärdenebene mit Parameterkonstellationen bekannter Gebärden, ergänzt fehlende Parameter oder korrigiert fehlerhaft erkannte Parameter. Hierfür sind die Parameter einer Gebärde zusammen mit Angaben über die Auftrittshäufigkeit dieser Gebärde und dem Zeitpunkt des letzten Auftretens in einer Datenbank gespeichert. Die Datenbank umfaßt zur Zeit ein Vokabular von 300 Gebärden. Anschließend erscheinen die Gebärden, nach Wahrscheinlichkeit sortiert, in einer Vorhersageliste. Der Benutzer wählt

[2] Eine ausführliche Beschreibung des SignPS Systems findet sich in [2]

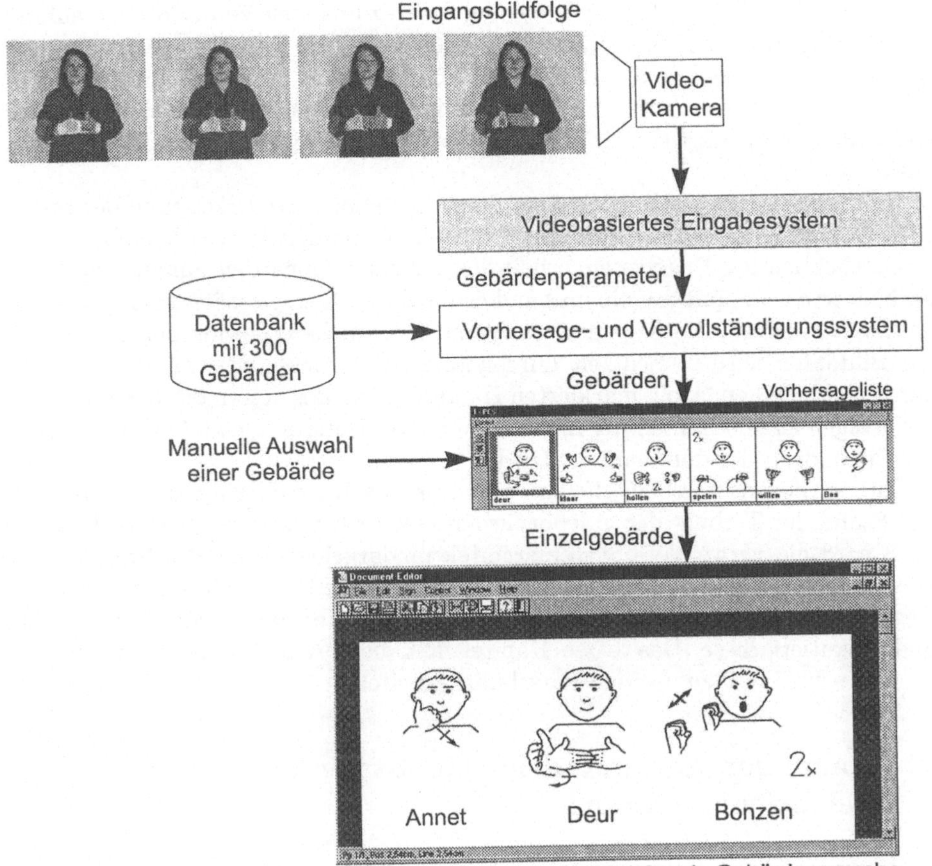

Abbildung 1. Gebärden schreiben mit Hilfe eines videobasierten Eingabesystems. Die Bildfolge auf der Eingabeseite zeigt, daß der Benutzer zur Zeit einen farbig markierten Handschuh an der dominanten Hand, einen einfarbigen Handschuh an der nichtdominanten Hand und eine Farbmarkierung am Ellenbogen trägt. Die Bildfolge zeigt beispielhaft vier Bilder der niederländischen Gebärde „deur (Tür)" des Satzes „Annet deur bonzen (Annet klopft an die Tür)". An der Ausgabeseite ist der Zeichensatz für Gebärdensprache (Sign Font), wie er im Rahmen des SignPS Projekts entwickelt wurde, dargestellt

eine Gebärde aus, die im Gebärdenfont auf dem Bildschirm im Gebärdentextverarbeitungsprogramm erscheint.

Ein Hauptproblem der automatischen Erkennung von Gebärden ist die Rekonstruktion dreidimensionaler Handpositionen aus zweidimensionalen Bildern. Die Lösung dieses Problems ist für die Berechnung der dreidimensionalen Bewegungstrajektorien von Hand und Arm erforderlich. Weiterhin treten in der zweidimensionalen Abbildung der realen Szene zum einen Verdeckungen auf, die den Erkennungsprozeß erschweren, zum anderen führen räumlich geringfügig gedrehte Ausführungen derselben Gebärde zu unterschiedlichen zweidimensionalen Abbildungen. Dieses Problem der Variabilität bei der Ausführung einer Gebärde tritt selbst dann auf, wenn ein und dieselbe Person die gleiche Gebärde mehrfach ausführt.

In dieser Arbeit wird ein System für die videobasierte Erkennung der manuellen Gebärdenparameter präsentiert, das die oben aufgeführten Randbedingungen berücksichtigt. Das System erfaßt den gesamten Gebärdenraum mit nur einer Farbkamera und läuft auf einem handelsüblichen PC mit zusätzlicher Bildverarbeitungshardware. Die Segmentierung und Merkmalsextraktion der digitalisierten Bilddaten wird in Echtzeit durchgeführt. Um dieses zu ermöglichen, trägt der Benutzer einen farbig markierten Handschuh an der dominanten Hand, einen einfarbigen Handschuh an der nicht-dominanten Hand und eine Farbmarkierung am Ellenbogen der dominanten Hand.

Die vorliegende Arbeit gliedert sich in sechs Kapitel. Kapitel 2 stellt kurz den Stand der Technik der videobasierten Gebärdenerkennung heraus. In Kapitel 3 wird die verwendete Systemarchitektur dargelegt. Eine Beschreibung der verschiedenen Module für die Erkennung der manuellen Gebärdenparameter ist Gegenstand des vierten Kapitels. Kapitel 5 beschreibt die durchgeführten Tests und diskutiert diese. Das letzte Kapitel faßt diese Arbeit zusammen und gibt einen Ausblick auf zukünftige Forschungsarbeiten.

2 Stand der Technik der videobasierten Gebärdenerkennung

In der Literatur werden verschiedene Systeme beschrieben, deren Ziel die videobasierte Gebärdenerkennung darstellt. Für die Erkennung werden unterschiedliche Verfahren, wie regelbasierte Systeme, Neuronale Netze oder Hidden Markov Modelle eingesetzt. Das erste bekannte System wurde 1988 von Tamura und Kawasaki [3] vorgestellt. Es ist in der Lage zwischen 10 verschiedenen japanischen Gebärden zu unterscheiden. Hierfür werden die manuellen Parameter Handposition, Handform und Bewegungsrichtung betrachtet und regelbasiert analysiert. Die Erkennung von Gebärden mit Hilfe Neuronaler Netze wurde 1993 von Wilson und Ansbach beschrieben [4]. Ihr Ziel war die Entwicklung eines Übersetzungssystems, um die Kommunikation zwischen Gehörlosen und Hörenden zu ermöglichen. Yamaguchi et al. [5] stellen ein System für die Erkennung von 16 japanischen Gebärden vor. Das System berechnet 2D Positionsdaten der Hand relativ zum Kopf. Diese werden für alle 16 Gebärden trainiert und in bidirektionalen Assoziativspeichern abgelegt. Starner und Pentland [6] verwenden Hidden Markov Modelle für die Erkennung kontinuierlicher Gebärden der amerikanischen Gebärdensprache. Als Merkmale dienen die absolute Position und die relative Geschwindigkeit der Hände. Die Orientierung findet durch die Richtung und die Exzentrizität der die Hände umgebenden Ellipsen Eingang in den Merkmalsvektor. Zwei weitere Merkmale bilden die jeweiligen Flächengrößen der Hände. Die gebärdende Person trägt zwei einfarbige Handschuhe unterschiedlicher Farbe. Bei einem Vokabular von 40 Gebärden und einer vorgegebenen syntaktischen Struktur wird eine Erkennungsrate von 99% angegeben. Ohne syntaktische Struktur erzielt das System eine Erkennungsrate von 91%. Grobel und Assan [7] präsentieren ein System, das die personenabhängige Erkennung isolierter Gebärden mit Hidden Markov Modellen durchführt. Unter Verwendung farbiger Handschuhe erzielt das System eine Erkennungsrate von 92% bei einer Vokabulargröße von 262 Gebärden.

3 Systemarchitektur

Abbildung 2 gibt einen Überblick über die Schritte der Bildverarbeitung, die für die Berechnung der manuellen Gebärdenparameter durchgeführt werden. Die Eingangsseite besteht aus einer einzelnen Farbvideokamera, die die Gebärde aufnimmt. Im Anschluß daran erfolgt die Umsetzung des analogen Signals in ein digitales Bildsignal durch ein Framegrabbersystem. Mit Hilfe eines echtzeitfähigen Segmentierungsalgorithmus wird anschließend die Segmentierung der Bilddaten durchgeführt. Das Ziel dabei ist zum einen eine Reduktion der zu verarbeitenden Daten und zum anderen die Unterteilung des Bildes in die Bereiche Hintergrund, Körper, Hautflächen sowie alle zehn Farbflächen der beiden Handschuhe und der Ellenbogenmarkierung [8]. In zwei weiteren Schritten werden aus den segmentierten Bilddaten Merkmale berechnet. Die Generierung der primären Merkmale erfolgt auf dem Framegrabbersystem mit einer Bildwiederholrate von 13 Bildern pro Sekunde. Die Berechnung der sekundären Bildmerkmale wird auf dem Host-PC durchgeführt. Sowohl die primären als auch die sekundären Merkmale formen den Merkmalsvektor, der für die abschließende Berechnung der manuellen Gebärdenparameter verwendet wird. Die Ausgabe des Systems bilden die erkannten Gebärdenparameter. Die Generierung der Merkmale muß in Echtzeit

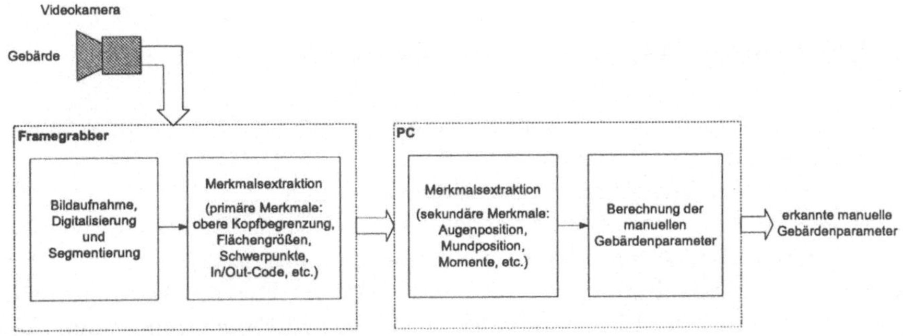

Abbildung 2. Überblick über die Bildverarbeitungsschritte für die Erkennung der manuellen Gebärdenparameter: Digitalisierung und Segmentierung, primäre und sekundäre Merkmalsextraktion, Berechnung der Gebärdenparameter

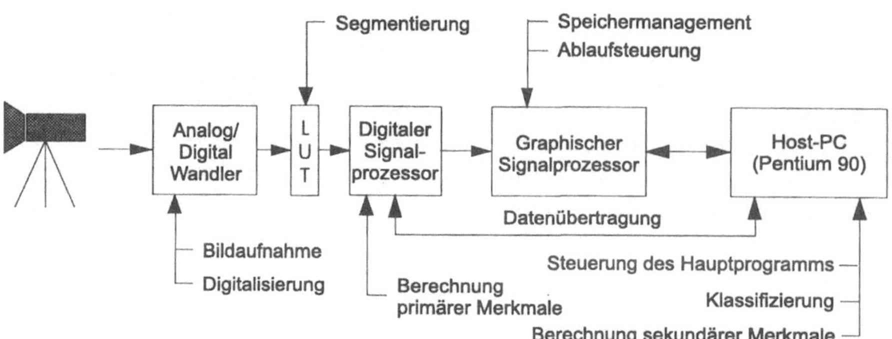

Abbildung 3. Bildverarbeitungshardware und Verteilung der Aufgaben auf die einzelnen Hardwarekomponenten

erfolgen, damit ausreichende Informationen für die Klassifikation zur Verfügung stehen. Ebenso muß die Klassifikation echtzeitfähig sein, um unerwünschte Zeitverzögerungen bei der Benutzung des Schreibsystems zu vermeiden und um die Akzeptanz des videobasierten Eingabesystems beim Benutzer zu gewährleisten.

Abbildung 3 zeigt die eingesetzte Bildverarbeitungshardware (PCprogress-M von Matrix Vision) sowie die Verteilung der verschiedenen Aufgaben auf die einzelnen Hardwarekomponenten. Das Bildverarbeitungssystem ist modular aufgebaut und besteht aus den folgenden Modulen: einem Aufnahmemodul für die Bilderfassung, einem Modul mit graphischem Signalprozessor für die Ablaufsteuerung und das Speichermanagement, sowie einem Modul mit digitalem Signalprozessor für die Verarbeitung der Bilder in Echtzeit. Weiterhin steht eine Hardware Look-Up-Tabelle zur Verfügung, die für die Segmentierung genutzt wird. Für die Übertragung der primären Merkmale zum HostPC existiert eine Datenverbindung zwischen DSP-Modul und Host-PC.

4 Erkennung der manuellen Gebärdenparameter

Dieses Kapitel beschreibt die Erkennung der manuellen Gebärdenparameter für ein- und zweihändige Gebärden.

In einem ersten Schritt findet eine Unterscheidung bezüglich ein- bzw. zweihändiger Gebärde statt. Da beide Hände jeweils durch verschiedene Farben markiert sind, ist das Auftreten der entsprechenden Farben das entscheidende Kriterium, d.h. eine Zweihandgebärde wird erkannt, wenn die Farbmarkierung der nicht-dominanten Hand im Bild detektiert wird. Anschließend findet eine Analyse der 2D-Bewegungstrajektorien mit dem Ziel statt, zwischen symmetrischer und unsymmetrischer Gebärde zu unterscheiden. Eine Basishandgebärde liegt vor, wenn die nicht-dominante Hand im Bild sichtbar ist und gleichzeitig keine Bewegung der Hand existiert. In diesem Fall wird die Berechnung der Handform (von möglichen sechs Grundhandformen [1]) der nicht-dominanten Hand aus

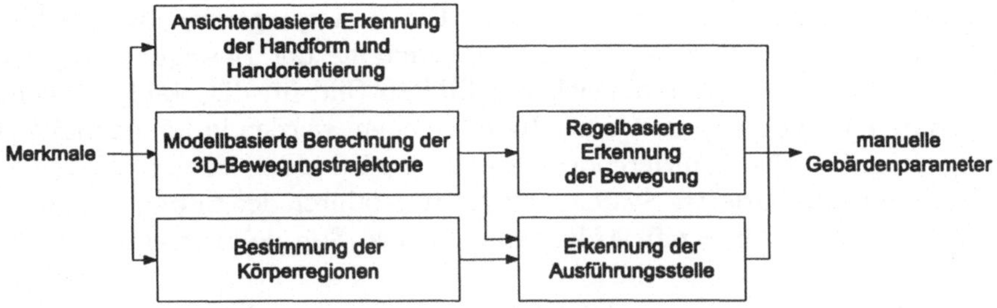

Abbildung 4. Ablaufstruktur für die Berechnung der manuellen Gebärdenparameter

dem Merkmalsvektor mit Hilfe einer Momentenberechnung durchgeführt. Andererseits, wenn eine symmetrische Gebärde erkannt wird, erfolgt eine weitere Charakterisierung der Bewegung der Hände relativ zueinander (parallel, spiegelsymmetrisch, punktsymmetrisch, alternierend) mit Hilfe von Korrelationsberechnungen. In diesem Fall ist keine separate Bestimmung der Handform der nicht-dominanten Hand erforderlich, da sie der Handform der dominanten Hand entspricht.

Die Verarbeitungsschritte für die Berechnung der manuellen Gebärdenparameter für die dominante Hand zeigt Abbildung 4. Die Bestimmung der Handform und Handorientierung ergibt sich durch einen Vergleich mit Handformprototypen. Zur Bestimmung der Handbewegung wird die 3D Trajektorie der Hand berechnet und mit Hilfe eines regelbasierten Systems klassifiziert. Dazu werden die 2D Koordinaten der Hand mit Hilfe eines Armmodells und eines Kameramodells in 3D Koordinaten transformiert. Für die Bestimmung der Ausführungsstelle einer Gebärde wird in einem ersten Schritt die 3D Position der Hand zur Schulter berechnet. Anschließend werden mit den berechneten Positionen der Schulter und der Augen sowie mit den Körperabmessungen der gebärdenden Person die Körperbereiche festgelegt, denen die Handposition zugeordnet wird.

Ansichtenbasierte Erkennung der Handform und Handorientierung: Ausgangspunkt für die ansichtenbasierte Erkennung der Handform und -orientierung ist die Tatsache, daß die zweidimensionale Abbildung der Hand Informationen sowohl über die Handform als auch die Handorientierung beinhaltet. Für die ansichtenbasierte Erkennung werden in einem Trainingsschritt Merkmalsvektoren für jede der 42 möglichen Handformen in verschiedenen Handorientierungen berechnet und abgespeichert. Auf diese Weise werden etwa 13000 Prototypen ermittelt. Während der Erkennung wird die zu klassifizierende Handform mit allen Ansichtenklassen der Referenzhandformen verglichen. Anschließend erfolgt eine Zuordnung zu der Handform, deren Repräsentant die größte Übereinstimmung aufweist. Die Idee des Verfahrens besteht darin, daß bei einer Bewegung der Hand im Raum immer unterschiedliche Prototypen erkannt werden, aber die zu klassifizierende Hand immer ein Element der unterschiedlichen Prototypen ist, während andere Handformen nur singulär enthalten sind [9].

Erkennung von Hand-Arm Bewegungen: Die Bewegungserkennung nutzt die dreidimensionale Position der Hand zur Aufnahme der Bewegungstrajektorie. Die Verschiebungsvektoren, die sich von Bild zu Bild für die dreidimensionalen Koordinaten des Schwerpunktes der Hand ergeben, werden in Länge und Orientierung normiert. Die resultierende Trajektorie wird anschließend auf ihre Form hin durch ein regelbasiertes System analysiert, wodurch der Bewegungspfad (gerade Linie, gerade Linie mit Abknickung, Kreis, Spirale) berechnet wird [10, 11].

Schätzung von Körperregionen und Bestimmung der Ausführungsstelle: Die Berechnung der Ausführungsstelle erfordert die Schätzung relevanter Körperregionen aus dem Videobild. Abbildung 5 zeigt ein Blockdiagramm für die Berechnung relevanter Regionen. Aus den digitalen Bilddaten werden Gesicht und Körperumriß segmentiert und in einen I/O-Code transformiert. Die Auswertung der einzelnen Segmente liefert die Positionen der Augen, der Schultern, der Körperachse und der oberen Kopfbegrenzung. Die Schulterpositionen werden mit Hilfe einer regelbasierten Analyse des Körperumrisses berechnet [12]. Die Augenerkennung wird auf einen rechteckförmigen Bereich innerhalb des Gesichts beschränkt, dessen Position und Größe aus den Positionen anderer, bereits bestimmter Gesichts- und Körpermerkmale (Gesichtsmittelpunkt, vorherige Augenposition) zu berechnen ist. In diese Berechnung geht auch das Ergebnis einer Plausibilitätsprüpfung ein, die auf die zuvor bestimmten Positionen angewendet wird. Gesichtsbereiche, die nicht mit Hilfe der Segmentierung zu lokalisieren sind (Stirn, Nase, Wangen, Mund, Kinn, Hals), ergeben sich aus allgemeinen Daten über die Gesichtsgeometrie durch Schätzung [13, 14]. Die Lage der Körperach-

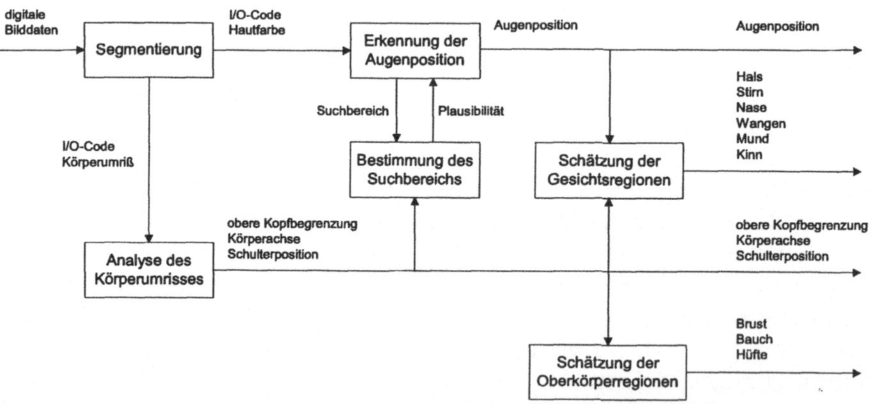

Abbildung 5. Berechnung relevanter Körperregionen. Relevante Körperregionen für die Gebärdenspracherkennung sind: Augen, Hals, Stirn, Nase, Wangen, Mund, Kinn, obere Kopfbegrenzung, Körperachse, Schulterposition, Brust, Bauch und Hüfte

se und der Schultern dient im weiteren als Bezugspunkt für die Rasterung des Oberkörperbereichs. Der Gesichtsbereich wird getrennt betrachtet, da dort eine feinere Auflösung notwendig ist. Häufig wird eine Gebärde so ausgeführt, daß sich nicht eindeutig festlegen läßt, ob sie beispielsweise vor dem Bauch oder vor der Brust ausgeführt wird. Um dennoch die Gebärde erfassen zu können, sind die Übergänge zwischen den Körperbereichen unscharf gestaltet. Hierfür wird der Oberkörperbereich mit einem Fuzzy-Raster modelliert, das quasi über das Bild der gebärdenden Person gelegt wird. Für die Aufteilung der Oberkörperbereiche in der Senkrechten gelten die linguistischen Variablen Schulter, Brust, Bauch und Hüfte; für die Aufteilung in der Waagerechten die linguistischen Variablen rechts, rechts vorne, Mitte, links vorne und links; für die Aufteilung der Entfernung die linguistischen Variablen Berührung nah, mittel und fern [15].

5 Evaluierung der videobasierten Eingabekomponente

Die videobasierte Eingabekomponente wurde getestet, um die Gebrauchstauglichkeit und die Erkennungsleistung zu bestimmen. Das System wurde mit insgesamt 19 Probanden (2 gehörlos, 2 schwerhörig, 15 hörend) getestet. 15 der 19 Versuchspersonen beherrschen die Gebärdensprache, d.h. sie benutzen die Gebärdensprache mindestens einige Male pro Woche. Für den Test wurde eine Testmenge von 33 Gebärden der niederländischen Gebärdensprache verwendet. Die Testmenge enstammt einer bekannten niederländischen Geschichte (Kom buiten kijken). Die Datenbank umfaßt ein Vokabular von 300 Gebärden. Jeder Proband verwendete eine neue Datenbank, so daß Auftrittshäufigkeiten und der Zeitpunkt des letzten Auftretens, welche beide vom PCS genutzt werden, nicht in die Bewertung eingehen. Für die Kalibrierung des Systems wird von jeder Versuchsperson die Länge des Unter-, des Oberarms und des Oberkörpers gemessen.

5.1 Aufbau der Experimentierumgebung

Die Versuchsperson steht in 1,85 m Abstand vor einer RGB-Farbkamera (Pulnix TMC-76). Das Objektiv hat eine Brennweite von 25 mm. Die Person ist weitgehend frei in der Wahl der Bekleidung und steht vor einem einfarbigen Hintergrund. Insgesamt leuchten sechs Halogenscheinwerfer, aus unterschiedlichen Richtungen, die Szene aus.

5.2 Experimentelle Ergebnisse und Auswertung

Die erhobenen Daten sind zum einen die Erkennungsrate für das Auftreten der richtigen Gebärde an der ersten Position der Vorhersageliste des PCS (top 1) und zum anderen die Erkennungsrate für das Auftreten der richtigen Gebärde innerhalb der ersten sechs Positionen der Vorhersageliste (top 6). Es wurden Tests für die personenabhängige wie auch personenunabhängige Erkennung durchgeführt. Die personenabhängigen Gebärden wurden von den Versuchspersonen selbst mit

Hilfe des Videosystems in die Datenbank eingegeben. Die Kodierung der Gebärden enthält dadurch die personenabhängigen Varianten. Tabelle 1 zeigt die

Tabelle 1. Erkennungsraten für personenabhängige und -unabhängie Erkennung

	top 6	top 1
personenabhängig	82,5%	56,5%
personenunabhängig	53,5%	24,0%

erzielten Erkennungsraten. Erwartungsgemäß liegen die Erkennungsraten für die personenabhängige Erkennung höher als bei der personenunabhängigen Erkennung. Im ersten Fall wird eine Erkennungsrate von 82,5% für top 6 und 56,5 % für top 1 erreicht. Für die personenunabhängige Erkennung erzielt das System eine Erkennungsrate von 53,5% für top 6 und 24,0% für top 1.

Die Tests haben gezeigt, daß das videobasierte Eingabesystem eine sehr geeignete Möglichkeit für die Eingabe der Gebärden in das Schreibsystem darstellt. Allerdings ist weiterer Forschungsbedarf erforderlich, bis ein derartiges System von Gehörlosen im Alltag verwendet werden kann. Die Erkennungsraten für die personenabhängige Erkennung sind gut, während für die personenunabhängige Erkennung keine zufriedenstellenden Ergebnisse erzielt wurden. Die Tests zeigten weiterhin, daß der Benutzer etwa sechs Gebärden pro Minute in das System eingeben kann. Da jede Gebärde einzeln eingegeben wird, fanden nahezu alle Versuchspersonen diese Situation unnatürlich.

6 Zusammenfassung und Ausblick

Diese Arbeit beschreibt ein Bildverarbeitungssystem für die personenabhängige und -unabhängige Erkennung von Gebärden der niederländischen Gebärdensprache. Die videobasierte Gebärdenerkennung stellt die natürlichste und intuitivste 3D Eingabekomponente für ein Schreibsystem für Gebärdensprache dar. Das Schreibsystem ermöglicht Gehörlosen den Zugang zu geschriebenen Informationen durch die schriftliche Darstellung der Gebärden. Der entwickelte Prototyp erlaubt die explizite Berechnung der vier manuellen Gebärdenparameter Handform, Handorientierung, Handbewegung und Ausführungsstelle sowohl von einals auch zweihändigen Gebärden. Das System wurde mit 19 Probanden validiert. Die Tests zeigen, daß die videobasierte Eingabekomponente eine geeignete Mensch-Maschine-Schnittstelle für das Schreibsystem darstellt.

Zukünftige Arbeiten sollten eine Erweiterung des Systems zur Erfassung nichtmanueller Ausdrucksmittel berücksichtigen, um die Erkennungsleistung weiter zu steigern. Die Erkennung kontinuierlicher Gebärdensprache sowie die Integration syntaktischer und semantischer Aspekte in das Erkennungssystem sind ebenfalls Bestandteil zukünftiger Forschung.

Literatur

1. P. Boyes Braem. *Einführung in die Gebärdensprache und ihre Erforschung.* Signum Press, Hamburg, 1995.
2. M. Soede (Eds.). *SignPS a System for Sign Writing: Final Report.* EEC TIDE Project No. 1202, 1997.
3. S. Tamura and S. Kawasaki. Recognition of sign language motion images. *Pattern Recognition*, Vol. 21(No. 4):343–253, 1988.
4. E. Wilson and G. Ansbach. *Neural Networks for Sign Language Translation.* Applications of Artificial Neural Networks, 1993.
5. T. Yamaguchi. *Japanese Sign Language Recognition System using Information Infrastructure.* IEEE International Conference on Fuzzy Systems and Fuzzy Engineering Symposium, Yokohama, Japan, 1995.
6. T. Starner and A. Pentland. *Real-Time American Sign Language Recognition from Video using Hidden Markov Models.* Technical Report No. 375, MIT Media Lab, Cambridge, USA, 1995.
7. K. Grobel and M. Assan. *Isolated Sign Language Recognition using Hidden Markov Models.* Proceedings of the IEEE International Conference on Systems, Man and Cybernetics, Orlando, USA, 1997.
8. H. Hienz, K.Grobel, and M. Tan. Ein Verfahren für die Berechnung von Farbclustern zur robusten Segmentierung von Farbflächen. In T. Lehmann, V. Metzler, K. Spitzer, and T. Tolxdorff, editors, *Workshop Bildverarbeitung für die Medizin*, pages 369–373, Aachen (Germany), 1998. Springer-Verlag Berlin.
9. M. Tan. *Ansichtenbasierte Handformerkennung in Bildfolgen.* Diplomarbeit, Rheinisch-Westfälische Technische Hochschule Aachen (RWTH), Lehrstuhl für Technische Informatik, 1997.
10. H. Hienz, K. Grobel, and G. Offner. *Real-Time Hand-Arm Motion Analysis using a single Video Camera.* Proceedings of the Second International Conference on Automatic Face and Gesture Recognition, Killington, USA, 1996.
11. G. Offner. *Entwicklung eines videobasierten Systems zur Charakterisierung von Hand-Arm Bewegungen in der deutschen Gebärdensprache in Echtzeit.* Diplomarbeit, Rheinisch-Westfälische Technische Hochschule Aachen (RWTH), Lehrstuhl für Technische Informatik, 1996.
12. S. Romainczyk. *Bestimmung der Schulterposition von Personen aus Videobildern.* Studienarbeit, Rheinisch-Westfälische Technische Hochschule Aachen (RWTH), Lehrstuhl für Technische Informatik, 1996.
13. B. Vetter. *Videobasierte Schätzung von Gesichtsbereichen in Echtzeit für die automatische Erkennung der deutschen Gebärdensprache.* Studienarbeit, Rheinisch-Westfälische Technische Hochschule Aachen (RWTH), Lehrstuhl für Technische Informatik, 1997.
14. H. Hienz and K.Grobel. Automatic estimation of body regions from video images. In I. Wachsmuth and M. Fröhlich, editors, *Gesture and Sign Language in Human-Computer Interaction, International Gesture Workshop Bielefeld 1997*, pages 135–145, Bielefeld (Germany), 1998. Springer-Verlag Berlin.
15. K. Grobel, H. Hienz, S. Romainczyk, S. Böken, and B. Vetter. Videobasierte Erkennung von Körperregionen zur Bestimmung der Ausführungsstelle einer Gebärde. In *Proceedings des 9. Aachener Kolloquiums Signaltheorie, Bild- und Sprachsignale*, pages 313–316, Aachen (Germany), 1997.

Interaktion, Körper und Realraum

Michael Hoch

ZKM I Institute for Visual Media
Lorenzstr. 19, 76135 Karlsruhe, Germany
mpunkt@zkm.de, www.khm.de/~micha

Zusammenfassung Dem Körper des Menschen kommt in der Wahrnehmung eine besondere Rolle zu. Bei einer Betrachtung der Vielzahl von Computeranwendungen läßt sich feststellen, daß der Mensch in zwei Welten arbeitet, die relativ wenig gemeinsam haben, der Computerwelt und der natürlichen Umgebung. Der Wunsch liegt also nahe, nach Ansätzen zu suchen, die nicht wie bisher den Menschen auffordern in der Welt der digitalen Maschine zu arbeiten, sondern den Computer so zu gestalten, daß er in unserer Welt arbeiten kann. Dabei wird bei den meisten Anwendungen der Körper nicht explizit in die Benutzerschnittstelle einbezogen. In diesem Beitrag wollen wir die Notwendigkeit der Einbeziehung des Körpers näher erläutern und anhand eines Beispielprojektes für gestische Interaktion im Realraum untersuchen. In diesem Beispielprojekt wurde ein Prototyp zur intuitiven Filmplanung entwickelt, der auf den Prinzipien der Intuitiven Schnittstelle basiert, eine Computerumgebung zur Planung bildkünstlerischer Prozesse, die den Körper und Realraum explizit berücksichtigt. Durch eine empirische Untersuchung werden Ergebnisse für die Anwendbarkeit von gestischer Interaktion präsentiert.

1 Einführung

Ein Computersystem, das mit den herkömmlichen technischen Accessoires für den Nutzer ausgestattet ist, ist weniger imstande, die Person wahrzunehmen, die mit ihm arbeiten möchte, als moderne Toiletten oder Außenlichter mit Bewegungsmeldern. Und obwohl die Erweiterung des Computers um die Fähigkeit, seine Umwelt zu registrieren und auf sie aktiv zu reagieren, bei einem solchen komplexen technischen System naheliegen würde, hat sich die Apparatur der Schnittstelle in den letzten 15 Jahren kaum verändert; die Kommunikation zwischen Nutzer und Computer geschieht in manueller Hinsicht fast ausschließlich über Maus und alphanumerische Tastatur. Dabei wäre es in vielen Anwendungssituationen sehr hilfreich, den Computer über die eigene Armlänge hinaus benutzen zu können. In der hier vorgestellten Arbeit werden Methoden skizziert und untersucht, die es gestatten, den Computer aus der herkömmlichen, wenig flexiblen Anordnung rund um den Monitor zu „befreien" und in die alltägliche Umgebung des Nutzers zu integrieren. Dazu soll der Rechner den Menschen wahrnehmen und auf seine äußeren Bewegungen und Artikulationen reagieren, ihn faktisch also sehen und hören können. Es soll das Konzept einer Schnittstelle geschaffen werden, die sich wegbewegt von Maus und Tastatur und der Bildschirmarbeit als primär einer Tätigkeit, die spezielle Fähigkeiten im Umgang mit Maschinen und Programmen voraussetzt; eine Schnittstelle, die in die Interaktion zwischen Mensch und Maschine den realen Raum und mögliche Bezüge zur Dingwelt einbezieht. Ziel ist also die Konstruktion einer Schnittstelle, die einen möglichst großen physischen Bewegungsspielraum des Benutzers erlaubt und die ihn nicht durch das Anlegen von technischen Prothesen (Datenhandschuhe, Brillen etc.) behindert.

Bei der Gestaltung von Mensch-Maschine-Schnittstellen beschäftigen sich Ingenieure, Gestalter und Informatiker hauptsächlich mit der Frage, mit welchen Mitteln es dem Benutzer erleichtert werden kann, den in seiner Konfiguration festgelegten Rechner zu benutzen und wie die Reaktionszeit der menschlichen Interaktion optimiert werden kann. Statt dessen könnte man sich aber auch umgekehrt fragen, wie der Computer so verändert werden kann, daß er adäquater mit den Benutzern umgehen könnte, damit der Mensch intuitiv auch ohne dazwischengeschalteten Lernvorgang und symbolische Interaktionen einen Computer bedienen könnte. Der Austausch fände so auf einer nichtlogischen Ebene statt. Eine Intuitive Schnittstelle, die sich in den alltäglichen Lebensraum des Menschen integriert – idealerweise eine Schnittstelle, die sich als solche gar nicht zu erkennen gibt –, kann dazu beitragen, den Umgang mit dem Rechner zu erleichtern und die Schwellenangst gegenüber der symbolischen Maschine abzubauen. Die Interaktion mit dem Interface geriete dadurch in den Hintergrund und würde nicht mehr im Fokus der Interaktion mit dem Medium stehen [5]. Neben Fragen der Ergonomie ermöglicht gerade die natürliche – im Sinne von gewohnter – Umgebung, in die der Computer integriert ist, einen ungezwungenen Umgang. Bei einer Betrachtung der Vielzahl von Computeranwendungen läßt sich jedoch feststellen, daß der Mensch in zwei Welten arbeitet, die relativ wenig gemeinsam haben, der Computerwelt und der natürlichen Umgebung. Der Wunsch liegt also nahe, nach Ansätzen zu suchen, die nicht wie bisher den Menschen auffordern, in der Welt der digitalen Maschine zu arbeiten, sondern den Computer so zu gestalten, daß er in unserer Welt arbeiten kann. Das Ergebnis wäre nicht nur einfach ein vergrößerter Interaktionsraum, sondern auch eine ergonomischere und natürlichere Arbeitsweise. Aus diesem Wunsch haben sich eine Vielzahl von interaktiven Systemen entwickelt, Systeme, die trotz verschiedener Zielrichtungen und diverser Benennungen stets das gleiche Ziel verfolgen. Diese Systeme unterteilen sich in Anwendungen der *Virtual Reality*, *Augmented Reality* [1] und sogenannte *Responsive Environments* [2]. Dabei wird bei den meisten Anwendungen der Körper nicht explizit in die Benutzerschnittstelle einbezogen. In diesem Beitrag wollen wir die Notwendigkeit der Einbeziehung des Körpers näher erläutern und anhand eines Beispielprojektes für gestische Interaktion im Realraum untersuchen. In diesem Beispielprojekt wurde ein Prototyp zur intuitiven Filmplanung entwickelt, der auf den Prinzipien der Intuitiven Schnittstelle basiert, eine Computerumgebung zur Planung bildkünstlerischer Prozesse, die den Körper und Realraum explizit berücksichtigt [6]. Hierbei werden durch eine empirische Untersuchung einerseits Ergebnisse für die Anwendbarkeit von gestischer Interaktion präsentiert und weiterhin auch Hinweise für eine weiterführende Untersuchung der Einbeziehung von Körper und Realraum in die Computerinteraktion gegeben.

2 Körper und Raum

Dem Körper des Menschen kommt in der Wahrnehmung ein besondere Rolle zu. Die Räumlichkeit des Körpers ist im Gegensatz zu der äußerer Gegenstände keine Positionsräumlichkeit, sondern eher eine Situationsräumlichkeit. Wenn ich mich auf einem Schreibtisch abstütze, so weiß ich nicht nur, wo meine Hand sich befindet, ich weiß auch genau, wo sich der Körper und jedes seiner Bestandteile befindet, und zwar nicht aufgrund eines Verhältnisses zu anderen Positionen oder äußeren Koordinaten, sondern aufgrund der Situation des Körpers selbst. Diese Situationsräumlichkeit ist mir gegeben, ohne mir als objektive Erkenntnis bewußt zu sein, das heißt ich kann mich in einer Umgebung einrichten, ohne Leib und Umgebung erst als Objekte im Kantischen Sinne aufnehmen zu müssen. So fällt es wesentlich leichter, beispielsweise die Nase zu greifen als auf sie zu zeigen. Ein Experiment mit einem Kranken zeigt, daß die Fähigkeit des Zeigens gänzlich verloren gehen kann, obwohl die des Greifens mit Erfolg ausgeführt werden kann: *„Was den Körperraum betrifft, so gibt es offenbar ein Wissen des Ortes, ... Von einer Mücke gestochen, muß der Kranke die gestochene Stelle nicht erst suchen, er findet sie unverzüglich, da es ihm nicht darum geht, sie in Bezug zum Koordinatensystem des objektiven Raums zu setzen, sondern nur darum, seine phänomenale Hand an eine schmerzende Stelle seines phänomenalen Leibes zu führen, ...“* [9, S. 128-131]. Etwas anders verhält es sich mit sogenannten abstrakten und virtuellen Bewegungen, d.h. z.B. Bewegungen, die ich ausführe, um die Form eines Gegenstandes in der Luft zu symbolisieren (abstrakt), oder Bewegungen, die einen Gegenstand erfahrbar machen allein aufgrund taktiler Reize (virtuelle). Abstrakte Bewegungen werden erst durch eine sogenannte Projektionsfunktion ermöglicht, die Zeichen erscheinen läßt und das Handeln orientiert (wie Schilder in einem Museum den Besucher leiten). Die menschliche Leistung besteht hier gerade darin, das natürliche Verhältnis von Leib und Umgebung umzukehren, sich von der Welt abwenden und seinen Körper besitzen zu können. Der Leib ist also nicht nur durch wirkliche Situationen in Bewegung zu setzen, er kann sich auch auf Experimente einlassen und sich im Virtuellen situieren. Genau diese Fähigkeit ist bei dem beschriebenen Kranken verloren gegangen, nicht jedoch das natürliche Verhältnis zu seinem Körperraum [9, S. 137-138]. In Bezug auf die Betrachtung von Bildern und Szenen auf einem Computerbildschirm bedeutet dies, daß der Mensch sich sehr wohl im Virtuellen situieren kann, dabei jedoch die Erfahrung der „Welt“ nicht aus einem natürlichen Körperschema heraus bezieht, sondern dies erst mittels seines Intellekts und der beschriebenen Projektionsfunktion möglich wird.

In der normalen Wahrnehmung haften bestimmte Eigenschaften, wie die Tiefe, Oben und Unten, Rechts und Links, nicht in erster Linie den Dingen an, sondern entstehen stets bezüglich eines Raumniveaus, das erst aus der Situation des Körpers zu seiner Umgebung entsteht. Aus dieser Überlegung heraus können sich die Dinge eines computergenerierten Bildes nur bezüglich eines Raumniveaus des Arbeitsplatzes konstituieren. Dies liegt an der Verankerung des Subjekts in der natürlichen Umgebung, der Umgebung, in der der Bildschirm situiert ist. Ein bei Merleau-Ponty [9, S. 290-293] beschriebener Versuch mit einem in einem Spiegel schräg dargestellten Zimmer zeigt jedoch, daß dies sehr wohl möglich ist, falls dem Subjekt die Verankerung nicht mehr gegenwärtig ist. Ein Effekt, der bei der computergestützten Generierung virtueller Welten als Immersion bezeichnet wird und im Apparat Kino sehr wohl funktioniert, bei den meisten computergestützten Anwendungen jedoch versagt, da nicht, wie beim Kino, eine narrative Umgebung vorliegt, in die der Mensch sich freiwillig begibt. Stattdessen wird eine zweite Welt geschaffen, die ein anderes als das konstituierte Raumniveau des Betrachters erfordern würde.

Diese Überlegungen lassen den Schluß zu, daß die traditionelle Arbeit mit dem Computer, mit Tastatur, Maus und Bildschirm, das Subjekt auf eine Weise seiner natürlichen Situation enthebt, auf eine andere Weise dieser Versuch aber scheitern wird, aufgrund seiner Verankerung in der Umgebung. Lediglich auf einer abstrakten Ebene, wie es beim Lesen eines Buches geschieht, oder nur, wenn die Verankerungspunkte „unsichtbar“ gemacht werden, wie es im Kino der Fall ist, wird hier Welt erfahren. Bestimmte Computeranwendungen versuchen durch Realismus und Detailreichtum Welt so zu vermitteln, wie wir sie naturgegeben gewohnt sind, sie können jedoch erst erfolgreich sein, wenn sie die Situation, das Situiertsein des Benutzers in seiner Umgebung berücksichtigen. Dazu muß sich eine Computeranwendung in die natürliche Umgebung integrieren, Raum, Bewegung, und Realobjekte einbeziehen, um uns mehr als nur die Vorstellung von einem Ding zu geben, kurz: der Mensch muß gegenüber der computergenerierten Welt situiert sein. Im folgenden wollen wir eine derartige Anwendung vorstellen: Die Umgebung der Intuitiven Schnittstelle, in der sich der Benutzer bewegt, ist hierbei nicht der Raum um den Computer, sondern der Realraum selbst, in den der Computer integriert ist, d.h. die gesamte Interaktionsumgebung wird zum Interface.

3 Anwendungsszenario

Der Prototyp zur intuitiven Filmplanung ist eine Beispielanwendung der Intuitiven Schnittstelle und realisiert einige wesentliche Komponenten eines interaktiven Filmplanungssystems [8], wie es in einem Projekt der Kunsthochschule für Medien Köln bereits als Idee entwickelt worden ist [3]. Ziel dieser Anwendung ist es u.a., in der Planungsphase eines Films unterschiedliche Kameraeinstellungen an einer computergenerierten Szene testen zu können. Auf einer Projektionsfläche wird eine computergenerierte Szene mit verschiedenen Objekten präsentiert. Der Benutzer kann die Objekte bewegen, indem er auf sie zeigt, sie mit einer sprachlichen Anweisung auswählt und anschließend auf der Projektion durch erneutes Zeigen an eine andere Stelle verschiebt (Abbildung 1). Zu diesem Zweck werden Kameras verwendet, welche die Szene beobachten.

Abbildung 1. Intuitive Schnittstelle mit Beispielanwendung zur Filmplanung

Zur Plazierung neuer Objekte werden diese aus einer Art Requisite, einem digitalen Archiv, ausgewählt. Hierbei wird davon ausgegangen, daß diese Objekte in einer Modellierungsphase an einem herkömmlichen Arbeitsplatz schon erstellt worden sind. Zur Auswahl von Objekten werden Menüs in Abhängigkeit von der Position des Benutzers im Raum eingeblendet. So können beispielsweise (virtuelle) Möbelstücke links hinten im Realraum positioniert werden, (virtuelle) Fahrzeuge rechts hinten. Zum Plazieren eines Stuhls in der 3D-Szene bewegt sich der Benutzer dann in den hinteren, linken Bereich des Realraumes, wodurch ein Auswahlmenü mit Möbelstücken auf der Projektion sichtbar wird. Mit einem gestischen Hinweis kann dann ein Stuhl ausgewählt werden. Diese nach dem Prinzip der „Ars Memoriae" [9] aufgebaute Gedächtnisfunktion ermöglicht einerseits das Aufrufen von Menüs auf intuitive Weise und ist zusätzlich einfacher zu erinnern als eine Funktion in einem hierarchisch aufgebauten Menüsystem.

Abbildung 2. Bühnenmetapher der Requisite für das Hinzufügen von Objekten zu der Szene. Verschiedene Objektgruppen sind über das untenliegende Fließband aufrufbar.

Zur weiteren Vereinfachung können im Realraum Objekte in Form von Platzhaltern verwendet werden, um die Position von Objekten der 3D-Szene und auch ihre relative Positionierung zueinander anzuzeigen. Die Platzhalterfiguren, deren Positionen durch farbliche Markierung und Videoverfolgung bestimmt werden, lassen sich über ein Sprachkommando an virtuelle Objekte koppeln. Anschließend werden die virtuellen Objekte entsprechend der Bewegung der Platzhalterfiguren im Realraum bewegt (Abbildung 3). Dadurch können räumliche Abhängigkeiten der computergenerierten Objekte im Realraum diskutiert und beurteilt werden, ohne auf Hilfsmittel wie orthographische Ansichten der 3D-Szene angewiesen zu sein, wie sie bei 3D-Animationssystemen verwendet werden.

Abbildung 3. Steuerung virtueller Objekte durch das Bewegen von Realobjekten

Weiterhin erhält der Benutzer durch das Gewicht der Holzfiguren eine haptische Rückmeldung beim Bewegen der virtuellen Objekte. Die virtuellen Objekte lassen sich hierbei innerhalb einer sensitiven Zone, die im Realraum markiert ist, steuern (siehe *ground area „room“* in Abbildung 4). Hierdurch ist das Arrangieren und Diskutieren der virtuellen Szene im Realraum möglich.

4 Systemaufbau

Für den Prototyp wurde eine Beispielszene mit mehreren Objekten entwickelt. Der Benutzer hat die Möglichkeit, die Objekte in der Szene zu arrangieren, d.h. es ist ein Bewegen, Rotieren oder Entfernen von Objekten möglich. Dabei interagiert er/sie typischerweise in einer Entfernung zwischen drei und fünf Metern. In Abbildung 4 ist die räumliche Situation der Schnittstelle für den Prototyp in einem Labor der Kunsthochschule für Medien Köln dargestellt. In einer Wand des Labors ist eine 2,60 Meter breite und 2,10 Meter hohe Rückprojektionswand eingelassen. Die Kameras des Stereoaufbaus befinden sich oberhalb der Projektionswand an den Positionen *cam1 = (0, 2.41, 0.177)* und *cam2 = (2.90, 2.41, 0.177)* (Angaben in Metern). Für die meisten Operationen wird ein Sprachkommando im Zusammenhang mit der Zeigeoperation verwendet, wobei das Bewegen von Objekten alternativ auch durch die Verwendung von realen Platzhalterfiguren möglich ist. Abbildung 4 zeigt die zugehörige sensitive Zone für das Arbeiten mit den Platzhalterfiguren (*ground area „room“*). Weiterhin können neue Objekte aus einer Art Requisite der Szene hinzugefügt werden, die entsprechende Funktion wird beim Überschreiten der Schwelle bei 4,20 Metern aufgerufen (*stage area* in Abb. 4). Ein Zurückschalten in die Szene geschieht erst beim erneuten Überschreiten der Schwelle bei 3,10 Metern, so ist sichergestellt, daß der Benutzer sich frei bewegen kann, ohne die Gefahr, ein ständiges Umschalten zwischen Szene und Requisite auszulösen. Für die Anwahl der Objektgruppen ist eine weitere sensitive Zone im hinteren Teil des Raumes definiert (*ground area „conveior“* in Abb. 4).

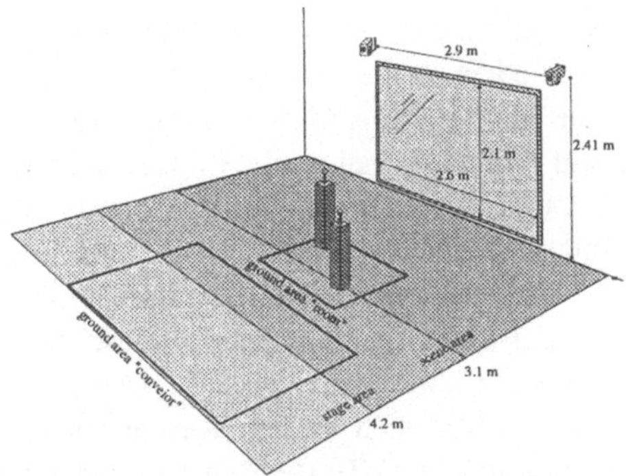

Abbildung 4. Räumliche Anordnung der Schnittstelle für den Prototyp

Für den Prototyp werden zwei PCs verwendet: einer für das Bildverarbeitungssystem und die Sprachverarbeitung, der andere für die Darstellung der Benutzerschnittstelle (200 MHz Pentium/Pro, 200 MHz Pentium). Beide PC sind über ein Netzwerk miteinander verbunden. Die Standard-Videosignale (FBAS) der beiden CCD-Kameras werden über zwei Grabber-Karten (Matrox Meteor), das Sprachsignal über einen Funkempfänger und eine Soundkarte in den PC geführt. Die Darstellung der Benutzerschnittstelle übernimmt ein 3-Linsen-Projektor. Vor dem Arbeiten mit dem System muß der Benutzer das Head-Set-Mikrofon aufsetzen und sich eine grüne Markierung mit einem Durchmesser von 11 cm anstecken. Von Seiten der Software wird ein für die Intuitive Schnittstelle entwickeltes Bildverarbeitungssystem verwendet [7], das auf die Bildverarbeitungsbibliothek MIL von Matrox zurückgreift. Weiterhin werden ein Sprachverarbeitungssystem und das Autorensystem Director von Macromedia verwendet. Als universelles Autorensystem, meist zur Produktion von CD-ROMs verwendet, eignet sich Director auch als Prototyping-Werkzeug zur Darstellung von Benutzerschnittstellen. Abläufe, Menüs und Interaktionen brauchen nicht programmiert werden, sondern können visuell definiert und ausgetestet werden. Zur Kontrolle von komplizierteren Abläufen steht eine Skriptsprache zur Verfügung.

5 Empirische Untersuchung

An dem vorgestellten Szenario wurde eine empirische Untersuchung durchgeführt. Ziel der Studie ist eine explorative Voruntersuchung der Intuitiven Schnittstelle. Als Untersuchungsmethode wurde das Intensivinterview ausgewählt [4], da über den gewählten Objektbereich in seiner speziellen Kombination keine vergleichbaren Untersuchungen vorliegen. Die Studie dient in erster Linie der Erlangung von Kenntnissen über den Objektbereich und ist daher eher beschreibender als analytischer, d.h. Hypothesen prüfender, Natur. Es wurden fünf Regisseure und eine Regisseurin aus verschiedenen Altersgruppen (31 bis 57 Jahre) und verschiedenen Berufszweigen der Filmregie befragt. Die von ihnen entwickelten Filme decken einen weiten Bereich von Autorenfilm und Spielfilm, über Dokumentarfilm und Musikverfilmungen bis hin zu experimentellen Filmen auch ohne Drehbuch ab. Entsprechend unterschiedlich fällt die Arbeitsweise der einzelnen Regisseure aus, wobei sich bestimmte Grundmuster bei der Planungsphase eines Films wiederholen und sich in die verschiedenen Filmkategorien einordnen lassen. So ist die Planung mit Storyboards und/oder eine genaue Besprechung mit Kameramann und Ausstatter bei (nicht improvisierten) Spielfilmen absolut notwendig, hingegen bei Dokumentarfilmen oft gar nicht möglich, da bestimmte Szenen, wie Interviews nicht geplant werden können und sollen. Die vorhandenen Vorkenntnisse im Bereich Computer waren ebenfalls stark unterschiedlich und variierten zwischen dem Benutzen des Computers als Schreibmaschine bis hin zur Erfahrung mit computergenerierten Szenen mit Hilfe von 3D-Animationsprogrammen. Die Auswertung der Interviews orientiert sich an den Kernaussagen und den Hypothesen des zugrundeliegenden Forschungsplans. Bei der Bewertung der einzelnen Aussagen ist stets zu berücksichtigen, daß sowohl die Teilnehmer, der Beobachter bzw. Interviewer, als auch das Angebot des Prototypen, die Ergebnisse determinieren.

5.1 Sinnliche Kommunikation und Realraum

Die Nutzung von Raum als Teil der Schnittstelle wurde unterschiedlich empfunden: Beim Aufrufen von Funktionen im Raum, wie das Heraustreten aus der Szene, ist die Meinung nicht einheitlich, sie schwankt zwischen einer Ablenkung bis hin zu einem Wohlfühlen. Einige Personen sind der Meinung, daß die Bewegung eine zusätzliche Konzentration erfordere und daher von der eigentlichen Aufgabe eher ablenken würde, andere empfanden den Raumeindruck eher angenehm. Beim Aufrufen von Requisiten im Raum (Gedächtnisfunktion) waren alle Befragten sich einig, daß dies eher mühsam sei und sie ein Menü, eine Auswahlleiste auf dem Bildschirm, bevorzugen würden, das dann durch Sprache oder auch Bewegung aufrufbar wäre. Von den meisten wurde das Stehen und physische Gehen als nicht angenehm betrachtet. Bei der Beurteilung dieser Aussage muß allerdings der befragte Personenkreis berücksichtigt werden, so gibt es auch Regisseure, die vorwiegend körperbetont arbeiten. Auch könnten sich vollständig andere Eindrücke und Antworten ergeben, wenn beispielsweise ein Regisseur für Actionfilme befragt werden würde. Trotz der negativen Aussage über die körperbetonte Bewegung, äußerten sich bis auf eine Ausnahme alle Personen positiv über das erfahrene Raumgefühl durch die Leinwand und die Positionierung des Benutzers. In Bezug auf die Bedienbarkeit konnte festgestellt werden, daß der Realraum allein den Umgang mit dem Computer nicht erleichtert. Dabei scheint es so, daß viele Menschen inzwischen schon auf die Arbeit mit Bildschirm und Maus sozialisiert sind, da auch Nicht-Computerleute durchaus Anwendungen mit Mausbedienung vorschlagen.

5.2 Adäquate Arbeitsumgebung

Bei der Auswertung bezüglich der Ähnlichkeit der Arbeitsumgebung der Intuitiven Schnittstelle mit der gewohnten Arbeitsweise eines Regisseurs läßt sich feststellen, daß die Schnittstelle im jetzigen Stadium noch erhebliche Aufmerksamkeit erfordert und lediglich die Schachfigur-ähnlichen Platzhalterfiguren uneingeschränkt funktionieren. Die Auswertung der Videoaufzeichnungen ergab außerdem, daß die Personen durchweg relativ steif stehen, was in der noch nicht perfekten Verfolgungssoftware begründet ist, die nicht bei jeder Körperhaltung befriedigende Ergebnisse liefert. Für eine Benutzerakzeptanz muß aber eine freie Beweglichkeit im Raum als solche auch gewährleistet sein, d.h. das alleinige Im-Raum-stehen reicht für eine Anwendung mit gestischer Interaktion nicht aus. Zusätzlich erscheinen das Stehen, das sich-Bewegen und eine Zeigegestik als Mausersatz der Arbeitssituation eines Regisseurs eher nicht ähnlich. Weiterhin wird deutlich, daß die Darstellung von Bewegungseindrücken sehr wichtig ist.

5.3 Praktischer Nutzen

Der Hauptnachteil, der von vier Personen gesehen wurde, ist die generelle Verwendung des Computers für diese Tätigkeit. Einerseits würde man sich durch ein Planungswerkzeug von dem prozeßhaften Arbeiten am Set entfernen, da sich stets Dinge aus den Menschen und der Gruppe ergeben würden, die nicht in den Einzelpersonen begründet sind sondern aus der Zusammenarbeit erst entstehen. Trotzdem konnten sich alle Befragten ein derartiges System besonders bei der Planung der Ausstattung und bei der Planung von Szenenauflösungen mit Ausstatter und Kameramann als sehr nützlich vorstellen. Besonders bei komplizierten Szenen könnte die Raumgestaltung inklusive Licht und Kameraeinstellung dargestellt werden. Der Beleuchter könnte dann direkt die Situation erkennen. Außerdem ließen sich, im Gegensatz zum Storyboard, Kameraeinstellungen überprüfen, denn oft, so meinte eine Person, würden Zeichner zu wenig darüber wissen. Die Nützlichkeit eines Planungssystems ist also bei komplexen Szenen und als Vorbereitung und Diskussionsgrundlage vorstellbar. In der vorliegenden Version ist mangels Kameraeinstellungsmöglichkeiten und der Totale als einzige Sicht auf die Szene eher eine Theateranwendung praktikabel. Das Abwenden vom prozeßhaften Arbeiten sowie die Gefahr der Illusion einer kinderleichten Regie durch den Computer sind bei der Überprüfung des praktischen Nutzens zu berücksichtigen.

6 Schlußfolgerungen

Zusammenfassend läßt sich feststellen, daß der untersuchte Prototyp der Arbeitssituation zumindest der hier befragten Regisseure eher nicht ähnlich ist. Die Verwendung von Raum zur Schaffung einer sinnlichen, körperlichen Kommunikation erscheint nicht zwingend notwendig, da Regie oft eine eher geistige Arbeit ist, obgleich eine Projektion für ein Raumgefühl hilfreich ist und die Nützlichkeit nach Einbeziehen von

Perspektiven und Kamerabewegungen erneut überprüft werden sollte. Für bestimmte Anwendungen der Filmplanung bietet es sich an, das System in Richtung einer traditionellen Desktop-Anwendung mit Maus und Bildschirm zu vereinfachen, wobei für bestimmte Situationen ein stationärer Aufbau mit Projektionswand verwendet werden kann. Diesbezügliche Aussagen der befragten Regisseure könnten ein Hinweis darauf sein, daß mit der Auswahl der Personen nicht die richtige Zielgruppe getroffen wurde. Die Interviews bestätigen, daß ein Regisseur ein Teil eines Teams ist, in dem besonders Kameramann und Ausstatter eine wichtige Rolle spielen. Alle Befragten konnten sich ein derartiges System besonders bei der Planung der Ausstattung und bei der Planung von Szenenauflösungen mit Ausstatter und Kameramann als sehr nützlich vorstellen. Die Befragung wurde somit nur mit einem kleinen Teil der Zielgruppe durchgeführt. Die Arbeit mit einem derartigen System dient eher der Vorbereitung und als Gesprächsgrundlage für Regisseur, Kameramann, Ausstatter und Beleuchter, weniger der direkten Arbeit mit den Schauspielern. Besonders bei komplexen Szenen erscheint dies sehr hilfreich, Szenen also, die eher bei großen Spielfilmen oder Actionfilmen die Regel sind, als beispielsweise bei einem Dokumentarfilm oder einem klassischen Autorenfilm. Somit kann der praktische Nutzen der Intuitiven Schnittstelle auf ein engeres Berufsfeld innerhalb der Filmplanung eingeschränkt werden. Eine erneute Untersuchung mit entsprechend gezielt ausgewählten Personen könnte nähere Aufschlüsse geben. Als absolut notwendig kann zuvor die Ergänzung um Kameraperspektiven und Bewegungseindrücke angesehen werden. Als Variante ist ein modellhaftes System mit kleinen Figuren sehr gut vorstellbar, welches besonders einfach zu bedienen wäre und nicht die Aufmerksamkeit des Benutzers erfordern würde.

Literatur

1. Azuma R, *A Survey of Augmented Reality*, Presence: Special Issue on Augmented Environments, Vol 6, Issue 4, August 1997, pp 355-385. http://www.cs.unc.edu/~azuma
2. Cooperstock J, Fels S, Buxton W, Smith K, *Reactive Environments*, Communications of the ACM, Vol. 40, No. 9, September 1997, pp 65-73.
3. Fleischmann G, Hoch M, Schwabe D, Barg W, Lampe G, *FilmPlan: ein interaktives Filmplanungssystem*, Lab 1, Magazin der Kunsthochschule für Medien Köln, 1994.
4. Friedrichs J, *Methoden empirischer Sozialforschung*, WV Studium Sozialwissenschaft, Westdeutscher Verlag, Opladen 1990.
5. Halbach WR, *Interfaces, Medien- und Kommunikationstheoretische Elemente einer Interface-Theorie*, Wilhelm Fink Verlag, München 1994.
6. Hoch M, *Intuitive Schnittstelle*, Lab, Jahrbuch 1996/97 für Künste und Apparate, Verlag Walther König, Köln 1997.
7. Hoch M, *Object Oriented Design of the Intuitive Interface*, 3D Image Analysis and Synthesis, Proceedings, Erlangen November 17-19, Infix 1997, pp 161-167.
8. Hoch M, *A Prototype System for Intuitive Film Planning*, Third IEEE International Conference on Automatic Face and Gesture Recognition (FG'98), April 14-16, Nara, Japan 1998, pp 504-509.
9. Merleau-Ponty M, *Phänomenologie der Wahrnehmung*, Walter de Gruyter & Co.
10. Yates FA, *The Art of Memory*, Routledge & Kegan Paul/PLC, London 1966.

Echtzeitfähige Gestikerkennung mit stochastischen Mustererkennungsverfahren

G. Rigoll, S. Eickeler, A. Kosmala, S. Müller

Gerhard-Mercator-Universität Duisburg
Fachgebiet Technische Informatik
Fachbereich Elektrotechnik
47057 Duisburg
e-mail: {rigoll,eickeler,kosmala,stm}@fb9-ti.uni-duisburg.de

Zusammenfassung In diesem Beitrag wird ein leistungsfähiges und robustes Echtzeitsystem zur Gestikerkennung vorgestellt. Dabei erfolgt die Gestikerkennung auf der Basis von mit der Kamera erfaßten Videosequenzen. Zur Klassifizierung der erkannten Geste werden stochastische Mustererkennungsverfahren verwendet. Eines der wesentlichen Bestandteile des Systems ist ein neuartiges Merkmalsextraktionsverfahren zur effektiven Verwendung von statistischen Methoden in der Videosequenzerkennung. Unter Verwendung der neuen Merkmalsextraktion wurde ein Gestenerkennungssystem aufgebaut, das hintergrund- und personenunabhängig arbeiten kann. Es stellte sich heraus, daß die neuen Merkmale nicht nur die Charakteristik der Gesten sehr gut beschreiben konnten, sondern auch zu Merkmalsvektoren mit sehr wenigen Dimensionen für die einzelnen Bilder führte. Durch diese Reduktion der Datenmenge kann das System echtzeitfähig Gesten erkennen.

1 Einleitung

Die Gestikerkennung hat sich in den letzten Jahren als neue und vielversprechende Disziplin im Bereich der visuellen Kommunikationstechnik entwickelt. Die Hauptanwendungsmöglichkeiten der Gestikerkennung liegen bei der Mensch-Maschine-Kommunikation mit folgenden Anwendungsszenarios:

- visuelle Kommunikation in virtuellen Umgebungen
- Kommunikation mit Robotern
- Kommunikation mit virtuellen Agenten
- Steuerung elektronischer Geräte der Konsumelektronik
- Kommunikation in geräuschbelasteten Umgebungen
- Zeigeoperationen in Präsentationen oder Video-Konferenzen
- Erkennung von Zeichensprache
- Kommunikation in Videospielen

Innerhalb der Gestikerkennung haben sich verschiedene Disziplinen herausgebildet. So unterscheidet man beispielsweise zwischen statischen und dynamischen Gesten. Ebenso werden meistens unterschiedliche Ansätze zur Erkennung von Hand- und Körpergesten verwendet. Die wichtigste Unterscheidung bei den verschiedenen Verfahren zur

Gestikerkennung liegt jedoch in der Akquisition und Verarbeitung der Merkmale zur Erkennung der Gesten. Hier kann man grob unterscheiden zwischen Erkennungssystemen, die bestimmte Hilfsmittel verwenden und rein videobasierten Gestikerkennungssystemen, die lediglich die mit der Kamera aufgenommene Geste mit Hilfe von Algorithmen der Bildverarbeitung auswerten. Die auf Hilfsmittel basierenden Systeme verwenden z.B. Datenhandschuhe, Leuchtsensoren oder Farbmarkierungen, um die Merkmale für die Erkennung besser extrahieren zu können. Dies erleichtert den Erkennungsprozeß erheblich, führt jedoch zu starken Einschränkungen für den Benutzer. Im folgenden sollen daher die videobasierten Systeme betrachtet werden, die aus Benutzersicht die größte Flexibilität und Bewegungsfreiheit bieten.

Es existieren unterschiedliche Ansätze zur Erkennung von Gesten in Videosequenzen. In [9] wird ein Verfahren beschrieben, das Gebärdensprache erkennen kann. Hier werden die Hände der handelnden Person mit verschiedenen Verfahren extrahiert. Die anschließende statistische Klassifizierung ist der in diesem Beitrag beschriebenen ähnlich. Das System in [1] überlagert die einzelnen Differenzbilder einer Videosequenz zu einem Bild und vergleicht dieses mit Referenzbildern. Das System kommt ohne ein Modell des menschlichen Körpers aus und kann positionsunabhängig und drehungsunabhängig arbeiten. Es kann jedoch nur drei unterschiedliche Gesten unterscheiden. In [8] wird ein Handgestikerkennungssystem zur Mensch-Rechner-Kommunikation vorgestellt. In [2] wird ein umfassender Überblick über bestehende Gestikerkennungssysteme gegeben.

Der Ansatz, der in [6,7] präsentiert wurde, verwendet statistische Methoden zur Videosequenzerkennung. In diesem Ansatz wird jedes Bild der Videosequenz in horizontale oder vertikale Streifen zerlegt. Diese Streifen bilden Vektoren, deren Zeilen die Grauwerte der Pixel enthalten. Die Vektoren werden mit einem Vektorquantisierer (VQ) in diskrete Indizes (Label) bezüglich des VQ-Codebooks umgewandelt. Auf diese Weise wird jedes Bild der Videosequenz durch eine Sequenz von Indizes dargestellt. Diese werden wiederum zu einer Gesamtsequenz aneinander gehängt, deren Länge die Anzahl der Bilder in der Videosequenz multipliziert mit der Anzahl von Streifen je Bild ist. Zur Erkennung wurden die Sequenzen von VQ-Indizes mit einem diskreten Hidden-Markov-Modell (HMM) klassifiziert. Alternativ konnte auch ein Probabilistisches Neuronales Netzwerk zur Klassifikation der Label-Sequenzen verwendet werden. Diese Methode zur Videosequenzerkennung war effektiv, hatte aber zwei große Nachteile: Der erste ist, daß die Merkmalsextraktion nicht die Charakteristik der Geste wiedergab. Der zweite ist die Mischung der zeitlichen und räumlichen Merkmale in der Merkmalssequenz. Das wichtigste Ergebnis des Systems in [7] ist jedoch die Tatsache, daß statistische Mustererkennungsmethoden sehr gut zur Videosequenzerkennung geeignet sind. Es wurde daher entschieden, sich weiterhin auf den statistischen Ansatz zur Bildsequenzerkennung zu konzentrieren und das System weiter zu verbessern. Das Ergebnis dieser Aktivitäten ist ein vollständig überarbeitetes Videosequenzerkennungssystem mit Verbesserungen, die in den folgenden Punkten zusammengefaßt werden können:

- Die Merkmalsextraktion ist zur Beschreibung der Charakteristik der Geste und der Dynamik der bewegten Bildteile geeignet und führt zu einer Reduzierung der Datenmenge für die Merkmalsvektoren auf 0.3% der ursprünglichen Datenmenge.

- Ausschließliche Verwendung von Hidden-Markov-Modellen anstelle von Neuronalen Netzwerken zur Erkennung von dynamischen Mustern.
- Der Wechsel von HMMs mit diskreter Ausgabeverteilung zu kontinuierlichen HMMs wurde durch die neue Merkmalsextraktion ermöglicht. Dieser Wechsel erhöhte die Robustheit des Systems gegenüber geringen Abweichungen in der Geste.
- Durch neue spezielle Dekodierungstechniken wurde die Erkennung spontaner Gesten ermöglicht.

2 Die Datenbasis und die Erkennungsaufgabe

Die Datenbasis zum Trainieren und Testen des Systems besteht aus Videosequenzen von unterschiedlichen Personen, die die gleichen Gesten vorführen. Insgesamt wurden 24 unterschiedliche Gesten (siehe Abb. 1) von zwölf Personen aufgenommen. Die Sequenzen wurden mit einer Bildauflösung von 96 x 72 Pixel und einer Bildrate von 16 fps aufgenommen. [1] Die Erkennungsaufgabe war das personenunabhängige Erkennen der Gesten. Hierzu wurden jeweils die Videosequenzen einer Person aus der Datenbasis herausgenommen, und das System mit der verbleibenden Datenbasis trainiert. Die herausgenommenen Gesten wurden anschließend zum Test des Systems verwendet. Um eine genauere Erkennungsrate zu erhalten, wurde dieses Verfahren für alle Personen wiederholt und der Mittelwert dieser einzelnen Erkennungsraten gebildet.

3 Beschreibung des Systems

Mit den hier beschriebenen Verbesserungen in der Merkmalsextraktion konnte ein Gestikerkennungssystem entwickelt werden, das eine Erkennungsrate von 92,9% für die vorher beschriebenen 24 Gesten erreicht. Das System hat die hohen Erkennungsraten nicht nur mit der aufgenommenen Datenbasis erreicht, sondern hat sich auch unter realistischen Einsatzbedingungen als sehr robust erwiesen. Es wurde als Forschungsprototyp auf zahlreichen Ausstellungen und Messen (darunter die Industriemesse in Hannover) vorgeführt und arbeitete auch bei Messebesuchern, die keine Erfahrung mit dem System hatten, sehr sicher.

Die Fähigkeiten des Systems sind auf zwei Tatsachen zurückzuführen: Die erste Tatsache ist die Verwendung von statistischen Methoden zur Erkennung dynamischer Muster. Die zweite Tatsache ist sicherlich die neue Merkmalsextraktion, die zu einer deutlichen Verbesserung des neuen Systems führte.
Das Erkennungssystem arbeitet in drei Stufen:

- Vorverarbeitung
- Merkmalsextraktion
- statistische Klassifizierung

[1] Beispiele der Gesten sind auf der Internetseite http://www.fb9-ti.uni-duisburg.de/projekte/video/video.html zu sehen.

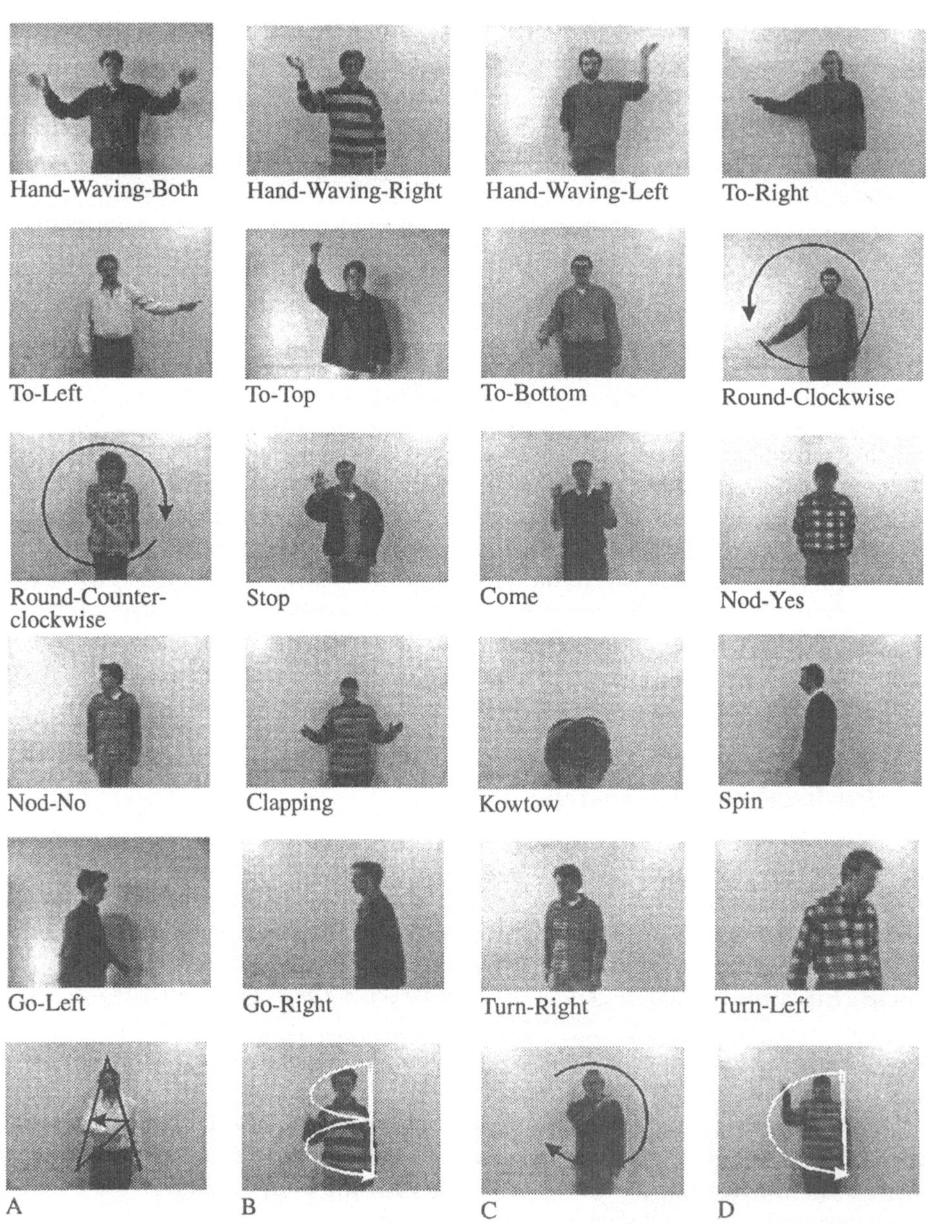

Abbildung 1. Beispielbilder aus den Gestensequenzen

3.1 Die Vorverarbeitung

Die Aufgabe der Vorverarbeitung ist die Vorbereitung der Videosequenz für die Erkennung. Es wurde bereits in [7] gezeigt, daß eine Differenzbildsequenz besser als die Originalsequenz zur Gestikerkennung geeignet ist. Die Differenzbildsequenz wird aus der Originalsequenz berechnet, indem die Differenz von den Bildpunkten aufeinanderfolgender Bilder $B(x, y)$ gebildet wird. Ein Bild der Differenzbildsequenz enthält nur die veränderten Bildteile und charakterisiert dadurch die Bewegung, die zwischen zwei Bildern stattgefunden hat. In der Differenzbildsequenz sind unbewegte Teile (z.B. Hintergrund) eliminiert. Dadurch kann die Erkennung hintergrund- und personenunabhängig arbeiten.

Der nächste Schritt in der Vorverarbeitung ist die Anwendung eines Schwellwertes. In der Differenzbildsequenz werden alle Pixel, deren Grauwertbetrag unter dem Schwellwert liegt, zu Null gesetzt.

3.2 Die Merkmalsextraktion

Aufgrund der in [7] und [6] gewonnenen Erkenntnisse war eine weitere wesentliche Verbesserung der Erkennungsleistung durch eine neue Merkmalsextraktion zu erwarten. Diese sollte folgende Anforderungen erfüllen:

- Vermeidung einer Mischung zwischen räumlicher und zeitlicher Information.
- Findung von Merkmalen, die die Dynamik in der Sequenz und damit die Geste charakterisieren.
- Robustheit gegenüber Abweichungen in der Geste und gegenüber unterschiedlichen Personen, die die Geste vorführen.
- Robustheit gegenüber unterschiedlichen Hintergründen.
- Reduktion der Datenmenge durch die Merkmalsextraktion unter Beibehaltung der zur Erkennung der Geste notwendigen Informationen.

Besonders wichtig für eine effektive Bildsequenzerkennung ist der letzte Punkt, da die zu verarbeitende Datenmenge schon bei statischen Bildern sehr hoch ist und sich diese bei Bildsequenzen vervielfacht.

Die Größe des Grauwertes $D(x, y, t)$ in den Differenzbildern ist ein Maß für die Bewegung in jedem Bildpunkt $B(x, y, t)$. Die Grauwerte können als Funktionsgebirge (siehe Abb. 2) der Funktion $D(x, y)$ über der (x, y)-Bildebene angesehen werden. Das Funktionsgebirge wird für jede Geste ein anderes Erscheinungsbild haben. Wenn es möglich ist, das Funktionsgebirge durch spezielle Merkmale zu beschreiben, dann sollten diese Merkmale auch eine gute Beschreibung der augenblicklichen Bewegung in der Differenzbildsequenz $D(x, y, t)$ sein. Zum Beispiel wird die Bewegung für eine Geste mit der rechten Hand in der linken oberen Ecke angeordnet sein und dort große Auslenkungen (Abweichungen vom Nullpunkt) im Funktionsgebirge bewirken. Eine Möglichkeit, dieses zu beschreiben, ist der Schwerpunkt $\boldsymbol{m}(t)^T = [m_x(t), m_x(t)]$ des Betragsdifferenzbildes $|D(x, y)|$.

$$m_x(t) = \frac{\sum\limits_{x,y} x|D(x,y)|}{\sum\limits_{x,y} |D(x,y)|} \qquad m_y(t) = \frac{\sum\limits_{x,y} y|D(x,y)|}{\sum\limits_{x,y} |D(x,y)|} \tag{1}$$

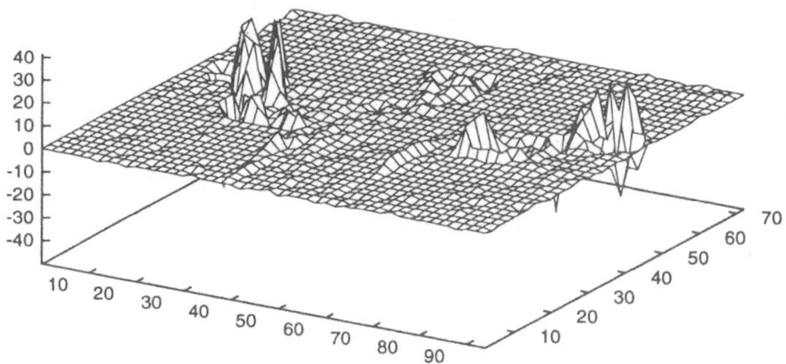

Abbildung 2. Funktionsgebirge eines Differenzbildes für die Geste "Hand-Waving-Both"

Der Vektor $m(t)$ kann auch als Bewegungsmittelpunkt angesehen werden. Dieser Mittelpunkt wird sich sicherlich bei einer rechtshändigen Geste auf der linken Seite des Bildes befinden.

Ein anderes nützliches Merkmal ist die mittlere Abweichung $\sigma(t)^T = [\sigma_x(t), \sigma_y(t)]$ der Bewegung aller Bildpunkte von diesem Bewegungsmittelpunkt. Sie ist folgendermaßen definiert:

$$\sigma_x(t) = \frac{\sum\limits_{x,y} |D(x,y)(x - m_x(t))|}{\sum\limits_{x,y} |D(x,y)|} \qquad \sigma_y(t) = \frac{\sum\limits_{x,y} |D(x,y)(y - m_y(t))|}{\sum\limits_{x,y} |D(x,y)|} \tag{2}$$

Dieses Merkmal ist nützlich, um Gesten mit Bewegungen von großen Körperteilen (z.B. ein Schritt zur Seite) von Gesten mit Bewegungen in einem kleineren Bereich (z.B. Kopfbewegungen) zu unterscheiden. Dieses Merkmal kann auch als Ausdehnung der Bewegung angesehen werden.

Ein weiteres wichtiges Merkmal wird die Intensität der Bewegung sein, welche als mittlere Höhe des Betragsfunktionsgebirges berechnet werden kann.

$$i(t) = \frac{\sum\limits_{x,y} |D(x,y)|}{\sum\limits_{x,y} 1} \tag{3}$$

Ein hoher Wert für $i(t)$ zeigt eine starke Bewegung an, während ein kleiner Wert ein stationäres Bild charakterisiert. Der Bewegungsschwerpunkt kann für die positiven und negativen Werte von $D(x, y, t)$ getrennt berechnet werden. Der Abstand zwischen den beiden Bewegungsschwerpunkten in x- und y-Richtung ist ein gutes Merkmal, um die schwer zu unterscheidenden Gesten Kopfnicken und Kopfschütteln zu erkennen.

$$dm_x(t) = \frac{\sum\limits_{x,y|D(x,y)<0} xD(x,y)}{\sum\limits_{x,y|D(x,y)<0} D(x,y)} - \frac{\sum\limits_{x,y|D(x,y)>0} xD(x,y)}{\sum\limits_{x,y|D(x,y)>0} D(x,y)}$$

$$dm_y(t) = \frac{\sum\limits_{x,y|D(x,y)<0} yD(x,y)}{\sum\limits_{x,y|D(x,y)<0} D(x,y)} - \frac{\sum\limits_{x,y|D(x,y)>0} yD(x,y)}{\sum\limits_{x,y|D(x,y)>0} D(x,y)} \tag{4}$$

Die Merkmale $m(t)$,$\sigma(t)$ und $i(t)$ können zu einer interessanten grafischen Darstellung der Geste genutzt werden. Eine Ellipse mit dem Mittelpunkt m und den Hauptachsen σ wird den Originalbildern oder den Differenzbildern überlagert. Die Intensität der Bewegung $i(t)$ wird als Helligkeit der Ellipse dargestellt. Abbildung 3 zeigt Beispielbilder der Gestensequenzen mit überlagerter Ellipse.

Abbildung 3. Bilder aus den Gesten Hand-Waving-Both, Go-Right und Round-Clockwise

Die Merkmale bilden für jedes Bild der Bildsequenz einen Merkmalsvektor ${x_t}^T = (m_x, m_y, \sigma_x, \sigma_y, dm_x, dm_y, i)$. Diese Merkmalsvektoren werden zu einer Vektorsequenz $\boldsymbol{X} = \boldsymbol{x}_1, ..., \boldsymbol{x}_T$ aneinandergehängt. Diese wird anschließend in der nächsten Verarbeitungsstufe klassifiziert.

3.3 Statistische Klassifizierung

Hidden-Markov-Modelle (HMM) [5] werden häufig zur Sprach- und Handschrifterkennung eingesetzt. Hier werden HMM zur Klassifizierung der Merkmalsvektorsequenzen verwendet. Ein Hidden-Markov-Modell λ besteht aus mehreren Zuständen, von denen einer aktiv ist. Der aktive Zustand erzeugt entsprechend einer zugeordneten Ausgabeverteilung ein Zeichen. Zu vorgegebenen Zeittakten ändert sich der aktuelle Zustand in Abhängigkeit von Übergangswahrscheinlichkeiten, die dem aktuellen Zustand zugeordnet sind. Abbildung 4 zeigt ein HMM mit vier Zuständen und einer kontinuierlichen Ausgabeverteilung. Die Übergangswahrscheinlichkeiten, die ungleich Null sind, sind als Pfeile zwischen den Zuständen eingezeichnet.

Die verwendeten HMMs besitzen eine kontinuierliche Ausgabeverteilungsfunktion, die mit einer Gaussfunktion modelliert wird. Das HMM λ für jede Geste wird durch den Baum-Welch-Algorithmus mit den Trainingssequenzen trainiert. Die Erkennung mit dem Forward-Algorithmus bestimmt das HMM mit der größten Bildungswahrscheinlichkeit $P(\boldsymbol{X}|\lambda_l)$. Bei den HMMs werden zwei unterschiedliche Topologien eingesetzt: Die ersten 16 Gesten werden mit zyklischen Modellen beschrieben, für die Gesten 17 bis 24 werden lineare Modelle verwendet.

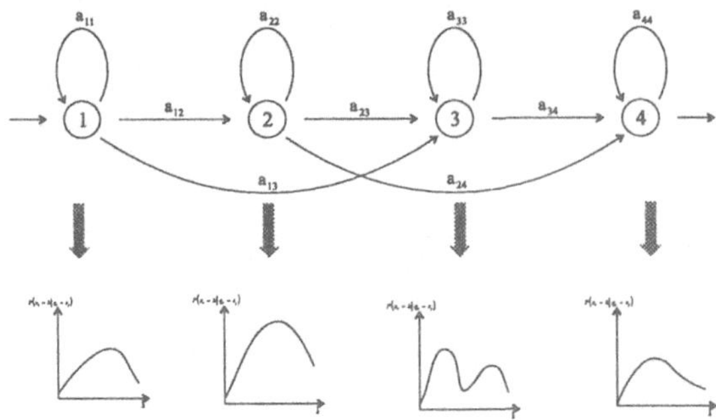

Abbildung 4. Aufbau eines HMM

4 Ergebnisse

Für die in Kapitel 2 beschriebene Erkennungsaufgabe erreicht das System eine Erkennungsrate von 92,9% . Dieses ist eine gute Erkennungsrate für die sehr komplexe Aufgabe, 24 verschiedene Gesten personenunabhängig zu erkennen. Eine genaue Betrachtung der fehlerhaft erkannten Gesten zeigt, daß einige Gesten relativ schlecht erkannt werden. Hierzu gehören die Buchstaben A-D, die nur zu 82% richtig erkannt werden. Gesten, die relativ schlecht erkannt werden, sind die Gesten Stop und Come. Die Bewegung dieser Gesten ist auf die Kamera gerichtet und nicht parallel zur Bildebene, wie bei den meisten anderen Gesten. Dieses Problem kann aber nur durch die Verwendung von Stereobildern zur Gestenerkennung gelöst werden.

Für die in [7] definierte Erkennungsaufgabe erreicht dieses System eine Erkennungsrate von 96,7%.Verglichen mit dem in [7] vorgestellten System, welches eine Erkennungsrate von 90% erreichte, bedeutet dieses eine relative Fehlerreduktion von 67%.

5 Systemverbesserungen

Im Zuge der Weiterentwicklung des Systems wurde besonderer Wert auf eine weitere Verbesserung der Benutzerfreundlichkeit gelegt. Zunächst wurden dabei zwei Gesichtspunkte verfolgt: Ein Aspekt, der zu einer wesentlich größeren Benutzerfreundlichkeit führt, ist die positionsunabhängige Gestikerkennung. Hierbei muß sich die Person nicht mehr in der Mitte des Kamerabildes befinden, was bei den vorhin beschriebenen Methoden noch notwendig ist, um die maximale Erkennungsleistung zu erzielen. Erreicht werden kann dies durch Maßnahmen zur Berechnung von Merkmalen, die normiert auf die relative Position des Benutzers im Bild sind und nicht mehr die absoluten Positionsdaten verwenden. Eine zweite wichtige Verbesserung der Benutzerfreundlichkeit ist die Erkennung von spontanen Gesten. Dabei soll der Benutzer in die Lage versetzt werden, sich relativ frei vor der Kamera zu bewegen, um sich zu positionieren und zu beliebigen Zeitpunkten eine Geste auszuführen. Die Gestikerkennung wird dann nicht mehr durch Knopfdruck initiiert, sondern der Erkennungsmechanismus ist ständig aktiv und darf die Positionierbewegung nicht mit der Ausführung einer Gestik verwechseln.

Das System muß selbst entscheiden, ob die momentane Bewegung eine Positionierbewegung oder eine Gestik ist, wobei Beginn und Ende dieses Vorgangs unbekannt sind. Somit kann der Benutzer seine Gesten zu beliebigen Zeitpunkten ausführen und sich zwischendurch vor der Kamera zwanglos bewegen oder aber alternativ dazu mehrere Gesten hintereinander ausführen. Dies stellt zweifellos eine deutliche Verbesserung der Kommunikationsmöglichkeiten für den Benutzer dar. Ein solches Problem ist jedoch sehr komplex und beispielsweise nicht durch eine einfache Bewegungsdetektion lösbar. Dies wäre nur dann der Fall, wenn keine Positionierbewegung des Benutzers zugelassen wäre und somit der Anfang und das Ende einer Gestik über eine Bewegungsdetektion (bzw. über Stillstandsdetektion) erkannt werden könnte. Es stellt sich heraus, daß diese Problematik nur lösbar ist, wenn der gesamte stochastische Dekodierungsprozess für den Erkennungsmechanismus so modifiziert wird, daß die Detektion von Gesten und von Positionierbewegungen beliebiger Länge in die Gesamtprozedur des zur Erkennung verwendeten Viterbi-Algorithmus integriert wird. Dies kann durch die in Bild 5 dargestellte HMM-Struktur erreicht werden, in der sich das System nun in einer kontinuierlichen Erkennungsschleife befindet. Dabei wird eine Positionierbewegung des Benutzers durch zusätzliche Markov-Modelle - sog. "Filler-Modelle" - repräsentiert, die extra mit Bewegungen trainiert wurden, die nicht den Gesten entsprechen. In Bild 5 sind 2 Filler-Modelle dargestellt, wobei das erste Modell hauptsächlich intensive Bewegungen des ganzen Körpers im gesamten Bild repräsentiert (z.B. Hin- und Hergehen, Drehen) und das zweite Modell mit Bewegungen von Körperteilen trainiert wurde (Arme verschränken, Oberkörper vorbeugen). Auch die Viterbi-Dekodierung selbst mußte wesentlich verändert werden, da üblicherweise entweder Anfangs- oder Endpunkt einer zu erkennenden Sequenz bekannt sein müssen, um den Viterbi-Dekodierungsprozeß zu starten. Eine Lösung kann jedoch realisiert werden, indem die Wahrscheinlichkeiten für alle Gesten parallel berechnet werden und ein gewisser Abfall in den akkumulierten Wahrscheinlichkeiten detektiert wird, der dann meistens sehr gut den Wechsel von einem Markov-Modell auf das andere HMM in Bild 5 anzeigt. Details zu dieser recht komplizierten Prozedur können in [3,4] gefunden werden. Mit dieser wesentlichen Neuerung konnte bereits erfolgreich die Echtzeiterkennung von spontan ausgeführten Gesten realisiert und somit das bestehende prototypische Gestikerkennungssystem entscheidend verbessert werden.

Eine vielversprechende Anwendung des Systems konnte in Zusammenarbeit mit dem Institut für Mechatronik in Moers realisiert werden. Dort wurde ein Großroboter, der für Spreng- und Ankerarbeiten im Bergbau eingesetzt wird, mit dem Gestikerkennungssystem gekoppelt. In diesem Fall wurde die visuelle Kommunikation zur Positionierung des Großmanipulators mit Hilfe von Gesten verwendet.

6 Zusammenfassung

In diesem Beitrag wurde ein leistungsfähiges videobasiertes Gestikerkennungssystem vorgestellt. Es wurde mit einer neuartigen Merkmalsextraktion gearbeitet, die die Datenmenge der Videosequenzen deutlich reduziert und dadurch eine Echtzeiterkennung ermöglicht. Das in diesem Beitrag beschriebene Verfahren hat zu einem sehr guten und robusten Gestikerkennungssystem geführt. Die Anzahl von 24 unterschiedlichen

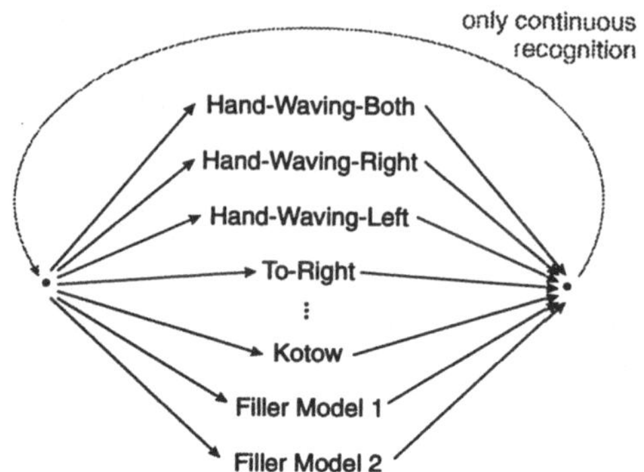

Abbildung 5. Netzwerk für die Gestikerkennung

Gesten stellt keine durch das System vorgegebene Höchstzahl dar. Zusätzliche Gesten würden jedoch die Erkennungsrate des Systems reduzieren. Das System eröffnet weitere Verbesserungsmöglichkeiten in der Vorverarbeitung, sowie in der statistischen Modellierung, und wird daher weiter verbessert werden. Zukünftige Forschungstätigkeiten beinhalten die Verbesserung der positionsunabhängigen Gestikerkennung und die kontinuierliche Erkennung von spontan ausgeführten Gesten. Für beide Aufgabenbereiche konnten bereits vielversprechende Ergebnisse erzielt werden.

Literatur

1. A. Bobick and J. Davis. An Apperance-Based Representation of Action. In *Proc. IEEE Int. Conf. on Pattern Recognition (ICPR-96)*, pages 307–312, Vienna, Austria, Aug. 1996.
2. C. Cédras and M. Shah. Motion-Based Recognition: A Survey. *Image and Vision Computing*, 13(2):129–155, 1995.
3. S. Eickeler, A. Kosmala, and G. Rigoll. Hidden Markov Model Based Continuous Online Gesture Recognition. In *International Conference on Pattern Recognition (ICPR)*, Brisbane, 1998.
4. S. Eickeler and G. Rigoll. Kontinuierliche Erkennung von spontan ausgeführten Gesten mit neuen stochastischen Dekodierverfahren. In *Workshop Dynamische Perzeption*, Bielefeld, June 1998.
5. L. R. Rabiner. A Tutorial on Hidden Markov Models and Selected Applications in Speech Recognition. *Proc. of the IEEE*, 77(2):257–285, 1989.
6. G. Rigoll, A. Kosmala, and M. Schuster. A New Approach to Video Sequence Recognition Based on Statistical Methods. In *Proc. IEEE Int. Conference on Image Processing (ICIP)*, Lausanne, 1996.
7. M. Schuster and G. Rigoll. Fast Online Video Image Sequence Recognition with Statistical Methods. In *Proc. IEEE Int. Conf. on Acoustics, Speech, and Signal Processing (ICASSP)*, pages 3450–3453, Atlanta, May 1996.
8. M. Stark, M. Kohler, and P. ZYKLOP. Video Based Gesture Recognition for Human Computer Interaction. In *Int. Workshop on Modeling, Virtual Worlds, Distributed Graphics*, Bad Honnef, Nov. 1995.
9. T. Starner and A. Pentland. Visual Recognition of American Sign Language Using Hidden Markov Models. In *International Workshop on Automatic Face and Gesture Recognition*, Zurich, Switzerland, 1995.

Laser-Display-Technologie Bilddarstellung der Zukunft

Dipl.-Ing. Christhard Deter
LDT GmbH & Co.
Laser-Display-Technologie KG
Fasaneninsel 1
D-07548 Gera

Tel.: +49 / 3 65 / 43 59 – 0
Fax: +49 / 3 65 / 4 38 03 95

1. Einführung

Durch die Entwicklung der Fernsehtechnik wurde es möglich, visuelle Bildinformationen in codierte elektronische Informationen zu wandeln und anschließend wieder in visuelle Bildinformationen umzusetzen. Damit wurde die Möglichkeit einer Bildfernübertragung geschaffen, die heute unterstützt durch die phantastischen Möglichkeiten der terrestrischen wie außerterrestrischen Informationsübertragungssysteme eine weltweite Verbreitung gefunden hat.
Durch die für die Fernübertragung erforderliche Wandlung einer realen Bildszene in codierte elektronische Informationen wurde gleichzeitig die Wurzel der heutigen Displaytechnik als Ausgabemedium der Computertechnik gelegt. Die Kathodenstrahlröhre (CRT) ist heute weltweit noch das meistverbreitetste Ausgabemedium in der Fernseh- sowie Displaytechnik in einer maximalen Bilddiagonale von 110 cm. Für die Erzeugung größerer Bilder hat sich in den letzten 20 Jahren das Prinzip der optischen Nachvergrößerung eines geräteinternen primären Bildes - das Projektionsprinzip - entwickelt. Vertreter dieser Technologie sind LCD-Projektoren, Projektoren auf der Grundlage eines Mikrospiegelarrays (DMD) sowie Lichtventilprojektoren. Bei all diesen Projektoren wird als Lichtquelle eine Projektionslampe eingesetzt, die auf Edisons Erfindung der Glühlampe aus dem vorigen Jahrhundert zurückgeht.

An der Schwelle des neuen Jahrtausends ist eine grundsätzlich neue Technologie zur Bilddarstellung auf dem Vormarsch. Diese Technologie bricht mit den elementaren Grundlagen jeder bekannten Bildprojektion durch:

- Ersatz des Temperaturstrahlers (Glühlampe) durch Laserlicht
- Ersatz des klassischen Projektorprinzips durch einen flächenhaft abgelenkten kollinearen Laserstrahl

2. Bild als Informationsträger

Die weiteren Betrachtungen beziehen sich auf elektronisch erzeugte zweidimensionale farbige Bewegtbilder. Für den menschlichen Gesichtssinn relevante Bildinformationen sind:

- Farbe (Chrominanz) — Farbton (dominante Wellenlänge des Farbreizes)
Sättigung (Farbbrillanz)
Helligkeit
- Leuchtdichte (verbunden mit Luminanz)
- Kontrast (Hell-Dunkelverhältnis)
- Gradation (Grauwertabstufung)
- Auflösung — Farbunterschiede
Helligkeitsunterschiede
Geometrische Auflösung
- Bildschärfe
- Pixelstruktur
- Konvergenz (Farbdeckung)
- Störmuster

3. Bilderzeugung beim klassischen Projektor

Als Lichtquelle dient eine Projektionslampe. Nach einer Kondensoroptik wird das Licht durch einen pixelorientierten RGB-Farbfilter in drei Teilstrahlengänge aufgeteilt. Dieses Licht wird durch eine Lichtmodulationseinheit geführt, die ebenso pixelorientiert sind. Die eingehenden seriellen elektronischen Videodaten werden zunächst so umgeformt, daß eine parallele Ansteuerung der Lichtmodulationseinheiten erfolgen kann. Bildweise erfolgt dann die Intensitätsmodulation parallel in allen Pixeln. Auf die optischen Wirkprinzipien dieser Modulation soll hier nicht eingegangen werden. Unmittelbar nach der Modulationseinheit liegt die vollständige Bildinformation – wenn auch noch in einem sehr kleinen Format – vor. Mit einem optischen System (Objektiv) erfolgt dann die vergrößerte Abbildung der Modulationsebene auf die Projektionsebene.
Der Informationsfluß durchläuft bei diesem Geräteprinzip folgende Etappen:

- serieller Eingang elektronischer Bilddaten
- Umsetzung in parallel verfügbare Daten
- Umsetzen der elektronischen Daten in optische Daten (Dateninhalt der elektronischen Bilddaten wird auf das Licht pixelweise aufmoduliert)
- das optische Abbildungssystem überträgt die noch in einem sehr kleinen Format vorliegenden optischen Bilddaten stark vergrößert auf die Projektionsebene

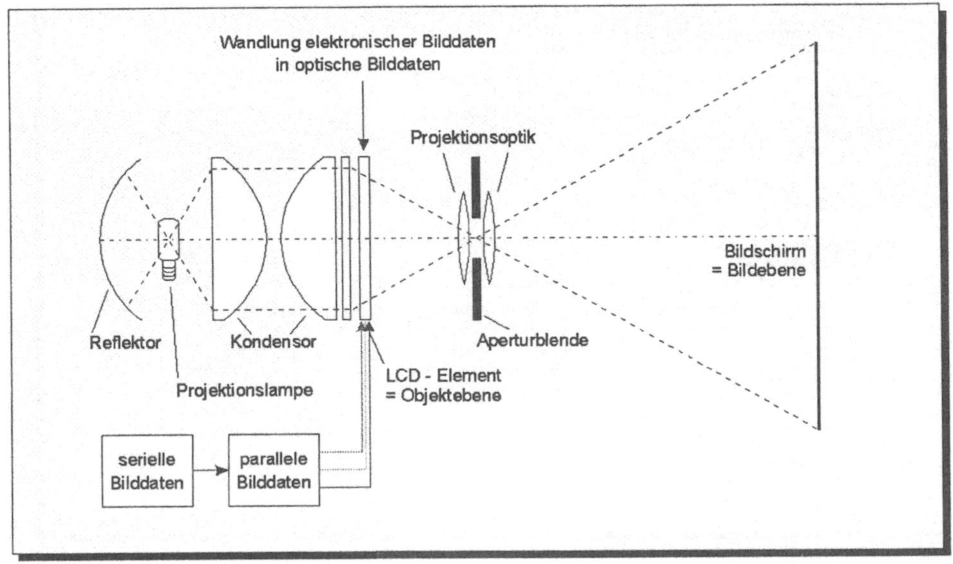

Bild 1   klassischer Projektor

4. Bilddarstellung mittels Laserlicht

Drei grundlegende Lösungselemente sind gegeben:

- Wandlung der seriellen-elektronischen Quelleninformation durch Amplitudenmodulation des Laserlichtes im Laserstrahl in optische Informationen
- Gesetz der additiven Farbmischung dreier Grundfarben unter Anwendung der Graßmannschen Gesetze
- Bewegen (Scannen) des Laserstrahles über ein gegebenes Bildformat

5. Grundprinzip der Laser-Display-Technologie

Die elektronische Eingangsplatine enthält Eingänge für die unterschiedlichsten Video-, Computer-, CAD-Normen. Der Mikrokontroller der Eingangsplatine programmiert selbständig die gesamte Steuerlogik des Systems gemäß der anliegenden Norm. Die Videoinformationen werden digitalisiert soweit sie nicht in digitaler Form vorliegen und im Bildspeicher zwischengespeichert.
Dem Ausgang des Bildspeichers folgen die Farbtransformation und die Lasermodulatoren. Die RGB-Videodaten basieren auf den durch Standards festgelegten Farbeigenschaften der Bildschirmphosphore der bekannten Kathodenstrahlröhre der TV-Empfänger. Die Farbeigenschaften der Laserstrahlen unterscheiden sich wesentlich von denen der Bild-

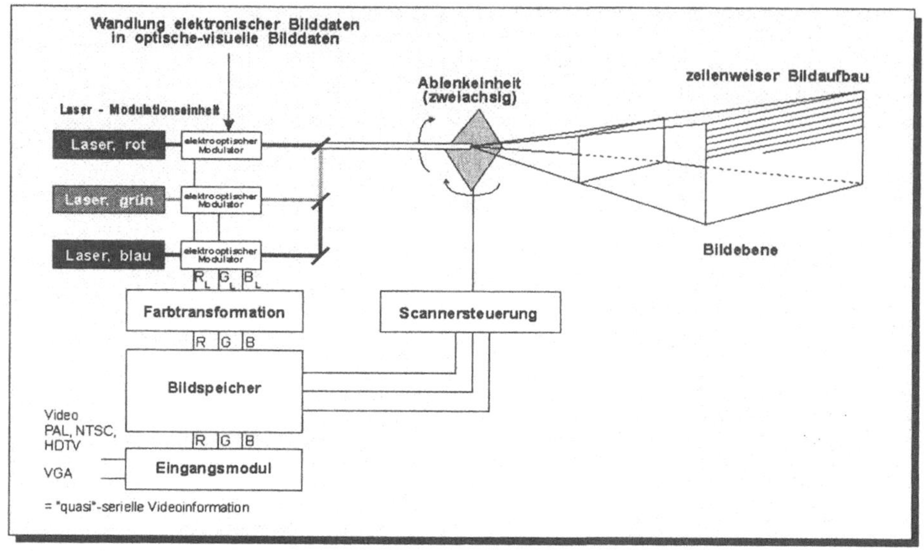

Bild 2 Grundprinzip der Laser-Display-Technologie

schirmphosphore. Eine direkte Ansteuerung der Lasermodulatoren würde zu farbverfälschten TV-Bildern führen. Die Farbtransformation hat die Aufgabe, die durch die RGB-Signale getragenen Farbinformationen vom Farbraum der Bildschirmphosphore in den Farbraum der Laserfarben umzusetzen. Diese Umsetzung erfolgt durch eine lineare Matrizentransformation in Echtzeit.
Die transformierten R_L, G_L, B_L-Signale übertragen nun die Farbinformationen auf die Lasermodulatoren, die durch Amplitudenmodulation des Laserstrahles die bis dahin in elektronischer Form vorliegenden Farbinformationen in optisch visuelle Farbinformationen umwandeln. An den Ausgängen der Lasermodulatoren stehen nun die drei intensitätsmodulierten Laserstrahlen zur Verfügung. Um gemäß des Gesetzes der additiven Farbmischung alle Farben des Laserfarbraumes zu erreichen, müssen die drei Laserstrahlen in einen kollinearen Laserstrahl vereinigt werden. Das erfolgt über dichroitische Spiegel. In dem nun vorliegenden Laserstrahl sind in serieller Form alle optisch visuellen Bildinformationen (als Summe der drei Farbinformationen, die zeitgleich addiert werden) enthalten. Dieser Laserstrahl bewegt sich mit Lichtgeschwindigkeit als ebene Welle mit einer Frequenz im Terahertzbereich. Da die Amplitudenmodulation des Laserstrahles in einem wesentlich geringeren Frequenzband arbeitet, werden auch die seriellen Bildinformationen entsprechend langsamer als die Lichtgeschwindigkeit transportiert.
Mit der Ablenkeinheit wird nun der Laserstrahl zeilenweise von links nach rechts und von oben nach unten abgelenkt. Aus einer Reihe von physikalischen Gründen ist das mit dem heutigen Stand von Wissenschaft und

Technik nur über eine oder mehrere bewegte Spiegelflächen realisierbar. Die Ablenkung erfolgt über einen sehr schnellen Polygonspiegel und einen Galvanometerspiegel.

6. Geometrisch-optischer Bildaufbau

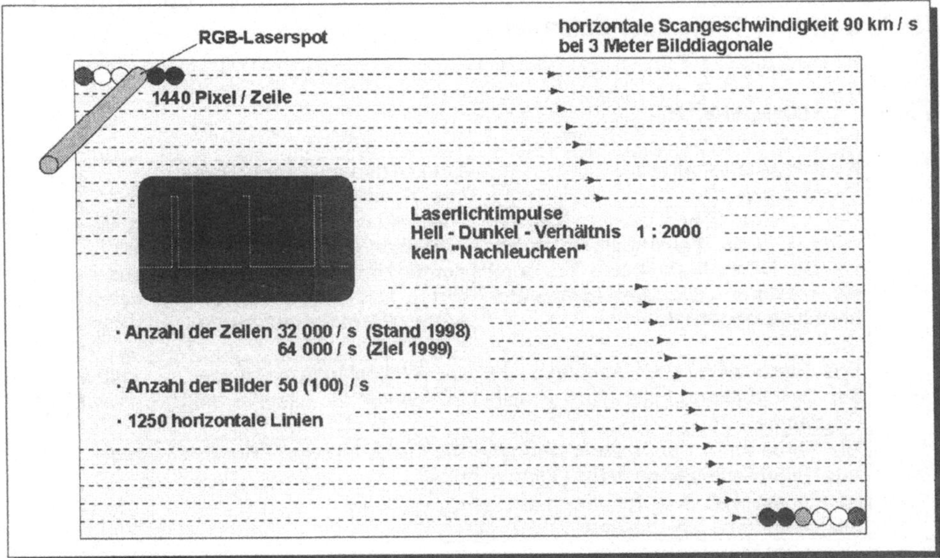

Bild 3 geometrisch-optischer Bildaufbau

Der Bildaufbau wird am Beispiel eines HDTV-Bildes erläutert.
Der Laserstrahl wird von links nach rechts über die Projektionswand geführt. Bei einer Bilddiagonale von 3 Metern beträgt die Geschwindigkeit des Laserspots auf der Projektionswand 90 km/s. Durch die Lasermodulation werden innerhalb einer Zeile 1440 unterschiedliche Laserspots erzeugt. Die Videobandbreite beträgt 30 MHz. Es werden je Bild 1250 Zeilen geschrieben. Die Bildwiederholfrequenz beträgt 50 Hz (interlaced).
Die Laserquelle arbeitet im Impulsbetrieb. Das Zeitverhältnis Licht zu kein Licht verhält sich wie 1 : 2000 ohne Nachleuchten. Die Repetitionsrate der Laserimpulse beträgt 85 MHz. Das Gleiche gilt dann ebenso für die Übertragung von Informationen. Dem menschlichen Gesichtssinn wird folgendes „Bild“ dargeboten. Der Laserspot (mit geringer Ausdehnung) befindet sich gerade an einer Stelle, die im Vergleich zum gesamten Bildformat eine sehr geringe Ausdehnung hat. Dabei wird nun das Licht in nur kurzen Lichtimpulsen angeboten. Statistisch gesehen befindet sich eigentlich überhaupt keine Bildinformation auf der Projektionswand. Der menschliche Gesichtssinn integriert jedoch diese selektiven Informationen zu einem in sich geschlossenen flimmerfreien Bild.

7. Eigenschaften und Vorteile der Laser-Display-Technologie

Die besonderen Eigenschaften und Vorteile der Laser-Display-Technologie sollen anhand von Technologievergleichen gegenüber schon am Markt erfolgreich eingeführten Projektionsverfahren dargestellt werden. Der Vergleich wird anhand der Projektionsverfahren geführt, die auf dem Prinzip des klassischen Projektors aufbauen.

7.1 Lichtquelle

Konkurrenzverfahren Projektionslampe	**Laser-Display-Technologie** Laserquelle
Der Einsatz herkömmlicher Lampen ruft eine hohe **Wärmebelastung** hervor. Die **Bildhelligkeit** wird u.a. durch die maximal zulässige Temperaturbelastung **begrenzt.**	Der Laser ist langfristig gesehen die **effektivste Lichtquelle** in Hinsicht auf die Umwandlung von elektrischem Strom in Lichtleistung. Es tritt dabei **keine Wärmebelastung** im optischen Kanal auf.
Das Farbspektrum ist abhängig von der Betriebstemperatur der Projektionslampe.	Die Wellenlänge der Laser ist unabhängig von der Laserleistung.
Die Farbe muß durch **verlustbehaftete Filter** erzeugt werden. Dadurch ist nur ein Teil des von der Lampe ausgesandten Lichts nutzbar.	Die **Farbe** ist ohne Filter **direkt gegeben.**
Das Licht der Lampe wird in einem **großen Raumwinkel** ausgestrahlt, wobei nur ein Teil dieses Winkels für die Beleuchtung des Objekts benötigt wird (Aperturverluste).	Lichtemission findet in **geringstmöglichen Raumwinkel** statt. Das gesamte erzeugte Laserlicht steht ohne Aperturverluste zur Verfügung.

7.2 Prinzip der Bilderzeugung

Konkurrenzverfahren klassisches optisches Abbildungsprinzip	**Laser-Display-Technologie**
Durch die klassische optische Abbildung ist die Tiefenschärfe stark eingeschränkt, die Abbildung muß wie beim Diaprojektor auf eine **bestimmte Entfernung scharfgestellt** werden. Die Projektion ist nur auf **ebene Flächen** möglich.	Durch den parallelen Laserstrahl ist das **Bild immer scharf,** unabhängig von der Projektionsentfernung. Die Tiefenschärfe ist praktisch unbegrenzt. Es kann ohne Schärfeverlust auf **gewölbte Flächen** z.B. Sphären oder Zylinder projiziert werden. Verzerrungen werden dabei elektronisch ausgeglichen.
Bei LCD oder DLP besteht das Objekt aus einer Pixelmatrix. Die statistisch verteilten **Ausfälle einzelner Pixel** sind im Bild störend wahrnehmbar.	Es gibt nur eine punktförmige Lichtquelle, Pixelausfälle sind **prinzipbedingt nicht möglich.**
Pixelgröße und -anzahl werden durch die zur Verfügung stehenden technologischen Verfahren **begrenzt.**	Das Verfahren ist **nicht pixelorientiert.**

7.3 Farbdarstellung

Konkurrenzverfahren	Laser-Display-Technologie
Die Farbe ist durch **Filter** gegeben. Diese haben einen bestimmte spektrale Bandbreite, d.h. sie lassen einen relativ breiten Wellenlängenbereich passieren, der die Sättigung der Farbe bestimmt. Man spricht dann von **entsättigten Farben**. Der darstellbare Farbraum ist dadurch eingeschränkt.	Die Farbe des Laserlichts ist physikalisch bedingt spektral sehr schmalbandig, die Farben sind **maximal gesättigt**. Ein großer Farbraum läßt sich darstellen. Dies ist z.B. für elektronisches Kino Voraussetzung.

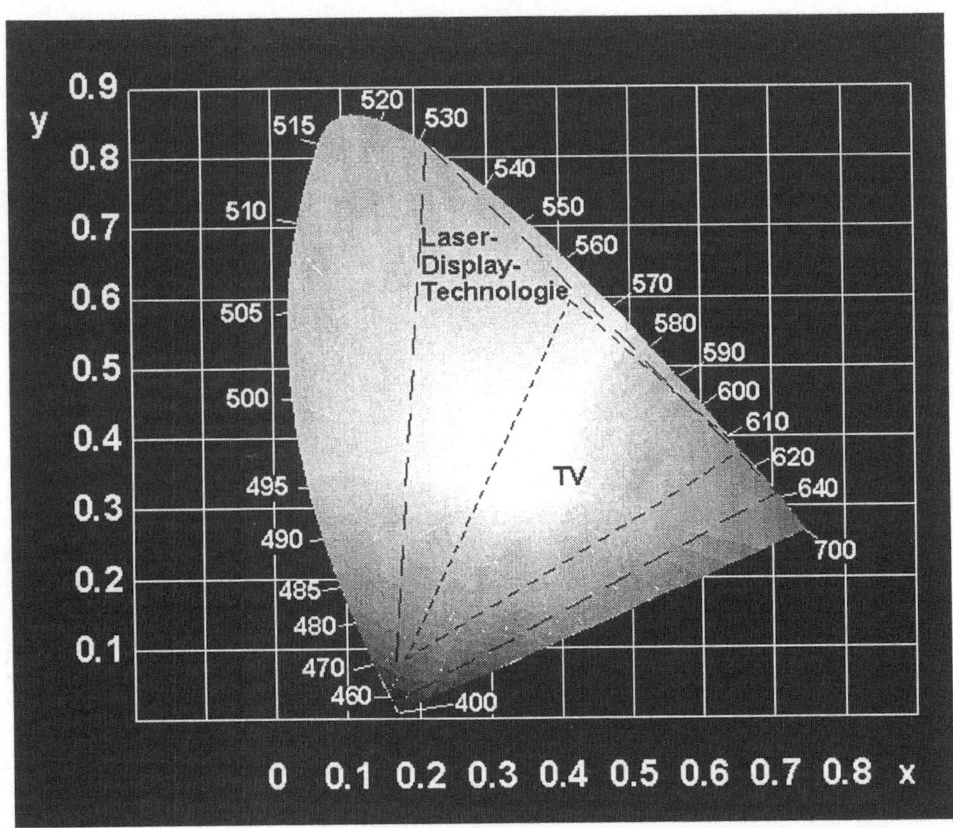

Bild 4 darstellbare Farbräume

7.4 Trennung von Lichtquelle und Projektionskopf

Konkurrenzverfahren	Laser-Display-Technologie
Die **Projektionsrichtung** ist durch die Ausrichtung des Gerätes **vorgegeben.** Sie läßt sich nur durch Bewegen des gesamten Gerätes verändern, was besonderes bei großen professionellen Geräten nicht praktikabel ist.	Lichtquelle und Projektionskopf sind durch eine **Lichtleitfaser** verbunden. Der Projektionskopf ist **leicht** und um zwei Achsen **drehbar**. Das bringt besonders dort Vorteile wo das Display mit bewegt werden muß (z.B. Simulatoren) oder bei der Projektion auf bewegliche Wände (z.B. Bühnenkulisse).

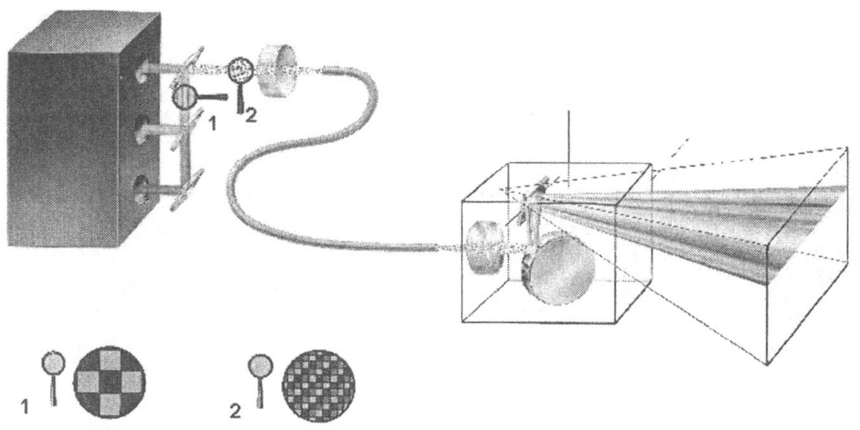

Bild 5 Trennung von Lichtquelle und Projektionkopf

Es gibt derzeit keine erkennbaren physikalischen oder technologischen Grenzen für die Laser-Display-Technologie, in Hinsicht auf Bildgröße, Auflösung (Schärfe), Kontrast und Farbrillanz. Sie hat deshalb die besten Chancen, die **Display-Technik der Zukunft** zu werden.

• Laser ist langfristig die effektivste Lichtquelle, dabei keine Wärmebelastung durch Temperaturstrahler im optischen Kanal • Farbe direkt ohne verlustbehafteten Filter gegeben • maximale Farbsättigung der Primärfarben gegeben • Lichtemission im geringstmöglichen Raumwinkel gegeben, dadurch keine Aperturverluste • erreichbarer Kontrast bei direkt moduliertem Laser maximal, bei schwarz keine Lichtemission durch die Quelle • keine Pixelbegrenzung durch materielle Elemente, dadurch keine Formatbegrenzung durch technologische Verfahrensgrenzen	• eine punktförmige Lichtquelle für ein Bild (Ausfall -Ausbeuteproblematik) • polarisiertes Licht ohne Filterverluste in der Laserquelle gegeben • durch das gewählte programmierbare Scannerprinzip Normunabhängigkeit bezüglich - Zeilenfrequenz - Bildfrequenz - interlaced/non interlaced mode - Seitenverhältnis - Videofrequenz • Farbstandards (durch Rücktransformation aus dem Laserfarbraum in den Normfarbraum) • Multinorm-/Multimediafähigkeit • Schärfentiefe unbegrenzt

Bild 6 Vorteile der Laser-Display-Technologie

Schwerpunkte in der Anwendung sind

- im professionellen Bereich
  - Simulatoren für LKW, Zug, Flugtrainer, Hubschrauber
  - Großbilddarstellung bei Messen, Werbung, Events
  - Kuppelprojektion für Planetarien, virtual reality
  - elektronisches Kino
- im Consumer Bereich
  Schrägprojektion im Wohnzimmerbereich

Bild 7 Schrägprojektion in einemWohnzimmerbereich

Schnelle computergraphische Hologrammberechnung für Displayzwecke

Oliver Deussen, Matthias König, Alf Ritter, Thomas Strothotte

Otto-von-Guericke Universität Magdeburg
Institut für Simulation und Graphik
{deussen,koenig,alf,tstr}@isg.cs.uni-magdeburg.de

Zusammenfassung Die Holographie ist eines der aussichtsreicheren Verfahren zur dreidimensionalen visuellen Darstellung. Leider werden hierbei extrem hohe Anforderungen sowohl an die räumliche Auflösung des Ausgabemediums als auch an die involvierten Kommunikationskomponenten gestellt, da große Datenmengen bewegt werden müssen. Für computererzeugte Hologramme kommt der immense Rechenaufwand zu ihrer Herstellung hinzu, der Realzeitanwendungen bisher verhindert hat. Im Beitrag wird ein Verfahren zur schnellen Generierung computererzeugter Hologamme vorgestellt, mit dem kleine und einfach geartete Hologramme in Echtzeit berechnet werden können, was neben der reinen Darstellung auch für eine Reihe optischer Prozesse interessant ist.

1 Motivation

Schon seit einer Reihe von Jahren wird an der Entwicklung dreidimensionaler Darstellungsmethoden gearbeitet, die Bewegtbilder ähnlich dem Fernsehen zeigen. Früh schon wurden Stereotechniken für Film und Fernsehen entwickelt, die auf der Basis von Rot/Grün- oder Polarisationsbrillen einen räumlichen Eindruck vermitteln. Diese Verfahren ermöglichen allerdings nur einen räumlichen Eindruck von einem Blickwinkel aus.

In einem Hologramm (siehe [1], aber auch [2,3]) wird jedoch das komplette von einem Objekt ausgehende Wellenfeld für einen ganzen Sichtbereich gespeichert, was erlaubt, das Objekt von verschiedenen Seiten zu betrachten.

Nach der Entdeckung des holographischen Prinzips durch Gabor [4] wurden zunächst Verfahren zur optischen Herstellung von Hologrammen entwickelt. Mitte der sechziger Jahre entstanden erste Versuche, Hologramme mit Rechnern zu erzeugen [5,6]. Heute existieren eine Reihe von Verfahren, die es ermöglichen, synthetische Hologramme der verschiedensten Eigenschaften zu erzeugen [7–9].

So können auf rechentechnisch relativ einfache Weise Hologramme erzeugt werden, die zweidimensionale Objekte auf verschiedenen Ebenen darstellen, oder solche, bei denen nur in der Horizontale eine Parallaxe entsteht. Stereogramme [10], eine weitere Art von Hologrammen, speichern eine Menge zweidimensionaler Ansichten eines Objektes auf eine Weise, daß der Betrachter einen räumlichen

Eindruck erhält. Oftmals wird auch hier eine Parallaxe unterschlagen, was die Hologrammgröße in einer Raumrichtung dramatisch reduziert [11].

Diese günstigen Eigenschaften erlaubten es in den letzten Jahren, Stereogramme mit Rechnern in Echtzeit zu erzeugen und darzustellen [12, 13]. Das am MIT entwickelte Holovideo-System [14] verwendet an verschiedenen Stellen Computergraphik und insbesondere Graphikhardware, um etwa die zweidimensionalen Objektansichten zu erzeugen (was auch in [15] getan wird) oder aber die bei der Berechnung anfallenden Beugungsgitter zu überlagern.

In unserer Arbeit haben wir diese Ideen erweitert, um allgemeine zweidimensionale komplexwertige Wellenfelder mit Hilfe von Graphikhardware zu interferieren [16–19]. Hierzu werden die Wellenfelder in Texturen [20] kodiert, die in der Computergraphik üblicherweise verwendet werden, um Objektoberflächen realistischer erscheinen zu lassen.

Solche Wellenfelder gehen beispielsweise von graphischen Grundprimitiven wie Punkten, Linien oder Kurven aus. Das Hologramm wird aus der Überlagerung dieser Grundprimitive zusammengestellt, ein Vorgehen, das in der Computergraphik an vielen Stellen angewendet wird.

Durch den Einsatz der Graphikhardware und die damit verbundene deutliche Beschleunigung des Verfahrens können kleine Hologramme mit durchaus akzeptablen Bildraten erzeugt werden, was ein wichtiger Schritt in Richtung der Erzeugung interaktiver Hologramme für Displayzwecke ist.

Im folgenden wird eine kurze Einführung in die Grundlagen synthetischer Hologramme gegeben, danach beschreiben wir unser Verfahren der texturbasierten Simulation von Interferenz für Punktmengen. Eine Erweiterung auf Strecken, Kurvenstücke und Dreiecksflächen soll die Generalität des Ansatzes demonstrieren. Schließlich werden die Resultate quantifiziert und analysiert, ein Ausblick schildert unsere Vorstellungen von weiteren wichtigen Arbeiten auf diesem Gebiet.

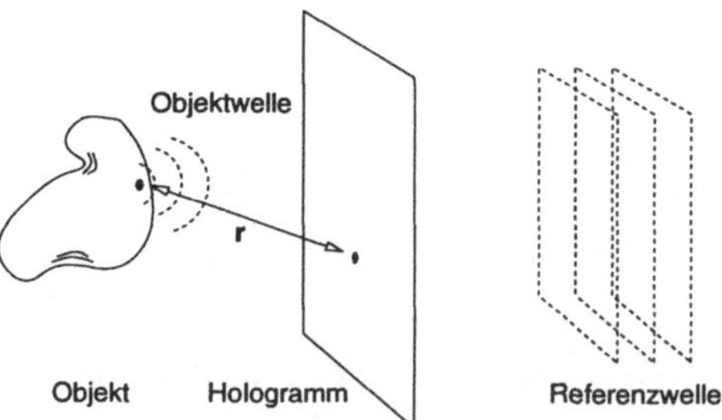

Abbildung1. Optische Aufnahme eines Hologramms. Objekt- und Referenzwelle überlagern sich zu einem Interferenzmuster, das im Hologramm gespeichert wird.

2 Synthetische Holographie

Grundlage für den holographischen Aufnahmeprozeß ist das Kirchhoffsche Beugungsintegral. Gegeben ist ein kohärent (also mit Licht einer Wellenlänge und zeitlich stabilem Schwingungszustand) beleuchteter Körper, der Licht auf eine Ebene abstrahlt[1], gesucht ist die Feldstärke auf einer entfernten Ebene. Der Zusammenhang ergibt sich nach Kirchhoff über

$$E(\mathbf{p}') = \frac{1}{i\lambda} \int_{\mathbf{p}}^{\mathbf{S}} E(\mathbf{p}) \; \frac{1}{r} \; e^{ikr} \; \cos(\alpha) \; d\mathbf{S} \tag{1}$$

wobei $E(\mathbf{p})$ die Feldstärke ist, die von Punkt $\mathbf{p}$ auf der Objektoberfläche $\mathbf{S}$ abgegeben wird , $E(\mathbf{p}')$ die Feldstärke in Punkt $\mathbf{p}'$ auf der Hologrammebene, λ die Wellenlänge, r der Abstand zwischen $\mathbf{p}$ und $\mathbf{p}'$ und α der Winkel zwischen dem Vektor $\mathbf{p}' - \mathbf{p}$ der Richtung des einfallenden Lichtes.

Wird das resultierende Wellenfeld mit einer ebenen Referenzwelle überlagert, bildet sich in der Hologrammebene eine Intensitätsverteilung, die mit einer photographischen Platte aufgezeichnet werden kann und das Hologramm ergibt.

Wird diese Platte mit kohärentem Licht beleuchtet, addieren sich die reflektierten Wellen zu genau dem Wellenfeld zusammen, welches das Ausgangsobjekt aussandte.

Soll ein synthetisches Hologramm erzeugt werden, muß Gleichung 1 diskret approximiert werden. Ein typisches Verfahren hierzu stellt die Oberfläche über eine Menge punktförmiger Lichtquellen dar

$$E(\mathbf{p}') = \frac{1}{i\lambda} \sum_{i}^{N} E(\mathbf{p}_i) \; \frac{1}{r} \; e^{ikr} \; \cos(\alpha). \tag{2}$$

Die von den einzelnen Lichtquellen ausgehenden Wellenfelder erzeugen hierbei in der Hologrammebene Muster, die, wenn mit einer ebenen Welle überlagert, sogenannte Fresnelsche Zonenplatten ergeben [21] (siehe auch Abbildung 2(a)).

Die Berechnung der Summe aus Gleichung 2 ist hierbei zeitaufwendig, da für jeden Hologrammpunkt alle Objektpunkte berücksichtigt werden müssen.

Tpische weitere Vereinfachungen in der Optik gehen daher von der Überlagerung paralleler Objektwellen aus, wobei die Hologrammebene ins Unendliche gelegt wird (Fourier-Hologramme), oder finden einfache, aber genauere Approximationen der Richtung (Fresnel-Hologramme).

In unserem Beitrag zeigen wir, wie die genaue Auswertung von Gleichung 2 mit Hilfe vorabberechneter Wellenfelder und Graphikhardware deutlich beschleunigt werden kann. Dies wird im nächsten Abschnitt näher erläutert.

[1] oftmals wird auch von zwei parallelen Ebenen ausgegangen, von denen eine in einem kompakten Bereich Licht abstrahlt und die Feldstärke auf der anderen berechnet wird.

3 Herstellung von Hologrammen mit Graphikhardware

Innerhalb unseres Verfahrens wird vorab eine Menge von Wellenfeldern über konventionelle Methoden berechnet. Diese Felder werden auf spezielle Art in Texturen kodiert. Texturen sind hierbei Bilddaten, die, wie in der Computergraphik üblich, vier Farbkanäle haben: rot, grün, blau und den Alpha-Kanal. Letzterer wird normalerweise für die Speicherung der Durchsichtigkeit einer Textur verwendet, hier allerdings als normaler Farbkanal behandelt.

Das Wellenfeld ist ein Feld komplexer Zahlen, deren positiver Realteil im roten Kanal der Textur, negativer Realteil im grünen, positiver Imaginärteil im blauen und negativer Imaginärteil im Alpha-Kanal gespeichert wird. Die entstehende Textur nennen wir im weiteren komplexe Textur.

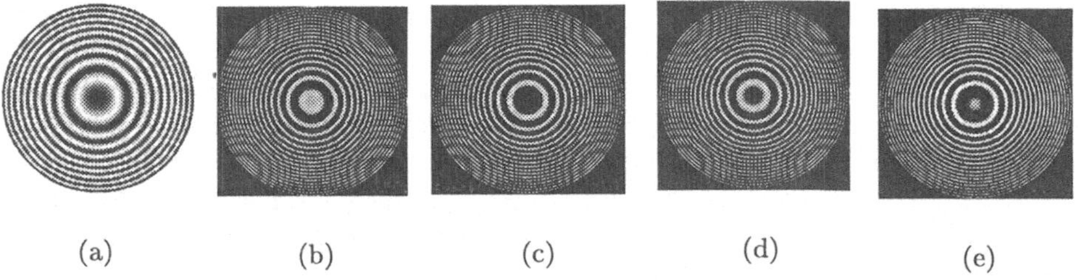

(a) (b) (c) (d) (e)

Abbildung2. Texturen von Wellenfeldern (a) Grauwerttextur zur Repräsentation einer Fresnelschen Zonenplatte, (b) bis (e) bilden eine komplexe Textur des zugrundeliegenden komplexen Wellenfeldes (b) rot, (c) grün, (d) blau, (e) Alpha-Kanal.

Im nächsten Schritt wird das Eingabeobjekt mit den Texturen verbunden. Besteht es beispielsweise aus einer Menge von Punktlichtquellen, so wird jede mit einer Textur verbunden, die dem aus einer Punktlichtquelle resultierenden Wellenfeld entspricht. Hierzu werden an die Orte der Punktlichtquellen Rechtecke plaziert die parallel zur Hologrammebene ausgerichtet sind. Auf diese Rechtecke werden die Texturen aufgebracht.

Um den Aufwand für die Vorabberechnung der Texturen zu begrenzen, macht man sich zunutze, daß die in der Hologrammebene resultierenden Wellenfelder unterschiedlich weit entfernter Objekte oftmals durch einfache Skalierung ineinander überführbar sind und demnach die gleichen Texturen durch unterschiedliche Skalierung der Rechtecke Wellenfelder unterschiedlich weit entfernter Punkte erzeugen. Die Kombination von Objektpunkten mit den komplexen Texturen läßt eine neue Datenstruktur entstehen, das holographische Äquivalent (siehe auch Abbildung 3).

Das Hologramm wird nun im letzten Schritt aus dem holographischen Äquivalent berechnet. Hierzu werden die Texturen in einer Parallelprojektion auf die Bildebene projiziert und überlagert. Dies umfasst die Interferenz zwischen den Texturen, die Interferenz mit einer anzugebenden Referenzwelle und die Be-

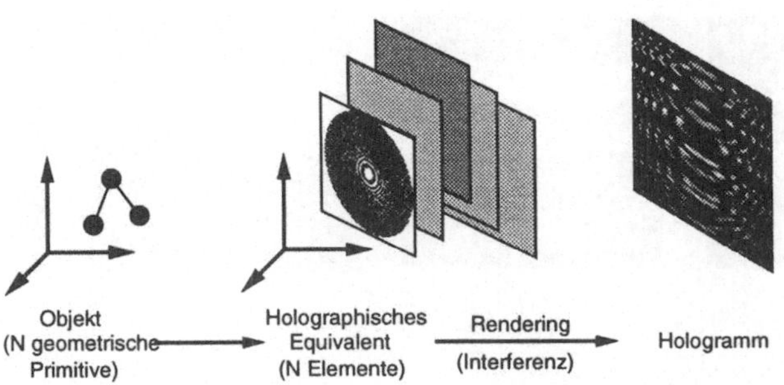

Abbildung3. Hologrammberechnung: Die Eingabeobjekte (links) werden in das holographische Äquivalent überführt (mitte), die Texturen werden zur Hologrammüberlagerung interferiert (rechts).

rechnung der gewünschten Intensitätsverteilung durch Benutzung von Look-up Tabellen. Weitere technische Details finden sich in [19, 25].

Alle diese Schritte werden über standardisierte Befehle der Graphikbibliotheken OpenGL [22] and IRIS Performer [23] ausgeführt, welche auf geeigneten Workstations komplett durch Graphikhardware unterstützt werden. Hierzu verwenden wir den Akkumulationspuffer [24] dieser Maschinen, der arithmetische Operationen mit ganzen Bildern erlaubt.

Typischerweise werden allerdings Hologrammgrößen benötigt, die die Größe der Graphikbildschirme und der maximal verwendbaren Fenster in OpenGL (heute 2000 x 2000 Bildpunkte) überschreiten. In diesen Fällen müssen die Hologramme gekachelt aufgebaut werden.

Fertige Hologramme können entweder optisch rekonstruiert werden, in dem man sie auf Film aufzeichnet und in einem geeigneten Laer-Setup sichtbar macht oder über Simulation. Letzteres führen wir mit dem optischen CAD-System DIGIOPT durch, das von Aagedal et al. [26] vorgestellt wurde und dessen Programmcode frei verfügbar ist.

Abbildung 4 zeigt Ergebnisse des Verfahrens. Das holographische Äquivalent des Eingabeobjekts wird einmal über Verblendung von Zonenplatten in ein Hologramm umgewandelt, was nur unbefriedigende Resultate ergibt. Werden jedoch komplexe Texturen interferiert, so entsteht ein typisches Muster welches das Eingabeobjekt rekonstruiert. Das hierbei entstehende Rauschen entsteht durch die verwendete Zufallsphase bei den Lichtquellen und ist ein inherentes Problem bei der Hologrammerzeugung und kann beispielwseise durch die Optimierung der Phasenverteilung vermindert werden [27]. Würden keine Zufallsphasen verwendet, so würde das Objekt spiegelnd erscheinen, was im Normalfall nicht gewünscht ist.

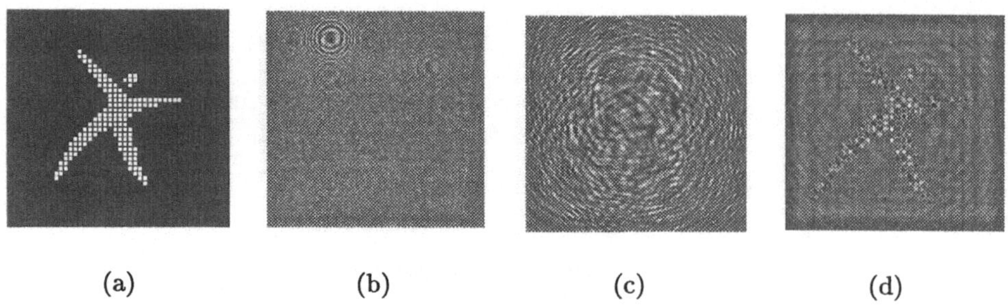

(a) (b) (c) (d)

Abbildung4. Herstellung eines Hologramms aus einer Menge von Punkten: (a) Eingabeobjekt; (b) Hologramm nach einfacher Addition von Zonenplatten; (c) Hologramm nach Interferenz komplexer Texturen (mit Zufallsphase der Punktlichtquellen) (d) Rekonstruktion

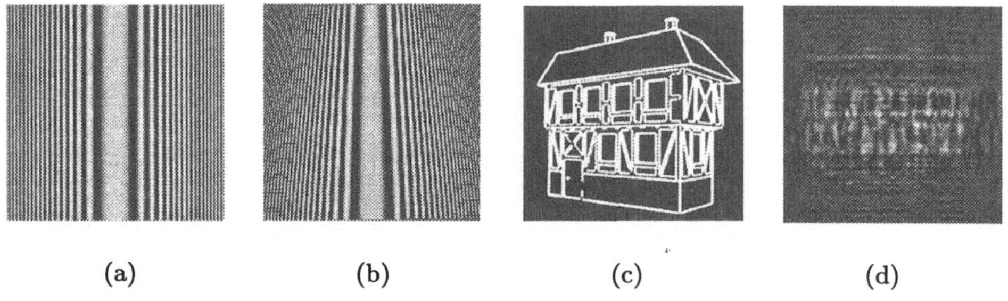

(a) (b) (c) (d)

Abbildung5. (a) Intensitätsmuster einer zylindrischen Welle ausgehend von einer Linie; (b) Konische Welle einer geneigten Linie, generiert aus (a) durch Texturtransformation; (c) Eingabeobjekt aus Linien; (d) Hologramm von (c) zusammengesetzt aus zylindrischen und konischen Wellen.

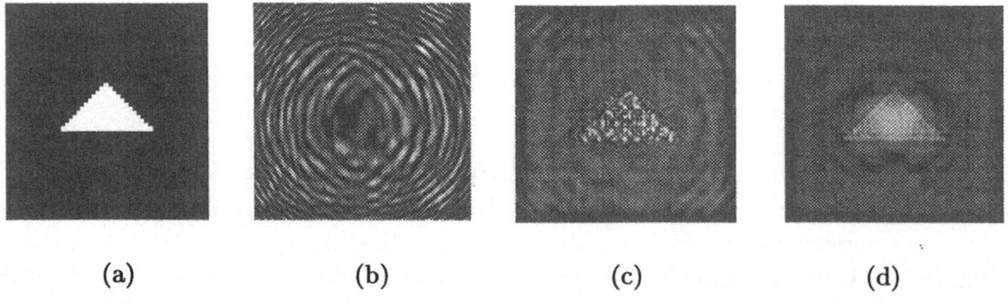

(a) (b) (c) (d)

Abbildung6. Hologramm einer Dreiecksfläche: (a) Eingabeobjekt, zerlegt in 144 Punkte; (b) Hologramm mit Zufallsphase; (c) Rekonstruktion; (d) Rekonstruktion bei einheitlicher Phase.

3.1 Strecken, Kurvenstücke und Flächen

Ein interessanter Aspekt des vorgestellten Verfahrens ist seine Erweiterbarkeit auf andere graphische Grundobjekte. Diese können in einigen Fällen direkt im holographischen Äquivalent mit einer oder mehreren Texturen verbunden werden, welche die Objekte rekonstruieren.

Punktlichtquellen emittieren sphärische Wellen, Linien hingegen zylindrische oder konische. Eine zylindrische Welle wird bei konstanter Phase entlang der Linie erzeugt, eine konische Welle bei linearer Änderung der Phase [28, 29].

Beide Wellenarten lassen sich (mit Einschränkungen) durch vorberechnete komplexe Texturen darstellen. So kann aus einer zylindrischen Welle eine konische durch Transformation der Texturkoordinaten approximiert werden (siehe Abbildung 5). Mit entsprechenden Phasenverteilungen entlang der Linie ist es möglich, Linien verschiedener Steigung darzustellen.

Auch die Darstellung von Kurven ist möglich. Dazu wird im holographischen Äquivalent das Kurvenobjekt in eine Reihe von kurzen Linienstücken zerlegt, die jeweils durch zylindrische oder konische Wellen dargestellt werden.

Es wurden desweiteren erste Versuche unternommen, auch Flächenstücke im Raum abzubilden. Ein Hologramm eines entsprechenden Wellenfeldes ist in Abbildung 6 exemplarisch zu sehen. Hier wurde ein Dreieck durch 144 Punkte im Raum approximiert. Weitere Untersuchungen hierzu müssen aber noch unternommen werden.

4 Bewertung der Methode

Im folgenden sollen ein paar Worte zur Numerik und etwas Statistik über die Rechenzeiten die Beschreibung der vorgestellten Methode abschließen.

Auf den verwendeten Graphikrechnern können Texturen von 8 bit pro Farbkanal definiert werden. Üblicherweise werden Hologramme und andere diffraktive Elemente jedoch mit wesentlich weniger als 255 Intensitätsstufen hergestellt, so daß der Wertebereich der komplexen Texturen ausreichend ist. Im Akkumulationspuffer werden Zahlen mit 25 bit pro Farbkanal gerechnet, was das Interferieren von 2^{17} Texturen ohne numerische Ungenauigkeiten ermöglicht. Hierzu trägt bei, daß innerhalb unserer Methode positive und negative Werte im Real- und Imaginärteil getrennt behandelt werden, was der Stabilität zugute kommt.

Tabelle 1 gibt Rechenzeiten zur Hologrammerzeugung wieder. Für verschiedene Hologrammgrößen und Punktmengen wurde die traditionelle Berechnungsmethode über die Auswertung von Gleichung 2 mit der texturbasierten Methode verglichen. Eine Beschleunigung um den Faktor 57 bis 91 wird in allen relevanten Fällen erreicht.

5 Zusammenfassung und Ausblick

In unserem Beitrag haben wir ein Verfahren zur schnellen Interferenz von zweidimensionalen diskreten komplexwertigen Wellenfeldern vorgestellt und seinen Einsatz in der optischen Holographie skizziert.

Tabelle1. Rechenzeit für die Herstellung von Hologrammen unterschiedlicher Größe (512 × 512, 1024 × 1024, 5120 × 5120 Pixel) und Komplexität (Anzahl abzubildender Punkte) in Sekunden. In der letzten Spalte ist der Beschleunigungsfaktor aufgetragen.

	Konventionell			Texturbasiert			Beschleunigung		
Punkte	512	1024	5120	512	1024	5120	512	1024	5120
1	2.5	9.9	255	0.19	0.75	18	13	13	14
10	4.8	19.3	483	0.21	0.84	20	23	23	44
100	28.5	113	2850	0.5	2.0	42	57	57	68
1000	250	1004	25000	3.6	15	275	69	67	91

Das Verfahren kann aber auch an anderen Stellen verwendet werden, an denen Felder ähnlicher Art zu verarbeiten sind, beispielsweise in der Elektrotechnik oder im Maschinenbau (Finite Element Technik). Denkbar sind auch Verschlüsselungstechniken für Live-Videodaten über holographische Abbildungsprozesse, bei denen Wissen über eine zeitlich sich ändernde Rekonstruktionswelle zur Entschlüsselung kodierter Bilddaten erforderlich ist.

Die hier nur angedeutete Erweiterung des Verfahrens auf einfache Flächenstücke ist ein spannendes Forschungsgebiet, da hiermit eine weitere Lücke zwischen Computergraphik und Holographie geschlossen werden kann und es unter Umständen möglich wird, Hologramme kompletter Körperoberflächen mittels Dreiecksnetzen effizient herzustellen.

Da das Ergebnis der Interferenz komplexer Texturen seinerseits als komplexe Textur gespeichert werden kann, tritt die Frage nach der Mehrfachverwendung von Modellteilen inklusive räumlicher Instanziierung in den Vordergrund. Verfahren hierfür könnten aus der konventionellen synthetischen Holographie bekannte Transformationsmethoden (Fresnel Transformation) verwenden, um Wellenfelder komplexer Objekte räumlich zu verschieben.

Desweitern ist die Kopplung unseres Verfahrens mit einem holographischen Display vorgesehen, das es in Zukunft erlauben soll, Bewegthologramme synthetisch zu erzeugen und in Echtzeit darzustellen.

Literatur

1. M. Born, E. Wolf. *Principles of Optics.* Pergamon Press, 6. Auflage, 1980.
2. S. A. Benton. Holograms: Giving pictures depth. *Scientific American*, 278(1):92, January 1998.
3. P. Heiß. *Die neue Holographie-Fibel.* Wittig Fachbuch, Hückelhoven, 4. Auflage, 1995.
4. D. Gabor. A new microscopic principle. *Nature*, 161(4098):777–778, Mai 1948.
5. B. R. Brown, A. W. Lohmann. Complex spatial filtering with binary masks. *Applied Optics*, 5(6):967–969, 1966.
6. B. R. Brown, A. W. Lohmann. Computer-generated binary holograms. *IBM J. Res. Develop.*, S. 160–168, März 1969.
7. D. Schreier. *Synthetische Holografie.* Physik-Verlag, Weinheim, 1984.

8. S. A. Benton. Holographic displays – a review. *Optical Engineering*, 14(5):402–407, 1975.
9. P. Hariharan. *Optical Holography*. Cambridge University Press, Cambridge, New York, Oakleigh, 1984.
10. S. A. Benton. Survey of holographic stereograms. *SPIE Processing and Display of Three-Dimensional Data*, 367:15–19, 1983.
11. M. Lucente. Interactive computation of holograms using a look-up table. *Journal of Electronic Imaging*, 2(1):28–34, 1993.
12. M. Lucente, T. A. Galyean. Rendering interactive holographic images. In R. Cook (Hrsg.), *Proceedings of SIGGRAPH '95 (Los Angeles, August 1995)*, Annual Conference Series, S. 387–394, New York, 1995. ACM Press.
13. M. Lucente. Interactive three-dimensional holographic displays: Seeing the future in depth. *ACM Computer Graphics*, 31(2):63–66, Mai 1997.
14. J. A. Watlington, M. Lucente, C. J. Sparrell, V. M. Bove, I. Tamitani. A hardware architecture for rapid generation of electro-holographic fringe patterns. In *Practical Holography IX*, Bd. 2406 of *SPIE Proceedings*, S. 23–34, Bellingham, 1995.
15. M. W. Halle, A. B. Kropp. Fast computer graphics rendering for full parallax spatial displays. In S. A. Benton (Hrsg.), *Practical Holography XI*, Bd. 3011 of *SPIE Proceedings*, S. 105–112, Bellingham, 1997.
16. A. Ritter, O. Deussen, H. Wagener, Th. Strothotte. Holographic imaging of lines: A texture-based approach. In P. Storms (Hrsg.), *International Conference on Information Visualization IV'97 (London, August 1997)*, S. 272–278, Los Alamitos, 1997. IEEE Computer Society.
17. A. Ritter, Th. Benziger, O. Deussen, Th. Strothotte, H. Wagener. Synthetic holograms of splines. In H.-P. Seidel, B. Girod, H. Niemann (Hrsg.), *3D Image Analysis and Synthesis '97 (Erlangen, November 1997)*, S. 11–18, Sankt Augustin, 1997. Infix-Verlag.
18. A. Ritter, J. Böttger, O. Deussen. Generierung Synthetischer Hologramme durch Texture Mapping. In B. Preim, P. Lorenz (Hrsg.), *Simulation und Visualisierung '98 (Magdeburg, March 1998)*, S. 171–180, Delft, Erlangen, Ghent, San Diego, 1998. SCS – Society for Computer Simulation Int.
19. A. Ritter, J. Böttger, O. Deussen, M. König, Th. Strothotte. Hardware-based rendering of full-parallax synthetic holograms. eingereicht zur Veröffentlichung.
20. M. J. Kilgard. Realizing OpenGL: Two implementations of one architecture. In S. Molnar, B.-O. Schneider (Hrsg.), *Proceedings of SIGGRAPH/EuroGraphics Workshop on Graphics Hardware*, S. 45–55, Los Angeles, August 1997.
21. J. P. Waters. Holographic image synthesis utilizing theoretical methods. *Applied Physics Letters*, 9(11):405–407, 1966.
22. J. Neider, T. Davis, M. Woo. *OpenGL Programming Guide: The Official Guide to Learning OpenGL*. Addison-Wesley, Bonn, Paris, Reading, 1993.
23. J. Rohlf, J. Helman. IRIS Performer: A high performance multiprocessing toolkit for real-time 3D graphics. In A. Glassner (Hrsg.), *SIGGRAPH 94 Conference Proceedings*, Annual Conference Series, S. 381–394, Orlando, August 1994.
24. J. S. Montrym, D. R. Baum, D. L. Dignam, C. J. Migdal. InfiniteReality: A real-time graphics system. In T. Whitted (Hrsg.), *SIGGRAPH 97 Conference Proceedings*, Annual Conference Series, S. 293–302, Los Angeles, August 1997.
25. A. Ritter, J. Böttger, O. Deussen, Th. Strothotte. Fast texture-based interference for synthetic holography. Preprint 3/98, Otto-von-Guericke-Universität Magdeburg, Fakultät für Informatik, Januar 1998.

26. H. Aagedal, Th. Beth, H. Schwarzer, S. Teiwes. Design of paraxial diffractive elements with the CAD system DigiOpt. In I. Cindrich, S. H. Lee (Hrsg.), *Diffractive and Holographic Optics Technology II*, Bd. 2404 of *SPIE Proceedings*, S. 50–58, Bellingham, 1994.
27. W. Lauterborn, Th. Kurz, M. Wiesenfeldt. *Coherent Optics, Fundamentals and Applications.* Springer-Verlag, Berlin, Heidelberg, New York, 1995.
28. C. Frère, D. Leseberg, O. Bryngdahl. Computer-generated holograms of three-dimensional objects composed of line segments. *Journal of the Optical Society of America (JOSA)*, 3(5):726–730, 1986.
29. D. Leseberg. Computer generated holograms: Cylindrical, conical, and helical waves. *Applied Optics*, 26(20):4385–4390, 1987.

The Physical Optics Design Problem

Frank Wyrowski and Harald Aagedal

Friedrich-Schiller-Universität, D-07743 Jena, Germany
wyrowski@iap.uni-jena.de

Abstract. The enormous progress which has been made in computer technology and science is of increasing impact on optics. In particular optical design seems to experience a drastic development with significant consequences. Besides the introduction of powerful software for the design of imaging systems an additional tendency may be observed. Physical optics is entering the design of optical systems and requires the development of new algorithms.

1 Wave Transformation by Inhomogeneous Media

In a homogeneous dielectric, that is a media with real valued and constant refractive index n, electromagnetic waves are solutions of Maxwell's equations. Air is, neglecting turbulences, an important example of a homogeneous dielectric. Glass is another one. Although an electromagnetic field is described by six scalar components, i.e. three coordinates of the electric field $\boldsymbol{E}$ and the magnetic field $\boldsymbol{H}$ respectively, the field in a homogeneous dielectric is completely specified by two independent scalar components $V^{(j)}(x,y,z,t)$ with $j \in \{1,2\}$. $V^{(j)}$ represents two of the six field components, for instance E_x and E_y.

By an arbitrary optical system which connects electromagnetic waves in homogeneous dielectric media, for instance air, the wave $V_{\text{in}}^{(j)}$ which enters the system is transformed into $V_{\text{out}}^{(j)}$. The general wave transformation may be expressed by the operator equation

$$
\begin{aligned}
V_{\text{out}}^{(1)} &:= \mathcal{W}^{(1)}(V_{\text{in}}^{(1)}, V_{\text{in}}^{(2)}), \\
V_{\text{out}}^{(2)} &:= \mathcal{W}^{(2)}(V_{\text{in}}^{(1)}, V_{\text{in}}^{(2)}) \ .
\end{aligned} \tag{1}
$$

The operator $\mathcal{W}^{(j)}$ depends on the incident wave and on the optical system. The function of the system relies on the interaction of the incident wave with the matter in the system during the propagation of the wave through the system. This interaction has to be properly described by physical models in order to predict the effect of a system on the incident wave.

Special cases of the general wave transformation (1) may be obtained. If $V_{\text{out}}^{(j)}$ only depends on $V_{\text{in}}^{(j)}$, i.e. $V_{\text{out}}^{(j)} := \mathcal{W}^{(j)} V_{\text{in}}^{(j)}$, the transformation is decoupled and both components may be treated independently of each other. If in addition $\mathcal{W}^{(1)} = \mathcal{W}^{(2)}$ the scalar case is obtained. Then, it is sufficient to analyse the wave transformation problem for one component. The result is directly applicable for the other one. Typically the general wave transformation problem for polychromatic waves $V^{(j)}$ is treated on the basis of transformations between monochromatic waves $V^{(j)}(x,y,z,t) = U^{(j)}(x,y,z)\exp[\mathrm{i}\omega t]$, that is the time dependence is separated.

It is remarkable, that the realization of a huge class of wave transformations (1) is at least theoretically possible on the basis of the interaction of waves with inhomogeneous, isotropic, and linear media [1]. A lens is an example of an optical element which mathematically represents nothing else than such an inhomogeneity. An antireflection layer for spectacles is another example.

Physical optics, that is the application of classical electrodynamics in optics, is in general necessary to describe the interaction of a wave with inhomogeneous media. It is common to introduce the complex refractive index function $\tilde{n}(x,y,z)$ with the real part $n(x,y,z)$ and the imaginary part $\kappa(x,y,z)$ to express the inhomogeneity. ***Physical optics design*** deals with the search for an optical system, that is the specification of an inhomogeneity $\tilde{n}(x,y,z)$, by means of physical optics. It is a rather new field in modern optics which becomes more and more attractive because of three main reasons. Firstly, the modelling of the optics of inhomogeneities demands high computer power and large computer memory. Today's computer technology starts to satisfy the minimum requirements. Secondly, on the basis of modern microstructure technology an ever increasing variety of inhomogeneities can be produced and therefore it becomes reasonable to mathematically search for general solutions of wave transformation problems. Thirdly, light is of increasing importance as carrier of information in communication and as carrier of energy in industrial and scientific applications. As a result novel techniques to generate, detect, and manipulate electromagnetic waves, mathematically represented by $V^{(j)}(x,y,z,t)$, are of particular concern. Physical optics design is the general approach to obtain optical systems which allow the realization of almost arbitrary wave transformations. In case of imaging optics very often geometrical optics may be used and the well-established optical design with ray-tracing is the appropriate method. However, general transformations, that are non-imaging optical functions, in general can only be treated on the basis of physical optics.

2 The Design Problem

The basis to tackle the general wave transformation (1) is the control of the monochromatic case for one scalar component. Then, the transformation reads as

$$U_{\mathrm{out}} := \mathcal{W}\, U_{\mathrm{in}} \quad . \tag{2}$$

In the design situation the input wave U_{in} and the desired signal wave U_{sig} are given in the planes z_{in} and an optical system specified by $\tilde{n}(x,y,z)$ is searched for which causes a $U_{\mathrm{out}}(x,y,z_{\mathrm{out}})$ with

$$U_{\mathrm{out}}(x,y,z_{\mathrm{out}}) \approx \alpha\, U_{\mathrm{sig}}(x,y,z_{\mathrm{out}}) \text{ for } (x,y) \in W \quad . \tag{3}$$

The scale factor $\alpha \leq 1$ should be as close to one as possible in order to maximize the efficiency η_{sig} with which the energy of the incident wave is transformed into signal energy. The signal window specifies the area in the plane z_{out} in which the signal wave is specified. A suitable measure of the quality of the representation of the signal information in U_{out} is the signal-to-noise-ratio (SNR). The theoretical solution of the design problem is a $\tilde{n}(x, y, z)$ which realizes the transformation according to (3) with an SNR greater than some reference value $\mathrm{SNR}_{\mathrm{ref}}$ and at the same time a maximization of η_{sig}. The physical optics design problem is illustrated in Fig. 1. In practice the theoretical solution has to be further modified in order to meet fabrication constraints. In particular a restriction of the modulation of The transfer of the theoretical solution encoding of a complex function in a function with restricted set of values [2].

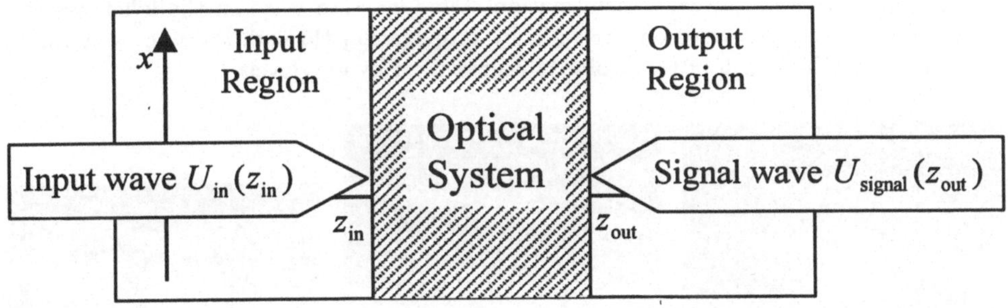

Fig. 1. Illustration of the design problem. The incident wave and a signal wave are given. An optical system which transforms the input wave into the signal wave is searched for.

A general analysis of the design problem as an inverse problem shows, that microstructured inhomogeneities are of fundamental concern to realize wave transformations. Because such microstructures also introduce diffraction phenomena, this field of modern optics is often called *diffractive optics* [2, 3]. Physical optics design for paraxial wave transformations is most matured [4]. An example of a paraxial beam shaping is illustrated in Fig. 2. The optical realization of it is demonstrated in Fig. 3. In the non-paraxial domain often rigorous electromagnetic theory has to be applied [5].

Physical optics design requires a thorough analysis of the interaction of waves with inhomogeneous media and corresponding algorithms are of particular concern. Moreover, the design demands the solution of the inverse problem which typically leads to nonlinear optimization problems. In order to obtain appropriate techniques a theoretical analysis of the design problem and its solution space is necessary. Although diffractive optics has been significantly developed in recent years, general physical optics design requires a new generation of optical design algorithms and software. This will be the next interdisciplinary step in the development of optical design techniques and corresponding effort may already be observed world-wide.

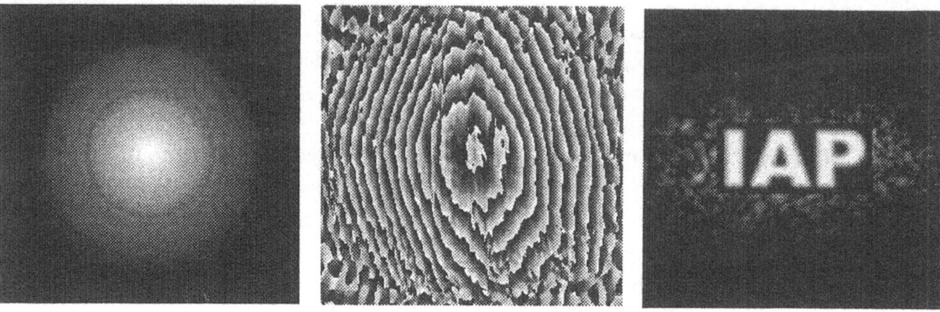

Fig. 2. Illustration of a wave transformation. The Gaussian wave on the left is transformed into the output wave on the right by propagating through the microstructure in the middle. The depth of the profile is represented by greylevels.

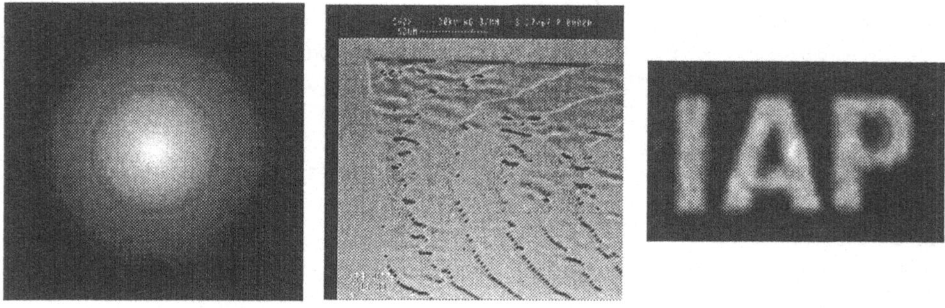

Fig. 3. Optical experiment of the example given in Fig. 2. On the left and the right the measured intensity distributions are given. The SEM picture in the middle illustrates a part of the microstructure.

References

1. J. Turunen and F. Wyrowski. Introduction to diffractive optics. In J. Turunen and F. Wyrowski, editors, *Diffractive optics for industrial and commercial applications*, chapter 1, pages 1–58. Akademie Verlag, Berlin, 1997.
2. O. Bryngdahl and F. Wyrowski. Digital holography-computer-generated holograms. In E. Wolf, editor, *Progress in Optics*, volume 28, chapter 1, pages 1–86. North-Holland, New York, 1990.
3. F. Wyrowski and O. Bryngdahl. Digital holography as part of diffractive optics. *Rep. Prog. Phys.*, 54:1481–1571, 1991.
4. H. Aagedal, F. Wyrowski, and M. Schmid. Paraxial beam splitting and shaping. In J. Turunen and F. Wyrowski, editors, *Diffractive optics for industrial and commercial applications*, chapter 6, pages 165–188. Akademie Verlag, Berlin, 1997.
5. J. Turunen. Diffraction theory of microrelief gratings. In H.P. Herzig, editor, *Micro-optics*, chapter 2, pages 31–52. Taylor & Francis, London, 1997.

Technologie-Diskussionen

Text, Bild, Ton, 3D-Modell und Animation – gleichberechtigte Partner in Digital Libraries

Dieter W. Fellner

Institut für ComputerGraphik, TU Braunschweig
d.fellner@tu-bs.de
http://www.cg.cs.tu-bs.de

Zusammenfassung 'Klassische', aber dennoch unverändert relevante Fragestellungen im Bereich des Dokumentenmanagements wie z.B. *Boolsches* versus *statistisches Volltext-Retrieval* oder *Relevance Ranking* beschäftigen sich fast ausschließlich mit traditionellen – sprich textbasierten – Inhalten von digitalen Bibliotheken.
Im Gegensatz zu dem eher konservativen Ansatz, den der Großteil der zur Zeit laufenden Digital Library Initiativen [8, 2, 5, 7, 6, 1] verfolgt, zielt das DFG Schwerpunktprogramm V^3D^2ganz speziell auf einen verallgemeinerten Dokumentenbegriff, der die Medientypen Text, Bild, Animation, 3D-Graphik, Ton, sowie softwaregestützte Simulationen und Teachware mit einschließt.
Dieser Beitrag gibt einen Überlick über die Ausrichtung des Schwerpunktprogramms V^3D^2 in Hinblick auf die Themenstellung der Jahrestagung und erläutert kurz die Fragestellungen, die in den entsprechenden Teilprojekten bearbeitet werden.

1 Einleitung

Allgemeines Ziel des seit Ende letzten Jahres von der Deutschen Forschungsgemeinschaft (DFG) geförderten Schwerpunktprogramms [3, 4] *„Verteilte Verarbeitung und Vermittlung Digitaler Dokumente“*, kurz V^3D^2, das mit dem Auftaktworkshop in der Bayrischen Staatsbibliothek im May dieses Jahres seine Arbeit voll aufgenommen hat, ist die Erforschung und Entwicklung neuer Techniken zur Erstellung, Verbreitung und Nutzung elektronischer Information zum Zwecke des *Aufbaus und der Nutzung „Digitaler Bibliotheken“* mit den zentralen Forschungsthemen

- Erstellung, Verwaltung und Vermittlung multimedialer digitaler Dokumente
- Netze, Kompression und Datenübertragung
- Multimediale Lehr- und Lernsysteme

Der sich wandelnde Dokumentenbegriff ist einer der stärksten Kräfte, die zu einer radikalen Veränderungen der Informationslandschaft beitragen. Verändern werden sich – und haben sich zum Teil schon – die *Informationsobjekte (Dokumente)*, ihre *Erstellung*, *Speicherung* und *Nutzung*.

Elektronisch gespeicherte Volltexte, Rasterbilder, 3D-Computermodelle (anstelle von 2D Konstruktionszeichnungen), Animationen dynamischer Vorgänge und multimediales Lehrmaterial inklusive von Tonaufzeichnungen werden künftig gleichberechtigt neben Zeitschriften und Büchern stehen. Diese neuen Darstellungsformen, die neben die herkömmliche Form der Informationsdarstellung treten werden, stellen eine technische Herausforderung dar. In praktisch allen Bereichen, in denen es um die Vermittlung von Wissen geht, bieten die neuen Darstellungsformen und ihre Verknüpfung große Chancen.

Elektronische „Bibliotheken" verstehen sich in diesem Kontext, unabhängig von dem konkreten institutionellen Begriff, als logische Datenhaltungs- und Datenvermittlungsräume. Sie lassen sich frei definieren und treten als elektronische Spezialbibliotheken gleichberechtigt neben klassische Universal- und Fachbibliotheken. Wesentlich ist hier vor allem, daß eine wie auch immer gewählte logische Kollektion von Datenbeständen Funktionen einer Bibliothek darstellen kann und wird.

Elektronische Bibliotheken, die neben textuellen Dokumenten auch umfangreiche Dokumente anderer Art wie Faktensammlungen, Still- und Bewegtbilder, Audio- und Videosequenzen sowie Animations- und Simulationsteile enthalten, verändern zunehmend auch das Lehren und Lernen an den Hochschulen.

Als Fernziel dient ein Szenario, das weit über die heutige traditionelle Form des Unterrichts hinausgeht und Studenten und Dozenten gleichermaßen den Zugriff und die Nutzung hypermedialer Informationssysteme erlaubt, die nicht nur lokal, sondern in globalen Rechnernetzen auf Servern abgelegt sein können. Man wird erwarten können, daß heute noch getrennte Entwicklungen wie mediengestütztes Lehren und Lernen, Computerpräsentation, Computerkonferenzsysteme, Computer-Supported-Cooperated-Work, Tele-Teaching und Computer-Aided-Instruction immer mehr zusammenwachsen.

Die Arbeiten im Schwerpunktprogramm sollten deshalb den folgenden Zielen dienen:

1. Entwicklung von Methoden und Werkzeugen für die Verarbeitung und Vermittlung verteilter multimedialer Dokumente,
2. Nutzbarmachung von Synergien durch engere Kooperation der Informatik mit den Bibliothekswissenschaften und der computergestützen Lehre,
3. Stärkung der Kooperation von Industrie, Bibliotheken und Hochschulen.

2 Verallgemeinerter Dokumentenbegriff

Digitale Dokumente umfassen neben der traditionellen, textlichen Form der Informationsdarstellung in zunehmendem Maß multimediale Objekte. Herkömmliche Datenverwaltungssysteme erweisen sich bei Anwendungen mit solchen Dokumenten als ebenso unzureichend wie klassische Dokument-Retrievalsysteme. Die resultierenden Fragestellungen bzw. Forschungsthemen sind:

- Verbindung von multimedia-tauglichen Datenbanksystemen mit Dokument-Retrievalsystemen

- Designkonzepte für Dokumentenserver als Bausteine einer digitalen Bibliothek
- Realisierung von Echtzeitanforderungen
- Zugriffsstrukturen für verschiedenartige Objekte bei bestimmten Anforderungsprofilen

Ein ganzes Bündel von grundlegenden Fragestellungen ergibt sich aus der Tatsache, daß Dokumente inhaltsorientiert gesucht werden. Es ist mit den heutigen technischen Mitteln sehr einfach, digitale Dokumente verschiedenster Art weltweit anzubieten. Das Auffinden von *relevanter* Information, die zur Lösung eines spezifischen Problems beitragen kann, wird immer schwieriger. Es fehlen Verfahren zur Reduktion der Datenflut nach inhaltlichen Kriterien. Gesucht sind Methoden und Techniken, die aus der Vielfalt des Informationsangebots die Inhalte auswählen, die für den Nutzer relevant und interessant sind. Der multimediale Aufbau der Dokumente verschärft das Problem, da die inhaltliche Charakterisierung von z.B. Audiodaten oder Videoclips ein ungelöstes Problem darstellt.

Zu den Forschungsthemen, die dazu im Rahmen des Schwerpunktprogramms behandelt werden, gehören:

- Retrieval von Bildern und 3D-Graphiken aufgrund von Skizzen, Beispielen oder inhaltsorientierter Information
- Automatische Indexierung und Abstract-Generierung von Videosequenzen und virtuellen Szenarien
- inhaltsbasierte Indexierung und Retrieval von Daten in digitalen Musikbibliotheken
- Weiterentwicklung von Vermittlungsdiensten zur Beherrschung umfangreicher und heterogener Informationsquellen
- Inhaltliche und formale Beschreibung von Datenbeständen als Basis für Vermittlungsdienste

Aber auch in Hinblick auf die effizientere Nutzung von Kommunikationskanälen müssen von Seiten der Datenproduktion große Anstrengungen unternommen werden.

Zu den wichtigen Fragestellungen gehören Methoden zur effizienten Erstellung höherdimensionaler Dokumente (Bilder, 3D-Szenen, Animationen) unter Berücksichtigung des Erhalts von semantischer Information und von Szenenhierarchien sowie der Berücksichtigung, daß einzelne Dokumentenbausteine in späteren Suchvorgängen wiedergefunden werden können und müssen.

Ein damit in Zusammenhang stehender und zur Zeit nur unbefriedigend behandelter Problembereich ist die Dokumentauszeichnung oder der *Markup* von beliebigen Dokumenttypen.

Ein ebenfalls sehr komplexer Problemkreis ist die Navigation in verteilten, dynamischen, multi-user Welten, wie sie zum Beispiel bei verschiedenen Formen der Telekooperation benötigt wird.

3 Multimediale Lehr- und Lernsysteme

Die Erstellung multimedialer Dokumente (mit Animationen, Simulationen, Ton, Integration von Still- und Bewegtbildern usw.) ist noch immer mit einem erheblichen finanziellen und zeitlichen Aufwand verbunden. Es sind zwar etliche Werkzeuge für verschiedene Rechnerplattformen vorhanden die eine große Zahl von für einen einzelnen Autor kaum noch zu beherrschenden Funktionalitäten anbieten. Dennoch sind sie von dem Leistungsstandard weit entfernt, den man inzwischen bei der Erstellung papiergebundener Dokumente mit Werkzeugen wie z.B. TEX, LATEX oder Framemaker gewöhnt ist.
Um das Fernziel einer multimediale Lehr- und Lernumgebung zu erreichen, in der Dozenten und Studenten gleichermaßen Zugriff auf hypermediale Informationssysteme haben, die weltweit verteilt sind, müssen noch zahlreiche technische Probleme gelöst werden:

- Fragen der Standardisierung und Transformation verschiedener Datenformate für Dokumente unterschiedlicher Art
- Kompressionsverfahren für großvolumige Daten wie Bilder, Filme usw.
- Editoren zur Integration verschiedener Medien, z.B. von Videoaufzeichnungen in elektronischen Skripten
- Synchronisation von Sprache mit anderen Ereignissen (z.B. Testpräsentation, Animation etc.)
- Entwicklung netzfähiger Produkte und Lösung des Verteilproblems (welche Daten sollen lokal, welche remote gehalten werden, was ist die geeignetere Form der Verteilung und Speicherung)

Es gibt bereits eine ganze Reihe von Versuchen, die zeigen, daß heute noch in der Regel getrennte Tätigkeiten, wie das Halten einer Vorlesung im Hörsaal, Computerpräsentation, Computerconferencing, Teleteaching und das Erstellen von für die Lehre geeigneten multimedialen Dokumenten künftig zusammenwachsen werden. Es hat sich allerdings auch herausgestellt, daß überzeugende Ergebnisse nur dann erreicht werden, wenn die zu vermittelnden Inhalte sehr sorgfältig auf die begrenzten Fähigkeiten der heute verfügbaren Werkzeuge abgestimmt sind. Dann kann man allerdings mit vertretbarem Aufwand multimediale Dokumente erzeugen, die deutlich über das hinausgehen, was ein nur papiergebundenes Dokument oder eine Videoaufzeichnung einer Vorlesung liefern könnte.

4 Die einzelnen Projekte

Den Bereich „Bild", konkret Graphik und Visualisierung, behandelt schwerpunktmäßig eine Gruppe von sieben Projekten, von denen drei Projekte dem Bereich *3D Graphik*, zwei Projekte dem Bereich *Visalisierung*, ein Projekt dem Bereich *Image Retrieval* und *Video-Indexierung* und ein Projekt dem Bereich *Digital Watermarking in Bild- und Audio-Daten* zugeordnet werden kann.

Der Problembereich **3D-Graphik** wird durch drei unterschiedliche Zugänge abgedeckt: einmal der Zugang über Szenen, die in Form von (komplexen) Polygonnetzen vorliegen, die für eine Nutzung erst mit *level-of-detail* Ansätzen (vor)verarbeitet werden müssen, zweitens der Zugang über neue Modellierungsansätze, die die „exakte" Repräsentation der einzelnen Objekte erhalten und ein „semantic level-of-detail" ermöglichen und drittens der Zugang über *image based rendering*, das auf einer Darstellung von 3D-Szenen aufbaut, von denen vorweg eine Menge von 2D-Bildaufnahmen erzeugt wurde (*plenoptic rendering*).

Effiziente Speicherung, Kompression und Übertragung komplexer polygonaler 3D-Modelle

Ziel dieses Projektes unter Leitung von Prof. Hans-Peter Seidel, Institut für Mathematische Maschinen und Datenverarbeitung der Universität Erlangen, ist die Entwicklung und Implementierung von Werkzeugen zur effizienten Speicherung, Kompression und Übertragung solcher komplexer polygonaler 3D-Modelle im World Wide Web (WWW). Hierbei ist grundsätzlich zwischen approximativen Verfahren (lossy compression) und Verfahren zur verlustfreien Darstellung und Übertragung (lossless compression) zu unterscheiden. Bei der ersten Klasse sollen vor allem wavelet-basierte Verfahren (beruhend auf Subdivision-Wavelets) Verwendung finden. Bei der verlustfreien Darstellung werden Verfahren, die auf der sukzessiven Entfernung von Kanten beruhen, im Vordergrund stehen. Insgesamt sollen die durchzuführenden Arbeiten zur Entwicklung eines interaktiven Web-Viewers in Formeines Netscape Plug-ins führen, der beide genannten Klassen von Verfahren unterstützt und einen raschen interaktivenZugriff auf 3D-Objekte über das WWW erlaubt.

Modellierung von und Navigation in 3D-Dokumenten

Das Vorhaben unter Leitung von Prof. Dieter W. Fellner, Institut für ComputerGraphik der TU Braunschweig, dient einerseits der Untersuchung und Entwicklung von Methoden zur effizienten Erstellung bzw. Mark-Up, zum Auffinden und zur Wiederverwendung dreidimensionaler Dokumente in großen, verteilten Datenbeständen. Dabei sollen duch Einsatz eines neuen Modellierungsansatzes, dem *generative modeling*, sowohl semantische Informationen über den Inhalt von 3D Dokumenten als auch Aufbau-Hierarchien erhalten und im Dokument abgelegt werden. Diese Informationen sollen die spätere Suche erstmals ermöglichen und die einfache Navigation in den Dokumenten unterstützen. Zur Kommunikation mehrerer Betrachter desselben Dokuments sollen in dem Projekt auch eine Server/Viewer-Architektur für verteilte multi-user Szenen entwickelt werden.

Begehbare 3D-Szenen in digitalen Dokumenten: Effiziente Repräsentation und Visualisierung durch geometriebasiertes Sampling der plenoptischen Funktion

Die Integration realitätsgetreuer dreidimensionaler Szenen in multimediale Dokumente, die in Informationssystemen bereitgehalten und über Netze ausgetauscht werden, verlangt Methoden zu deren effizienter Repräsentation und Visualisierung. Herkömmliche Modelliertechniken reichen zur Modellierung von komplexen natürlichen Szenen nicht aus oder produzieren unhandhabbar große Datenmengen. Eine Alternative stellt das inzwischen weitverbreitete bildbasierte Quicktime-VR-Verfahren und Datenformat dar, das jedoch die Wahl des Beobachtungspunktes einschränkt oder ebenfalls zu viel Speicherplatz und Rechenzeit benötigt. Ziel dieses Projektes unter Leitung von Prof. Wolfgang Straßer und Dr. Reinhard Klein, Fakultät für Informatik der Universität Tübingen, ist die Entwicklung neuer Verfahren sowohl zur komprimierten Speicherung und Übertragung als auch zur Echtzeitvisualisierung hoch komplexer dreidimensionaler digitaler Szenen. Der Schwerpunkt der Aktivitätensoll auf der Entwicklung einer redundanzfreien Repräsentation von dreidimensionalen Szenen durch geeignete Kombination von Geometrie und Bilddaten liegen, die auch die Integration realer Modelle in synthetische Szenen erlaubt.

Im Bereich **Visualisierung** beschäftigen sich zwei Projekte mit der Integration von Graphiktechnologie in die Anwendungsbereiche Geographic Information Systems (GIS) und Chemie.

ATLAS 2000: Entwicklung neuer Datenzugriffs-, Visualisierungs- und Aufbereitungstechniken zum Einsatz in digitalen Atlanten der Zukunft

Die neuen Instrumente müssen eine interaktive, individuelle, problembezogene Darstellung, Kombination, Modellierung sowie den Austausch von vieldimensionalen raumbezogenen Datensätzen erlauben. Dazu sind eine grosse Zahl theoretischer und praktischer Aufgaben zu bewältigen, die vor allem in den Problemkreisen Durchdringung und Füllung des Raum-Zeit-Kontinuums, Betrachtung von Daten verschiedener Skalen, Anwendung fachspezifischer und didatktischer Modelle und Aufbereitung didaktischer Konzepte zur Erschließung der Daten angesiedelt sind. In diesem Rahmen sind Ziele dieses Projektes unter Leitung von Prof. Dietmar Saupe, Institut für Informatik der Universität Freiburg, und Prof. Hermann Goßmann, Institut für Physische Geographie der Universität Freiburg, die Entwicklung neuer Methoden der Komprimierung, der Visualisierung und des Datenzugriffes zur besseren Handhabung verteilter Resourcen in weltweiten Datenund Rechnernetzen, sowie die Bereitstellung didaktischer Konzepte für die Nutzung wissenschaftlicher Modelle und Verfahren durch einen breiten Nutzerkreis. Das Vorhaben ist ein Gemeinschaftsprojekt des Institutes für Informatik und des Institutes für Physische Geographie der Universität Freiburg in Zusammenarbeit mit dem Deutschen Wetterdienst in Offenbach.

Chemische Visualisierungen im Internet: Eingebettete dynamische und interaktive Hochleistungsgraphik in digitalen Dokumenten zur Visualisierung komplexer Sachverhalte

Ziel des Projekts unter Leitung von Dr. Wolf-Dietrich Ihlenfeldt, Computer-Chemie-Centrum, Institut für Organische Chemie, und Prof. Thomas Ertl, Lehrstuhl für Graphische Datenverarbeitung der Universität Erlangen, ist die Entwicklung eines portablen, sich an Internet-Standards orientierenden Systems zur Einbettung von dynamischen Visualisierungen aus dem Bereich der Chemie in digitale Dokumente. Anhand konkret implementierter Beispiele soll der Nachweis geführt werden, daß mit einem solchen System gegenüber statischen 3D-Szenen oder Video das Verständnis komplexer Phänomene, die aktuelle Forschungsthemen der Chemie sind, wesentlich erleichtert oder sogar erst ermöglicht werden. Wichtige Effekte sind zum Beispiel von der räumlichen Geometrie, der Zeitachse und Feldeinflussen abhängig und sind kaum durch einzelne statische Punktansichten zu vermitteln. Die Kopplung und Echtzeitmanipulation von 3D-Visualisierungen, gesteuert von durch den Benutzer geänderte Darstellungsattribute, Raum/Zeitparameter oder andere Einflußfaktoren erlaubt es, eine neue Qualität und Dichte der Information zu realisieren, die mit der Komplexität der Forschungsgegenstände Schritt hält. Verschiedene Modelle der Szenenmanipulation werden einen breiten Rahmen der Einsatzmöglichkeiten und -voraussetzungen solcher dynamischer Szenarios ausleuchten.

Im Bereich **Video-Indexierung und -Retrieval** beschäftigt sich ein Projekt mit der automatischen syntaktischen und semantischen Erschließung von Videoinhalten für ein späteres effizientes Wiederauffinden von Videoclips.

Algorithmen und Methoden für die syntaktische und semantische Annotation und für ein integriertes Retrieval von Texten, Bildern und Videos in verteilten, elektronischen Bibliotheken

Ziel des Projektes unter Leitung von Prof. Otthein Herzog, Technologie-Zentrum Informatik, FB 3 der Universität Bremen, ist die Entwicklung von neuen Methoden und Algorithmen zur syntaktischen und semantischen Analyse von Videosequenzen und deren Umsetzung in ein System zur Unterstützung der Annotation dieser digitalen Dokumente. Die Funktionalität des aus den Entwicklungen resultierenden Systems umfaßt zusätzlich zur Annotierung die inhaltsbasierte Suche, die zur Suche über Bilder und Videos auch die Suche über Texte integriert. Die Anwendung wird in Zusammenarbeit mit Radio Bremen realisiert, um eine im Vergleich zu bisher verfügbarer Technologie, bei der für eine Stunde Video *acht* Stunden Erschließungsarbeit investiert werden müssen, effektivere Archivierung und Suche in Fernseharchiven zu unterstützen.

Das letzte Projekt im Themenbereich „Bild" befaßt sich mit dem vor allem aus kommerzieller Sicht äußerst wichtigen **Digital Watermarking**, der Fragestellung, wie in Bildern und Videosequenzen die Urheberrechte von Autoren nachhaltig geschützt werden können.

Einbettung von digitalen Wasserzeichen in Text-, Bild und Videodokumente

Eine Folge der digitalen Verarbeitung und Vermittlung von Text-, Bild- und Videodokumenten ist die Möglichkeit zur unbegrenzten Vervielfältigung ohne Qualitatseinbußen. Dies ist bei urheberrechtbehafteten, wirtschaftlich verwertbaren

Text-, Bild- und Videodokumenten unerwünscht, da dem Urheber kommerzielle Nachteile entstehen können. In dem Projekt unter Leitung von Prof. Bernd Girod, Lehrstuhl für Nachrichtentechnik der Universität Erlangen-Nürnberg, werden einfache und robuste Verfahren zur Einbettung digitaler Wasserzeichen in Text-, Bild- und Videodokumente entwickelt. Die Einbettung digitaler Wasserzeichen ermöglicht durch die Anbringung von Herkunfts- und Bestimmungsinformationen die Identifikation des Urhebers und eines möglichen Urheberrechtsverletzers. Das Wasserzeichen soll einerseits für den Menschen nicht störend bemerkbar sein, und andererseits nicht oder nur mit erheblichem Aufwand wieder zu entfernen oder zu manipulieren sein. Der zu untersuchende Ansatz zur Einbettung digitaler Wasserzeichen beruht auf Konzepten der Spreizbandmodulation. In diesem Vorhaben wird dieser Ansatz auf Postscript-codierte Textdokumente und erstmals auf bereits komprimierte Bild- und Videodokumente erweitert, wie sie in verteilten Systemen zur Speicherung und Vermittlung digitaler Dokumente vorliegen. Dabei soll die Berücksichtigung der visuellen Wahrnehmung des Menschen und die Einbeziehung fehlerkorrigierender Codes zur Optimierung der Verfahren beitragen.

Der Themenbereich **Ton** ist im Schwerpunktprogramm leider nur mit einem Projekt vertreten, was sicherlich daran liegt, daß die Fragestellung der Integration von Audiodaten in digitale Bibliotheken bzw. der Aufbau dedizierter Audioarchive zur Zeit auch international von nur sehr wenigen Forschungsgruppen behandelt wird.

MiDiLiB: Inhaltsbasierte Indexierung, Retrieval und Kompression von Daten in digitalen Musikbibliotheken

Im Projekt *MiDiLiB* unter Leitung von Prof. Michael Clausen, Institut für Informatik der Universität Bonn, geht es um die Lösung zweier fundamentaler, offener Probleme im Bereich „Digitale Musikbibliotheken". Einerseits sollen automatische Indexierungsverfahren und Retrievaltechniken für Musikdaten entworfen und implementiert werden, so daß insbesondere für verschiedene Arten von Audiodaten eine effiziente inhaltliche Suche möglich ist. Zunächst soll dieses Ziel für MIDI-Dateien erreicht und durch eine geeignete Linkstruktur auf gedrucktes Notenmaterial übertragen werden. Da inhaltliche Anfragen hier oft nur vage gestellt werden können, muß das Retrieval-System effizient eine Rangliste approximativer Matchings generieren. Andererseits sollen perceptuell stabile Kompressionsverfahren entwickelt werden, die eine Bearbeitung sowie häufige Kodierung und Dekodierung einer Audiodatei – etwa zu Editierzwecken – erlauben, ohne daß es zuhörbaren Qualitätsverlusten kommt. Die entwickelten Verfahren werden allgemein dort einsetzbar sein, wo multimediale Dokumente eine Audiokomponente enthalten.

Weitere Informationen Online Informationen zu diesem Schwerpunkt wie auch zu weiteren Digital Library Projekten finden sich unter der Adresse:

`http://www.cg.cs.tu-bs.de/DigLib`

Literatur

1. Barth A., Breu M., Endres A., de Kemp A. (Eds.): *Digital Libraries in Computer Science*, vol. 1392 of *Lecture Notes in Computer Science*. Springer, 1998.
2. Davis J. R., Lagoze C.: Dienst: An architecture for distributed document libraries. *Commun. ACM 38*, 4 (Apr. 1995), 47.
3. Fellner D. W.: DFG Schwerpunktprogramm Verteilte Verarbeitung und Vermittlung digitaler Dokumente. *Informatik Forschung und Entwicklung 12*, 1 (1997), 38–42.
4. Fellner D. W.: DFG Schwerpunktprogramm V^3D^2 – Verteilte Verarbeitung und Vermittlung digitaler Dokumente. http://www.cg.cs.tu-bs.de/dfgspp/V3D2, 1998.
5. French J., Fox E., Maly K., Selman A.: Wide area technical report service: Technical reports online. *Commun. ACM 38*, 4 (Apr. 1995), 45.
6. Global Info Consortium: Global Info. http://www.global-info.org.
7. Networked computer science technical reports library (NCSTRL). http://cs-tr.cs.cornell.edu.
8. NSF/DARPA/NASA: US Digital Library Initiative. http://www.cise.nsf.gov/iis/dli_home.html.

Methoden und Werkzeuge zur Unterstützung der medienwissenschaftlichen Analyse audiovisueller Informationen

B. Freisleben, M. Grauer, T. Kamphusmann, U. Kelter, U. Merten, D. Platz, G. Rößling

Universität-GH Siegen, Hölderlinstr. 3, D–57068 Siegen

Zusammenfassung Der Beitrag ist als Übersicht zum Teilprojekt Z2 "Methoden und Werkzeuge zur rechnergestützten medienwissenschaftlichen Analyse" im Sonderforschungsbereich 240 "Ästhetik, Pragmatik und Geschichte der Bildschirmmedien" an der Universität-GH Siegen zu verstehen. Ziel dieses von der DFG geförderten Projektes ist die Unterstützung medienwissenschaftlicher Methoden zur Analyse von Bildschirmmedien durch computergestützte Informationssysteme.
Drei Schwerpunkte werden bearbeitet: die integrierte Verwaltung multimedialer Informationen, die Entwicklung geeigneter Analyseverfahren sowie flexibler Benutzeroberflächen für den Medienwissenschaftler. Die anstehenden Arbeitsfelder werden in den medienwissenschaftlichen Kontext eingeordnet und Ansätze zur Problemlösung skizziert.

1 Einleitung

Gegenstand des Teilprojekts ist der Entwurf und die prototypische Implementierung eines rechnergestützten Arbeitsplatzsystems für Medienwissenschaftler [FGK97]. Hierfür bieten die langjährigen Erfahrungen mit audiovisuellen Medien verschiedener Art und die entstandenen Analysemethoden im Sonderforschungsbereich 240 (*sfb*) eine gute Plattform. Bisher wurden die empirischen Arbeiten in den einzelnen Teilprojekten vorwiegend manuell durchgeführt. Für viele Forschungsbereiche existieren folglich Datenbanken zu den Ergebnissen, die den Stand der Forschung reflektieren aber auch über die Laufzeit und den Gegenstand des sfb reichende Bedeutung haben.

Die bisherigen Erkenntnisse gestatten, die relevanten und größtenteils digital vorliegenden Daten in fünf Klassen zu unterteilen:

1. formatierte Daten, z.B. über Verfilmungen, Aussendungen, Literaturvorlagen, beteiligte Personen, Kritiken, Nachrichteninhalte, Standorte von Aufzeichnungen usw.
2. Texte wie Veröffentlichungen des sfb, Literaturquellen, Hintergrundmaterial,
3. digitalisierte Bilder,
4. digitalisierte Videos, die am sfb im Umfang von ca. 10.000 Stunden vorliegen, sowie
5. Analysedaten zu den digitalisierten Videos als Ergebnis der medienwissenschaftlichen Arbeit.

In Kooperation der Fachgebiete Praktische Informatik, Parallele Systeme und Wirtschaftsinformatik wird ein funktionsfähiger Prototyp entworfen und realisiert. Das resultierende integrierte System dient als Arbeitsplatz eines Medienwissenschaftlers. Dabei werden im wesentlichen drei Aufgabenkomplexe bearbeitet: (I) die konsistente Verwaltung mono- und multimedialer primärer und sekundärer Datenbestände, (II) die (semi-)automatische Erzeugung relevanter sekundärer Daten im Sinne von Analyseergebnissen sowie (III) die Bereitstellung flexibler Benutzerschnittstellen für die Speicherung, Manipulation und Präsentation sowohl der Primär- als auch der Sekundärdaten.

Hierzu ist auch die Entwicklung von Methoden für die semantische und inhaltbasierte Suche nach audiovisuellen Daten notwendig. Inhaltsbasierte Zugriffsmöglichkeiten auf multimediale Daten erlauben die Extraktion und Analyse von grundlegenden Elementen, Merkmalen und Strukturen in digitalen Videos und sind daher für die im Sonderforschungsbereich verfolgten medienwissenschaftlichen Untersuchungen wichtig.

Nach einer Einleitung in den medienwissenschaftlichen Projektkontext am sfb und die Fokussierung auf die Analyse von Nachrichten werden die Zielsetzungen des Teilprojektes Z2 skizziert. Dabei wird einer zeitlich orientierten Einteilung nach abgeschlossenen Projekten mit vorliegenden Ergebnissen bzw. aktuellen Forschungen gefolgt.

2 Medienwissenschaftlicher Hintergrund des Vorhabens

Im folgenden wird zunächst der sfb mit seinen vielfältigen Projekten charakterisiert und das Teilprojekt Z2 eingeordnet. Am Beispiel der Nachrichtenanalyse wird in den konkreten Aufgabenkontext eingeführt.

2.1 Übersicht zum Sonderforschungsbereich

Der Sonderforschungsbereich 240 "Ästhetik, Pragmatik und Geschichte der Bildschirmmedien; Schwerpunkt: Fernsehen in der Bundesrepublik Deutschland" existiert seit 1986 an der Universität Siegen; hinzu kommen Kooperationspartner an anderen Standorten. Ziel des sfb ist es, die Theorie, die Geschichte, die Präsentationsformen sowie die sich verändernden Handlungsrollen in den Bildschirmmedien zu erforschen. In rund 30 Teilprojekten wurden und werden unterschiedlichste geisteswissenschaftliche Fragestellungen im Zusammenhang mit Bildschirmmedien, speziell dem Fernsehen und rechnergestützten neuen Medien, untersucht. Es wurden sowohl theoretisch/konzeptionelle Grundlagen entwickelt als auch die sozialen, kulturellen, politischen oder wirtschaftlichen Auswirkungen und Begleitphänomene des Medieneinsatzes empirisch untersucht. Beispiele für frühere und laufende Teilprojekte bzw. Themenkomplexe sind [sfb95]:

- Nachrichten im Fernsehen,
- Fernsehen für Kinder und der Medienmarkt der 90er Jahre,
- interaktive Mediennutzung,

- Fernsehen und neue Medien im Europa der 90er Jahre,
- Hybridkultur,
- historische Rolle der Eurovision sowie
- Medienwertungsforschung

Erheblichen Raum nimmt dabei die Klassifizierung und Systematisierung der AV-Materialien ein, wobei unterschiedliche Perspektiven eingenommen und teilweise konkurrierende Ansätze verfolgt werden.

Rechner wurden bei den bisherigen Untersuchungen nur punktuell eingesetzt: Manche Untersuchungsgegenstände sind durch automatische Verfahren nicht sinnvoll unterstützbar. Bei anderen Untersuchungen, speziell bei der Bild- und Videospeicherung und -Analyse, erscheint ein Rechnereinsatz wünschenswert, allerdings lagen die Kosten der erforderlichen Rechner und Netzwerke bisher in einer völlig unrealistischen Größenordnung; infolge der Leistungssteigerung bei der Hardware in den letzten Jahren ist dieses Problem inzwischen lösbar. Es fehlt allerdings immer noch spezielle Software, die die Medienforschung geeignet unterstützt.

2.2 Einordnung des Teilprojekts Z2

Infolgedessen wurde für die letzte Bewilligungsphase des sfb, die sich über den Zeitraum 1998-2000 erstreckt, das Teilprojekt Z2 mit dem Titel "Methoden und Werkzeuge zur rechnergestützten medienwissenschaftlichen Analyse" beantragt und bewilligt. Hauptziele dieses Projekts sind:

- Realisierung eines Informationssystems, das die vorhandenen und entstehenden Datenbestände des sfb (Texte, Bilder und Videos) integriert und innerhalb des sfb, aber auch über die Dauer des sfb hinaus für Forschung und Lehre verfügbar macht.
- Realisierung eines Video-Analysesystems, das für spezielle medienwissenschaftliche Fragestellungen geeignete Analysealgorithmen bereitstellt; hierdurch sollen Untersuchungen, die bisher mit hohem Aufwand von Hand durchgeführt wurden, (teil-) automatisiert werden; gleichzeitig sollen hierdurch quantitativ umfangreichere und damit qualitativ bessere Ergebnisse ermöglicht werden.
- Realisierung von diversen dedizierten Schnittstellen zur Eingabe, Korrektur und Präsentation von Daten; in Kooperation mit einzelnen Teilprojekten soll auch der Frage nachgegangen werden, ob völlig neue Darstellungen medienwissenschaftlicher Sachverhalte (graphisch, hypertextartig usw.) sinnvoll sind; hierzu sind unterstützende Werkzeuge und Anwendungsexperimente mit diesen erforderlich.

Das System soll evolutionär und mit intensiver Benutzerbeteiligung (also in Kooperation mit anderen Teilprojekten des sfb) entwickelt werden: dies gilt für alle Komponenten des Systems (Benutzungsschnittstellen, Retrievalfunktionen und Analysefunktionen). Benutzeranforderungen werden als explizite Arbeitsergebnisse festgehalten werden.

2.3 Nachrichtenforschung im Fernsehen und in Online-Medien

Die Besonderheiten der medienwissenschaftlichen Analyseanforderungen werden an einem Beispiel aus der Forschungsarbeit des Nachrichtenanalyseprojekts deutlich. Eine aktuelle Fragestellung dieses Projekts ist die Präsentation von Staatsoberhäuptern und "einfachen Leuten" in Nachrichtensendungen der USA, BRD und DDR.

Bei der Analyse im Rahmen des Teilprojekts "Umbrüche in der Medieninformation" wird versucht, einen Zusammenhang zwischen gesellschaftlich-politischen Veränderungen und der Darstellung beispielsweise von Staatsoberhäuptern in den Medien aufzuzeigen. Die Mediendarstellung ist durch das sozio-kulturelle Umfeld der Berichterstatter aber auch durch entsprechende Weisungen geprägt. Ein wesentliches Element der Forschungsarbeit in diesem Kontext ist die Reduktion von Beiträgen in Nachrichtensendungen aber auch Onlinemedien auf sogenannte Schlüsselbilder bzw. kurze Sequenzen solcher Bilder.

Historisch wird die Entwicklung von Schlüsselbildern auf die Notwendigkeit zurückgeführt, für die zunehmende Menge audiovisueller Medien Entschlüsselungsmechanismen bereitzustellen [Lud98]. Sie sind analog zu Schlagworten, Schlüsselwörtern, Schlagzeilen u.ä. für Printmedien zu sehen. Im (audio-)visuellen Umfeld werden Schlüsselbilder als Überordnung visueller Stereotypen und Images gesehen.

Die Schlüsselbildforschung am sfb konzentriert sich auf die systematische Typisierung von Schlüsselbildern in den einzelnen Medien. Seit 1988 wurden bereits die Hauptfernsehnachrichten in den USA, der Bundesrepublik Deutschland sowie der DDR analysiert. Die Analyse erfolgte manuell, die Selektionsstrategien für Schlüsselbilder waren in einer systematischen Codieranweisung operationalisiert (s. dazu [Lud93)]. Der Zeitaufwand für die Analyse wird mit etwa 10 Stunden pro Nachrichtensendung beziffert. Dies motiviert die Auseinandersetzung mit automatisierten Vorgehensweisen in diesem Forschungsbereich.

3 Aufgabenstellungen und Problemlösungsansätze

Die Aufgaben am Sonderforschungsbereich beziehen sich im wesentlichen auf zwei Komplexe: Erstens sind die in abgeschlossenen Teilprojekten erzielten Ergebnisse und Datenbestände für weitere Forschungsergebnisse zu archivieren und für die Recherche zugänglich zu machen. Zweitens ist die aktuelle Forschung zu unterstützen, indem wissenschaftliche Methoden der Analyse audiovisuellen Medienmaterials auf Rechnersysteme abgebildet werden.

3.1 Verfügbarkeit abgeschlossener Forschungsarbeiten

Da die Grundlage der medienwissenschaftlichen Arbeit Informationen unterschiedlicher Herkunft und Art sind, liegt das Hauptziel in einer integrierten Behandlung der korrespondierenden Datenbestände. Dies beinhaltet Text- und Bilddaten ebenso wie Bewegtbilddaten in Form von digitalisierten Videos.

Grundsätzlich besteht ein enger Bezug zwischen den Informationen, der in einem geeigneten Datenbankschema Eingang finden muß. Als Beispiel sei eine Textpublikation genannt, die audiovisuelles Belegmaterial referenziert. Diese Primärdatenbestände sind für die weitere Recherche aufzubereiten und zugänglich zu machen. Im Vorfeld werden sie über die bisherige Laufzeit des sfb von einem Ringprojekt nach Relevanz beurteilt und aufgearbeitet. Die im Sinne eines medienwissenschaftlichen Archivs verfügbaren Informationen sind damit einem öffentlichen interessierten Publikum zur Verfügung zu stellen.

Die Datenbestände liegen i.a. in unterschiedlichen proprietären Datenbankformaten vor. Entsprechend sind sie zu extrahieren und in ein integriertes Schema einzupassen. Da den Einzelschemata nicht zwingend eine einheitliche Codierung, d.h. Bezeichung und Verwendung von Attributbezeichnungen und -semantiken zugrunde liegt, muß bei der Überführung eine zumindest teilweise automatisierte Bereinigung erfolgen.

Als Basis für den Systemprototypen dient das strukturell objekt-orientierte H-PCTE (s. z.B. [Kel92] und [KeDä96]) als Datenbankmanagementsystem. Es stellt Mechanismen zur Datenverwaltung sowie zur Abfrage und Manipulation von Datenobjekten bereit. Für die Aufgaben im Rahmen des Projektes ist es um Eigenschaften multimedialer DBMS zu erweitern. Die Problemfelder, die dabei tangiert werden, sind z.B. in [RNL96] und [GrMe97] skizziert. Ein Aspekt ist dabei die Schaffung einer integrierten Abfragesprache für die ggf. multimedialen Objekte. In einem ersten Schritt dient P-OQL als mengenorientierte Sprache, die auch einen navigierenden Zugriff ermöglicht (s. [Hen98] und [HeKe96]).

3.2 Unterstützung der aktuellen medienwissenschaftlichen Arbeit

In den vergangenen Jahren war das Gebiet der Methoden zur Darstellung von und Suche nach visuellen Medien Gegenstand intensiver Forschung. Dieser Sachverhalt korrespondiert mit der zunehmenden Nachfrage nach derartigen Überlegungen für eine Reihe von Anwendungen wie Bild- und Videodatenbanken, geographische Informationssysteme (GIS) und Multimediasysteme. Die inhaltsbasierte Suche nach visuellen Medien basiert auf Zusatzinformationen, die durch das Parsen des Videostroms gewonnen werden können. Dies kann zwar manuell erfolgen, die (semi-)automatische Generierung ist jedoch effizienter sowohl bezogen auf den Zeit- als auch auf den Kostenaufwand.

Ein wesentliches Einsatzgebiet für Videoanalysen ist im Teilprojekt "Umbrüche in der Medieninformation" zu sehen. Hier besteht die konkrete Aufgabe in der Unterstützung des Medienwissenschaftlers bei der Sichtung von Videos für die Schlüsselbildforschung. Diese kann durch die Reduktion des potentiell zu sichtenden Videomaterials erreicht werden. Der Versuch einer vollständigen Automatisierung der Selektion von Schlüsselbildern scheint in diesem Kontext nicht aussichtsreich zu sein. Denoch ist aus der Analysesicht die Problemstellung zunächst auf die ähnlichkeitsbasierte Suche reduzierbar. Sie ermöglicht die Suche nach Objekten in einem Video. Dabei lassen sich die Suchkriterien kontextspezifisch eingrenzen, insbesondere bei der Suche nach Staatsoberhäuptern.

Die Analyse läßt sich prinzipiell in drei Phasen unterteilen: (I) Gewinnung von Rohdaten im Sinne der Lokalisierung von Objekten bezogen auf Frames im Videostrom, (II) die Verdichtung dieser Daten durch sekundäre Analyseprozesse zu inhaltlich relevanten Segmenten sowie (III) die manuelle Nachbearbeitung der Analyseergebnisse.

Die Analysen in Phase 1 und teilweise auch in Phase 2 sind sehr rechenzeitaufwendig. Hier ist ein eigenes System zur Verwaltung und Überwachung und ggf. Wiederaufsetzen von Analysejobs vorgesehen. Ferner werden frühere Analysejobs, die dabei angewandten Analyseparameter, die Brauchbarkeit der Ergebnisse und ggf. der Archivierungsort protokolliert. Dies dient der Vermeidung doppelter Analysen und bei erfolgreichen Analysen die Herkunft von Daten in der Datenbank zu dokumentieren.

Die in der oben erwähnten Phase 1 (Gewinnung von Rohdaten) einzusetzenden Analysealgorithmen sind teilweise schon bekannt, teilweise sind in Absprache mit den Medienwissenschaftlern völlig neue Algorithmen zu realisieren.

Bekannte Verfahren sind insbesondere künstliche neuronale Netze zur Klassifikation von Objekten oder Personen, pixel- oder blockorientierte Verfahren zum Abgleich von Elementen innerhalb der zeitlichen Abfolge des Videomaterials sowie merkmalsbasierte Segmentierung (s. z.B. [May97]). Für die einzelnen Analyseverfahren ist dabei im einzelnen noch zu prüfen, welche Verfahren bzw. Kombinationen von Verfahren einen guten Kompromiß zwischen Aufwand und Präzision liefern.

Neben der Objekt- und Personenerkennung muß – für ausgewählte Beispiele, etwa "Redner vor Pult" oder "Händeschütteln" – auch der Inhalt des Materials bestimmt werden, d.h. man muß sich auf semantischer Ebene mit den audiovisuellen Daten auseinandersetzen.

Geplant ist daher ein "Baukasten", der die vorhandenen implementierten Algorithmen enthält und es dem Benutzer erlaubt, sich eine "persönliche" Analyse durch Verbindung dieser Algorithmen zu "bauen". Durch die Verwendung einer gemeinsamen, exakt definierten objektorientierten Vererbungshierarchie ist dabei auch der Einsatz externer, benutzerprogrammierter Algorithmen denkbar.

3.3 Integration zum medienwissenschaftlichen Arbeitsplatz

Die Realisierung des Arbeitsplatzsystems gestaltet sich als interdisziplinäre Aufgabe zwischen den Arbeitsgruppen der Informatik und den Medienwissenschaften. Wichtige grundlegende Eigenschaften des Systems sind die Erweiterbarkeit und eine evolutionäre Entstehung, um den Bedürfnissen der Medienwissenschaftler, die im Vorfeld der Realisierungsarbeiten nicht alle spezifiziert werden können, Rechnung zu tragen.

Ausgehend von einem integrativen Ansatz für einen medienwissenschaftlichen Arbeitsplatz wurde das Internet/WWW als grundlegende Kommunikationsplattform gewählt. Ein den Anforderungen genügendes WWW-Informationssystem hat somit folgende Aufgaben: (I) die Anbindung des Datenbanksystems und damit die Verfügbarkeit der Primär- und Sekundärdatenbestände, (II) die

Bereitstellung projekt- und benutzerspezifischer Benutzerschnittstellen unter Berücksichtigung der Öffentlichkeit bzw. Geschlossenheit der Informationen sowie (III) die Nutzbarmachung des Arbeitsplatzes für eine Vielzahl von Arbeitsplätzen vor Ort und ggf. weltweit.

Aus der Sicht des Medienforschers sind dabei insbesondere geeignete Schnittstellen einerseits für die Ansicht und Bearbeitung von Medien verschiedener Typen zu schaffen. Andererseits ist eine kontextspezifische Oberfläche für alle Tätigkeiten im Bereich der Analyse bereitzustellen. Dies betrifft die Formulierung von Analysen ebenso wie deren Ansicht und Bearbeitung. In beiden Fällen sind die benutzer- bzw. projektspezifischen Restriktionen einzuhalten.

Das System basiert auf WWW-Diensten und Javamoduln, um den Forschern einen Zugriff von einer größtmöglichen Anzahl von Plattformen zu gestatten. Zum Zugriff auf die Datenbank wurde bereits ein Java-API entsprechend der PCTE-Spezifikation entwickelt (s. dazu http://pi.informatik.uni-siegen.de und [pcte93]). Weiterhin sind Komponenten zur Verwaltung der "multimedialen" Informationen in Realisierung. Für große Datenmengen wird hierzu derzeit eine neue Version des Hauptspeicher-DBMS H-PCTE realisiert, die 64-Bit-Adreßräume ausnutzt. Die Videoaufzeichnungen und -sequenzen werden in einem Videoarchiv gespeichert und zugegriffen, das stream- und framebasierte Mechanismen beinhaltet. Die Sekundärdaten (Metadaten) werden ebenfalls vom Objektmanagementsystem verwaltet.

Die Benutzerschnittstelle stellt Funktionalitäten zur Abfrage, Ansicht und Bearbeitung von Informationen zur Verfügung sowie zur Konfiguration von Analysen, die asynchron vom System bearbeitet werden. Die Methoden zur Analyse audio-visueller Informationen sind vom spezifischen Forschungskontext der Medienwissenschaftler abhängig. Entsprechend ist die Repräsentation im Front-end flexibel zu halten.

4 Zusammenfassung und Ausblick

Die Realisierung eines medienwissenschaftlichen Arbeitsplatzes erfordert die Auseinandersetzung mit vielschichtigen Forschungsfeldern, die insbesondere aus der Informatik heraus zu bearbeiten sind. Die Eingliederung in den Sonderforschungsbereich stellt darüberhinaus ein relevantes Anwendungsgebiet dar.

Insbesondere stehen derzeit operative Aspekte im Vordergrund, so z.B. die Integration von vorhandenen Datenbeständen als Ergebnis früherer medienwissenschaftlicher Arbeit. Diese liegen teilweise in proprietären Formaten vor oder führen zu Problemen bzgl. ihrer Vollständigkeit, Konsistenz und Korrektheit. Entsprechend müssen sie vor der Übernahme in das Gesamtsystem manuell bearbeitet werden. Die Lösung dieses Schrittes bildet die Grundlage der weiteren inhaltlichen Auseinandersetzung mit den methodischen Problemstellungen.

Das Projekt hat eine Gesamtlaufzeit von drei Jahren. Im laufenden ersten Jahr ist bereits die Realisierung eines operativen Prototypen mit den genannten Anforderungen anvisiert. In der Folgezeit stehen insbesondere Arbeiten zur Videoanalyse im Vordergrund.

Literatur

[FGK97] Freisleben, B.; Grauer, M.; Kelter, U.: *Teilprojekt Z2.* In: Fortsetzungsantrag für den fünften Bewilligungsabschnitt 1998-2000, Siegen 1997, S. 385-421.

[GrMe97] Grauer, M.; Merten, U.: *Multimedia - Entwurf, Entwicklung und Einsatz in betrieblichen Informationssystemen.* Springer, Berlin/Heidelberg 1997.

[HeKe96] Henrich, A.; Kelter, U.: *Integration von Zugriffsparadigmen in einem Repository.* In: Mayr, H.C. (ed.): Beherrschung von Informationssystemen. Proc. Informatik'96, Klagenfurt, 25.-27.09.1996 , R. Oldenbourg, Wien 1996, S. 307-326.

[Hen98] Henrich, A.: *Retrieval-Dienste für Software-Entwicklungsumgebungen.* Shaker Verlag, Aachen 1998.

[Kam96] Kammer, M.: *Entwicklung und Struktur der Sendungsdatenbank 'Fernsehsendungen nach literarischer Vorlage'.* In: Schanze, H. (Hrsg.): Fernsehgeschichte der Literatur. Voraussetzungen - Fallstudie - Kanon, Wilhelm Fink Verlag, München 1996, S. 43-73.

[KeDä96] Kelter, U.; Däberitz, D.: *An Assessment of Non-Standard DBMSs for CASE Environments.* In: Proc. of the Int. Conf. on Extending Database Technology, Springer, Berlin/Heidelberg 1996.

[Kel92] Kelter, U.: *H-PCTE - A High Performance Object Management System for System Development Environments.* In: Proc. of 13th Annual International Computer Software and Application Conference, IEEE Computer Science Press, 1992, S. 45-50.

[Lud93] Ludes, P.: *Orientierungs und Unterhaltungsmittel.* In: Ludes, P.: Orientierungsmittel im Fernsehen. Arbeitsheft Nr. 37, DFG-Sonderforschungsbereich 240, Siegen 1993, S. 3-39.

[Lud98] Ludes, P. (Hrsg.): *Schlüsselbilder von Staatsoberhäuptern. Pressefotos, Spielfilme, Fernsehnachrichten, CD-ROMs und World Wide Web.* Arbeitsheft Nr. 72, DFG-Sonderforschungsbereich 240, Siegen 1998.

[May97] Maybury, M.T. (Ed.): *Intelligent Multimedia Retrieval.* MIT Press, 1997.

[pcte93] o.V.: *Portable Common Tool Environment - Abstract Specification.* Standard ECMA-149, 2nd edition und ISO DIS 13719-1, 1993.

[RNL95] Rakow, T.C.; Neuhold, E.J.; Löhr, M.: *Multimedia Database Systems - The Notions and the Issues.* In: Proc. of BTW'95, Springer, Berlin/Heidelberg 1995, S. 1-29.

[sfb95] o.V.: *Ästhetik, Pragmatik und Geschichte der Bildschirmmedien. Projektübersicht.* Arbeitsheft Nr. 55, DFG-Sonderforschungsbereich 240, Siegen 1995.

The HERON Project — Multimedia Database Support for History and Human Sciences

Werner Kießling, Katharina Erber-Urch, Wolf-Tilo Balke, Thomas Birke, Matthias Wagner

Universität Augsburg

Abstract. The interdisciplinary HERON project investigates the impact of multimedia applications from the humanities, in particular heraldry, on future database technology. We present first evaluation results of querying image databases by visual content. Also the requirements of a digital workbench for art historians are described. Here we present an approach how to tackle the complex problem of exchanging multimedia documents over the internet.

1 Introduction

Images were always used to bear complex information. Though they tend to be even the most intuitive kind of information, image interpretation requires a lot of semantic knowledge and consequently is a time-consuming, difficult task. According to their complexity, so far little database support for image retrieval and evaluation has been established. Currently research efforts draw upon two orthogonal approaches for the retrieval of images based on their content: The conservative way is to manually index an image's content using predefined vocabulary. Queries then are specified using the predefined vocabulary [8, 3]. A more recent approach attempts an automatic content-based image retrieval based on generic features like color, texture, shape or spatial layout. There are numerous projects and (commercial) systems dealing with database support for multimedia data and content-based retrieval, such as QBIC [5], Photobook [9] or Virage [6]. This emerging technology opens up the opportunity for challenging applications in the humanities, where large and precious collections of images exist.

At the University of Augsburg computer scientists and art historians have initiated the interdisciplinary research project HERON[1] (HERaldry ONline). Today the use of digital libraries in arts, history and humanities is still exceptional. Though images are essential in almost all historic sciences, their use in heraldry is outstanding. The HERON project is set up with the target of building a very large multimedia database for heraldic research in art history. Heraldry

[1] Since the beginning of 1998 HERON is funded by the DFG (Deutsche Forschungsgemeinschaft) as part of the DFG program "Verteilte Verarbeitung und Vermittlung digitaler Dokumente".

is one of the oldest ancillary sciences and useful for the classification of a wide variety of medieval historical documents, epitaphs, paintings or other pieces of art. Especially when it comes to the identification of particular persons or personal possessions, results can often only be achieved by the means of heraldry. To classify coats of arms depicted on historical objects, historians still have to go through various large works of reference, some containing more than 100,000 different shields [11, 10]. Thus existing technologies for content-based image retrieval have to be evaluated seriously w.r.t. the requirements of heraldry.

The integration into the internet together with efficient online access is crucial for HERON. From an art historian's viewpoint the WWW can be characterized as a world wide compound of multimedia document servers delivering historical documents relevant to his/her work. However, the art historian's requirements dramatically influence the profile of online multimedia databases: The intensive use of multimedia documents in a variety of formats and at different levels of quality demands an optimized storage of multimedia documents, together with the integration of knowledge on multimedia formats into web servers and clients.

The rest of this paper is organized as follows: An overview of the science of heraldry together with new challenges for heraldic databases is presented in Sect. 2. First results on the retrieval by image content are presented in Sect. 3. Section 4 discusses the impact of an art historian's requirements on the design of HERON's prospective server architecture and its integration into a networked environment. We will draw conclusions in Sect. 5 and point out future research directions of the HERON project.

2 Heraldic Databases

2.1 Basic Issues in heraldry

The beginnings of heraldry date back to the late eleventh century when nobles began to fight in armour. As it became more and more impossible to recognize strongly armoured fighters, pictorial representations were used to identify individuals, and later on entire families (cf. Fig. 1). By the Middle Ages heraldry had blossomed into a complex system with the growing tendency to crystallize vague guiding principles into exact rules [4].

Three principal elements characterize a coat of arms: the field, tinctures and charges. The field is the ground of the shield and may be divided by horizontal, perpendicular or diagonal lines and by any combination of these. Thus smaller partitions arise that can be divided or emblazoned with charges like the original shield. Each partition or charge is of a specific tincture. The tinctures comprise two metals – gold and silver (often represented by yellow and white), seven colors – red, blue, green, purple, black, orange and brown and three furs – ermine, vair and potent. In drawings or engravings tinctures are mostly represented by dots or differently arranged lines (hatchings). There are lots of charges or symbols that can emblazon a shield, even overlaying several partitions. The art of correct descriptions of bearings (blazonings) is a very complex matter requiring a specific

Praun (Tafel 125)
schweizerischer Uradel, hiessen dort »die Prunen von Schenwerd« und sassen bereits im XIII. Jahrhundert im Rathe der Stadt Zürch. Einer des Geschlechts siedelte im XIV. Jahrhundert nach Nürnberg über, wo das Geschlecht mit der Zeit auch ins Patriziat kam.

Ihr Stammwappen zeigte in S. einen r. Stern, und auf dem Helm einen ebensolchen, an den Spizen mit g. Kugeln besteckt. Dies Wappen wurde den Nürnberger Praun i. J. 1474 von Kaiser Friedrich verändert, aus welchen Ursachen unbewusst, und bildet diese Umänderung ein merkwürdiges Beispiel in der Geschichte der Heraldik.

Das neue, jezt noch übliche Wappen zeigt in S. einen abgehauenen Ast mit drei r. Lindenblättern, oben 2, unten 1. — Auf dem Helm ein r. und s. Wulst, daraus hervorwachsend ein s. Arm, mit dem Ast in der Hand. — Decken: r. und s. Im vorigen Jahrhundert führte die Familie auch die beiden Wappen vereint in einem gevierteten Schilde mit zwei Helmen, wie die Abbildung auf der Tafel zeigt.

Fig. 1. Image of a shield with blazoning from [11]

vocabulary. Not only partitions, colors and charges are named individually, but also particular postures and several ways of depiction.

Considering the portrait shown in Fig. 2, the identity of the person portrayed is not apparent. The only realizable hint is given by the coat of arms painted in the upper right corner, which is supposed to be the bearing of the person depicted. Using one of the main works of reference [11] for German heraldry, the manual search for this bearing produced the result shown in Fig. 1. Though the form of the shield differs, the charge and colors used are the same. Besides the illustration of the arms, there is a short text containing genealogical information as well as the blazoning. Finding particular coat of arms in works of reference has been a difficult matter so far, because most works are ordered by topographic aspects, i.e. any volume only contains arms of a regionally restricted area. Furthermore there are far too many different collections of arms, preventing a complete sequential scan. For instance [11] consists of more than a hundred volumes, together containing about 130,000 different arms. So it is easy to verify assumptions, but finding arms without any knowledge of their provenance or the bearer's name is far too often - despite time consuming searches - unsuccessful.

2.2 Querying Heraldic Databases

Traditional digital image archives have in common that they only allow conventional query by keyword or full text search on only a few categories (name of the artist, iconographic subject, depository or even physical attributes like format or size). From the beginning of image processing standardized grammars like [13] have been used for description of almost any kind of images, but for any searches using unanticipated keywords or subjective descriptions – e.g. shades of colors – good results cannot be expected. Though blazonings are standardized by particular rules and use a special vocabulary of graphical elements occurring that could be translated into a grammar, major experiences in describing images correctly would be necessary, due to the complexity of art historical sciences.

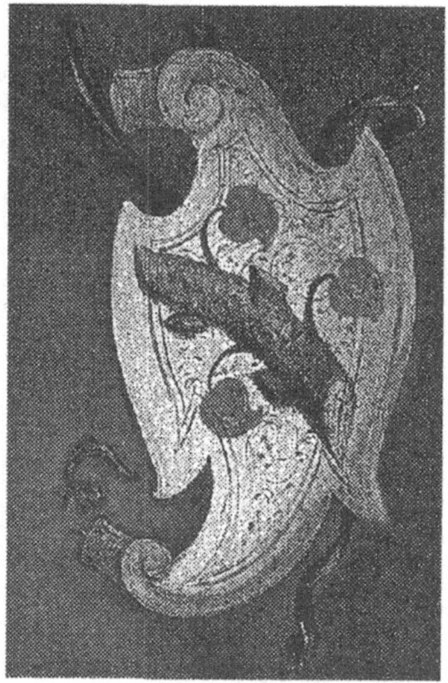

Fig. 2. 17th **Century portrait and magnification of the upper right corner**

Moreover, using language-bound descriptions only is far too obstructive to interdisciplinary research as well as to queries in other languages. In most cases the descriptions are done without using a standard vocabulary or thesaurus and even if so, the problem of specialized terminology in each discipline as well as often missing multilingual descriptions remain as a barrier to interdisciplinary communication. Retrieval by image content has the potential to make archives accessible to a far larger group of users, as only the visual impression and not the exact definition of what is shown is needed to retrieve certain images. However, experts in the field may still want to use traditional retrieval capabilities as full text search on blazonings. Therefore a combination of both conventional and visual approaches of retrieval is going to be adopted by the HERON project.

3 Query by Image Content in Heraldic Databases

3.1 Building a Heraldic Database

One problem in content-based querying is to determine the exact set of appropriate attributes or features that describes the content of each image in the database adequately. The complete process of querying is illustrated in Fig. 3.

The future HERON database will consist of images of about 32,000 coat of arms. High quality scanners are used for the monochrome digitization of images. As it is not necessary to have high quality for just fastly browsing the images, low quality images or thumbnails are sufficient to choose the relevant ones. Due to important details of the original, it is necessary to get at least an average quality image on the screen, which must also be available in high quality for zooming or printing. The high quality images (original size about 1.5×2 inches)

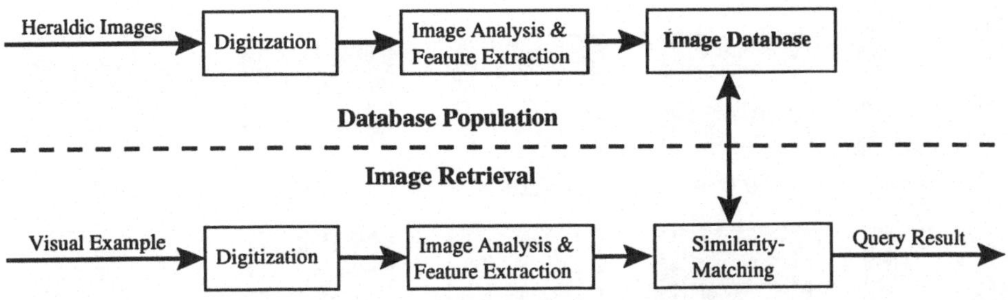

Fig. 3. Image processing and retrieval

are scanned at 600dpi using TIFF5.0 format. Every coat of arms is divided in two heraldic images, one showing the complete coat of arms, the other one presenting the shield only. About twelve coat of arms per person and hour can be scanned and postprocessed on the average. Furthermore thumbnails (50dpi) and the images in medium quality (300dpi) of all those images showing shields only, will be stored in the online retrieval database together with full text blazonings of the corresponding coat of arms resulting in a database at the total size of approximately 9GB. For the purpose of zooming, the high quality images can be stored in a nearline CD-ROM database with a size of about 50GB.

3.2 First Results

There are lots of different features, algorithms and similarity measures that have been proposed, but an optimal set can only be chosen considering the field of application. To get a first feeling about the specific problems in heraldry, a small database containing 100 shields has been created using IBM's Ultimedia Manager [5] that offers a variety of different features including color – histograms as well as average color –, texture, position and shape of images and the objects they contain. Since charges are essential to compare coats of arms, shape has proven to be the by far most important feature. Secondary are colors and textures that are both used to determine tinctures and position features that can be used to compare regionally restricted areas of shields. In [1] these features have been analyzed with respect to heraldry.

Shape Features: Retrieval by shape is known to be one of the most complex problems in image retrieval. A wide variety of shape features have been proposed in machine vision literature, but similarity strongly depends on the particular field of application. The Ultimedia Manager determines shape features by area, circularity, eccentricity and major axis orientation as well as a set of algebraic moment invariants [12]. The resulting feature vectors are accessed using conventional R*-trees [2] as feature indexes. To retrieve similar images a weighted Euclidean distance is computed for matching the query vector with all the vectors in the database. We have studied the retrieval of both simple geometric structures (circles, rectangles, etc.) and complex shapes (lions, eagles, etc.).

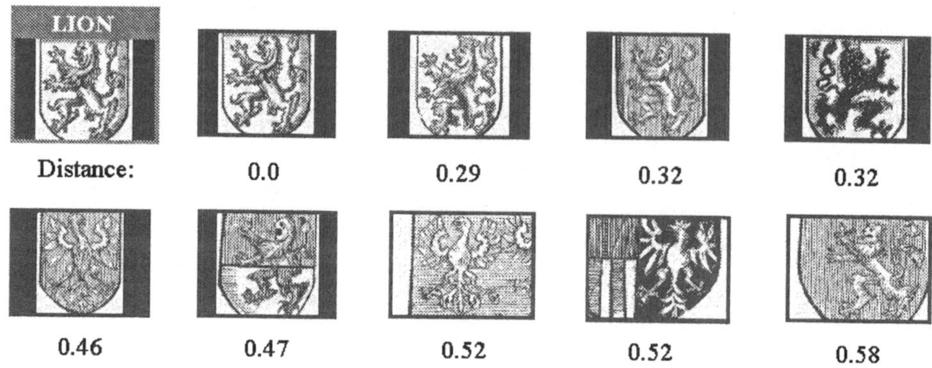

Fig. 4. Query by shape: complex shape

Of course, the quality of retrieval may differ with the sample chosen. A query result for complex shapes is shown in Fig. 4. The visual example is shown in the upper left corner. Obviously there are many false retrievals here. But all images of lions in the database are retrieved within a tolerable distance that is determined matching the features of each image in the database to the visual example.

Though there are lots of quite similar, but different charges in heraldry to emblazon a shield, their planarity, stylized depiction and clear recognizable borders encourage the further use of query by shape.

Color Features: In many applications best content-based query results have been achieved using color features. But whereas histogram color has proven to be rather useful, average color has no real application in heraldic databases, because it is impossible to distinguish clearly between shields only using their average color, e.g. a crest containing red and blue parts may have the same average color values as a purple one. Though comparing histograms is an effective way to distinguish between even similar shields, the relevancy of mere colors in heraldry is quite limited. Thus queries by color will only be useful in combination with additional features, such as shape or texture. Unfortunately colors cannot be used directly for querying, as most books of reference merely reproduce monochrome prints of shields, where each color is shown as a certain hatching. Therefore the problem of segmentation - in particular the distinction between areas of different color - is going to become more and more important, since this is the only way to take advantage of queries by color in heraldic applications.

Texture Features: The main application of texture features in heraldry is to find areas covered by furs. In the case of the Ultimedia Manager contrast, coarseness and directionality features are evaluated to represent textures of images. A sample query result is shown in Fig. 5. A visual example of an area covered with ermine (upper left) is compared to all images of the database. Since the example was taken from the database, the original image has been found first, followed by all those containing areas covered with ermine. The last image shown does not contain any ermine. Note that the distance measured for the last retrievals

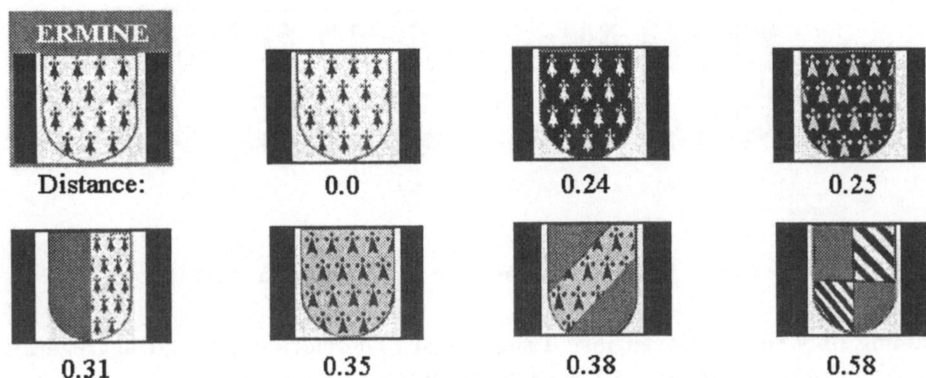

Fig. 5. Query by texture

displayed in Fig. 4 and Fig. 5 have the same value. But the latter image is a false retrieval, whereas the former image is relevant. This is due to the meaning of absolute values of distances strongly differing w.r.t. the particular feature.

Contour of Objects: Whereas color and texture features are extracted automatically, in most present systems the contour of any object has to be outlined manually to extract shapes or any other feature restricted to a specific object. This manual identification is time-consuming, expensive and an inhibition to a more widespread use of digital image libraries. To segment shields by manually outlining the shape of charges, an average of merely 3-4 shields can be processed per person and hour. Thus advanced capabilities of auto-segmentation of shields are absolutely necessary. Especially when it comes to segmentation of monochrome prints of crests, the representation of different colors by particular hatchings prevents the use of conventional algorithms for auto-segmentation.

Invariance to Rotation: Parallel to human perception both texture and shape features have generally been implemented invariant with respect to affine transformations such as translation, scaling and rotation [5]. Though invariance to scaling and translation is necessary in heraldic applications, invariance to rotation causes some serious problems, as neither the direction of hatchings nor the orientation of ordinaries and subordinaries or the specific posture of animals, etc. that are relevant parts in retrieving most similar images, can be recognized. Considering for instance the moon as a charge, unless the moon is shown full, the horns can point in different directions as shown in Fig. 6.

Positional Aspects: It is a necessity to determine the position of specific charges towards each other, since their exact topological arrangement is important to distinguish between coats of arms, e.g. there are different ways to arrange three lions: they may be arranged one above two, two above one or three in a row. All these coats of arms would be different, although showing three lions.

Aggregational Aspects: Charges often have to be counted. For instance, shields containing five stars have strictly to be distinguished from those con-

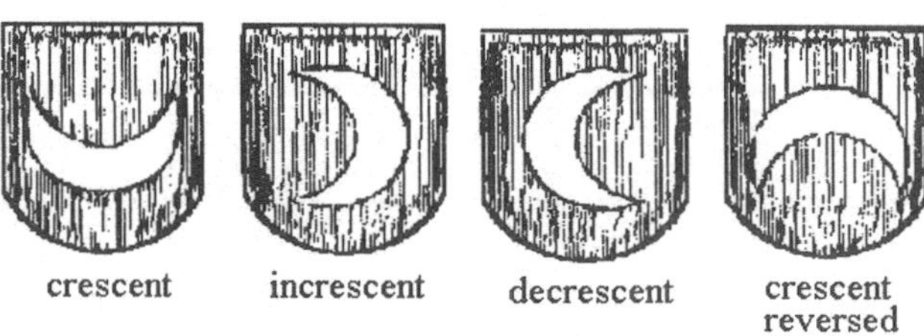

Fig. 6. Different bearings due to rotation of a charge

taining only three or even just a single star. Therefore additional aggregation capabilities on all images retrieved are required.

4 Heraldry Online

4.1 A Digital Workbench for Art Historians

What sets the research of art historians apart from other humanities is an intensive and varied use of images. Art historical research is based on voluminous reference works containing high quality reproductions of art collections like museum catalogues or on numerous monographies. Additionally photographic material in various forms (transparencies, reverse prints, etc.), either collected and archived by the individual researcher himself or by public art institutions, represent an important source. Scientific analysis of works of art is not conceivable without permanent use of reproductions primarily for the purpose of comparison. Therefore, it seems promising to use the possibilities of new media in art research at a large scale: a plurality of different material either printed, photographic or on continuous media can be stored in online multimedia databases.

Today large systematically arranged image archives especially addressed to art historians or historians, which allow research at any computer with internet-connection, are built up just to a small extent. They are available more often offline (CD-ROM) than online. The future "digital workbench" for art historians, consisting of a personal computer usually fed with digitized material from traditional sources which is connected to a network of (multimedia) databases, is depicted in Fig. 7. HERON is intended to line up with existing online databases, but it is strongly tailored to the needs of art historians by providing an intuitive visual query engine for the retrieval of a very large stock of historical multimedia documents together with a storage optimization for the digitized material aiming at a good quality of service.

4.2 Optimization of Document Delivery Costs

Future HERON users will extensively use image material in a large variety of formats. As mentioned above, multimedia objects in several formats and at different levels of quality are required. However, image formats are not independent from

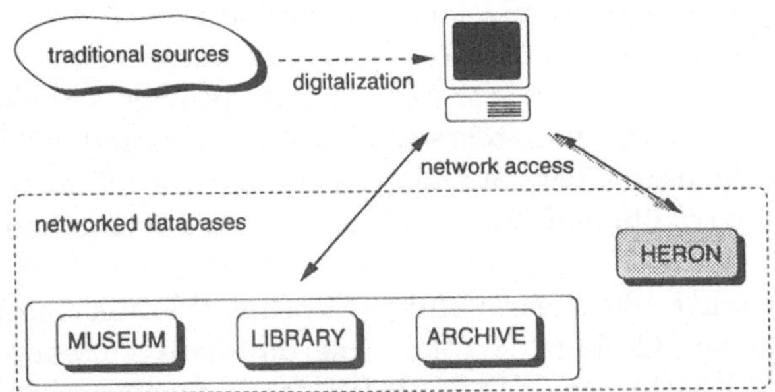

Fig. 7. A digital networked workbench for art historians

each other but interrelated by conversion tools and may differ in some aspects such as compression, color depth and resolution.

The Optimization Problem: To determine an optimal choice of stored image formats is a non-trivial optimization problem subject to parameters such as query profile, available disk storage, server load and network bandwidth. In [7] we have addressed this problem formally and proposed to integrate the conversion tools into database and proxy servers aiming at a dynamic optimization of multimedia document exchange. Format interrelations between images are modelled as a graph of functional constraints. An acyclic graph of functional constraints, where every computed format has a unique functional composition, is called a functional base. These functional bases are used to model sequences of potential online conversions. Since the number of potential functional bases grows exponentially in the number of functional constraints, determining an optimal functional base is non-trivial. Functional bases allow storage optimization by partitioning multimedia formats into physically stored and computed ones.

A prototypical implementation using the most popular HTTP server Apache has shown first promising results in the reduction of multimedia storage costs and the increase of server performance. This result will be published elsewhere.

5 Summary and Outlook

In this paper we have outlined the goals of the interdisciplinary HERON project at the University of Augsburg. The necessity of combining database technology with advanced content-based query methods was pointed out regarding the requirements of art history. Given the capabilities of modern internet technology, an efficient integration of the HERON into the WWW is mandatory.

First results concerning heraldic queries by image content and client-server optimization of multimedia documents have been presented. Though especially the results in content-based retrieval are encouraging, the IBM Ultimedia Manager has some serious disadvantages due to a highly restricted range of possible queries or a missing database support. Currently other commercially available products like Excalibur Image DataBlade Module by INFORMIX Software Inc. and DB2 Relational Extender by IBM Inc. are evaluated on IBM RS6000/AIX.

Our further research will mainly focus on performance issues, scalability and advanced visual retrieval capabilities. Query by image content uses similarity measures, hence content based searches can only provide a ranked list of query results. This set of successful matches can get very large and will ultimately have to be refined by the user. Therefore another crucial aim will be to minimize false retrievals in query results by fully exploiting all semantic knowledge in heraldry.

Acknowledgements: We are grateful to Dr. Rudolf Frankenberger, co-director of HERON, and Dr. Gerhard Köstler. The database software applied in the project is granted within the "INFORMIX for Innovation Educational Grant Program" and the program "DB2 For Educational Purpose".

References

1. W.-T. Balke. Untersuchungen zur bildinhaltlichen Datenbank-Recherche in einer Wappensammlung anhand des IBM Ultimedia Managers. Master's thesis, Universität Augsburg, November 1997.
2. N. Beckmann, H.-P. Kriegel, R. Schneider, and B. Seeger. R-tree. an efficient and robust access method for points and rectangles. *SIGMOD Record (ACM Special Interest Group on Management of Data)*, 19(2):322–331, June 1990.
3. T. Birke, M. Wagner, and W. Kießling. Classification of Late Roman Bronze Coins Using an Object-Oriented Database. In M. Yoshikawa, editor, *Proceedings of the International Symposium on Digital Media Information Base (DMIB'97)*, pages 39–48. Nara, Japan, November 1997.
4. C. Boutell. *Heraldry*. Frederick Warne & Co. Ltd., London UK, rev. ed. by j. p. brooke-little edition, 1958.
5. C. Faloutsos, R. Barber, M. Flickner, J. Hafner, W. Niblack, D. Petkovic, and W. Equitz. Efficient and effective querying by image content. *Journal of Intelligent Information Systems*, 3:231–262, 1994.
6. V. Inc. Virage Media Management Solutions. http://www.virage.com/, 1997.
7. G. Köstler, W. Kowarschick, and W. Kießling. Client-Server Optimization for Multimedia Document Exchange. In *Proceedings of the Fifth International Conference on Database Systems for Advanced Applications*, pages 135–144, Melbourne, Australia, April 1997.
8. V. E. Ogle and M. Stonebraker. Chabot: Retrieval from a relational database of images. *Computer*, 28(9):40–48, Sept. 1995.
9. A. Pentland, R. W. Picard, and S. Sclaroff. Photobook: Tools for content-based manipulation of image databases. In *Proc. SPIE Conf. on Storage and Retrieval of Image and Video Databases II*, pages 34–47, San Jose, CA, Feb. 1994.
10. J. B. Rietstap. *Armorial général: précédé d' un dictionnaire des termes du blason.* Heraldry Today, London UK, reprod. from the 2nd ed. 1884/87 edition, 1950.
11. J. Siebmacher. *Siebmachers großes Wappenbuch.* Bauer & Raspe, Neustadt a.d.Aisch, reprint edition, 1856.
12. G. Taubin and D. B. Cooper. Object recognition based on moment (or algebraic) invariants. In *Geometric Invariance in Computer Vision.* MIT Press, 1992.
13. S. van Roelof. *Iconography Indexing Iconclass.* Foleor Pub., Leiden, 1994.

The SFB 603 — Model Based Analysis and Visualization of Complex Scenes and Sensor Data

H. Niemann, B. Girod, H.-P. Seidel, B. Heigl, W. Heidrich, M. Magnor

University of Erlangen–Nuremberg
http://sfb-603.uni-erlangen.de

Abstract. This special research area combines visualization and interpretation of sensor data by exploring the central subjects "models", "optimization", "hierarchies", and "data fusion". This article describes the structural and thematic organization of the research project and illustrates first results of one sub–project as an example.

1 Introduction

The Sonderforschungsbereich (SFB, special research area) 603 "model based analysis and visualization of complex scenes and sensor data" has been established by the German Research Foundation in the beginning of 1998, and for the first research period it is granted until the end of 2000. At the moment, it is divided into twelve sub–projects in which seven institutes of the Technical Department of the University of Erlangen–Nuremberg and two clinics are involved.

This article describes the thematic questions and goals for which section 2 gives an overview. The whole SFB is divided into sub–projects, which are explained in section 3. In section 4 first results of one sub–project are shown as an example. Because of thematic linkage, three institutes directly cooperate within this project.

2 Overview

In the fields of information theory, computer science, production engineering, and medicine the technological process has enabled the utilization of images with high resolution and precision and their integration in system solutions. This results in innovative, economically interesting products and applications, requiring the visualization of more and more complex scene and sensor data. So the formerly orthogonal issues pattern recognition, computer graphics, and image communication more and more converge. System solutions increasingly necessitate methods from several, or from all these issues. Their common investigation is not only reasonable but also objectively necessary. Complex applications require high specialization which is achievable only in cooperation of several experts.

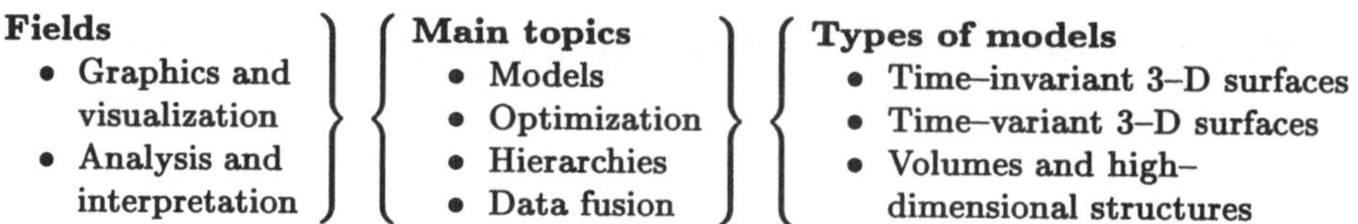

Fig. 1. Fields and topics

In cooperation of visualization and interpretation of sensor data, the SFB 603 examines fundamental principles, motivated by problems arising in the fields of engineering and medicine. The long–term goal is the development and the theoretical justification of new solutions which are to be validated by tests of practical problems in both fields. In the long term, new formulations should lead to a complete, uniform, and practically tested method for the analysis and development of systems, for the interpretation and visualization of images, sensor data, and descriptions of complex realistic scenes.

The four main topics of the SFB are model–based principles, development of solutions by optimization, use of resolution hierarchies, and fusion of sensor data. These topics characterize the common scientific issue of the sub–projects, each contributing to some of the main topics. The scientific goal in the first period is the examination of different types of models for time–invariant and time–variant 3–D surfaces and for volumes and high–dimensional structures (see Fig. 1).

We generally assume, that the properties of a system for the analysis and/or visualization are contained within a model (see Fig. 2). It must represent those aspects of reality accurately enough which are relevant for the application. Its structure must be designed such that efficient algorithms for its utilization can be developed and that it can be constructed almost automatically. The automatic construction of a model and its efficient use mainly will be based on optimization methods. For obtaining the required efficiency, hierarchical approaches are used. The necessity for multiple sensors results from requirements given by concrete applications.

The long–term scientific goals are:

- To examine similarities and differences of the models and the use of model–based methods for analysis and/or visualization.
- To construct models almost automatically from observations and to describe and to solve model construction by optimization.
- To formulate and solve the fusion of sensor data as an optimization problem.
- To use hierarchical representations as main component for achieving high efficiency and robustness of algorithms and data–structures.
- To derive a common and practically tested method for analyzing and developing systems which interpret and visualize sensor data and scene descriptions with sufficient complexity.

These goals are covered by the twelve sub–projects which are described in the next section.

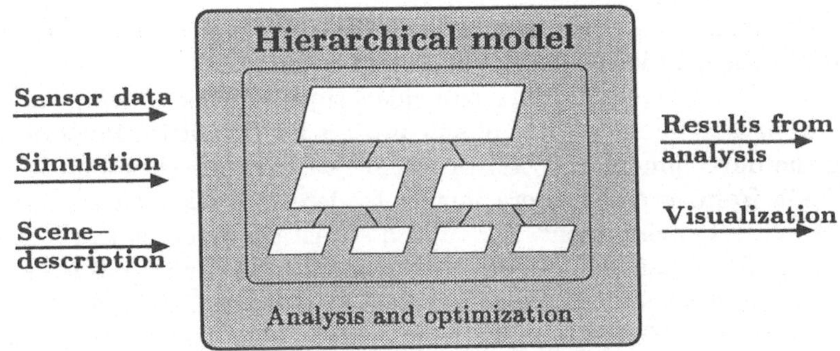

Fig. 2. A hierarchical model is the central element in a system for analysis and/or visualization of multi–sensor data.

3 The Sub–Projects

The main topic described above is the common goal of the single sub–projects, listed in this section. In each sub–project, models and model based approaches for different tasks for visualization and analysis are to be evolved and examined. Here, we have to take into account the aspects of acquisition, representation, and application of models.

Project Area A examines the acquisition and efficient use of arbitrary time–invariant 3–D surfaces, mainly based on geometry. In sub–project A1 (Chair for Optics) the goal is to build a system of 3–D sensors and algorithms to record different views of an object and to combine them automatically or by minimal interaction. A mesh of curved triangles is generated to describe the surface. Based on this, sub–project A2 (Chair for Computer Graphics) calculates surfaces from discrete measurements. The surfaces should meet given tolerances and curvature properties and be made available in a CAD–compatible format. The goal of sub–project A3 (Chair for Computer Graphics) is the development of an extensive simulation system for illumination including surfaces with specular and glossy properties. In sub–project A4 (Chair for Quality Management and Production Metrology) a system is developed to measure and evaluate form deviations of cutting tools. Relying on a CAD model of the cutting tools with specified cutting edge, their complex forms of wear are to be measured with appropriate resolution using optical sensors. Modules are to be realized to visualize these deviations for workers. On the basis of an optical system for recording 3–D images, in sub–project A5 (Chair for Manufacturing Technology) a fast and exact control of forming processes (e.g. laser bending) of metal parts with complex geometry is realized.

Project Area B deals with models for time–variant 3–D surfaces, including the additional aspect of the recognition and localization of objects as well as the interpretation of images. This requires the representation of information about typical ranges of parameters, invariants together with geometry and time variant properties within the model. In sub–project B1 (Chair for Communications Engineering I) the goal is the development and systematic test of new methods of the combined processing of audio– and video–signals for recognizing and tracking moving acoustical sources. Goal of sub–project B2 (Chair for Pattern Recognition) is the development and test of optimization approaches for the fusion of sensor data from several camera images to detect, track, and classify objects within a natural environment. For that, a statistical model is to be developed. Sub–project B3 (Chair for Pattern Recognition) follows the goal to develop an expert system to rehabilitate facial paralysis by planned interaction between patient and system. Different functional areas of the face, the type of paralysis and its degree are analyzed from an image stream and the expert system develops a training program for the patient. The models used here cover anatomy as well as rehabilitation strategy.

Models and high–dimensional structures are examined in Project Area C. Here, new models are developed for visualization and interpretation, for the combination of simulation and analysis of huge amounts of data, for the interactive planning of surgery, as well as for the discovery of interesting regularities in multi–sensor data. The goal of sub–project C1 (Chair for Computer Graphics) is the development of integrated algorithms for data analysis and visualization and the data models they are based on. The interaction and control by the user has to be possible even for extremely large amounts of data. The sub–project C2 (Chairs for Pattern Recognition, Communications Engineering I, and Computer Graphics) deals with image–based models, and is shown in more detail in section 4 as one example of a project. The problems of dealing with a huge amount of data is in the main interest of sub–project C3 (Chair for Fluid Mechanics). Its goal is the direct numerical simulation of data sets describing turbulent flows by the combination technique. The size of data is to be reduced, compressed, and to be visualized properly. In sub–project C4 (Chair for Communications Engineering I, Chair for Optics, and Department of Maxillofacial Surgery) the goal is the development and clinical testing of new methods for the interactive, photo–realistic visualization of soft tissue deformations caused by craniofacial surgery. This requires corresponding volume models and in long–term also time–variant models for animation.

Additionally, the three following working groups have been installed:

1. The working group for optimization methods.
   Optimization is one central topic which is important for many sub–projects. For example for global optimization, for the optimization of structure or for estimating parameters, the techniques often do not depend on one concrete application. So methods are easy to be exchanged.
2. The working group for visualization and interpretation.
   In most of the sub–projects, both visualization as well as interpretation of sensor data commonly belong to the goals, even though their main interests are different. The intensive exchange of experiences and algorithms between these two disciplines therefore is important.
3. The working group for quality criteria.

The evaluation of the quality of results is either subjective (e.g. "the synthesized scene looks like in reality") or objective (e.g. "the error rate for object recognition is 10%"). This leads to statements which are not comparable. The elaboration of quality criteria, which are useful for different algorithms and applications is the precondition for the proof of progress.

The main goal of each working group is to work out principles which are common for many sub–projects. So they support the cooperation between the institutes. Beside the working groups, institutes directly collaborate within single sub–projects, as the following section shows.

4 One Exemplary Sub–Project: Analysis, Coding, and Processing of Light Fields

4.1 Description

The efficient acquisition of model data for the photo–realistic representation and analysis of 3–D objects is still a big problem for the use of three–dimensional computer graphics and image processing. Above all, traditional surface–based models are inadequate for representing natural objects usually having complex spatial reflection properties (e.g. fur, cloth, tree). The goal of the sub–project C2 is the image–based acquisition and visualization of object models from image streams without the necessity to reconstruct the geometry explicitly. This approach is based on the light field of a scene describing the optical flow at every point and in every direction. The Lumigraph is an image–based representation of a light field and can be reconstructed from image streams [7]. In this sub–project, we not only reconstruct the light field and visualize it directly. Our aim is also to infer optical and geometric properties of an object from the light field. The sub–project is divided into the three main parts "reconstruction of light field and geometry" (Chair for Pattern Recognition), "hierarchical coding of light fields" (Chair for Communications Engineering I) and "reconstruction of reflection properties and rendering" (Chair for Computer Graphics). In this section, we show first results of all three parts.

To understand the following results, we introduce the concept of the Lumigraph representation. In correspondence to [3], one way to represent a light field is to define each viewing ray by two points on two specified planes, as illustrated in Fig. 3. The Lumigraph consists of a collection of such viewing rays with the corresponding color values. We call the (s,t) plane the image plane, because when fixing one point on the (u,v) plane and taking all rays through the (s,t) plane, we get a ray bundle which can be seen as one image of the scene. Therefore, a Lumigraph can be represented as a two–dimensional array of images. It is possible to render images from all arbitrary positions if they are within the range which is described by the representation. Combining more pairs of planes the viewing range can be expanded.

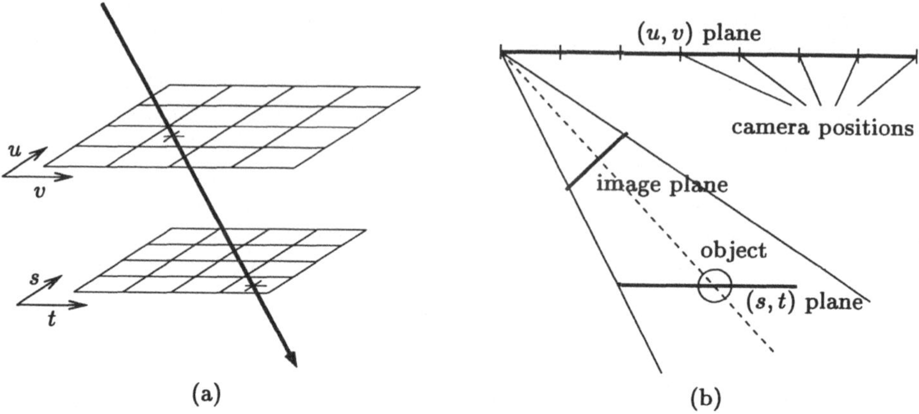

Fig. 3. Parameterization of a Lumigraph (a) and recording configuration (b)

4.2 Light Field Recording

There exist two different possibilities for recording a Lumigraph. One is to use a fixed system for moving a camera around an object, the other one is to take a hand–held camera, to move it around the scene manually, and to record an image sequence finally used for reconstructing the Lumigraph representation. The second possibility is the final aim, requiring the determination of camera movement out of image streams. In a first step we chose the first possibility for the acquisition of real Lumigraphs using a camera mounted on a robot's arm. The hand–eye and camera calibration already has been done in former work, so first realistic Lumigraphs have been available very soon, and we were able to test coding methods and visualization tools as described below.

Fig. 3(b) shows our recording configuration which is in correspondence to the Lumigraph definition. The center of projection of the camera is moved to discrete positions of the (u, v) plane, whereas the optical axis always intersects the object center. The recorded images are resampled such that the changing image plane is transformed to the same (s, t) plane for each camera position. The whole array of these transformed images corresponds to the Lumigraph representation.

4.3 Image Synthesis Using Light Fields

Light fields in the parameterization described above can be used to efficiently reconstruct images from arbitrary viewpoints. To this end, the discrete data stored in the Lumigraph has to be resampled for the new camera position. The most straightforward way of achieving this is by using a simple ray–casting approach [7].

A ray is shot from the new camera position through each pixel of the desired image and the intersection points with the two planes of the Lumigraph are recorded. The intersection point on the (u, v) plane lies within a grid cell of the

Lumigraph, which is delimited by the four closest camera positions in the (u, v) plane. On the other hand, the intersection point on the (s, t) plane lies within a grid cell formed by four pixels of the images on the (s, t) plane. See Fig. 3(a) for illustration. The Lumigraph data structure stores the radiance values for rays going from each of the four camera points to each of the four pixels. This makes for a total of 16 radiance values, from which the radiance of the pixel in the new image can be computed via quadri–linear interpolation. With this software approach interactive frame rates ($\approx$ 10 frames per second) are possible for relatively small window sizes ($\approx 320 \times 200$ pixels).

Another approach for rendering Lumigraphs has been proposed in [3]. This method heavily relies on the texture mapping capabilities of modern 3D computer graphics hardware. Linear interpolation within the (s, t) plane is achieved using bilinear texture filtering which is available on almost any modern graphics system, while the interpolation in the (u, v) plane is done by blending together multiple images with appropriately chosen blending factors. With this approach, we are able to achieve high frame rates ($>$ 20 frames per second) at very high resolutions (1280×1024 pixels) on low–end workstations (SGI O2).

4.4 Hierarchical Coding of Light Fields

Image-based rendering techniques require huge amounts of data. Even moderate light fields can easily reach sizes of one gigabyte or more, which have to be stored in local RAM for fast access during rendering. Therefore, an efficient compression scheme is needed that allows for fast decoding of arbitrary data segments.

Correlation within light field images (*intra*-redundancy, i.e. in the (s, t) plane) as well as similarity between adjacent recordings (*inter*-redundancy in the (u, v) plane) cause high overall redundancy in the four-dimensional Lumigraph data structure. Exploiting these dependency relations is the key to an efficient coder for light field information.

Hierarchical coding of the data structure allows for faster access to light field data at reduced quality, e.g., to enable interactive rendering. By applying the entire light field information, the scene can also be rendered at optimum quality. Inspired by the ITU-T standard H.263 for video compression [4], a coder has been developed that takes into account light field specific compression opportunities and rendering demands. A number of light field images in the (u, v) plane are *intra-frame* coded, i.e. they are compressed using solely a discrete cosine transform (DCT) quantization scheme similar to the JPEG compression standard [1]. Thus, intra frames can be decoded quickly and independently of other images. For hierarchical decoding, the intra frames form the reduced quality light field representation.

The intra frames also serve as reference images for prediction of all remaining light field images, the *inter frames*. For coding, an inter frame is divided into square blocks of 16×16 or 8×8 pixels. All blocks are then approximated by similar regions within the reference images. Since the recording geometry of the light field is known, the search for the best-matching region can be constrained along a one-dimensional epipolar line (disparity compensation) [2], improving coding

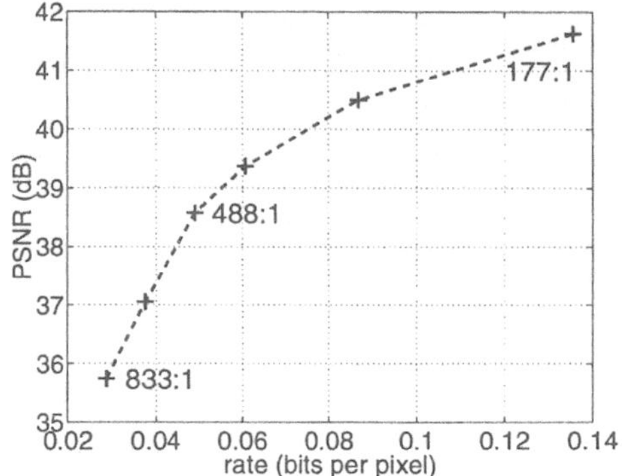

Fig. 4. Rate-distortion curve of light field *feather chick* with corresponding data compression ratios Light field data: (U, V) 17×17 images, (S, T) 256×256 pixels per image, 24-bit RGB color depth, 54 MB total.

Fig. 5. (a) Original light field image from *feather chick*; (b) corresponding decompressed light field image of (a); compression ratio 395:1, decompressed image quality 39.5 dB PSNR.

speed and compression efficiency. Compression efficiency is further enhanced by considering block-matching from a number of reference images. The difference between the original block and its best match (the residual error) is then coded using DCT quantization. By distributing the intra frames uniformly over the (u, v) plane, the similarity relations to adjacent inter frames can be efficiently exploited.

During rendering, many small segments from different light field images need to be accessed. The block-oriented coding/decoding scheme allows for independent decoding of arbitrary regions of 16×16 (8×8) pixel, accelerating rendering performance. Varying the coder's quantizer levels, different compression rates and corresponding decompressed image qualities can be achieved. Fig. 4 depicts the coder's rate-distortion curve measured for the light field *feather chick*. The distortion is defined here as the peak signal to noise ratio of the 8-bit luminance component, averaged over all light field images. For our test sequence, the decompressed light field images show little visual degradation from the original recording up to compression ratios of about 400:1 (Fig. 5). Due to the rendering process's inherent low pass filtering property, the loss of some high frequency components has little effect on reconstruction quality.

The current coder is based on the notion of light fields consisting of a number of two-dimensional images. Future work will exploit approximate three-dimensional geometry models of the objects in the scene in order to improve disparity compensation.

4.5 Applications to Global Illumination

We have also implemented support for light fields in the rendering system "Vision" [9]. Lumigraphs are available as geometric primitives for ray–tracing and

Fig. 6. Office scene rendered with two different Canned Lightsources based on different lamp sizes. The blurring due to nearfield effects is very prominent in both images.

interactive, OpenGL based viewing. Due to the architecture of the Vision system, this also allows us to use Lumigraphs in global illumination computations based on Radiosity and Monte–Carlo ray–tracing techniques. For example, light fields can now be used as light-sources in the Vision system.

We have developed a new method for using realistic light–sources for image synthesis. For a given lamp geometry and luminary, the outgoing light field is computed using standard global illumination methods, and stored away in a Lumigraph data structure. Later the light field can be used to illuminate a given scene while abstracting from the original lamp geometry. We call a light source stored and used in this fashion a "Canned Lightsource" [5] (see Fig. 6).

Our method speeds up the rendering process by factoring out the computation of the internal reflections and refractions of the light-source into a separate preprocessing step. As a consequence, realistic light-sources can be efficiently used in applications where a complete global illumination solution would be too expensive. Also, the cost of computing the global illumination within the lamp can be amortized over a large number of lamp instances and frames. It is interesting to note that the hardware rendering of Lumigraphs can be extended to Canned Lightsources as well. Projective textures and 3D texturing hardware can be used to speed up the rendering of scenes illuminated by Canned Lightsources [5]. This for the first time allows interactive walkthroughs for scenes with complex luminaries.

4.6 Applications to Statistical Object Recognition

One application of the Lumigraph arises from statistical pattern recognition. For the training of statistical object models, a large sample of images must be available which are recorded from known positions with different illuminations. As it is a very time–consuming task to do this by moving a robot around the object, it would be better to have a system for producing such views. One way is to use geometric object models to produce scene views by methods known from computer graphics. This solution may be feasible for the statistical modeling of geometric properties described by segmentation objects. But in the case of appearance based strategies, this way fails, because actually it is impossible to model the surface reflectance of complex objects adequately enough. Now the idea is to use the Lumigraph to produce this training set. Since the illumination is fixed within one Lumigraph, we recorded several Lumigraphs with changing light sources.

We used the appearance based statistical object model described in [8], and compared the results after training with the reconstructed views with those after training with real recorded images. The test views always have been real views. As shown in [6], the error rates increased from 12% to 23%. This result shows that in principle this approach is feasible, but at the time the reality is not covered accurately enough. The main reason seems to be that the errors made by interpolation during the reconstruction of new unknown views are too large. Especially sharp edges appear blurred. Therefore, we work on improving our interpolation methods to attain sufficient accuracy. If we can achieve this, we get a virtual environment for doing experiments for object recognition. The advantages are that one can use one exactly calibrated constellation for recording the Lumigraph and is able to render arbitrarily many views at arbitrary positions with arbitrary camera parameters like focus or radial distortion in a short time.

References

1. ISO/IEC JTC1 CD 10918. Digital compression and coding of continuous–tone still images — part 1: Requirements and guidelines, 1993. http://www.jpeg.org /public/jpeglinks.htm.
2. O. Faugeras. *Three Dimensional Computer Vision.* MIT Press, Cambridge, 1993.
3. S. J. Gortler, R. Grzeszczuk, R. Szelinski, and M. F. Cohen. The Lumigraph. In *Computer Graphics (SIGGRAPH '96 Proceedings)*, pages 43–54, New Orleans, Louisiana, USA, August 1996.
4. ITU-T Recommendation H.263. Video coding for low bitrate communication, December 1995. Draft, http://www.itu.ch/ITU-T/index.html.
5. W. Heidrich, J. Kautz, P. Slusallek, and H.-P. Seidel. Canned Lightsources. In *Rendering Techniques '98 (Proceedings of the Eurographics Workshop on Rendering '98) (to appear)*, Vienna, Austria, Europe, June 1998.
6. B. Heigl, J. Denzler, and H. Niemann. On the application of light field reconstruction for statistical object recognition. In *EUSIPCO 98 Proceedings (to appear)*, Rhodes, Greece, 1998.
7. M. Levoy and P. Hanrahan. Light field rendering. In *Computer Graphics (SIGGRAPH '96 Proceedings)*, pages 31–45, New Orleans, Louisiana, USA, August 1996.
8. J. Pösl and H. Niemann. Wavelet features for statistical object localization without segmentation. In *Proceedings of the International Conference on Image Processing (ICIP)*, volume 3, pages 170–173, Santa Barbara, Kalifornien, USA, Oktober 1997. IEEE Computer Society Press.
9. P. Slusallek and H.-P. Seidel. Vision: An architecture for global illumination calculations. *IEEE Transactions on Visualization and Computer Graphics*, 1(1):77–96, March 1995.

The MoCA Project
Movie Content Analysis Research at the University of Mannheim

Silvia Pfeiffer, Rainer Lienhart, Gerald Kühne, and Wolfgang Effelsberg

University of Mannheim, Praktische Informatik IV, 68131 Mannheim, Germany
{pfeiffer, lienhart,kuehne,effelsberg}@pi4.informatik.uni-mannheim.de

1 Introduction & Project Overview

In 1994, an ambitious project in the multimedia domain was started at the University of Mannheim under the guidance of Prof. Dr. W. Effelsberg. We realized that multimedia applications using continuous media like video and audio data absolutely require access to semantic contents of these media types similar to that for textual and numerical data. Imagine the existence of large digital collections of textual data such as books, articles etc. without anyone being able to search for pertinent keywords. Content analysis of continuous data, especially of video data, currently relies mainly on manual annotations. This implies reduction of the searchable content is reduced to the annotated content, which usually does not contain the required information. The MoCA project therefore aims to extract structural and semantic content of videos automatically.

Recently, different applications have been implemented and the scope of the project has concentrated on the analysis of movie material such as can be found on TV, in cinemas and in video-on-demand databases. This has provided access to a great amount of input data for our algorithms. The algorithms developed for video and audio analysis thus concentrate on movie material. However, they are also applicable to general video and audio material.

Analysis features developed and used within the MoCA project fall into four different categories:

1. features of single pictures (frames) like brightness, colors and text,
2. features of frame sequences like motion and video cuts,
3. features of the audiotrack like audio cuts and loudness, and
4. combination of features of the three classes to extract e.g. scenes.

The first two categories are usually regarded together and called video features. We have implemented a large number of well-known and new features in all four categories. Details can be found in our publications.

In order to facilitate our research, we also implemented a workbench in Tcl/Tk, the MoCA-WB, with capabilities for visualizing feature values and for rapid prototyping of demos and new applications. So far, we have examined the following application areas using either audio (A) features, video (V) features or both (AV):

- commercial segmentation & recognition (A,V),

- text segmentation & recognition (V),
- VisualGREP (V, also applied to audio event retrieval), and
- video abstracting (AV).

These will be presented in the sections following the next one, which introduces the MoCA Workbench.

2 The MoCA Workbench

2.1 Motivation

The MoCA-WB is a software environment for the development and rapid prototyping of audio and video content analysis algorithms. The workbench answered our need for support in handling the vast amounts of data resulting from the execution of content analysis algorithms. We also wanted to be able to combine results from picture track and audio track analysis. The aim was to shield researchers from technical details and to provide interactivity and sophisticated visualization possibilities, thus allowing them to concentrate on the development of new algorithms.

2.2 Key Concepts

Key design and implementation concepts of the MoCA-WB include:

1. Definition of orthogonal image, video, and audio operators:
   There is no room for creativity if there are too many technical restrictions and too few possibilities. Thus, a large set of basic algorithms is prerequisite to the development of more elaborate image, video and audio algorithms.
2. Combination of operators:
   In addition to providing a set of pre-coded operators, the MoCA-WB lets the user combine existing operators freely and easily to create new operators. Information from both channels (video and audio) can be combined to find higher semantics in films, in order to classify a movie into a certain genre.
3. Clear presentation of extracted data:
   Human beings are good at building new associations and deriving new ideas, but creativity depends to a large degree on the clear presentation of the objects of thought. If we apply this insight to a researcher working in the field of automatic movie content analysis, the need for a clear presentation of derived values and content indicators is obvious. Thus, we allow the researcher to control at any resolution/aggregation level the original and derived data to be displayed.
4. Rapid prototyping:
   The MoCA-WB makes it possible to translate new ideas quickly into action. This speeds up development of features, demos and applications, and motivates the researcher to try out new ideas/operators. Rapid prototyping leads us to two requirements: calculations should be fast in order to keep the system interactive, and operators should be able to be defined and edited at run-time, i.e. recompilation should be avoided. This is feasible due to an interpreter interface based on Tcl/Tk and low-level functionality implemented in C/C++.

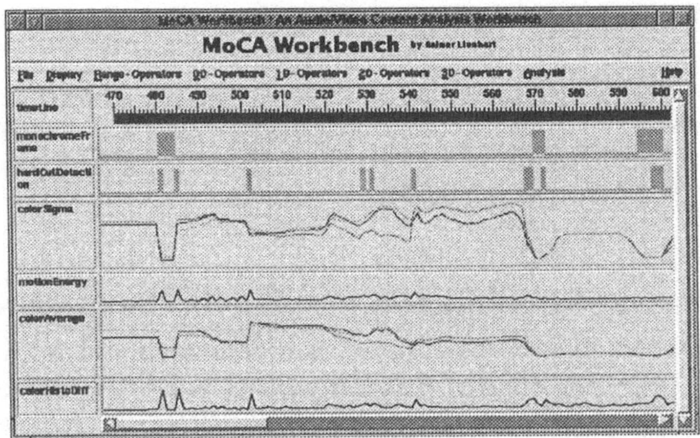

Fig. 1. Analysis example of the MoCA-WB

5. Validation of the output of new operators:
   Visualizing the results of operators often is not enough. The question of how well an operator performs its task is also of interest. We have therefore incorporated qualitative and quantitative means for validating results of operators into our workbench. The user generates reference streams for the automatically calculated results which contain the correct information. These reference streams are then used to evaluate the performance of (new) operators.

2.3 User Interface

A timeline-based interface was implemented on top of the interpreter interface. The timeline-interface includes the following features:

- control over the visible video segments – uninteresting parts can be made invisible and interesting parts can be shown at different levels of resolution,
- control over the visible operators and
- control over the visualization function.

An example of content analysis which has been investigated on the MoCA-WB is shown in Figure 1.

2.4 Status

The MoCA-WB has been implemented on a SUN Ultra 2 under Solaris 2.6 using C++ and Tcl/Tk 8.0. It has also been ported to DEC alpha under OSF1. The implementation, currently, comprises about 2000 lines of Tcl/Tk code and 13000 lines of C++ code. For the MoCA Workbench a new Tcl interpreter has been created, extended by our image- and video-processing algorithms, the Vista library 1.3, the DEC AudioFile V3.0 and a JPEG image viewer. Currently, we are developing new fast 2D and 3D visualization widgets for our Tcl/Tk interpreter.

The MoCA Workbench has been used successfully in different MoCA subprojects. See [8] for more details.

3 Commercial Segmentation and Recognition

3.1 Motivation

TV commercials are interesting in many respects: advertisers and psychologists are interested in their influence on purchasing habits, while parents might be interested in shielding their children from their influence.

3.2 Approach

Three approaches have been implemented within the MoCA project:

1. The first method detects and segments commercial blocks from a TV broadcast. It is based on statistics of measurable features like the cut frequency, the existence of monochrome frames between spots, the length of the shots (spots) and the amount of action (detected via the edge change ratio and the motion vector length).
2. The second method detects and recognizes known commercial spots which are stored in a database. It uses a video fingerprint of the commercial images that is based on a color feature called color coherence vector[10].
3. The third method also indexes and retrieves commercial spots which are stored in a database. It uses a fingerprint of the audio tracks of the commercials that is based on intensity statistics of frequency bands.

These approaches can be combined into a self-learning system which automatically identifies individual spots and stores them in a database.

3.3 Experimental results

The video and the audio methods were analyzed separately. For the video analysis, we digitized 200 commercial spots from several German TV channels. For the audio analysis, 100 commercial spots were used. These sets contained a number of new spots as well as spots from the sample video, but recorded from different TV channels and/or at different times. All commercial blocks were recognized with an average difference between the precise and detected location of only 5 frames. The recognition worked perfectly for both the video and the audio fingerprints: all were recognized, none was missed and none was falsely detected. See [7, 6, 11, 1] and http://www.informatik.uni-mannheim.de/informatik/pi4/projects/-MoCA/Project-commercialDetectionAndRecognition.html for more details.

4 Text Segmentation and Recognition

4.1 Motivation

There is no doubt that video is an increasingly important modern information medium. Setting free its complete potential and usefulness requires efficient content-based indexing and access. One powerful high-level index for retrieval is the text contained in videos. This index can be built by detecting, extracting and recognizing such text. The index enables the user to submit sophisticated queries such as a listing of all movies featuring John Wayne or those produced by Steven Spielberg. Or it can be used to jump to news stories about a specific topic, since captions in newscasts often provide a condensation of the underlying news story. Many useful high-level applications are imaginable if text can be recognized automatically and reliably in digital video.

Unlike other systems using text for the indexing of videos, ours does not take advantage of close-captions that might be transmitted on some television channels; rather, our system extracts the text from the video itself. We discriminate between scene text and artificial text. Text appearing, for example, on street signs or T-shirts belongs to the former, while the latter like the movie title and actor names is carefully directed and overlaid on the images in a post processing step. The algorithms we propose make use of typical characteristics of artificial text in videos to enable and enhance segmentation and recognition performance. Our video retrieval application also demonstrates their suitability for indexing and retrieval by our video retrieval application.

4.2 Approach

Our feature-based text recognition approach is performed in two steps:

- text segmentation and
- text recognition.

Text Segmentation The first step, text segmentation, extracts all pixels out of the video that are part of text characters and discards all pixels which do not belong to characters. The process starts reducing the number of different colors used in each video frame. This transformation does not affect the outline of the characters since characters are assumed to be monochrome and to have a high contrast highly to their background. However, the transformation generates larger homogeneous regions, thereby reducing the complexity of each frame, easing subsequent processing. The following steps reduce the number of candidate character regions: Some regions are too large and others too small to be instances of characters. Consequently, such regions are removed. Since we are analyzing text in videos, the same text typically appears in a number of consecutive frames. Thus, by analyzing motion we should be able to find the same text characters in consecutive frames. If we are unable to re-detect characters in the next frame, the region is regarded as a non-character segment and discarded. Since characters either remain stationary or move linearly, this condition is loosely checked over five consecutive frames for candidate character regions. Text produced by video title machines is made to be read. Thus, such text must contrast with the background. So each remaining candidate character region is checked for contrast with its surroundings. If insufficient contrast is found, we conclude that the region cannot belong to a character and discard the region. As a result we are left with candidate character regions which most probably are characters or parts of characters.

Text Recognition The second step, text recognition, then tries to recognize the characters contained in the candidate character regions by applying optical character recognition techniques. In principle, any standard OCR software can be used. However, our experience with the candidate character regions in the segmented frames reveals that most OCR software packages available today will

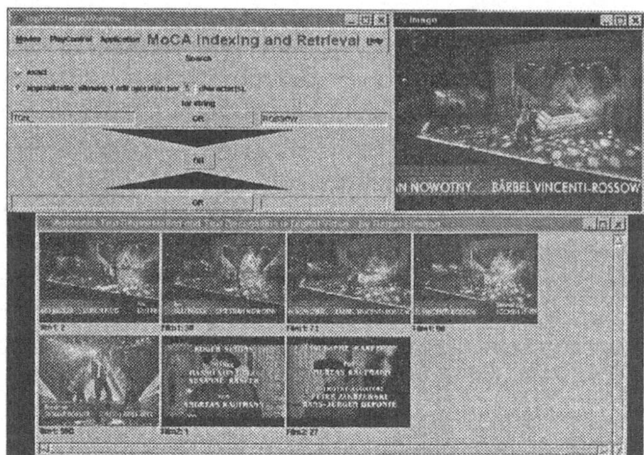

Fig. 2. User interface of the query-by-text application

have significant difficulty recognizing the text. Therefore, we have implemented our own OCR software.

4.3 Experimental results

Upon the described algorithms we built an indexing and retrieval application for digital videos. The indexing scheme is quite simple. Each video sample is processed by the text recognition software. Then, for each frame the recognized characters are stored after deletion of all text lines with fewer than 3 characters. The reason for this deletion is that as experience shows, text lines with up to two characters are produced mainly by background objects and, even if not, consist of semantically weak words such as "a", "by", "in", "to".

Video sequences are retrieved by specifying a search string. Two search modes, exact substring matching and approximate substring matching, are supported. The segmentation performance on our video test set was about 98%. The average character recognition rate was about 80%. Figure 2 shows the user interface of the video retrieval application on the segmented and recognized text.

4.4 Status of the Project

We are currently investigating new ideas on motion segmentation and a refined second segmentation step. Also, we are developing algorithms that will extract the bitmaps of the text appearances such as the title in feature films for inclusion in our automatic video abstracting system. See [9, 3] and http://www.informatik.-uni-mannheim.de/informatik/pi4/projects/MoCA/Project-textSegmentationAnd-Recognition.html for more details.

5 VisualGREP

5.1 Motivation

Any kind of video database retrieval task requires a systematic method to compare and retrieve video sequences. Retrieval based on single images is investigated in many other projects like QBIC, VisualSeek and Virage. We concentrate on the task of performing queries based on video sequences. Therefore, the problem of similarity between different video sequences must be addressed in detail. With our VisualGREP system, users may specify a video sample and the type of similarity they are interested in, and VisualGREP searches the video database for similar video sequences.

5.2 Approach

Three basic questions must be raised and answered by this system. Firstly, at what temporal resolution can video sequences be compared? The frame, shot, scene and video levels are identified. Secondly, given some image or video feature, what are the requirements on its distance measure and how can it be "easily" transformed into the visual similarity desired by the inquirer? We found that the distance measures must be normalized to the extent that two perceptual thresholds for the distance measures must be given by the user: a threshold which signifies complete similarity and one that signifies complete dissimilarity. In between, the similarity decreases linearly. Thirdly, how can video sequences be compared at different levels? A general approach based on either a set or sequence representation with variable degrees of aggregation is implemented and applied recursively over the different levels of temporal resolution. It allows the inquirer to fully control the importance of temporal ordering and duration.

5.3 Experimental Results

The performance of any indexing and retrieval system is usually measured by its recall and precision values. In our case, recall specifies the ratio of the number of relevant video sequences found to the number of relevant video sequences in the database. Precision specifies the ratio of the number of relevant video sequences to the total number of returned video sequences. The ground truth, i.e. the decision whether a video sequence is relevant or not, has to be determined by humans and their judgement of similarity.

The system was tested on a database of 4 hours of video from different sources. Two properties were shown: Firstly, the sequence representation performs better on sequences with motion since it takes into account the temporal development. For calm scenes, however, the set and sequence representations perform similarly. Secondly, there seems to be no difference in retrieval performance for non-aggregated and slightly aggregated sequences. The retrieval results improved with the size of the database. This suggests that the proposed algorithms are appropriate for large video archives of thousands of hours. See [5, 4] and http://www.informatik.uni-mannheim.de/informatik/pi4/projects/-MoCA/Project-visualGREP.html for more details.

6 Video Abstracting

6.1 Motivation

In current video marketing, it is common to produce a trailer (a short summary) of a video in order to get people interested in the film. With a vast number of stored videos in a video archive, it is not possible to produce by hand a trailer for each of the stored films. It is, however, interesting for a customer to browse the content of video before ordering to gain an overview of the content of the film. Therefore, we have developed ways to create video abstracts automatically.

6.2 Approach

The purpose of an abstract varies widely; for example, viewers of documentaries may want to be told all about the content of the full-length video, whereas a Hollywood film trailer seeks to lure the audience into a movie theater. Thus, a documentary abstract should give a good overview of the contents of an entire video, whereas a movie trailer should be entertaining in itself without revealing the end of the story. When we began the MoCA project, we made a basic decision about the type of material we would use as input. For example, different types of material can be used for producing a movie trailer: unchanged material from the original movie, revised material, and outtakes not used in the movie's final version. However, we use only unchanged material from the original movie, enabling our system to work with any video archive, independent of additional sources of information.

The abstracting algorithm we developed can be subdivided into three consecutive steps (see Figure 3). In the first step, video segmentation and analysis, the input video is segmented into its shots and scenes. Shot detection is performed by calculating an edge change ratio with global motion compensation. Scenes are determined by calculating audio cuts, which are detected as big changes of the frequency composition of the audio track. If audio cuts and shot limits coincide, they are labeled scene breaks. Identified at the same time are frame sequences containing special events, such as text appearing in the title sequence, close-up dialogs by the main actors, explosions, and gunfire. Text is determined as described in the previous section. Close-ups of main actors are determined via a face detection of upright and frontal faces using a neural network, tracking them in consecutive frames and determining typical shot/reverse-shot dialogs in these frame sets. Explosions and gunfire are determined by using the presented VisualGREP algorithms on audio features.

In the second step, clip selection, video clips are selected for inclusion in the abstract. The user specifies a target length for the abstract. In order not to reveal the end of the movie, the final 20% of the movie is not used. 50% of the abstract's length is composed of selections from aforementioned special events, distributed in equal shares. The other 50% is composed of selections from the remaining parts, equally distributed.

In the third and last step, clip assembly, the clips are assembled into their final sequence and the presentation layout is produced; this step involves determining the order of the video clips, the type of video transitions between them, and the assembly of the audio track.

6.3 Experimental results

For evaluation purposes, we ran a series of experiments with video sequences recorded from German television. We quickly found that there is no absolute

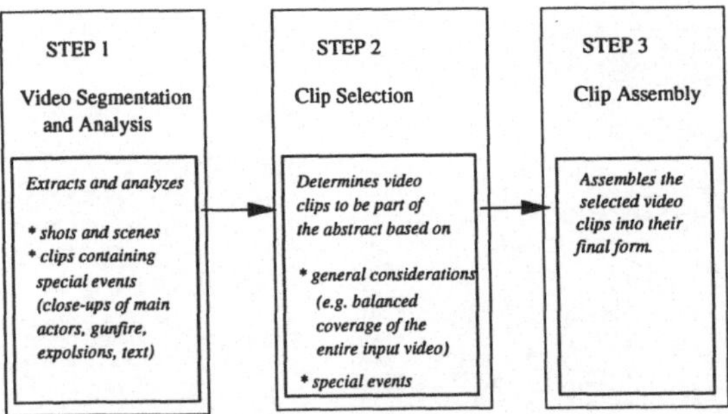

Fig. 3. The three abstracting steps

measure of the quality of an abstract; even experienced movie directors told us that making good trailers for a feature film is an art, not a science. It is interesting to note that the shots extracted by a human for an abstract depend on the purpose of the abstract. For example, a trailer for a movie often emphasizes thrill and action without giving away the ending; a preview of a documentary on television attempts to capture the essential contents as completely as possible; and a review of last week's soap opera highlights the most important events in that particular episode. We conclude that automatic abstracting should be controlled by a parameter describing the purpose of the abstract.

For commercial applications, we suggest our algorithms to be used for precomputing interesting scenes for abstracts. This data may then be integrated into a professional video editing environment such as Adobe Premiere of Ulead MediaStudio and a professional video abstract editor may then produce an abstract with our precomputed clips. An example of such data is shown as an html-page in Figure 4.

We expect our tools to be used for large multimedia archives in which video abstracts would constitute the basis of a browsing technique much more powerful than textual abstracts. For example, broadcast stations today sit on a gold mine of archived, difficult-to-access video material. Another application of our technique is to create an online TV guide on the Web, with short abstracts of upcoming shows, documentaries, and feature films. Just how well the generated abstracts capture the essentials of all kinds of videos remains to be seen in a larger series of practical experiments. See [12, 13, 2] and http://www.informatik.uni-mannheim.de/informatik/pi4/projects/MoCA/MoCA/Project-videoAbstracting.-html for more details.

7 Conclusion and Outlook

We have presented an overview of the MoCA project, which performs analysis tasks on different types of video material and has investigated many new application areas in the multimedia field. This is an ongoing project and more promising results are to be expected in the future.

Fig. 4. Result of video abstracting, compiled into an HTML page

References

[1] *Handbook of Multimedia Computing*, chapter Isolating and Identifying Commercials in TV Programs. CRC Press, 1998.

[2] *Handbook of Multimedia Computing*, chapter Automatic Trailer Production. CRC Press, 1998.

[3] Rainer Lienhart. Automatic text recognition for video indexing. In *Proc. ACM Multimedia*, pages 11–20, Bosten, MA, Nov 1996.

[4] Rainer Lienhart, Wolfgang Effelsberg, and Ramesh Jain. Visualgrep: A systematic method to compare and retrieve video sequences. Technical Report TR-97-005, Praktische Informatik IV, University of Mannheim, Oct 1997.

[5] Rainer Lienhart, Wolfgang Effelsberg, and Ramesh Jain. Towards a Visual Grep: A systematic analysis of various methods to compare video sequences. In Ishwar. K. Sethi and Ramesh C. Jain, editors, *Storage and Retrieval for Image and Video Databases VI, Proc. SPIE 3312*, pages 271–282, 1998.

[6] Rainer Lienhart, Christoph Kuhmünch, and Wolfgang Effelsberg. Aufspüren und Erkennen von Werbung in laufenden Fernsehsendungen. In Erwin Paulus and Friedrich M. Wahl, editors, *Mustererkennung 1997, 19. DAGM-Symposium*, pages 435–445, Braunschweig, September 1997.

[7] Rainer Lienhart, Christoph Kuhmünch, and Wolfgang Effelsberg. On the detection and recognition of television commercials. In *Proc. IEEE Conf. on Multimedia Computing and Systems*, pages 509 – 516, Ottawa, Canada, June 1997.

[8] Rainer Lienhart, Silvia Pfeiffer, and Wolfgang Effelsberg. The MoCA workbench: Support for creativity in movie content analysis. In *Proc. IEEE Conf. on Multimedia Computing and Systems*, pages 314 – 321, Hiroshima, Japan, June 1996.

[9] Rainer Lienhart and Frank Stuber. Automatic text recognition in digital videos. In *Image and Video Proc. IV 1996, Proc. SPIE 2666-20*, pages 180–188, Jan 1996.

[10] Greg Pass, Ramin Zabih, and J. Miller. Comparing images using color coherence vectors. In *Proc. ACM Multimedia*, pages 65–73, Boston, MA, nov 1996.

[11] Silvia Pfeiffer, Stephan Fischer, and Wolfgang Effelsberg. Automatic audio content analysis. In *Proc. ACM Multimedia*, pages 21–30, Boston, MA, nov 1996.

[12] Silvia Pfeiffer, Rainer Lienhart, Stephan Fischer, and Wolfgang Effelsberg. Abstracting digital movies automatically. *Journal of Visual Communication and Image Representation*, 7(4):345–353, Dec 1996.

[13] Silvia Pfeiffer Rainer Lienhart and Wolfgang Effelsberg. Video abstracting. *Communications of the ACM*, 40(12):55–62, Dec 1997.

SFB 340: "Linguistic Foundations for Computational Linguistics"

Christian Rohrer

University of Stuttgart

Participating Institutions:
University of Stuttgart and University of Tübingen
Participating Subject Areas:
Computational Linguistics, Computer Science, Logic, Theoretical Linguistics

1 Introduction

The SFB starts from two assumptions: on the one hand a theoretically well-founded linguistic analysis is a necessary prerequisite for the development of computational linguistics and its applications. On the other hand problems and results of natural language processing provide new insights and challenges for theoretical linguistics.

One can interpret the statement: "linguistic analysis of natural language is a prerequisite for computational linguistics" in a narrow sense or in a wide sense. In a narrow sense it means that the results achieved in theoretical linguistics are used and implemented by computational linguists. The syntax projects of our SFB for instance are GB-based [2]. The analyses of German which come out of these syntax projects, are reinterpreted in the framework of unification-based grammars like HPSG or LFG. These unification-based grammar formalisms constitute the basis of our implementations. Typical examples of such a 'reuse' of GB analyses is the treatment of long distance dependencies, the verbal complex in German, DP analysis vs NP analysis, analysis of parenthetical constructions.

The universities of Tuebingen and Stuttgart have been centers of excellence in theoretical and descriptive syntax of German for many years. The close interaction with computational linguists working in HPSG and LFG has lead to efficient grammar development environments (B4, B8) and implemented grammars of German with large coverage (B12).

Besides purely symbolic theories of syntax we also use statistical theories, or to be more precise, theories of grammar which combine statistical with structural information. We develop robust parsing technologies based on such theories and use them to induce lexica from corpora (B7). The grammar development project (B12) will use the valence information contained in the lexica thus induced in order to fulfill the subcategorization requirements of LFG.

From the very beginning of the SFB there was a close connection between theoretical semantics and natural language processing. The theoretical framework for semantics is Discourse Representation Theory (DRT). This theory was developed by Hans Kamp, who also directed the main semantics projects in the SFB. Already in its first version [14] DRT contained an algorithm for mapping syntactic structures into semantic representations. The implementation of DRT and its later variant UDRT (underspecified DRT) plays an important role in our SFB (A10, A12). We have now reached the stage where we can produce underspecified semantic representations (UDRSs) for a large fragment of German (B9).

The projects mentioned so far illustrate contributions of theoretical linguistics to computational linguistics. In a wider sense theoretical linguistics produces results, whose direct relevance for computational linguistics is not yet obvious. It would be a mistake to expect all linguists to be able to specify in which area of computational linguistics their results are relevant. The short history of computational linguistics offers already enough examples of results in basic research whose pratical relevance was discovered only decades later. Finite state parsing uses results from the theory of finite automata which go back to the fifties. In statistical parsing Church and Gale use 'Good-Turing Smoothing'. The original paper about 'Good-Turing Smoothing' had no direct connection to computer science. It was about population modelling.

Since this presentation at the annual meeting of the GI addresses computer scientists with an interest in natural language processing, we will nevertheless describe only those projects where the possible practical applications are already obvious or where we at least have produced some prototypical implementations.

2 Projects B4/B8 "From Constraints to Rules: Efficient Compilation of HPSG Grammars"

The aim of the B4 project "From Constraints to Rules: Efficient Compilation of HPSG Grammars" was the development of a computational system to process HPSG constraint grammars. While computational feature structure systems generally offer phrase structure rules as the main building block for a grammar, linguists conceive of an HPSG grammar as a set of implicational constraints, a set of linear precedence constraints, and a set of lexical rules.

There are at least two motivations for implementing HPSG theories close to the way they are formulated in linguistics. From a computational point of view a complex theory serves well as a test for the feature logic systems being developed. It can illustrate performance and theoretic devices, such as named disjunction or full negation, or more specific mechanisms, like definite clause attachments on lexical entries. The intention of a linguist on the other hand is to use the development of an implementation as a tool to provide feedback for a rigid and complete formalization of a linguistic theory.

The ConTroll system [11] which was developed in the project uses strongly typed feature structures as data structure and offers definite relations, universal constraints, and lexical rules to express grammar constraints. The system thus allows a direct implementation of HPSG grammars without forcing the grammar writer to introduce a phrase structure backbone or to provide a relational encoding of the theories as logic programs. In addition, the availability of universal constraints in ConTroll also allows for a more modular encoding of traditional grammars using a relational backbone. In a purely relational encoding, all principles need to be folded into all phrase structure rules for which the principles are applicable. In ConTroll, on the other hand, the universal constraints generalize over all occurrences of some data structure.

As formal foundations, the system builds on the set theoretic logic of [16, 1994]. The practical effect of this is that ConTroll implements an exhaustive typing strategy which provides the stronger kind of inferencing over descriptions [5, 1994] required by standard HPSG theories.

Fig 1 provides an overview of the ConTroll system and highlights some of the key ideas behind its implementation. First, the complex antecedents of the universal constraints and the occurrences of negation are eliminated, which is possible due to the exhaustive typing we assume. The resulting type constraints are then compiled into definite clauses using the method described in [7]. For the second kind of grammar constraints, the definite relations, the compiler detects the places in arguments of the definite relations in which constrained types can occur and integrates the type constraints into the code by adding calls to the relational encoding of the universal constraints. As described in [8], the universal constraints are integrated in a lazy fashion, i.e. only in case the argument of a relation is specific enough to cause a conflict with a universal constraint does the compiler attach a call to the universal constraint. Such lazy interpretation has a significant efficiency payoff, especially for large grammars, since it results in preferred processing of those constraints in the large constraint pool which are specific enough to fail. As third kind of linguistic constraints, lexical rules are dealt with by a separate compiler which translates a set of lexical rules and their interaction into a definite clause encoding [24]. The disjunctive possibilities arising from lexical rule application are encoded as systematic covariation in the specification of lexical entries. The final output of the compiler constitutes an efficient computational counterpart of the linguistic generalizations captured by lexical rules and allows "on the fly" application of lexical rules. Finally, program transformation techniques such as constraint propagation are used to advance the encoding [25].

Special mechanisms are included to allow the grammar writer to specify how the universal constraints and definite clauses are intended to interleave in processing [10]. Most importantly, the delay mechanism of ConTroll supports coroutining of both universal constraints and definite clauses, and it offers a variety of control statements to fine tune the execution strategy. This is a prerequisite to efficient processing with constraint grammars.

The system is fully implemented and has been used as workbench to develop and test the large HPSG grammar for German developed in the project B8 "Ein HPSG-Syntaxfragment für das Deutsche – Sprachtheoretische Grundlagen und computerlinguistische Implementierung" [12]. The grammar was developed in a distributed fashion by eight linguists and consist of > 8000 lines of code in 57

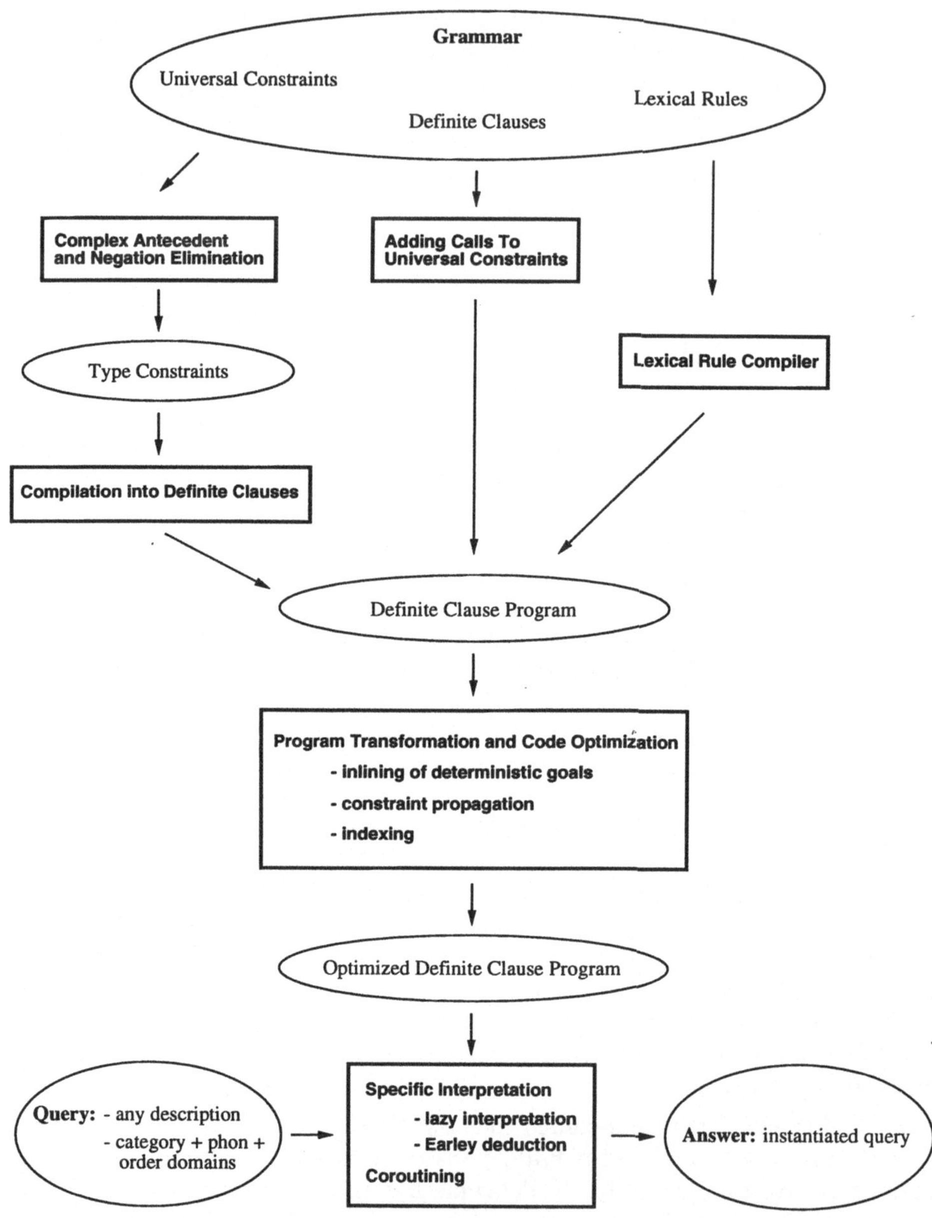

Fig. 1. Overview of the ConTroll system

files. It provides an analyses for simple and complex verb-second, verb-first and verb-last sentences with scrambling in the Mittelfeld, extraposition of nominal and sentential complements, Wh-Movement and Topicalization, integrated verb-first parentheticals, and an interface to an illocution theory, as well as the three kinds of infinitive constructions (coherent, incoherent, third-construction), nominal phrases, and adverbials. To support development of such large grammars, as described in [9] the ConTroll system provides a graphical user interface for data structure visualization and interactive debugging and tracing, tools supporting a modular grammar organization and automatic macro generation, as well as incremental compilation, global grammar optimization and arbitrary multiple indexing of grammar constraints.

3 Project B7 "Statistical Models of Grammar and the Lexicon"

This project is concerned with models of natural language grammars and lexicons which combine statistical with structural information, with the development of robust parsing technologies based on such theories, and with the application of these parsing technologies in inducing lexicons from text corpora. The grammar formalism employed is head-lexicalized probabilistic context free grammar. A lexicalized probabilistic grammar differs from an ordinary one in that all choices made in constructing a tree analysis are conditioned on the lexical head of a parent node. For instance, in generating the verb phrase "*ask a perfectly reasonable question*", the rule [VP→V NP] used in expanding the parent node VP is conditioned on the head of the phrase, namely *ask*. This can be used to represent the fact that *ask* takes a transitive valence frame with high probability. Further, each terminal word is conditioned on a synactically governing head: *question* is conditioned on *ask*, *reasonable* is condioned on *question*, and *perfectly* is conditioned on *reasonable*. Such syntactic word-pair collocates are useful in comparing competing syntactic analyses because they represent very specific frequency information which can be induced from examples of use via an unsupervised learning algorithm.

Algorithms employed include tabular parsing for the construction of parse forests (and-or graphs representing a set of tree analyses); the probabilistic inside-out algorithm for the computation of probabilities of constituents and rules; a graph flow algorithm for the estimation of rule frequencies; a modified EM algorithm for the estimation of the probability model; and latent class clustering. Programs are packaged into a probabilistic parsing and lexicon-induction system known as Gramotron. The system includes a graphical grammar development environment involving a probabilistic chart display. Parsers for lexicalized and unlexicalized probabilistic grammars are included. The implementation in C++ is based on a library for parsers, probability models, and linguistic objects which is similar to the Standard Template Library.

The methodology employed combines linguistic knowledge in the form of a hand-written grammars and morphology (word-terminal category relation) with computational induction of probability parameters.

Languages being studied are English and German, and in a dissertation project, Portuguese. Lexicon induction involves iterations of parsing in order to collect event freqencies, followed by re-estimation of a probability model. In an experiment performed on English described in [1], a 50 million word text corpus was mapped to a probabilistic lexicon; subsequent experiments on English involved a 90 million word corpus. Similar experiments have been performed with a more restricted German grammar on a 3 million word corpus. The probabilistic parser can be used to produce a graph representation of all the tree analyes of a sentence and their probabilities, or to map a sentence to a maximum-probability tree analysis. It provides a probabilistic language model, assigning probabilities to sentences. Such probabilistic models for sentences and their grammatical analyses are useful in a variety of applications where ambiguity is a problem.

4 Project B9 "Computational Semantics"

There is quite a range of commercial products on the market which promise to assist humans to retrieve and to organize textual information. In general, these products are based on knowledge-poor stochastic methods. In order to get a grasp on the evergrowing wealth of information, there is a need for methods which take into account the knowledge which is rendered by a text - not just its surface appearance. Methods for building semantic representations of texts are becoming currently established. Similarly, efficient inference engines for predicate logic are available. However, still, a serious, computationally prohibitive problem of natural language utterances is their ambiguity. Humans can react to a text or to utterances in a meaningful manner, even though they may not be able to assign to it a single formal interpretation.

The major goal of the project B9 is to realize an *inference-based method of computational semantics* without making the conventional assumption that all, or at least most, of the premises be available in an unambiguous, fully specified manner. In the previous phases of the SFB, a system has been implemented which constructs the semantic representations for a wide range of syntactic constructions and which is able to draw inferences from representations which are underspecified with respect to quantifier scope and with respect to the distributive/collective distinction, cf. [20], [26], [19]. Currently, we are extending the representations and the theorem prover component in order to cover additional phenonema of natural language ambiguity like syntactic ambiguity and ambiguity of contextual reference, cf. [3], [27]. This involves the elaboration of the linguistic theories and the design and implementation of specialized theorem proving mechanisms.

In addition to the design of explicit inference rules for underspecified representations, we want to take advantage of the fact that our linguistic descriptions are implemented in a *constraint logic programming language* (CUF) [4], [18]. Syntactic, semantic and pragmatic properties of natural language are described as a set of constraints. Linguistic processing is thus *concurrent processing* of constraints. We develop heuristics how to control the processing of such constraints in order to obtain a reasonable run-time behaviour.

One further issue of B9 is to pursue the development of our system as a *'semantic workbench'* where researchers from more theoretically oriented neighbour projects can test their ideas. For this purpose and for the sake of portability to the alternative syntactic approaches of the projects B8 and B 12, it is of foremost importance that the system be built in a well-organized, modular manner and that guidelines for the organization of linguistic descriptions are being developed.

5 Project B12 "How to Write, Maintain and Optimize a Large-Coverage Grammar of German"

The aim of the B12 project is to write a linguistically well motivated unification-based grammar which is easy to maintain and runs fast. There have been quite a number of projects in the past with this aim and which failed. Why should we be more successful?

1. We already have a fairly large grammar. In a recent experiment we parsed more than 70% of the subordinate clauses in a newspaper text [22].
2. Our dictionary contains about 42 000 lemmata, which allow to analyze roughly 2,2 million inflected forms. In addition we have special lexicons for verbs, adjectives and nouns which contain the relevant subcategorization information: 14 274 readings for 13 328 verbs, 11 368 readings for 8744 nouns and 2913 readings for 2274 adjectives.
3. We develop our lexical resources in tandem with the grammar and use very large corpora (more than 200 million running words) to test our hypotheses about syntactic classes and/or syntactic constructions.
4. We use a state of the art development system, designed for industrial applications [15].

The bigger the grammar and lexica get the more difficult it is to successfully manage the huge amount of information. With each new grammar rule that gets added there might be unwanted interactions with existing rules. Therefore we have to use and adapt methods from software engineering to grammar engineering. One area where we already can report progress is testing. We have developed large test suites containing pairs of sentences and readings (analyses). Thus we can automatically detect whether changes in the grammar affect the number of readings of a given sentence [21]. In the future we want to speed up the construction of testsuites using a generator. To support distributed grammar development we have implemented tools which are based on RCS and CVS, but which should make it easier for the linguist to merge his grammar file with the master file. We also enforce obligatory tests before check-in. To cope at least partially with massive ambiguity we use a version of optimality theory which allows us to express a preference (or dispreference) ranking of possible readings of a sentence [23]. Optimality theory is also used in our project to detect sources of inefficiency in the grammar.

At the moment it is still unclear whether it is possible to write a UG of German which allows us to parse 95% of a newspaper like Stuttgarter Zeitung or

Handelsblatt, where parse correctly means 'assign the correct predicate-argument structure(s). Will we reach a point of 'diminishing returns' where adding a new rule causes other analyses to fail? At the moment the lexicon seems to be the main bottleneck. As long as there is no comprehensive electronic dictionary of German, NLP of German will be fragmentary.

References

1. Glenn Carroll and Mats Rooth. Valence induction with a Head-lexicalized PCFG. In *Third Conference on Empirical Methods in Natural Language Processing*, 1998.
2. Noam Chomsky. *The Minimalist Program.* MIT Press, Cambridge, Mass., 1995.
3. Jochen Dörre. Efficient construction of underspecified semantics under massive ambiguity. In *Proceedings of the Association for Computational Linguistics*, 1997.
4. Jochen Dörre and Michael Dorna. CUF - a formalism for linguistic knowledge representation. Deliverable R.1.2A, DYANA 2, August 1993.
5. Dale Gerdemann and Paul John King. Typed feature structures for expressing and computationally implementing feature cooccurence restrictions. In *Proceedings of 4. Fachtagung der Sektion Computerlinguistik der Deutschen Gesellschaft für Sprachwissenschaft*, pages 33–39, 1993.
6. Dale Gerdemann and Paul John King. The correct and efficient implementation of appropriateness specifications for typed feature structures. In *Proceedings of COLING-94*, Kyoto, Japan, 1994.
7. Thilo Götz and Walt Detmar Meurers. Compiling HPSG type constraints into definite clause programs. In *Proceedings of the Thrirty-Third Annual Meeting of the ACL*, Boston, 1995. Association for Computational Linguistics.
8. Thilo Götz and Walt Detmar Meurers. The importance of being lazy - using lazy evaluation to process queries to HPSG grammars. In Philipe Blache, editor, *Actes de la troisième conférence anuelle sur le traitment automatique du langage naturel*, 1996.
9. Thilo Götz and Walt Detmar Meurers. The ConTroll system as large grammar development platform. In *Proceedings of the ACL/EACL post-conference workshop on Computational Environments for Grammar Development and Linguistic Engineering*, Madrid, Spain, 1997.
10. Thilo Götz and Walt Detmar Meurers. Interleaving universal principles and relational constraints over typed feature logic. In *Proceedings of the 35th Annual Meeting of the ACL and the 8th Conference of the EACL*, Madrid, Spain, 1997.
11. Thilo Götz, Walt Detmar Meurers, and Dale Gerdemann. *The ConTroll Manual (ConTroll v.1.0.β, Xtroll v.5.0.β).* Universität Tübingen, Seminar für Sprachwissenschaft, Tübingen, 1997.
12. Erhard Hinrichs, Detmar Meurers, Frank Richter, Manfred Sailer, and Heike Winhart. Ein HPSG-Fragment des Deutschen, Teil 1: Theorie. Arbeitspapiere des SFB 340 Nr. 95, Universität Tübingen, 1997.
13. IMS Stuttgart. CUF home page. `http://www.ims.uni-stuttgart.de/cuf/`.
14. Hans Kamp. A theory of truth and semantic representation. In Jeroen Groenendijk, T. Janssen, and Martin Stokhof, editors, *Formal Methods in the Study of Language*, pages 277–321. Mathematical Centre, Amsterdam, 1981. Reprinted in: Groenendijk, J., Janssen, T. and Stokhof, M. (eds): Truth, Interpretation and Information, pp. 1-41. Dordrecht, Foris, 1984.

15. Ron Kaplan and Paula Newman. Lexical resource reconcilation in the Xerox Linguistic Environment. In D. Estival, A. Lavelli, K. Netter, and F. Pianesi, editors, *Computational Environments for Grammar Development amd Linguistic Engineering, ACL Workshop*, pages 54–61, Madrid, Spain, 1997.
16. Paul John King. *A logical formalism for Head-driven Phrase Structure Grammar.* PhD thesis, University of Manchester, 1989.
17. Paul John King. An expanded logical formalism for Head-driven Phrase Structure Grammar. Arbeitspapiere des SFB 340 Nr. 59, Universität Tübingen, 1994.
18. Esther König. A CUF tutorial. Technical report, Institut für Maschinelle Sprachverarbeitung, Universität Stuttgart, 1997. See [13].
19. Esther König and Uwe Reyle. A general reasoning scheme for underspecified representations. In Hans-Jürgen Ohlbach and Uwe Reyle, editors, *Logic and its Applications. Festschrift for Dov Gabbay. Part I.* Kluwer, 1997.
20. Peter Krause, Hans Kamp, and Christian (eds) Rohrer. Ein UDRS-basiertes Semantikfragment für das Deutsche. Dokumentation der Implementierung. Arbeitspapier des Sonderforschungsbereich 340, Institut für Maschinelle Sprachverarbeitung, Universität Stuttgart, October 1997.
21. Jonas Kuhn. Towards data-intensive testing of a broad-coverage LFG grammar. In *Proceedings of KONVENS 1998*, Bonn, Germany, October 1998.
22. Jonas Kuhn, Judith Eckle-Kohler, and Christian Rohrer. Lexicon acquisition with and for symbolic NLP-systems – a bootstrapping approach. In *Proceedings of the First International Conference on Language Resources and Evaluation (LREC98)*, Granada, Spain, 1998.
23. Jonas Kuhn and Christian Rohrer. Approaching ambiguity in real-life sentences – the application of an Optimality Theory-inspired constraint ranking in a large-scale LFG grammar. In *Proceedings of DGfS-CL 1997*, Heidelberg, Germany, 1997.
24. W. Detmar Meurers and Guido Minnen. A computational treatment of lexical rules in HPSG as covariation in lexical entries. *Computational Linguistics*, 23(4):543–568, 1997.
25. Walt Detmar Meurers and Guido Minnen. Off-line constraint propagation for efficient HPSG processing. In Gert Webelhuth, Jean-Pierre Koenig, and Andreas Kathol, editors, *Lexical and Constructional Aspects of Linguistic Explanation.* CSLI, Stanford, 1998.
26. Uwe Reyle. Dealing with ambiguities by underspecification: Construction, representation, and deduction. *Journal of Semantics*, 10(2):123–179, 1993.
27. Michael Schiehlen. Disambiguation of Underspecified Discourse Representation Structures under anaphoric constraints. In *International Workshop on Computational Semantics*, Tilburg, 1997.

CAVE: Ein High-End-Konzept der audiovisuellen räumlichen Mensch-Rechner-Interaktion

Heinrich Müller[1], André Hinkenjann[1], Roland Blach[2], Martin Göbel[3], Ulrich Lang[4], Stefan Müller[5]

[1] Informatik VII, Universität Dortmund, 44221 Dortmund
[2] Competence Center Virtual Reality, FhG IAO, Nobelstraße 12, 70569 Stuttgart
[3] IMK - VSMD, GMD, 53757 Sankt Augustin
[4] HLRS, Universität Stuttgart, Allmandring 30, 70550 Stuttgart
[5] FhG IGD, Rundeturmstraße 6, 64283 Darmstadt

Zusammenfassung Das CAVE-Konzept zur raumorientierten Mensch-Rechner-Interaktion, das Anfang der Neunzigerjahre vorgestellt wurde, findet trotz des damit verbundenen erheblichen technischen Aufwands zunehmend Verbreitung. Dieser Beitrag gibt eine Einführung in die CAVE-Technik und geht auf existierende Installationen und Anwendungen ein. Ferner wird eine Einordnung in andere Techniken zur audiovisuellen räumlichem Interaktion gegeben.

1 Einleitung

Ein Trend der Mensch-Rechner-Interaktion ist die Schaffung "*virtueller Umgebungen*", indem über synthetische Signale auf die Sinne des Benutzers so eingewirkt wird, daß physikalische oder abstrakte Gegebenheiten so an ihn vermittelt werden, daß er den Eindruck erhält, als wären sie real vorhanden. Durch gleichzeitige Verwendung von Seh-, Hör- und eventuell auch Tastsinn kann ein besonders hoher Grad der Einbettung des Benutzers in das Geschehen erreicht werden.

Heutige VE-Systeme (VE = Virtual Environments) bieten anwendungsunabhängige Möglichkeiten zur Synthese des visuellen, akustischen und haptischen Eindrucks, auf die konkrete Anwendungen abgebildet werden. Für die Qualität eines VE-Systems spielt neben den hardware- und softwaretechnischen Aspekten der Grad der Immersion, also des Eindrucks des Eintauchens in die virtuelle Welt, eine zentrale Rolle. Die Immersion wird durch den Einsatz von Stereotechniken für Visualisierung und Akustik zu maximieren versucht. Zum Stereosehen werden dem linken und dem rechten Auge getrennte Bilder geliefert. Geräusche werden über 3D-Klangcomputer generiert und können in Richtung und Position frei gewählt werden. Zur räumlichen Navigation und Manipulation werden spezielle Geräte eingesetzt, deren Lage und Orientierung im Raum festgestellt werden können.

Ein Konzept für ein VE-System, das trotz des damit verbundenen erheblichen technischen Aufwands zunehmend Verbreitung findet, ist die CAVE. CAVE steht für *C*ave *A*utomatic *V*irtual *E*nvironment, das englische Wort "cave" bedeutet "Höhle" oder "Grube". Das CAVE-Konzept wurde an der University of Illinois von Carolina Cruz-Neira, Dan Sandin und Tom DeFanti und deren Studenten entwickelt. Die erste CAVE wurde auf der SIGGRAPH '92 gezeigt [6]. Mittlerweile kümmert sich die amerikanische Firma Pyramid Systems Inc. um die kommerzielle Vermarktung dieses Systems, der Name "CAVE" ist ein geschütztes Warenzeichen der University of Illinois. Inzwischen wurden etliche weitere Systeme weltweit, häufig mit eigener Konzeption und Technik der Betreiber, aufgebaut. In Europa hat sich die Firma Tan in Düsseldorf der CAVE-Technik angenommen, viele existierende Installationen wurden von ihr realisiert. Interessant ist, daß gerade Deutschland die wohl höchste Dichte CAVE-artiger Systeme weltweit aufzuweisen hat. Dies ist ein Grund, hier über den Stand der Technik und deren Anwendungsfelder zu informieren, mit dem Ziel, Interesse zu wecken, die Diskussion über Möglichkeiten dieser Techniken zu stimulieren und so auch weitere Anwendungsgebiete zu erschließen.

Im folgenden Kap. 2 wird der Aufbau von CAVE-Systemen beschrieben. In Kap. 3 sind CAVE-Standorte und dort betriebene Anwendungen zusammengestellt, wobei insbesondere auf die Situation in Deutschland eingegangen wird. Diese Zusammenstellung basiert auf Daten aus dem World-Wide-Web und persönlich eingeholten Informationen[1]. Dabei wird kein Anspruch auf Vollständigkeit erhoben, da insbesondere Informationen über CAVEs in militärischen Einrichtungen unvollständig sind. In Kap. 4 werden weitere gebräuchliche Möglichkeiten für die Realisierung von VE-Systemen zusammengestellt und mit dem CAVE-Ansatz verglichen. Kapitel 5 geht auf Zukunftsperspektiven ein.

2 Aufbau und Funktionsweise von CAVEs

Kern einer CAVE ist ein würfelförmiger Raum, in dem sich der Benutzer aufhält (Abbildung 1). Die Kantenlänge des Würfels orientiert sich an der üblichen Höhe von Innenräumen, d.h. zwischen etwas mehr als 2 m und 3 m. Eine der senkrechten Wände und die Decke sind üblicherweise offen. Auf jede der anderen senkrechten transparenten Wände wird von außen, auf den Boden meist von oben, so wie im Bild gezeigt, mit je einem Stereovideoprojektor die von einem Rechner generierte Stereographik aufprojiziert (eine Alternative ist, den CAVE-Würfel im Raum aufzuhängen, um so von unten auf den Boden projizieren zu können). Dies wird so gemacht, daß sich die Bilder zu einer einheitlichen Rundumdarstellung zusammenfügen. Der Benutzer sieht sich bei der Betrachtung der Wände durch eine Stereobrille in die projizierte Graphik räumlich eingebettet. Damit er die gezeigte Umwelt und deren Gegenstände aus verschiedenen Blickrichtungen inspizieren kann, wird seine aktuelle Blickposition über Sensoren, häufig auf elektromagnetischen Feldern beruhend, erfaßt, die meist mit der Brille verbun-

[1] Dank an Randy Smith (General Motors) und Tom Coffin (NCSA)

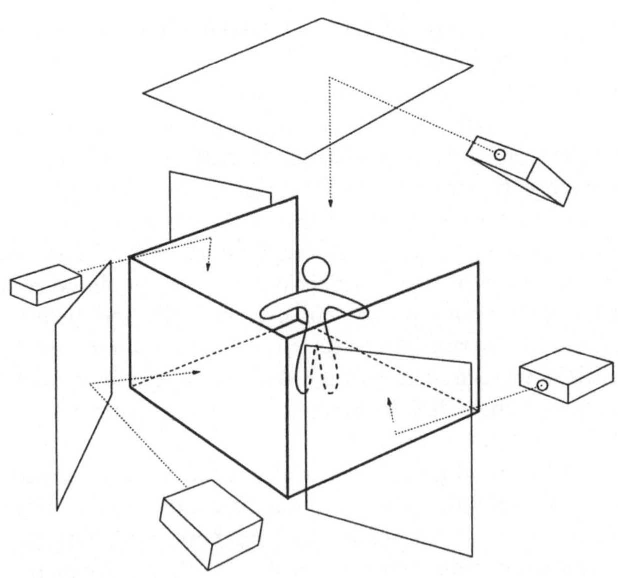

Abbildung 1. Schematische Darstellung einer CAVE

den sind. Aufgrund der empfangenen Sensorinformation baut der Rechner das projizierte Bild entsprechend der aktuellen Blickrichtung des Benutzers auf.

Zur Interaktion mit der dargestellten Graphik verfügt der Benutzer über ein Zeigeinstrument, dessen Lage im Raum der Rechner ebenfalls über Sensoren erfährt. Das Zeigeinstrument kann auch zur Auswahl von Menüpunkten verwendet werden, die in den Raum projiziert werden.

In einer CAVE wirken eine Reihe von Komponenten zusammen, die besonderen Anforderungen genügen müssen.

Der *Graphikcomputer* hat die üblicherweise realitätsnah zu wirkende Graphik on-line in Echtzeit zu generieren. Die Qualität der graphischen Darstellung kann etwa durch die Möglichkeiten von OpenGL [26] charakterisiert werden, die zur Zeit wohl wichtigste 3D-Graphikbibliothek, die in Kombination mit entsprechenden 3D-Graphikkarten inzwischen auch in der PC-Welt Einzug gehalten hat. Da die Graphik mit mindestens 15–20 Bilder pro Sekunde in Stereo auf mehreren Projektionsflächen generiert werden muß, ist eine besonders hohe Anforderung an die Graphikleistung gegeben.

Über die graphische Darstellung hinaus hat die Rechnerausstattung einer CAVE noch die Aufgabe der Tongenerierung und Erfassung der Eingabegeräte. Hinzu kommt noch die Rechenleistung, die für die Anwendungsrechnung beziehungsweise für die Kommunikation mit dem Rechnersystem, auf dem die Anwendungsberechnung abläuft, zu erbringen ist.

Aufgrund dieser Anforderungen werden in CAVEs üblicherweise die jeweils leistungsfähigsten verfügbaren Graphikrechner eingesetzt, die über die Graphikhardware hinaus meist über besonders hohe Rechenleistung, bereitgestellt durch mehrere Prozessoren, verfügen.

Für die *Projektion* werden stereofähige Videoprojektoren verwendet. Die Bilder der Projektoren werden über Umlenkspiegel (vgl. Abb. 1) auf die Projektionsflächen projiziert, um Raum zu sparen. Wichtig ist, daß die Projektoren eine möglichst konsistente Helligkeit und Kontrast sowie geringe Verzerrung garantieren. Dazu sind Projektoren hoher Lichtstärke wünschenswert, auch um eine hinreichende Sättigung und Helligkeit der Farben zu erreichen. Ein besonderes Problem stellen die Kanten des Würfels dar, an denen die verschiedenen Projektionen nahtlos aneinander passen müssen und die möglichst nicht sichtbar sein sollten. Eine Verbesserung kann durch Verweben der Projektionsflächen an den Kanten erreicht werden. Die geringe Auflösung heutiger Rastergraphik und die Interreflexion zwischen den Wänden können Artefakte beziehungsweise ein verschwimmendes Bild zur Folge haben.

Der Stereoeindruck wird üblicherweise mit *Shutterbrillen* erreicht. Dabei handelt es sich um LCD-Kristallflächen, die das linke und rechte Auge abwechselnd verdunkeln und die in eine Brillenfassung eingebaut sind. Voraussetzung für eine gute Bildqualität ist eine hinreichend große Wechselfrequenz zwischen den beiden Augenbildern. Derzeit ist eine Frequenz von 60 Hz üblich.

Zur *Verfolgung* (Tracking) des Benutzers werden in der Regel elektromagnetische Verfolgungssysteme eingesetzt, da sie im Vergleich zu optik- und ultraschallbasierten Systemen keinen Abtastschatten aufweisen. Nachteil der elektromagnetischen Verfolgungssysteme ist deren mit der Entfernung Sender/Empfänger wachsende Ungenauigkeit, die zudem zeitlich nicht konstant ist. Dies kann durch den Einsatz sogenannter „long range transmitter" kompensiert werden, die ein erheblich stärkeres Magnetfeld aufbauen als die Standard-Transmitter. Zusätzlich treten häufig Magnetfeldverzerrungen auf, die insbesondere durch metallische Gegenstände hervorgerufen werden. Bei der CAVE-Konstruktion kann dies vermieden werden, indem etwa der CAVE-Rahmen aus nichtmetallischem Material, z.B. Holz, gebaut wird. Ein Nachteil von Holz kann darin bestehen, daß es sich verzieht, mit negativen Auswirkungen gerade in den für die Projektion kritischen Kanten der Projektion, so daß es auch CAVE-Installationen mit Metallrahmen gibt. Auch ist Metall, das im umgebenden Gebäude, etwa in Stahlbetonkonstruktionen verwendet wird, nicht immer zu vermeiden. Durch Kalibrierung kann dieser Effekt soweit gemindert werden, daß er für Interaktionszwecke tolerierbar wird [14].

Gebräuchliche *Interaktionsgeräte* in CAVEs sind „free flying joystick" oder „wand". Es handelt sich dabei um Interaktionsgeräte für die Hand mit Aktionsknöpfen, die frei belegbar sind. Die Bewegung des Instruments im Raum wird in der Regel über ein Verfolgungssystem erfaßt, wie es im vorigen Abschnitt beschrieben wurde. Eine andere Möglichkeit sind *Datenhandschuhe*, um Objekte greifen oder verformen zu können. Auch fest installierte Geräte, die z.B. Teil eines virtuellen Gegenstandes sein können, sind denkbar. So kann der Benutzer beispielsweise in einem echten Cockpit eines Rennwagens sitzen, wobei auf die Projektionswände die aktuelle Rennszene projiziert wird.

Der Aufbau der Projektionseinrichtung (Leinwand, Projektoren, Spiegel) einer CAVE kann finanziell im Bereich um 400 000 DM angesetzt werden. Der Preis des Graphikrechners hängt von der Ausbaustufe ab, liegt aber heute typischerweise im Millionen DM-Bereich.

3 CAVE-Standorte und -Anwendungen

Die meisten CAVE-Standorte sind in den USA auszumachen. Dort gab es Anfang 1998 etwa 18 Installationen an 16 verschiedenen Labors. In Europa konnten derzeit mindestens 11 CAVE-Einrichtungen gezählt werden, während 6 Institutionen in Japan eine CAVE betrieben. In Deutschland werden bei der Großforschungseinrichtung GMD – Forschungszentrum Informationstechnik in St. Augustin, beim Fraunhofer-Institut für Graphische Datenverarbeitung (FhG IGD) in Darmstadt, beim Fraunhofer Institut für Arbeitswirtschaft und Organisation (FhG IAO) in Stuttgart und am Bundeshöchstleistungsrechenzentrum Universität Stuttgart (HLRS) CAVEs betrieben. Ferner gibt es mindestens drei Installationen in der Industrie.

Die vier explizit genannten Installationen in Deutschland unterscheiden sich in ihrem technischen Aufbau. Die CyberStage der GMD, die CAVEE des FhG IAO und der CUBE des HLRS haben vier Projektionsflächen: drei Wände und den Boden. Die CAVE des FhG IGD hingegen hat zusätzlich eine Decke, auf die projiziert wird. Um dennoch eine Bodenprojektion zu ermöglichen, ist der CAVE etwa 2 m angehoben. Die Projektion auf den Boden geschieht von unten. Der Boden besteht aus einer 30 mm dicken Paraglas-Platte, einem speziellen Acrylglas, das fest genug ist, um 10 Personen ohne signifikante Deformation tragen zu können und keine beobachtbare Lichtabsorption zeigt.

Die CAVE mit Deckenprojektion weitet die Möglichkeiten auf Anwendungen aus, für die ein Blick nach oben typisch ist, beispielsweise die Betrachtung von Innenräumen wie die von Kirchen. Ferner entfällt der möglicherweise störende, durch die Projektion von oben auf den Boden bewirkte Schattenwurf durch den Benutzer. Schließlich erlaubt die Verwendung der Deckenprojektion die geringere Kantenlänge von 2.40 m, im Unterschied zu den bei den anderen Systemen verwendeten 3 m. Eine große Kantenlänge kompensiert den Nachteil einer fehlenden Deckenprojektion etwas durch die erweiterte Sicht schräg nach oben, ferner können sich mehr Personen gleichzeitig in der CAVE aufhalten. Nachteilig ist allerdings, daß sich bei größerer Kantenlänge die Auflösung verschlechtert, da dieselbe Anzahl von Bildpunkten auf eine größere Fläche projiziert wird.

Die Installationen des FhG IGD, des HLRS und der GMD verwenden Holzrahmen, wohingegen am FhG IAO ein Metallrahmen verwendet wird.

Bei der CyberStage der GMD wurde besonderes Augenmerk auf die Akustik gelegt. Sie verfügt über einen akustischen Boden, mit dem Vibrationen erzeugt werden können. Ferner ist ein 8-Kanal-Surround-Sound-System installiert. Zur Tongenerierung wird die Raumakustiksoftware Spatilisateur von IRCAM eingesetzt [9], mit der lokalisierte Tonquellen im Raum generiert werden können.

Als Rechnerplattform werden in allen vier Installationen Onyx-Systeme der Firma Silicon Graphics (SGI) mit einer größeren Anzahl an Prozessoren und mehreren Graphik-Pipes eingesetzt. Hingegen wird von allen Betreibern eigene VE-Kernsoftware entwickelt: AVOCADO [24] bei der GMD, Virtual Design II beim FhG IGD [11], Lightning [23] beim FhG IAO und COVISE [5] beim HLRS. Diese Software baut typischerweise direkt auf OpenGL oder auf dem Basissystem "Performer" von SGI auf, das eine effiziente Schnittstelle zur Graphikhardware bietet. Da an allen Standorten neben CAVEs auch andere Systeme zur Realisierung virtueller Umgebungen betrieben werden, ist die Kernsoftware so allgemein angelegt, daß sie auch für andere Geräte nutzbar ist.

Alle vier Einrichtungen beschäftigen sich mit anwendungsnaher Forschung. Bezüglich der CAVE-Installationen zielt sie dahin, dieses System für Anwendungsfelder zu erschließen [15]. Das Spektrum ist praktisch identisch zum generellen Trend weltweit. Prinzipiell ist die CAVE für praktisch alle Anwendungen der virtuellen Umgebungen einsetzbar.

Als Einsatzfeld für CAVEs, das besondere Aufmerksamkeit erfährt, hat sich die *virtuelle Prototypentwicklung*, insbesondere im mechanischen, maschinenbaulichen Umfeld, erwiesen. Speziell in der Automobilindustrie werden CAVEs zur Betrachtung und Bewertung von Karosserieteilen eingesetzt. Ein solcher Anwender ist die Fa. General Motors, Detroit, USA, aber auch deutsche Automobilhersteller setzen diese Technik ein. Schwerpunkte sind hier die Evaluation des Designs und der Konstruktionsdaten. Ersteres kann eine visuelle Beurteilung nach ästhetischen Kriterien bedeuten. Techniker können Teile eines CAD-Modells daraufhin überprüfen, ob sie nahtlos zusammenpassen oder sich ein komplexes Modell aus Einzelteilen überhaupt kollisionsfrei zusammensetzen läßt.

Weitergehende Möglichkeiten, die die virtuelle Prototypentwicklung bietet, sind funktionale Analysen und Ergonomiestudien. In einem Fahrzeug-Cockpit kann beispielsweise die Bedienbarkeit und Funktionalität der Cockpit-Elemente untersucht werden, indem diese graphisch dreidimensional dargestellt werden. Der Luftstrom im Innern des Fahrzeugs, das Gegenstand des Entwurfs ist, kann simuliert und visualisiert werden, etwa mittels virtueller Partikel-Quellen an den Fingerspitzen einer Person, die sich in der CAVE aufhält.

Die technischen Anforderungen sind bei den genannten Anwendungen recht unterschiedlich. Dies kann die bloße Visualisierung vorberechneter Daten sein, aber auch die graphische on-line-Interaktion mit einem anwendungsbezogenen Simulationsprozeß. Bei sehr aufwendigen Anwendungssimulationen kann es notwendig werden, die Anwendungsrechnung auf einem anderen als dem CAVE-Rechner durchzuführen. Dazu ist die schnelle Anbindung an Höchstleistungsrechner erforderlich, die die Simulationsdaten liefern [7]. So sind etwa die CAVE des Argonne National Laboratory und der CUBE des HLRS über HIPPI und ATM an Großrechner angebunden. Die verteilte Software-Umgebung COVISE (Collaborative Visualization and Simulation Environment [5]) des HLRS ist besonders auf die Integration von Visualisierung und Simulation hin entwickelt worden.

Ein weiterer Aspekt bei der virtuellen Prototyp-Entwicklung, aber auch bei anderen Anwendungen, ist die Zusammenarbeit mehrerer Personen. Die Möglichkeit, daß gleichzeitig mehrere Personen vor Ort den Gegenstand des Interesses gemeinsam in Stereodarstellung betrachten und manipulieren können, ist ein wesentlicher Vorteil der CAVE gegenüber diversen anderen Systemen. Durch Kopplung von CAVEs über schnelle Netze können Forscher darüber hinaus an verschiedenen Standorten gemeinsam anhand der virtuellen Präsentation des Untersuchungsgegenstandes miteinander kommunizieren und interagieren. Am Electronic Visualization Lab (EVL) der University of Illinois werden solche Versuche unter dem Namen „collaborative environments“, „collaborative architectural layout“ unternommen, am Argonne National Laboratory unter dem Namen „CAVEComm“ [10]. Entsprechendes ist vor dem Hintergrund des Sonderforschungsbereichs "Rapid Prototyping" mit den beiden CAVEs in Stuttgart geplant, die über ATM miteinander verbunden sind.

Ein weiterer Schritt ist, neben dem Gegenstand der Untersuchung die entfernt wirkenden Partner virtuell im eigenen CAVE vor Ort repräsentiert zu haben. Dies kann dadurch geschehen, daß die entfernt agierenden Teilnehmer mit einer Stereokamera aufgenommen werden und die Stereoaufnahme als Textur in die CAVE eingespielt wird, so wie dies bei der GMD getan wird [22]. Die externen Teilnehmer können aber auch als modellierte Figuren, sogenannte Avatars, in Erscheinung treten, auf die ihr Verhalten abgebildet wird.

Die Ergänzung oder der Ersatz der klassischen durch die virtuelle Prototypentwicklung macht die konzeptionelle Integration von virtuellen Umgebungen in Arbeitsabläufen notwendig, einem Thema, dem sich etwa das FhG IAO besonders angenommen hat.

Die Prototypentwicklung ist nicht auf mechanische Systeme beschränkt. Ein wichtiges Feld ist auch die *Architektur*. Die CAVE ermöglicht das Durchschreiten modellierter virtueller Gebäude, Städte und Landschaften mit einer besonders starken Wahrnehmung des Raums in Relation zum eigenen Körper, das das Gefühl der Anwesenheit vermittelt. Als besonders komplexes Beispiel ist hier das Modell des neuen Terminals 1 des Frankfurter Flughafens vom FhG IGD zu nennen. Der realitätsnahe Eindruck wird dabei noch durch die Radiosity-Darstellung verstärkt, die die diffuse Interreflexion von Licht im Raum bei der Darstellung berücksichtigt.

Der *Entwurf von Molekülen* (molecular modeling) kann als weiteres verbreitetes Beispiel für virtuelle Prototypentwicklung verstanden werden [8, 1]. Beispiele hierfür sind auf internationaler Ebene das Argonne National Laboratory, die Virginia Tech University und die Iowa State University.

In der *Medizin* gibt es ein weites Spektrum von Anwendungen, das Diagnose, Therapie und Training umfaßt und das in verschiedener Weise von den vier genannten deutschen Forschungseinrichtungen bearbeitet wird. Interessant ist, daß virtuelle Umgebungen auch zu Zwecken der Erforschung menschlicher Verhaltensweisen und zur Therapie von Verhaltenskrankheiten beitragen können [4].

Ein völlig anderes Feld ist *Unterhaltung und Bildung*, das "Edutainment". Hier scheinen die großen Firmen die Möglichkeiten des Einsatzes von CAVEs zu testen. Die Firma Sega, Japan, soll laut NCSA eine CAVE bestellt haben. Als ein besonderes Projekt ist hier das virtuelle Ozeaneum zu nennen, das am FhG IGD entwickelt wurde. Es basiert auf einer Echtzeitsimulation der Form und des Verhaltens von Fischen, etwa die Bildung von Schwärmen und das Angriffsverhalten betreffend. Der Betrachter wird von einem virtuellen Schauspieler durch das Szenario geführt und bekommt die wichtigsten Fakten des Ozeans erklärt. Das virtuelle Ozeaneum wird auf der EXPO'98 in Portugal auf einer Projektionsleinwand gezeigt, um eine größere Besucherzahl gleichzeitig bedienen zu können.

In der Kunst existieren Installationen beim Ars Electronica Center in Linz, Österreich, sowie bei der japanischen NTT (Nippon Telegraph and Telephone Corp.), Tokyo [16].

Neben der Realisierung von Anwendungsideen dienen CAVE-Installationen auch der Erforschung von grundsätzlichen Prinzipien. Dies betrifft die technische Optimierung, um Unzulänglichkeiten, wie sie in Kap. 2 genannt wurden, zu reduzieren. Gegenstand des Interesses sind auch psychologische und ergonomische Fragestellungen. Ein Beispiel sind Untersuchungen zur Größenschätzung von Objekten, in denen am FhG IAO verschiedene virtuelle Repräsentationen und die Realität miteinander verglichen wurden. Eine andere Aufgabe ist das Auffinden geeigneter visueller Repräsentationen für konkrete und abstrakte Prozesse sowie dazu passende Interaktionsmetaphern.

4 Alternativen

CAVEs stellen eine aufwendige High-End-Lösung für die Visualisierung und Manipulation virtueller Welten dar. Nicht immer ist derartig hoher Aufwand zwingend notwendig, gerechtfertigt oder machbar.

Als kostengünstige Alternative bieten sich herkömmliche Monitore zur graphischen Darstellung und Tastatur und Maus zur Eingabe und Interaktion an. Daß dies durchaus auch heute noch im weiteren Sinn der VE zugeordnet werden kann, wird am Beispiel des Internet mit VRML (Virtual Reality Modeling Language) ersichtlich [18].

Der nächste Schritt in Richtung höherer Immersion ist die Nutzung von 3D-Brillen, die den Augen getrennte Bilder liefern, so daß ein Tiefeneindruck entsteht. Bekannt sind solche Arbeitsplätze etwa aus dem Moleküldesign.

Eine weitere Stufe sind die sogenannten *helmet mounted displays* (HMD). Dies sind Datensichtgeräte, die in einen Helm integriert auf dem Kopf getragen werden. Bei den HMDs wird das Bild direkt über eine spezielle Optik, deren Träger der Helm ist, an die beiden Augen herangeführt, etwa indem vor jedem Auge ein kleiner Monitor angebracht ist. Das erste HMD wurde bereits 1965 von Evans&Sutherland vorgestellt (vgl. [3]).

HMDs werden üblicherweise in einem VE-Szenario eingesetzt, das freie Bewegung des Benutzers zuläßt. Die Lage des Helms wird mit Hilfe des Tracking-Systems verfolgt, so daß der Bildaufbau wie bei der CAVE abhängig vom aktuellen Blick des Benutzers stattfindet. Damit kann der Benutzer sich frei in dem gezeigten virtuellen Raum bewegen. Auch die Eingabe erfolgt wie bei der CAVE über verfolgte 3D-Eingabegeräte. Die erzielte Wirkung ist damit ähnlich wie bei der CAVE. Der wesentliche Nachteil ist der mangelnde Tragekomfort des Helms und die enge Verknüpfung des Benutzers mit dem Display, das einen schnellen Ausstieg erschwert. Ferner muß jeder teilnehmende Benutzer einen eigenen Helm haben, während sich in der CAVE mehrere Benutzer gleichzeitig aufhalten können, wenn auch nur einer mit der korrekten Projektion, was sich jedoch als nicht zu großer Nachteil erweist. Diese Probleme haben den Nutzungswillen von HMDs reduziert.

Eine Alternative zu HMDs ist der *BOOM*. "BOOM" steht für *B*inocular *O*mni-*O*rientation *M*onitor. Er wird von der amerikanischen Firma Fakespace produziert und bietet dem Benutzer eine Stereosicht in die virtuelle Welt. Zwei Bildröhren sind dabei in einem Gehäuse untergebracht, das, mit Gegengewichten ausbalanciert, an einem Gestänge hängt. Direkt an dem Gehäuse befinden sich Tasten für Interaktionsfunktionen. Da das Tracking über die Mechanik geschieht, sind die Daten frei von Störeinflüssen, wie beispielsweise fremde Magnetfelder. Ein Nachteil des Booms ist, daß die freie Bewegung im Raum eingeschränkt ist.

Neben der CAVE gibt es andere projektionsbasierte Umgebungen, die weniger aufwendig sind und für manche Anwendungen ausreichend sind. Zu nennen sind die ***Responsive Workbench*** [21], die ***Infinity Wall*** und der ***ImmersaDesk*** [12]. Nur die CAVE bietet jedoch eine räumliche Rundumvisualisierung und damit den wohl höchsten Immersionsgrad der genannten Umgebungen.

Insgesamt stellt die CAVE die wohl zur Zeit umfassendste menschgerechte und intuitive Realisierung für die Aufgabe der räumlichen Mensch-Rechner-Interaktion dar.

5 Ausblick

VE-Systeme werden sich wie in der Vergangenheit mit mindestens dem gleichen Tempo weiterentwickeln wie der allgemeine Fortschritt in Punkto Rechnerleistung und -kapazität.

Auf dem Feld der Darstellungsgeräte sind durch direkt auf die Netzhaut projizierende Laserprojektoren bei den HMDs deutliche Verbesserungen in Auflösung und Schärfe zu erwarten [20]. In der Videoprojektionstechnik werden die heute noch verwendeten Röhrenprojektoren in ihrer Leistung und vor allem im Preis zunehmend von kleinen, sogar tragbaren Videoprojektoren, etwa auf LCD-Basis, eingeholt. Auch die in Deutschland entwickelten und ausgezeichneten Laserprojektoren können die herkömmlichen Projektionen verbessern. Für einen Überblick über die Entwicklung in der Displaytechnik siehe [12].

Eine Ideallösung hinsichtlich der Darstellung wäre die rechnergenerierte dreidimensionale Laserholographie [13]. Trotz der schon lange auf diesem Gebiet stattfindenden Forschung gibt es noch eine Vielzahl von zu lösenden Problemen, die dieses Medium in nächster Zeit nicht als leistungsmäßig adäquat zu den existierenden Techniken erwarten läßt.

Ein Defizit der heute verbreiteten VE-Systeme gegenüber der realen Welt ist, daß die Gegenstände keine Materie haben, sie also beliebig durchdringbar sind. Diesem Defizit wird mit den sogenannten haptischen Displays Rechnung getragen. Dabei handelt es sich um Geräte, die, vom Rechner gesteuert, dem Benutzer physischen Widerstand entgegensetzen können. Trotz vieler kreativer Schöpfungen, die für beschränkte Anwendungsbereiche durchaus geeignet sind, steht eine allgemeine, breit anwendbare Lösung noch aus. Gewisse Verbreitung hat zum einen das PHANToM der Firma SensAble Technologies gefunden [25, 27], das eine räumlich begrenzte Kraftrückkopplung über Motoren zuläßt. Zum andern gibt es die sogenannten *shape forming devices*, welche die Oberflächen der virtuellen Gegenstände mit Hilfe von Stangenmatrizen oder Flüssigkeiten veränderlicher Viskosität simulieren [17]. Einen guten Überblick über haptische Displays gibt [28].

Wünschenswert wäre die Entkabelung der Benutzer durch den Einsatz von drahtloser Übertragung der Verfolgungsdaten oder der komplette Verzicht auf aktive Verfolgungshardware, etwa durch Übergang zu videobasiertem Tracking. Forschung im Bereich Gestenerkennung macht einen Verzicht auf flying joysticks o.ä. denkbar, vgl. etwa [19]. Für einfachere Befehle ist die Spracheingabe nutzbar (siehe z.B. [2] für eine medizinische Anwendung). Sie ist idealerweise mit anderen Eingabemöglichkeiten gekoppelt.

Graphikleistungen, die vor ein paar Jahren nur auf Graphikhöchstleistungsrechnern anzutreffen waren, sind nun auf PCs mit entsprechenden 3D-Karten verfügbar. Der technische Fortschritt läßt spezialisierte CAVEs, die auf PCs basieren, in nicht allzu ferner Zukunft als machbar erscheinen. Es ist zu erwarten daß dadurch die heute noch aufwendige Technologie von VE-Systemen und insbesondere die CAVE-Technologie in Zukunft weitere Verbreitung finden wird.

Literatur

1. Akkiraju, N., Edelsbrunner, H., Ping, F., and Jiang, Q.: Viewing geometric protein structures from inside a CAVE; IEEE Computer Graphics and Applications, 16(4), pp 58-61, 1996
2. Billinghurst, M., Savage, J., Oppenheimer, P., Edmond, C.: The Expert Surgical Assistant: An Intelligent Virtual Environment With Multimodal Input; Medicine Meets Virtual Reality Iv, 1996.
3. Burdea, G., Philippe C.I.: Virtual Reality Technology, 1994, NY, J. Wiley & Sons.
4. CACM: Special Issue on VR and Health Care, CACM 1997(8).
5. COVISE: http://www.hlrs.de/structure/organisation/vis/covise/ und http://www.hlrs.de/people/rantzau/ipt98_rantzau.pdf
6. Cruz-Neira, C., Sandin, D.J., DeFanti, T.A., Kenyon, R.V., and Hart, J.C.: The CAVE: Audio Visual Experience Automatic Virtual Environment, Communications of the ACM, Vol. 35, No. 6, pp 67–72, June 1992.
7. Cruz-Neira, C: Steering a High Performance Computing Application from a Virtual Environment, in Presence: Teleoperations and Virtual Environments, Vol. 4, No. 2, MIT Press, pp 121-129, Spring 1995.
8. Cruz-Neira, C., Langley, R., and Bash, P. A.: VIBE: a Virtual Biomolecular Environment for interactive molecular modeling; Computers & Chemistry, 20(4), pp 469-477, 1996

9. Dechelle, F., DeCecco, M.: The IRCAM Real-Time Platform and Applications; Proceeding of the 1995 Interbational Computer Music Conference, International Computer Music Association, San Francisco, 1995
10. Disz, T.L., Papka, M.E., Pellegrino, M., and Stevens, R.: Sharing Visualization Experience among Remote Virtual Environments; in Proc. of the International Workshop on High Performance Computing for Computer Graphics and Visualization, Swansea, United Kingdom, Juli 1995.
11. Fraunhofer-Institut für Graphische Datenverarbeitung, Abteilung Visualisierung und Virtuelle Realität: www.igd.fhg.de/www/igd-a4
12. FOCUS: Next Generation Visual Displays, Computer Graphics 31(2), May 1997
13. Lucente, M.: Interactive Three-dimensional Holographic Displays: Seeing the Future in Depth, Computer Graphics 31, p. 63, May 1997
14. Ghazisaedy, M., Adamczyk, D., Sandin, D. J., Kenyon, R. V., and DeFanti, T. A.: Ultrasonic calibration of a magnetic tracker in a virtual reality space; In Proceedings of the Virtual Reality Annual International Symposium '95 (pp. 179-188). Los Alamitos, CA, USA: IEEE Comput. Soc. Press, 1995
15. Encarnacao, J., Knöpfle, Chr., Müller, S., Unbescheiden, M.: Experiments and Applications with 3-, 4- and 5-sided CAVEs, Presentation at Digital Convergence - The Future of the WWW, 20-23. April 1998
16. Hegedüs, A., Shaw, J., Lintermann, B., Stuck, L.: conFIGURING the CAVE; permanent installation at ICC, Japan; URL: http://www.ntticc.or.jp/permanent/cave/cave_e.html
17. Hirota, K., Hirose, M.: Providing Force Feedback in Virtual Environments; IEEE Computer Graphics and Appl., 15(5), pp. 22-30, 1995
18. Information technology – Computer graphics and image processing – The Virtual Reality Modeling Language (VRML) – Part 1: Functional specification and UTF-8 encoding. URL: http://www.vrml.org/Specifications/VRML97/
19. Kohler, M., Schröter, S.: Handgestenerkennung durch Computersehen; Informatik '98, in diesem Band
20. Kollin, J.: A Retinal Display for Virtual-Environment Applications; In Proceedings of the Society for Information Display, 1993 International Symposium, Digest of Technical Papers, Vol. XXIV. (p. 827). Playa del Rey, CA: Soc. for Inf. Display
21. Krüger, W., Fröhlich, B: The Responsive Workbench; Computer Graphics and Applications 14(3), pp. 12–15, 1994
22. Lalioti, V., Garcia, Ch., Hasenbrink, F.: Meet.Me@Cyberstage: towards Immersive Telepresence; "Virtual Environments: Conference and 4th Eurographics Workshop, Eurographics Workshops Proceedings Series, ISSN 1024-0861, 1998
23. Landauer, J., Blach, R., Bues, M., Roesch, A., Simon, A.: Toward Next Generation Virtual Reality Systems, In: Proc. IEEE International Conference on Multimedia Computing and Systems, Ottawa, 1997
24. Avocado 1997, URL: http://http://viswiz.gmd.de/ hase/Avocado.html
25. Massie, T. H., J. K. Salisbury: The PHANToM Haptic Interface: A Device for Probing Virtual Objects; International Mechanical Engineering Exposition and Congress. Chicago (pp. 295-302) ASME (1994)
26. OpenGL Architecture Review Board: OpenGL Reference Manual: The Official Reference Document for OpenGL, Release 1, Addison-Wesley, Reading, Massachusetts, 1992.
27. Sensable Technologies, URL: http://www.sensable.com
28. Ziegler, R.: Haptic Displays – How can we feel Virtual Environments?; in Proceedings: Eurographics'96, France, 1996

Minisymposium: Neue Entwicklungen in der Informatikausbildung

Stefan Conrad Gunter Saake Ingo Schmitt

Universität Magdeburg, Fakultät für Informatik,
Institut für Technische und Betriebliche Informationssysteme,
Postfach 4120, D-39016 Magdeburg, Germany
symp98@iti.cs.uni-magdeburg.de

Noch vor wenigen Jahren schienen sich Studienformen und -inhalte in Informatikstudiengängen langfristig stabilisiert zu haben. Die Rahmenprüfungsordnung und die Aktivitäten des Fakultätentages garantieren seit längerem die Vergleichbarkeit und gegenseitige Anerkennung der Studienleistungen. Die Wirtschaftsinformatik wurde in der Regel unabhängig von den bestehenden Informatikstudiengängen aufgebaut und etabliert — mit erstaunlich geringer Rückwirkung auf die „klassische" Informatik. Auch die deutsche Wiedervereinigung brachte betreffend Studiengängen nur kleinere Variationen, so Studiengänge mit Praxissemester und Fernstudiengänge mit Präsenzveranstaltungen, die vom Inhalt her jedoch an die Rahmenprüfungsordnung angelehnt sind.

In den letzten Jahren zeichnen sich nun jedoch Veränderungen ab, die diese wohlgeordnete Landschaft verändern könnten:

- Der dramatische Rückgang der Studienanfänger in den technischen Disziplinen einschließlich der Informatik motivierte die Einführung neuer Studiengänge und Studienformen, um Studienanfänger zu gewinnen. Es hat sozusagen der Wettbewerb um die potentiellen Studierenden begonnen. Anwendungsbezogene Studiengänge sollen gerade diejenigen erreichen, die unter anderem aufgrund der verbreiteten Technikphobie vom 'reinen' Informatikstudium abgeschreckt werden könnten.
  An diesem Wettbewerb beteiligen sich nicht nur die Informatik-Fachbereiche — auch Ingenieurfakultäten versuchen mit Studiengängen wie Informationstechnik oder Technische Informatik am Reservoir der potentiellen Informatikstudenten zu partizipieren.
- Die neuen Medien und die globale Vernetzung haben zu neuen Berufsfeldern geführt, die bisher von der reinen Informatik nicht abgedeckt werden. Studiengänge wie Computervisualistik, Informationswirtschaft, Medieninformatik und Medientechnik versuchen auf diese neuen Anforderungen zu reagieren.
- Nicht erst durch die Anstrengungen für ein neues Hochschulrahmengesetz sind internationale Abschlüsse und internationale Vergleichbarkeit von Studienleistungen ein wichtiges Thema der aktuellen Hochschullandschaft. Stichworte wie Master-Studiengänge, Bachelor-Abschlüsse, Kreditpunktsysteme und deren Einführung an Fachhochschulen und Universitäten beschäftigen alle Hochschultypen.

Das Symposium „Neue Entwicklungen in der Informatikausbildung" auf der Informatik'98 beabsichtigt, Beiträge zu den genannten Themenkreisen zu sammeln und die Diskussion innerhalb der Gesellschaft für Informatik zu aktivieren. Welche der neuen Studiengänge rechnen wir unserer Fachgesellschaft zu? Sind es nur Modeerscheinungen, die man aussitzen kann, oder wird es Rückwirkungen auf das Profil der Informatik geben? Diese und andere Fragen werden in drei Fachsitzungen und einer Podiumsdiskussion behandelt.

Mit der Einrichtung dieses Symposiums im Rahmen der GI-Jahrestagung Informatik'98 trägt das Programmkomitee diesen aktuellen Entwicklungen und Diskussionen hinsichtlich der Ausbildung von Informatikerinnen und Informatikern Rechnung. Zu den verschiedenen Themen wurden Vortragende gewonnen, die an ihren jeweiligen Hochschulen mit der Umsetzung neuer Entwicklungen befaßt sind oder durch ihre Funktion in speziellen Gremium bzw. Verbänden einen fundierten Überblick über die aktuellen Entwicklungen haben.

Studiengänge mit Multimedia-Bezug

Im Rahmen dieses Vortragsschwerpunktes werden verschiedene Studiengänge an Hochschulen vorgestellt, in denen in unterschiedlicher Form und Ausprägung Multimedia als zentrales Element verstanden wird. Bei diesen Studiengängen handelt es sich einerseits um Abwandlungen des klassischen Informatikstudiums und andererseits auch um konsequente Neukonzeptionen. In den Vorträgen werden im einzelnen die folgenden Themen behandelt:

- Medieninformatik an Hochschulen (ein Überblick)
- Der Studiengang Computervisualistik an der Universität Magdeburg als Beitrag zur Diskussion universitärer Ausbildung im Bereich Multimedia (ist als regulärer, begutachteter und angenommener Beitrag der Informatik'98 in diesem Band enthalten)
- Medienwissenschaften: Ein interdisziplinärer Studiengang an der TU Braunschweig mit Informatik
- Erfahrungen der FH Furtwangen mit dem Studiengang Medieninformatik

Durch diese Vorträge wird das Spektrum der unterschiedlichen Umsetzungsformen aufgezeigt, das an den Hochschulen zu finden ist.

Podiumsdiskussion: Quo vadis — Informatikstudium

Unter der Moderation von R. Gunzenhäuser diskutieren Vertreter der Hochschulen und der Industrie über die drei Themenschwerpunkte des Symposiums:

- Neue Medien
- Anforderungen der Industrie an das Informatikstudium
- Internationalisierung der Studiengänge

Im Rahmen der Podiumsdiskussion sollen kontroverse Fragen zu diesen Themenschwerpunkten aufgeworfen werden, zu denen sich die Diskussionsteilnehmer dann positionieren.

Neue Studienabschlüsse

Eines der gegenwärtig besonders kontrovers diskutierten Themen ist die Einrichtung neuer Studienabschlüsse. Ausgangspunkt ist die Frage, ob das bisherige Studiensystem, das auf den Diplomgrad als berufsqualifizierenden Abschluß ausgerichtet ist, den Anforderungen insbesondere in Hinblick auf die internationale Vergleichbarkeit und die Flexibilisierung der Abschlüsse zur Ermöglichung eines früheren berufsqualifizierenden Abschlusses gerecht werden kann. Eine Variante ist die Ergänzung des bisherigen Angebots durch zusätzliche, international ausgerichtete Masters-Programme. Eine andere Qualität zeigt sich in der Einführung von Bachelor- und Master-Abschlüssen parallel zu dem bisherigen Diplomgrad. Eine darüber hinausgehende Variante ist die völlige Abschaffung des gegenwärtigen Diplomabschlusses bei Einführung von Bachelor- und Master-Graden. In den verschiedenen Varianten, die in vielen Hochschulen diskutiert werden, zeigt sich auch eine uneinheitliche Bewertung hinsichtlich der Wertigkeit von Diplom und Master im direkten Vergleich. Neben den neuen Abschlüssen ist auch die Einführung von Kreditpunktsystemen ein häufig genanntes Mittel, um eine auch internationale Kompatibilität und damit Anrechenbarkeit von Studienleistungen zu garantieren.

In den Vorträge zu diesem Themenschwerpunkt werden verschiedene Modelle der Einführung neuer Studienabschlüsse vorgestellt. Der abschließende Vortrag zeigt die aktuelle Bewertung dieser Thematik aus der Sicht des Fakultätentags auf:

- Informatik in Paderborn: Ein dreistufiger Diplomstudiengang mit international kompatiblen Abschlüssen
- Studienschwerpunkt Technische Informatik - Ein neues Studienangebot an der Universität Gesamthochschule Kassel
- Computational Logic - Ein internationales Masters-Programm an der TU Dresden
- Kreditpunktsysteme und neue Abschlüsse aus der Sicht des Fakultätentags Informatik

Natürlich kann im Rahmen dieser Veranstaltung nur eine Auswahl aktueller Bestrebungen zur Einführung neuer Abschlüsse an den Hochschulen aufgezeigt werden. Aufgrund der hohen Dynamik dieses Themas ist zu erwarten, daß in der nächsten Zeit weitere Hochschulen ähnliche oder auch ganz andere Modelle vorlegen werden, so daß eine Vollständigkeit anstrebende Darstellung in diesem Rahmen weder möglich noch gegenwärtig sinnvoll erscheint. So sind die in den Vorträgen dargestellten Varianten als exemplarisch zu verstehen.

Weitere Entwicklungen

Neben den zuvor schon beschriebenen teilweise kontrovers diskutierten Themenbereichen wie etwa der Einführung neuer Studienabschlüsse gibt es noch eine Vielzahl weiterer relevanter aktueller Entwicklungen. So wird beispielsweise mit dem Modellstudiengang Softwaretechnik eine moderne inhaltliche Fokussierung als Alternative zum bisherigen Informatikstudiengang angeboten. Auch Fragestellungen der kooperierenden Ausbildung über Staatsgrenzen hinweg werden zukünftig eine immer größere Rolle spielen. Eine neue Variante, deren Umsetzung und Erfolg von vielen in der nächsten Zeit aufmerksam beobachtet werden dürfte, ist die Einrichtung neuer, in der Regel privat getragener Universitäten, die die Ausbildung nach dem angelsächsischen System durchführen, um insbesondere für ausländische Studenten attraktiv zu sein. Vorträge werden im einzelnen zu den folgenden Themen gehalten:

- Softwaretechnik in Stuttgart - Ein konstruktiver Informatik-Studiengang
- Konzepte und Erfahrungen zur länderübergreifenden Zusammenarbeit in der Informatikausbildung
- Das Konzept einer internationalen Universität in Deutschland

Zu diesem Themenschwerpunkt lassen sich problemlos noch viele weitere konkrete Projekte (besondere Studiengänge, kooperative Ausbildung mehrere Hochschulen, etc) angeben, so daß hier nur exemplarisch über solche Konzepte und die Erfahrungen mit deren Umsetzung berichtet werden kann.

Weitere Informationen

Weitere Informationen zu diesem Symposium sind über die URL der GI-Jahrestagung Informatik'98 (http://fuzzy.cs.uni-magdeburg.de/gi98) bzw. direkt über die URL http://wwwiti.cs.uni-magdeburg.de/GI98-Symp.html verfügbar. Insbesondere das endgültige Programm mit der Angabe aller Vortragenden und Teilnehmer an der Podiumsdiskussion wird dort veröffentlicht, da zum Zeitpunkt der Anfertigung dieses Beitrages noch nicht alle Vortragenden namentlich feststanden.

Zu diesem Symposium wird ein einfacher Tagungsband als technischer Bericht herausgegeben. In diesem Band sind zu (fast) allen Vorträgen ausführliche Beiträge enthalten. Nähere Informationen dazu sind auch über die zuvor angegebene Web-Seite erhältlich.

Computervisualistik: Ein Beitrag zur Diskussion universitärer Ausbildung im Bereich Multimedia

Thomas Strothotte, Jörg R.J. Schirra

ISG, FIN, Otto-von-Guericke-Universität Magdeburg
{tstr,joerg}@isg.cs.uni-magdeburg.de

Abstract. Vorgestellt werden Motivation und Struktur des Diplomstudiengangs Computervisualistik, der seit 1996 an der Universität Magdeburg angeboten wird. Die Konzeption ist dreigliedrig und enthält neben der informatischen Methodik die Säulen "Reflexion" und "Anwendung". Die Aufteilung ist motiviert von einer modernen Auffassung der Ingenieurausbildung, die weniger auf einen Experten für etwas, denn einen Experten für jemanden abzielt und entsprechend kommunikative und soziale Kompetenzen verstärkt fördert. Thematisch umfaßt die Computervisualistik die Vielzahl von Möglichkeiten, Bilder digital zu erzeugen oder zu verarbeiten.

1 Motivationen

Zu den seit Anfang der 70'er Jahre an vielen Hochschulen etablierten Diplomstudiengängen zur „(Kern-) Informatik" traten im Laufe der Zeit immer mehr Studiengänge in sogenannten „Bindestrich-Informatiken", wie z.B. Medieninformatik, aber auch Medizinische Informatik oder Wirtschaftsinformatik. Es ist bei solchen Ausbildungsrichtungen keine leichte Aufgabe, die beiden Konstituenten – informatischer und nicht-informatischer Teil – thematisch und methodologisch aufeinander abzustimmen. Computervisualistik an der Otto-von-Guericke-Universität Magdeburg, ein Studiengang, der ebenfalls informatische und nicht-informatische Anteile umfaßt, versucht hier eine besonders dichte Verzahnung, eine einheitliche Linie der curricularen Struktur, wie sie in Bindestrich-Informatiken nicht immer zu finden ist: Es gibt einerseits ein zentrales Thema, der Umgang/das Kommunizieren mit Bildern, dem sich die verschiedenen Gebiete auf je eigene Weise nähern. Die unterschiedlichen Methoden unter diesem gemeinsamen Bezugspunkt zu betrachten führt andererseits zu einem methodologischen Synergieeffekt: Die Betrachtungsweisen, die etwa Geisteswissenschaftler oder Designer zu den diversen Formen der Bildverwendung entwickelt haben, flankieren die für den Studiengang zentralen informatischen Methoden in mehr als einer Hinsicht. Zunächst eröffnen sie eine umfassendere und damit präzisere Sicht auf das zentrale Thema; sie erlauben aber auch, die informatischen Methoden selbst unter allgemeineren Gesichtspunkten zu betrachten und die eigene Tätigkeit aus unterschiedlicher Perspektive zu reflektieren. Schließlich erleichtern die damit verbundenen kommunikativen Fertigkeiten den Umgang mit fachfremden Klienten. Mit dieser starken Verzahnung ihrer informatischen und nicht-informatischen Anteile soll Computervisualistik als ein Vorschlag verstanden werden, der die Diskussion über innovative Ideen in der Informatikausbildung anregt.

a Das neue Bild vom Ingenieur

> If the computer scientist is a toolsmith [...] we must partner with those who will use our tools, those whose intelligence we hope to amplify. [Brooks 96, S. 64]

Ingenieure aller Fachrichtungen sind sich in den letzten Jahren verstärkt einer bestimmten gesellschaftlichen Forderung bewußt geworden: Es genügt nicht, einfach gemäß den eigenen, d.h. fach-internen Kriterien gute Lösungen für entsprechende ingenieur-wissenschaftliche Probleme vorzulegen. Darüber hinaus ist zu berücksichtigen, daß Ingenieure sich vor allem mit Problemen beschäftigen, die von fachfremden Klienten aufgeworfen werden, in deren Sprache abgefaßt sind, von deren Rahmenbedingungen abhängen, und die dem Ingenieur zur Lösung im Sinne einer Dienstleistung übergeben werden. Die Kriterien für die Güte einer Lösung werden also auch von fach-externen Faktoren wesentlich abhängen. Um diese in die eigene Arbeit zu integrieren, bedarf der Ingenieur vor allem einer gut entwickelten *sozialen Kompetenz*. Für die *Gesellschaft für Informatik* hat deren Präsident W. Stucky soziale Kompetenz als grundlegend auch für eine moderne Informatikausbildung in seinem Vorwort zur *Informatik-Spektrum* 20:1-2 (S. 1f., 97) bezeichnet. International ist vor allem D. Denning als Befürworter einer entsprechenden Revision der Ingenieursausbildung hervorgetreten: Er charakterisiert unter dem aufschlußreichen Titel „*Educating a New Engineer*“ [Denning 92] das traditionelle Selbstverständnis der Ingenieure als Experten vor allem *für etwas*, für ein bestimmtes Fachgebiet, wie etwa Maschinenbau, Elektrotechnik oder Informationsverarbeitung; als jemand, der Prinzipien für die Konstruktion gewisser Artefakte – Maschinen, Programme etc. – sucht. Das neue Bild vom Ingenieurberuf verstehe Ingenieure hingegen vor allem als Experten *für jemanden*: Sie sollen die Bedürfnisse eines in der Regel fachfremden Klienten bedienen, in dessen Kontext sich Fragestellungen ergeben, die in das Fachgebiet des Ingenieurs fallen. Beispielsweise mag ein Werkstoffwissenschaftler im Rahmen seiner Tätigkeit mit Problemen konfrontiert sein, bei denen Information aufgenommen, automatisch verarbeitet oder über elektronische Medien verbreitet und dargestellt werden soll. Denning leitet daraus eine Empfehlung ab für eine konzeptuelle Neugestaltung der Ingenieurausbildung – weg von einer Auffassung der „*l'art pour l'art*“-Expertise hin zu einer breit angelegten kommunikativen Kompetenz:

> *[A] curriculum capable of preparing students for the shifting world must incorporate new elements emphasizing design, demonstrated proficiency, effective interaction with others, and greater sensitivity toward the historical and cultural spaces in which we all live and work.* [Denning 92, S. 83]

b Der Bedarf an Bildexperten

Ein in diesem Zusammenhang zur Zeit besonders aufschlußreiches Gebiet von Ingenieursexpertise ist durch den computerisierten Umgang mit Bildmaterial gegeben: Das Medium „Bild“ wird in unserer Gesellschaft zunehmend als Darstellungs-, wie auch als Argumentations- oder Überzeugungsmittel benutzt. Besonders in den letzten Jahren hat der technische Fortschritt — und zwar nicht nur unter dem Schlagwort

„Multimedia" — geradezu eine Explosion der Verfügbarkeit von bildlich dargestelltem Datenmaterial bewirkt. Erinnert sei hier nur beispielsweise an die riesige Menge von Bilddaten, die die erdnahe Fernerkundung permanent liefert. Daß diese Daten in der Regel in digitaler Form vorliegen, zieht allerdings auch ihre (fast) unbegrenzte Manipulierbarkeit nach sich.

Die Konstruktion künstlicher visueller Darstellungen bis hin zu sogenannten „virtuellen Realitäten" könnte gesellschaftlich auf lange Sicht sogar noch weitreichendere Folgen haben, als die bildliche Präsentation von Wirklichkeit. Prominentestes Beispiel für den Einsatz digitaler Bilderzeugung in der Unterhaltungsindustrie sind die Filme „Jurassic Park" und „Toy Story". Die Verwendung von bildgebenden Verfahren und von maschinell erzeugten Bildern nimmt aber auch in der Medizin eine zunehmend wichtige Position ein, sowohl in der bildgestützten Diagnostik oder der Operationsplanung, wie in der Lehre. Die Fülle des Bildmaterials droht hier ebenfalls zum Problem zu werden. Ferner ist die Authentizität der erzeugten Bilder in diesem Bereich offensichtlich von besonderer Brisanz: Fehler der Visualisierung betreffen unmittelbar Leben und Gesundheit von Menschen.

Die wachsende Menge der dieser Bilderflut zugrunde liegenden Verfahren ergeben mittlerweile einen eigenen Teilbereich von Ingenieursexpertise, die von den verschiedensten Anwendungsgebieten — Medizin, Werkstoffwissenschaft, Geo- und Astrophysik, Architektur, Design, Film und Fernsehen, den Printmedien, etc. — in Anspruch genommen werden muß. Allerdings kann kaum erwartet werden, daß jede Ärztin oder jeder Geophysiker diese Expertise selbst erwirbt: Ein Architekt mag zwar die photorealistisch erzeugte interaktive Ansicht eines geplanten Bauwerks zur Visualisierung seines Entwurfs für seine Auftraggeber benötigen. Aber er dürfte in der Regel kaum selbst über entsprechende Fertigkeiten verfügen (und darüber in einer hochgradig arbeitsteiligen Gesellschaft, wie der unsrigen, auch gar nicht verfügen müssen). Gebraucht wird eine „Bild-Ingenieurin" oder ein „Bild-Ingenieur", d.h. jemand, der den Anwendern gezielt eine solche Expertise im neuen Bereich *Computervisualistik* zur Verfügung stellt und zugleich speziell hin zur dabei unabdingbaren sozialen Kompetenz ausgebildet wurde.

Ein Beispiel für das Zusammenwirken von digitaler Bilderflut und neuem Verständnis des Ingenieurberufs bildet der Diplomstudiengang Computervisualistik, wie er seit Herbst 1996 an der Fakultät für Informatik der Otto-von-Guericke-Universität Magdeburg angeboten wird. Er führt in 10 Semestern zum Abschluß „Diplomingenieurin" bzw. „Diplomingenieur" und kreist thematisch um all die Verfahren zum Erzeugen, Bearbeiten, Archivieren oder Übertragen von Bildmaterial mit Hilfe des Computers.

Im folgenden wird zunächst auf das zugrunde liegende pädagogische Konzept eingegangen. Darauf aufbauend werden Inhalte und Anliegen der drei Säulen des Studiengangs etwas ausführlicher vorgestellt (Abschn. 2). Weitere Details der inhaltlichen und formalen Ausgestaltung in der Prüfungsordnung sowie ein Vergleich mit dem Diplomstudiengang Informatik an der Magdeburger Universität schließen sich an (Abschn. 3). Nach einer kurzen Präsentation des assoziierten internationalen Aufbaustudiengangs (Abschn. 4) folgt ein Bericht über die ersten praktischen Erfahrungen (Abschn. 5). Ein Ausblick mit Perspektiven für Studiengang und Absolventen beendet die Vorstellung (Abschn. 6).

2 Das pädagogische Konzept

Folgt man modernen erziehungswissenschaftlichen Analysen (cf. etwa [Girmes 97]), so ergibt sich die Medienkompetenz, die das primäre Ausbildungsziel des Studiengangs Computervisualistik darstellt, nicht alleine aus dem Erwerb bestimmter Techniken und Methoden – also eines bestimmten Handlungsrepertoires, das den Lernenden bei Erfolg zusätzlich zur Verfügung stehen soll (siehe Abb. 1): Da Handlungen stets in bestimmten Anwendungskontexten vorkommen, deren Eigenheiten bei der jeweiligen Tätigkeit berücksichtigt werden müssen, gehören die spezifischen Strukturen des Handlungsfeldes, wie auch die daran anknüpfende reflexive Fähigkeit zur Einschätzung der Bedingungen dafür, daß die Handlung erfolgreich ausgeführt, die Technik mit Erfolg angewandt werden kann, ebenfalls notwendig zu dem, was vermittelt werden muß. Schließlich ist es nötig, daß jeder, der eine Kompetenz erwerben soll, auch über entsprechende Intentionen verfügt, an denen letztlich die Qualität einer zugehörigen Handlungsausführung (und damit auch des Kompetenzerwerbs insgesamt) zu messen ist. Die dreigliedrige Konzeption der Magdeburger Computervisualistik folgt dieser Analyse:

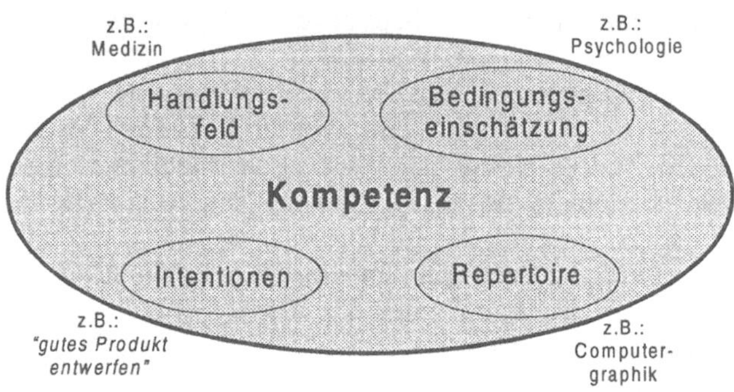

Abbildung 1: Vier Aspekte von Kompetenz

- **Methodik:**
  die algorithmische Behandlung bildhafter Datenstrukturen in der Informatik
- **Allgemeine Visualistik:**
  humanwissenschaftliche Aspekte des Umgangs mit Bildern
- **Anwendungsfach:**
  ein exemplarisches Anwendungsfeld, z.B. Medizin, Werkstoffwissenschaft

Allgemein gesagt dienen die Veranstaltungen der Säule *Allgemeine Visualistik* vor allem zur Vermittlung der Bedingungseinschätzungen für das gelernte Repertoire. Letzteres wird offenbar durch die Techniken und Methoden der Informatik gebildet, der ersten Säule also, die tatsächlich auch zeitlich die umfangreichste ist. Zum Einüben in die praktische Umsetzung der informatischen Techniken stellt schließlich die dritte Säule, das Anwendungsfach, ein konkretes Handlungsfeld exemplarisch zur Verfügung, wobei die verstärkt vermittelte kommunikative Kompetenz, der Fundus an Methoden und die Allgemeinheit der geisteswissenschaftlichen Betrachtungen zum Umgang mit Bildern es den Absolventen auch ermöglichen soll, im späteren Berufsleben ohne extremen Aufwand die Grenzen dieses Beispiels zu verlassen und sich leicht auf andere Anwendungsgebiete einzulassen.[1]

[1] Der erwähnte Kompetenzaspekt „Intention“ ist nicht einem einzelnen Bereich zugeordnet, da die Intentionen sich individuell mit dem jeweiligen Studierenden entwickeln müssen.

Im Einzelnen: Die **Informatik** mit ihren Subdisziplinen liefert sozusagen das „Handwerkszeug" der Computervisualistik: Insbesondere stehen hier neben den Grundlagen spezifische bildthematische Inhalte im Vordergrund. Beispielsweise geht es im Bereich **Computergraphik** vor allem um das Erzeugen von realistisch wirkenden Bildern meist fiktiver Gegenstände. Diese Bilder können photorealistisch sein, d.h. so, als würde es sich um eine photographische Reproduktion einer wirklichen Ansicht handeln. Aber auch andere gestalterische Mittel können eingesetzt werden, so daß Graphiken etwa im Stil von Kohlezeichnungen oder Kupferstichen entstehen (cf. auch [Strothotte 98]).

Ein zweiter, für die Computervisualistik bedeutsamer Bereich der Informatik ist das Fach **'Mensch-Computer-Interaktion'**, in dem gerade auch Überlegungen zur „Interpretierbarkeit" einer Graphik eine wichtige Rolle spielen. Neben zum Teil ergonomisch ausgerichteten Untersuchungen zur Verwendung von Fenstern, Graphiken, Menüs, Piktogrammen und anderen Darstellungen auf dem Bildschirm gehört hierher die Forschung zu immersiven Systemen, populärer auch als *„virtual reality"* bezeichnet. Das Interesse des Computervisualisten richtet sich dabei vor allem auf Auswirkungen und Anforderungen an graphische Benutzungsoberflächen, die sich aus dem Einsatz besonderer Techniken zur Bedienung von Computern – etwa *head-mounted display* oder Datenhandschuhe – oder durch spezielle Einschränkungen – wie kleine, niedrig auflösende Bildschirme – ergeben (cf. etwa auch [Strothotte^2 97]).
Diese beiden Gebiete mögen hier als ausführlichere Beispiele genügen. Erwähnt seien aber als weitere, spezifisch computervisualistische Themen der Informatik (ohne Anspruch auf Vollständigkeit) noch Bildverarbeitung (Methoden der Bildverbesserung, auch Bilddatenkompression), Mustererkennung und Bildverstehen (Verfahren zur automatischen Extraktion von bedeutungstragenden Aspekten), algorithmische Geometrie (Effizienzbetrachtungen) und Multimedia-Datenbanken.

Daneben treten wahlobligatorisch Standardfächer der Informatikausbildung, die keinen direkten Bezug zu Bildern aufweisen, insbesondere aus der Praktischen und Angewandten Informatik. Theoretische Informatik wird vollständig anhand der algorithmischen Geometrie vorgestellt.

Die Säule **Allgemeine Visualistik** hat im Studiengang Computervisualistik die Funktion, die Studierenden einerseits mit den theoretischen und praktischen Grundlagen des (nicht-informatischen) Umgehens mit Bildern und den entsprechenden Handlungskontexten aus verschiedener Perspektive vertraut zu machen; dazu zählen sowohl analytische Gesichtspunkte, wie sie beispielsweise in Psychologie oder Philosophie behandelt werden, wie auch konstruktive Aspekte, wie im Fach Industriedesign. Andererseits soll zugleich die Kommunikationskompetenz der Studierenden durch den intensiven argumentativen Umgang mit Nicht-Ingenieuren gefördert werden. Beides zusammen erlaubt den Absolventen, neben informatischen auch eine Fülle anderer Faktoren bei der Beurteilung der eigenen Arbeit zu berücksichtigen. Es ist angestrebt, daß Computervisualisten in der Lage sind, bei ihrer späteren Tätigkeit schnell zu erkennen, welche Aspekte der Allgemeinen Visualistik jeweils relevant sind und wo entsprechendes Vertiefungsmaterial zu finden ist. Durch die vermittelten Grundlagen sollen sie sich jenes Material ohne extremen Aufwand aneignen und auf die aktuelle Situation anwenden können. Darüber hinaus soll das Studium im Gebiet Allgemeine Visualistik die Motivation schüren, diese Vertiefung auch tatsächlich durchzuführen und sich nicht in den Elfenbeinturm des Ingenieurtechnokraten zurückzuziehen.

Derzeit werden im Grundstudium die folgenden fünf Fächer angeboten: Psychologie, Erziehungswissenschaft, Politikwissenschaft, Philosophie und Industriedesign.

Das **Anwendungsfach** ergänzt das Studium, indem von Beginn an die Kooperationsproblematik im späteren Tätigkeitsfeld der Computervisualisten beispielhaft behandelt wird. Absolventen des Diplomstudiengangs Computervisualistik sollen in ihrer Tätigkeit als Experten für das informatische Bearbeiten von bildhaftem Material auftreten. Das heißt, daß sie von Experten anderer Gebiete, die Aufgabenstellungen haben, bei denen Bilddaten verarbeitet werden sollen, zu deren angemessenen Lösung im Sinne einer Dienstleistung engagiert werden können. Die Kommunikation zwischen den beiden Expertengruppen mit ihren meist recht unterschiedlichen Begrifflichkeiten, Ausbildungswegen, wissenschaftlichen Erfahrungen, Sichtweisen auf Probleme und vor allem auch Vorstellungen über das jeweils andere Gebiet stellt dabei bekanntlich einen besonders komplexen „Flaschenhals" dar, der effektive Lösungen erschwert. Dieser Problemtyp muß frühzeitig bewußt gemacht, Lösungsstrategien eingeübt werden.

Ein typisches Anwendungsgebiet ist die Werkstoffwissenschaft mit ihrem reichen Arsenal an modernen bildgebenden Verfahren von der Röntgendiffraktometrie (REM) bis zur Konfokalen Laserrastermikroskopie (CLSM). Neben den physikalischen Grundlagen dieser bildgebenden Verfahren bilden Einführungen in die Theorie von Struktur und Gefüge von Werkstoffen die Basis, auf der dann spezielle computervisualistische Fragestellungen innerhalb der Werkstoffwissenschaft, etwa zum Einsatz von Fraktalen bei der Modellierung und Analyse von Werkstoffoberflächen, behandelt werden können.

Medizin, Werkstoffwissenschaft und Bildinformationstechnik sind derzeit in Magdeburg als Anwendungsfächer installiert;[2] weitere sind in Vorbereitung. Die Wahl erfolgt zu Beginn des Studiums.

3 Die Prüfungsordnung des Studiengangs im Überblick

Die Prüfungsordnung fordert von den Studierenden bei einer Regelstudienzeit von 10 Semestern die Teilnahme an Veranstaltungen im Umfang von 168 Semesterwochenstunden (s. Tab. 1, nächste Seite). Die Veranstaltungen zur Mathematik und zur Einführung in die Informatik sind dabei identisch mit den für die Diplom-Informatiker vorgeschriebenen.

Im Rahmen des Hauptstudiums ist ein Berufspraktikum von 20 Wochen Dauer abzulegen, das mit einer öffentlich zu verteidigenden Studienarbeit dokumentiert wird. Abgeschlossen wird das Studium mit der Verteidigung der Diplomarbeit, zu deren Erstellung fünf Monate in der Regelstudienzeit vorgesehen sind. Verliehen wird dann der akademische Grad „Diplomingenieurin" bzw. „Diplomingenieur".

Der äußere Rahmen entspricht genau dem des Diplomstudiengangs Informatik an der Otto-von-Guericke-Universität Magdeburg. Das Volumen der abgeprüften Veran-

[2] In Zusammenarbeit mit den Fakultäten für Medizin, Maschinenbau resp. Elektrotechnik.

staltungen im Hauptstudium ist geringfügig größer. Im Grundstudium sind vor allem aufgrund der Allgemeinen Visualistik deutlich mehr Scheine vorzulegen (Differenz: sieben). Ähnliches gilt in geringerem Umfang auch für das Hauptstudium, allerdings wird in Computervisualistik eine Prüfung weniger verlangt.

Das Angebot in Allgemeiner Visualistik umfaßt derzeit die Fächer *Industriedesign, Psychologie, Erziehungswissenschaft, Philosophie und Politikwissenschaft.* Von diesen sind im Grundstudium vier auszuwählen und mit jeweils vier Semesterwochenstunden zu belegen. Im Hauptstudium folgt eine weitere Konzentration auf drei Fächer, von denen zwei als Schwerpunkte gelten mit je acht Semesterwochenstunden. Das dritte Fach schlägt mit der Hälfte zu Buche. Damit ergibt sich insgesamt die in Abbildung 2 gezeigte zeitliche Verteilung der Veranstaltungen auf die drei Säulen.

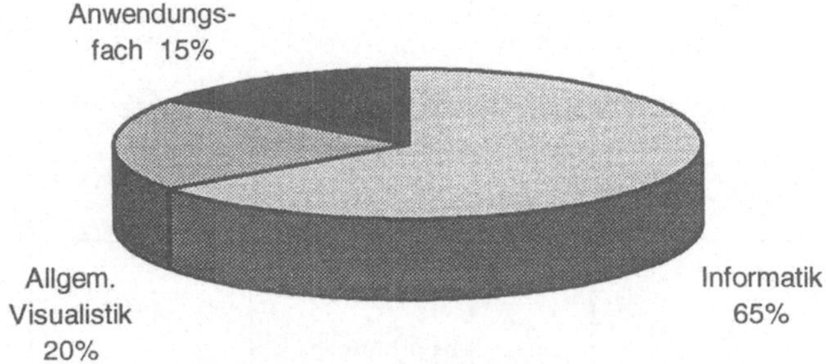

Abbildung 2: Zeitanteile der „Säulen" am Diplomstudiengang Computervisualistik

4 Ein Beitrag zur Internationalisierung der deutschen Universitätsausbildung

Der Erfolg des Diplomstudiengangs und das internationale Interesse an seiner Konzeption haben die Otto-von-Guericke-Universität Magdeburg dazu bewogen, ab dem Herbst 97 auch ausländischen interessierten Akademikern eine Vertiefung im Bereich der Computervisualistik zu ermöglichen. Es handelt sich hierbei um einen Aufbaustudiengang, der mit dem Titel »Master of Science« abschließt, dem akademischen Grad also, der in angelsächsischen Ländern etwa dem Niveau des deutschen Universitätsdiploms entspricht. Die Regelstudienzeit beträgt drei Semester, inklusive eines Berufspraktikums. Verfügt eine Bewerberin oder ein Bewerber bereits über einschlägige Arbeitserfahrung, so ist das Praktikum nicht obligatorisch: Die Regelstudienzeit reduziert sich auf zwei Semester. Ab dem Wintersemester 1998/99 wird Englisch die Lehrsprache sein, wobei Studierende natürlich auch in deutscher Sprache gehaltene Lehrveranstaltungen belegen können. Die Prüfungen können auf Deutsch oder Englisch abgelegt werden. Studierende nehmen an etwa acht Lehrveranstaltungen zu je vier Stunden pro Woche teil, die über zwei Semester verteilt sind (cf. Tab. 2). Davon gehören 16 zu dem Fach *Computational Visualistics* (aufgeteilt in die Bereiche *graphics*, *vision*, *geometry* und *medical imaging*); acht Stunden kommen ergänzend aus der übrigen Informatik; acht weitere sind der Allgemeinen Visualistik zugeordnet.

Tabelle 1: Auszug aus der Prüfungsordnung zum Diplomstudiengang Computervisualistik (vereinfacht, mit Vergleichzahlen des Diplomstudiengangs Informatik an der Otto-von-Guericke-Universität Magdeburg gemäß PO 1996, siehe „Summen"):

Fach	SWS	Prüfungen	Prüf.-vorleist.	Studienleist.
Grundstudium				
Mathematik	24	2 x K 4h	2 Scheine	--
Praktische Informatik	12	K 4h	1 Schein	--
Technische Informatik	8	M 30min	1 Schein	--
Theoretische Informatik	6	K 2h	1 Schein	--
Computervisualistik[3]	12	M 40min	1 Schein	--
Softwarepraktikum	4	--	--	1 Schein
Allgemeine Visualistik	16	--	--	8 Scheine
Anwendungsfach	8	K 2h	--	2 Scheine
Summe Grundstudium (4 Semester)	**90**	**7 Prüfungen**	**6 Scheine**	**11 Scheine**
[Informatik]	*[90]*	*[7]*	*[5]*	*[5]*
Hauptstudium:				
Computervisualistik[4]	20	M 60min	--	2 Scheine
Prakt. u. Angew. Informatik	20	3 x M 30min	--	2 Scheine
Technische Informatik	6	--	--	1 Schein
Studienarbeit		Studienarbeit	--	--
Allgemeine Visualistik	20	2 x {M 30min o. K 4h}	2 Scheine	2 Scheine
Anwendungsfach	12	M30	--	1 Schein
Summe Hauptstudium (6 Semester)	**78**	**4 Prüfungen + Studienarbeit**	**2 Scheine**	**8 Scheine**
[Informatik]	*[75]*	*[5]*	*[0]*	*[8]*

Legende: K: Klausur M: mündliche Prüfung SWS: Semesterwochenstunden
(die Zahl gibt jeweils die geforderte Dauer der Prüfung an);

[3] Das Gebiet „Computervisualistik" umfaßt im Grundstudium Einführungen in Computergraphik, Bildverarbeitung und graphische objektorientierte Programmierung.

[4] Das Gebiet „Computervisualistik" umfaßt im Hauptstudium Vertiefungen zu Computergraphik, Bildverarbeitung, sowie die Fächer Visualisierung, geometrische Modellierung, Animation und Simulation.

Tabelle 2: Auszug aus der Prüfungsordnung des Aufbaustudiengangs zum M.Sc.

Fachgebiet	SWS/ Credit points	Prüfung
Computervisualistik	16	4 x M 30min
Praktische & Angewandte Informatik	8	2 x M 30min
Allgem. Visualistik	8	M 60min
Master's Thesis	--	Master' Thesis Verteidigung
Summe	32	

In den vorlesungsfreien Zeiten wird an einer Master's Thesis (kleine Diplomarbeit) gearbeitet; insgesamt sind drei Monate dafür vorgesehen. Gegebenenfalls wird das fünfmonatige Berufspraktikum absolviert (s.o.). Bewerbung setzt einen ersten Hochschulabschluß voraus. Das ist bei Bewerbern aus deutschsprachigen Ländern generell das Diplom (FH oder Universität), während bei allen anderen allgemein der *Bachelor's degree* zählt.

5 Erste Erfahrungen

Der Diplomstudiengang wurde im März 96 genehmigt und zum folgenden Wintersemester erstmals angeboten. War die Universität bei ihren Kapazitätsplanungen von maximal 30 Anfängern ausgegangen, so wurde sie bereits im Laufe des August 96 eines Besseren belehrt: Tatsächlich hatten sich im Oktober über 60 Frauen und Männer zum Diplomstudiengang Computervisualistik eingeschrieben. Besonders erfreulich war dabei, daß der Frauenanteil für ein ingenieurwissenschaftliches Studium recht hoch war: Mit fast 25% lag der Studiengang an der Spitze der Ingenieurwissenschaften der Universitätsstatistik. Das große Interesse hielt auch im zweiten Jahr mit einer Steigerung auf rund 150% an; die Computervisualistik stellt im Jahrgang 97 damit nicht nur die Hälfte der Neuimmatrikulationen in Diplomstudiengängen an der Fakultät für Informatik, sondern hat ingesamt diese Anfängerzahl gegenüber der recht stabilen Zahl in den anderen Studiengängen verdoppelt (siehe auch Tab. 3.) Die durch diese zunächst unerwartete Flut ausgelösten organisatorischen Probleme konnten – nicht zuletzt durch großzügige und prompte Reaktionen des zuständigen Kultusministeriums – schnell behoben werden: Ein Computervisualistik-Rechnerlabor mit speziellen Graphikrechnern ist inzwischen eröffnet worden; mehrere Stellen zur

Tabelle 3: Entwicklung der Immatrikulationszahlen an der Fakultät für Informatik der Otto-von-Guericke-Universität Magdeburg: Aufgeführt sind die drei Diplomstudiengänge der FIN

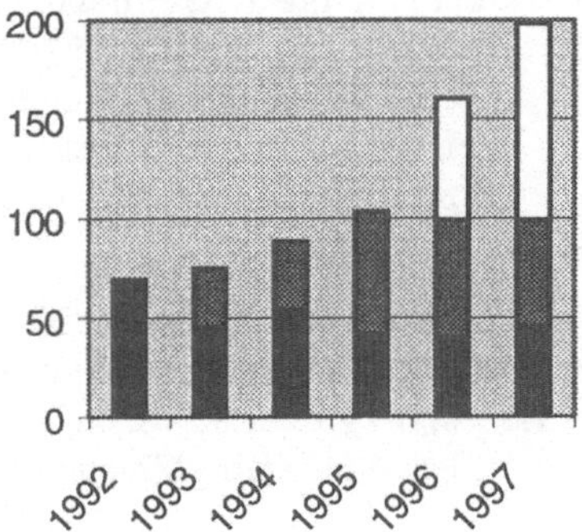

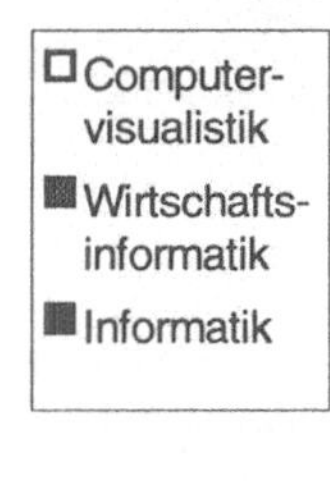

Unterstützung von Forschung und Lehre wurden geschaffen (gebündelt in der *Interdisziplinären Forschungsstelle für Computervisualistik*) und eine C4-Professur für Computervisualistik ausgeschrieben, deren Besetzung noch für das laufende Jahr erwartet wird.

Für den ersten Jahrgang liegen mittlerweile auch schon Abschätzungen zur Abbrecherquote vor. Sie liegt mit über 40% zwar recht hoch, aber durchaus noch im durch die Informatik vorgegebenen Bereich (dort: etwa 40-50%). Berücksichtigt werden muß bei diesem ersten Jahrgang auch, daß eine Reihe von Anfängern (trotz umfangreichen Informationsmaterials) nur unzureichende Vorstellungen über den Studieninhalt aufwiesen und insbesondere vom Schwergewicht auf ingenieurwissenschaftlichen Grundlagen im Grundstudium überrascht und überfordert wurden: Mehrere wechselten nach dem ersten Semester zum Designstudium an eine FH. Tatsächlich stellt auch die geistige Integration so verschiedener Fachgebiete mit ihren unterschiedlichen Blickrichtungen und Methodologien, wie sie von den Studierenden dieses hochinterdisziplinären Fachs gefordert wird, keine geringe Anforderung dar. Erleichtert wird diese Integration durch eine Verstärkung der fachübergreifenden Anteile in den Veranstaltungen, die dem Bedarf folgend nun zunehmend ausgebaut werden. So wird beispielsweise in die Einführungsveranstaltung zur Erziehungswissenschaft für Computervisualisten ein Video-Grundkurs eingefügt: Der entsprechende Schein kann (außer durch Klausur oder Hausarbeit) erlangt werden, indem in der vorlesungsfreien Zeit in kleinen Gruppen kurze Videofilme über in der Vorlesung behandelte erziehungswissenschaftliche Themen erstellt werden. Geplant ist auch, im Hauptstudium einen abgestimmten Doppelschwerpunkt in Philosophie und Erziehungswissenschaft zum Thema „Film“ aufzubauen.

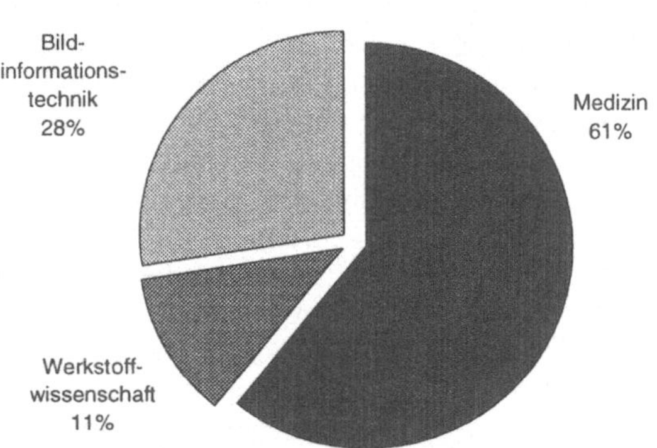

Abbildung 3: Anteile der Anwendungsfächer (Jahrgang 97)

Nachdem im ersten Jahrgang Medizin das einzige Anwendungsfach war, konnten dem zweiten Jahrgang zusätzlich Werkstoffwissenschaft und Bildinformationstechnik angeboten werden. Die Aufteilung auf diese drei Fächer ist in Abb. 3 wiedergegeben. Wegen der relativ großen Nachfrage in Medizin, die die ursprünglichen Kapazitätsberechnungen weit hinter sich läßt, ist derzeit daran gedacht, eine lokale Zugangsbeschränkung für dieses Anwendungsfach zu installieren.

Genaue Daten zur Wahl in den Fächern der Allgemeinen Visualistik liegen zur Zeit noch nicht vor. Ein deutliches Schwergewicht im Interesse der Studierenden gilt aber offenkundig in beiden Jahrgängen dem Bereich Industriedesign (größer 60%), wo neben einer Einführung zur Zeit insbesondere die Themen „Gestaltungslehre/Zeichnen“ und „Bildgestaltung/Photographie“ angeboten werden.

6 Die Zukunft der Computervisualisten und der Computervisualistik

Zur Arbeitsmarktsituation können gegenwärtig offensichtlich noch keine Erfahrungswerte vorliegen. Doch erlauben allgemeine Prognosen aus Politik und Wirtschaft es zumindest, eine grobe Tendenz anzugeben: Der am 7. Februar 1996 vom Deutschen Bundestag verabschiedete Bericht *„Info 2000: Deutschlands Weg in die Informationsgesellschaft“* (cf. [Info 2000]) konstatiert beispielsweise, daß bis zum Jahr 2010 in Europa im Bereich der Informations- und Kommunikationstechniken rund sechs Millionen zusätzliche Arbeitsplätze geschaffen werden könnten. Davon würden unter optimalen Bedingungen rund 1,5 Millionen in Deutschland entstehen. Zu deren Besetzung wäre aber insbesondere eine entsprechende höhere Qualifikation von Nöten, eine Qualifikation, so kann wohl hinzugefügt werden, wie sie der Studiengang Computervisualistik anstrebt.

Die Zukunft des Fachs kann zur Zeit durchaus als gut bezeichnet werden. Das Volumen an Anfragen von Interessenten für einen Studienbeginn im Herbst 98 entspricht in etwa dem des Vorjahres. Besonders gefreut hat uns zu erfahren, daß die Universität Koblenz-Landau im März 98 als zweite bundesdeutsche Universität den Entschluß gefaßt hat, einen Diplomstudiengang Computervisualistik zu installieren, der sich an die Magdeburger Konzeption anlehnt. Das geplante Curriculum umfaßt je 80 Semesterwochenstunden im Grund- und Hauptstudium und führt zum Abschluß Diplom-Informatiker(in) (cf. Tab. 4 und [Kob/Lan]). Eine intensive Zusammenarbeit ist von beiden Seiten beabsichtigt. So sollen regelmäßige Koordinierungstreffen der Studienfachbetreuer stattfinden. Studienleistungen und Vordiplome werden wechselseitig anerkannt. Darüber hinaus ist eine gemeinsame Studienwerbung ins Auge gefaßt. Auf diese Weise soll sichergestellt werden, daß die Computervisualistik an allen Standorten mit einem einheitlichen charakteristischen Profil erkennbar bleibt.

Tabelle 4: Computervisualistik in Koblenz-Landau: geplanter Lehrplan (schematisch)

Grundstudium	SWS
Informatik	44
Technische Informatik	9
Mathematik	15
Interdisziplinär (ähnlich Allgem. Visualistik)	12 (10 Pflicht)
Hauptstudium	
Informatik	50 (34 Pflicht)
Interdisziplinär	30 (14 Pflicht)
Summe	160

* * *

Wir möchten an dieser Stelle die Gelegenheit nutzen, um den Kollegen, der Hochschulleitung und dem Ministerium für den Mut, ein solches neues Ausbildungskonzept umzusetzen, ganz herzlich zu danken.

Literatur

Brooks 96: F.P. Brooks, Jr.: The computer scientist as a toolsmith (II), Acceptance lecture of the first recipient of the ACM Allen Newell Award, *CACM* 39/3, 1996, S. 61—68.

Denning 92: P.J. Denning: Educating a New Engineer. *CACM* 35/12, 1992, p. 83-97.

Girmes 97: R. Girmes (Hg.): *Studium – Berufsentwicklung – Persönlichkeitsbildung: Ansätze zu einem biographieorientierten Hochschulstudium.* Münster: Waxmann, 1997.

Info 2000: *Deutschlands Weg in die Informationsgesellschaft*, Bonn, Bundesministerium für Wirtschaft, 1996 (auch: *http://www.kp.dlr.de/BMWi/gip/programme/info2000/index.html*).

Kob/Lan: Materialien zum Studiengang Computervisualistik an der Universität Koblenz-Landau siehe unter: *http://www.uni-koblenz.de/~lb/visualistik/vis/vis.html* (Juni 98).

Strothotte² 97: C. Strothotte, Th. Strothotte: *Seeing between the pixels*, Berlin: Springer, 1997.

Strothotte 98: Th. Strothotte (Hg.): *Abstraction in interactive computational visualization.* Berlin: Springer, 1998, in Vorbereitung.

Stucky 97: W. Stucky, Editorial, *Informatik-Spektrum* 20:1-2, 1997.

[zur Magdeburger Computervisualistik siehe auch:
http://isgnw.cs.uni-magdeburg.de/~joerg/compvis/compvis.htm]

Podiumsdiskussion: Electronic Commerce — welche Rolle spielt die universitäre Informatik?

Ralf Cordes

debitel – Strategisches Marketing, Schelmenwasenstraße 37–39, D-70567 Stuttgart, Germany
Ralf.Cordes@de.debitel.com

Die Zielsetzung dieser Podiumsdiskussion ist einerseits eine Standortbestimmung der (universitären) Informatik im Bereich Electronic Commerce vorzunehmen und andererseits ihre mögliche zukünftige Rolle zu diskutieren. An Hand von fünf Fragekomplexen versuchen wir dieses Thema näher zu annalysieren.

1. *Wo steht die heutige Informatik oder Wirtschafts-Informatik im Bezug auf Electronic Commerce?*

Electronic Commerce oder Business Digital ist ein komplexer Prozeß, der mit Mitteln der IT-Industrie effizient unterstützt werden kann. Er geht über eine reine Darstellung von Katalogen auf web-pages im heißgeliebten Internet weit hinaus. Gerade die Wirtschafts-Informatik lieferte mit Arbeiten an Universitäten wie Münster / Frankfurt/Oder (Prof. Kurbel), Saarbrücken (Prof. Scheer), Würzburg (Prof. Thomé), Erlangen (Prof. Mertens), Freiburg (Prof. Müller) oder Konstanz (Prof. Kuhlen) Beiträge zu der Entwicklung von Electronic Commerce. Dennoch war, ist und bleibt Electronic Commerce ein Bereich, der durch Beraterideen, Anwendungsszenarien und Machbarkeitsstudien geprägt ist.

Es drängt sich somit die Frage nach weiteren wesentlichen Beiträgen der universitären Informatik zu den bisherigen Entwicklungen auf. Sind es Entwicklungen zu intelligenten Agenten, ist es die Verbindung von Retrievaltechniken und Hypertext oder sind es Arbeiten, die rein in universitären Prototypen mündeten? Welche Rolle kann heute und in Zukunft die Integration von intelligenter Bild- und Sprachverarbeitung spielen?

2. *Sind die IT-Hersteller und Anbieter treibende Kräfte für die Umsetzung von Electronic Commerce Konzepten?*

Betrachtet man sich die Situation bei Herstellern und Anwendern der IT-Industrie, so scheint E-Commerce ein neues Marketing-Vehikel zu sein, um bekannte Produkte in ein neu geschnittenes Produktportfolio zu ordnen oder um neue Upgrades und Features an bestehender Software zu etablieren.

Anwenderseitig zeigten sich erste Lösungen wie My World von Karstadt. Geht es darum, unter E-Commerce neue Vertriebskanäle oder effizientere Abwicklungsformen zwischen Kunde und Lieferant zu etablieren, so gibt es verheißungsvolle Ergebnisse nicht nur bei amazon.com, sondern auch bei IT- Herstellern wie hp oder CISCO.

Die Frage, wie sich anwendungstechnisch sogenannte Mall-Anbieter durchsetzen werden bleibt offen, weil erst mit T-Mart oder Primus Online sehr junge geschäftliche Anbieter tätig sind. Regionalkonzepte wie Regio Online Basel,

Bodensee-Mall oder City Web sind wichtige Bestandteile und Prüfsteine einer solchen Entwicklung.

Es gibt hier dennoch die Frage zu klären: Ist E-Commerce technischer Hype, geschäftliche Nutzung oder eine neue Dienste- und Anbieterform?

3. *Wo sind Synergien oder Kooperationen zwischen Hochschule und Industrie und welche universitären Evolutionen gibt es?*

Schaut man sich noch junge Firmen an wie Intershop, Brokat oder Broadvisison, Start- up Companies also, so stellt sich die Frage nach Synergien oder Kooperationen im Umfeld Electronic Commerce zwischen Hochschule und Industrie. Einerseits werden bei diesen Firmen gezielt Geschäftsmodelle und technische Lösungen umgesetzt, die nach eingehender Analyse ein hohes Potential verheißen, andererseits sind es Evolutionen aus dem Hochschulumfeld, die zu Erfolgsstories werden.

Sind es Verbindungen einer Universität Saarbrücken mit einer IDS zur SAP, die Innovationen im Großen voranbringen können? Oder sind es die vielen kleinen Firmen in Gründerzentren, Technologieparks oder als Institut an der Universität geführt, die für einen Transfer von universitärer Informatik in Produkte und Anwendungen des Electronic Commerce tätig sind?

4. *Müssen neue Akzente in der Informatikausbildung gelegt werden?*

Haben diese neuen Anwendungen der Informatik im Umfeld handelsorientierter Prozesse eine Rückwirkung auf neue Studienschwerpunkte und -inhalte? Oder können bereits heute diese Inhalte in übergreifenden Fächern wie Wirtschaftsinformatik und Medieninformatik abgedeckt werden?

Wo werden sowohl Web-Design mit Security Management und Netzwerkprotokollen angeboten? Wo bekomme ich gleichzeitig Einsicht in Materialwirtschaft, Logistik, elektronischen Zahlungsverkehr und dem Erstellen von Stroylines für interaktive online Auftritte? Was liefert die klassische Informatik zu diesen neuen Herausforderungen?

5. *Welche Rolle spielt die Informatik in einer zukünftigen Welt des Electronic Commerce?*

Gehen wir von einer medienorientierten zukünftigen vernetzten Welt aus, so stellt sich natürlich die Frage nach einer Positionierung des Electronic Commerce. Nimmt man an, daß Electronic Commerce eine bedeutende Anwendung in diesem Umfeld wird, so stellt sich natürlich die Frage nach der Rolle der Informatik. Wird Sie Nischenlieferant sein oder universeller Dienstleister oder kann die Informatik wesentliche Impulse für eine Fortentwicklung von Electronic Commerce liefern?

Wird die Informatik die technische Basis liefern und somit Zulieferer zu Prozessen sein, die durch Werbung, Handel und Marketing gesteuert werden? Kann die Informatik eine eigenen Identität durch Schwerpunkte wie Wirtschafts- und Medieninformatik aufbauen? Wird es gar zu noch neuen Berufsbildern für Informatiker führen oder aber wird Electronic Commerce eine Fortentwicklung nehmen wie Künstliche Intelligenz oder Multimedia?

Workshops, Tutorien, Computer Animation Festival

Workshop: Abstract State Machines

Uwe Glässer[1] and Peter H. Schmitt[2]

[1] Heinz Nixdorf Institut, Universität-GH Paderborn,
D-33102 Paderborn, Germany
glaesser@uni-paderborn.de
[2] Institut für Logik, Komplexität und Deduktionssysteme Universität Karlsruhe,
D-76128 Karlsruhe, Germany
pschmitt@ira.uka.de

The Abstract State Machine (ASM) Project (formerly known as the Evolving Algebras Project) was started by Yuri Gurevich almost exactly a decade ago as an attempt to bridge the gap between formal models of computation and practical specification methods.

The ASM thesis is that any algorithm can be modeled at its natural abstraction level by an appropriate ASM. Based upon this thesis, members of the ASM community have sought to develop a methodology based upon mathematics which would allow algorithms to be modeled naturally; that is, described at their natural abstraction levels. Here the term algorithm is taken in a broad sense including programming languages, architectures, distributed and real-time protocols, *etc.*. The result is a simple but efficient methodology allowing to formalize the behaviour of arbitrary algorithms in terms of simple abstract machines.

ASMs have been used to specify languages (*e. g.* C, Prolog and VHDL), to specify real and virtual architectures (*e. g.* Java VM, PVM, and Transputer), to validate standard language implementations (*e. g.* of Java, Occam, Prolog), to validate distributed protocols, to prove complexity results, *etc.*. A description of a semantics of Java using ASMs will be presented at the workshop by the invited speaker Wolfram Schulte from the University of Ulm.

For further general information and a thorough introduction we refer the reader to [2], the authoritative guide to ASMs. A comprehensive survey of papers related to ASMs can be found in the annotated bibliography [1].

International workshops on ASMs have become regular annual events. The first workshop was held during the IFIP World Computer Congress in Hamburg, September 1994. The second one at Schloß Eringerfeld in May 1996, the third and the fourth near Cannes in June 1997, and June 1998. This workshop at the annual conference of the German Society of Computer Science (GI) is thus already the second ASM workshop in 1998. June 1998. Plans are already under way for a meeting of the ASM User Group at FM'99, the World Congress on Formal Methods in Toulouse in September 1999.

What are the current issues pursued by the ASM community and presented at this workshop?

There are, of course, and hopefully will continue to be, applications. We are looking forward to the invited talk by Dr. Peter Päppinghaus from Siemens AG, München to hear more on this topic. Speaking about recent specific application project we want to point out a talk on authentication protocols, an area that is only now being subjected to rigorous formal treatment. Another domain that has already received much attention by the ASM community is the specification and verification of compilers. Efforts continue here with two noticable novelties: The project that will be reported at the workshop is much closer to practice and is done by people that have been working in the area of compiler construction for many years. The second trend is the use of automated reasoning methods and systems to proof properties of ASM specifications. In the case at hand the PVS systems from SRI International is used. Other approaches did employ model checking or the KIV (Karlsruhe Interactive Verifier) system. Both papers are contained in the special issue on ASMs in JUCS, Vol. 3(4), 1997.

Another prominent issue is the extension of the ASM programming language. Mainly, researchers are trying to incorporate constructs for modelling interacting and communicating processes. But also the treatment of object-oriented specification and programming are on the agenda.

Practical experience clearly shows that there still is an enormous potential for innovations in modelling and validating complex computer-based systems, especially when the ASM method is used in an industrial or scientific design context.

However, in order to make ASM appealing to a wider user group something important seems to be missing: a challenging vision how to transform the ASM method into the *ASM Technology* complete with a sufficient variety of practical tools. Work towards this end has already started at various institutions. A project conducted at the university of Tromso will be presented. It remains an important goal of this workshop to combine efforts and shape ideas for future developments in this area.

For further and up to date information you may want to check the ASM home pages `http://www.eecs.umich.edu/gasm/` and `http://www.uni-paderborn.de/cs/asm/`.

References

1. E. Börger & J. Huggins. Abstract State Machines 1988-1998: Commented ASM Bibliography. *Bulletin of EATCS*, 64:105–127, February 1998.
   The most recently published version of the annotated bibliography of papers which deal with or use ASMs, as of the end of 1997.
2. Y. Gurevich. Evolving Algebras 1993: Lipari Guide. In E. Börger, editor, *Specification and Validation Methods*, pages 9–36. Oxford University Press, 1995.
   For a recent update *May 1997 Draft of the ASM Guide* see the Technical Report CSE-TR-336-97, EECS Dept., University of Michigan.

Workshop: Componentware — Schlüsseltechnologie für moderne Krankenhausinformationssysteme?

Alfred Winter

Institut für Medizinische Informatik, Statistik und Epidemiologie, Universität Leipzig, Liebigstraße 27, D-04103 Leipzig, Germany
winter@imise.uni-leipzig.de

Krankenhausinformationssysteme modular aus Bausteinen aufzubauen ist Stand der Technik. Dies beschränkt sich bislang allerdings in der Regel auf autonome Anwendungssysteme, die auf der Basis von Kommunikationsstandards wie z. B. HL7 und Kommunikationsservern verbunden werden. Diese Technologie erlaubt zwar weitgehende Datenintegration, bietet aber keine ausreichende Lösung für die erforderliche Funktionsintegration an klinischen Arbeitsplatzsystemen. Für die optimale Gestaltung der Architektur eines Krankenhausinformationssystems wäre darüber hinaus die Nutzung und Austauschbarkeit 'kleinerer' Komponenten von Anwendungssoftwareprodukten wünschenswert.

Unter dem Stichwort „Middleware" zusammengefaßte Integrationsplattformen wie z. B. CORBA oder COM/DCOM erlauben das Design von Anwendungssoftware in Form zusammenfügbarer „Business Objects". Damit kann „Componentware" als 'Rohstoff' für den Zusammenbau großer, heterogener Informationssysteme bereitgestellt werden.

In dem u. a. von dem GI-Arbeitskreis und der GMDS-Arbeitsgruppe „Methoden und Werkzeuge für das Management von Krankenhausinformationssystemen" und den GMDS-Arbeitsgruppen „Klinische Arbeitsplatzsysteme" und „Kommunikationsstandards" getragenen Workshop sollen z. B. folgende Fragen diskutiert werden:

- Gibt es einen evolutionären Weg von vorhandenen Krankenhausinformationssystemen, die z. B. mit Kommunikationsservern integriert sind, zu solchen, die aus Componentware unter Nutzung moderner Middleware zusammengebaut sind?
- Welche Rolle spielen Kommunikationsstandards wie HL7 bei der Kommunikation zwischen Business Objects?
- Welche Granularität und Funktionalität müssen Business Objects aus Sicht klinischer Arbeitsplatzsysteme anbieten?
- Werden Referenzmodelle zur Beschreibung der funktionalen Anforderungen von Krankenhausinformationssystemen an Componentware benötigt und wie müssen diese Referenzmodelle aufgebaut sein?

Ziel des Workshops ist die Zusammenführung aktueller Diskussionen zu Componentware in Informatik, Wirtschaftsinformatik und Medizinischer Informatik, um den Nutzen dieser Technologie für die Weiterentwicklung von Krankenhausinformationssystemen besser abschätzen und erfolgversprechende Entwicklungsstrategien ableiten zu können.

Grundlage der Diskussion der zuvor angesprochenen Fragen sind die folgenden Beiträge:

- *Winter, A.*: Referenzmodelle und Bausteinkataloge für Krankenhausinformationssysteme.
- *Blobel, B.*: Componentenware für KIS — erläutert am Beispiel der CORBA-med-Architektur.
- *Heinrich, A., Berse, H.*: Objektorientierter Entwurf und Entwicklung eines Krankenhausinformationssystems auf Basis von CORBA: Lösen Komponenten das Entwicklungsdilemma der Standardsoftware?
- *Hasselbring, W.*: Top-Down Integration of Components for Hospital Information Systems based an HL7 and SGML.

Der erste Beitrag beschäftigt sich mit der Frage, wie auf der Basis von Referenz-Informationssystemmodellen für Krankenhausinformationssysteme die Grundlage geschaffen werden kann, Bausteinkataloge zu realisieren. Aus solchen Bausteinkatalogen sollten sich Manager von Krankenhausinformationssystemen unter den für ihr jeweiliges Anwendungssproblem geeigneten kommerziell verfügbaren Bausteinen das jeweils präferierte Angebot auswählen können. Die entsprechenden Bausteine sind dann Softwareprodukte, mit denen sich autonome Anwendungssysteme als Komponenten eines heterogenen Krankenhausinformationssystems realisieren lassen.

Voraussetzung hierfür ist eine geeignete Architektur für Krankenhausinformationssysteme. Der zweite Beitrag befaßt sich mit den Bemühungen, den allgemeinen Ansatz der CORBA-Architektur für die speziellen Belange von Krankenhausinformationssystemen zu konkretisieren; dies umfaßt die Berücksichtigung der speziellen Datenschutz- und Datensicherheitsanforderungen im Krankenhaus. Hierbei fließen u. a. Vorarbeiten aus dem Bereich des Kommunikationsstandards HL7 ein.

Nicht nur das Krankenhausinformationssystem als Ganzes sondern auch die kommerziell angebotenen Anwendungssoftwareprodukte selbst sind aus Komponenten aufgebaut. Im dritten Beitrag wird darüber berichtet, welche Erfahrungen ein Softwarehersteller mit dem Einsatz dieser Technologie bei der Produktion von Anwendungssoftware für Krankenhausinformationssysteme gemacht hat und welche Perspektiven sich ergeben. Hierbei wird insbesondere die Frage nach einer verbesserten Spezialisierung und Arbeitsteilung zwischen Softwareherstellern diskutiert.

Im vierten Beitrag geht es wieder um die Integration von Komponenten, die autonome Anwendungssysteme sind. Es wird ein Konzept vorgestellt, bei dem Methoden der standardisierten Kommunikation und föderierter Datenbanken kombiniert werden mit neueren Ansätzen auf der Basis von SGML. SGML wird hierbei zur Beschreibung der (Teil-) Datenbankschemata eingesetzt, die sich die zu integrierenden Komponenten teilen.

Bei der Vorbereitung des Workshops wirkten mit: A. Winter (Leipzig), B. Blobel (Magdeburg), J. Dudeck (Gießen), M. Dugas (München), G. Herrmann (Leipzig), A. Oberweis (Frankfurt), A. Winter (Koblenz-Landau).

Workshop: Data Mining und Data Warehousing als Grundlage moderner entscheidungsunterstützender Systeme

Rudolf Kruse und Gunter Saake

Otto-von-Guericke-Universität Magdeburg, Fakultät für Informatik,
Universitätsplatz 2, D-39106 Magdeburg

In vielen Bereichen leiden Anwender heute unter eine Flut von Daten. Aus diesem Grund werden Analysewerkzeuge entwickelt, die im Rahmen einer Wertschöpfungskette zunächst aus Daten Information destillieren. Die so gewonnenen Informationen werden weiter analysiert und schließlich modelliert, um unterstützendes Wissen für Entscheidungsprozeße bereitzustellen. Data Mining ist ein neues Forschungsgebiet, das Ergebnisse und Werkzeuge für diesen auch als *Knowledge Discovery from Databases* (KDD) bezeichneten Prozeß zur Verfügung stellt. Zum KDD-Prozeß gehören als Einzelschritte unter anderem: Data Warehousing, Datenvorverarbeitung, Datenreduktion, Data Mining, Modellauswahl sowie Bewertung und Interpretation.

Ein populärer Ansatz zur Bereitstellung entscheidungsrelevanter Daten ist das sogenannte *Data Warehousing*. Ein Data Warehouse ist eine aus einer oder mehreren operativen Datenbanken extrahierte Datenbank, die alle für den Geschäftsprozeß relevanten Daten eines Unternehmens zusammenfaßt, aufbereitet und aggregiert. Die Aufbereitung und Aggregierung der entstehenden sehr großen Datenbestände bildet die Kopplung zu dem Gebiet des Data Minings, dessen Methoden in Data Warehouses zum Einsatz kommen können.

Im Rahmen des Workshops sollen Ansätze und Verfahren vorgestellt werden, die es ermöglichen, aus Datenbanken jene Informationen zu gewinnen, die notwendig sind, um das Treffen von Entscheidungen wirksam zu unterstützen. Diese komplexe Aufgabe kann nur interdisziplinär gelöst werden. Zur Zeit werden vornehmlich Methoden aus dem Datenbankbereich, dem Maschinellen Lernen sowie der Statistik verwendet. Wegen des großen Interesses der Anwender entwickelt sich dieses neue Gebiet extrem schnell und bietet deshalb auch vielen anderen Forschungsrichtungen, wie z.B. der Visualistik, der Datenanalyse oder der Wissensrepräsentation ausgezeichnete Perspektiven. Aus diesem Grund wird der Workshop auch gemeinsam von den GI-Gruppen Datenbanken (FG 2.5.1), Fuzzy Systeme (FG 1.2.4), Maschinelles Lernen (FG 1.1.3) und Management Support Systems (AK 5.5.2) veranstaltet.

Das Programm umfaßt 14 Präsentationen. Neben zwei eingeladenen Vorträgen und einem gemeinsamen Vortrag mit dem Workshop *Molekulare Bioinformatik* gibt es elf weitere Vorträge zu begutachteten Beiträgen. Das Programm gliedert sich in drei Abschnitte: Data-Warehousing-Techniken, Data-Mining-Anwendungen und Data-Mining-Methoden.

Data-Warehousing-Techniken

- Paulo Marques, Paula Furtado, Peter Baumann (FORWISS München): *An Efficient Strategy for Tiling Multidimensional OLAP Data Cubes.*
- Dirk Bergemann, Elke Hickethier, Thomas Wittmann (Uni Jena): *Lösungsansaetze zurAnbindung eines KDD-Systems an ein Data Warehouse.*
- Wolfgang Lehner, Jens Albrecht (Uni Erlangen): *Modellierung, Verwaltung und Verwendung multidimensionaler Aggregate.*
- Werner Emde (NCR, Augsburg): *Data Mining in einer Data Warehouse Umgebung.*

Data-Mining-Anwendungen

- Gholemreza Nakhaeizadeh (Daimler Benz AG, Ulm): *Data Mining: Theoretische Aspekte und Anwendungen.*
- Daniela Krahl (SIZ GmbH, Bonn): *Nutzungsmöglichkeiten von Data Mining im Bankenwesen.*
- Edgar Wingender (GBF, Braunschweig): *Eine Hierachie molekularbiologischer Datenbanken zur Beschreibung genregulatorischer Prozesse.*
- Jörg Gebhardt (TU Braunschweig): *Data Mining for the Prognosis of Parts and Components in the Automotive Industry.*
- Thomas Runkler et al. (Siemens AG, München): *Compression of Industrial Process Data Using Fast Cluster Estimation.*

Data-Mining-Methoden

- Thomas Wittmann, Johannes Ruhland (Uni Jena): *Fallstudie zum Knowledge Discovery in Databases mit Neuro-Fuzzy Systemen.*
- Peter Chamoni, Steffen Stock (Uni Duisburg): *Modellierung temporaler multidimensionaler Daten in Analytischen Informationssystemen.*
- Frank Lemke, Johann-Adolf Mueller (Uni Dresden): *Self-Organizing Data Mining.*
- Annette Keller (DLR Braunschweig), Frank Klawonn (FH Emden): *Regelerzeugung mit Fuzzy-Clusteranalyse.*

Im Programmkomitee haben mitgewirkt: Peter Baumann (FORWISS München), Peter Chamoni (Uni Duisburg), Werner Emde (NCR, Augsburg), Jörg Gebhardt (TU Braunschweig), Andreas Heuer (Uni Rostock), Daniel Keim (Uni Halle), Rudolf Kruse (Uni Magdeburg, cochair), Peter Lockemann (Uni Karlsruhe), Katharina Morik (Uni Dortmund), Gholamreza Nakhaeizadeh (Daimler Benz), Claus Rautenstrauch (Uni Magdeburg), Michael M. Richter (Kaiserslautern), Bodo Rieger (Uni Osnabrück), Gunter Saake (Uni Magdeburg, cochair), Bernd Schürmann (Siemens), Rudi Studer (Uni Karlsruhe), Richard Weber (MIT Aachen), Rüdiger Wirth (Daimler Benz Ulm), Hans Wolff (Uni Ulm), Stefan Wrobel (GMD, Bonn).

Weitere Informationen zum Workshop sind unter der WWW-Adresse `http://fuzzy.cs.uni-magdeburg.de/dm98` abrufbar.

Workshop: Informatikanwendungen in afrikanischen Ländern

Nazir Peroz

Fachbereich Informatik, Technische Universität Berlin, Franklinstr. 28/29, 10587 Berlin, Germany
nazir@cs.tu-berlin.de

1 Einleitung

Es gibt keine generelle Antwort auf die Frage, ob die Anwendung der Computertechnologie eine Chance für Entwicklungsländer darstellt, oder ob man damit nicht dazu beiträgt, die Hürde zwischen Arm und Reich zu erweitern. Informationstechnologie (IT) und Technologietransfer (TT) sind problematisch für afrikanische Länder. Es fehlt u. a. Wissen darüber, wie ein bestimmtes System funktioniert, wie damit umzugehen ist, wie es zu warten ist, wie Applikationen zu entwickeln sind oder wie die Komponenten des Systems herzustellen und zusammenzusetzen sind.

Fakt ist aber, daß z. B. seit Juni 1995 die Association of African Universities mit Sitz in Accra, Ghana, 119 afrikanische Universitäten und Forschungseinrichtungen aus 42 Ländern per e-mail verbindet. 1995 wurde von der Weltbank im Rahmen ihres InfoDev-Programms die African Virtual University (AVU) initiiert und finanziert. Hierbei handelt es sich um ein Satelliten basiertes Projekt zur distance education. Es soll Länder des südlichen Afrikas in der Universitätsausbildung im Bereich von Naturwissenschaft und Ingenieurwesen unterstützen und damit die Zahl der Studenten afrikaweit erhöhen. Erste Demonstrationsprojekte der AVU wurden bereits Anfang 1997 in Addis Abeba vorgestellt und englischsprachige Kurse in Naturwissenschaften, Mathematik und Technik für Studenten des Grundstudiums aus sechs Ländern, Simbabwe, Tansania, Uganda, Äthiopien, Kenia und Ghana, durchgeführt. Das Kursmaterial stammte aus den USA und Irland. Vom 20.–22. 05. 98 fand in Ghana eine Konferenz zum Thema „Computer Literacy & distance education“ statt, was die Bedeutung des Internets für Afrika dokumentiert.

Die Einführung dieser Computertechnologie sollte sehr behutsam erfolgen. Dazu brauchen diese Länder Fachkräfte, die informationstechnologische Fähigkeiten und Fertigkeiten besitzen. Sie müssen geschult sein und über eigene Erfahrung verfügen. Weitere Aspekte sind, ländliche Gebiete bei der Anwendung deren einzubeziehen, da ein bedeutender Teil der Bevölkerung dort lebt.

2 Resümee

Informationstechnologie gewinnt zunehmend an Bedeutung in afrikanischen Ländern. Die Studentenzahl soll damit erhöht werden, um Fachkräfte heranzubilden, die das Land zur Weiterentwicklung dringend benötigt. Aber unzureichende Bildung und Ausbildung stellt nur eines der zentralen Probleme Afrikas dar. Nicht einmal die Grundbedürfnisse nach Nahrung, Wohnung, Arbeit und Frieden sind gewährleistet. Was können da neue Informationstechnologien helfen? Werden durch solche Projekte nicht noch zudem die Hürden zwischen Arm und Reich größer? Wer kann es sich schon leisten, mittels Computerhardware am Programm der AVU teilzunehmen? Verlieren afrikanische Länder nicht an kultureller Identität? Die Kurse sind englisch- oder französisch-sprachig, afrikanische Sprachen werden nicht berücksichtigt. Werden bei der Konzipierung von Systemen für einen bestimmten Einsatzbereich vor Ort Feldforschungen durchgeführt, um ein System zu entwickeln, das auch die Bedürfnisse abdeckt?

3 Ziele des Workshops

Ziel des Workshops ist es, die Entwicklung der Informatik und Informationstechnologien nicht aus Sicht der Industrieländer zu sehen, sondern Chancen und Möglichkeiten dieser Technologien insbesondere für Afrika zu diskutieren.

Es sollen im Rahmen des Workshops die Bedeutung und Perspektive von Anwendungsbereichen der Informatik für afrikanische Länder erörtert werden. Im besonderen Interesse stehen Wege des Technologietransfers wie, z. B. Erwerb von Wissen, technische Hilfe, Ausbildung und Training.

Zum Abschluß des Workshops sollen die oben genannten Fragen in einer Podiumsdiskussion reflektiert und Vorschläge zusammengefaßt werden.

4 Beschreibung des Workshops

Im ersten Teil des Workshops wird über die Verfügbarkeit von Information als der neue Weg in die partizipative Gestaltung einer zivilen Gesellschaft in Afrika referiert. Es wird zudem Einblick in Forschungsbereiche des Fachbereichs Informatik der TU Berlin gewährt, die sich mit der Anwendung von Computertechnologie in Afrika befassen.

Im zweiten Teil des Workshops wird ein „Verkehrssimulationssystem“ vorgestellt. Es entstand nach intensiver Recherche über die Verkehrsproblematik eines Testgebietes und dient als Diskussionsbasis zum besseren Verständnis für Problembehandlungen zwischen Entwicklern und Anwendern.

Quellentext

1. Afemann, U.: Internet als Chance für den Bildungsbereich in Entwicklungsländern? Workshop-Beitrag bei der Jahrestagung der GI in Stuttgart, 1998.
2. `http://www.zamet.zm/zamnet/aau/aau.htm`
3. `http://www.avu.org/`

Workshop: Integration Heterogener Softwaresysteme (IHS'98)

Stefan Conrad[1] und Wilhelm Hasselbring[2]

[1] Universität Magdeburg, Fakultät für Informatik, Institut für Technische und Betriebliche Informationssysteme, Postfach 4120, D-39016 Magdeburg
[2] Tilburg University, Department of Information Management and Computer Science, INFOLAB, 5000 LE Tilburg, Niederlande

Typische Anwendungsbereiche, in denen heterogene Software-Systeme zusammenarbeiten müssen, sind Informationssysteme in der produzierenden Industrie und im Dienstleistungsbereich. Die technische Integration derartiger heterogener Informationssysteme stellt eine aktuelle Herausforderung dar, wobei die beteiligten Teilsysteme weitgehend ihre Autonomie bewahren sollen. Bestehende Anwendungen (legacy systems) sollen dann weiterhin auf ihre lokalen Daten zugreifen können, so daß bereits getätigte Investitionen in Informationssysteme gesichert bleiben und eine sanfte Migration hin zu modernen Systemen ermöglicht wird.

Solche technischen Probleme treten z. B. häufig bei der Kopplung verteilter Software-Systeme innerhalb von Organisationen oder auch zwischen verschiedenen Organisationen für Anwendungen im Bereich 'Electronic Business' auf. Sogenannte Middleware-Systeme, wie z. B. CORBA, und Datenbankschnittstellen, wie etwa JDBC, bieten hier eine technische Plattform zur Realisierung der Integration. Derartig komplexe Systeme, die aus verschiedenen Teilsystemen bestehen, erfordern einen systematischen Entwicklungsprozeß.

Ziel dieses Workshops ist es, ein Diskussionsforum für Ansätze und Verfahren zur Integration von komplexen Softwaresystemen aus verschiedenen Bereichen zu bieten. Insbesondere sollen die beiden lebhaften Forschungsgebiete und -gemeinden auf dem Gebiet der Integration von Datenbanken und Datenbanksystemen einerseits und auf dem Gebiet der Systemintegration innerhalb des Software Engineering andererseits zusammengebracht werden. Aus diesem Grund wird der Workshop auch von den Fachgruppen 2.1 (Softwaretechnik und Programmiersprachen) und 2.5 (Rechnergestützte Informationssysteme) der Gesellschaft für Informatik e. V. (GI) unterstützt, was sich auch in der Zusammensetzung des Programmkomitees ausdrückt.

Neben konzeptionellen Beiträgen ist auch vorgesehen, Anwendungsberichte über die praktische Umsetzung von Integrationskonzepten in den Workshop zu integrieren. Das für diesen Workshop angestrebte Themenspektrum wird durch die folgenden Themen umrissen:

- Methodische Aspekte der Integration heterogener Softwaresysteme
- Integration von Datenbankschemata
- Verfahren für die Datenintegration
- Wissensbasierte Verfahren für die Softwareintegration
- Software-Architekturen für die Integration

- Reengineering für die Integration bestehender Systeme
- Inkrementelle Integration
- Integration und Migration
- Vergleich von Ansätzen aus dem Software-Engineering und dem Datenbankbereich
- Praxiserfahrungen bei der Durchführung der Integration
- Standards und Schnittstellen
- Vorgehensmodelle

Das Programm des Workshops besteht im wesentlichen aus drei Komponenten: einem eingeladenen Übersichtsvortrag, sechs Langbeiträgen und einigen zusätzlichen Kurzbeiträgen. Die Lang- und Kurzbeiträge wurden aus den eingegangenen Einreichungen ausgewählt. Hierzu wurde jede Einreichung von mehreren Programmkomitee-Mitgliedern und gegebenenfalls weiteren Experten begutachtet. Der Übersichtsvortrag von W. Emmerich (University College London) gibt einen Überblick über Entwicklungen im Bereich Komponentensysteme, wie z.B. *CORBA Business Object Facilities* und *Enterprise JavaBeans*.

Die Langbeiträge bilden das inhaltliche Gerüst des Workshops. Ihre Themen spannen ein großes Spektrum relevanter Aspekte auf, von allgemeinen Grundlagen und Architekturen bis hin zu konkreten Lösungen in speziellen Anwendungsbereichen. Als Anwendungsbereiche werden beispielsweise Electronic Commerce, CAx-Entwicklungsumgebungen und Umweltkatalogsysteme betrachtet. Für die Integration von Individual- und Standardsoftware werden unterschiedliche Architekturen diskutiert. Als eine technische Plattform wird etwa CORBA betrachtet, um daraus Entwurfsanforderungen für Datenbankzugriff abzuleiten. Auch die Nutzung des Web als Integrationstechnologie ist Gegenstand der Betrachtung.

Die Kurzbeiträge ergänzen das Programm durch Darstellung spezieller Aspekte aus verschiedenen Bereichen. Hier wird die Integration heterogener Workflowmanagementsysteme genauso betrachtet wie die Integration heterogener Werkzeuge für die Planung von Materialflußanlagen. Weitere Betrachtungsgegenstände sind Aspekte der Integration von Informationssystemen im Bereich der Bioinformatik sowie der Verwendung von Metadaten für die kontinuierliche Weiterentwicklung heterogener verteilter Informationssysteme.

Weitere Informationen zu diesem Workshop, insbesondere das endgültige Programm sowie voraussichtlich der Workshop-Band in elektronischer Fassung, sind unter `http://wwwiti.cs.uni-magdeburg.de/~conrad/IHS98` zu finden.

Programmkomitee: W. Benn (TU Chemnitz), S. Conrad (Uni Magdeburg, co-chair), J. Ebert (Uni Koblenz), M. Goedicke (UniGH Essen), W. Hasselbring (Uni Tilburg, co-chair), A. Heuer (Uni Rostock), A. Kotz-Dittrich (Union Bank of Switzerland), B. Krämer (FernUni Hagen), K. Küspert (Uni Jena), G. Ruhe (FhG IESE Kaiserslautern), M. Schrefl (Uni Linz), F. Toenniessen (congenio GmbH, München).

Workshop: Molekulare Bioinformatik

Ralf Hofestädt

Otto-von-Guericke-Universität Magdeburg
Institut für Technische und Betriebliche Informationssysteme
Universitätsplatz 2, D-39106 Magdeburg
hofestaedt@iti.cs.uni-magdeburg.de

Die Anwendung der Methoden und Konzepte der Informatik in den Forschungsbereichen der molekularen Biologie wird heute mit dem Begriff der Molekularen Bioinformatik umschrieben. Der umfassende Begriff der Bioinformatik repräsentiert darüber hinaus innovative Aspekte der Biologie in der Informatik. Hier sind u. a. die modernen Bereiche des Molecular Computing (DNA-Computing, Genetische Algorithmen etc.) in der Informatik von primärer Bedeutung. In der Molekularen Bioinformatik dominieren heute zwei wesentliche Forschungsschwerpunkte. Zum einen spielt die Sequenzanalyse eine zentrale Rolle. Dies wurde in den letzten Jahren vor allem durch die enormen technologischen Fortschritte bezüglich der Automatisierung der Protein- und Nukleotidsequenzierung verstärkt. Die in diesen Bereichen der Biotechnologie anfallenden exponentiellen Datenbestände müssen strukturiert und elektronisch verfügbar gemacht werden. Für die bereits sequenzierten und analysierten Proteine, Gene und metabolischen Pathways sind gegenwärtig Informationssysteme verfügbar. Um die spezifischen Fragestellungen der Anwender klären zu können, sind entsprechende Algorithmen zu entwickeln und zu implementieren. So ist die erste Frage eines jeden Biochemikers, der eine molekulare Struktur sequenziert hat, ob diese Sequenz oder eine dazu ähnliche Sequenz bereits in einer der Datenbanken verfügbar ist. Für die Klärung solcher oder ähnlicher Fragestellungen wurden differenzierte Werkzeuge (Algorithmen) entwickelt und implementiert. Die Aufgabe besteht heute darin, der Biotechnologie die informationstechnologische Infrastruktur verfügbar zu machen. Dies umfaßt, neben dem Zugriff auf die relevanten Datenbanken, vor allen Dingen auch in Kombination damit den Zugriff und die Benutzung der verfügbaren Analysetools. Wenn wir uns den Stand der Dinge in diesem Bereich der Forschung vor Augen führen und auch die Analysealgorithmen berücksichtigen, so stellt sich die Welt der Molekularen Bioinformatik im Bereich der Sequenzanalyse heute wie folgt dar: Eine Vielzahl von molekularen Datenbanksystemen wurde bereits entwickelt und implementiert. Eine hohe Zahl dieser Systeme ist auch über Internet verfügbar (u. a. EMBL, GENBANK, PIR, SWISSPROT). Darüber hinaus wird eine Vielzahl — eine für den Benutzer heute nicht überschaubare Menge — von bereits implementierten Analysetools über Internet angeboten. Das Problem dieser Tools liegt darin, daß in den meisten Fällen die Bedienung sehr schwierig ist. Außerdem ist die Dokumentation dieser Methoden mangelhaft.

Hier zeichnet sich eine wichtige Aufgabe der Molekularen Bioinformatik für die nächsten Jahre ab: Die Entwicklung Molekularer Informationssysteme. Dies umfaßt die Implementierung von Multi-Datenbanken, die letztlich die verteilten heterogenen molekularen Datenbanken für den Nutzer unter einer uniformen Schnittstelle zusammenfassen. Dadurch wird die Informationsfusion im molekularen Bereich unterstützt.

Der zweite aktuelle Forschungsschwerpunkt der Molekularen Bioinformatik liegt im Bereich des Protein Designs. Hier werden Werkzeuge entwickelt, um die Konstruktion neuer oder modifizierter Wirkstoffe im Rechner zu unterstützen. Das Konstruieren solcher Wirkstoffe basiert heute weitgehend auf Heuristiken, da die Modellierung der zugrunde liegenden biochemischen Prozesse erst rudimentär gelungen ist.

Der Workshop wird neben der Sequenzanalyse und dem Molecular Design das breite Spektrum der Molekularen Bioinformatik erfassen und anhand ausgewählter Fachvorträge zur Diskussion stellen. Dabei bilden die Modellierung und Simulation der Genregulation und Metabolic Pathways einen ausgezeichneten Schwerpunkt des Workshops. Auf dem Workshop werden folgende eingeladene Sprecher erwartet: Prof. Dr. F. Brandenburg (Universität Passau), Dr. R. Drees (Universität Stuttgart), Dr. O. Deussen (Universität Magdeburg), N. Grabe (Universität Magdeburg), Prof. Dr. Dr. H.-G. Lipinski (FH Dortmund), F. Meineke (Universität Leipzig), Dr. G. Michal (Tutzingen), U. Ohler (Universität Erlangen), Dr. T. Werner (GSF München), Prof. Dr. W. Wiechert (GH Siegen), Dr. E. Wingender (GBF Braunschweig)

Im Zuge des vom BMBF veröffentlichten Biotechnologie 2000 Reports wurde 1992 die GI FG 4.0.2 Informatik in den Biowissenschaften in Bonn gegründet. Die erste Fachtagung fand 1993 in Bonn statt (R. Hofestädt, F. Krückeberg und T. Lengauer: Informatik in den Biowissenschaften, Informatik Aktuell, Springer Verlag 1993). Seit 1994 findet die jährliche Fachtagung in enger Kooperation mit der Arbeitsgruppe Computereinsatz in den Biowissenschaften der DECHEMA statt. Die erste gemeinsame internationale Fachtagung wurde 1996 in Leipzig durchgeführt (R. Hofestädt, T. Lengauer, M. Löffler und D. Schomburg: Bioinformatics, LNCS 1278, Springer Verlag 1997). Neben diesen Fachtagungen wurden zahlreiche nationale und internationale Workshops organisiert und ausgetragen (u. a. vier Dagstuhl-Seminare). Die Bedeutung der Bioinformatik hat in den vergangenen Jahren permanent zugenommen. Dies ist anhand der Vielzahl der geförderten Forschungsschwerpunkte (in Deutschland u. a. BMBF und ab 1998 DFG-Schwerpunkt Bioinformatik) und nicht zuletzt an der Vielzahl der Firmengründungen im Bereich der Bioinformatik abzulesen.

Workshop: Multimedia-Systeme

Hans-Jürgen Appelrath[1] und Klaus Meyer-Wegener[2]

[1] Informatik-Institut OFFIS, Universität Oldenburg, Fachbereich Informatik, Abteilung Informationssysteme, Escherweg 2, D-26121 Oldenburg
appelrath@offis.uni-oldenburg.de
[2] Technische Universität Dresden, Fakultät Informatik, Institut für Betriebssysteme, Datenbanken und Rechnernetze, D-01062 Dresden
kmw@inf.tu-dresden.de

1 Inhalt und Ziele

Ziel des Workshops „Multimedia-Systeme" ist es, aktuelle Forschungs- und Entwicklungsergebnisse im Bereich der Multimedia- und Internet-Technologien vorzustellen, Erfahrungen auszutauschen und offene Probleme zu diskutieren. Der Workshop gliedert sich dabei in die zwei Teilbereiche „Multimedia-Systeme in Wissenschaft und Technik" und „Multimedia-Datenbanken und -Informationssysteme".

1.1 Multimedia-Systeme in Wissenschaft und Technik

Durch die Kombination von Text, Bild, Ton und Bewegtbild sowie deren Kopplung mit Interaktionsformen ermöglichen Multimedia-Systeme in vielen Anwendungsfeldern eine realitätsnähere und verständlichere Vermittlung sowie einen flexibleren Austausch von Informationen als herkömmliche Print-Medien. Dies gilt in besonderem Maße auch für den naturwissenschaftlich-technischen Bereich:

- Inhaltliche Grundlagen können hypermedial dargestellt werden. Durch Navigationsmechanismen und Suchhilfen lassen sich so benötigte Informationen schnell nachschlagen bzw. auffinden.
- Mit Hilfe von Internet-Technologien lassen sich multimediale Informationen schnell austauschen.
- Die Bedienung komplexer Geräte sowie die Abläufe wissenschaftlicher Experimente können per Video demonstriert werden.
- In „virtuellen Laboren" lassen sich reale Experimente simulieren bzw. gezielt vorbereiten; hierdurch können Materialien und Zeit eingespart, in speziellen Anwendungen auch Tierversuche reduziert werden.
- Experimente können in einem elektronischen Verbund mehrerer Forschungsgruppen unabhängig von Raum und Zeit durchgeführt werden.

Ziel dieses Teils des Workshops ist die Präsentation und Diskussion von Konzepten, Methoden, Modellen, Werkzeugen und Anwendungsbeispielen für die

Entwicklung von Multimedia-Systemen, die primär Naturwissenschaftler, Ingenieure und Mediziner bei ihrer täglichen Arbeit unterstützen. Insbesondere stellen Projekte des BMBF-Förderprogramms „Weiterentwicklung des wissenschaftlichen und technischen Buches zur multimedialen Wissensrepräsentation" erste Ergebnisse vor.

1.2 Multimedia-Datenbanken und -Informationssysteme

Der Begriff „Multimedia-Datenbanken" wurde 1985 in einem von S. Christoudoulakis geleiteten Panel auf der ACM-SIGMOD-Konferenz erstmals *offiziell* verwendet. Inzwischen ist die Entwicklung so weit gediehen, daß 1996 mindestens sechs Fachbücher zu diesem Thema erschienen sind. Dabei sind die Proceedings der verschiedenen Workshops noch gar nicht mitgerechnet.

Inhaltlich hat sich sehr viel getan im Bereich der Medien-Server, bei denen es ja auch schon etliche Produkte gibt, die aber meist dateibasiert sind und Datenbank-Technik nur in Ansätzen verwenden. Es sind auch etliche Verfahren zur Unterstützung der inhaltsorientierten Suche vorgeschlagen worden, die allerdings meist nur eine bestimmte Art der Suche unterstützen (z. B. räumliche).

Dieser Teil des Workshops soll dazu beitragen, diese Entwicklungen zu sichten, sie an einem gemeinsamen Ziel für Multimedia-Datenbanken zu messen und offene Probleme zu identifizieren. In den Beiträgen werden sowohl konkrete Anwendungen als auch spezielle Techniken im Bereich Multimedia-Datenbanken vorgestellt. Insbesondere wird der Workshop dazu dienen, alle Gruppen im deutschsprachigen Raum, die sich mit Multimedia-Datenbanken befassen (und das sind inzwischen einige), wieder mal an einem Ort zusammenzubringen und den Austausch von Ideen zu fördern.

1.3 Programm- und Organisationskomitee

Prof. Dr. H.-J. Appelrath (Universität Oldenburg)
Dipl.-Inform. D. Boles (Universität Oldenburg)
Prof. Dr. A. Brüggemann-Klein (Technische Universität München)
Prof. Dr. W. Effelsberg (Universität Mannheim)
Prof. Dr. H. Kopp (Fachhochschule Regensburg)
Prof. Dr. K. Meißner (Technische Universität Dresden)
Prof. Dr. K. Meyer-Wegener (Technische Universität Dresden)
Prof. Dr. T. Ottmann (Universität Freiburg)
Prof. Dr. R. Steinmetz (Technische Hochschule Darmstadt)

Workshop: Sportinformatik

Heinz Bayen[1] und Jürgen Perl[2]

[1] c/o Software AG, Uhlandstraße 12,
D-64297 Darmstadt, Germany
heinz_bayen@software.ag.de
[2] Institut für Informatik, Fachbereich 17, Universität Mainz, Staudingerweg 9,
D-55099 Mainz, Germany
perl@informatik.uni-mainz.de

Die besonderen Problemstellungen, Anforderungen und Lösungsansätze des Sportes und der Sportwissenschaft im Bereich EDV und Informatik haben in den letzten Jahren zunehmend wissenschaftlichen Charakter angenommen. Diese Entwicklung war aus der Sicht des Sports Anlaß, die Kooperation mit der Informatik nicht nur zu fördern, sondern auch zu institutionalisieren. Eine Konsequenz war 1995 die Einrichtung der Sektion „Sportinformatik" in der Deutschen Vereinigung für Sportwissenschaft. Zu den Aufgaben der Sportinformatik gehören — neben der Entwicklung eigener Arbeitsfelder, wie sie z. B. im Programm dieses Workshops angesprochen werden — die Erkennung wissenschaftsrelevanter Informatikaspekte im Sport und die Beobachtung der sich entwickelnden Informatik im Hinblick auf deren möglichen Nutzen für den Sport. Der Nutzen einer solchen interdisziplinären Kooperation liegt im Abgleich von Anforderung und Angebot, wobei im Fall der Sportinformatik i. d. R. der Sport die Probleme liefern und von der Informatik die Lösungsansätze erwarten wird; umgekehrt ist aber auch die Formulierung neuer Probleme und Lösungsanforderungen für eine Servicewissenschaft wie die Informatik von Nutzen.

So hat die Bereitstellung sportwissenschaftlicher Literatur in Datenbank- und Informationssystemen sicherlich kaum etwas mit Sportinformatik zu tun. Eine Multimedia-Datenbank oder -Anwendung mit Text, Bildern, Videosequenzen, Videoanalysen und Animationen kann dagegen Arbeitsgegenstand der Sportinformatik sein, wenn die Realisierung einer solchen multimedialen Kombination informatische Konzepte oder Werkzeuge erfordert oder umgekehrt der Informatik neue Impulse liefert. Auch der Einsatz oder die Entwicklung von Expertensystemen oder etwa die Verwendung neuer Modellbildungsparadigmen („Softcomputing") müssen im Einzelfall sportinformatische Bedeutung erst nachweisen, können aber so auch der Informatik Anregungen für weiterführende Entwicklungen geben. Was genau „nur" Sportwissenschaft bzw. Informatik ist, und was sich zu Arbeitsfeldern der Sportinformatik entwickeln kann, ist gegenwärtig natürlich nicht geklärt und sollte u. a. Diskussionsgegenstand dieses Workshops sein. Erfreulich wäre es auch, wenn durch den Workshop weitere Informatiker motiviert werden könnten, Beiträge zur Sportinformatik zu leisten und so die interdisziplinäre Kooperation von der Seite der Informatik zu intensivieren.

Der Workshop basiert auf einer Reihe von Workshops über Sport & Informatik seit 1989 und internationalen Konferenzen seit 1992 in Israel (Netanya), Spanien (Torremolinos), 1997 in Paris und Köln. Vier eingeladene Vorträge von den Wissensbasierten Systemen an der Universität Bielefeld, der Trainings- und Bewegungslehre an der Deutschen Sporthochschule Köln (DSHS), der Informatik an der Universität Mainz und der Sportinformatik an der Technischen Universität Darmstadt geben einen Überblick über wichtige Gebiete der Sportinformatik wie Verhaltensanalyse, Medien und Präsentation, Modellbildung und Ausbildung. Fünf begutachtete Beiträge aus der Sportmedizin an der DSHS Köln, dem Institut für Angewandte Trainingslehre Leipzig, Nachfolger der Deutschen Hochschule für Körperkultur, der Bewegungswissenschaft an der Universität Oldenburg und der Bewegungs- und Trainingswissenschaft an der Universität Saarbrücken zeigen aktuelle Arbeiten der Sportinformatik.

Nicht gezeigt werden in diesem Workshop etablierte Anwendungen wie Videoanalyse und Sportspielsimulation. Nicht gezeigt werden auch Anwendungen, die mehr mit Spiel allein als mit Sport zu tun haben, auch wenn z. B. die Gruppe Künstliche Intelligenz der Humboldt-Universität Berlin 1997 Weltmeister im Roboter-Fußball wurde. Die nachfolgend aufgeführten Beiträge bieten, wie oben schon angesprochen, sicher Stoff für kontroverse Diskussionen: Ist das noch Sport, noch Informatik, ginge das nicht eleganter, gibt es das nicht auch außerhalb des Sports? Wir erhoffen uns Antworten und sehen der Vorstellung der Sportinformatik im Rahmen der Jahrestagung der Gesellschaft für Informatik mit gespannter Erwartung entgegen.

Das Programm gliedert sich in folgende vier Abschnitte:

Verhaltensanalysesysteme

- Wachsmuth (Universität Bielefeld): *Hauptvortrag.*
- Brück, Weper, Müller, Reiser, Daugs (Universität Saarbrücken): *Optische Flugbahnaufnahme und -auswertung zur Unterstützung des Wurftrainings im Basketball.*

Medien und Präsentation

- Mester (Deutsche Sporthochschule Köln): *Hauptvortrag.*
- Wagner, Krug (Institut für Angewandte Trainingswissenschaft Leipzig): *Bildreihen — eine interessante Möglichkeit der Gestaltung von Informationsprozessen beim motorischen Lernen.*

Modellbildung

- Perl (Universität Mainz): *Hauptvortrag.*
- Mader, Ulmer (Deutsche Sporthochschule Köln): *Der Mechanismus der aktiven Belastungsadaptation und das Phänomen von Überlastung und Übertraining auf der Ebene der Muskulatur, dargestellt in einem Simulationsmodell.*

Ausbildung

- Wiemeyer (TU Darmstadt): *Hauptvortrag.*
- Rockmann (Universität Oldenburg): *Zur Lernleistungskontrolle beim Einsatz von Computerlernmaterialien.*
- Daugs, Schmidt, Igel, Bernarding (Universität Saarbrücken): *Virtuelle Kommunikation in Sport und Sportwissenschaft — ein europäisches Modellprojekt.*

Verfahren zur photorealistsichen und nicht-photorealistischen Bilderzeugung

Thomas Strothotte, Oliver Deussen, Bernhard Preim

Otto-von-Guericke Universität Magdeburg
Institut für Simulation und Graphik
{tstr,deussen,bernhard}@isg.cs.uni-magdeburg.de

1 Motivation

Die Computergraphik ist in den letzten 20 Jahren dem Ziel der Generierung täuschend echt wirkender Bilder sehr nahe gekommen. Eine Fülle von Techniken und Werkzeugen wurde entwickelt, die die Generierung, Modellierung und Abbildung geometrischer Daten ermöglicht[3]. Integrierte Systeme ermöglichen die Herstellung kompletter Animationen von der Geometrieerzeugung über Simulationsverfahren zur Bewegungsgenerierung bis zur Integration von Videobildern mit synthetischen Objekten. Spezielle Hardwarekomponenten in Graphikrechnern unterstützen die Bilderzeugung und erlauben die Echtzeitvisualisierung selbst komplexer Daten.

Oftmals sind aber nicht photorealistische Bilder die beste Darstellungsmethode, sondern abstraktere Abbildungen. Dies ist der Fall bei Lehr- und Lernsystemen oder zu Dokumentationszwecken und zur Entscheidungsunterstützung. Beispiele finden sich in Atlanten, technischen Handbüchern, Anleitungen und Dokumentationen. Die Erzeugung solcher Bilder mit dem Rechner wurde lange vernachlässigt, hat aber in den letzten Jahren zunehmend an Beachtung gewonnen.

Das Tutorial richtet sich an interessierte Forscher, Entwickler und Anwender der Computergraphik. Es soll Basis- und Zusammenhangswissen aus beiden Bereichen vermittelt werden, das es dem Zuhörer ermöglicht, neue Produkte, Standards und Trends besser einschätzen zu können.

2 Inhalt des Tutorials

Im Tutorial werden neben den theoretischen Grundlagen Standards zur Darstellung graphischer Daten besprochen sowie Werkeuge zur Herstellung von Modelldaten und zur Erzeugung von Bildern vorgestellt. Das Tutorium gliedert sich wie folgt:

1. **Hardwarenahe Graphikstandards**
   Im Zusammenhang mit Graphikhardware, die in vielen Workstations und einer zunehmenden Zahl von PCs vorhanden ist, haben sich Standards wie OpenGL [5] und Performer [6], herausgebildet, die überall dort eingesetzt werden, wo komplexe Graphikdaten in Echtzeit ausgegeben werden sollen. Unterstützt werden sie durch Hight-Level Bibliotheken wie Inventor[7].

2. **Photorealistische Bilderzeugungsmethoden**
   Auf dem Markt finden sich eine Reihe von Programmen, mit denen photorealistische Bilder erzeugt werden können. Wir demonstrieren Raytracing [10], Radiosity [1] und Radiance und geben Hinweise auf deren Benutzung sowie Bildbeispiele.

3. **Nicht-photorealistische Bilderzeugung**
   Zur Herstellung von Illustrationen und graphisch abstrakten Bildern gibt es inzwischen ebenfalls Software wie etwa den "Fractal Design Painter" oder Plug-Ins zu verschiedenen Animationssystemen. Diese werden vorgestellt und der Stand der Forschung anhand eigener und auswärtiger Arbeiten besprochen[8, 9].

4. **Modellierung**
   Die Herstellung von geometrischen Modelldaten ist ein zentrales Problem der Computergraphik. Hierzu zählen auch Materialien, Oberflächeneigenschaften und zeitliche Veränderungen der Geometrie.
   Es werden Programmsysteme zur Modellierung und Animation wie Maya und 3D-Studio vorgestellt. Speziell wird auf Generierungsmethoden zur Herstellung komplexer natürlicher Objekte und Szenen[2] eingegangen.

Literatur

1. M. F. Cohen and J. R. Wallace. *Radiosity and Realistic Image Synthesis.* Academic Press Professional, San Diego, 1993.
2. O. Deussen, P. Hanrahan, B. Lintermann, R. Mech, M. Pharr, and P. Prusinkiewicz. Realistic modeling and rendering of plant ecosystems. In *SIGGRAPH 98 Conference Proceedings*, ACM SIGGRAPH, 1998 (im Druck)
3. J. D. Foley, A. van Dam, S. K. Feiner, and J. F. Hughes. *Computer Graphics. Principle and Practice.* Addison-Wesley, Bonn, Paris, Reading, 2. Auflage, 1990.
4. J. T. Kajiya. The rendering equation. In *SIGGRAPH '86 Conference Proceedings*, S. 143–150, ACM SIGGRAPH, 1986.
5. J. Neider, T. Davis, and M. Woo. *OpenGL Programming Guide: The Official Guide to Learning OpenGL.* Addison-Wesley, Bonn, Paris, Reading, 1993.
6. J. Rohlf and J. Helman. IRIS Performer: A high performance multiprocessing toolkit for real-time 3D graphics. In *SIGGRAPH 94 Conference Proceedings*, S. 381–394, ACM SIGGRAPH, 1994.
7. P. S. Strauss and R. Carey. An object-oriented 3D-graphics toolkit. In *SIGGRAPH 92 Conference Proceedings*, S. 341–349, ACM SIGGRAPH, 1992.
8. T. Strothotte (Hrsg.). *Abstraction in Interactive Computer Visualizations: Exploring Complex Information Spaces.* Springer-Verlag, 1998
9. T. Strothotte, B. Preim, A. Raab, J. Schumann, and D. R. Forsey. How to render frames and influence people. *Computer Graphics Forum (Proc. Eurographics)*, 13(3):455–466, 1994.
10. A. Watt. *3D Computer Graphics.* Addison-Wesley, Bonn, Paris, Reading, 2. Auflage, 1993.

Tutorium „Maschinelle Sprachverarbeitung“

Günther Görz

IMMD (Informatik), Universität Erlangen-Nürnberg, Martensstraße 3,
D-91058 Erlangen, Germany
goerz@informatik.uni-erlangen.de

Das Tutorium gibt einen Überblick über die wichtigsten Methoden und Verfahren der maschinellen Sprachverarbeitung. Dabei wird eine systemorientierte Sichtweise im Vordergrund stehen, d. h. der Schwerpunkt liegt bei den Aspekten der Verarbeitung, und hier insbesondere im Hinblick auf Dialogsysteme. Vorausgesetzt werden elementare Kenntisse der Schulgrammatik und Grundkenntnisse in der formalen Logik. Weitergehendes Wissen über linguistische und formalsprachliche Sachverhalte wird im Rahmen des Tutoriums vermittelt.

Für jede der im folgenden aufgezählten linguistischen Abstraktionsebenen, die zugleich auch modulare Verarbeitungsschichten in Sprachverarbeitungssystemen bezeichnen, wird exemplarisch ein moderner algorithmischer Ansatz eingeführt. Das Tutorium ist in die folgenden Abschnitte gegliedert:

1. Sprache und Kognition
2. Lexikon und Morphologie
3. Syntax: Grammatikformalismen und Strukturanalyse
4. Semantische Verarbeitung
5. Pragmatik, Diskurs und Dialoggestaltung
6. Sprachgenerierung
7. Sprachsignalverarbeitung, Erkennung und robuste Verabeitung
8. Architekturen und Anwendungen sprachverarbeitender Systeme

Nach einem einführenden Abschnitt, der die besondere Problemlage der maschinellen Sprachverarbeitung im Spannungsfeld zwischen Linguistik, Kognitionswissenschaft und Anforderungen der Anwendung vorstellt, wird das Lexikon als eine grundlegende linguistische Ressource behandelt. Die maschinelle Darstellung lexikalischen Wissens schließt die algorithmische Behandlung der Bildung und Analyse von Wortformen mithilfe von endlichen Automaten ein. Um die syntaktische Zerlegung von Sätzen algorithmisch behandeln zu können, werden zunächst geeignete Formalismen zur Darstellung der Grammatik eingeführt. Exemplarisch stützen wir uns hierbei auf einen Ansatz aus dem Bereich der constraint-basierten (auch: Unifikations-) Grammatiken. Als generisches Analyseverfahren wird dann das „Chart-Parsing“ Algorithmenschema behandelt. Um die in sprachlichen Äußerungen ausgedrückte Bedeutung verarbeitungsgerecht ausdrücken zu können, wird ein Verfahren zur Konstruktion bedeutungsdarstellender formaler Ausdrücke auf der Basis der Diskursrepräsentationstheorie eingeführt. Dieser Ansatz gestattet, auch Einzelsätze übergreifende Bedeutungen in einem umfassenden Dialogkontext zu behandeln. Mit Wissen über den Anwendungsbereich — denkt man beispielsweise an ein Auskunftssystem über

Verkehrsverbindungen — können die solchermaßen formal dargestellten Bedeutungen dann anwendungsbezogen interpretiert und für Anfragen an ein Datenbanksystem oder einen anderen Problemlöser aufbereitet werden. Um Dialoge — etwa Auskunftsdialoge mit einem Informationssystem — in kohärenter Weise führen zu können, so daß der Informationsbedarf der Benutzer befriedigt werden kann, bedarf es der Steuerung durch eine Dialogkomponente. Die Ausgaben des Problemlösers, in unserem Beispiel etwa eine Verbindungsauskunft, müssen dann durch eine Generierungskomponente wieder in eine umgangssprachliche Antwort umgesetzt werden. Besondere Anforderungen stellt die Forderung, daß ein Sprachverbeitungssystem mit gesprochenen Eingaben bedient werden soll. Neben der Analyse von Sprachsignalen und Verfahren zur Worterkennung muß gerade hier der Robustheit der Verarbeitung besondere Aufmerksamkeit gewidmet werden. Den Abschluß des Tutoriums bildet eine Übersicht über wichtige Anwendungen der Sprachverarbeitung, zu denen neben Dialogsystemen u. a. auch die maschinelle Übersetzung, die Informationsgewinnung aus Textkorpora und und die Einbettung in multimodale und multimediale Systeme gehört, sowie eine Diskussion hierzu geeigneter Systemarchitekturen.

Literatur

1. Allen, J.: *Natural Language Understanding.* Reading, Mass.: Addison-Wesley, 1995
2. Charniak, E: *Statistical Language Learning.* Cambridge, Mass.: MIT Press, 1993
3. Görz, G. (Hg.): *Einführung in die Künstliche Intelligenz.* (Kapitel über Sprachverarbeitung) Bonn: Addison-Wesley, 1995

Entwicklung sicherheitskritischer eingebetteter Systeme: Der ESPRESS-Ansatz

Maritta Heisel[1], Rainer Mackenthun[2], Thomas Neustupny[3], Sadegh Sadeghipour[4], Matthias Weber[4]

[1] Otto-von-Guericke-Universität Magdeburg, heisel@cs.uni-magdeburg.de
[2] Fraunhofer-Institut für Software- und Systemtechnik Berlin, rainer.mackenthun@isst.fhg.de
[3] GMD FIRST Berlin, thomas@first.gmd.de
[4] Daimler-Benz AG Berlin, {weber, Sadegh.Sadeghipour}@dbag.bln.daimlerbenz.com

Überblick

Software wird heute in zunehmendem Maße in sicherheitskritischen Bereichen eingesetzt, wo Fehler katastrophale Folgen haben können. Deshalb muß sicherheitskritische Software besonders sorgfältig entwickelt werden.

Das Tutorium stellt einen Ansatz zur Entwicklung von Software für sicherheitskritische eingebettete Systeme vor, der im Projekt ESPRESS entwickelt wurde. ESPRESS ist ein vom Bundesministerium für Bildung, Wissenschaft, Forschung und Technologie (BMBF) gefördertes Verbundprojekt mit Partnern aus Industrie, Forschungseinrichtungen und Universitäten.

Der ESPRESS-Ansatz verwendet formale Spezifikationstechniken, da formale Spezifikationen genauer analysiert werden können als informelle und weil eine formale Spezifikation zur werkzeuggestützten Ermittlung von Testfällen und Testdaten und zur automatischen Testauswertung herangezogen werden kann. Die verwendete Spezifikationssprache ist eine Integration der Statemate-Sprachen [HLN+90] und der Z-Notation [Spi92], die in der Industrie vergleichsweise weit verbreitet sind.

Ein Nachteil formaler Techniken liegt darin, daß sie für Softwareingenieure in der Regel nicht einfach zu handhaben sind. Oftmals werden Benutzer formaler Techniken mit einem reinen Formalismus konfrontiert, für den es keine "Bedienungsanleitung" gibt. Der ESPRESS-Ansatz legt deshalb besonderen Wert auf eine angemessene methodische Unterstützung seiner Benutzer.

Ein weiterer Schwerpunkt des ESPRESS-Ansatzes ist die angemessene Werkzeugunterstützung des Entwicklungsprozesses. Hier wurden verschiedene kommerzielle Werkzeuge mit speziellen ESPRESS-Werkzeugen zum Editieren von Spezifikationen, zur Typüberprüfung und zur Validation integriert.

Bild 1 gibt einen Überblick über den von der ESPRESS-Methodik abgedeckten Teil des Systementwicklungsprozesses, nämlich die Entwicklung einer sicherheitskritischen Softwarekomponente.

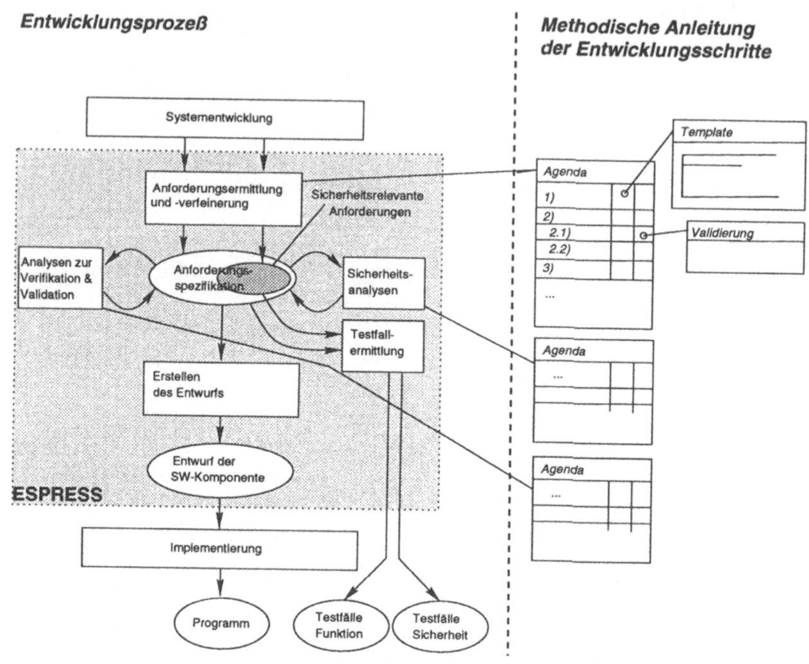

Abbildung1. ESPRESS Prozeßmodell

Gliederung

Das Tutorium gliedert sich wie folgt:

1. Einführung
   Nach einer Motivation der in ESPRESS verfolgten Vorgehensweise und einem Überblick über das Projekt wird hier die industrielle Fallstudie eingeführt, mit der der ESPRESS-Ansatz im weiteren Verlauf des Tutoriums illustriert wird. Dies ist eine Anwendung aus dem Automobilbereich, nämlich ein intelligenter Fahrgeschwindigkeitskonstanter (Tempomat).
2. Einführung in die Spezifikationssprache [BDG+96]
   Die Grundlagen der kombinierten Sprachen werden erläutert. Dabei werden drei Sichten auf das Softwaresystem unterschieden: die Architektursicht, die reaktive Sicht und die funktionale Sicht.
3. Methodische Konzepte [Hei98]
   Methoden zur Durchführung der in Bild 1 gezeigten Tätigkeiten werden als *Agenden* ausgedrückt. Eine Agenda besteht aus einer Liste von Tätigkeiten, die zur Erfüllung einer Softwareentwicklungsaufgabe durchgeführt werden müssen. Sie gibt den Entwicklern somit substantielle Anleitung zur Lösung dieser Aufgabe.
   Referenzarchitekturen repräsentieren bewährte Entwurfsprinzipien für sicherheitskritische eingebettete Systeme. Agenden unterstützen jeweils eine konkrete Referenzarchitektur.

4. Agenda für zyklische Softwarekomponenten [GHD98]
   Eine Agenda für die Referenzarchitektur „zyklische Softwarekomponente" wird vorgestellt und ihre Anwendung am Beispiel des Fahrgeschwindigkeitskonstanters illustriert.
5. Sicherheitsanalyse [KM97]
   Hier werden bekannte Ansätze zur Sicherheitsanalyse skizziert und ihre Anwendung in ESPRESS unter Verwendung einer Agenda erläutert.
6. Konsistenzanalysen
   Die entwickelte Spezifikation wird mit deduktiven Methoden analysiert, um wichtige Qualitätsanforderungen garantieren zu können.
7. Testmethodik [HNS97,SCS97]
   Aus der formalen Spezifikation können Testfälle, Testsequenzen und Testdaten systematisch und werkzeugunterstützt generiert werden.
8. Werkzeugüberblick [KSW96]
   Die in ESPRESS entwickelten Werkzeuge bauen u.a. auf Statemate [HLN+90] und Isabelle [Pau94] auf.
9. Abschluß

Literatur

[BDG+96] R. Büssow, H. Dörr, R. Geisler, W. Grieskamp und M. Klar. μSZ – ein Ansatz zur systematischen Verbindung von Z und Statecharts. Technischer Bericht TR 96-32, Technische Universität Berlin, 1996.

[GHD98] Wolfgang Grieskamp, Maritta Heisel und Heiko Dörr. Specifying safety-critical embedded systems with Statecharts and Z: An agenda for cyclic software components. In E. Astesiano, Hsg., *Proc. ETAPS-FASE'98*, LNCS 1382, S. 88–106. Springer-Verlag, 1998.

[Hei98] Maritta Heisel. Agendas – a concept to guide software development activites. In R. N. Horspool, Hsg., *Proc. Systems Implementation 2000*, S. 19–32, London, 1998. Chapman & Hall.

[HLN+90] D. Harel, H. Lachover, A. Naamad, A. Pnueli, M. Politi, R. Sherman, A. Shtull-Trauring und M. Trakhtenbrot. Statemate: A working environment for the development of complex reactive systems. *IEEE TSE*, 16 No. 4, April 1990.

[HNS97] S. Helke, T. Neustupny und T. Santen. Automating test case generation from Z specifications with Isabelle. In J. Bowen, M. Hinchey und D. Till, Hsg., *ZUM '97: The Z Formal Specification Notation*, LNCS 1212, S. 52–71. Springer-Verlag, 1997.

[KM97] Christian Kelling und Rainer Mackenthun. Fehlermodell und Sicherheitsanalysen bei der Anforderungsspezifikation. Technischer Bericht 43, Fraunhofer ISST Berlin, 1997.

[KSW96] Kolyang, T. Santen und B. Wolff. A structure preserving encoding of Z in Isabelle/HOL. In J. von Wright, J. Grundy und J. Harrison, Hsg., *Theorem Proving in Higher-Order Logics*, LNCS 1125. Springer-Verlag, 1996.

[Pau94] L. C. Paulson. *Isabelle*. LNCS 828. Springer-Verlag, 1994.

[SCS97] H. Singh, M. Conrad und S. Sadeghipour. Test case design based on Z and the classification-tree method. In M. G. Hinchey und S. Liu, Hsg., *Proceedings of First Internationsl Conference on Formal Engineering Methods*, S. 81–90. IEEE Computer Society, 1997.

[Spi92] J.M. Spivey. *The Z Notation – A Reference Manual*. Prentice Hall, 1992.

Computer Animation Festival

Stefan Schlechtweg, Thomas Strothotte

Institut für Simulation und Graphik
Otto-von-Guericke-Universität Magdeburg
{stefans,tstr}@isg.cs.uni-magdeburg.de
http://isgwww.cs.uni-magdeburg.de/caf/caf.html

Das Motto der diesjährigen GI-Jahrestagung „Informatik zwischen Bild und Sprache" birgt die Möglichkeit, mit einem kulturellen Ereignis der besonderen Art ein breites Publikum zu erreichen und einen Aspekt der Informatik anzusprechen, der bisher allgemeinhin eher der Kunst als der Wissenschaft zugeordnet wird: Computer-Animationen. Das Festival soll dabei zum einen die Brücke zwischen Kunst und Wissenschaft schlagen und andererseits an die Tradition solcher Veranstaltungen auf anderen Tagungen (insbesondere im Bereich der Computergraphik, wie beispielsweise SIGGRAPH oder Graphics Interface) anknüpfen.

Zur Mitarbeit im Programmkomitee konnten folgende Personen gewonnen werden:

- Prof. John Buchanan, University of Alberta, Kanada,
- Uwe Büchler, Werkleitz Gesellschaft e.V.,
- Prof. Dieter W. Fellner, Rheinische Friedrich-Wilhelms-Universität Bonn,
- Prof. Thomas Hägele, Filmakademie Baden-Württemberg, Ludwigsburg,
- Prof. Heinrich Müller, Universität Dortmund,
- Prof. Thomas Strothotte, Otto-von-Guericke-Universität Magdeburg.

Die Themen der einzureichenden Beiträge sind bewußt nicht auf bestimmte Bereiche beschränkt, um das breite Anwendungsgebiet zu demonstrieren. Somit werden Videos zu verschiedensten Themen präsentiert, die die Anwendung von Techniken der Computergraphik und -animation auf einem sehr breiten Gebiet demonstrieren. Darunter sind sowohl künstlerische Arbeiten als auch Computeranimationen, die neue Techniken der Computergraphik oder neue Erkenntnisse in anderen wissenschaftlichen Bereichen demonstrieren.

Die eingereichten und von der Jury ausgewählten Animationen zeigen sehr gut, welchen Beitrag die Entwicklung der Computergraphik und -animation in den letzten Jahren geleistet hat, um neue künstlerische Ausdrucksformen zu schaffen, aber auch den Wissenschaftlern neuartige Techniken zur Präsentation ihrer Forschungsergebnisse bereitzustellen.

Diese interessante Verbindung von Kreativität und Wissenschaft stellt eine wichtige Grundlage dar, die zukunftsweisend in unserer heutigen multimedialen Informationsgesellschaft eingesetzt werden muß. Gerade Magdeburg ist als Austragungsort für das Computer Animation Festival besonders prädestiniert, da hier mit dem innovativen Studiengang „Computervisualistik" Studierenden die Möglichkeit gegeben wird, genau in diesem Sinne die Basis für ihren zukünftigen Beruf zu gestalten.

Autorenverzeichnis